abled. Plaintiffs primarily used the Rehabilitation Act of 1973 (29 U.S.C.A. § 701 et seq.), the earliest law of this type. But the Rehabilitation Act has a limited scope: it applies only to federally funded workplaces and institutions, and says nothing about those that do not receive government money.

With passage of the ADA in 1990, Congress gave broad protection to people with AIDS who work in the private sector. In general, the ADA is designed to increase access for disabled persons, and it also forbids discrimination in hiring or promotion in companies with fifteen or more employees. Specifically, employers may not discriminate if the person in question is otherwise qualified for the job. Moreover, they cannot use tests to screen out disabled persons, and they must provide reasonable accommodation for disabled workers. The ADA, which took effect in 1992, has quickly emerged as the primary means for bringing AIDS-related discrimination lawsuits.

AIDS and Health Care Closely related to work is the issue of health care. In some cases, the two overlap: health insurance, Social Security, and disability benefits for AIDS victims were often hard to obtain during the 1980s. Insurance was particularly difficult because employers feared rising costs and insurance companies did not want to pay claims. To avoid the costs of AIDS, insurance companies used two traditional industry techniques: they attempted to exclude AIDS coverage from general policies, and they placed caps (limits on benefits payments) on AIDS-related coverage.

In January 1995, the settlement in a lawsuit brought by a Philadelphia construction worker with AIDS illustrated that the ADA can be used to fight caps on coverage. In 1992, the joint union-management fund for the Laborers' District Council placed a $10,000 limit on AIDS benefits, in stark contrast to the $100,000 allowed for other catastrophic illnesses. At that time, the fund said the cap on AIDS benefits was designed to curb all health costs. In 1993, the EEOC ruled that it violated the ADA, and, backed by the AIDS Law Project of Philadelphia, the worker sued. Rather than fight an expensive lawsuit, the insurance fund settled.

AIDS and Education Issues in the field of education include the rights of HIV-positive students to attend class and of HIV-positive teachers to teach, the confidentiality of HIV records, and how best to teach young people about AIDS. A few areas have been settled in court: for instance, the right of students to attend classes was of greater concern in the early years of the epidemic, and no longer remains in dispute.

Certain students with AIDS may assert their right to public education under the Education for All Handicapped Children Act of 1975 (EAHCA), but the law is only relevant in cases involving special education programs. More commonly, students' rights are protected by the Rehabilitation Act.

Schools play a major role in the effort to educate the public on AIDS. Several states have mandated AIDS prevention instruction in their schools. But the subject is controversial: it evokes personal, political, and moral reactions to sexuality. During the 1980s, those who often criticized liberal approaches to sex education argued that AIDS materials should not be explicit, encourage sexuality, promote the use of contraceptives, or favorably portray gays and lesbians.

Civil Litigation TORT law has seen an explosion of AIDS-related suits. This area of law is used to discourage individuals from subjecting others to unreasonable risks, and to compensate those who have been injured by unreasonably risky behavior. The greatest number of AIDS-related LIABILITY lawsuits has involved the receipt of HIV-infected blood and blood products. A second group has concerned the sexual transmission of HIV. A third group involves AIDS-related psychic distress. In these cases, plaintiffs have successfully sued and recovered damages for their fear of having contracted HIV.

CROSS-REFERENCES
Disabled Persons; Discrimination; Food and Drug Administration; Gay and Lesbian Rights; Health Care; Patients' Rights; Physicians and Surgeons; Privacy.

Cross-references at end of article

BIOGRAPHY

Gloria Allred

Biography of contributor to American law

ALLRED, GLORIA Gloria Allred, born July 3, 1941, in Philadelphia, is a flamboyant, widely recognized lawyer, feminist, activist, and radio talk show host. Though her critics dismiss her as a publicity monger and a dilettante, Allred has received praise from others who believe that she is a master at using the power of the news media to draw attention to the day-to-day struggles of ordinary people.

Born Gloria Rachel Bloom, Allred grew up in Philadelphia with her parents, Morris Bloom, a door-to-door salesman, and Stella Davidson Bloom, a homemaker. Her conventional middle-class childhood gave no hint of the outspoken activist to come. Allred graduated with honors from the University of Pennsylvania in 1963 with a bachelor's degree in English. She moved to New York to pursue a master's degree in teaching at New York University. While she was interested in the CIVIL RIGHTS movement, which was beginning to gain momentum, she received her master's degree in 19[...]

Timeline for subject of biography, including general historical events and life events

GLORIA ALLRED 1941–

1977 U.S. Supreme Court upheld *Roe v. Wade*, legalizing abortion

1966 Received master's in teaching from NYU, moved to Los Angeles to teach in Watts

1974 Received J.D. from USC, formed law partnership with Nathan Goldberg and Michael Maroko

1965 Watts riots in Los Angeles

1986 Sued L.A. County to stop shackling of pregnant inmates during labor and delivery

Graduated from Univ. Pennsylvania, with honors

1941 Born Philadelphia, Pa.

1965–68 Martin Luther King active in civil rights movement

1988 Sued Friars Club; L.A. for sex discrimination

Wrote "Protection of Prostitution" for *L.A. Times*, advocating legalization of prostitution

1925   1950   1975   2000

Philadelphia to teach at a high school with a predominantly black enrollment.

Allred says her interest in the struggle for equal rights arose from personal experiences. While she was in college, she married, gave birth to a daughter, and divorced. Unable to collect CHILD SUPPORT from her former husband, she was forced to return to her parents' home. She also recalls being paid less than a man for what she considered equal work. The reason given was that the man had a family to support, but at the time, Allred was the single mother of an infant.

After moving to California, Allred taught in the turbulent Watts section of Los Angeles and became the first full-time female staff member in United Teachers of Los Angeles, the union representing Los Angeles teachers. The experience stirred her interest in CIVIL RIGHTS and collective bargaining and prompted her to go to law school. She received her law degree, with honors, from Loyola Marymount University, Los Angeles, Law School in 1974. Soon after, she entered a law firm partnership with her classmates Nathan Goldberg and Michael Maroko.

Allred is probably the most flamboyant and well known member of her firm. She has achieved notoriety and name recognition through staged press conferences and demonstrations publicizing and dramatizing the cause she is championing at the time. She also accepts controversial cases that naturally attract media attention. During her years in practice, she has successfully sued Los Angeles County to stop the practice of shackling and chaining pregnant inmates during labor and delivery; put a halt on the city of El Segundo's quizzing job applicants about their sexual histories (*Thorne v. City of El Segundo*, 802 F.2d 1131 [9th Cir. 1986]); represented a client who was turned down for a job as a police officer after a six-hour lie detector exam that included questions about her sex life; and sued a dry cleaning establishment for discrimination because it charged more to launder women's shirts than men's.

Allred relishes confrontation, and her showy tactics have earned her both praise and criticism.

Internal cross references

"THERE ARE ENOUGH HIGH HURDLES TO CLIMB, AS ONE TRAVELS THROUGH LIFE, WITHOUT HAVING TO SCALE ARTIFICIAL BARRIERS CREATED BY LAW OR SILLY REGULATIONS."

Quotation from subject of biography

Full cite for case

Defending what many have called self-promoting publicity stunts, Allred says she tries to use the few moments she is in the spotlight to make her point as forcefully as possible. Her detractors say that she wastes her time and energy on trivial issues that do not advance any worthwhile cause and deflect attention away from serious issues. Yet, she points out, she is often stopped on the street by people who recognize her and want to thank her for taking on the small fights that no one else wants.

Some critics say she is all show and no substance. But Allred has many supporters as well. Among them is Justice Joan Dempsey Klein, of the California Court of Appeal, who credits Allred with moving women's issues forward. Klein also points out that Allred saves her dramatics for outside the courtroom and always observes proper decorum when before the bench. According to Klein, Allred is always well-prepared and, for that reason, is quite successful.

Dressed in her trademark reds and electric blues, her striking black hair set off by deep red lipstick, Allred is a potent combination of scholarship and theatrics. Her keen intelligence and shrewd understanding of the power of the media have made her a contemporary success story in the world of law and politics.

ARBITER [Latin, *One who attends something to view it as a spectator or witness.*] Any person who is given an absolute power to judge and rule on a matter in a dispute.

Definition enclosed in book logos with Latin translation provided

WEST'S
ENCYCLOPEDIA
of
AMERICAN
LAW

WEST'S ENCYCLOPEDIA *of* AMERICAN LAW

Volume 4

WEST GROUP

This encyclopedia is the result of efforts by numerous individuals and entities from the Twin Cities and around the United States. West Group wishes to thank all who made this publication, its quality and content, a priority in their lives.

In addition to the individuals who worked on *West's Encyclopedia of American Law*, West Group recognizes Harold W. Chase (1922–1982) for his contributions to *The Guide to American Law: Everyone's Legal Encyclopedia*.

COPYRIGHT ©1998 By
    WEST GROUP
    610 Opperman Drive
    P.O. Box 64526
    St. Paul, MN 55164-0526
All rights reserved
Printed in the United States of America
05 04 03 02 01 00 99 98   8 7 6 5 4 3 2 1 0
Library of Congress Cataloging in
    Publication Data
ISBN: 0-314-20157-2 (Hard)

West's encyclopedia of American law.
        p.   cm.
    Includes bibliographical references and
    indexes.
    ISBN 0-314-20157-2 (hard   :
    alk. paper)
    1. Law—United States—Encyclopedias.
    2. Law—United States—Popular works.
    I. West Publishing Company.
KF154.W47   1997
348.73'03—dc20
[347.30803]   96-34350
                            CIP

PRODUCTION CREDITS

Cover, interior design, and page layout:
    David J. Farr, ImageSmythe
Composition: Carlisle Communications
Proofreading: Maureen Meyer
Photo research: Elsa Peterson Ltd.
Art research: Nanette E. Bertaut
Editorial research: Pat Lewis
Artwork: Patricia Isaacs, Parrot Graphics;
    Alice B. Thiede/William A. Thiede,
    Carto-Graphics
Indexing: Schroeder Indexing Services

This publication is designed to provide information on the subjects covered. It is sold with the understanding that the publisher is not engaged in rendering legal or other professional advice. If legal advice or other professional assistance is required, the services of a competent professional person should be sought.

WEST'S COMMITMENT TO THE ENVIRONMENT

In 1906, West Publishing Company began recycling materials left over from the production of books. This began a tradition of efficient and responsible use of resources. Today, 100 percent of our legal bound volumes are printed on acid-free, recycled paper consisting of 50 percent new paper pulp and 50 percent paper that has undergone a de-inking process. We also use vegetable-based inks to print all of our books. West recycles nearly 27,700,000 pounds of scrap paper annually—the equivalent of 229,300 trees. Since the 1960s, West has devised ways to capture and recycle waste inks, solvents, oils, and vapors created in the printing process. We also recycle plastics of all kinds, wood, glass, corrugated cardboard, and batteries, and have eliminated the use of polystyrene book packaging. We at West are proud of the longevity and the scope of our commitment to the environment.

West pocket parts and advance sheets are printed on recyclable paper and can be collected and recycled with newspapers. Staples do not have to be removed. Bound volumes can be recycled after removing the cover.

Production, printing, and binding by West Group.

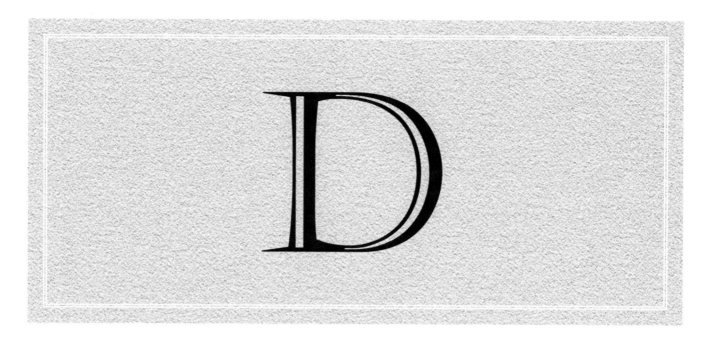

DALLAS, ALEXANDER JAMES

Alexander James Dallas achieved prominence as a jurist, statesman, and author. Dallas was born June 21, 1759, in Jamaica, British West Indies. He relocated to the United States, becoming a citizen in 1783.

In 1785, Dallas was admitted to the Pennsylvania bar and began his judicial career as counselor of the Pennsylvania Supreme Court. Six years later he acted as secretary of the Commonwealth of Pennsylvania. He also performed editorial duties on the first series of the U.S. Supreme Court Reports and served as U.S. district attorney from 1801 to 1814, before entering the federal government system.

Dallas became secretary of the treasury in 1814 and remained in the cabinet of President JAMES MADISON for two years. He gained recognition during his tenure for his policies advocating protective TARIFFS, public credit, and the formation of the Second BANK OF THE UNITED STATES. His programs were responsible for restoring the United States to a strong financial position after several years of depression. In addition to these duties, he served concurrently as acting secretary of war from 1815 to 1816.

BIOGRAPHY

Alexander James Dallas

"OVER THEIR REPRESENTATIVES THE PEOPLE HAVE A COMPLETE CONTROL, AND IF ONE SET TRANSGRESS THEY CAN APPOINT ANOTHER SET, WHO CAN RESCIND AND ANNUL ALL PREVIOUS BAD LAWS."

As an author, Dallas wrote many noteworthy publications, including *Features of Mr. Jay's Treaty* (1795); *Laws of the Commonwealth of Pennsylvania*, four volumes (1793 to 1801); *Reports of Cases Ruled and Adjudged in the Several Courts of the United States and Pennsylvania*, four volumes (1790 to 1807); and *Treasury Reports: An Exposition of the Causes and Character of the War* (1815).

Dallas died January 16, 1817, in Trenton, New Jersey.

DALLAS, GEORGE MIFFLIN

George Mifflin Dallas was born July 10, 1792 to statesman ALEXANDER JAMES DALLAS. He graduated from Princeton University in 1810 and was admitted to the bar three years later.

In 1813, statesman Albert Gallatin was dispatched to Russia for the purpose of securing Russian aid in negotiating an end to the War of 1812 between the United States and Great Britain. Dallas performed the duties of secretary to Gallatin and was commissioned in 1814 by the American delegates at the Ghent Peace Conference to relay the terms of peace to the British.

Dallas returned to Philadelphia and served as

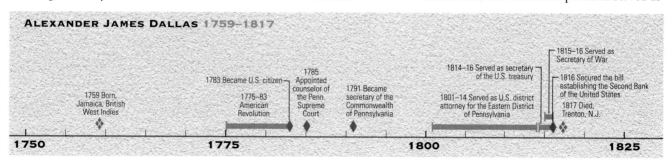

ALEXANDER JAMES DALLAS 1759–1817

1759 Born, Jamaica, British West Indies

1775–83 American Revolution

1783 Became U.S. citizen

1785 Appointed counselor of the Penn. Supreme Court

1791 Became secretary of the Commonwealth of Pennsylvania

1801–14 Served as U.S. district attorney for the Eastern District of Pennsylvania

1814–16 Served as secretary of the U.S. treasury

1815–16 Served as Secretary of War

1816 Secured the bill establishing the Second Bank of the United States

1817 Died, Trenton, N.J.

1750   1775   1800   1825

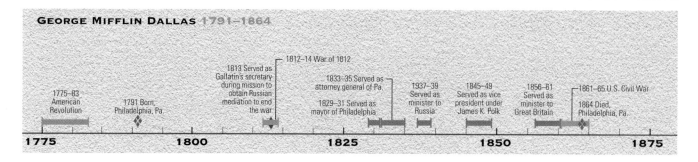

1812–14 War of 1812

1813 Served as Gallatin's secretary during mission to obtain Russian mediation to end the war

1833–35 Served as attorney general of Pa.

1775–83 American Revolution

1791 Born, Philadelphia, Pa.

1829–31 Served as mayor of Philadelphia

1937–39 Served as minister to Russia

1845–49 Served as vice president under James K. Polk

1856–61 Served as minister to Great Britain

1861–65 U.S. Civil War

1864 Died, Philadelphia, Pa.

1775   1800   1825   1850   1875

deputy attorney general before becoming mayor in 1829 for a three-year period. He also acted as U.S. district attorney, and in 1831, he entered the federal government.

Dallas filled a vacancy in the U.S. Senate and represented Pennsylvania until 1833; in that same year, he also performed the duties of attorney general of Pennsylvania and continued in this capacity until 1835.

In 1837, Dallas again acted as a diplomat, serving as emissary to Russia. Eight years later, he was elected as U.S. vice president during the administration of JAMES K. POLK. His term lasted until 1849, and in 1856, he returned to foreign service, acting as minister to Great Britain until 1861. During his tenure Dallas was instrumental in the negotiations that resulted in the formation of the Dallas-Clarendon Convention of 1856, for the purpose of arbitrating disputes concerning Central America between the United States and Great Britain.

Dallas died December 31, 1864, in Philadelphia, Pennsylvania.

DAMAGES 📖 Monetary compensation that is awarded by a court in a CIVIL ACTION to an individual who has been injured through the wrongful conduct of another party. 📖

Damages attempt to measure in financial terms the extent of harm a plaintiff has suffered because of a defendant's actions. Damages are distinguishable from COSTS, which are the expenses incurred as a result of bringing a lawsuit and which the court may order the losing party to pay. Damages also differ from the VERDICT, which is the final decision issued by a jury.

The purpose of damages is to restore an injured party to the position the party was in before being harmed. As a result, damages are generally regarded as remedial rather than preventive or punitive. However, PUNITIVE DAMAGES may be awarded for particular types of wrongful conduct. Before an individual can recover damages, the injury suffered must be one recognized by law as warranting redress and must have actually been sustained by the individual.

Three major categories of damages are recognized: compensatory, which are intended to

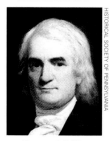

HISTORICAL SOCIETY OF PENNSYLVANIA

George Mifflin Dallas

restore what a plaintiff has lost as a result of a defendant's wrongful conduct; nominal, which consist of a small sum awarded to a plaintiff who has suffered no substantial loss or injury but has nevertheless experienced an invasion of rights; and punitive, which are awarded not to compensate a plaintiff for injury suffered but to penalize a defendant for particularly egregious, wrongful conduct. In specific situations, two other forms of damages may be awarded: treble and liquidated.

Compensatory Damages With respect to COMPENSATORY DAMAGES, a defendant is liable to a plaintiff for all the natural and direct consequences of the defendant's wrongful act. Remote consequences of a defendant's act or omission cannot form the basis for an award of compensatory damages.

CONSEQUENTIAL DAMAGES, a type of compensatory damages, may be awarded where the loss suffered by a plaintiff is not caused directly or immediately by the wrongful conduct of a defendant, but instead results from the defendant's act. For example, if the defendant carried a ladder and negligently walked into the plaintiff, a model, injuring the plaintiff's face, the plaintiff could recover for the loss of income resulting from the injury. These consequential damages are based on the resulting harm to the plaintiff's career. They are not based on the injury itself, which was the direct result of the defendant's conduct.

The measure of compensatory damages must be real and TANGIBLE, although it can be difficult to fix the amount with certainty, especially in cases involving claims such as pain and suffering or emotional distress. In assessing the amount of compensatory damages to be awarded, a trier of fact (the JURY or, if no jury exists, the judge) must exercise good judgment and common sense, based on general experience and knowledge of the economic and social affairs of life. Within these broad guidelines, the jury or judge has wide discretion to award damages in whatever amount is deemed appropriate, so long as the amount is supported by the EVIDENCE in the case.

A plaintiff can recover for a number of different injuries suffered as a result of another person's wrongful conduct. The plaintiff can recover for a physical impairment if it results directly from a harm caused by the defendant. The jury, in determining damages, considers the present as well as long-range effects of the disease or injury on the physical well-being of the plaintiff, who must demonstrate the disability with reasonable certainty.

Compensatory damages can be awarded for mental impairment, such as a loss of memory or a reduction in intellectual capacity suffered as a result of a defendant's wrongful conduct.

A plaintiff may recover compensatory damages for both present and future physical pain and suffering. Compensation for future pain is permitted when there is a reasonable likelihood that the plaintiff will experience it; the plaintiff is not permitted to recover for future pain and suffering that is speculative. The jury has broad discretion to award damages for pain and suffering, and its judgment will be overturned only if it appears that the jury abused its discretion in reaching the award.

Mental pain and suffering can be considered in assessing compensatory damages. Included in mental pain and suffering are fright, nervousness, grief, emotional trauma, anxiety, humiliation, and indignity. Historically, a plaintiff could not recover damages for mental pain and suffering without an accompanying physical injury; today, most JURISDICTIONS have modified this rule, allowing recovery for mental anguish alone where the act precipitating the anguish was WILLFUL or intentional or done with extreme carelessness or recklessness. Ordinarily, mental distress brought on by sympathy for the injury of another will not warrant an award of damages, although some jurisdictions may allow recovery if the injury was caused by the willful or MALICIOUS conduct of the defendant. For instance, if an individual wrongfully and intentionally injures a child in the presence of the child's mother, and as a result, the mother suffers psychological trauma, the defendant can be liable for the mother's mental suffering. In some jurisdictions, a bystander can recover damages for mental distress caused by observing an event in which another negligently, but not intentionally, causes harm to a family member.

Compensatory damages of a more economic nature may also be recovered by an injured party. A plaintiff may recover for loss of earnings resulting from an injury. The measure of lost earnings is the amount of money that the plaintiff might reasonably have earned by work-

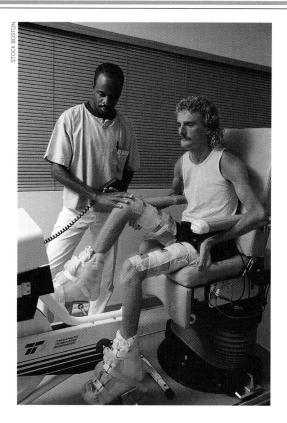

Compensatory damages may be due to this man to pay for physical therapy if he suffered an injury because of the negligence of another.

ing in her or his profession during the time the plaintiff was incapacitated because of the injury. In the case of a permanent disability, this amount can be determined by calculating the earnings the injured party actually lost and multiplying that figure out to the age of retirement—with adjustments. If the amount of earnings actually lost cannot be determined with certainty, as in the case of a salesperson paid by commission, the plaintiff's average earnings or general qualities and qualifications for the occupation in which she or he has been employed are considered. Evidence of past earnings can also be used to determine loss of future earnings. As a general rule, lost earnings that are speculative are not recoverable, although each case must be examined individually to determine if damages can be established with reasonable certainty. For example, a plaintiff who bought a restaurant for the first time immediately before suffering an injury could not recover damages for the profits he might have made running it, because such profits would be speculative. A plaintiff unable to accept a promotion to another job because of an injury would stand a better chance of recovering damages for loss of earnings, because the amount lost could be established with more certainty.

Individuals injured by the wrongful conduct of another may also recover damages for impairment of earning capacity, so long as that impairment is a direct and foreseeable consequence of a disabling injury of a permanent or lingering nature. The amount of damages is determined by calculating the difference between the amount of money the injured person had the capacity to earn prior to the injury and the amount he or she is capable of earning after the injury, in view of his or her life expectancy.

Loss of profits is yet another element of compensatory damages, allowing an individual to recover if such a loss can be established with sufficient certainty and is a direct and probable result of the defendant's wrongful actions. Expected profits that are uncertain or are contingent upon fluctuating conditions would not be recoverable, nor would they be awarded if no evidence existed from which they could be reasonably determined.

A plaintiff can recover all reasonable and necessary expenses brought about by an injury caused by the wrongful acts of a defendant. In a CONTRACT action, for example, the party who has been injured by another's breach can recover compensatory damages that include the reasonable expenses that result from reliance on the CONTRACT, such as the cost of transporting perishable goods wrongfully refused by the other contracting party. In other actions, expenses awarded as part of compensatory damages may include medical, nursing, and prescription drug costs; the costs of future medical treatment, if necessary; or the costs of restoring a damaged vehicle and of renting another vehicle while repairs are performed.

Interest can be awarded to compensate an injured party for money wrongfully withheld from her or him, as where an individual defaults on an obligation to pay money owed under a contract. Interest is ordinarily awarded from the date of DEFAULT, which is set by the time stated in the contract for payment; the date a demand for payment is made; or the date the lawsuit alleging the breach of the contract is initiated.

Nominal Damages   NOMINAL DAMAGES are generally recoverable by a plaintiff who successfully establishes that he or she has suffered an injury caused by the wrongful conduct of a defendant, but cannot offer proof of a loss that can be compensated. For example, an injured plaintiff who proves that a defendant's actions caused the injury but fails to submit medical records to show the extent of the injury may be awarded only nominal damages. The amount awarded is generally a small, symbolic sum, such as one dollar, although in some jurisdictions, it may equal the costs of bringing the lawsuit.

Punitive Damages   Punitive damages, also known as exemplary damages, can be awarded to a plaintiff in addition to compensatory damages where a defendant's conduct is particularly willful, wanton, malicious, vindictive, or oppressive. Punitive damages are awarded not as compensation, but to punish the wrongdoer and to act as a deterrent to others who might engage in similar conduct.

The amount of punitive damages to be awarded lies within the discretion of the trier of fact, which must consider the nature of the wrongdoer's behavior, the extent of the plaintiff's loss or injury, and the degree to which the defendant's conduct is repugnant to a societal sense of justice and decency. An award of punitive damages will usually not be disturbed on the ground that it is excessive, unless it can be shown that the jury or judge was influenced by PREJUDICE, BIAS, passion, partiality, or corruption.

In the late twentieth century, the constitutionality of punitive damages has been considered in several U.S. Supreme Court decisions. In 1989, the Court held that large punitive damages awards did not violate the EIGHTH AMENDMENT prohibition against the imposition of excessive FINES (*Browning-Ferris Industries of Vermont v. Kelco Disposal*, 492 U.S. 257, 109 S. Ct. 2909, 106 L. Ed. 2d 219). Later, in *Pacific Mutual Life Insurance Co. v. Haslip*, 499 U.S. 1, 111 S. Ct. 1032, 113 L. Ed. 2d 1 (1991), the Court held that unlimited jury discretion in awarding punitive damages is not "so inherently unfair" as to be unconstitutional under the Due Process Clause of the FOURTEENTH AMENDMENT to the U.S. Constitution. And in *TXO Production Corp. v. Alliance Resources Corp.*, 509 U.S. 443, 113 S. Ct. 2711, 125 L. Ed. 2d 366 (1993), the Court ruled that a punitive damages award that was 526 times the compensatory award did not violate DUE PROCESS. Both *Haslip* and *TXO Production* disappointed observers who hoped that the Court would place limits on large and increasingly common punitive damages awards. In a 1994 decision, the Court did strike down an amendment to the Oregon Constitution that prohibited JUDICIAL REVIEW of punitive damages awards, on the ground that it violated due process (*Honda Motor Co. v. Oberg*, 512 U.S. 415, 114 S. Ct. 2331, 129 L. Ed. 2d 336).

In a jury proceeding, although the amount of damages to be awarded is an issue for the jury to decide, the court may review the award. If the court determines that the verdict is excessive in view of the particular circumstances of the case, it can order REMITTITUR, which is a procedural process in which the jury verdict is reduced. The opposite process, known as ADDI-TUR, occurs when the court deems the jury's award of damages to be inadequate and orders the defendant to pay a greater sum. Both *remit-titur* and *additur* are employed at the discretion of the trial judge, and are designed to remedy a blatantly inaccurate damages award by the jury without the necessity of a new trial or an APPEAL.

Treble Damages In some situations, where provided by statute, treble damages may be awarded. In such situations, a statute will authorize a judge to multiply by three the amount of monetary damages awarded by a jury and to order that a plaintiff be paid the tripled amount. The Clayton Anti-Trust Act of 1914 (15 U.S.C.A. § 12 et seq.), for example, directs that TREBLE DAMAGES be awarded for violations of federal ANTITRUST LAWS.

Liquidated Damages LIQUIDATED DAM-AGES constitute compensation agreed upon by the parties entering into a contract, to be paid by a party who breaches the contract to a nonbreaching party. Liquidated damages may be used when it would be difficult to prove the actual harm or loss caused by a breach. The amount of liquidated damages must represent a reasonable estimate of the actual damages a breach would cause. A contract term fixing unreasonably large or disproportionate liqui-dated damages may be VOID because it consti-tutes a PENALTY, or punishment for default. Furthermore, if it appears that the parties have made no attempt to calculate the amount of actual damages that might be sustained in the event of a breach, a liquidated damages provi-sion will be deemed unenforceable. In deter-mining whether a particular contract provision constitutes liquidated damages or an unenforce-able penalty, a court will look to the intention of the parties, even if the terms *liquidated dam-ages* and *penalty* are specifically used and defined in the contract.

DAMNUM [*Latin, Damage.*] The loss or reduction in the value of property, life, or

BIOGRAPHY

Richard Henry Dana

"IN ORDER THAT JUSTICE MAY BE DONE TO THE WEAKEST, AND THAT IN ANY HOUR OF FRENZY OR MISTAKE, WE MAY NOT TOUCH THE HAIR OF [HIS] HEAD, WE WILL GIVE HIM A TRIBUNAL WHICH SHALL BE INDEPENDENT OF THE FLUCTUATIONS OF OUR OPINIONS OR PASSIONS."

health of an individual as a consequence of FRAUD, carelessness, or ACCIDENT.

The phrase *ad damnum*, "to the damage," is the name of a clause in a COMPLAINT that states the damages for which the individual seeks judicial relief.

DANA, RICHARD HENRY Richard Henry Dana achieved prominence as a lawyer and author, and for his knowledge of the sea.

Dana was born August 1, 1815, in Cam-bridge, Massachusetts. A student at Harvard University, he interrupted his studies in 1834 and spent two years as a sailor. In 1836, he returned to Harvard, graduating in 1837. He subsequently received an honorary doctor of laws degree in 1866.

Before entering a legal career Dana taught elocution at Harvard from 1839 to 1840. He was admitted to the bar in 1840 and established a successful legal practice, demonstrating his expertise in admiralty cases.

Dana entered politics in 1848 as an organizer of the Free-Soil party, which opposed the prin-ciples of slavery. He attended the party's conven-tion of that same year, held in Buffalo, New York.

In 1861, Dana performed the duties of U.S. attorney for the district of Massachusetts, serv-ing in this capacity until 1866. From 1867 to 1868, he participated in the TREASON trial against confederate President Jefferson Davis, acting as attorney for the United States. During 1866 and 1868, he also returned to Harvard as a lecturer at the law school. In 1877, Dana was selected to represent the United States as senior counsel at the fisheries commission held at Halifax, Nova Scotia.

Dana is regarded as an eminent writer, as is evidenced by the enduring popularity of *Two Years Before the Mast*, published in 1840. In this book, Dana described his experiences as a sailor, recounting his voyage from Boston around Cape Horn to California from 1834 to 1836. He also authored *The Seaman's Friend* (1841) and *To Cuba and Back* (1859), and he edited *Wheaton's Elements of International Law* (1866).

He died January 6, 1882, in Rome, Italy.

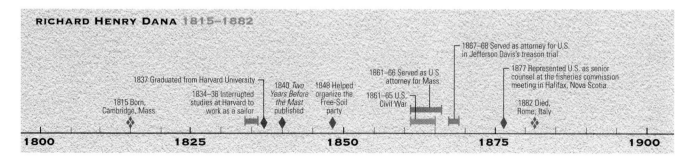

DANELAGE A system of law introduced into England as a result of its invasion and conquest by the Danes during the eighth and ninth centuries, which occurred primarily in some of the midland counties and on the eastern coast.

Danelage provided basic values and customs to which the later Norman conquerors of England added their customs to provide the foundation of English law.

DANGEROUS INSTRUMENTALITY

Any article that is inherently hazardous or has the potential for harming people through its careless use.

Examples of a dangerous instrumentality include EXPLOSIVES and electrically charged wires. Statutes and case law must be consulted to determine what items are regarded as dangerous instrumentalities.

When dealing with dangerous instrumentalities, some JURISDICTIONS require that due CARE be exercised to prevent harm to those who are reasonably expected to be in proximity with them. Others impose STRICT LIABILITY for injuries and losses caused by them.

DANIEL, PETER VIVIAN

Peter Vivian Daniel served as an associate justice of the U.S. Supreme Court from 1841 to 1860. A prominent lawyer and Democratic politician from Virginia, Daniel adhered to a Jeffersonian political philosophy that favored states' rights and disfavored large economic institutions. A minor figure in the history of the Supreme Court, Daniel joined the majority in *Dred Scott v. Sandford*, 60 U.S. (19 How.) 393, 15 L. Ed. 691 (1857), which held that freed black slaves could not be citizens under the Constitution because they had originally been property, not citizens.

Daniel was born in Stafford County, Virginia, on April 24, 1784. He came from a wealthy family and was educated at Princeton University, graduating in 1805. He read the law in the Richmond offices of Edmund Randolph, who helped draft the Constitution. He was admitted to the Virginia bar in 1808.

Although Daniel maintained a law practice, his focus was on politics and government. He

"THE MERE GRANT OF POWER TO THE [FEDERAL] GOVERNMENT CANNOT . . . BE CONSTRUED TO BE AN ABSOLUTE PROHIBITION TO THE EXERCISE OF ANY POWER OVER THE SAME SUBJECT BY THE STATES."

BIOGRAPHY

Peter Vivian Daniel

was elected to the Virginia House of Delegates in 1809. In 1812 he was appointed by the house to serve on the privy council, which acted as an advisory board for the state governor. Daniel remained on the council for twenty-three years, serving as lieutenant governor for much of his term.

Daniel was active in the Democratic party and was a strong supporter of President ANDREW JACKSON. In 1836 Jackson appointed Daniel as a judge to the U.S. District Court for Eastern Virginia. Five years later President MARTIN VAN BUREN appointed Daniel to the U.S. Supreme Court. This move sparked controversy because it occurred at the end of Van Buren's term of office. The Whig party's presidential candidate, WILLIAM HENRY HARRISON, was elected president. Whigs in Congress tried to block the appointment of Daniel so Harrison could choose a justice. Daniel was confirmed by the Senate on March 3, 1841, in the last moments of the Van Buren administration.

Throughout his years on the Supreme Court, Daniel maintained his commitment to Jeffersonian government. THOMAS JEFFERSON's view of republican government valued an agricultural economy and a limited role for government. Daniel also adopted the Jacksonian variation, which included hostility to banks, corporations, and the federal government. A southerner and a believer in STATES' RIGHTS, he supported the right of states to maintain the institution of SLAVERY.

Daniel was known more for his dissents than for crafting majority opinions. He did, however, join the majority in the *Dred Scott* case. Dred Scott was a slave owned by an army surgeon, John Emerson, who resided in Missouri. In 1836 Emerson took Scott to Fort Snelling, in what is now Minnesota but was then a territory where slavery had been expressly forbidden by the MISSOURI COMPROMISE legislation of 1820. In 1846 Scott sued for his freedom in Missouri state court, arguing that his residence in a free territory released him from slavery. The Missouri Supreme Court rejected his argument, and Scott appealed to the U.S. Supreme Court.

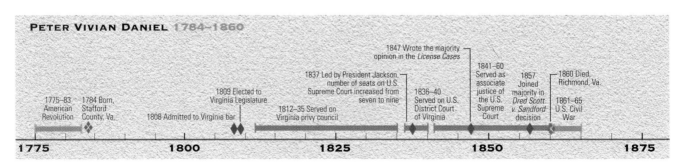

PETER VIVIAN DANIEL 1784–1860

1775–83 American Revolution

1784 Born, Stafford County, Va.

1808 Admitted to Virginia bar

1809 Elected to Virginia Legislature

1812–35 Served on Virginia privy council

1837 Led by President Jackson, number of seats on U.S. Supreme Court increased from seven to nine

1836–40 Served on U.S. District Court of Virginia

1847 Wrote the majority opinion in the *License Cases*

1841–60 Served as associate justice of the U.S. Supreme Court

1857 Joined majority in *Dred Scott v. Sandford* decision

1860 Died, Richmond, Va.

1861–65 U.S. Civil War

1775 1800 1825 1850 1875

The Court heard arguments on *Dred Scott* in 1855 and 1856. A key issue was whether African Americans could be CITIZENS of the United States, even if they were not slaves. Daniel was a loyal southerner, holding in his concurring opinion that African Americans who had been freed since the enactment of the Constitution could never be citizens. The Framers had not contemplated the prospect of granting citizenship to persons who were legally recognized as property when the Constitution was drafted.

During his term on the Supreme Court, Daniel's adherence to his principles led him to drift further from the mainstream. As the national economy expanded, and with it both big business and the federal government, Daniel's Jeffersonian beliefs lost relevance.

Daniel died May 31, 1860, in Richmond, Virginia.

See also DRED SCOTT V. SANDFORD.

DARROW, CLARENCE   Lawyer and social reformer Clarence Darrow was the most famous and controversial defense attorney of the early twentieth century. He won unprecedented fame in momentous courtroom battles where he championed the causes of labor, liberal social thought, and the use of scientific criminology. His aggressive legal tactics as well as his outspoken denunciations of industrial capitalism, political corruption, and popular religion aroused animosities throughout his life. But in the end, his compassion for oppressed persons as well as his winsome personality compelled friends and foes alike to honor his unparalleled legal career as attorney for the damned.

Darrow was the master of the courtroom drama. One striking and effective aspect of his legal style was his physical appearance in the courtroom. He wore rumpled suits—often bared to shirtsleeves and suspenders—and let his tousled hair hang into his face. He had a halting walk and slouching stance, and his habits of smoking long cigars slowly during the proceedings and even reading and writing during the prosecution's presentation were endlessly arresting for juries and distracting for opponents.

BIOGRAPHY

Clarence Darrow

Darrow was born poor, on April 18, 1857, near Kinsman, Ohio. His mother died when he was fourteen, and his father, an embittered seminary student–turned–undertaker, bore the stigma of the village atheist in an intensely religious rural community. As a child, Darrow hated formal schooling, but with his father's encouragement, he read widely from the extensive family library to educate himself. As his father's intellectual companion, Darrow grew to love reading, to hate being poor, and to willingly embrace unpopular causes. Once, Darrow's father went to observe a public hanging to see what it was like, but left before the moment of execution and reported to Darrow how he felt a terrible shame and guilt for being any part of such a "barbaric practice." This report was not lost on Darrow, who would become a fierce public opponent of the popular practice of CAPITAL PUNISHMENT, defending fifty murderers in his legal career and losing only one such case.

Darrow's entrance into the practice of law was strained by poverty. He left his studies at Allegheny College after one year for lack of money. After three years teaching in a rural one-room schoolhouse and one year at the Michigan University law school, where he again withdrew for lack of tuition, Darrow gained an apprenticeship with a law firm in Youngstown, Ohio. There, he read the law and passed the bar exam in 1878 at the age of twenty-one. Returning home, he married his childhood sweetheart, Jessie Ohl, began his own practice in the rural Ohio towns of Andover and Ashtabula, and fathered his only child, a son. In search of a better income for his family and eager for opportunity, Darrow accepted an invitation from his brother Everett Darrow to move to Chicago—then the commercial and cultural center of the Midwest—in 1887.

Darrow's path from the country to the city was well-worn by millions of others at the end of the nineteenth century. The lure of jobs and opportunities following the Civil War combined with mass migrations from Europe added 31 million residents to U.S. cities between 1860

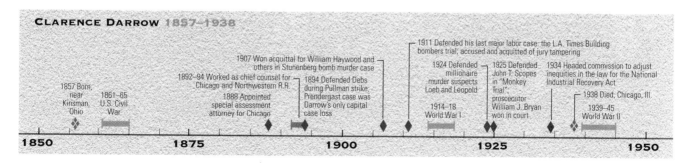

CLARENCE DARROW 1857–1938

1857 Born, near Kinsman, Ohio

1861–65 U.S. Civil War

1892–94 Worked as chief counsel for Chicago and Northwestern R.R.

1888 Appointed special assessment attorney for Chicago

1894 Defended Debs during Pullman strike; Prendergast case was Darrow's only capital case loss

1907 Won acquittal for William Haywood and others in Stuhenberg bomb murder case

1911 Defended his last major labor case: the L.A. Times Building bombers trial; accused and acquitted of jury tampering

1924 Defended millionaire murder suspects Loeb and Leopold

1914–18 World War I

1925 Defended John T. Scopes in "Monkey Trial"; prosecutor William J. Bryan won in court

1934 Headed commission to adjust inequities in the law for the National Industrial Recovery Act

1938 Died; Chicago, Ill.

1939–45 World War II

1850   1875   1900   1925   1950

and 1930. Chicago, which barely existed in 1830, had by 1900 grown to 3 million inhabitants. Along with other large U.S. cities such as New York and Boston, Chicago was unprepared for this overwhelming influx of urban immigrants. The result was poverty, crime, and corruption spawning human misery on a grand scale.

When Darrow moved his hopes and his family to Chicago, the city was in the midst of both a population and an industrial boom. With its being the railroad center of the nation, the meatpacking, lumber, steel, and agricultural industries were rapidly expanding. A devastating fire in 1871 had leveled much of the city and helped inspire new building programs and fresh commercial initiatives. The city had also become a magnet for social reformers, artists, and intellectuals, including JANE ADDAMS, Lincoln Steffens, Sinclair Lewis, Edgar Lee Masters, and Theodore Dreiser, who viewed the human suffering of the great city with outrage.

Darrow found Chicago both fascinating and troubling. While he saw opportunity for himself to advance, he was moved by the evident suffering of laboring families, poor people, and those who were imprisoned. His passion for the lower class only increased as he witnessed the economic contrasts of industry and labor. Throughout the city, industrial tycoons were striking it rich off the backs of laborers—often uneducated and poor—who earned poverty wages under hazardous conditions. Similarly, the prisons were filled with poor and broken people who had little means of defending themselves.

Having read the prison reform writings of Judge John P. Altgeld of Illinois, Darrow shortly introduced himself to this social reformer who would one day become governor. He began a mentorship in the law and politics of reform under Altgeld that would last until Altgeld's death. When Darrow became outraged by the heavy sentences laid upon four anarchist defendants in the Haymarket Square bombing of 1887, Altgeld urged him to join the alliance for their AMNESTY. In turn, Darrow later successfully implored Altgeld as governor to commute their sentences.

In 1888, after being impressed by Darrow's public speaking ability, Mayor DeWitt Cregier, of Chicago, offered him an appointment as a special assessment attorney. Within a year, Darrow rose to chief corporation counsel—becoming the head of the legal department for the entire city of Chicago at age thirty-three. From this vantage, he observed firsthand the plight of the city's working class in industries where labor had little power to organize and government had little power to regulate.

After four years, with his city appointment about to be terminated, Darrow accepted an offer to become chief counsel for the Chicago and Northwestern Railway (CNR), which he had recently defeated in court. He imposed one condition: that he be allowed to continue his outside legal assistance work as long as it did not conflict with his loyalty to the company. Within two years, a decisive conflict was staring Darrow in the face: the Pullman STRIKE of 1894. This bitter dispute pitted the workers of the newly formed American Railway Union (ARU) against the powerful Pullman Company and its railroad industry allies. The conflict was so violent that President GROVER CLEVELAND sent in Army troops to protect the trains.

Darrow resigned his corporate position with CNR despite enticing offers of higher pay. Instead, he took the case of the ARU's national leader Eugene V. Debs, who was charged with violating a strike INJUNCTION. Darrow's defense strategy was not to quibble about the violation of an injunction order but to expose the working conditions imposed upon railroad workers by the industry—in this case, the enormously wealthy and ruthless Pullman Company. To do this, Darrow boldly subpoenaed company president George M. Pullman to testify, but the tycoon went into hiding rather than appear. So, after describing the abysmal working conditions of Pullman's railroad workers and their families, he argued fervently that people had a right to strike for just causes, and that inadequate wages and unsafe working conditions were such causes.

Darrow defended Debs in two trials—taking an appeal to the U.S. Supreme Court before finally losing and seeing his client sentenced to six months in prison. In this defense of the underdog against the powerful, Darrow had found his calling. In just six years, Darrow had moved from positions of political power and financial security to that of gladiator in the nation's emerging class struggle.

In 1894 Darrow handled his first criminal case in Chicago, defending Eugene Prendergast. Prendergast was a mentally deranged drifter who had murdered Mayor Carter H. Harrison, Sr., of Chicago, then walked to a police station and confessed to the crime. Darrow attempted an INSANITY defense and failed, and Prendergast was executed. Of the fifty murder defendants Darrow represented in his lifetime, this was the first and last one he lost to execution.

In 1897 Darrow divorced his wife of seventeen years. In 1903 he married Ruby Hamerstrom, a Chicago newspaper journalist. This second marriage for Darrow lasted his lifetime, but produced no children.

In 1907 the former governor of Idaho Frank Stuenenberg was killed by a booby trap bomb on his front gate. Stuenenberg had been a powerful supporter of the mining industry. WILLIAM ("Big Bill") HAYWOOD, leader of the Western Federation of Miners union, and several others were abducted by PINKERTON AGENTS from other states and brought to Boise, where they were charged with CONSPIRACY to murder. The miners' union hired Darrow for the defense, and he traveled with Ruby to Idaho and assembled a defense team.

The prominence of the individuals involved and the violent nature of the crime drew national attention to the trial. Darrow was able to crack the government's case with painstaking cross-examination of its star witness, the self-confessed perpetrator of the crime, Harry Orchard. Darrow exposed Orchard to be a man bent on personal revenge who had implicated the labor leaders only after being prompted to do so by the prosecutors. Darrow's moving summation in defense of the labor movement—"for the poor, for the weak, for the weary—who, in darkness and despair, have borne the labors of the human race"—drew tears in the courtroom, and Haywood and the others were acquitted.

Thanks to Darrow, labor was again vindicated over opponents in government and industry. But the cost to Darrow was considerable. After the trial, he was broke and in poor health. His legal fees from the union had already been spent, and he suffered from an acute ear infection. When he returned to Chicago, the financial crash of 1907 had wiped out all his savings, and he started back into his law practice.

Darrow reluctantly entered the limelight again in 1911 when he agreed to defend the accused in what newspapers called the crime of the century. At one o'clock in the morning on October 10, 1910, Los Angeles was rocked by two explosions that blew apart the Los Angeles Times Building with over one hundred people inside. Twenty-one people were killed and forty injured in the concussion and the fire that followed. The *Times*'s prominent and antiunion editor, Harrison Gray Otis, managed to get out an edition with the headline "Unionist Bombs Wreck Times."

Under pressure from Otis, the mayor of Los Angeles hired a private detective agency to investigate and abduct labor movement suspects living in Indiana and Michigan and return them to Los Angeles to stand trial. Labor movement members appealed to Darrow, but he resisted, still drained and wary from the Haywood defense. Renowned labor leader Samuel Gompers, then president of the American Federation of Labor (AFL), visited Darrow in Chicago and appealed to him to defend labor, the innocent, and due process. Gompers promised in return that a nationwide AFL union war chest would generously compensate his services. Darrow agreed.

By the time Darrow arrived in Los Angeles, the three defendants had already confessed to the crime. Darrow pleaded them guilty in a plea bargain to at least save them from execution. The shock and outrage from labor supporters were devastating. Darrow was jeered by a waiting crowd and shunned by Gompers and other labor leaders. The promised fees evaporated.

Within days, Darrow was charged with attempting to bribe the jury and was brought to trial. Away from home, without funds or allies to make a strong defense, Darrow fell into a depression that lasted through most of the proceedings. But in the CLOSING ARGUMENTS, he arose to defend himself to the jury with such force and poignancy that he again brought the jury, the audience, the press, and even the judge to tears. When the VERDICT came, and Darrow was acquitted, the courtroom burst into sustained cheers and embraces. Darrow never again took a major labor case.

Darrow continued to take the unpopular route in his court cases. When the United States entered World War I despite a strong pacifist movement, Darrow managed to offend people on both sides of the war issue by personally supporting the war while professionally defending pacifists who refused to serve.

Darrow's choice of defense in a notorious murder case further outraged popular sentiments. In 1924 two Chicago adolescents from millionaire families—Richard Loeb, age eighteen, and Nathan Leopold, Jr., age nineteen—decided to commit a murder for the thrill of it. Loeb had graduated with honors from the University of Michigan and was on his way to Harvard Law School. Leopold was a Phi Beta Kappa already attending law school. They thought they were clever enough that they would not get caught. Luring a fourteen-year-old friend named Bobby Franks into their car, Loeb killed Franks with a chisel. The two then stuffed his body into the trunk before sending ransom notes to the boy's millionaire family. Two days after the boys had been caught, had been charged, and had confessed, three members of the Loeb family came to Darrow's home

"I DO NOT CONSIDER IT AN INSULT, BUT RATHER A COMPLIMENT TO BE CALLED AN AGNOSTIC. I DO NOT PRETEND TO KNOW WHERE MANY IGNORANT MEN ARE SURE—THAT IS ALL AGNOSTICISM MEANS."

in the early morning before he had yet awakened and insisted on making their way to his bedside to beg him to take the case. As a friend of the family, and because of their desperation, Darrow accepted.

Hoping to save the boys from execution, Darrow had his clients plead guilty and then presented expert scientific testimony from fourteen psychiatrists and psychologists. These witnesses contended that the boys suffered from a mental illness that caused them to commit the crime. Loeb and Leopold received life sentences. This verdict was extremely unpopular with the public, for many had called for the death penalty for this unusually grisly murder. Darrow was attacked in the press and threatened in the mail, and the millionaire families who had begged him to save their children balked at paying the agreed-upon legal fees. Darrow, now age sixty-seven, spoke of retiring from legal work unless he could really "have some fun" doing it. The next year, he got his chance.

Intent on stemming the influence of Modernist thinking in the schools, in 1925, the Tennessee legislature passed a law making it illegal to teach anything that contradicted the account of the Creation portrayed in the Bible's book of Genesis. With the help of local citizens and the support of the AMERICAN CIVIL LIBERTIES UNION (ACLU), a twenty-four-year-old biology teacher in rural Dayton, a Tennessee native named John T. Scopes, challenged the law by teaching the evolutionary theories of Charles R. Darwin in his high school classroom. When Scopes was arrested and charged with violating the law, WILLIAM JENNINGS BRYAN, a well-known former representative from Nebraska and presidential candidate, offered his services for the prosecution. At Scopes's insistence, the ACLU recruited the most controversial defense attorney and atheist in the country, Darrow.

For nearly a century, European scholars in linguistics and geology, as well as in Darwin's biology, had contested certain beliefs about the Bible, which left many of the faithful anxious. The Fundamentalists in the Tennessee legislature had attempted one solution to this problem: forbid the teaching of anything in conflict with creationism in the public schools. Since Darrow passionately opposed this in principle and was no friend of religion, he happily took the case.

The trial drew enormous media attention in the form of international newspaper coverage and live nationwide radio broadcast. The popular Henry L. Mencken covered the story and joined other major newspaper reporters in calling it the Monkey Trial. Since the weather was hot and muggy, and the trial had drawn more than two thousand visitors, the judge moved the proceedings outside the courthouse onto a platform built for the occasion. Here, the two masters of law and rhetoric sparred before a stirred crowd and an international audience. The trial was ostensibly to determine whether Scopes had violated the law, which he clearly had purposely done. But the exchanges between Bryan and Darrow quickly revealed deeper issues, such as the constitutional guarantee of free speech and the struggle between Fundamentalist and Modernist interpretations of the Bible.

This time, Darrow's favorite strategies of elevating the crime to a context of higher issues and presenting expert scientific evidence did not work. The presiding judge repeatedly upheld objections to these defense tactics. So, knowing that the local folk were overwhelmingly Fundamentalist and saw Bryan as their champion, Darrow took a masterful gamble and put Bryan himself on the stand as a Bible expert for the defense. In a series of deft and probing questions about the Bible, Darrow managed to so befuddle the champion of Fundamentalism that the crowds were finally laughing with Darrow and at Bryan. To many observers, Bryan and his cause were humiliated.

Although the jury voted to convict, the judge imposed only a nominal fine of $100 on Scopes, who was immediately rehired by the school board. Five days later, after eating a characteristically heavy meal, Bryan died in his sleep. Many believed that the devastating cross-examination by Darrow and Bryan's failure to win a larger judgment against Scopes were the cause of Bryan's death. Darrow responded tersely, "No such thing—he died of a broken belly."

After the Scopes trial, Darrow became a public celebrity once again. He received many invitations to speak and to debate the issue of religion. As he had in the Pullman case, Darrow lost in the courts but seemingly won before a wider audience.

A year later, the NATIONAL ASSOCIATION FOR THE ADVANCEMENT OF COLORED PEOPLE asked Darrow to defend eleven blacks in Detroit who were being charged in the death of a single white during an ugly racial incident. Darrow again, at age sixty-nine, called upon his powerful defense skills to prove that none of the accused had fired the fatal bullet but that all were instead the target of racial prejudice. All charges were dismissed.

In 1934 President FRANKLIN D. ROOSEVELT appointed Darrow, at age seventy-seven, to head a commission to adjust inequities in the law for the NATIONAL INDUSTRIAL RECOVERY ACT, a program intended to relieve the Depression. Darrow's work proved successful when the Supreme Court declared the law unconstitutional, and the necessary revisions were made. The same year, Darrow was asked to chair the opening session of the American Inquiry Commission, a citizens' committee to study the darkening events in Germany. He emerged to tell Mayor Fiorello La Guardia, of New York, at lunch that "Herr Hitler is a very dangerous man and should be destroyed."

Darrow died in Chicago in 1938, at the age of eighty-one. He had asked his friend Judge William H. Holly to deliver his eulogy because, as Darrow put it, "he knows everything about me, and has the sense not to tell it." As Darrow's body lay in state in Chicago for two days, thousands from every sector of humanity lined up in a driving rain to say good-bye. The tributes to Darrow were bountiful. He was commended for his courage and compassion; his public service and his private practice; his support for labor, minority groups, poor people, and criminals; and, always, his defense of freedom. Although his popularity rose and fell during his lifetime, Darrow's memory has received the highest accolades. Popular and scholarly biographies as well as theater, cinema, and television dramatizations of his impassioned career and complex life have won for Darrow a legendary stature in U.S. law and history.

Despite wavering public opinion, fickle allies, and powerful opponents, he was an uncommonly skillful and courageous warrior for justice in the courts and in public life. The secret of his courage was revealed in a memorial comment by the eminent attorney JOSEPH N. WELCH: Darrow was "so brave and fearless that he never seemed to realize he was either."

CROSS-REFERENCES

Haymarket Riot; Labor Union; Leopold (Nathan) and Loeb (Richard); Scopes, John T.

DARTMOUTH COLLEGE CASE   See TRUSTEES OF DARTMOUTH COLLEGE V. WOODWARD.

Angela Yvonne Davis

DAVIS, ANGELA YVONNE   Angela Yvonne Davis, political activist, author, professor, and Communist party member, was an international symbol of the black liberation movement of the 1960s and 1970s.

Davis was born in Birmingham, Alabama, on January 26, 1944, the eldest of four children. Her family was relatively well-off among the blacks in the city. Her father and mother were teachers in the Birmingham school system, and her father later purchased and operated a service station.

When Davis was four years old, the family moved out of the Birmingham projects and bought a large wooden house in a nearby neighborhood. Other black families soon followed. Incensed white neighbors drew a dividing line between the white and black sections and began trying to drive the black families out by bombing their homes. The area soon was nicknamed Dynamite Hill. Davis's mother had in college been involved in antiracism movements that had brought her into contact with sympathetic whites. She and Davis's father tried to teach their daughter that this hostility between blacks and whites was not preordained.

All of Birmingham was segregated during Davis's childhood. She attended blacks-only schools and theaters and was relegated to the back of city buses and the back door of shops, which rankled her. On one occasion, as teenagers, Davis and her sister Fania entered a Birmingham shoe store and pretended to be non-English-speaking French visitors. After receiving deferential treatment by the salesmen and other customers, Davis announced in English that black people only had to pretend to be from another country to be treated like dignitaries.

Davis later wrote that although the black schools she attended were much poorer than the white schools in Birmingham, her studies of black historical and contemporary figures such as Frederick Douglass, Sojourner Truth, and Harriet Tubman helped her develop a strong positive identification with black history.

The CIVIL RIGHTS MOVEMENT was beginning to touch Birmingham at the time Davis entered

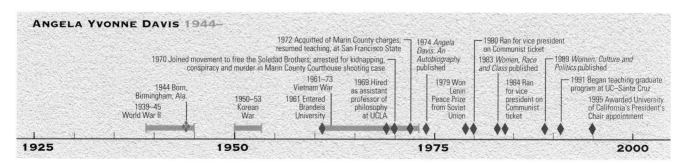

ANGELA YVONNE DAVIS 1944–

1925 — 1950 — 1975 — 2000

1939–45 World War II

1944 Born, Birmingham, Ala.

1950–53 Korean War

1961 Entered Brandeis University

1961–73 Vietnam War

1969 Hired as assistant professor of philosophy at UCLA

1970 Joined movement to free the Soledad Brothers; arrested for kidnapping, conspiracy and murder in Marin County Courthouse shooting case

1972 Acquitted of Marin County charges; resumed teaching, at San Francisco State

1974 *Angela Davis: An Autobiography* published

1979 Won Lenin Peace Prize from Soviet Union

1980 Ran for vice president on Communist ticket

1983 *Women, Race and Class* published

1984 Ran for vice president on Communist ticket

1989 *Women, Culture and Politics* published

1991 Began teaching graduate program at UC–Santa Cruz

1995 Awarded University of California's President's Chair appointment

high school. Her parents were members of the NATIONAL ASSOCIATION FOR THE ADVANCEMENT OF COLORED PEOPLE (NAACP). In her junior year of high school, Davis decided to leave what she considered to be the provincialism of Birmingham. She applied for an early entrance program at Fisk University, in Nashville, Tennessee, and an experimental program developed by the American Friends Service Committee (AFSC) through which black students from the South could attend integrated high schools in the North. Although Davis was admitted to Fisk—which she viewed as a stepping-stone to medical school, where she could pursue a childhood dream of becoming a pediatrician—she chose the AFSC program. At fifteen, she boarded a train for New York City. There, she lived with a white family headed by an Episcopalian minister who had been forced from his church after speaking out against Senator JOSEPH R. McCARTHY's anti-Communist witch-hunts. Davis attended Elisabeth Irwin High School, located on the edge of Greenwich Village. The school originally had been a public school experiment in progressive education; when funding was cut off, the teachers turned it into a private school. Here, Davis learned about socialism and avidly studied the *Communist Manifesto*. She also joined a Marxist-Leninist youth organization called Advance, which had ties to the Communist party.

In September 1961, Davis entered Brandeis University, in Waltham, Massachusetts, on a full scholarship. One of only three black first-year students, she felt alienated and alone. The following summer, eager to meet revolutionary young people from other countries, Davis attended a gathering of Communist youth from around the world in Helsinki. Here, she was particularly struck by the cultural presentations put on by the Cuban delegation. She also found that the U.S. Central Intelligence Agency had stationed agents and informers throughout the festival. Upon her return to the United States, Davis was met by an investigator from the Federal Bureau of Investigation (FBI), who questioned her about her participation in a Communist event.

Meeting people from around the world convinced Davis of the importance of tearing down cultural barriers like language, and she decided to major in French at Brandeis. She was accepted in the Hamilton College Junior Year in France Program, and studied contemporary French literature at the Sorbonne, in Paris. Upon her return to Brandeis, Davis, who had always had an interest in philosophy, studied with the German philosopher Herbert Marcuse. The following year, she received a scholarship to study philosophy in Frankfurt, where she focused on the works of the Germans IMMANUEL KANT, GEORG HEGEL, and Karl Marx.

During the two years Davis spent in Germany, the black liberation and black power movements were emerging in the United States. The BLACK PANTHER PARTY for Self-Defense had been formed in Oakland to protect the black community from police brutality. In the summer of 1967, Davis decided to return home to join these movements.

Back in Los Angeles, Davis worked with various academic and community organizations to build a coalition to address issues of concern to the black community. Among these groups was the Black Panther Political Party (unrelated to Huey Newton and Bobby Seale's Black Panther Party for Self-Defense). During this period, Davis was heavily criticized by black male activists for doing what they considered to be men's work. Women should not assume leadership roles, they claimed, but should educate children and should support men so that they could direct the struggle for black liberation. Davis was to encounter this attitude in many of her political activities.

By 1968, Davis had decided to join a collective organization in order to achieve her goal of organizing people for political action. She first considered joining the Communist party. But because she related more to Marxist groups, she decided instead to join the Black Panther Political Party, which later became the Los Angeles branch of the Student Nonviolent Coordinating Committee (SNCC). SNCC was soon embroiled in internal disputes. After her longtime friend Franklin Kenard was expelled from his leadership position in the group because of his Communist party membership, Davis resigned from the organization. In July 1968, she joined the Che-Lumumba Club, the black cell of the Communist party in Los Angeles.

In 1969 Davis was hired as an assistant professor of philosophy at the University of California, Los Angeles. In July 1969, Davis joined a delegation of Communist party members who had been invited to spend a month in Cuba. There, she worked in coffee and sugarcane fields, and visited schools, hospitals, and historical sites. Davis remarked that everywhere she went in Cuba, she was immensely impressed with the gains that had been made against racism. She saw blacks in leadership positions throughout the country, and she concluded that only under a socialist system such as that established by Cuban leader Fidel Castro could the fight against racism have been so successful.

When she returned to the United States, she discovered that several newspaper articles had been published detailing her membership in the Communist party and accusing her of activities such as gunrunning for the Black Panther party. Governor RONALD REAGAN, of California, invoked a regulation in the handbook of the regents of the University of California that prohibited the hiring of Communists. Davis responded by affirming her membership in the Communist party, and she began to receive hate mail and threatening phone calls. After she obtained an INJUNCTION prohibiting the regents from firing her, the threats multiplied. Soon, she was receiving so many bomb threats that the campus police stopped checking her car for explosives, forcing her to learn the procedure for doing so herself. By the end of the year, the courts had ruled that the regulation prohibiting the hiring of Communists was unconstitutional. However, in June 1970, the regents announced that Davis would not be rehired the following year, on the grounds that her political speeches outside the classroom were unbefitting a university professor.

During this time, Davis became involved with the movement to free three black inmates of Soledad Prison in California: George Jackson, John Clutchette, and Fleeta Drumgo. The men, known as the Soledad Brothers, had been indicted for the murder of a prison guard. The guard had been pushed over a prison railing when he inadvertently stumbled into a rebellion among black prisoners caused by the killing of three black prisoners by another prison guard. Although Jackson, Clutchette, and Drumgo claimed there was no evidence that they had killed the guard, they were charged with his murder. Davis began corresponding with Jackson and soon developed a personal relationship with him. She attended all the court hearings relating to the Soledad Brothers' indictment, along with many other supporters, including Jackson's younger brother, Jonathon Jackson, who was committed to freeing his brother and the other inmates. On August 7, 1970, using guns registered to Davis, Jonathon attempted to free his brother in a shoot-out at the Marin County Courthouse. Four people were killed, including Jonathon and superior court judge Harold Haley.

Davis was charged with KIDNAPPING; CONSPIRACY; and MURDER, which was punishable in California by death. She fled, traveling in disguise from Los Angeles to Las Vegas, Chicago, Detroit, New York, Miami, and finally back to New York. In October 1970, she was arrested by the FBI, which had placed her on its most wanted list. In December, after two months in jail, Davis was extradited to California, where

she spent the next fourteen months in jail. She later said that this period was pivotal to her understanding of the black political struggle in the United States. Having worked to organize people in communities and on campuses against political repression, Davis now found herself a victim of that repression. In August 1971, while incarcerated in the Marin County Jail, she was devastated to learn that George Jackson had been killed by a guard in San Quentin Prison, allegedly while trying to escape.

In February 1972, Davis was released on BAIL following the California Supreme Court's decision to abolish the death penalty (*People v. Anderson*, 6 Cal. 3d 628, 100 Cal. Rptr. 152, 493 P.2d 880). Previously, bail had not been available to persons accused of crimes punishable by death. Her trial began a few days later, and lasted until early June 1972, when a jury acquitted her of all charges.

After her ACQUITTAL, Davis resumed her teaching career, at San Francisco State University. She continued her affiliation with the Communist party, receiving the Lenin Peace Prize from the Soviet Union in 1979 and running for vice president of the United States on the Communist party ticket in 1980 and 1984. She is a founder and cochair of the National Alliance against Racist and Political Repression. She is on the national board of the National Political Congress of Black Women and on the board of the Atlanta-based National Black Women's Health Project. She has authored five books, including *Angela Davis: An Autobiography* (1974), *Women, Culture, and Politics* (1989), and *Women, Race, and Class* (1983). In 1980, she married Hilton Braithwaite, a photographer and faculty colleague at San Francisco State. The marriage ended in divorce several years later.

In 1991, Davis began teaching an interdisciplinary graduate program titled "The History of Consciousness," at the University of California, Santa Cruz. In 1995 she found herself again surrounded by controversy when she was awarded a prestigious University of California President's Chair by university president Jack Peltason. The appointment provides $75,000 over several years to develop new ethnic studies courses. Some state lawmakers were outraged over the award and unsuccessfully demanded that Peltason rescind the appointment. Davis said she planned to use the stipend to create programs dealing with the criminalization and incarceration of women and with issues concerning women of color.

CROSS-REFERENCES

Carmichael, Stokely; Cleaver, Eldridge; Communism; Marx, Karl.

"WE HAVE ACCUMULATED A WEALTH OF HISTORICAL EXPERIENCE WHICH CONFIRMS OUR BELIEF THAT THE SCALES OF JUSTICE ARE OUT OF BALANCE."

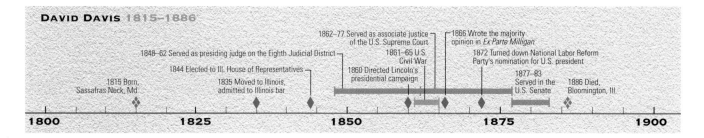

DAVID DAVIS 1815–1886

1862–77 Served as associate justice of the U.S. Supreme Court

1866 Wrote the majority opinion in *Ex Parte Milligan*

1848–62 Served as presiding judge on the Eighth Judicial District

1861–65 U.S. Civil War

1872 Turned down National Labor Reform Party's nomination for U.S. president

1844 Elected to Ill. House of Representatives

1860 Directed Lincoln's presidential campaign

1877–83 Served in the U.S. Senate

1815 Born, Sassafras Neck, Md.

1835 Moved to Illinois, admitted to Illinois bar

1886 Died, Bloomington, Ill.

1800   1825   1850   1875   1900

DAVIS, DAVID

David Davis served as an associate justice of the U.S. Supreme Court from 1862 to 1877. An Illinois attorney and judge, Davis acted as Abraham Lincoln's campaign manager in the 1860 election, working tirelessly to win the Republican party nomination and the general election for Lincoln.

Davis was born in Sassafras Neck, Maryland, on March 9, 1815. He attended Kenyon College at the age of thirteen. Following graduation he read the law in a Massachusetts law firm, before attending New Haven Law School for less than a year. In 1835 he moved to Illinois and was admitted to the bar, and opened a law firm in Pekin. In 1836 he purchased a law practice in Bloomington, Illinois, where he remained a resident the rest of his life.

He was soon drawn into politics. After losing a bid for a seat in the Illinois Senate in 1840, he was elected to the Illinois House of Representatives in 1844. He participated in the Illinois Constitutional Convention, which convened in 1847. A force for judicial reform, Davis was elected to Illinois's Eighth Judicial Circuit, where he served as presiding judge until 1862.

During his years as a practicing attorney and judge, Davis became a close friend and adviser to ABRAHAM LINCOLN. Ignoring the traditional concept of judicial neutrality concerning politics, Davis acted as Lincoln's campaign manager during the 1860 election. His actions have been credited with securing the Republican party nomination for Lincoln.

In 1862 Lincoln rewarded his friend with an appointment to the U.S. Supreme Court. Davis's tenure encompassed both the Civil War and Reconstruction. He is best remembered for his 1866 majority opinion in *Ex parte Milligan*,

ARTIST: JON M ISAACS. COLLECTION OF THE SUPREME COURT OF THE UNITED STATES.

David Davis

NEW YORK PUBLIC LIBRARY

John Chandler Bancroft Davis

71 U.S. 2, 18 L. Ed. 281. In 1864 Lamdin Milligan was arrested and tried for TREASON by a military commission established by order of President Lincoln. He was convicted and sentenced to death, but the sentence was not carried out.

In his majority opinion, Davis noted that the civilian courts were open and operating in Indiana when Milligan was arrested and tried by the military. In ordering Milligan's release, Davis condemned Lincoln's directive establishing military jurisdiction over civilians outside of the immediate war area. He strongly affirmed the fundamental right of a civilian to be tried in a regular court of law, with all the required procedural safeguards.

In 1872 Davis was nominated for president by the National Labor Reform party, but he turned down the opportunity. However, political ambition led him to resign from the Supreme Court in 1877 and run for the Senate, representing Illinois. He was elected as an independent and served one six-year term. From 1881 to 1883, he served as president pro tempore of the Senate.

Davis died June 26, 1886, in Bloomington, Illinois.

See also MILLIGAN, EX PARTE.

DAVIS, JOHN CHANDLER BANCROFT

John Chandler Bancroft Davis enjoyed a long and prolific career as a diplomat, jurist, and legal historian.

The son of John Davis, a Massachusetts governor and U.S. senator, Davis was born December 29, 1822, in Worcester, Massachusetts. He entered Harvard College in 1840 but was suspended (unjustly, by some accounts) in his senior year. He then studied law and was

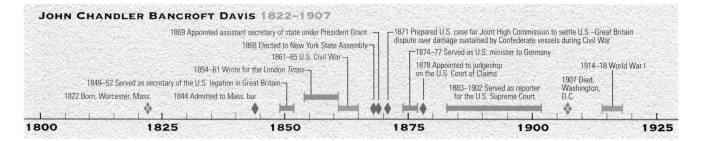

JOHN CHANDLER BANCROFT DAVIS 1822–1907

1869 Appointed assistant secretary of state under President Grant

1871 Prepared U.S. case for Joint High Commission to settle U.S.–Great Britain dispute over damage sustained by Confederate vessels during Civil War

1868 Elected to New York State Assembly

1861–65 U.S. Civil War

1874–77 Served as U.S. minister to Germany

1854–61 Wrote for the London *Times*

1878 Appointed to judgeship on the U.S. Court of Claims

1914–18 World War I

1849–52 Served as secretary of the U.S. legation in Great Britain

1883–1902 Served as reporter for the U.S. Supreme Court

1907 Died, Washington, D.C.

1822 Born, Worcester, Mass.

1844 Admitted to Mass. bar

1800   1825   1850   1875   1900   1925

admitted to the Massachusetts bar in 1844. Three years later, he received his degree from Harvard.

Davis practiced law in New York City until August 1849, when he was appointed secretary of the U.S. legation in Great Britain. He was also acting chargé d'affaires of the embassy for a brief time. Davis left his diplomatic post in November 1852 to resume his law practice and become U.S. correspondent for the London *Times*. Illness forced him to give up his law practice, and in 1862, he and his wife settled on a farm in rural New York State.

Six years later, after regaining his health, Davis was elected to the New York state assembly. In 1869, he left the legislature to accept an appointment as assistant secretary of state under President ULYSSES S. GRANT. As the assistant secretary, Davis arbitrated a dispute between Portugal and Great Britain over their African possessions. In 1871, a Joint High Commission was created to settle a dispute between the United States and Great Britain over damages sustained by Confederate vessels during the Civil War. Davis resigned his position with the State Department to become U.S. secretary to the commission. Davis prepared the case for the United States and wrote a five-hundred-page book, *The Case of the United States*, in which the government demanded compensation for losses sustained by Confederate cruisers and for injuries to commerce. The Tribunal of Arbitration at Geneva later awarded the United States over $15 million in gold for damages.

Davis was reappointed assistant secretary of state in January 1873 but resigned six months later to succeed his uncle, George Bancroft, as minister to Germany.

After six years in Berlin, Davis gave up his diplomatic career to become a judge on the U.S. Court of Claims. He sat on the court for five years, and then served for nearly twenty years as REPORTER of decisions for the U.S. Supreme Court. As reporter for the Court, he edited over seventy-five volumes of the *United States Reports*, the official publication of the Court's opinions. Davis also classified important historical data on the federal judiciary. At

BIOGRAPHY

John William Davis

"THERE IS NOTHING I RESENT MORE THAN THE IDEA THAT A LAWYER SELLS HIMSELF BODY AND SOUL TO HIS CLIENTS."

the time of his death in 1907 at age eighty-five, he had authored significant works on diplomacy, religion, and history, including *The Massachusetts Justice* (1847), *Mr. Fish and the Alabama Claims* (1893), and *Origin of the Book of Common Prayer of the Protestant Episcopal Church in the United States of America* (1897).

DAVIS, JOHN WILLIAM John William Davis was born April 13, 1873, in Clarksburg, West Virginia. Davis earned a bachelor of arts degree from Washington and Lee University in 1892, a bachelor of laws degree in 1895, and a doctor of laws degree in 1915. He also received doctor of laws degrees from numerous other institutions, including the University of Birmingham, England, 1919; Yale, 1921; Dartmouth, 1923; Princeton, 1924; and Oberlin College, 1947. Three doctor of civil law degrees were bestowed upon Davis, by Oxford University in England, 1950; Columbia, 1953; and Hofstra College, 1953.

After his admission to the bar in 1895, Davis returned to his alma mater, Washington and Lee University, as an assistant professor of law, teaching from 1896 to 1897. In the latter year, he established his law practice in Clarksburg, West Virginia, serving as counselor until 1913.

Davis entered politics in 1899 by participating in the West Virginia House of Delegates. He was a member of the Democratic National Conventions from 1904 to 1932.

In 1911, he served the federal government as a congressman, representing West Virginia until 1915. Davis left this post to perform the duties of solicitor general from 1913 to 1918.

The next phase of Davis's career encompassed foreign service. He was appointed ambassador to Great Britain in 1918 and acted in this capacity until 1921. Also in 1918, Davis was chosen as an American delegate to Berne, Switzerland, to the conference with Germany regarding prisoners of war captured during World War I.

In 1924, Davis was the Democratic candidate for president of the United States; he was defeated by CALVIN COOLIDGE.

Davis died March 24, 1955, in Charleston, South Carolina.

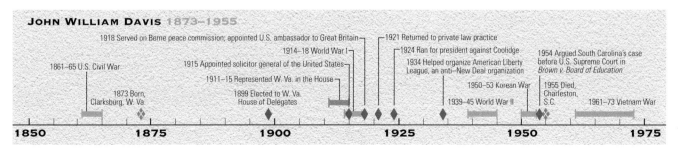

JOHN WILLIAM DAVIS 1873–1955

1918 Served on Berne peace commission; appointed U.S. ambassador to Great Britain — 1921 Returned to private law practice

1914–18 World War I — 1924 Ran for president against Coolidge

1915 Appointed solicitor general of the United States — 1934 Helped organize American Liberty League, an anti–New Deal organization

1861–65 U.S. Civil War

1911–15 Represented W. Va. in the House — 1954 Argued South Carolina's case before U.S. Supreme Court in *Brown v. Board of Education*

1873 Born, Clarksburg, W. Va.

1899 Elected to W. Va. House of Delegates

1950–53 Korean War

1955 Died, Charleston, S.C.

1939–45 World War II

1961–73 Vietnam War

1850   1875   1900   1925   1950   1975

DAVIS-BACON ACT 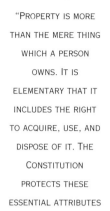 A federal law that governs the MINIMUM WAGE rate to be paid to laborers and mechanics employed on federal public works projects.

The Davis-Bacon Act (40 U.S.C.A. §§ 276a to 276a-5), was enacted on March 3, 1931, and has subsequently been amended over the years. Its purpose is to preserve local wage standards and promote local employment by preventing contractors who bid on PUBLIC CONTRACTS from basing their bids on the use of cheap labor recruited from foreign sources.

When controversies arise under the Davis-Bacon Act, they are first submitted to the federal agency that is in charge of the project. Thereafter, if the dispute is not satisfactorily resolved, the matter is submitted to the secretary of labor. The Wage Appeals Board of the LABOR DEPARTMENT acts on behalf of the secretary in reviewing questions of law and fact made in wage determinations issued under the act and its related prevailing wage statutes. The board has discretion in selecting the controversies that it will review. Following these administrative procedures, a dissatisfied party may seek relief in the FEDERAL COURTS. The courts, however, will only review whether there has been compliance with the constitutional, statutory, and procedural requirements of the practices and procedures of the agencies involved in the dispute.

See also LABOR LAW.

DAY, WILLIAM RUFUS William Rufus Day served as an associate justice of the U.S. Supreme Court from 1903 to 1922. Day served on a Court dominated by Justice OLIVER WENDELL HOLMES, JR., yet Day played a key role during a period when the federal government began to extend its police and regulatory powers.

Day was born April 17, 1849, in Ravenna, Ohio. He graduated from the University of Michigan in 1870 and attended its law school for one year. He was admitted to the Ohio bar in 1872 and entered practice in Canton, Ohio.

Ohio was a hotbed of Republican party politics in the late nineteenth century. Day became active in the party and, more important, be-

"PROPERTY IS MORE THAN THE MERE THING WHICH A PERSON OWNS. IT IS ELEMENTARY THAT IT INCLUDES THE RIGHT TO ACQUIRE, USE, AND DISPOSE OF IT. THE CONSTITUTION PROTECTS THESE ESSENTIAL ATTRIBUTES OF PROPERTY."

BIOGRAPHY

William Rufus Day

ARTIST ROLF STOLL. COLLECTION OF THE SUPREME COURT OF THE UNITED STATES

came a trusted friend and adviser to WILLIAM McKINLEY, who was elected president in 1896. McKinley appointed Day secretary of state in April 1898. Five months later Day was chosen to head the U.S. Peace Commission to negotiate an end to the Spanish-American War with Spain. He left his cabinet post to fulfill this duty.

McKinley rewarded Day for his friendship, political counsel, and service as secretary of state with an appointment in 1899 to the U.S. Sixth Circuit Court of Appeals. With McKinley's assassination in 1901, Vice President THEODORE ROOSEVELT assumed the presidency. In 1903 Roosevelt appointed Day to the Supreme Court, in part because Roosevelt needed to strengthen his ties with Ohio Republicans.

Day held a centrist position on the Supreme Court. More liberal justices such as Holmes and LOUIS D. BRANDEIS sought to allow more active government involvement in the national economy. Conservative justices continued to restrict government regulation of business and the growth of federal power. Day took a middle course, though some commentators believe he tilted more to supporting STATES' RIGHTS.

His most famous opinion, *Hammer v. Dagenhart*, 247 U.S. 251, 38 S. Ct. 529, 62 L. Ed. 1101 (1918), illustrates his more conservative tendencies. In the early 1900s, Congress sought to regulate the use of child labor, passing a child labor act in 1916 (39 Stat. 675, c. 432, formally known as the Keating-Owen Act). The act prohibited the movement in interstate commerce of goods that were made by children. In *Hammer*, a manufacturer was charged with violating the act. Under the Constitution's COMMERCE CLAUSE, Congress has the right to regulate interstate commerce. Day gave the clause a restrictive reading, ruling that commerce did not include manufactured goods that were themselves harmless. In addition, he said, Congress had intruded into an area of regulation that was reserved to the states. To allow Congress to regulate industry would destroy FEDERALISM and the system of government set out in the Constitution.

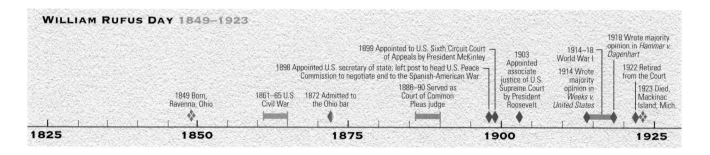

WILLIAM RUFUS DAY 1849–1923

1849 Born, Ravenna, Ohio

1861–65 U.S. Civil War

1872 Admitted to the Ohio bar

1886–90 Served as Court of Common Pleas judge

1898 Appointed U.S. secretary of state; left post to head U.S. Peace Commission to negotiate end to the Spanish-American War

1899 Appointed to U.S. Sixth Circuit Court of Appeals by President McKinley

1903 Appointed associate justice of U.S. Supreme Court by President Roosevelt

1914 Wrote majority opinion in *Weeks v. United States*

1914–18 World War I

1918 Wrote majority opinion in *Hammer v. Dagenhart*

1922 Retired from the Court

1923 Died, Mackinac Island, Mich.

1825   1850   1875   1900   1925

Despite this hostility to the Child Labor Act, Day upheld the federal government's power to regulate interstate commerce in other cases that involved the shipment of impure food, drugs, and liquor. He was also supportive of federal ANTITRUST prosecutions that involved RESTRAINT OF TRADE.

In addition, Day's opposition to federal regulation of the workplace did not carry over to state regulation of industry. This is revealed in his dissent in *Lochner v. New York*, 198 U.S. 45, 25 S. Ct. 539, 49 L. Ed. 937 (1905). In *Lochner* the Court, on a 5–4 vote, struck down a New York state law that specified a maximum sixty-hour week for bakery employees. The Court ruled that the law was a "meddlesome interference" with business, concluding that the regulation of work hours was an unjustified infringement on "the right to labor, and with the right of free contract on the part of the individual, either as employer or employee." Although Holmes's dissent has received more attention, Day's made clear that the state had the right to promote public welfare, even if it came in conflict with the concept of liberty of contract.

Finally, Day authored the opinion in *Weeks v. United States*, 232 U.S. 383, 34 S. Ct. 341, 58 L. Ed. 652 (1914), which established the federal EXCLUSIONARY RULE for criminal evidence seized in violation of the FOURTH AMENDMENT. Day's opinion suggested that exclusion of tainted evidence was implicit in the requirement of the Fourth Amendment. If illegally seized evidence could be admitted in a criminal trial, he said, "the protection of the 4th Amendment . . . is of no value . . . and might as well be stricken from the Constitution."

Day retired from the Court in 1922. He died on Mackinac Island, Michigan, on July 9, 1923.

CROSS-REFERENCES

Child Labor Laws; Labor Law; *Lochner v. New York.*

DAY CERTAIN A specified date. A term used in the rules of civil and criminal procedure to designate a particular time by which all MOTIONS for a new TRIAL must be submitted to the court.

DAY IN COURT The opportunity afforded an individual to have a CLAIM litigated in a judicial setting.

A person is said to have his or her day in court when he or she is given notice to appear and has the opportunity to defend his or her rights, seek relief, or set forth his or her claims. When someone has had his or her day in court with reference to a particular matter, that individual will generally be prevented from reliti-

gating the claim in a subsequent action unless grounds exist that warrant an APPEAL of the matter.

DAYS OF GRACE An extension of the time originally scheduled for the performance of an act, such as payment for a DEBT, granted merely as a GRATUITOUS favor by the person to whom the performance is owed.

In old English practice, days of grace allowed a person an extra three days beyond the date specified in a WRIT summoning him or her before a court in which to make an appearance without being subject to punishment for failure to appear. This allowance of time was granted in consideration of the far distances that had to be traveled to court.

The laws and customs that regulate the commercial affairs of merchants have recognized days of grace as a means of facilitating various transactions. Three days of grace were originally allowed to give a MAKER or acceptor of a NOTE, BILL, or DRAFT, in which the person is ordered to make payment according to its terms, a longer time to pay than specified by the date in the document. This practice was begun merely as a favor to those who regularly engaged in business with each other, but it soon became a custom between merchants. Eventually, the courts recognized this right, often as a result of statute; in some cases, it has become a right that must be demanded.

The phrase *days of grace* is sometimes used interchangeably with GRACE PERIOD, a term used in INSURANCE law to denote an extension of time within which to pay a PREMIUM due on a policy, but the terms do not have identical meanings.

DEAD BODY A corpse; the physical remains of expired human beings prior to complete decomposition.

Property and Possession Rights In the ordinary use of the term, a PROPERTY RIGHT does not exist in a dead body. For the purpose of burial, however, the dead body of a human being is considered to be property or quasi-property, the rights to which are held by the surviving spouse or NEXT OF KIN. This right cannot be conveyed and does not exist while the DECEDENT is living. Following burial, the body is considered part of the ground in which it was placed. Articles of PERSONAL PROPERTY that have been buried with the body, such as jewelry, may be taken by their rightful owner as determined by traditional property rules or laws relating to DESCENT AND DISTRIBUTION or WILLS, since they are material objects independent of the body.

A body may not be retained by an undertaker as SECURITY for unpaid funeral expenses, particularly where a body has been kept without authorization and payment is demanded as a CON-DITION precedent to its release.

At times, the need to perform an AUTOPSY or postmortem examination gives the local CORO-NER a superior right to possess the dead body until such an examination is performed. The general rule is that such examinations should be performed with the exercise of discretion and not routinely. Some state statutes regulate when an autopsy may be performed, which may require the procurement of a court order and written permission of a designated person, usually the one with property rights in the corpse.

Burial Rights The right to a decent burial has long been recognized at COMMON LAW, but no universal rule exists as to whom the right of burial is granted. Generally, unless otherwise provided before death by the deceased, the right will go to the surviving spouse, or if there is none, it will go to the next of kin. When a controversy arises concerning the right of burial, each case will be considered on its own merits. The burial right per se is a sacred trust for those who have an interest in the remains.

Although the surviving spouse usually has the principal right to custody of the remains and to burial, special circumstances undermine this right, such as the absence or neglect of the surviving spouse or the separation of the parties at the time of death.

When there is no surviving spouse, the next of kin, in order of age, have the burial rights, unless a friend or remote relative is found by the court to have a superior right. The caretaker of an elderly childless decedent who lived with the decedent for years prior to his or her death and to whom the ESTATE was bequeathed might have a burial right superior to that of relatives.

In the case of the death of a child of divorced parents, the paramount privilege of burial is awarded to the parent who had CUSTODY.

The preference of the deceased concerning the disposition of his or her body is a right that should be strictly enforced. Some states confer this right, considering a decedent's wishes as of foremost importance.

In most instances, the courts will honor the wishes of the decedent, even in the face of opposition by the surviving spouse or next of kin. If for some reason a decedent's wishes cannot be carried out, direction should be sought by the court. The court will decide how the body shall be disposed of and will most likely do so according to the wishes of the surviving spouse or next of kin, provided those wishes are reasonable and not contrary to PUBLIC POLICY.

When an individual wishes to direct the disposition of his or her remains, no formality is required. Oral directions are considered to be sufficient, and an individual's last wish will ordinarily be the controlling factor, provided it is within the limits of reason and decency.

Duties as to Burial Public policy favors the concept of what is colloquially referred to as a "decent burial." There is a strong societal interest in the proper disposition of the bodies of deceased persons. It is universally recognized that a duty is owed to both society and the deceased that the body be buried without any unnecessary delay. This duty rests upon whoever has the right to bury the decedent. At common law, the duty was imposed upon the person under whose roof the deceased died.

Some state statutes specifically name those people who are charged with the duty of having a decedent buried. Statutes of this kind have been enacted for various policy reasons, such as the general interests of public health and the protection of public welfare, as well as the relief of anxiety that some people might experience concerning the proper disposition of their remains.

Rights to Disinterment After a body has been buried, it is considered to be in the custody of the law; therefore, disinterment is not a matter of right. The disturbance or removal of an interred body is subject to the control and direction of the court.

The law does not favor disinterment, based on the public policy that the sanctity of the grave should be maintained. Once buried, a body should not be disturbed. A court will not ordinarily order or permit a body to be disinterred unless there is a strong showing of necessity that disinterment is within the interests of justice. Each case is individually decided, based on its own particular facts and circumstances.

The courts frequently allow a change of burial place in order to enable people who were together during life to be buried together as well, such as husbands and wives, or family members. Disinterment for the purposes of reburial in a family plot acquired at a later date is generally authorized by law, particularly if the request is made by the surviving members of the decedent's family.

Disinterment may be allowed under certain circumstances, such as when a CEMETERY has been abandoned as a burial place or when it is condemned by the state by virtue of its EMINENT DOMAIN power for a public improvement.

Instrumental in a decision of a court as to whether or not a body should be disinterred is the consideration of the deceased's wishes as to his or her burial place. Such wishes are of paramount importance but are not necessarily controlling in all cases, such as when subsequent circumstances require a change of burial.

In states that have statutes regulating the exhumation or removal of the dead, such statutes are controlling.

Purchasing a lot in a cemetery entails a contract that obligates the purchaser and his or her survivors to abide by and observe the laws, rules, and regulations of the cemetery as well as those of the religious group that maintains it. When a dispute over the right to disinter a dead body arises, the court must make a finding of fact as to whether or not the rules or regulations of the cemetery forbid it.

Rights of Particular Persons to Disinterment The surviving spouse or next of kin of a deceased person has the right to have the body remain undisturbed. This right, however, is not absolute and can be violated when it is in conflict with the public good or when it is required by the demands of justice.

The right to change the place of burial is also not absolute, and the courts take various factors into consideration when deciding whether a body should be removed for burial elsewhere, such as the occurrence of unforeseen events. If an elderly woman's husband died and was buried in New York and she subsequently moved to California, she might be allowed to have his remains removed to a different location to facilitate her visits to his grave.

The consent of the surviving spouse of a decedent to the decedent's original resting place is another factor that the court will consider in determining whether a body may be disinterred, particularly if it is against the wishes of the next of kin. Once consent has been shown, the burial will usually not be disturbed in the absence of strong and convincing evidence of new and unforeseen events.

If a body is improperly buried—that is, buried in a grave belonging to someone else who has not consented to the burial—the court will order the body removed for reburial.

An owner of land who allows the burial of a deceased person on his or her property cannot later remove the body against the will of the surviving spouse or next of kin. On the other hand, the landowner is entitled to object to the removal of the remains from his or her land. A landowner may not assert that a burial was made without his or her consent if he or she fails to raise any objections within a reasonable time after the interment of the decedent.

Disinterment for Autopsies The disinterment of a body may be ordered by the courts for the purpose of an autopsy. Courts occasionally permit a body to be exhumed and an autopsy to be performed under certain circumstances in order to discover truth and promote justice. If disinterment for the purpose of examination is to be allowed, good cause and exigent circumstances must exist to make such action necessary, such as where there is controversy over the cause of death or to determine in an heirship proceeding whether or not a decedent ever gave birth to a child.

Disinterment for an autopsy should not be granted arbitrarily. The law will only search for facts by this method in the rarest of cases and when there is a reasonable probability that answers will be found through disturbing interment.

Civil Liabilities A CIVIL ACTION for breach of CONTRACT as to the care and burial of a dead body may be brought under certain circumstances. An individual who makes an agreement to properly bury a dead body may be subject to a lawsuit if he or she gives the body an improper burial, negligently allows the body to be taken from his or her custody, or allows the body to suffer indignities while in his or her possession.

General rules that govern DAMAGES for breach of contract have similarly been applied in these actions.

In one case, an undertaker was sued for failure to embalm a body in such a manner that it would be preserved for a reasonably long time. The plaintiff recovered damages for illness and disability suffered when he found out that the body had disintegrated and become infested with insects as a result of the undertaker's breach of contract. Exemplary or PUNITIVE DAMAGES in such cases, however, are not recoverable.

The right to a decent burial has long been recognized. This person's casket is draped with a U.S. flag because he or she served in the armed forces.

Funeral or Burial Expenses Even in the absence of contract or statute, a person may be liable for funeral or burial expenses based on his or her relationship to the decedent, such as a husband and wife, or a parent and child. Statutes may also dictate LIABILITY. Some statutes designate the persons charged with the duty of burial but do not impose financial responsibility for burial or funeral expenses. Others impose financial liability on designated people in the order in which they are named in the statute.

Liability for burial expenses is not ordinarily imposed on someone merely because that person received a financial benefit as a result of the decedent's death. A joint tenant will not be charged with funeral expenses merely as a result of the joint ownership of property with the deceased.

Contractual Liability An individual who would not ordinarily be obligated to pay for burial or funeral expenses may accept responsibility to do so by contract. The terms of such an agreement must be very clear. The mere direction to furnish funeral services does not automatically create a contract for their payment. Liability for funeral services cannot be imposed arbitrarily. The obligation to pay the costs of a decent burial will be enforced by the law on those who should properly pay.

Although there is a lack of authority on the question of who should bear the costs of disinterment and reburial, it has generally been held to be the responsibility of the person who caused it to be done.

Torts In the law of TORTS, there are a large number of cases involving the mishandling of dead bodies. These cases are concerned with mutilation, unauthorized disinterment, interference with proper burial, and other types of intentional disturbance. The breach of any duty as well as the unlawful invasion of any right existing with regard to a dead body is a tort for which an ACTION may be commenced. For example, if the wrong body is delivered to a funeral home and the family discovers this when they attend the wake, they may be able to recover damages for mental suffering. Thus, the right of recovery is not necessarily based directly on injury to the dead body per se. Exemplary damages may be awarded in cases where the injury to plaintiffs was either MALICIOUS or resulting from gross NEGLIGENCE.

The award of damages is subject to APPELLATE COURT review, and the adequacy or excessiveness of the amount awarded is dependent upon the particular circumstances of each case.

A tort action for damages in such cases may be maintained to protect the personal feelings of the survivors and, mainly, to compensate for the mental distress that has been caused.

Mutilation, Embalmment, and Autopsy An important component of the right to decent burial is the right to possession of the body in the same condition in which it is left by death. There is no additional basis for recovery where MUTILATION is caused simultaneously with death, as in the case of a person who dies in a train crash or who is fatally stabbed.

Some statutes authorize the delivery of dead bodies to medical colleges for dissection under certain conditions. It is mandatory, however, that the consent of relatives be obtained if such relatives can be found. Only a reasonable inquiry is necessary, the duty of which is on the school and on those delivering the body.

The mere unauthorized embalming of a body alone does not necessarily support a cause of action for damages based upon mutilation or mishandling. When such unauthorized embalming occurs, combined with the resulting mental suffering of the next of kin and other such factors, a legal action may be brought. If, for example, an unauthorized embalming contrary to the decedent's religious beliefs is performed, an actionable wrong occurs for which damages may be granted.

Generally, an unauthorized autopsy is a tort. No liability exists, however, when an autopsy is performed in accordance with the consent of the individual having burial rights or pursuant to statute or the proper execution of the duties of the coroner.

Offenses and Prosecutions Several varied offenses with respect to dead bodies are recognized both at common law and under statute. At common law, it is an offense to treat a dead body indecently by keeping, handling, and exposing it to view in order to create the impression that the deceased is still alive. The attempt to dispose of a dead body for gain and profit is a MISDEMEANOR punishable at common law. Ordinarily, it is a misdemeanor for the individual possessing the duty of having a body buried to refuse or neglect to do so, or to dispose of the corpse indecently. The burning of a dead body in such a way as to incite the feelings of the public is a common-law offense.

At common law and often under statute, interfering with another person's right of burial or neglecting to bury or cremate a body within a reasonable time after death is an offense. It is also a crime to detain a body as security for the payment of a debt.

The mutilation of a corpse is an offense at common law, and under some statutes, the unauthorized dissection of a dead body is a specific criminal offense. Someone who receives a body for the purpose of dissection with the knowledge that it has been unlawfully removed is subject to prosecution.

The unauthorized disturbance of a grave is indictable at common law and by statute as highly contrary to acceptable community conduct. Similarly, the unauthorized disinterment of a body is a criminal offense under some statutes and at common law.

Some statutes make disinterment for specified purposes an offense; therefore, an offense is not committed unless disinterment was done for such purposes. However, a case where a body was exhumed and a portion of the body was removed by the next of kin for use as evidence in a malpractice trial did not warrant prosecution for removal of the body because of mere wantonness, as set forth in a statute.

Under laws that make it an offense to open a grave to remove anything interred, the act is forbidden per se and is conclusive as to the intent with which it is done. In such cases no specific intent, whether felonious or otherwise, needs to be shown.

Statutes making disinterment an offense do not apply to exhumations made by public officials attempting to ascertain whether a crime has been committed. Similarly, statutes are not directed against cemetery authorities who wish to change the place of burial and who are authorized to do so; nor are they directed against people who had obtained the permission of those having burial rights or against those who, under necessary permit, remove the dead body of a relative for reinterment.

DEADLY FORCE 📖 An amount of force that is likely to cause either serious bodily injury or death to another person. 📖

Police officers may use deadly force in specific circumstances when they are trying to enforce the law. Private citizens may use deadly force in certain circumstances in SELF-DEFENSE. The rules governing the use of deadly force for police officers are different from those for citizens.

During the twelfth century, the COMMON LAW allowed the police to use deadly force if they needed it to capture a FELONY suspect, regardless of the circumstances. At that time, felonies were not as common as they are now and were usually punishable by death. Also, law officers had a more difficult time capturing suspects because they did not have the technology and weaponry that are present in today's world. In modern times, the courts have restricted the use of deadly force to certain, dangerous situations.

In police jargon, deadly force is also referred to as shoot and kill. The Supreme Court has ruled that, depending on the circumstances, if an offender resists arrest, police officers may use as much force as is reasonably required to overcome the resistance. Whether the force is REASONABLE is determined by the judgment of a reasonable officer at the scene, rather than by hindsight. Because police officers can find themselves in dangerous or rapidly changing situations where split second decisions are necessary, the judgment of someone at the scene is vital when looking back at the actions of a police officer.

The Supreme Court has defined the "objective reasonableness" standard as a balance between the rights of the person being arrested and the government interests that allow the use of force. The FOURTH AMENDMENT protects U.S. citizens from unreasonable SEARCHES AND SEIZURES, the category into which an arrest falls. The Supreme Court has said that a search and seizure is reasonable if it is based on PROBABLE CAUSE and if it does not unreasonably intrude on the rights and privacy of the individual. This standard does not question a police officer's intent or motivation for using deadly force during an arrest; it only looks at the situation as it has happened.

For deadly force to be constitutional when an arrest is taking place, it must be the reasonable choice under all the circumstances at the time. Therefore, deadly force should be looked at as an option that is used when it is believed that no other action will succeed. The Model Penal Code, although not adopted in all states, restricts police action regarding deadly force. According to the code, officers should not use deadly force unless the action will not endanger innocent bystanders, the suspect used deadly force in committing the crime, or the officers

A sniper fired on police officers during a riot in Miami in 1991, and they responded with deadly force.

STARR/STOCK BOSTON

believe a delay in arrest may result in injury or death to other people.

Circumstances that are taken into consideration are the severity of the offense, how much of a threat the suspect poses, and the suspect's attempts to resist or flee the police officer. When arresting someone for a MISDEMEANOR, the police have the right to shoot the alleged offender only in self-defense. If an officer shoots a suspect accused of a misdemeanor for a reason other than self-defense, the officer can be held liable for criminal charges and damages for injuries to the suspect. This standard was demonstrated in the Iowa case of *Klinkel v. Saddler*, 211 Iowa 368, 233 N.W. 538 (1930), where a sheriff faced a WRONGFUL DEATH lawsuit because he had killed a misdemeanor suspect during an arrest. The sheriff said he had used deadly force to defend himself, and the court ruled in his favor.

When police officers are arresting someone for a felony, the courts have given them a little more leeway. The police may use all the force that is necessary to overcome resistance, even if that means killing the person they are trying to arrest. However, if it is proved that an officer used more force than was necessary, the officer can be held criminally and civilly liable. In *Tennessee v. Garner*, 471 U.S. 1, 105 S. Ct. 1694, 85 L. Ed. 2d 1 (1985), the Supreme Court ruled that it is a violation of the Fourth Amendment for police officers to use deadly force to stop fleeing felony suspects who are nonviolent and unarmed. The decision, with an opinion written by Justice BYRON R. WHITE, said, in part, "We conclude that such force may not be used unless it is necessary to prevent the escape and the officer has probable cause to believe that the suspect poses a significant threat of death or serious physical injury to the officer or others."

When deadly force is used by a private citizen, the reasonableness rule does not apply. The citizen must be able to prove that a felony occurred or was being attempted, and that the felony threatened death or bodily harm. Mere suspicion of a felony is considered an insufficient ground for a private citizen to use deadly force.

This was demonstrated in the Michigan case of *People v. Couch*, 436 Mich. 414, 461 N.W.2d 683 (1990), where the defendant shot and killed a suspected felon who was fleeing the scene of the crime. The Michigan supreme court ruled that Archie L. Couch did not have the right to use deadly force against the suspected felon because the suspect did not pose a threat of injury or death to Couch.

DEAD MAN'S STATUTES ▣ State rules of EVIDENCE that make the oral statements of a DECEDENT inadmissible in a civil lawsuit against the EXECUTOR or ADMINISTRATOR of the decedent's ESTATE when presented by persons to bolster their claims against the estate. ▣

Dead man's statutes are designed to protect the estate of a deceased person from fraudulent claims made by a person who had engaged in transactions with the decedent. These laws do not permit the claimant to TESTIFY as to what terms a decedent verbally accepted, since the decedent is unable to testify and give his or her version of the transaction.

Such statutes are derived from COMMON-LAW principles that disqualified WITNESSES from testifying in an ACTION if they would be affected by the outcome of the case. Many states admit such TESTIMONY as evidence under specific statutory conditions, such as if the decedent's statements can be corroborated by the testimony of other disinterested witnesses.

The Federal Rules of Evidence govern the use of oral statements made by decedents in federal cases.

DEATH AND DYING ▣ *Death* is the end of life. *Dying* is the process of approaching death, including the choices and actions involved in that process. ▣

Death has always been a central concern of the law. The many legal issues related to death include laws that determine whether a death has actually occurred, as well as when and how it occurred, and whether or not another individual will be chargeable for having caused it. Increasingly, the law has had to deal with complex issues regarding the termination of medical care—such as when an artificial respirator or a feeding tube is withdrawn from a comatose person, or when chemotherapy is withheld from a terminally ill cancer patient. With the development of increasingly complex and powerful medical procedures and devices in the middle and late twentieth century, the U.S. legal system has established rules and standards for the removal of life-sustaining medical care. These laws and judicial decisions have established, for example, the right of individuals to refuse medical treatment—sometimes called the right to die—as well as the boundaries of that right, particularly as regards the state's interest in protecting life and the medical profession's right to protect its standards. The issues involved in death and dying have often pitted patients' rights groups against physicians' professional organizations as each vies for control over the decision of how and when people die.

Defining Death in the Law The law recognizes different forms of death, not all of them meaning the end of physical life. The term *civil death* is used in some states to describe the circumstance of an individual who has been convicted of a serious crime or sentenced to life imprisonment. Such an individual forfeits his or her civil rights, including the ability to marry, the capacity to own property, and the right to contract. *Legal death* is a presumption by law that a person has died. It arises following a prolonged absence, generally for a prescribed number of years, during which no one has seen or heard from the person and there is no known reason for the person's disappearance that would be incompatible with a finding that the individual is dead (e.g., the individual had not planned to move to another place). *Natural death* is death by action of natural causes without the aid or inducement of any intervening instrumentality. *Violent death* is death caused or accelerated by the application of extreme or excessive force. *Brain death*, a medical term first used in the late 1960s, is the cessation of all functions of the whole brain. *Wrongful death* is the end of life through a willful or negligent act.

In the eyes of the law, death is not a continuing event but something that takes place at a precise moment in time. The courts will not wield authority concerning a death. The determination of whether an individual has died, and the way in which this is proved by the person's vital signs, is not a legal decision but rather a medical judgment. The opinion of qualified medical personnel will be taken into consideration by judges when a controversy exists as to whether an individual is still alive or has died.

Legal Death and Missing Persons There is a legal presumption that an individual is alive until proved dead. In attempting to determine whether a person has died after having been missing for a certain period of time, the law assumes that the person is alive until a reason exists to believe otherwise.

The common-law rule is that where evidence indicates that the absent person was subject to a particular peril, she or he will be legally presumed dead after seven years unless the disappearance can be otherwise explained. The seven-year interval may be shortened if the state decides to enact legislation to change it. Some states may permit the dissolution of a marriage or the administration of an estate based on a mysterious disappearance that endures for less than seven years. A majority of states will not make the assumption that a missing person is dead unless it is reasonable to

assume that the person would return if still alive.

A special problem emerges in a situation where a person disappears following a threat made on his or her life. Such an individual would have a valid reason for voluntarily leaving and concealing his or her identity. Conversely, however, the person would in fact be dead if the plot succeeded. A court would have to examine carefully the facts of a particular case of this nature.

In some states, the court will not hold that an individual has died without proof that an earnest search was made for her or him. During such a search, public records must be consulted, wherever the person might have resided, for information regarding marriage, death, payment of taxes, or application for government benefits. The investigation must also include questioning of the missing person's friends or relatives as to her or his whereabouts.

Death Certificates The laws of each state require that the manner in which an individual has died be determined and recorded on a death certificate. CORONERS or medical examiners must deal with issues establishing whether someone can be legally blamed for causing the death. Such issues are subsequently determined by CRIMINAL LAW in the event that someone is charged with HOMICIDE, and by TORT law in the event of a civil suit for WRONGFUL DEATH.

Dying and End-of-Life Decisions Because of the many changes in modern medicine, the nature of death and dying has changed greatly in the past several centuries. A majority of people in industrial societies such as the

The case of Karen Ann Quinlan, who died ten years after her parents removed her respirator, raised legal and ethical questions about end-of-life decisions made by patients and their families.

AP/WIDE WORLD PHOTOS

United States no longer perish, as they once did, from infectious or parasitic diseases. Instead, life expectancies range above seventy years and the major causes of mortality are illnesses such as cancer and heart disease. Medicine is able to prolong life by many means, including artificial circulatory and respiratory systems, intravenous feeding and hydration, chemotherapy, and antibiotics.

The cultural circumstances of death have changed as well. A 1988 study indicated that 85 percent of deaths in the United States occur in health care institutions, and of those, about 70 percent involve withholding some type of life-sustaining medical care. In 1990, it was estimated that of the 2 million deaths each year in the United States, 1.3 million followed decisions to withhold life support. The law has had to change and adapt in order to cope effectively with the new realities involved in death and dying in the United States.

Since the landmark decision of the New Jersey Supreme Court *In re Quinlan*, 70 N.J. 10, 355 A.2d 647, in 1976, the law has been greatly concerned with establishing the precise circumstances in which it is legal to withhold or withdraw various forms of life-supporting medical treatment. *Quinlan* established the first guidelines governing the removal of life-support systems from patients who no longer have the mental capacity, or competence, to make their own decisions. (See The Right to Die: Individual Autonomy and State Interests later in this article for details of the *Quinlan* case.)

Euthanasia   Allowing people to die by withdrawing or withholding life support is a form of *euthanasia* (a Greek word meaning "easy or good death") and is the only legally protected alternative in the United States to maximum health care treatment. Euthanasia is the act of killing an incurably ill person out of concern and compassion for that person's suffering. It is sometimes called mercy killing, but many advocates of euthanasia define mercy killing more precisely as the ending of another person's life without his or her request. Euthanasia is usually separated into two categories: *passive euthanasia* and *active euthanasia*. Withholding or withdrawing life-sustaining medical care is often classified as a form of passive euthanasia. Active euthanasia, sometimes called aid in dying, on the other hand, can consist, for example, of a physician's giving a patient a lethal injection of medication. It can also consist of a physician's providing the means for a patient to take his or her own life, as when a doctor prescribes a drug knowing that it will be used by the patient to commit SUICIDE. This last form of active euthanasia is also called *physician-assisted suicide* (see Assisted Suicide later in this article). In the United States, active euthanasia is generally recognized as MURDER or MANSLAUGHTER, whereas passive euthanasia is accepted by professional medical societies and the law in certain circumstances.

Euthanasia is a divisive topic, and different interpretations of its meaning, practice, and morality abound. Those who favor active euthanasia and a patient's right to die do not acknowledge a distinction between active and passive euthanasia. They assert that the withdrawal of life-sustaining treatment cannot be distinguished in principle from affirmative steps to hasten a patient's death. In both situations, they argue, a person intends to cause the patient's death, acts out of compassionate motives, and causes the same outcome. In their view, turning off a life-sustaining respirator switch and giving a lethal injection are morally equivalent actions.

Opponents of active euthanasia argue that it undermines the value of, and respect for, all human life; erodes trust in physicians; desensitizes society to killing; and contradicts many people's religious beliefs. Moreover, they maintain that the intentions and natures of active and passive euthanasia are not essentially the same. In active euthanasia, a person *directly intends* to cause death and uses available means to achieve this end. In passive euthanasia, a person decides against using a certain form of treatment and then directs that such treatment be withdrawn or withheld, *accepting but not intending* the patient's death, which is caused by the underlying illness.

The American Medical Association (AMA), in its Code of Medical Ethics, considers euthanasia to be different from the removal of life-sustaining medical care. Although accepting the removal of life support as a sometimes necessary duty of the physician to relieve suffering and obey the principle of patient self-determination, the AMA considers euthanasia—which it defines as "the administration of a lethal agent by another person to a patient"—to be a breach of professional ethics (Code of Medical Ethics, rule 2.21 [1994]).

Brain Death   In traditional Western medical practice, death was defined as the cessation of the body's circulatory and respiratory (blood pumping and breathing) functions. With the invention of machines that provide artificial circulation and respiration, that definition has ceased to be practical and has been modified to include another category of death called brain death. People can now be kept alive using such machines even when their brains have effectively died and are no longer able to control their bodily functions. Moreover, in certain medical procedures, such as open-heart surgery, individuals do not breathe or pump blood on their own. Since it would be wrong to declare as dead all persons whose circulatory or respiratory systems are temporarily maintained by artificial means (a category that includes many patients undergoing surgery), the medical community has determined that an individual may be declared dead if brain death has occurred—that is, if the whole brain has ceased to function, or has entered what is sometimes called a persistent vegetative state. An individual whose brain stem (lower brain) has died is not able to maintain the vegetative functions of life, including respiration, circulation, and swallowing. According to the Uniform Determination of Death Act (§ 1, U.L.A. [1980]), from which most states have developed their brain death statutes, "An individual who has sustained either (1) irreversible cessation of circulatory and respiratory function, or (2) irreversible cessation of all functions of the entire brain, including the brain stem, is dead."

Brain death becomes a crucial issue in part because of the importance of organ transplants. A brain-dead person may have organs—a heart, a liver, and lungs, for example—that could save other people's lives. And for an individual to be an acceptable organ donor, she or he must be dead but still breathing and circulating blood. If a brain-dead person were maintained on artificial respiration until her or his heart failed, then these usable organs would perish. Thus, the medical category of brain death makes it possible to accomplish another goal: saving lives with organ transplants.

The Right to Die: Individual Autonomy and State Interests The first significant legal case to deal with the issue of termination of life-sustaining medical care was *Quinlan*. This 1976 case helped resolve the question of whether a person could be held liable for withdrawing a life-support system even if the patient's condition is irreversible. In 1975, Karen Ann Quinlan unexplainedly became comatose and was put on a mechanical respirator. Her parents authorized physicians to use every possible means to revive her, but no treatment improved her condition. Although doctors agreed that the possibility of her recovering consciousness was remote, they would not pronounce her case hopeless. When her parents themselves lost all hope of Quinlan's recovery, they presented the hospital with an authorization for the removal of the respirator and an

exemption of the hospital and doctors from responsibility for the result. However, the attending doctor refused to turn off the respirator on the grounds that doing so would violate his professional oath. Quinlan's parents then initiated a lawsuit asking the court to keep the doctors and the hospital from interfering with their decision to remove Quinlan's respirator.

In a unanimous decision, the New Jersey Supreme Court ruled that Quinlan had a constitutional right of PRIVACY that could be safeguarded by her legal GUARDIAN; that the private decision of Quinlan's guardian and family should be honored; and that the hospital could be exempted from criminal liability for turning off a respirator if a hospital ethics committee agreed that the chance for recovery is remote. Quinlan was removed from the respirator, and she continued to live in a coma for ten years, nourished through a nasal feeding tube.

In cases following *Quinlan*, courts have ruled that life-sustaining procedures such as artificial feeding and hydration are the legal equivalent of mechanical respirators and may be removed using the same standards (*Gray v. Romeo*, 697 F. Supp. 580 [D.R.I. 1988]). Courts have also defined the right to die according to standards other than that of a constitutional right to privacy. The patient's legal right to refuse medical treatment has been grounded as well on the common-law right of bodily integrity, also called bodily self-determination, and on the liberty interest under the Due Process Clause of the FOURTEENTH AMENDMENT. These concepts are often collected under the term *individual autonomy*, or *patient autonomy*.

Subsequent cases have also defined the limits of the right to die, particularly the state's interest in those limits. The state's interests in cases concerning the termination of medical care are the preservation of life (including the prevention of suicide), the protection of dependent third parties such as children, and the protection of the standards of the medical profession. The interests of the state may, in some cases, outweigh those of the patient.

In 1990, the U.S. Supreme Court issued its first decision on the right-to-die issue, *Cruzan v. Director of Missouri Department of Health*, 497 U.S. 261, 110 S. Ct. 2841, 111 L. Ed. 2d 224. *Cruzan* illustrates the way in which individual and state interests are construed on this issue, but leaves many of the legal questions on the issue still unresolved. Nancy Cruzan was in a persistent vegetative state as a result of severe brain injuries suffered in an automobile accident in 1983. She had no chance of recovery, although with artificial nutrition and hydration

PHYSICIAN-ASSISTED SUICIDE

Imagine that you are suffering from a disease that is terminal, debilitating, and very painful. Should you have the right to die when you wish to rather than live in continued agony? Should your doctor be legally free to help you take your own life, perhaps by prescribing some pills and telling you their fatal dosage? Or should the law forbid anyone, including doctors, to assist the suicide of another human being? These are just some of the questions that surround the issue of physician-assisted suicide, a widely debated ethical issue in modern medicine.

IN FOCUS

Physician-assisted suicide is a form of voluntary euthanasia—in other words, it involves the patient's voluntarily acting to end his or her life. Such action usually consists of taking a lethal overdose of prescription medication. However, the twenty patients who were assisted by Jack Kevorkian between 1990 and 1994 chose to press a button that delivered a lethal poison into their veins or to put on a mask that emitted carbon monoxide into their lungs. Physician-assisted suicide differs from conventional suicide in that it is facilitated by a physician who confirms the patient's diagnosis, rules out conditions such as depression that may be clouding the patient's judgment, and finally provides the means for committing suicide. Assisted suicide is a felony offense in

most states and is also expressly forbidden in the American Medical Association's (AMA's) Code of Medical Ethics.

The debate surrounding physician-assisted suicide in the United States has been influenced by medical practices in other countries, particularly the Netherlands. In the Netherlands, both active euthanasia, which can include the physician's administration of a lethal agent such as an overdose of morphine, and physician-assisted suicide have been legalized in a series of court decisions that protect the physician from prosecution. Physician-assisted suicide in the Netherlands is conducted within established guidelines that include the following requirements: the patient's request for assisted suicide must be voluntary, the patient must be experiencing intolerable suffering, all other alternatives for treatment must have been explored, and the physician must consult another independent physician before proceeding. A 1991 study commissioned by the Dutch government indicated that 400 deaths, or 0.3 percent of the 130,000 deaths that occurred in the Netherlands each year, were caused by physician-assisted suicide. About 2,300 deaths, or 1.8 percent—including those that occurred by physician-assisted suicide—occurred by active euthanasia, which the study

defined as the termination of life at the patient's request. Polls conducted in 1988 indicated that popular support for such liberal euthanasia policies ran as high as 81 percent, and support among physicians ran even higher.

In the United States, the debate on legalizing assisted suicide began in earnest in the 1970s. On one side of the debate have been patients' rights groups that have lobbied for what they have called the right to die—or the right to choose to die, as some have clarified it—of terminally ill patients. The strongest opposition to the legalization of physician-assisted suicide has come from physicians' groups such as the AMA and from religious groups that are morally opposed to the practice.

One person who has done much to make the case for physician-assisted suicide is Derek Humphry, a former journalist who founded the Hemlock Society in 1980 after seeing the pain and suffering his first wife experienced in her death from cancer. With its motto Good Life, Good Death, the Hemlock Society has advocated for the right of terminally ill people to choose voluntary euthanasia, or what Humphry has termed self-deliverance. By 1990, the organization claimed to have thirty-eight thousand members and seventy chapters. Humphry has written several books on the subject of voluntary euthanasia, including *Jean's Way* (1978),

could have lived another thirty years. Her parents' attempts to authorize removal of Cruzan's medical support were first approved by a trial court and then denied by the Missouri Supreme Court. Her parents then appealed the case to the U.S. Supreme Court.

The Court held that the guarantee of liberty contained in the Fourteenth Amendment to the Constitution does not prohibit Missouri from insisting that "evidence of the incompetent [patient's] wishes as to the withdrawal of treatment be proved by clear and convincing evidence." The Court left other states free to adopt this "clear-and-convincing evidence" standard but

did not compel them to do so. Thus, existing state laws remained the same after the *Cruzan* decision. Although the Court affirmed that a COMPETENT patient has a constitutionally protected freedom to refuse unwanted medical treatment, it emphasized that an INCOMPETENT person is unable to make an informed choice to exercise that freedom. The Court explained that the state has an interest in the preservation of human life and in safeguarding against potential abuses by surrogates and is therefore not required to accept the "substituted judgment" of the patient's family. The Court agreed with the Missouri Supreme Court ruling that state-which recounts his struggle to assist his wife's death in 1975; *Final Exit: The Practicalities of Self-Deliverance and Assisted Suicide for the Dying* (1991), a controversial book that gives detailed advice on how terminally ill people may take their own life; and *Lawful Exit: The Limits of Freedom for Help in Dying* (1993), which contains Humphry's own recommendations for legislation that would legalize physician-assisted suicide and active voluntary euthanasia. In Humphry's words, the "right to choose to die" is "the ultimate civil liberty."

Humphry presents physician-assisted suicide as a merciful, dignified option for people whose illness has eroded their quality of life beyond the limits of tolerance. He also points out that what he calls beneficent euthanasia occurs every day in medical facilities as physicians make decisions regarding the end of life. Others, including some medical ethicists, go so far as to claim that a decision to withhold antibiotics, oxygen, or nutrition from a terminally ill patient is no less "active" a form of euthanasia than is administering a fatal dose of morphine. Indeed, they see the common practice of withholding life support as more open to potential abuse than the practice of physician-assisted suicide. The former, they argue, is a less visible, less easily regulated decision. Proponents of physician-assisted suicide also claim that diseases kill people in far more cruel ways than would any means of death that a physician might provide for an irreversibly ill patient. As a result, they see the action

of assisting in suicide as entirely compatible with the physician's duty to the patient.

Humphry has been an open critic of Kevorkian's work. He has described Kevorkian's theory and practice of assisted suicide as open-ended euthanasia. Noting Kevorkian's lack of precautionary measures such as the use of waiting periods and second opinions, Humphry sees any wider application of Kevorkian's methods as potentially leading to abuse and tragedy. "The thinking people in our movement are appalled by it," Humphry said. "If you have Kevorkian's type of euthanasia, it will be a slippery slope. Kevorkian's is a recipe for skiing down a glacier."

On the opposite side of the issue, the AMA, in its Code of Medical Ethics, condemns physician-assisted suicide as incompatible with the fundamental role of the physician as healer. According to this view, allowing the doctor to assist in the suicide of a patient would diminish the trust that must exist in the patient-doctor relationship. Patients should not have to worry that their doctor will make a value judgment that their life is not worth living. Others have asked whether doctors might begin to counsel patients to commit suicide, therefore making assisted suicide less "voluntary" than its proponents claim.

Detractors of physician-assisted suicide also use the familiar "slippery slope" argument, proposing that once physician-assisted suicide is legalized, other forms of euthanasia will more likely be practiced as well. They see

assisted suicide as potentially leading to situations in which elderly, chronically ill, and handicapped people, along with others, are killed through active, nonvoluntary euthanasia. Related to this idea is the view that widespread practice of physician-assisted suicide might claim the lives of those whose intolerable suffering is caused by treatable depression. They point out that terminally ill people or others in pain are often also suffering from depression, and that despite their illness, their feelings of hopelessness can often be addressed through means such as counseling and antidepressant medication.

The Catholic Church is one of many religious organizations that opposes euthanasia and assisted suicide. In Pope John Paul II's words, medical killings such as those caused by assisted suicide are "crimes which no human law can claim to legitimize." Basing its arguments on passages from the Bible, Catholic theology has for many centuries opposed all forms of suicide. Catholicism argues that innocent human life may not be destroyed for any reason whatsoever.

Ultimately, the voters and representatives of the states and the legal system itself will have to decide whether or not physician-assisted suicide will be legalized. Regardless of what side prevails in the debate, the exchange of ideas that it creates may lead to a greater understanding of the difficult choices surrounding death in our time.

See also Physicians and Surgeons; Suicide

---

ments made by Cruzan to a housemate a year before her accident did not amount to "CLEAR AND CONVINCING PROOF" that she desired to have hydration and nutrition withdrawn. Cruzan had allegedly made statements to the effect that she would not want to live should she face life as a "vegetable." There was no testimony that she had actually discussed withdrawal of medical treatment, hydration, or nutrition.

After the Court's decision, Cruzan's parents went back to the Missouri probate court with new evidence regarding their daughter's wishes. On December 14, 1990, a Missouri judge ruled that clear evidence of Cruzan's wishes existed,

and permitted her parents to authorize withdrawing artificial nutrition and hydration. Cruzan died on December 27, twelve days after feeding tubes were removed.

A court must consider many factors and standards in right-to-die cases. It must determine, for example, whether a patient is *competent* or *incompetent*. A competent patient is deemed by the court to be able to give INFORMED CONSENT or refusal relative to the treatment under consideration, whereas an incompetent patient (e.g., a patient in a coma) lacks the decision-making capacity to do so. According to the principle of individual autonomy, the court must honor the informed consent of competent patients regarding their medical care. For incompetent patients who cannot make informed decisions regarding their care, an *advance directive* may provide a means of decision making for the termination of life-supporting treatment.

An advance directive gives patients some control over their health care after they have lost the ability to make decisions owing to a medical condition. It may consist of detailed instructions about medical treatment, as in a living will; or the appointment of a proxy, or substitute, who will make the difficult choices regarding medical care with the patient's earlier directions in mind. The appointment of a proxy is sometimes called a *proxy directive* or *durable* POWER OF ATTORNEY. Sometimes, the patient appoints a proxy decision maker when he or she is competent; often, the physician appoints a proxy. Usually, a relative such as a spouse, adult child, or sibling is chosen as a proxy. Sometimes, the court appoints a legal guardian who acts on behalf of an incompetent person. If an advance directive provides adequate evidence of a patient's wishes, a decision about the termination of life support can often be made without involving a court of law.

For an incompetent patient whose preferences regarding medical care are known from prior oral statements, the patient's proxy may make a *substituted judgment*—that is, a judgment consistent with what the patient would have chosen for herself or himself. If no preference regarding medical treatment is known, the standard for the proxy's decision is the "best interests of the patient." According to that standard, the proxy's decision should approximate what most reasonable individuals in the same circumstances as the patient would choose.

By 1991, over forty states had living-will statutes, and all fifty states had durable-power-of-attorney statutes that allowed an individual to appoint a proxy decision maker. By the early 1990s, proxy directives had become a preferred alternative to living wills. Most living-will statutes are applicable only to patients who are terminally ill, limit the types of treatment that can be refused, and require a person to predict accurately his or her final illness and what medical interventions might be available at that time. Only a small minority of adults in the United States have executed advance directives.

Assisted Suicide   Despite the many advances in medicine's ability to control pain, some terminally or chronically ill patients experience what they consider to be an intolerable decline in quality of life. This situation has led to a call for a practice known as physician-assisted suicide, in which a doctor helps a patient take her or his own life. However, assisted suicide, even by a physician, is a FELONY offense in most states. Moreover, the AMA

Jack Kevorkian has assisted in the suicides of many people suffering from serious illnesses. He uses a machine that allows the patient to decide when to begin ingestion of a poison.

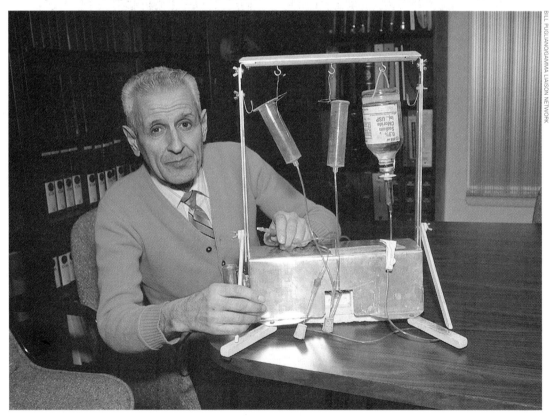

considers physician-assisted suicide a violation of professional ethics (Code of Medical Ethics, rule 2.22 [1994]).

Physician-assisted suicide received greater public attention after Jack Kevorkian, a retired pathologist from Michigan, participated in his first such procedure in 1990. Kevorkian set up a machine that allowed a fifty-four-year-old woman suffering from Alzheimer's disease (a degenerative neurological condition) to press a button that delivered a lethal poison into her veins. Kevorkian went on to assist in the suicides of dozens of individuals suffering from terminal, debilitating, or chronic illnesses. In 1992, Michigan passed an assisted suicide bill (Mich. Comp. Laws § 752.1021) specifically designed to stop Kevorkian's activities, but technicalities and questions as to its constitutionality delayed its implementation, allowing Kevorkian to continue assisting suicides—often in direct opposition to court INJUNCTIONS.

Kevorkian has been charged with murder several times but has never been found guilty. When murder charges were brought against him for his first three assisted suicides, for example, they were dismissed because Michigan at that time had no law against assisted suicide. In 1994, Kevorkian was tried and found not guilty of assisting in the August 1993 suicide of Thomas W. Hyde, Jr. However, in December 1994, Michigan's supreme court ruled in *People v. Kevorkian*, 447 Mich. 436, 527 N.W.2d 714, that there is no constitutional right to commit suicide, with or without assistance, and upheld the Michigan statute making assisted suicide a crime. The following year, the U.S. Supreme Court refused to hear Kevorkian's appeal from the state supreme court's ruling (*Kevorkian v. Michigan*, __U.S.__, 115 S. Ct. 1795, 131 L. Ed. 2d 723).

Observers disagree about the humanity of Kevorkian's activities. Some see him as a hero seeking to give suffering people greater choice and dignity in dying. Others point to his lack of procedural precautions and fear that the widespread practice of assisted suicide will lead to the unnecessary death of people who may have been helped by other means, including treatment for depression. Many opponents of assisted suicide find the same faults in the practice that they see in other forms of euthanasia. They envision its leading to a devaluation of human life and even a genocidal killing of vulnerable or so-called undesirable individuals.

More than thirty states have passed statutes criminalizing assisted suicide. The statutes forbid a person to knowingly assist or aid another in committing suicide. Some also prohibit solic-

iting, advising, or encouraging another to commit suicide. Some statutes penalize assisted suicide under guidelines established for murder or manslaughter, whereas others make it a unique offense with separate penalties. Few courts have interpreted the assisted suicide statutes, because prosecutions for assisted suicide are rare. In cases of assisted suicide, a state usually prosecutes individuals for murder or manslaughter.

See also PHYSICIANS AND SURGEONS.

DEATH PENALTY See CAPITAL PUNISHMENT.

DEATH WARRANT 📖 An order from the executive, the governor of a state, or the president directing the warden of a prison or a sheriff or other appropriate officer to carry into execution a SENTENCE of death; an order commanding that a named person be put to death in a specified manner at a specific time. 📖

See also CAPITAL PUNISHMENT.

DEBENTURE 📖 [*Latin, Are due.*] A PROMISSORY NOTE or BOND offered by a CORPORATION to a CREDITOR in exchange for a loan, the repayment of which is backed only by the general creditworthiness of the corporation and not by a MORTGAGE or a LIEN on any specific property. 📖

Debentures are usually offered in issues under an INDENTURE, a document that sets the terms of the exchange. A debenture is usually a BEARER instrument. When it is presented for payment, the person in possession of it will be paid, even if the person is not the original creditor. COUPONS representing annual or semi-annual payments of interest on the debt are attached, to be clipped and presented for payment on their due dates. They may be deposited in, and collected by, the banks of holders of the debentures, the creditors of the corporation.

A *convertible debenture* is one that can be changed or converted, at the option of its holder, into shares of STOCK, usually COMMON STOCK, at a fixed ratio as stated in the indenture. The ratio can be adjusted in light of STOCK DIVIDENDS; otherwise the value of converting the debt into securities would be worth less than retaining the debenture until its date of maturity.

A *subordinate debenture* is one that will be repaid only after other corporate debts have been satisfied.

A *convertible subordinate debenture* is one that is subject or subordinate to the prior repayment of other debts of the corporation but which can be converted into another form of security.

A *sinking fund debenture* is one whereby repayment is secured by periodic payments by the corporation into a sinking fund, an amount of money made up of corporate assets and earn-

THE _____ CORPORATION

Issue of _____ debentures, of $_____ each, numbered _____ to _____, bearing interest at _____ per cent per annum, payable on the _____ day of _____ and the _____ day of _____ in each year.

Debenture No. _____

§ **1.1** The _____ Corporation (herein called the "Corporation"), in consideration of the sum of $_____ paid to the Corporation, hereby binds itself to pay to the bearer of this debenture on the _____ day of _____, 19_____, or on such earlier day as the principal moneys hereby secured may become payable by the conditions of this debenture, the sum of $_____, and until payment of the said sum of $_____ to pay interest thereon at the rate of _____ per cent per annum by equal half-yearly payments on the _____ day of _____ and the _____ day of _____ in each year in accordance with the coupons annexed hereto.

§ **1.2** The Corporation as beneficial owner hereby charges with such payments its undertaking and all its property and assets whatsoever and wheresoever, both present and future, including therein the uncalled capital of the Corporation for the time being.

§ **2.1** This debenture is one of a series of like debentures, numbered _____ to _____, issued or about to be issued by the Corporation. All the debentures of this series are payable pari passu, and will rank equally as a first charge upon the property and assets of the Corporation comprised therein, without any preference or priority one over another.

§ **2.2** The said charge shall constitute a floating security only, not hindering any sale or other dealings in the ordinary course of business by the Corporation with the property or assets comprised in the charge, but the Corporation shall not be at liberty to create any mortgage or charge upon the property or assets comprised in the security, either in priority to or to rank equally with the charge hereby created, without the consent of holders of [*two thirds*] in value of the outstanding debentures of this issue.

§ **2.3** The principal moneys hereby secured shall become immediately payable in any of the following events:

(a) If the Corporation defaults for [*two months*] in the payment of any interest hereby secured, and the holder before such interest is paid by notice in writing to the Corporation calls the said principal.

(b) If a distress or execution, either by writ or appointment of a receiver, is levied on any part of the property or assets charged, and the debt for which such levy is made or receiver appointed is not paid off within seven days.

(c) If an order is made or a special resolution passed for the dissolution and winding up the Corporation.

§ **2.4** This debenture is a negotiable instrument, with all the incidents of negotiability.

§ **2.5** The Corporation is entitled at any time after the _____ day of _____, 19_____, to redeem this debenture [*at a premium of _____ per cent*] on giving [*six*] months' notice by advertisement of its intention so to do.

§ **2.6** The principal moneys secured by this debenture will be paid at the _____ Bank, or at other of the Corporation's bankers for the time being. On application for payment this debenture must be produced and surrendered, together with any coupons for future interest.

Given under the seal of the _____ Corporation this _____ day of _____, 19_____.

[*Corporate Seal*]

[*Name of Corporation*]

By _____

ings that are set aside for the repayment of designated debentures and long-term debts.

DEBIT 📖 A sum charged as due or owing. An entry made on the ASSET side of a LEDGER or ACCOUNT. The term is used in bookkeeping to denote the left side of the ledger, or the charging of a person or an account with all that is supplied to or paid out for that person or for the subject of the account. Also, the balance of an account where it is shown that something remains due to the party keeping the account.

As a noun, an entry on the left-hand side of an account. As a verb, to make an entry on the left-hand side of an account. A term used in ACCOUNTING or bookkeeping that results in an increase to an asset and an expense account and a decrease to a liability, revenue, or owner's equity account. 📖

DE BONIS NON ADMINISTRATIS 📖 [*Latin, Of the goods not administered.*] When an ADMINISTRATOR is appointed to succeed another who has left the ESTATE partially unsettled, the administrator is said to be granted "administration *de bonis non,*" that is, of the goods not already administered. 📖

DEBT 📖 A sum of money that is owed or due to be paid because of an express agreement; a specified sum of money that one person is obligated to pay and that another has the legal right to collect or receive.

A fixed and certain OBLIGATION to pay money or some other valuable thing or things, either in the present or in the future. In a still more general sense, that which is due from one person to another, whether money, goods, or services. In a broad sense, any duty to respond to another in money, labor, or service; it may even mean a moral or honorary obligation, unenforceable by legal action. Also, sometimes an aggregate of separate debts, or the total sum of the existing claims against a person or company. Thus we speak of the "national debt," the "bonded debt" of a corporation, and so on. 📖

DEBT, ACTION OF 📖 One of the oldest common-law FORMS OF ACTION available to private litigants seeking to collect what is owed to them because of a harm done to them by another. 📖

Originally, the ACTION was allowed for any plaintiff who claimed an OBLIGATION owed by another person, but the courts gradually began to recognize two forms of action: DETINUE, an action to collect a specific item of property, and a debt for a sum of money. The distinction had become clear in England by the early thirteenth century. In debt, as in detinue, a defendant who lost the case had the option of either paying a sum of money for the judgment or giving back

the property that gave rise to the debt. Later in the thirteenth century, courts began to permit REPLEVIN, an action for the return of goods wrongfully taken or withheld, and COVENANT, an action for DAMAGES from someone who broke an agreement. Gradually, judges began to demand firm proof of the agreement, and finally they would accept nothing less than a CONTRACT made under SEAL. Later the action in ASSUMPSIT enlarged the rights of a disappointed party to a contract by allowing monetary damages for any breach. This action enjoyed growing popularity and supplanted the action of debt for a time because it permitted the defendant to prove his or her case by swearing in open court and by bringing along eleven neighbors who would proclaim their belief in their neighbor's truthfulness. When this procedure, called the WAGER

Federal Debt, 1945–1994

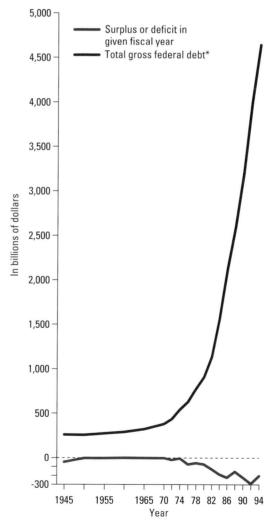

*Gross federal debt includes money borrowed by the U.S. Treasury and various federal agencies.

Source: U.S. Office of Management and Budget, *Historical Tables*, annual.

OF LAW, was abolished during the reign of King William IV (1830–1837), the action of debt again became important as an action to enforce a simple contract.

As long as COMMON-LAW forms of action were the required modes for PLEADING civil actions, the action of debt continued to be useful. Relief was available only for those whose claims fit exactly into its form, however, and there was criticism of its rigidity and technicalities. By the end of the nineteenth century most states had passed laws to replace the old forms of action with CODE PLEADING. Today, the law of CIVIL PROCEDURE recognizes only one form for a lawsuit, the CIVIL ACTION. An individual can still sue to collect what is due on a debt, but no longer is it necessary to draw the COMPLAINT in the form of the ancient action of debt.

DEBTOR One who owes a DEBT or the performance of an obligation to another, who is called the CREDITOR; one who may be compelled to pay a CLAIM or demand; anyone liable on a claim, whether due or to become due.

In BANKRUPTCY law, a person who files a voluntary petition or person against whom an involuntary petition is filed. A person or municipality concerning which a bankruptcy case has been commenced.

DEBT POOLERS Individuals or organizations who receive and apply monthly funds from a person owing money to several CREDITORS and who make arrangements to pay these creditors less than what is actually owed.

Debt poolers, also known as *debt adjusters* or *consolidators*, are helpful to consumers, particularly when they are nonprofit organizations that provide their services free or for a reasonable fee. In other cases, however, their usefulness to consumers is lessened when they charge fees that would make it less costly for consumers to make similar arrangements with creditors on their own.

DECALOGUE SOCIETY OF LAWYERS Founded in 1934, the Decalogue Society of Lawyers is an association of attorneys of the Jewish faith who seek to advance and improve the law, the legal profession, and the administration of justice; to foster friendly relations among its members, and between its members and other members of the bar, the courts, and the public; to cooperate as lawyers and citizens in worthy movements for the public welfare; to maintain vigilance against public practices that are antisocial or discriminatory; and to cooperate with other bar associations for the attainment of those objectives. Activities include a forum on legal topics of general and Jewish interest, lectures and seminars on recent decisions and legislation, and the presentation of

awards. The society provides a placement service for members and maintains a welfare fund. Meetings are held annually in June.

The society has several active committees including those on arbitration, civic affairs, civil rights, family law, lawyer counseling, legal education, legislation, and professional relations.

The society publishes *The Decalogue Journal* (quarterly) and a membership directory (annually).

DECEDENT An individual who has died. The term literally means "one who is dying," but it is commonly used in the law to denote one who has died, particularly someone who has recently passed away.

A decedent's ESTATE is the real and personal property that an individual owns upon his or her death.

DECEIT A MISREPRESENTATION made with the express intention of defrauding someone, which subsequently causes injury to that person.

In order for a statement to be deceit, it must be untrue, made with knowledge of its falsity, or made in reckless disregard of the truth. The misrepresentation must be such that it causes harm to another individual.

DECENNIAL DIGEST® One of the volumes of the American Digest System that classifies by topic the summaries of court decisions that were reported chronologically in the various units of the National Reporter System.

Each of the four hundred subject classifications corresponds to a general legal concept—TORTS, for example—and all cases found under a specific topic discuss similar points of law. Summaries of cases decided during the period from 1897 to 1905 and for every ten-year period until 1976 and every five years thereafter.

DECISION A conclusion reached after an evaluation of facts and law.

As a generic term, *decision* refers to both administrative and judicial determinations. It includes final JUDGMENTS, rulings, and INTERLOCUTORY or provisional orders made by the court pending the outcome of the case. Frequently, a decision is considered the initial step in a rendition by a court of a judgment in an ACTION.

When referring to judicial matters, a decision is not the same as an OPINION, although the terms are sometimes used interchangeably. A decision is the pronouncement of the solution of the court or judgment in a case, while an opinion is a statement of the reasons for its determination made by the court.

DECISION ON THE MERITS An ultimate determination rendered by a court in an ACTION that concludes the status of legal rights contested in a controversy and precludes a later lawsuit on the same CAUSE OF ACTION by the parties to the original lawsuit. 📖

A decision on the merits is made by the application of SUBSTANTIVE LAW to the essential facts of the case, not solely upon technical or procedural grounds.

DECLARATION 📖 The first PLEADING in a lawsuit governed by the rule of COMMON-LAW PLEADING. In the law of EVIDENCE, a statement or narration made not under oath but simply in the middle of things, as a part of what is happening. Also, a PROCLAMATION. 📖

A declaration is the PLAINTIFF's statement of a claim against the DEFENDANT, formally and specifically setting out the facts and circumstances that make up the case. It generally is broken into several sections, which describe the different COUNTS of the CAUSE OF ACTION. The declaration should give the title of the action, the court and place of trial, the basis for the claim, and the relief demanded. The defendant then answers with a PLEA. Common-law pleading has been abolished in the United States, and modern systems of CODE PLEADING and rules based on federal CIVIL PROCEDURE now provide for a COMPLAINT to accomplish the same purpose as did the declaration in former times.

Under some circumstances, statements made out of court by one person may be repeated in court by someone else even though the HEARSAY rule ordinarily forbids secondhand TESTIMONY. For example, a DYING DECLARATION is a statement in which a homicide victim names his or her killer on his or her deathbed. If the victim had known who had attacked him or her, had abandoned all hope of recovery, and had in fact died

of the wounds, a person who heard the dying declaration can repeat it in court at the time the killer is brought to trial. The theory is that a deceased person would not have lied just before dying.

A *declaration against interest* is another type of statement received into evidence even though it is being repeated by someone who heard it out of court. It is any comment that admits something harmful to the rights of the person who made the statement. For example, a driver says to his or her passenger just before the car misses a curve and ends up in a ditch, "I know the brakes are bad, but don't worry." Later when suing to recover compensation for injuries, the passenger can testify that he or she heard the driver make a declaration against his or her interest even though that testimony is hearsay.

Customs law requires all persons entering the United States to provide officers with a list of merchandise they are bringing into the country. This list is also called a declaration.

REAL PROPERTY laws in various states require the filing of statements to disclose plans that establish certain rights in particular buildings or parcels. For example, a homeowners' association formed by neighbors to maintain a recreation center owned by all of them together may file a declaration of COVENANTS. A builder may be required to file a declaration of CONDOMINIUM before beginning to sell new units.

As a preliminary step before becoming naturalized U.S. citizens, ALIENS must file a declaration of intention which states that they are honestly trying to become CITIZENS and that they formally renounce all allegiance to any other nation where they were ever citizens or subjects.

The DECLARATION OF INDEPENDENCE was a formal announcement on July 4, 1776, by which the Continental Congress of the United States of America proclaimed the independence of the people of the colonies from the rule of Great Britain. It explained the reasons for their assertion of political autonomy and announced to the world that the United States was a free and independent nation.

INTERNATIONAL LAW recognized that nations may formally and publicly proclaim a condition of armed conflict by a declaration of war, which in effect forbids all persons to aid or assist the enemy. In the United States, the Congress has the authority to declare war, and a declaration fixes a beginning date for the war.

A *declaration of a dividend* is an act of a CORPORATION in setting aside a portion of net or surplus income for proportional distribution as a DIVIDEND to those who hold shares of STOCK.

President George Bush clenched his fist as he spoke with reporters about unsuccessful meetings with Iraqi officials. Later that month a declaration of war by the United States and other nations marked the start of the Persian Gulf War.

DECLARATION OF INDEPENDENCE

A formal announcement executed by the Continental Congress on July 4, 1776, on behalf of the people living in the American colonies, that asserted and proclaimed their freedom from Britain.

Since its creation in 1776, the Declaration of Independence has been considered the single most important expression of the ideals of U.S. democracy. As a statement of the fundamental principles of the United States, the Declaration is an enduring reminder of the country's commitment to popular government and equal rights for all.

The Declaration of Independence is a product of the early days of the Revolutionary War. On July 2, 1776, the Second Continental Congress—the legislature of the American colonies—voted for independence from Great Britain. It then appointed a committee of five—JOHN ADAMS, Benjamin Franklin, THOMAS JEFFERSON, ROGER SHERMAN, and ROBERT R. LIVINGSTON—to draft a formal statement of independence designed to influence public opinion at home and abroad. Because of his reputation as an eloquent and forceful writer, Jefferson was assigned the task of creating the document, and the final product is almost entirely his own work. The Congress did not approve all of Jefferson's original draft, however, rejecting most notably his denunciation of the slave trade. Delegates from South Carolina and Georgia were not yet ready to extend the notion of inalienable rights to African Americans.

On July 4, 1776, the day of birth for the new country, the Congress approved the Declaration of Independence. The Declaration served a number of purposes for the newly formed United States. With regard to the power politics of the day, it functioned as a propaganda statement intended to build support for American independence abroad, particularly in France, from which the Americans hoped to have support in their struggle for independence. Similarly, it also served as a clear message of intention to the British. Even more important for the later Republic of the United States, it functioned as a statement of governmental ideals.

In keeping with its immediate diplomatic purposes, most of the Declaration consists of a list of thirty grievances against acts of the British monarch George III. Many of these were traditional and legitimate grievances under British constitutional law. The Declaration firmly announces that British actions had established "an absolute Tyranny over these States."

Britain's acts of despotism, according to the Declaration's list, included taxation of Americans without representation in Parliament; imposition of standing armies on American communities; establishment of the military above the civil power; obstruction of the right to trial by jury; interference with the operation of colonial legislatures; and cutting off of trade with the rest of the world. The Declaration ends with the decisive resolution that "these United Colonies are, and of Right ought to be Free and Independent States; that they are Absolved from all Allegiance to the British Crown, and that all political connection between them and the State of Great Britain, is and ought to be totally dissolved."

The first sentences of the document and their statement of political ideals have remained the Declaration's most memorable and influential section. Among these sentences are the following:

> We hold these truths to be self-evident, that all men are created equal, that they are endowed by their Creator with certain unalienable Rights, that among these are Life, Liberty and the pursuit of Happiness.— That to secure these rights, Governments are instituted among Men, deriving their just powers from the consent of the governed,—That whenever any Form of Government becomes destructive of these ends, it is the Right of the People to alter or to abolish it, and to institute new Government.

Ever since their creation, these ideas have guided the development of U.S. government, including the creation of the U.S. CONSTITUTION in 1787. The concepts of equal and unalienable rights for all, limited government, popular consent, and freedom to rebel have had a lasting effect on U.S. law and politics.

Scholars have long debated the relative importance of the different sources Jefferson used for his ideas in the Declaration. Most agree that the natural rights philosophy of English philosopher JOHN LOCKE greatly influenced Jefferson's composition of the Declaration. In particular, Locke advanced the ideas that a just government derives its legitimacy and power from the consent of the governed, that people possess inalienable rights that no legitimate government may take away, and that the people have the right and duty to overthrow a government that violates their rights. Jefferson also paralleled Locke in his identification of three major rights—the rights to "Life, Liberty and

DECLARATION OF INDEPENDENCE

IN CONGRESS, JULY 4, 1776
THE UNANIMOUS DECLARATION of the thirteen united STATES OF AMERICA

WHEN in the Course of human events, it becomes necessary for one people to dissolve the political bands which have connected them with another, and to assume among the powers of the earth, the separate and equal station to which the Laws of Nature and of Nature's God entitle them, a decent respect to the opinions of mankind requires that they should declare the causes which impel them to the separation.—We hold these truths to be self-evident, that all men are created equal, that they are endowed by their Creator with certain unalienable Rights, that among these are Life, Liberty and the pursuit of Happiness.—That to secure these rights, Governments are instituted among Men, deriving their just powers from the consent of the governed.—That whenever any Form of Government becomes destructive of these ends, it is the Right of the People to alter or to abolish it, and to institute new Government, laying its foundation on such principles and organizing its powers in such form, as to them shall seem most likely to effect their Safety and Happiness. Prudence, indeed, will dictate that Governments long established should not be changed for light and transient causes; and accordingly all experience hath shown, that mankind are more disposed to suffer, while evils are sufferable, than to right themselves by abolishing the forms to which they are accustomed. But when a long train of abuses and usurpations, pursuing invariably the same Object evinces a design to reduce them under absolute Despotism, it is their right, it is their duty, to throw off such Government, and to provide new Guards for their future security.—Such has been the patient sufferance of these Colonies; and such is now the necessity which constrains them to alter their former Systems of Government. The history of the present King of Great Britain is a history of repeated injuries and usurpations, all having in direct object the establishment of an absolute Tyranny over these States. To prove this, let Facts be submitted to a candid world.—He has refused his Assent to Laws, the most wholesome and necessary for the public good.—He has forbidden his Governors to pass Laws of immediate and pressing importance, unless suspended in their operation till his Assent should be obtained; and when so suspended, he has utterly neglected to attend to them.—He has refused to pass other Laws for the accommodation of large districts of people, unless those people would relinquish the right of Representation in the Legislature, a right inestimable to them and formidable to tyrants only.—He has called together legislative bodies at places unusual, uncomfortable, and distant from the depository or their public Records, for the sole purpose of fatiguing them into compliance with his measures.—He has dissolved Representative Houses repeatedly, for opposing with manly firmness his invasions on the rights of the people.—He has refused for a long time, after such dissolutions, to cause others to be elected; whereby the Legislative powers, incapable of Annihilation, have returned to the People at large for their exercise; the State remaining in the mean time exposed to all the dangers of invasion from without, and convulsions within.—He has endeavored to prevent the population of these States; for that purpose obstructing the Laws for Naturalization of Foreigners; refusing to pass others to encourage their migration hither, and raising the conditions of new Appropriations of Lands.—He has obstructed the Administration of Justice, by refusing his Assent to Laws for establishing Judiciary powers.—He has made Judges dependent on his Will alone, for the tenure of their offices, and the amount and payment of their salaries.—He has erected a multitude of New Offices, and sent hither swarms of Officers to harrass our people, and eat out their substance.—He has kept among us, in times of peace, Standing Armies, without the Consent of our legislatures.—He has affected to render the Military independent of and superior to the Civil power.—He has combined with others to subject us to a jurisdiction foreign to our constitution, and unacknowledged by our laws; giving his Assent to their Acts of pretended Legislation:—For quartering large bodies of armed troops among us:—For protecting them, by a mock Trial, from punishment for any Murders which they should commit on the Inhabitants of these States:—For cutting off our Trade with all parts of the world:—For imposing Taxes on us without our Consent:—For depriving us in many cases, of the benefits of Trial by Jury:—For transporting us beyond Seas to be tried for pretended offences:—For abolishing the free System of English Laws in a neighbouring Province, establishing therein an Arbitrary government, and enlarging its Boundaries so as to render it at once an example and fit instrument for introducing the same absolute rule into these Colonies:—For taking away our Charters, abolishing our most valuable Laws, and altering fundamentally the Forms of our Governments:—For suspending our own Legislatures, and declaring themselves invested with power to legislate for us in all cases whatsoever.—He has abdicated Government here, by declaring us out of his Protection and waging War against us.—He has plundered our seas, ravaged our Coasts, burnt our towns, and destroyed the lives of our people.—He is at this time transporting large Armies of foreign Mercenaries to compleat the works of death, desolation and tyranny, already begun with circumstances of Cruelty & perfidy scarcely paralleled in the most barbarous ages, and totally unworthy the Head of a civilized nation.—He has constrained our fellow Citizens taken Captive on the high Seas to bear Arms against their Country, to become the executioners of their friends and Brethren, or to fall themselves by their Hands.—He has excited domestic insurrections amongst us, and has endeavored to bring on the inhabitants of our frontiers, the merciless Indian Savages, whose known rule of warfare, is an undistinguished destruction of all ages, sexes and conditions. In every state of these Oppressions We have Petitioned for Redress in the most humble terms. Our repeated Petitions have been answered only by repeated injury. A Prince, whose character is thus marked by every act which may define a Tyrant, is unfit to be the ruler of a free people. Nor have We been wanting in attentions to our British brethren. We have warned them from time to time of attempts by their legislature to extend an unwarrantable jurisdiction over us. We have reminded them of the circumstances of our emigration and settlement here. We have appealed to their native justice and magnanimity, and we have conjured them by the ties of our common kindred to disavow these usurpations, which would inevitably interrupt our connections and correspondence. They too have been deaf to the voice of justice and consanguinity. We must, therefore, acquiesce in the necessity, which denounces our Separation, and hold them, as we hold the rest of mankind, Enemies in War, in Peace Friends.—

WE, THEREFORE, the REPRESENTATIVES of the UNITED STATES OF AMERICA, in General Congress, Assembled, appealing to the Supreme Judge of the world for the rectitude of our intentions, do, in the Name, and by Authority of the good People of these Colonies, solemnly publish and declare, That these United Colonies are, and of Right ought to be FREE AND INDEPENDENT STATES; that they are Absolved from all Allegiance to the British Crown, and that all political connection between them and the State of Great Britain, is and ought to be totally disolved; and that as Free and Independent States, they have full Power to levy War, conclude Peace, contract Alliances, establish Commerce, and to do all other Acts and Things which Independent States may of right do.—And for the support of this Declaration, with a firm reliance on the protection of Divine Providence, we mutually pledge to each other our Lives, our Fortunes and our sacred Honor.

John Hancock	Benj. Harrison	Lewis Morris
Button Gwinnett	Thos. Nelson, Jr.	Richd. Stockton
Lyman Hall	Francis Lightfoot Lee	Jno. Witherspoon
Geo. Walton	Carter Braxton	Fras. Hopkinson
Wm. Hooper	Robt. Morris	John Hart
Joseph Hewes	Benjamin Rush	Abra. Clark
John Penn	Benj. Franklin	Josiah Bartlett
Edward Rutledge	John Morton	Wm. Whipple
Thos. Heyward, Jr.	Geo. Clymer	Saml. Adams
Thomas Lynch, Jr.	Jas. Smith	John Adams
Arthur Middleton	Geo. Taylor	Robt. Treat Paine
Samuel Chase	James Wilson	Elbridge Gerry
Wm. Paca	Geo. Ross	Step. Hopkins
Thos. Stone	Caesar Rodney	William Ellery
Charles Carroll of	Geo. Read	Roger Sherman
Carrollton	Tho. M: Kean	Sam. Huntington
George Wythe	Wm. Floyd	Wm. Williams
Richard Henry Lee	Phil. Livington	Oliver Wolcott
Th. Jefferson	Frans. Lewis	Matthew Thornton

The Declaration of Independence was signed July 4, 1776. This artist has surrounded the text of the document by portraits of John Hancock, George Washington, and Thomas Jefferson and representations of the thirteen original states.

the pursuit of Happiness"—though the last of his three is a change from Locke's right to "property."

Jefferson himself minimized the Declaration's contribution to political philosophy. In a letter that he wrote in 1825, fifty years after the Declaration was signed, he described the document as "an appeal to the tribunal of the world." Its object, he wrote, was

> [n]ot to find out new principles or new arguments, never before thought of, not merely to say things which had never been said before; but to place before mankind the common sense of the subject, in terms so plain and firm as to command their assent, and to justify ourselves in the independent stand we are compelled to take. Neither aiming at originality of principle or sentiment, nor yet copied from any particular and previous writing, it was intended to be an expression of the American mind, and to give to that expression the proper tone and spirit called for by the occasion.

Although the Declaration of Independence stands with the Constitution as a founding document of the United States of America, its position in U.S. law is much less certain than that of the Constitution. The Declaration has been recognized as the founding act of law establishing the United States as a sovereign and independent nation, and Congress has placed it at the beginning of the U.S. Code, under the heading "The Organic Laws of the

United States of America." The Supreme Court, however, has generally not considered it a part of the ORGANIC LAW of the country. For example, although the Declaration mentions a right to rebellion, this right, particularly with regard to violent rebellion, has not been recognized by the Supreme Court and other branches of the federal government. The most notable failure to uphold this right occurred when the Union put down the rebellion by the Southern Confederacy in the Civil War.

Despite its secondary authority, many later reform movements have quoted the Declaration in support of their cause, including movements for universal suffrage, abolition of SLAVERY, WOMEN'S RIGHTS, and CIVIL RIGHTS for African Americans. Many have argued that this document influenced the passage and wording of such important developments in U.S. law and government as the THIRTEENTH and FOURTEENTH AMENDMENTS, which banned slavery and sought to make African Americans equal citizens. In this way, the Declaration of Independence remains the most outstanding example of the spirit, as opposed to the letter, of U.S. law.

DECLARATION OF TRUST 📖 An assertion by a property owner that he or she holds the property or estate for the benefit of another person, or for particular designated objectives. 📖

The term also signifies the DEED or other instrument that contains the statement—which may be either written or oral, depending upon the applicable state law.

DECLARATORY JUDGMENT 📖 Statutory remedy for the determination of a JUSTICIABLE controversy where the PLAINTIFF is in doubt as to his or her legal rights. A binding ADJUDICATION of the rights and status of litigants even though no consequential RELIEF is awarded. 📖

Individuals may seek a declaratory JUDGMENT after a legal controversy has arisen but before any DAMAGES have occurred or any laws have been violated. A declaratory judgment differs from other judicial rulings in that it does not require that any action be taken. Instead, the judge, after analyzing the controversy, simply issues an opinion declaring the rights of each of the parties involved. A declaratory judgment may only be granted in justiciable controversies—that is, in actual, rather than hypothetical, controversies that fall within a court's jurisdiction.

A declaratory judgment, sometimes called declaratory relief, is conclusive and legally binding as to the present and future rights of the parties involved. The parties involved in a declaratory judgment may not later seek another court resolution of the same legal issue unless they appeal the judgment.

Declaratory judgments are often sought in situations involving CONTRACTS, DEEDS, LEASES, and WILLS. An insurance company, for example, might seek a declaratory judgment as to whether a policy applies to a certain person or event. Declaratory judgments also commonly involve individuals or parties who seek to determine their rights under specific regulatory or criminal laws.

Declaratory judgments are considered a type of preventive justice because, by informing parties of their rights, they help them to avoid violating specific laws or the terms of a contract. In 1934 Congress enacted the Declaratory Judgment Act (28 U.S.C.A. § 2201 et seq.), which allows for declaratory judgments concerning issues of federal law. At the state level, the National Conference of Commissioners on Uniform State Laws passed the Uniform Declaratory Judgments Act (12 U.L.A. 109) in 1922. Between 1922 and 1993, this act was adopted in forty-one states, the Virgin Islands, and the Commonwealth of Puerto Rico. Most other states have varying laws that provide for declaratory judgments. Most declaratory judgment laws grant judges discretion to decide whether or not to issue a declaratory judgment.

DECREE 📖 A JUDGMENT of a court that announces the legal consequences of the facts found in a case and orders that the court's decision be carried out. A decree in EQUITY is a SENTENCE or ORDER of the court, pronounced on hearing and understanding all the points in issue, and determining the rights of all the parties to the suit, according to equity and good conscience. It is a declaration of the court announcing the legal consequences of the facts found. With the procedural merger of law and equity in the federal and most state courts under the Rules of Civil Procedure, the term *judgment* has generally replaced *decree*. 📖

A *divorce decree* sets out the conclusions of the court relating to the facts asserted as grounds for the DIVORCE, and it subsequently dissolves the marriage.

Decree is sometimes used interchangeably with DETERMINATION and order.

DEDICATION 📖 In COPYRIGHT law the first publication of a work that does not comply with the requirements relating to copyright notice and which therefore permits anyone to legally republish it. The GIFT of land—or an EASEMENT, that is, a right of use of the property of another—by the owner to the government for public use, and accepted for such use by or on behalf of the public. 📖

The owner of the land does not retain any rights that are inconsistent with the complete exercise and enjoyment of the public uses to which the property has been committed.

A dedication is express where the gift is formally declared, but it can also be implied by OPERATION OF LAW from the owner's actions and the facts and circumstances of the case.

A dedication may be made under COMMON LAW or pursuant to the requirements of statute. A common-law dedication is not subject to the STATUTE OF FRAUDS, an English law adopted in the United States, which provides that certain agreements must be in writing. Therefore, a common-law dedication does not have to be expressed in writing to be effective; it is based on ESTOPPEL. If the landowner indicates that his or her land is to be used for a public purpose and public use then occurs, the landowner is estopped, or prevented, from refuting the existence of the public right.

An *express common-law dedication* is one in which the intent is explicitly indicated—such as by ordinary DEEDS or recorded PLATS, which are maps showing the locations and boundaries of individual land parcels subdivided into lots—but the execution of the dedication has not been in accordance with law or certification of it has been defective so as not to constitute a statutory dedication.

A *statutory dedication* is necessarily express, since it is executed pursuant to, and in conformity with, the provisions of a statute regulating the subject. It cannot be implied from the circumstances of the case.

A dedication can result from the contrary exclusive use of land by the public pursuant to a claim of right with the knowledge, actual or attributed, and the acceptance of the owner. This method is known as *dedication by adverse user.*

DEDUCTIBLE 📖 That which may be taken away or subtracted. In TAXATION, an item that may be subtracted from GROSS INCOME or ADJUSTED GROSS INCOME in determining taxable income (e.g., interest expenses, charitable contributions, certain taxes).

The portion of an insured loss to be borne by the insured before he or she is entitled to recovery from the insurer. 📖

Automotive INSURANCE policies frequently include a deductible, such as $250 or $500, which the insured must pay before receiving reimbursement under the policy. Usually, the insured motorist chooses among several levels of deductible, with the policy payment being somewhat lower when the insured chooses a higher deductible.

Many types of insurance policies include a deductible amount.

DEDUCTION 📖 That which is deducted; the part taken away; ABATEMENT; as in deductions from GROSS INCOME in arriving at net income for tax purposes.

In CIVIL LAW, a portion or thing that an HEIR has a right to take from the mass of the SUCCESSION before any PARTITION takes place. 📖

A contribution to a CHARITY can be used as a deduction to reduce income for INCOME TAX purposes if the taxpayer meets the requirements imposed by law.

DEED 📖 A written instrument, which has been signed and delivered, by which one individual, the GRANTOR, conveys TITLE to REAL PROPERTY to another individual, the GRANTEE; a CONVEYANCE of land, TENEMENTS, or HEREDITAMENTS, from one individual to another. 📖

At COMMON LAW, a deed was an instrument under SEAL that contained a COVENANT or CONTRACT delivered by the individual who was to be bound by it to the party to whom it was granted. It is no longer required that such an instrument be sealed.

Transfer of Land Land can only be transferred from one individual to another in the legally prescribed manner. Historically speaking, a written deed is the instrument used to convey ownership of real property.

A deed is labeled an instrument of conveyance. Under Spanish law, which was in effect at an early date in areas of the western United States, a written deed was not necessary to convey title to land. A verbal grant was sufficient to complete the transaction, provided that it was accompanied by a transfer of POSSESSION. Verbal grants of land in Texas have, therefore, been given recognition in U.S. courts.

A deed must describe with REASONABLE certainty the land that is being conveyed. The conveyance must include operative words of GRANT; however, technical terms do not need to be used. The grantor must be adequately identified by the conveyance, although it is not required that the grantor's name be specifically mentioned. State laws sometimes require that the deed indicate the RESIDENCE of the grantor by town, city, county, and state.

In order for title to property to pass, a deed must specify the grantee with sufficient certainty to distinguish that individual from the rest of the world. Some statutes mandate that the deed list the grantee's residence by town, city, county, and state.

Execution In order for a deed to be properly executed, certain acts must be performed to create a valid conveyance. Ordinarily, an essential element of EXECUTION is the SIGNATURE of the grantor in the proper place. It is not necessary,

however, that the grantee sign the deed in order for it to take effect as a conveyance. Generally state statutes require that the deed be signed in the presence of WITNESSES, attesting to the grantor's request.

Delivery Proper DELIVERY of a deed from the grantor to the grantee is an essential element of its effectiveness. In addition, the grantor must make some statement or perform some act that implies his or her intention to transfer title. It is insufficient for a grantor to have the mere intention to transfer title, in the absence of further conduct that consummates the purpose.

There is no particular prescribed act, method, or ceremony required for delivery, and it is unnecessary that express words be employed or used in a specified manner. The deed need not be physically delivered to the grantee. It is sufficient to mail it to the grantee. Delivery of the deed by the attorney who has written the instrument for the grantor is also adequate. Unless otherwise provided by statute, a deed becomes effective upon its delivery date. The mere fact that the grantee has physical possession of the deed does not constitute delivery unless it was so intended by the grantor.

Acceptance A deed must be accepted by the grantee in order for proper transfer of title to land to be accomplished. There are no fixed principles regarding what acts are sufficient to effect ACCEPTANCE, since the issue is largely dependent upon the party's intent.

Acceptance of a deed need not be made by express words or in writing, absent a contrary statutory provision. A deed is ordinarily accepted when the grantee retains it or obtains a MORTGAGE on the property at issue.

Recording Legal policy mandates that a deed to real property be a matter of public record; therefore, subsequent to delivery and acceptance, a deed must be properly recorded.

The recording process begins when the deed is presented to the clerk's or recorder's office in the county where the property is located. The entire instrument is duplicated, ordinarily by photocopying. The copy is inserted into the current book of official RECORDS, which consists exclusively of copies of documents that are maintained and labeled in numerical order.

A properly recorded deed provides constructive NOTICE of its contents, which means that all parties concerned are considered to have notice of the deed whether or not they actually saw it. A majority of JURISDICTIONS place the burden upon home buyers to investigate any suspicious facts concerning the property of which they have actual or constructive notice. If, for example, there is a reference to the property for sale in the records to other deeds, the purchaser might be required to determine whether such instruments give rights in the property to other individuals.

A map referred to in a recorded deed that describes the property conveyed becomes part of the document for identification purposes.

The original copy of a deed is returned to the owner once it has been duplicated, recorded, and filed in the office of the recorder. See also RECORDING OF LAND TITLES.

A records or clerk's office maintains a set of indexes, in addition to official records, in which information about each deed is recorded, so that upon a search for a document such information can be disclosed. A majority of states have a GRANTOR-GRANTEE INDEX, a set of volumes containing a reference to all documents recorded alphabetically according to the grantor's name. The index lists the name of the grantor first, followed by the name of the grantee, then ordinarily a description of the instrument and sometimes of the property, and ultimately a reference to the volume and page number in the official record where the document has been copied. A grantee-grantor index has the identical information, but it is listed alphabetically according to the grantees' names. A *tract index* arranges all of the entries based upon the location of the property.

Indexes are frequently classified according to time periods. Therefore separate sets of indexes covering various periods of time may be available.

A significant problem can result in the event that a deed cannot be located through the indexes. This could be due to a mistake in the recording process, such as indexing the deed under the wrong name. In a number of states,

A sample grant deed

THIS INDENTURE, made the _____ day of _____, nineteen hundred and _____ BETWEEN _____, residing at _____, party of the first part, and _____, residing at _____, party of the second part,

WITNESSETH, that the party of the first part, in consideration of Ten Dollars and other valuable consideration paid by the party of the second part, does hereby grant and release unto the party of the second part, the heirs or successors and assigns of the party of the second part forever,

ALL that certain plot, piece or parcel of land, with the buildings and improvements thereon erected, situate, lying and being in the _____

_____

TOGETHER with all right, title and interest, if any, of the party of the first part of, in and to any streets and roads abutting the above-described premises to the center lines thereof; TOGETHER with the appurtenances and all the estate and rights of the party of the first part in and to said premises; TO HAVE AND TO HOLD the premises herein granted unto the party of the second part, the heirs or successors and assigns of the party of the second part forever.

AND the party of the first part covenants that the party of the first part has not done or suffered anything whereby the said premises have been encumbered in any way whatever, except as aforesaid.

AND the party of the first part, in compliance with Section _____ of the _____ Law, covenants that the party of the first part will receive the consideration for this conveyance and will hold the right to receive such consideration as a trust fund to be applied first for the purpose of paying the cost of improvement and will apply the same first to the payment of the cost of improvement before using any part of the total of the same for any other purpose.

The word "party" shall be construed as if it read "parties" whenever the sense of this indenture so requires.

IN WITNESS WHEREOF, the party of the first part has duly executed this deed the day and year first above written.
In presence of:

_____

_____

[Acknowledgment]   [Signature of Grantor]

A sample quitclaim deed

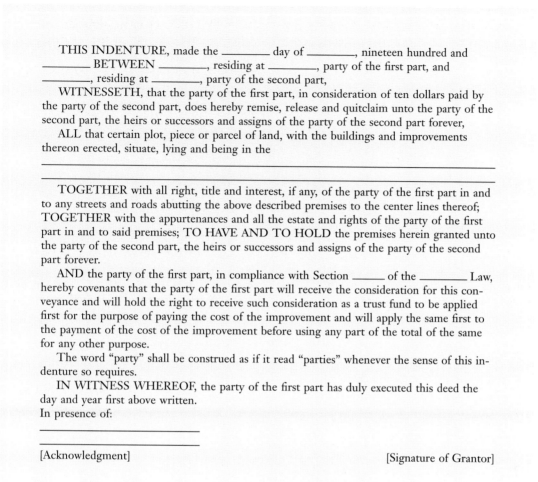

THIS INDENTURE, made the _____ day of _____, nineteen hundred and
_____ BETWEEN _____, residing at _____, party of the first part, and
_____, residing at _____, party of the second part,

WITNESSETH, that the party of the first part, in consideration of ten dollars paid by the party of the second part, does hereby remise, release and quitclaim unto the party of the second part, the heirs or successors and assigns of the party of the second part forever,

ALL that certain plot, piece or parcel of land, with the buildings and improvements thereon erected, situate, lying and being in the

_____

TOGETHER with all right, title and interest, if any, of the party of the first part in and to any streets and roads abutting the above described premises to the center lines thereof; TOGETHER with the appurtenances and all the estate and rights of the party of the first part in and to said premises; TO HAVE AND TO HOLD the premises herein granted unto the party of the second part, the heirs or successors and assigns of the party of the second part forever.

AND the party of the first part, in compliance with Section _____ of the _____ Law, hereby covenants that the party of the first part will receive the consideration for this conveyance and will hold the right to receive such consideration as a trust fund to be applied first for the purpose of paying the cost of the improvement and will apply the same first to the payment of the cost of the improvement before using any part of the total of the same for any other purpose.

The word "party" shall be construed as if it read "parties" whenever the sense of this indenture so requires.

IN WITNESS WHEREOF, the party of the first part has duly executed this deed the day and year first above written.

In presence of:

_____

[Acknowledgment]   [Signature of Grantor]

the courts will hold that such a deed was never recorded inasmuch as it was not indexed in such a manner as to provide notice to someone properly conducting a check on the title. In these jurisdictions, all grantees have the duty to return to the recorder's office after filing to protect themselves by checking on the indexing of their deeds. A purchaser who lives in a state with such laws should protect himself or herself either by consulting an attorney or returning to the recorder's office to ascertain that the deed is properly recorded and indexed. Other state statutes provide that a document is considered recorded when it is deposited in the proper office even if it is improperly recorded such that it cannot be located. In these states, there are no practical steps for subsequent buyers to take to circumvent this problem.

Types of Deeds   Three basic types of deeds commonly used are the grant deed, the QUITCLAIM DEED, and the warranty deed.

Grant Deed   By use of a *grant deed*, the conveyor says, "I grant (convey, bargain, or sell) the property to you." In a number of jurisdictions a representation that the conveyor actually owns the property he or she is transferring is implied from such language.

Quitclaim Deed   A *quitclaim deed* is intended to pass any title, interest, or claim that the grantor has in the property but makes no representation that such title is valid. In effect, this type of deed states that if the grantor actually owns the premises described or any interest therein, it is to be conveyed to the grantee. For this type of deed, some state statutes require a WARRANTY by the grantor, stating that neither the grantor nor anyone associated with him or her has encumbered the property, and that the grantor will defend the title against any defects that arise under and through him or her, but as to no others.

Warranty Deed   In a *warranty deed* the grantor inserts convenants for title, promising that such title is good and clear. The customary covenants of title include warranty of SEISIN, QUIET ENJOYMENT, the right to convey, freedom from ENCUMBRANCES, and a defense of the title as to all claims.

Validity   If a deed is to have any validity, it must be made voluntarily. The test of the CAPACITY of an individual to execute a VALID deed is based upon that person's ability to comprehend the consequences of his or her act. If a deed is not made through the conscious act of the grantor, it can be set aside in court. Relevant factors for the determination of whether or not a particular individual is capable of executing a valid deed are his or her age, and mental and physical condition. Extreme physical weakness resulting from old age or disease is a proper element for consideration in establishing capacity. Mental capacity, however, is the most important factor. If an individual is deemed to be mentally capable of disposing of his or her own property, the deed is ordinarily valid and would withstand objections made to it.

If FRAUD is committed by either the grantor or grantee, a deed can be declared invalid. For example, a deed that is a FORGERY is completely ineffective.

The exercise of UNDUE INFLUENCE also ordinarily serves to invalidate a deed. The test of whether such influence has been exerted turns upon the issue of whether or not the grantor executed the deed voluntarily. Undue influence is wrongful, and serves to confuse the judgment and to control the will of the grantor. Ordinary influence is insufficient to invalidate a deed. Deeds between parties who share a CONFIDENTIAL RELATIONSHIP are frequently examined by the courts for undue influence. For example, the courts might place a deed under close scrutiny if the grantor's attorney or physician is named grantee. In addition, if the grantor is a DRUNKARD or uses DRUGS AND NARCOTICS to excess, such would be circumstances for consideration when a court determines whether undue influence was exercised upon the grantor.

Defects   In a number of jurisdictions, an individual selling a house is required to disclose any material DEFECT known to him or her but not to the purchaser. A failure to disclose gives the buyer the right to cancel the deed, sue for DAMAGES, and in some instances, recover for personal injuries incurred as a result of such defect.

DEED OF TRUST 📖 A document that embodies the agreement between a lender and a borrower to transfer an interest in the borrower's land to a neutral third party, a TRUSTEE, to secure the payment of a DEBT by the borrower. 📖

A deed of trust, also called a TRUST DEED or a Potomac Mortgage, is used in some states in place of a MORTGAGE, a transfer of interest in land by a mortgagor-borrower to a mortgagee-lender to secure the payment of the borrower's debt. Although a deed of trust serves the same purpose as a type of security, it differs from a mortgage. A deed of trust is an arrangement among three parties: the borrower, the lender, and an impartial trustee. In exchange for a loan of money from the lender, the borrower places LEGAL TITLE to REAL PROPERTY in the hands of the trustee who holds it for the benefit of the lender, named in the deed as the beneficiary. The borrower retains EQUITABLE title to, and possession of, the property.

The terms of the deed provide that the transfer of legal title to the trustee will be VOID on the timely payment of the debt. If the borrower DEFAULTS in the payment of the debt, the trustee is empowered by the deed to sell the property and pay the lender the proceeds to satisfy the debt. Any surplus will be returned to the borrower.

The right of the trustee to sell the premises is called FORECLOSURE by POWER OF SALE. It differs in several respects from the power of a mortgagee to sell mortgaged property upon default, which is called a judicial foreclosure. A foreclosure by power of sale is neither supervised nor confirmed by a court, unlike a judicial foreclosure. While the rights received by a purchaser at a foreclosure by power of sale are the same as those obtained at a judicial foreclosure, there is a practical difference. Since the sale has not been judicially approved, there is a greater possibility of litigation over TITLE, thereby making title to the purchased premises less secure than one purchased at a judicial foreclosure. In addition, the lender may purchase the property for sale under the provisions of a deed of trust, since the neutral trustee conducts the sale. This is not the case in a foreclosure, unless contract or statute provides otherwise, since the mortgagee must act impartially in selling the property to satisfy the debt. Some mortgages may, however, provide for foreclosure by power of sale.

The procedure for a foreclosure by power of sale is regulated by statute, a characteristic shared by a judicial foreclosure. All interested parties must be given NOTICE of the sale, which must be published in local newspapers, usually in the public notice columns, for a certain period of time as required by statute. The sale is usually open to the public to ensure that the property will be sold at its FAIR MARKET VALUE.

DEEM 📖 To hold; consider; adjudge; believe; condemn; determine; treat as if; construe. 📖

To deem is to consider something as having certain characteristics. If an act is deemed a

A sample deed of trust

_____ BANK & TRUST COMPANY
DEED OF TRUST

STATE OF NORTH CAROLINA
COUNTY OF

THIS INDENTURE, made this ____ day of _____, 19____, by and between _____,
hereinafter referred to as "Trustor," whether one or more; _____,
hereinafter referred to as "Trustee," whether one or more; and _____, a North Carolina banking corporation, hereinafter called "Beneficiary":

WITNESSETH:

WHEREAS, Trustor is justly indebted to Beneficiary in the principal sum of _____
_____ Dollars ($_____) as evidenced by a Note of even date herewith, payable with interest as specified therein, at _____, North Carolina, or at such other place as the holder thereof from time to time may designate in writing, said Note being due or having a final payment due on _____, 19____; and,

WHEREAS, the property hereinafter described is conveyed herein to secure the payment of the indebtedness, interest, taxes, charges, assessments, insurance premiums and other obligations of Trustor as herein expressly provided;

NOW, THEREFORE, for and in consideration of the premises and the sum of One Dollar ($1.00) to Trustor paid by Trustee, the receipt of which is hereby acknowledged, Trustor has bargained, sold, granted and conveyed, and by these presents does bargain, sell, grant and convey to Trustee, his heirs, assigns, and successors in trust, all of the following described property, to-wit:

Together with all the buildings, fixtures and improvements thereon, and all rights, easements, hereditaments and appurtenances thereunto belonging, including all heating, plumbing, ventilating, lighting goods, equipment and other tangible and intangible property now or hereafter acquired, attached to or reasonably necessary to the use of such premises. COLLATERAL IS OR INCLUDES FIXTURES.

[continued on page 44]

TO HAVE AND TO HOLD the same, with all rights, privileges and appurtenances thereunto belonging, to said Trustee, his heirs, assigns and successors in trust, upon the trust and for the uses and purposes hereinafter set forth, and no other;

AND TRUSTOR covenants to and with Trustee and Beneficiary that Trustor is seized of said premises in fee; that Trustor has the right to convey same in fee simple; that the same are free and clear from all encumbrances and restrictions not specifically mentioned herein; and that Trustor does hereby forever warrant and will forever defend the title to same against the lawful claims of all persons whomsoever;

AND TRUSTOR FURTHER COVENANTS AND AGREES AS FOLLOWS:

1. PAYMENT—To pay the sum or sums specified above and as more particularly provided in the note or notes evidencing same, with interest thereon.

2. TAXES AND CHARGES—To pay, within sixty (60) days after they shall come due and payable, and before any penalty or interest shall be charged thereon, all general and special taxes, charges, and assessments of every kind and nature that may be levied, assessed or be or become a lien on the premises and property herein described, whether the same be for state, county, or city purposes, and to furnish annually to Beneficiary, immediately after payment, certificates or receipts of the proper authorities showing full payment of same.

That in the event of failure of Trustor to pay all of the aforesaid taxes, assessments and charges as hereinabove provided, Beneficiary shall have the option to advance the necessary funds to pay said taxes, assessments and charges; and all amounts so expended by Beneficiary for taxes, charges and assessments, as herein provided, shall be charged hereunder as principal money secured by this Deed of Trust and shall bear interest at the same rate as the principal indebtedness secured hereby, payable upon demand or otherwise as Beneficiary may determine. After any such advances are made, Beneficiary may apply any funds received hereunder to principal, advances or interest as Beneficiary may determine and Beneficiary will not be held to have waived any rights accruing to Beneficiary by the payment of any sum hereunder and particularly the right to declare this Deed of Trust in default by the reason of failure of performance of this condition or the non-payment of the indebtedness secured.

3. INSURANCE—To secure, maintain and keep in force with an insurance company or companies approved by Beneficiary an insurance policy or policies providing fire, extended coverage, malicious mischief and vandalism coverage and such other insurances as may be required by Beneficiary from time to time upon the buildings, fixtures and improvements now or hereafter situate upon the premises in an amount equal to the maximum insurable value of same or such amount as shall be approved by Beneficiary, whichever shall be the lesser sum; and to keep the policy or policies therefor constantly assigned and delivered to Beneficiary with subrogation clauses satisfactory to Beneficiary providing the right and power in Beneficiary to demand, receive and collect any and all money becoming payable thereunder and to apply same toward the payment of the indebtedness hereby secured, unless the same is otherwise paid.

That in the event of failure of Trustor to pay all of the aforesaid insurance premiums, as hereinabove provided, Beneficiary shall have the option to advance the necessary funds to pay said insurance premiums, and all amounts so expended by Beneficiary for insurance premiums, as herein provided, shall be charged hereunder as principal money secured by this Deed of Trust and shall bear interest at the same rate as the principal indebtedness secured hereby, payable upon demand or otherwise as Beneficiary may determine. After any such advances are made, Beneficiary may apply any funds received hereunder to principal, advances or interest as Beneficiary may determine and Beneficiary will not be held to have waived any rights accruing to Beneficiary by the payment of any sum hereunder and particularly the right to declare this Deed of Trust in default by the reason of failure of performance of this condition of the non-payment of the indebtedness secured.

4. REPAIRS—To keep all buildings and improvements now or hereafter situate upon the premises in good order and repair, to comply with all governmental requirements respecting the premises or their use, and to neither commit nor permit any waste, nor to alter, add to or remove any of said buildings or improvements without the written consent of Beneficiary.

5. TITLE DEFECTS—To pay to Beneficiary any and all sums, including costs, expenses, and reasonable attorneys' fees, which Beneficiary may incur or expend in any proceeding, legal or otherwise, which Beneficiary shall deem necessary to sustain the lien of this Deed of Trust or its priority.

6. ACCELERATION—That in the event (a) Trustor shall default in any respect in the performance of any one or more covenants, conditions, or agreements specified herein; or, (b) for any reason Trustor's covenant to pay all taxes specified above shall be or become legally inoperative or unenforceable in any particular; or, (c) for any reason Trustor shall fail to provide and maintain the necessary insurance as hereinabove required; or, (d) any lien, charge, or encumbrance prior to or affecting the validity of this Deed of Trust be found to exist, or proceedings be instituted to enforce any lien, charge or encumbrance against any of said premises; or, (e) the removal or demolition of any of the buildings or improvements now or hereafter situate upon the premises is threatened; or, (f) Trustor be declared bankrupt or insolvent, or abandon the premises; or (g) for any reason Trustor shall default in any respect in the performance of any one or more of the covenants, agreements or conditions specified herein; then upon the occurrence of any such event, the entire balance of the principal, advances and interest, shall become due and payable immediately at the option of Beneficiary, and neither the advance of funds by Beneficiary under any of the terms and provisions hereof nor the failure of Beneficiary to exercise promptly any right to declare the maturity of the debt under any of the foregoing conditions shall operate as a waiver of Beneficiary's right to exercise such option thereafter as to any past or current default.

7. CASUALTY LOSS OR CONDEMNATION—In the event of any loss covered by insurance assigned to Beneficiary hereunder, or in the event that the premises hereby conveyed, or any part thereof, shall be condemned and taken under power of eminent domain, Trustor shall give immediate written notice to Beneficiary and Beneficiary shall have the right to receive and collect any proceeds of such insurance and all damages awarded by reason of such taking, and the right to such proceeds and damages is hereby assigned to Beneficiary who shall have the discretion to apply the amount so received, or any part thereof, toward the principal indebtedness due hereunder or toward the alteration, repair or restoration of the premises by Trustor.

8. ASSIGNMENT OF RENTS—Trustor hereby assigns to Beneficiary any and all rents or emoluments from the premises herein described and, in the event of any default hereunder, Trustor hereby authorizes Beneficiary or Beneficiary's agents to enter upon and take possession of the premises or any part thereof, to rent same for the account of Trustor at any rent satisfactory to Beneficiary, to deduct from such rents or emoluments received all necessary and reasonable costs and expenses of collection and administration, and to apply the remainder on account of the indebtedness hereby secured.

9. APPOINTMENT OF RECEIVER—Beneficiary, immediately upon default herein, or upon proceedings being commenced for the foreclosure of this Deed of Trust, may apply ex parte for and as a matter of right be entitled to the appointment of a receiver of the rents and emoluments of the premises, without notice, and without reference to the value of the premises or the solvency of any persons or entities liable hereunder.

10. SUBSTITUTION OF TRUSTEE—Beneficiary and the successors or assigns of same are hereby authorized and empowered at any time or times hereafter, at Beneficiary's sole option, without notice and without specifying any reason for such action, to remove any Trustee or successor hereunder, and in such event or in the event of the death, resignation or other incapacity of any Trustee, to appoint a successor in his place by an instrument duly recorded in the office of the Register of Deeds of the County in which this Deed of Trust is recorded and such substitute Trustee or Trustees shall thereupon become vested with all the rights, powers, duties and obligations herein conferred upon the Trustee: it being expressly understood that the rights and powers herein conferred shall be in addition to, and not in derogation of, any other rights, powers and privileges under then existing law with reference to the substitution of Trustees.

[continued on page 46]

11. ADVANCES—Beneficiary and the successors or assigns of same, upon default of Trustor in any respect in the performance of any one or more of the covenants or agreements specified herein, may perform, at its option, such defaulted covenant or agreement and may advance such funds as it may deem necessary for this purpose, and all such advances and other funds expended by Beneficiary under the terms and provisions hereof shall be payable upon demand or otherwise as Beneficiary shall determine, shall bear interest at the maximum lawful rate until repaid, and shall be secured by this Deed of Trust and any other security interest given to secure the loan secured by this Deed of Trust. After any such advances are made, Beneficiary may apply any funds received hereunder to principal, advances or interest as it, in its sole discretion, may determine.

12. CONVEYANCE—DEFAULT—In the event Trustor conveys to any other party an interest in said premises or any part thereof without the prior written consent of Beneficiary or its successors or in the event Trustor shall sell or otherwise dispose of the said premises or any part thereof without the prior written consent of Beneficiary, Beneficiary at its election may declare the entire indebtedness hereby secured to be immediately due and payable, without notice to Trustor or its successor, which notice said Trustor and any successor to Trustor in interest hereby expressly waives, and upon such declaration the entire indebtedness hereby secured shall be immediately due and payable, anything herein or in the said promissory note to the contrary notwithstanding.

13. CROSS DEFAULT—In the event of default by Trustor in the performance (1) of Trustor's obligations under this deed of trust, (2) of any other obligation of Trustor to the holder of the note secured by this deed of trust, whether at the same branch or otherwise, (3) of default or failure to perform any of the conditions or covenants of the note secured by said deed of trust or any security agreement given to secure said note, such default may be deemed, at the option of the holder of the note secured by this deed of trust, a default in all indebtedness due said holder and the whole sum of the principal and interest of the debt evidenced by the note secured by this deed of trust and all of the other indebtedness due to holder by Trustor shall, at the option of the holder of the said note, become due and payable immediately, and this deed of trust and all other security interest for the benefit of or held by the holder may be foreclosed at once.

14. TERMS—The term "Trustor" as used herein shall include, jointly and severally, all parties hereinbefore named as "Trustor," whether one or more and whether individual, corporate or otherwise, and their heirs, legal representatives and assigns, and any subsequent owners of the property hereby conveyed, and the term "Beneficiary" as used herein shall include any lawful owner or holder of the indebtedness secured hereby whether one or more.

BUT THIS CONVEYANCE IS MADE UPON THIS SPECIAL TRUST that if Trustor shall pay or cause to be paid to Beneficiary the aforesaid indebtedness in accordance with the terms and conditions of the note or notes evidencing the same, and at the time and place therein mentioned for the payment thereof, together with all interest thereon and all taxes, charges, assessments and any premiums for insurance hereby secured, as hereinabove expressly agreed, and shall perform and observe all the covenants, conditions and agreements herein, then and in that event this Deed of Trust shall become null and void and shall be canceled or released of record.

BUT IF DEFAULT shall occur in the payment of said indebtedness, interest or any part of either, of any note or bond given in renewal in whole or in part thereof, or of any taxes, charges, assessments or insurance premiums, or other default as hereinabove provided, or by reason of the failure of Trustor to perform and observe each and every covenant, condition and agreement specified in this Deed of Trust, then in all or any of said events, the full principal sum, advances and interest thereon, at the option of Beneficiary as hereinabove provided, shall become immediately due and payable without further notice, and it shall be lawful for and upon the request of Beneficiary, it shall become the duty of Trustee hereby authorized, empowered and directed, to advertise and sell under this Deed of Trust the land and property herein described, at public sale, to the highest bidder for cash and in one or more parcels, after first giving such notice of hearing as to commencement of foreclosure proceedings and obtaining such findings or leave of court as then may be required by applicable law, and thereafter giving such notice and advertising of the time and place of such sale

A sample deed of
trust (continued)

in such manner as then may be required by applicable law; and upon such sale and any re-sales in accordance with the law then relating to foreclosure proceedings, and upon collection of the purchase money arising therefrom, to make and deliver to the purchaser or purchasers, their heirs, successors or assigns, a proper deed or deeds therefor, and to pay from the proceeds arising from such sale: first, all costs and expenses incident to said sale, including as compensation for his services an amount equal to five per cent (5%) of the gross proceeds of such sale or $150 whichever is greater, together with reasonable attorneys' fees for legal services actually performed; second, all taxes or assessments then constituting a lien against said premises other than those advertised and sold subject to; third, the unpaid principal, interest, and such sums advanced by Beneficiary as herein provided; and fourth, the balance to Trustor or such other person entitled thereto, or to the Clerk of Court of the County in which said foreclosure proceedings were instituted, or as then may be authorized or directed by applicable law.

It is further provided that in the event foreclosure is terminated upon the request of Trustor prior to delivery of the deed of Trustee as aforesaid, Trustor shall pay unto Trustee all costs and expenses incident to said foreclosure, including as compensation for his services an amount equal to 50 per cent of the compensation to which he would have been entitled upon delivery of the deed as aforesaid if such termination is prior to any hearing then required by applicable law; 75 per cent of such amount if such termination is after such hearing but before any sale hereunder; and the full amount if such termination is at any time after such sale; together with reasonable attorneys' fees for legal services actually performed to the date of such termination and reasonable attorneys' fees, if any, as provided in the evidence of indebtedness secured by this Deed of Trust.

It is further provided that the compensation herein allowed to Trustee shall constitute a lien on said property immediately upon request of sale as aforesaid, and that said Trustee shall suffer no liability by virtue of Trustee's acceptance of this trust, except such as may be incurred by Trustee's failure to advertise and sell said property if so requested or a failure to account for the proceeds thereof.

The covenants herein contained shall bind and the benefits and advantages shall inure to the respective heirs, executors, administrators, successors or assigns of the parties hereto.

IN TESTIMONY WHEREOF, Trustor has caused this instrument to be executed in its corporate name by its _____ President, attested by its _____ Secretary, and its corporate seal to be hereto affixed, all by order of its Board of Directors duly given, the day and year first above written.

_____
                        Name of Corporation
By: _____
_____ President

ATTEST: _____
_____ Secretary

IN TESTIMONY WHEREOF, each Trustor has hereunto set his hand and adopted as his seal the word "SEAL" appearing beside his name, the day and year first above written.

_____ (SEAL)
_____ (SEAL)
_____ (SEAL)
_____ (SEAL)

[continued on page 48]

A sample deed of trust (continued)

STATE OF NORTH CAROLINA
COUNTY OF

I, _____,
a Notary Public in and for said County and State, do hereby certify that _____
_____ personally appeared before me this day and
acknowledged the due execution of the foregoing instrument.

WITNESS my hand and notarial seal, this _____ day of _____, 19_____.

_____
Notary Public

My Commission expires:

STATE OF NORTH CAROLINA
COUNTY OF

I, _____,
a Notary Public in and for said County and State, do hereby certify that on the _____ day
of _____, 19_____ before me personally came_____
with whom I am personally acquainted, who, being by me duly sworn, says that
_____ is the _____ President and that
_____ is the _____ Secretary of
_____, the corporation described in and which executed the foregoing instru-
ment; that he knows the common seal of said corporation; that the seal affixed to the foregoing instrument is said common seal; and the name of the corporation was subscribed thereto
by said _____ President, and that said _____
President and _____ Secretary subscribed their names thereto, and said common seal
was fixed, all by order of the Board of Directors of said corporation; and that said instrument is the act and deed of said corporation.

WITNESS my hand and notarial seal, this _____ day of _____, 19_____

_____
Notary Public

My Commission expires:

STATE OF NORTH CAROLINA
COUNTY OF

The foregoing certificate of _____,
a Notary Public of the County of _____, State of North
Carolina, is certified to be correct. This instrument was presented for registration this day
and hour and duly recorded in the office of the Register of Deeds of _____
County, North Carolina, in Book _____, at Page _____.

This _____ day of _____, 19_____, at _____ o'clock _____.M.

_____
Register of Deeds

crime by law, then it is held to be a crime. If someone is deemed liable for damages, then he or she will have to pay them.

DE FACTO 📖 [*Latin, In fact.*] In fact, in deed, actually. 📖

This phrase is used to characterize an officer, a government, a past action, or a state of affairs that must be accepted for all practical purposes, but is illegal or illegitimate. Thus, an office, position, or status existing under a claim or color of right, such as a de facto corporation. In this sense it is the contrary of *de jure*, which means rightful, legitimate, just, or constitutional. Thus, an officer, king, or government *de facto* is one that is in actual possession of the office or supreme power, but by usurpation, or without lawful title; while an officer, king, or governor *de jure* is one who has just claim and rightful title to the office or power, but has never had plenary possession of it, or is not in actual possession. A wife *de facto* is one whose marriage is voidable by decree, as distinguished from a wife *de jure*, or lawful wife. But the term is also frequently used independently of any

CARL PURCELL/PHOTO RESEARCHERS

The fact that this Girl Scout troop is all African American is de facto (actual) segregation but not de jure (intentional) segregation.

distinction from *de jure;* thus a blockade *de facto* is a blockade that is actually maintained, as distinguished from a mere paper blockade.

A de facto CORPORATION is one that has been given legal status despite the fact that it has not complied with all the statutory formalities required for corporate existence. Only the state may challenge the validity of the existence of a de facto corporation.

De facto segregation is the separation of members of different races by various social and economic factors, not by virtue of any government action or statute.

DEFALCATION 📖 The misappropriation or EMBEZZLEMENT of money. 📖

Defalcation implies that funds have in some way been mishandled, particularly where an officer or agent has breached his or her FIDUCIARY duty. It is commonly applied to public officers who fail to account for money received by them in their official capacity, or to officers of CORPORATIONS who misappropriate company funds for their own private use.

Colloquially, the term is used to mean any type of BAD FAITH, DECEIT, misconduct, or dishonesty.

DEFAMATION 📖 Any intentional false communication, either written or spoken, that harms a person's reputation; decreases the respect, regard, or confidence in which a person is held; or induces disparaging, hostile, or disagreeable opinions or feelings against a person. 📖

Defamation may be a criminal or civil charge. It encompasses both written statements, known as libel, and spoken statements, called slander.

The probability that a plaintiff will recover DAMAGES in a defamation suit depends largely on whether the plaintiff is a public or private figure in the eyes of the law. The public figure law of defamation was first delineated in *New York Times v. Sullivan,* 376 U.S. 254, 84 S. Ct. 710, 11 L. Ed. 2d 686 (1964). In *Sullivan,* the plaintiff, a police official, claimed that false allegations about him appeared in the *New York Times,* and sued the newspaper for libel. The Supreme Court balanced the plaintiff's interest in preserving his reputation against the public's interest in freedom of expression in the area of political debate. It held that a public official alleging libel must prove actual MALICE in order to recover damages. The Court declared that the FIRST AMENDMENT protects open and robust debate on public issues even when such debate includes "vehement, caustic, unpleasantly sharp attacks on government and public officials." A public official or other plaintiff who has voluntarily assumed a position in the public eye must prove that defamatory statements were made with knowledge that they were false or with reckless disregard of whether they were false.

Where the plaintiff in a defamation action is a private citizen who is not in the public eye, the law extends a lesser degree of constitutional protection to defamatory statements. Public figures voluntarily place themselves in a position that invites close scrutiny, whereas private citizens who have not entered public life do not relinquish their interest in protecting their reputation. In addition, public figures have greater access to the means to publicly counteract false statements about them. For these reasons, a private citizen's reputation and PRIVACY interests tend to outweigh free speech considerations and deserve greater protection from the courts. (See *Gertz v. Robert Welch, Inc.,* 418 U.S. 323, 94 S. Ct. 2997, 41 L. Ed. 2d 789 [1974]).

Distinguishing between public and private figures for the purposes of defamation law is sometimes difficult. For an individual to be considered a public figure in all situations, the person's name must be so familiar as to be a household word—for example, Michael Jordan. Because most people do not fit into that category of notoriety, the Court recognized the limited-purpose public figure, who is voluntarily injected into a public controversy and becomes a public figure for a limited range of issues. Limited-purpose public figures, like public figures, have at least temporary access to the means to counteract false statements about them. They also voluntarily place themselves in the public eye and consequently relinquish some of their privacy rights. For these reasons, false statements about limited-purpose public figures that relate to the public controversies in which those figures are involved are not considered defamatory unless they meet the actual-malice test set forth in *Sullivan*.

Determining who is a limited-purpose public figure can also be problematic. In *Time, Inc. v. Firestone*, 424 U.S. 448, 96 S. Ct. 958, 47 L. Ed. 2d 154 (1976), the Court held that the plaintiff, a prominent socialite involved in a scandalous divorce, was not a public figure because her divorce was not a public controversy and because she had not voluntarily involved herself in a public controversy. The Court recognized that the divorce was newsworthy, but drew a distinction between matters of public interest and matters of public controversy. In *Hutchinson v. Proxmire*, 443 U.S. 111, 99 S. Ct. 2675, 61 L. Ed. 2d 411 (1979), the Court determined that a scientist whose federally supported research was ridiculed as wasteful by Senator William Proxmire was not a limited-purpose public fig-

ure because he had not sought public scrutiny in order to influence others on a matter of public controversy, and was not otherwise well-known.

See also FREEDOM OF THE PRESS; LIBEL AND SLANDER; NEW YORK TIMES V. SULLIVAN.

DEFAULT 📖 An omission; a failure to do that which is anticipated, expected, or required in a given situation. 📖

Default is distinguishable from NEGLIGENCE in that it does not involve carelessness or imprudence with respect to the discharge of a duty or obligation but rather the intentional omission or nonperformance of a duty.

To default on a debt is to fail to pay it upon its due date. Default in CONTRACT law implies failure to perform a contractual obligation.

A *default* JUDGMENT is one that may be entered against a party in a lawsuit for failure to comply with a procedural step in the suit, such as failure to file an ANSWER to a COMPLAINT or failure to file a paper on time. A default judgment is not one that goes to the MERITS of a lawsuit but is procedural in nature.

DEFAULT JUDGMENT 📖 Judgment entered against a party who has failed to defend against a claim that has been brought by an-

A sample default judgment entered by the clerk upon failure to appear

SUPREME COURT OF THE STATE OF _____

COUNTY OF _____

_____

_____.

                   Plaintiff.

-against-

_____.

                   Defendant.

DEFAULT JUDGMENT
Index No. _____

The summons and complaint (*or the summons with notice*) in the above entitled action having been personally served upon the defendant, _____, on the _____ day of _____, 19___, and the time for said defendant to appear, answer or raise an objection to the complaint in point of law having expired, and said defendant not having appeared, answered or raised an objection to the complaint in point of law, [and the notice required by the last paragraph of CPLR 308 having been duly mailed.]

Now, upon the summons and complaint and proof of service thereof, [the notice required by the last paragraph of CPLR 308 and proof of mailing thereof,] the affidavit of _____, sworn to on the _____ day of _____, 19___, and upon motion of _____ attorney for plaintiff, it is

ORDERED, ADJUDGED AND DECREED, that the plaintiff, _____, residing at No._____ _____ St., _____, _____, do recover of the defendant, _____, residing at No. _____ _____ St., _____, _____, the sum of _____ ($_____) Dollars, the amount claimed with interest, with _____ ($_____) Dollars costs and disbursements, amounting in all to the sum of _____ ($_____) Dollars, and that plaintiff have execution therefor.

Judgment signed this _____ day of _____, 19___ .

                   Clerk

other party. Under rules of civil procedure, when a party against whom a judgment for affirmative relief is sought has failed to plead (i.e., answer) or otherwise defend, the party is in default and a judgment by default may be entered either by the clerk or the court. ▥

DEFEASANCE CLAUSE ▥ A provision of a MORTGAGE—an interest in land given to a mortgagee-lender to secure the payment of a DEBT—which promises that the mortgagor-borrower will regain title to the mortgaged property when all the terms of the mortgage have been met. ▥

Defeasance clauses are found in mortgages in the few states that still follow the COMMON-LAW theory of mortgages. At early English common law, a mortgagee who lent money to a mortgagor received in exchange a deed of defeasible fee to the property, offered as security for the payment of the debt. Such TITLE was subject to defeat or cancellation upon payment of the debt on the law day, that is, at its maturity, and the mortgagor would at that time regain title to the property. If the mortgagor failed to pay the debt, even by only one day, the mortgagee's title became an estate in FEE SIMPLE absolute, which gave the mortgagee absolute

of a certain specified event, for example, the death of the person holding such an interest.

DEFECT ▥ Imperfection, flaw, or deficiency. ▥

That which is subject to a defect is missing a requisite element and, therefore, is not legally binding. Defective SERVICE OF PROCESS, for example, is service that does not comply with a procedural or jurisdictional requirement. A defective WILL is one that has not been properly drawn up, has been obtained by unlawful means, or does not comply with a particular law. In some cases, however, defects can be cured; for example, defective service of process can be cured by the service of an amended COMPLAINT.

In PRODUCT LIABILITY, a defective product is one that cannot be used for the purposes intended or is made dangerous as a result of a flaw or imperfection. Such a defect might exist in the entire design of a product or in the production of a particular individual product. A *latent defect* is one that is not readily observable by the buyer of an item, whereas a *patent defect* is obvious or immediately apparent upon observation.

A *fatal defect* is one that, due to its serious nature, serves to nullify a CONTRACT.

A typical
defeasance clause

Upon condition, however that upon payment of the indebtedness hereby secured, this conveyance to be void, payment of taxes and insurance, the satisfaction of prior incumbrances and other loans and advances to the mortgagor by the mortgagee before the full settlement and payment of this mortgage and all expenses of recording are to be a part of this mortgage indebtedness.

ownership of the property. A defeasance clause embodies these common-law principles that govern this type of mortgage agreement.

Defeasance clauses are not found in mortgages based upon the LIEN theory, observed in most states. The mortgage creates a lien for the mortgagee on the mortgaged property, which gives the mortgagee the right to its possession only after the mortgage has been foreclosed. Since the mortgage has not been given defeasible title, there is no need for a defeasance clause.

DEFEASIBLE ▥ Potentially subject to defeat, termination, or annulment upon the occurrence of a future action or event, or the performance of a CONDITION *subsequent*. ▥

The most common legal application of the term is with respect to estates as interest in land, such as in the case of a CONVEYANCE or a LIFE ESTATE, which is defeasible upon the happening

DEFENDANT ▥ The person defending or denying; the PARTY against whom relief or recovery is sought in an ACTION or suit, or the ACCUSED in a criminal case. ▥

In every legal action, whether civil or criminal, there are two sides. The person suing is the PLAINTIFF and the person against whom the suit is brought is the defendant. In some instances, there may be more than one plaintiff or defendant.

If an individual is being sued by his or her neighbor for TRESPASS, then he or she is the defendant in a civil suit. The person being accused of murder by the state in a HOMICIDE case is the defendant in a criminal action.

DEFENSE ▥ The forcible repulsion of an unlawful and violent attack, such as the defense of one's person, property, or country in time of war.

The totality of the facts, law, and contentions presented by the party against whom a civil action or ciminal prosecution is instituted in order to defeat or diminish the plaintiff's cause of action or the prosecutor's case. A reply to the claims of the other party, which asserts reasons why the claims should be disallowed. The defense may involve an absolute denial of the other party's factual allegations or may entail an AFFIRMATIVE DEFENSE, which sets forth completely new factual allegations. Pursuant to the rules of federal CIVIL PROCEDURE, numerous defenses may be asserted by MOTION as well as by ANSWER, while other defenses must be pleaded affirmatively. ▦

A *frivolous defense* is one that entails a vacuous assertion, which is not supported by argument or EVIDENCE. The rules of federal procedure provide that on motion such defense may be ordered stricken from the PLEADINGS.

A *meritorious defense* is one that involves the essence or substance of the case, as distinguished from technical objections or delaying tactics.

With respect to a criminal charge, defenses such as alibi, consent, duress, entrapment, ignorance or mistake, infancy, insanity, intoxication, and SELF-DEFENSE can result in a party's ACQUITTAL.

DEFENSE DEPARTMENT The Department of Defense (DOD) is the executive department in the federal government that is responsible for providing the military forces needed to deter war and protect the security of the United States. The major elements of the military forces under its control are the Army, Navy, Marine Corps, and Air Force, consisting of about 1.5 million men and women on active duty. They are backed, in case of emergency, by 1 million members of reserve components. In addition, about nine hundred thousand civilians are employees in the DOD.

Every state in the Union has some defense activities. The central headquarters of the DOD is at the Pentagon, the "world's largest office building."

The DOD is the successor agency to the National Military Establishment, created by the National Security Act of 1947 (50 U.S.C.A. § 401). It was established as an executive department of the government by the National Security Act Amendments of 1949, with the secretary of defense as its head (5 U.S.C.A. § 101). Since 1949, many legislative and administrative changes have occurred, evolving the department into the structure under which it currently operates.

Structure The DOD is composed of the Office of the Secretary of Defense; the military departments and the military services within those departments; the chair of the Joint Chiefs of Staff and the Joint Staff; the unified combatant commands; the DOD agencies; the DOD

field activities; and such other offices, agencies, activities, and commands as may be established or designated by law or by the president or the secretary of defense.

Office of the Secretary The secretary of defense is the principal adviser on defense policy to the president. The secretary is responsible for the formulation of general defense policy and DOD policy and for the execution of approved policy. Under the direction of the president, the secretary exercises authority, direction, and control over the DOD. The deputy secretary of defense is delegated full power and authority to act for the secretary of defense.

Three positions are designated as under secretary of defense. The under secretary of defense for acquisition and technology chairs the Defense Acquisition Board and advises the secretary of defense on all matters relating to the acquisition system, research and development, test and evaluation, production, logistics, military construction, procurement, and economic affairs.

The under secretary of defense for policy advises the secretary of defense on policy matters relating to overall international security and political-military affairs, including NORTH ATLANTIC TREATY ORGANIZATION affairs, arms limitations agreements, and international trade and technology.

The under secretary of defense for personnel and readiness develops policies and administrative processes to ensure that the military forces have sufficient readiness to execute the National Military Strategy; develops civilian and military personnel policies including health and drug policies, equal opportunity programs, and family issues and support; and oversees matters concerning the reserve components.

The comptroller and chief financial officer of the DOD is the principal adviser and assistant to the secretary of defense for budgetary and fiscal matters, including financial management, accounting policy, and systems and budget formulation and execution.

The director of operational test and evaluation serves as a staff assistant and adviser to the secretary of defense, prescribing policies and procedures for the conduct of operational test and evaluation within the department, including assessments of operational effectiveness and of the suitability of major defense acquisition programs.

The assistant secretary of defense for command, control, communications, and intelligence (C³I) is the principal staff assistant and adviser to the secretary of defense for C³I, information management, counterintelligence, and security countermeasures matters.

The assistant secretary of defense for legislative affairs is responsible for maintaining a direct liaison with Congress, coordinating departmental actions relating to congressional consideration of the legislative program of the department, coordinating responses to requests for information by members of Congress, and arranging for witnesses from the DOD and the various military departments at congressional hearings on defense matters.

The general counsel is the chief legal officer of the DOD and is responsible for the preparation and processing of legislation, executive orders, and proclamations, and reports and comments thereon. The general counsel also serves as director of the Defense Legal Services Agency, providing legal advice and services for the Office of the Secretary of Defense, its field activities, and the defense agencies. The general counsel also administers the Defense Industrial Security Clearance Review Program and the Standards of Conduct Ethics Program.

The inspector general serves as an independent and objective official in the DOD. The inspector general is responsible for conducting, supervising, monitoring, and initiating AUDITS, investigations, and inspections relating to programs and operations of the department. The inspector general coordinates activities designed to promote economy, efficiency, and effectiveness in the administration of such programs and operations, and to prevent and detect FRAUD and abuse in them.

The assistant to the secretary of defense for public affairs is responsible for the functional areas of the DOD, which include public and internal information, audiovisual activities, community relations, and security clearance. The assistant secretary also reviews information intended for public release, and implements programs under the FREEDOM OF INFORMATION ACT (5 U.S.C.A. § 552) and Federal Privacy Act (5 U.S.C.A. § 552a) within the DOD.

The assistant to the secretary of defense for intelligence oversight conducts independent oversight inspections of DOD intelligence and counterintelligence operations to ensure compliance with legal requirements, and reviews all allegations that raise questions of legality or propriety involving intelligence and counterintelligence activities.

The director of administration and management serves as the principal staff assistant to the secretary and deputy secretary of defense on matters concerning departmentwide organizational and administrative management, and also serves as the director of the Washington Headquarters Service.

Joint Chiefs of Staff The Joint Chiefs of Staff consists of a chair and vice chair, the chief of staff of the U.S. Army, the chief of naval operations, the chief of staff of the U.S. Air Force, and the commandant of the Marine Corps.

The chair of the Joint Chiefs of Staff is the principal military adviser to the president, the NATIONAL SECURITY COUNCIL, and the secretary of defense. While serving, the chair holds the grade of general or admiral and outranks all other officers of the armed forces.

The chair of the Joint Chiefs of Staff helps the president and the secretary of defense provide for the strategic direction and planning of the armed forces, including resource allocation, the assessment of the military strength of potential adversaries, and the preparation of both contingency plans and joint logistic and mobility plans. In addition, the chair coordinates military education and training, represents the United States on the Military Staff Committee of the United Nations, and convenes and presides over regular meetings of the Joint Chiefs of Staff.

Field Activities The American Forces Information Service, established in 1977 under the supervision of the assistant to the secretary of defense for public affairs, is responsible for the department's internal information program and visual information policy. The Armed Forces Radio and Television Service and Broadcast Center and the American Forces Press and Publications Service (which includes among its many products the *Current News Early Bird*) function under the director of the American Forces Information Service. (*Current News Early Bird* is a Pentagon-produced newspaper

General John Shalikashvili, Chair of the Joint Chiefs of Staff, testified before the Senate Armed Forces Services Committee in 1995.

STEPHEN JAFFE/THE IMAGE WORKS

Defense Department

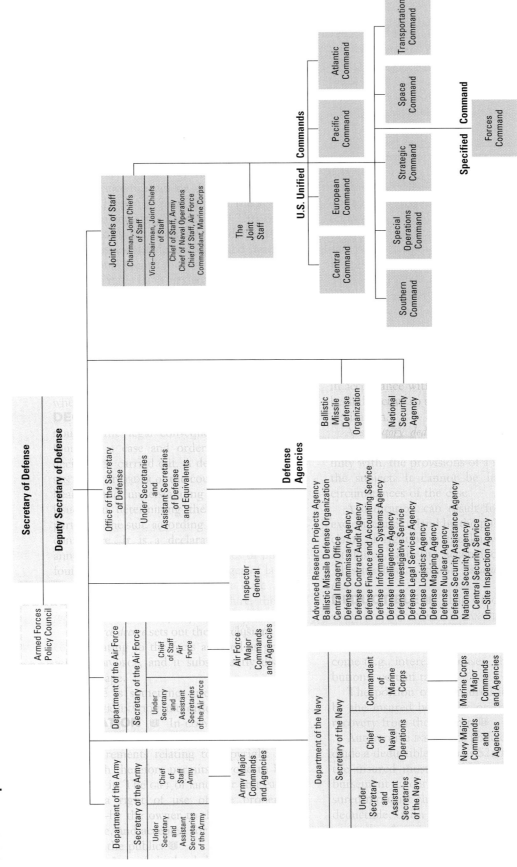

Secretary of Defense

Deputy Secretary of Defense

Armed Forces Policy Council

Joint Chiefs of Staff

Chairman, Joint Chiefs of Staff
Vice–Chairman, Joint Chiefs of Staff
Chief of Staff, Army
Chief of Naval Operations
Chief of Staff Air Force
Commandant, Marine Corps

The Joint Staff

U.S. Unified Commands

Central Command
European Command
Pacific Command
Atlantic Command

Southern Command
Special Operations Command
Strategic Command
Space Command
Transportation Command

Specified Command

Forces Command

Office of the Secretary of Defense

Under Secretaries and Assistant Secretaries of Defense and Equivalents

Defense Agencies

Ballistic Missile Defense Organization

National Security Agency

Advanced Research Projects Agency
Ballistic Missile Defense Organization
Central Imagery Office
Defense Commissary Agency
Defense Contract Audit Agency
Defense Finance and Accounting Service
Defense Information Systems Agency
Defense Intelligence Agency
Defense Investigative Service
Defense Legal Services Agency
Defense Logistics Agency
Defense Mapping Agency
Defense Nuclear Agency
Defense Security Assistance Agency
National Security Agency/
Central Security Service
On–Site Inspection Agency

Inspector General

Department of the Army

Secretary of the Army

Under Secretary and Assistant Secretaries of the Army

Chief of Staff Army

Army Major Commands and Agencies

Department of the Air Force

Secretary of the Air Force

Under Secretary and Assistant Secretaries of the Air Force

Chief of Staff Air Force

Air Force Major Commands and Agencies

Department of the Navy

Secretary of the Navy

Under Secretary and Assistant Secretaries of the Navy

Chief of Naval Operations

Commandant of Marine Corps

Navy Major Commands and Agencies

Marine Corps Major Commands and Agencies

that contains clippings and analysis of defense-related articles from newspapers around the country.) The American Forces Information Service provides policy guidance and oversight for departmental periodicals and pamphlets, the *Stars and Stripes* newspapers, military command newspapers, and the Defense Information School, among other projects.

The Department of Defense Civilian Personnel Management Service was established August 30, 1993, and functions under the authority, direction, and control of the under secretary of defense for personnel and readiness. It provides services in civilian personnel policy, support, functional information management, and civilian personnel administration to DOD components and their activities.

The Department of Defense Education Activity (DODEA) was established in 1992 and also functions under the authority, direction, and control of the under secretary of defense for personnel and readiness. It consists of three subordinate entities: the DOD dependents schools, the DOD section 6 schools, and the Continuing Adult and Post-Secondary Education Office. The DODEA formulates, develops, and implements policies, technical guidance, and standards for the effective management of defense activities and programs both stateside and overseas.

The Office of Civilian Health and Medical Program of the Uniformed Services (OCHAMPUS) was established as a field activity in 1974. The office administers a civilian health and medical care program for retired service members and the spouses and dependent children of active duty, retired, disabled, and deceased service members, and also administers a program for payment of emergency medical and dental services provided to active duty service members by civilian medical personnel.

The Defense Medical Programs Activity develops and maintains the department's Unified Medical Program to provide resources for all medical activities, including planning, programming, and budgeting construction projects for medical facilities and also providing information systems and related communications and automated systems in support of the activities of the DOD Military Health Services System (MHSS), the Defense Enrollment Eligibility and Reporting System, the Tri-Service Medical Information System, the Reportable Disease Database, and other departmentwide automated MHSS information systems.

The Defense Prisoner of War/Missing in Action Office was established July 16, 1993, under the authority, direction, and control of the assistant secretary of defense for international security affairs. It provides centralized management of prisoner of war–missing in action (POW-MIA) affairs with the DOD. The office provides DOD participation in negotiations with officials of foreign governments to achieve the fullest possible accounting of missing U.S. servicemen and -women and also assembles and administrates information and databases on U.S. military and civilian personnel who are, or were, prisoners of war or missing in action. The office declassifies DOD documents and maintains open channels of communication between the department, Congress, POW-MIA families, and veterans' organizations.

The Defense Technology Security Administration was established May 10, 1985, and functions under the control, direction, and authority of the under secretary of defense for policy. The administration is responsible for reviewing the international transfer of defense technology, goods, services, and munitions, consistent with U.S. foreign policy and national security objectives.

The Office of Economic Adjustment is responsible for planning and managing the department's economic adjustment programs and for assisting federal, state, and local officials in cooperative efforts to alleviate any serious social and economic side effects resulting from major departmental realignments or other actions. The office supports the secretary of defense in her or his capacity as chair of the Economic Adjustment Committee, an interagency group established to coordinate federal economic adjustment activities.

The Washington Headquarters Service is headed by the director of administration and management. It provides administrative and operational support to certain DOD activities in the national capital region. Such support includes budgeting and accounting, personnel management, office services, security, travel aid, information and data systems, and other services as required.

CROSS-REFERENCES

Armed Services; Arms Control and Disarmament; Military Law.

DEFENSE RESEARCH INSTITUTE The Defense Research Institute (DRI) was founded in 1960 to limit the abuse of legal processes for PERSONAL INJURY compensation through a program of education and information. The institute seeks to improve the knowledge and ability of defense attorneys, and the fairness of the ADVERSARY SYSTEM of justice. The institute provides research facilities such as files of speeches,

A sample
deficiency
judgment

JUDGMENT
Index No. _____

WHEREAS, an order made by Mr. Justice _____, at a Special Term, Part _____, of this Court, and entered and filed in the office of the Clerk of the County of _____, on the _____ day of _____, 19___, confirmed the referee's report in the above entitled action, and directed the entry of a deficiency judgment in this action in favor of the plaintiff, _____, and against the defendants, _____, as Executrix and _____, as Executor of the Last Will and Testament of _____, deceased, in the sum of _____ ($_____) Dollars, with interest thereon from _____, 19___, it is

ADJUDGED, that the plaintiff, _____, whose address is No. _____ _____ Street, Borough of _____, City and State of _____, do recover from the defendants _____, whose address is No. _____ _____ Street, Borough of _____, City and State of _____, as Executrix and _____, whose address is No. _____ _____ Street, Borough of _____, City and State of _____, as Executor of the Last Will and Testament of _____, deceased, the sum of _____ ($_____) Dollars, with interest thereon from _____, 19___, in the sum of _____ ($_____) Dollars, amounting in all to the sum of _____ ($_____) Dollars, and that plaintiff have execution therefor.

Dated, _____, 19___.

_____
Clerk of the County of _____

briefs, and names of expert witnesses, plus a small library. Activities include institutes and programs for legal, law student, general public, and special interest groups. Its members are attorneys, claims investigators, adjusters, insurance companies, trade associations, corporations, and groups of frequently targeted defendants such as doctors, pharmacists, engineers, and manufacturers.

The institute is organized into three separate divisions: the Arbitration Program, the Individual Research Service, and Transcripts of Economists' Testimony. DRI also has various committees including those with the following titles: Admiralty Law, Congressional Liaison, Environmental Law, Manufacturers' Corporate Counsel, Medical-Legal, Product Liability, Professional Liability, Property and Liability Insurance, and Workers' Compensation.

The institute publishes *For the Defense* (monthly), *Brief Bank Index* (annually), and a membership directory.

DEFICIENCY 📖 A shortage or insufficiency. The amount by which federal INCOME TAX due exceeds the amount reported by the taxpayer on his or her return; also, the amount owed by a taxpayer who has not filed a return. The outstanding balance of a DEBT secured by a MORTGAGE after the mortgaged property has been sold to satisfy the obligation at a price less than the debt. 📖

DEFICIENCY JUDGMENT 📖 An assessment of personal liability against a mortgagor, a person who pledges TITLE to property to secure a DEBT, for the unpaid balance of the MORTGAGE debt when the proceeds of a FORECLOSURE sale are insufficient to satisfy the debt. 📖

Legislation enacted during the Depression still restricts the availability of deficiency judgments in several states. In some JURISDICTIONS, deficiency judgments are proscribed in certain situations, while in other states, they are limited to the amount by which the debt exceeds the FAIR MARKET VALUE of the property. WAIVER, the intentional relinquishment of a known right, of the benefits conferred by antideficiency legislation contravenes PUBLIC POLICY and is ineffective.

DEFICIT 📖 A deficiency, misappropriation, or DEFALCATION; a minus balance; something wanting. 📖

Deficit is commonly used to mean any kind of shortage, as in an ACCOUNT, a number, or a balance due. Deficit spending or financing involves taking in less money than the amount that is paid out.

See also FEDERAL BUDGET.

DEFINITIVE 📖 Conclusive; ending all controversy and discussion in a lawsuit. 📖

That which is definitive is capable of finally and completely settling a legal question or action.

A *definitive judgment* is final and not provisional; a *definitive sentence* mandates imprisonment for a certain specified period of time.

DEFORCEMENT ◻ The COMMON-LAW name given to the wrongful possession of land to which another person is rightfully entitled; the detention of DOWER from a widow. ◻

Although the term includes disseisin, ABATEMENT, discontinuance, and intrusion, deforcement especially applies to situations in which a person is entitled to a LIFE ESTATE or absolute ownership of land but has never taken possession.

DEFRAUD ◻ To make a MISREPRESENTATION of an existing MATERIAL fact, knowing it to be false or making it recklessly without regard to whether it is true or false, intending for someone to rely on the misrepresentation and under circumstances in which such person does rely on it to his or her damage. To practice fraud; to cheat or trick. To deprive a person of property or any interest, estate, or right by FRAUD, deceit, or artifice. ◻

Intent to defraud means an intention to deceive another person, and to induce such other person, in reliance upon such deception, to assume, create, transfer, alter, or terminate a right, obligation, or power with reference to property.

DEGREE ◻ Extent, measure, or scope of an action, condition, or relation. Legal extent of guilt or negligence. Title conferred on graduates of school, college, or university. The state or civil condition of a person.

The grade or distance one thing may be removed from another; i.e., the distance, or number of removes that separate two persons who are related by CONSANGUINITY. Thus, a sibling is in the second degree of kinship but a parent is in the first degree of kinship. ◻

DE JURE ◻ [*Latin, In law.*] Legitimate; lawful, as a matter of law. Having complied with all the requirements imposed by law. ◻

De jure is commonly paired with *de facto*, which means "in fact." In the course of ordinary events, the term *de jure* is superfluous. For example, in everyday discourse, when one speaks of a CORPORATION or a government, the understood meaning is a de jure corporation or a de jure government.

A de jure corporation is one that has completely fulfilled the statutory formalities imposed by state corporation law in order to be granted corporate existence. In comparison, a de facto corporation is one that has acted in GOOD FAITH and would be an ordinary corporation but for failure to comply with some technical requirements.

A de jure government is the legal, legitimate government of a state and is so recognized by other states. In contrast, a de facto government is in actual possession of authority and control of the state. For example, a government that has been overthrown and has moved to another state will attain de jure status if other nations refuse to accept the legitimacy of the revolutionary government.

De jure segregation refers to intentional actions by the state to enforce racial segregation. The JIM CROW LAWS of the southern states, which endured until the 1960s, are examples of de jure segregation. In contrast, de facto racial segregation, which occurred in other states, was accomplished by factors apart from conscious government activity.

DEL CREDERE ◻ [*Italian, Of belief or trust.*] An arrangement in which an AGENT or FACTOR— an individual who takes possession and agrees to sell goods for another—consents for an additional fee to guarantee that the purchaser, to whom CREDIT has been extended, is financially solvent and will perform the CONTRACT. ◻

As the result of a *del credere agency*, the *del credere agent* becomes a SURETY of the purchaser. If the purchaser DEFAULTS, the agent is responsible to the principal for the outstanding amount. A *del credere commission* is the extra fee paid to the agent for such promises.

DELECTUS PERSONAE ◻ [*Latin, Choice of the person.*] By this term is understood the right of partners to exercise their choice and preference as to the admission of any new members to the PARTNERSHIP, and as to the persons to be so admitted, if any. The doctrine is equally applicable to close and family CORPORATIONS and is exemplified in the use of restrictions for the transfer of shares of stock. ◻

DELEGATE ◻ A person who is appointed, authorized, delegated, or commissioned to act in the place of another. Transfer of authority from one to another. A person to whom affairs are committed by another.

A person elected or appointed to be a member of a representative assembly. Usually spoken of one sent to a special or occasional assembly or convention. Person selected by a constituency and authorized to act for it at a party or state political convention.

As a verb, it means to transfer authority from one person to another; to empower one to perform a task in behalf of another, e.g., a landlord may delegate an AGENT to collect rents. ◻

DELEGATION ◻ A sending away; a putting into commission; the assignment of a debt to another; the entrusting of another with a general power to act for the good of those who depute him or her; a body of delegates. The transfer of authority by one person to another.

The body of delegates from a state to a national nominating convention or from a county to a state or other party convention. The whole body of delegates or representatives sent to a convention or assembly from one district, place, or political unit is collectively spoken of as a *delegation*. 📖

Delegation of powers, for example, is the impartation of authority by a particular governmental branch, in which such authority is placed, to another branch or to an ADMINISTRATIVE AGENCY. The U.S. Constitution delegates different powers to the three branches of government: the executive, legislative, and judicial. However, certain powers may not be transferred from one branch of government to another, such as the congressional power to declare war.

DELIBERATE 📖 Willful; purposeful; determined after thoughtful evaluation of all relevant factors; dispassionate. To act with a particular intent, which is derived from a careful consideration of factors that influence the choice to be made. 📖

When used to describe a crime, deliberate denotes that the perpetrator has weighed the motives for the conduct against its consequences and the criminal character of the conduct before deciding to act in such a manner. A deliberate person does not act rashly or suddenly but with a preconceived intention.

Deliberate is synonymous with premeditated.

DELICTUM 📖 [*Latin, A fault.*] An injury, an offense, or a TORT—a wrong done to the property or person of another that does not involve breach of CONTRACT.

Culpability; blameworthiness of a criminal nature, as in the Latin phrase *in pari delicto*—in equal fault or equally criminal—used to describe ACCOMPLICES to a crime. 📖

An *actio ex delicto* is a lawsuit based upon the commission of a tort, as opposed to an *actio ex contractu*, an action for breach of contract.

DELIVERY 📖 The transfer of possession of REAL PROPERTY or PERSONAL PROPERTY from one person to another. 📖

Two elements of a valid GIFT are delivery and donative intent. Delivery is not restricted to the actual physical transfer of an item—in some cases delivery may be symbolic. Such is the case where one person gives land to another person. Land cannot be physically delivered, but delivery of the DEED constitutes the transfer if coupled with the requisite intent to pass the land on to another.

Similarly, delivery can take place in a situation where goods are set apart and notice is given to whoever is scheduled to receive them. This is known as CONSTRUCTIVE delivery.

DEMAND 📖 Peremptory ALLEGATION or assertion of a legal right. 📖

A demand is an emphatic claim, which presumes that no doubt exists regarding its legal force and effect. It is a request made with authority.

A *money demand* is a demand for a fixed sum of money that arises out of an agreement or CONTRACT. COMMERCIAL PAPER is frequently payable on demand or immediately upon request.

A *legal demand* is one that is made by a lawfully authorized individual and is proper as to form, time, and place.

DEMEANOR 📖 The outward physical behavior and appearance of a person. 📖

Demeanor is not merely what someone says but the manner in which it is said. Factors that contribute to an individual's demeanor include tone of voice, facial expressions, gestures, and carriage.

The demeanor of this witness will affect whether the jury finds his testimony credible.

The term *demeanor* is most often applied to a witness during a trial. Demeanor EVIDENCE is quite valuable in shedding light on the CREDIBILITY of a WITNESS, which is one of the reasons why personal presence at trial is considered to be of paramount importance and has great significance concerning the HEARSAY rule. To aid a jury in its determination of whether or not it should believe or disbelieve particular TESTIMONY, it should be provided with the opportunity to hear statements directly from a witness in court whenever possible.

DE MINIMIS 📖 An abbreviated form of the Latin maxim *de minimis non curat lex*, "the law cares not for small things." A legal doctrine by which a court refuses to consider trifling matters. 📖

In a lawsuit, a court applies the *de minimis* doctrine to avoid the resolution of trivial matters that are not worthy of judicial scrutiny. Its application sometimes results in the dismissal of an ACTION, particularly when the only redress sought is for a nominal sum, such as one dollar. APPELLATE COURTS also use the *de minimis* doctrine when appropriate.

DEMISE 📖 Death. A CONVEYANCE of property, usually of an interest in land. 📖

The term *demise* originally meant a posthumous grant but is now commonly applied to a conveyance that is made for a definitive term, such as an estate for a term of years. A LEASE is a common example, and demise is sometimes used synonymously with "lease" or "let."

DEMOCRATIC PARTY The modern Democratic party is the descendant of the Democratic-Republican party, an early-nineteenth-century political organization led by THOMAS JEFFERSON and JAMES MADISON. Also known as the Jeffersonians, the Democratic-Republican party began as an antifederalist group, opposed to strong, centralized government. The party was officially established at a national nominating convention in 1832. It dropped the Republican portion of its name in 1840.

Despite destructive struggles and philosophical shifts, the Democratic party remains a dominant political force in the United States. The Democrats compete for office with the Republicans, their counterparts in the United States' de facto two-party system.

The Democratic party of the late 1990s supports liberal government policies in social and economic matters. The early party disapproved of federal involvement. Jefferson, Madison, and James Monroe—Virginians who were each elected president of the United States—favored limited powers for the national government.

The fundamental change in Democratic philosophy was the result of fluid coalitions and historical circumstance. The master coalition builder and founder of the modern Democratic party was ANDREW JACKSON, a populist president portrayed as a donkey by political satirists. Jackson transformed presidential politics by expanding party involvement. (The donkey later became the symbol for the Democratic party.)

The transformation began after Jackson's first unsuccessful bid for the White House. In the 1824 presidential election, Jackson won the popular vote but failed to win a majority in the ELECTORAL COLLEGE. The U.S. Constitution requires the House of Representatives to select the president under these circumstances. When the House chose JOHN QUINCY ADAMS, Jackson was incensed—and began a four-year campaign to win the next presidential election.

With help from political adviser and future president MARTIN VAN BUREN, Jackson won the presidency in 1828.

Jackson had benefited from growth in the nation's population and from laws that increased the number of U.S. citizens eligible to vote. In the 1824 presidential election, about 365,000 votes had been counted. In the 1828 election, over 1 million votes were cast, an increase that clearly helped Jackson, the so-called people's president.

In reaching his goal, Jackson laid the groundwork for a strong party system. He set up an efficient Democratic political organization by forming committees at the local, district, and state levels; holding rallies and conventions; generating publicity; registering new voters; and getting people to the POLLS.

Jackson also backed the newly created convention system for nominating presidential candidates—and was himself nominated for re-election at the 1832 Democratic convention. The original purpose of conventions was to allow local input in the political process. In Jackson's time conventions were forums for debate and deal making.

As the Democratic party changed in form and purpose, alliances became more difficult. Relations between southern and northern Democrats were increasingly strained. Southern states sought the reduction of TARIFFS, or taxes on imports, whereas northern states favored tariffs to safeguard their manufactured goods. Some southern Democrats suggested that individual states could nullify federal tariff laws.

Even more troublesome was the issue of STATES' RIGHTS and SLAVERY. The regional split within the party widened over the designation of new territories as free or slave states. The breaking point was the 1860 national convention. The Democrats were divided—the southern faction favored John C. Breckinridge, and the northerners selected STEPHEN A. DOUGLAS. Although Douglas advocated limited national control, or popular sovereignty, the southern delegates were not appeased. Republican nominee ABRAHAM LINCOLN capitalized on the dissension in the Democratic party and won the election.

Following Lincoln's election came a twenty-four-year spell with no Democrat in the White House. After the Civil War, Democrats were renounced in the North because they had not supported legislation to finance the war or enlist new soldiers. Meanwhile, the South became solidly Democratic in response to the Republicans' unpopular Reconstruction policies.

During the nineteenth century, the Democrats also created powerful urban political machines such as New York City's TAMMANY HALL. In these systems, people were offered political jobs or money in exchange for voter loyalty. Immigrants tended to support the Democratic party and machine politics as a way to gain a foothold in their new country. Unfortunately, the machines became sources of corruption and graft.

In 1884 Democratic nominee GROVER CLEVELAND, of New York, was elected U.S. president with a pledge to end political patronage and support for the gold standard. Again, factionalism undermined Democratic strength. WILLIAM JENNINGS BRYAN, a powerful Democratic orator, supported free coinage of silver currency. He tapped into the discontent of southern and western farmers who sought government assistance. He also drew support from the labor movement. With Bryan as the unsuccessful Democratic presidential nominee in 1896, 1900, and 1908, the party's original position on limited government was all but abandoned.

Factionalism was the party's strength as well as its weakness. On the one hand, it gave minority interests a chance to be heard. However, successful coalitions among the different interests were difficult to achieve. The traditional Democratic alliance consisted of labor supporters, immigrants, farmers, urban interests, and southern populists. Later, African Americans and northern liberals joined the coalition.

After Bryan's losses, the Democrats were determined to regain the White House. In 1912 former Princeton University president WOODROW WILSON won the nomination on the forty-sixth ballot of the Democratic convention. A liberal reformer, Wilson defeated Republican WILLIAM HOWARD TAFT and third-party candidate THEODORE ROOSEVELT. Wilson's accomplishments as president included lowering tariffs, establishing the Federal Trade Commission, backing ANTITRUST legislation, and leading the country during World War I. However, the Republicans regained the presidency in 1920 with a huge victory by WARREN G. HARDING.

The Republicans prevailed for the next decade. Finally, in 1932, the Democratic party triumphed at the polls with the election of New York's FRANKLIN D. ROOSEVELT. The Roosevelt era marked the complete conversion of the Democrats' position on government interven-

Democratic Party

Democratic National Political Convention Sites, 1832 to 1996

Year	Site
1832	Baltimore
1836	Baltimore
1840	Baltimore
1844	Baltimore
1848	Baltimore
1852	Baltimore
1856	Cincinnati
1860	Baltimore*
1864	Chicago
1868	New York City
1872	Baltimore
1876	St. Louis
1880	Cincinnati
1884	Chicago
1888	St. Louis
1892	Chicago
1896	Chicago
1900	Kansas City, MO
1904	St. Louis
1908	Denver
1912	Baltimore
1916	St. Louis
1920	San Francisco
1924	New York City
1928	Houston
1932	Chicago
1936	Philadelphia
1940	Chicago
1944	Chicago
1948	Philadelphia
1952	Chicago
1956	Chicago
1960	Los Angeles
1964	Atlantic City
1968	Chicago
1972	Miami Beach
1976	New York City
1980	New York City
1984	San Francisco
1988	Atlanta
1992	New York City
1996	Chicago

*An earlier convention, held in Charleston, South Carolina, had resulted in a split ticket in the party. The official nomination was made at the Baltimore convention.
SOURCE: The World Almanac, 1996 (copyright).

tion. Roosevelt introduced his sweeping New Deal to pull the nation out of the Great Depression. Ambitious government programs helped put many businesses and millions of people back on their feet. The Roosevelt administration openly embraced social welfare programs and economic regulation. Elected president in 1932, 1936, 1940, and 1944, Roosevelt has been the only president in U.S. history to win four terms in office. He also steered the nation through World War II.

After Roosevelt's death in 1945, Vice President HARRY S. TRUMAN assumed office. In 1948, after Truman had supported key civil rights legislation, a cadre of southern Democrats rebelled by joining the Dixiecrat party, a group advocating states' rights and segregation. The

Dixiecrats eventually disbanded, and some southern Democrats switched to the Republican party. This shift began in earnest with the election of DWIGHT D. EISENHOWER in 1952 and peaked with the election of RONALD REAGAN in 1980 and 1984.

In 1960 Democratic nominee JOHN F. KENNEDY became the first Roman Catholic to achieve the Oval Office. Kennedy's administration, called the New Frontier, established the Peace Corps; weathered the CUBAN MISSILE CRISIS, in which it convinced the Soviet Union to dismantle long-range nuclear missile sites in Cuba and return the missiles to Russia; and lent support to integration efforts in the South. After Kennedy's assassination in 1963, Vice President LYNDON B. JOHNSON was sworn in as president. He later defeated Republican BARRY M. GOLDWATER for the chief executive position in the 1964 general election.

Johnson strongly supported civil rights, a position that further eroded the Democrats' base of southern whites and northern labor and ethnic voters. Johnson's policies for U.S. military involvement in Southeast Asia made him unpopular at home and abroad. In 1968, after Johnson declined a reelection bid, the Democrats held a tumultuous convention in Chicago that tarnished the image of party leaders and Chicago police. As protesters and police officers clashed on the streets, convention delegates nominated Minnesota's HUBERT H. HUMPHREY, despite a groundswell of support for Vietnam War critic Eugene McCarthy. Humphrey lost the general election to Republican RICHARD M. NIXON.

In 1976 Governor Jimmy Carter, of Georgia, reclaimed the White House and the South for Democrats. Carter served one term, losing the 1980 election to Republican Reagan. Another southern Democrat, Governor BILL CLINTON, of Arkansas, won the presidency in 1992 and again in 1996, becoming the first Democratic president to win reelection since Franklin D. Roosevelt.

Many political observers believe that the current Democratic party is adopting a more centrist stance on social issues such as WELFARE, which may be a response to Republican gains tied to calls for reducing the federal deficit and lowering taxes.

See also ELECTIONS; REPUBLICAN PARTY.

DEMONSTRATIVE EVIDENCE   Evidence other than TESTIMONY that is presented during the course of a civil or criminal TRIAL.

Demonstrative evidence includes actual EVIDENCE (e.g., a set of bloody gloves from a murder scene) and illustrative evidence (e.g., photographs and charts). Demonstrative evidence may affect the jurors' sense of hearing in combination with another of their senses, like sight or touch: thus, courts may allow jurors to view videotaped reenactments of accidents or to visit the scene of an alleged crime.

Many trial attorneys view the presentation of evidence to the jury as analogous to the presentation of information by a teacher to students. As in the classroom, the involvement of more than one of a juror's senses in the courtroom increases the amount of information retained by that juror. Combining verbal testimony from witnesses with before and after X rays, or a defective machine part that jurors can hold in their hands for inspection, makes for compelling courtroom activity. In a modern, "show-me" society, the ability of a trial lawyer to use demonstrative evidence effectively can make the difference between winning and losing a case.

One common and effective example of demonstrative evidence is the still photograph. Photographs of a plaintiff's bruises taken immediately after an accident can help a JURY understand those injuries in a trial that occurs months or even years after the accident, when the injuries may have healed. Aerial photographs of the scene of a vehicular accident can show how a particular intersection is laid out, and can make more clear an ambiguous description of a blind intersection given by a witness.

X rays and medical models and illustrations can be very helpful to a jury in physical injury cases. These examples of demonstrative evidence help the jury "see inside" the victim to understand the nature and extent of the injuries. X rays can show not only fractures but also permanent metal pins and plates. Accurate models of a plaintiff's head and neck can show the interaction between the cervical area of the spine and the surrounding muscle and tissues in a soft-tissue injury case. Sometimes, partial or full skeletons are brought into courtrooms to demonstrate losses or restrictions of movement due to injuries. Modern computer-generated illustrations can show the exact injury to a specific plaintiff, as opposed to the generic injury represented in a stock medical illustration.

Graphs and charts are perhaps the most useful forms of demonstrative evidence. These tools can vividly illustrate a loss of earnings, a decrease in life expectancy, and past and future medical bills. Clear and concise charts can help a jury to arrange a complex set of events in a chronological fashion. These time lines can be crucial in organizing evidence, whether in a criminal trial or in a complex securities litigation. Often, maps and other geographic charts are used to show water flow, elevation, and other physical characteristics of real property (land).

Graphs and charts can be presented to a jury in a variety of ways. In addition to offering the standard large prepared poster board on an easel, some attorneys prefer to create charts as they speak to the jury, using large blank pieces of poster board and colored marker pens. Other attorneys like the dramatic effect of dimming the courtroom lights and using an overhead projector to focus visual attention on their illuminated charts and graphs. Whatever the style of presentation, well-constructed charts and graphs that make good use of color and are clear and easy to understand are appreciated by jurors and can have a big effect during deliberations.

Articles and objects are also forms of demonstrative evidence. In addition to actual evidence that is introduced at trial (like the knife from a murder scene), other physical articles and objects can be used to help the jury understand the testimony. For example, in a PRODUCT LIABILITY action based on a defective artificial hip, giving the jury models of ball-and-socket joints to manipulate and examine with their own hands can clarify testimony regarding the replacement joint that is still inside the plaintiff. Three-dimensional models and mock-ups of roadways, accident sites, or proposed buildings can simulate the outside world inside the courtroom to give proportion and scale to a witness's testimony.

With the permission of the judge, attorneys may be allowed to take the jurors to the scene of the crime or accident. Here, all a juror's senses are at work, and testimony presented in court can be compared to and contrasted with the physical scene. A list prepared by both

attorneys of items to "notice" may be read by the bailiff at the scene. Many juries appreciate not only the chance to get outside the courtroom but also the opportunity to see for themselves the place where it all happened.

With the advent of low-cost videocassette players and recorders, it has become more and more common to see videotape in the courtroom. A "day in the life of . . ." video can graphically demonstrate the activities of a plaintiff living with debilitating injuries: for example, a plaintiff witness may say, "I can't pick up my children," whereas a video can actually show the plaintiff's young children milling about with the plaintiff able only to sit by and watch them. Videotapes can also show the traffic volume at a busy intersection or provide a driver's-eye view of a road sign obstructed by brush and leaves. If a jury is unable to leave the courtroom to visit the scene of a fire, a video camera can provide a tour through the burned-out remains of the family's residence. Some attorneys have actually begun hiring stuntpersons to re-create vehicular accidents, driving comparable vehicles at the speeds they were going when the accidents occurred, and filming the results. Unlike a controlled dramatic re-creation, this kind of actual re-creation, with its inherent danger yet accurate representation of accident conditions, can be an effective tool at trial.

Though waning in popularity owing to the greater availability and lower cost of computers, slide projectors and human-created animation are still used by some attorneys. By taking two slide projectors, superimposing their projections, and connecting them with a sophisticated mechanical device, an attorney can make a before picture fade into an after picture with dramatic results. As with a presentation using an overhead projector, the dark courtroom and brightly lit screen of a slide presentation focus the jury's visual attention. Animated cartoon shorts, hand inked by artists, are eye-catching and can portray exactly what the attorney wants to emphasize to the jury: for example, a cutaway "operating" engine might show how a defective part can cause the engine to break down.

Computers and computer-generated displays are at the cutting edge of demonstrative evidence. One CD-ROM disk can contain thousands of still photos, graphs, charts, digitized video clips, and even three-dimensional computer animations. A courtroom presentation coordinated by a computer can combine many different forms of demonstrative evidence into a cohesive and dramatic presentation. Still photos of an injury can be followed by a digitized video showing limited physical abilities after the in-

Illustrative evidence includes charts that explain complicated information, such as matching DNA samples, that is being disputed by the two sides in a trial.

DAVID TAYLOR/SIPA

jury. X ray images can fade into graphs showing a loss of earning capacity. All these exhibits can be contained in a laptop computer and presented with minimal setup and distraction to the jurors. The attorney making the presentation can instantly return to a particular demonstrative exhibit when making a point during closing arguments.

Virtual reality—where individuals see and hear computer-generated images and sounds, and through body sensors "see" their hands and body within the simulation—may soon move from arcades and nightclubs into the courtroom.

No matter the technology, demonstrative evidence must still conform to standard evidentiary rules. Any item of demonstrative evidence that is inaccurate or incomplete may be disallowed by the trial court. Courts can also strike evidence if it is unnecessarily cumulative: for example, thirty photographs of one bruise that can be clearly seen in one or two photographs constitute evidence that is unnecessarily cumulative.

An attorney must keep in mind that demonstrative evidence is not real evidence: it merely illustrates the points being argued to the jury and court. Computer-generated animation may only portray evidence that has been properly presented to the jury through testimony or as physical evidence. A chart or graph may only present numbers and amounts that have been properly calculated and proved. No matter how exciting the "show," the attorney must remember that items of demonstrative evidence are merely props, and that the WITNESSES and their testimony are still the primary method of presenting evidence to a jury.

DEMONSTRATIVE LEGACY A gift by WILL of money or other personal property that is to be paid to an HEIR from a fund designated in the provisions of the will but, in any event, is to be paid if there are sufficient available assets in the ESTATE.

A demonstrative legacy differs from a SPECIFIC LEGACY, a gift of particular PERSONAL PROPERTY by will. A demonstrative legacy is payable from the general assets of the estate that have not been specifically devised or bequeathed if its designated source has been adeemed or no longer exists or if it is inadequate to satisfy the gift. In the case of a specific legacy the ADEMPTION of property revokes the gift completely so that the heir receives nothing. However, if the value of the gift has only been reduced, the heir receives the decreased value.

Courts often interpret provisions of a will that appear to grant specific legacies of money or shares of stock as demonstrative legacies to avoid the consequences of ademption where it is clear that the TESTATOR intended the gift to be made in any event.

DEMUR To dispute a legal PLEADING or a statement of the facts being alleged through the use of a DEMURRER.

DEMURRAGE A separate freight charge, in addition to ordinary shipping costs, which is imposed according to the terms of a carriage contract upon the person responsible for unreasonable delays in loading or unloading cargo.

In maritime law, demurrage is the amount identified in a charter contract as DAMAGES payable to a shipowner as compensation for the detention of a ship beyond the time specified by a charter party for loading and unloading or for sailing.

Demurrage is intended to serve the public interest by facilitating the flow of commerce through the prompt loading and unloading of cargo. In general, the person liable for demurrage is the one who assumed the duty to unload or load the cargo but failed to fulfill it. A consignee who agrees to unload a shipment but unreasonably delays in doing so is liable for the charge.

Demurrage

Waterborne Commerce in the United States, by Type of Commodity, in 1993. U.S. domestic trade includes all commercial movements between U.S. ports and on inland rivers, Great Lakes, and connecting channels of the United States, Puerto Rico, and U.S. Virgin Islands.

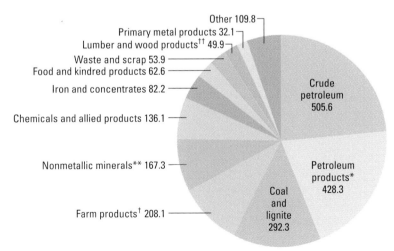

Total tonnage: 2,128.2
(in millions)

Other 109.8
Primary metal products 32.1
Lumber and wood products†† 49.9
Waste and scrap 53.9
Food and kindred products 62.6
Iron and concentrates 82.2
Chemicals and allied products 136.1
Nonmetallic minerals** 167.3
Farm products† 208.1
Crude petroleum 505.6
Petroleum products* 428.3
Coal and lignite 292.3

*Includes gasoline, fuel oils, and other refined petroleum products.

**Includes sand, gravel, limestone, phosphate rocks, and other nonmetallic minerals. Does not include fuels.

†Includes, but is not limited to, corn, wheat, and soybeans.

††Excludes furniture.

Source: U.S. Army Corps of Engineers, *Waterborne Commerce of the United States,* annual.

Payment of demurrage is excused only if the delay was unavoidable, such as a delay caused by a natural disaster or the fault of the CARRIER. *Reciprocal demurrage* may be imposed upon a carrier who unreasonably delays in providing transportation to customers. The practical effect of reciprocal demurrage is a reduction in the customer's shipping charges unless the contractual amount exceeds that figure. If a person against whom demurrage is imposed fails to pay, the carrier might have a right to keep the goods until payment is made. This is known as demurrage lien, enforceable only if authorized by statute, contract, or custom.

See also SHIPPING LAW.

DEMURRER ▯ An assertion by the DEFENDANT that although the facts alleged by the PLAINTIFF in the COMPLAINT may be true, they do not entitle the plaintiff to prevail in the lawsuit. ▯

The PLEADINGS of the PARTIES to a lawsuit describe the dispute to be resolved. The plaintiff sets out the facts that support the claim made in the complaint, and the defendant then has an opportunity to respond in an ANSWER.

A demurrer is a type of answer used in systems of CODE PLEADING, established by statute to replace the earlier common-law FORMS OF ACTION. While a demurrer admits the truth of the plaintiff's set of facts, it contends that those facts are insufficient to grant the complaint in favor of the plaintiff. A demurrer may further contend that the complaint does not set forth enough facts to justify legal relief or it may introduce additional facts that defeat the legal effectiveness of the plaintiff's complaint. A demurrer asserts that, even if the plaintiff's facts are correct, the defendant should not have to answer them or proceed with the case.

Under the modern rules of pleading established by the rules of federal CIVIL PROCEDURE and followed in a number of states, the demurrer has been abolished as a formal type of answer. The same argument against the plaintiff's cause of action can be, however, made by MOTION to dismiss the plaintiff's action on the ground that he or she has failed to state a claim on which relief can be granted. Even where the formal demurrer is no longer used, lawyers and judges often use the old term for an argument of the same type.

DENNIS v. UNITED STATES ▯ A 1951 decision of the Supreme Court, *Dennis v. United States*, 341 U.S. 494, 71 S. Ct. 857, 95 L. Ed. 1137, that upheld criminal convictions under the SMITH ACT (18 U.S.C.A. § 2385 [1940]), which proscribed teaching and advocating the violent and forcible overthrow of the U.S. government. ▯

Eugene Dennis was one of a number of persons convicted in federal district court for violation of the Smith Act. He and the others were alleged to have engaged in a CONSPIRACY to form the Communist party of the United States to teach and advocate the overthrow of the United States government by force and violence. Such conduct was in direct contravention with the provisions of the Smith Act. Dennis unsuccessfully appealed his conviction and was granted CERTIORARI by the Supreme Court.

The Court focused its review on two issues: whether the particular provisions of the Smith Act violated the FIRST AMENDMENT and the Bill of Rights and whether the sections in question were unconstitutional because they were indefinite in describing the nature of the proscribed conduct. The Court relied upon the determination of the Court of Appeals that the objective of the Communist party in the United States was to bring about the overthrow of its government by force and violence. From this perspective, it reasoned that Congress was empowered to enact the Smith Act, which was designed to safeguard the federal government against terrorist and violent revolution. Peaceable and lawful change was not proscribed, however. The power of Congress to so legislate was not in question, but the means it used to do so created constitutional problems.

The defendants argued that the statute inhibited a free and intelligent discussion of Marxism-Leninism, in violation of the defendants' rights to free speech and press. The Court countered that the Smith Act prohibits *advocacy*, not intellectual discussion, which is admittedly protected by the First Amendment. It continued, however, that the rights given by the First Amendment are not absolute and unqualified, but must occasionally yield to other concerns and values in society.

The Court decided that the "clear and present danger" test, first formulated by the Supreme Court in 1919 in *Schenck v. United States*, 249 U.S. 47, 39 S. Ct. 247, 63 L. Ed. 470, applied to the case and set out to explain its applicability. The forcible and violent overthrow of the government constituted a substantial enough interest to permit the government to limit speech that sought to cause it. The Court then reasoned that "If [the] Government is aware that a group aiming at its overthrow is attempting to indoctrinate its members and to commit them to a course whereby they will strike when the leaders feel the circumstances permit, action by the Government is required." The likelihood of success or success itself is not necessary, provided the words and proposed actions posed a CLEAR AND PRESENT DANGER to the government. The Court based its rationale upon the majority opinion in *Gitlow v. New York*, 268 U.S. 652, 45 S. Ct. 625, 69 L. Ed. 1138 (1925), " 'In each case [courts] must ask whether the gravity of the "evil," discounted by its improbability, justifies such invasion of free speech as is necessary to avoid the danger.' "

Concerning the issue of indefiniteness, the Court concluded that since the defendants were found by the jury to have intended the forcible overthrow of the government as soon as the circumstances permitted, there was no need to reverse their convictions because of the possibility that others might, in the future, be unaware of its proscriptions. When possible "borderline" cases arise, the Court would at that time strictly scrutinize the convictions.

The *Dennis* decision so broadly expanded the parameters of the "clear and present danger" test that the Supreme Court eventually rejected it in favor of a test that balances First Amendment freedom against the substantial interests of the government.

CROSS-REFERENCES

Communism; Freedom of Speech; Freedom of the Press; *Gitlow v. New York*; *Schenck v. United States.*

DE NOVO 📖 [*Latin, Anew.*] A second time; afresh. A TRIAL or a HEARING that is ordered by an APPELLATE COURT that has reviewed the record of a hearing in a lower court and sent the matter back to the original court for a new trial, as if it had not· been previously heard nor decided. 📖

DENY 📖 To refuse to acknowledge something; to disclaim connection with or responsibility for an action or statement. To deny someone of a legal right is to deprive him or her of that right. 📖

A *denial* is a part of a legal PLEADING that refutes the facts set forth by the opposing side. A *general denial* takes exception to all the material elements of the COMPLAINT or PETITION, and a specific denial addresses a particular ALLEGATION in issue.

DEPENDENT 📖 A person whose support and maintenance is CONTINGENT upon the aid of another. CONDITIONAL. 📖

A dependent is someone who is sustained by another person, such as a child supported by his or her parents.

In an INSURANCE policy, the term *legal dependent* generally includes all of those people whom the insured person is under a legal duty to support, such as a spouse and minor children. A *lawful dependent* includes someone whom an

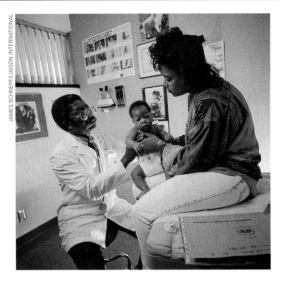

This young baby is a dependent of her parents, who are responsible for her care.

insured person is permitted, but not required, to support.

That which is dependent is conditional upon the occurrence of another event. A *dependent contract* is an agreement between two parties that is conditional upon another agreement. For example, one person agrees to deliver goods to another person only after that person CONTRACTS to purchase such goods from the first person only for a certain designated period.

DEPENDENT RELATIVE REVOCATION

📖 The doctrine that regards as mutually interrelated the acts of a TESTATOR destroying a WILL and executing a second will. In such cases, if the second will is either never made or improperly executed, there is a REBUTTABLE PRESUMPTION that the testator would have preferred the former will to no will at all, which allows the possibility of PROBATE of the destroyed will. 📖

Some JURISDICTIONS decline to apply the doctrine of dependent relative revocation to cases to eliminate a written revocation of a will, but apply it to declare the ineffectiveness of a physical act of revocation. The justification for the distinction is that the physical act is inherently equivocal. The court has the power to interpret the ambiguous act to ascertain what the testator did but not to disregard an express statement of the testator and substitute its own conception of what the testator should have done.

The doctrine of dependent relative revocation contravenes the strict interpretation of and demand for rigid adherence to the specific language of the statutes concerning the execution and revocation of wills and the theory of the PAROL EVIDENCE rule. In deciding whether to apply the doctrine, the court considers the TESTAMENTARY pattern of the decedent, the terms of the prior wills, the respective identities and shares of the BENEFICIARIES under the previous will and the new will in question, the nature of the defect that prevents the new will from taking effect, the trustworthiness of the proof of the reasons for the testator's desire to make the desired objective to the former testamentary plans as contrasted to the application of the laws of DESCENT AND DISTRIBUTION. The court will not execute a new will, but it will eradicate revocations to infuse new life into a prior will that achieves the same objective.

DEPENDENT STATES States can be classified into two general categories: dependent and independent. A dependent state does not exercise the full range of power over external affairs that an independent state possesses under INTERNATIONAL LAW. The controlling or protecting state may also regulate some of the internal affairs of the dependent state. Formal treaties and the conditions under which the status of dependency has been recognized by other states govern the balance of sovereign powers exercised by the protecting state and the dependent state. Various terms have been used to describe different types of dependent states, such as CONDOMINIUM, MANDATE, PROTECTORATE, and vassal state. Since 1945 there has been strong international pressure to eliminate forms of dependency associated with colonialism.

DEPLETION ALLOWANCE 📖 A tax deduction authorized by federal law for the exhaustion of oil and gas wells, mines, timber, mineral deposits or reserves, and other natural deposits. 📖

Frequently, the ownership of such resources is split so that the depletion deduction is allotted among the various owners. Rights to ROYALTY payments, LEASES, and subleases are not the same as ownership but the holders of such rights may be entitled to depletion deductions under the theory of "economic interest" formulated by the courts to ascertain the right to depletion allowances. Such economic interest, which signifies an investment interest in the minerals that furnish the sole resource for recouping the investment, is usually determined by the parties according to the provisions of their contract.

The cost method and the percentage, or statutory, method represent the two ways of calculating the depletion allowance.

Cost depletion, like DEPRECIATION, bases the allowance on the original cost of the income-generating property. For example, a taxpayer who purchases rights to extricate oil for $2 million should be permitted to regain the capital tax-free when he or she extracts and markets the oil. The earnings from the depletable property should be viewed as encompassing a return

of the taxpayer's capital investment. A proportionate segment of such receipts each year should be exempt from taxation as income. When oil is viewed as a "wasting asset," cost depletion permits yearly deductions for the receipt of $2 million tax-free over the duration of the pumping operations. The tax law permits the taxpayer to divide the cost of the investment by the estimated total of recoverable units in the natural deposit. This cost per unit is subsequently multiplied by the number of units sold annually, which results in the depletion deduction permitted for that year.

The percentage, or statutory, method does not employ recovery of cost in the computation of the deduction. A percentage of annual income, rather than cost, is deductible each year, even if the owner has recovered all cost or discovery value of the depletable asset. The federal tax laws vary from year to year in regard to the percentage depletion allowable for oil and some other deposits, and the categories of producers entitled to such allowances.

Percentage depletion, which applies to other mineral deposits or energy sources such as geothermal steam, provides an extremely profitable allowance as an alternative to cost depletion. The taxpayer calculates a fixed percentage of his or her GROSS INCOME and deducts that amount from gross income annually for as long as the property generates income, even after he or she has completely recovered the actual cost. Some taxpayers employ cost depletion at the outset of operations, when a large number of units of the deposit are extracted and sold, and then convert to percentage depletion upon recoupment of cost in other circumstances—when percentage depletion yields a more sizable deduction.

The owners of this copper mine are allowed a depletion allowance on their taxes because the mine has been exhausted.

Percentage depletion furnishes an additional tax subsidy to detection, development, and dissipation of qualified reserves. The subsidy approach began during World War I to induce exploration for minerals. Cost depletion had been expanded to permit discovery value rather than cost to serve as the gauge of tax-exempt recovery. A problem in estimating the quantity of depletable units prior to extraction existed, however, and percentage depletion was enacted in 1924 as the solution. This method was subsequently extended to include additional minerals and other deposits and to raise rates of depletion in some instances. It was eventually diminished due to excessive profits and tax benefits obtained by some companies. Only depletion, rather than percentage depletion, may be used for gas, water, soil, timber, and oil.

For percentage depletion, gross income must be restricted to income from extracting and selling the deposit, not from refining, processing, or manufacturing it.

The option to deduct present exploration and development expenditures rather than capitalizing them represents an additional tax advantage for the industries entitled to depletion allowances. A more substantial tax benefit ensues if such expenses are deducted immediately, since they would never be recovered through the application of percentage depletion, which is based on gross income and not the cost of the capital invested in the enterprise.

See also INCOME TAX; MINE AND MINERAL LAW.

DEPONENT An individual who, under oath or affirmation, gives out-of-court TESTIMONY in a DEPOSITION. A deponent is someone who gives EVIDENCE or acts as a WITNESS. The testimony of a deponent is written and carries the deponent's signature.

DEPORTATION Banishment to a foreign country, attended with CONFISCATION of property and deprivation of CIVIL RIGHTS.

The transfer of an ALIEN, by exclusion or expulsion, from the United States to a foreign country. The removal or sending back of an alien to the country from which he or she came because his or her presence is deemed inconsistent with the public welfare, and without any punishment being imposed or contemplated. The grounds for deportation are set forth at 8 U.S.C.A. § 1251, and the procedures are provided for in §§ 1252-1254.

DEPOSE To make a DEPOSITION; to give EVIDENCE in the shape of a deposition; to make statements that are written down and sworn to; to give TESTIMONY that is reduced to writing by a duly qualified officer and sworn to by the deponent.

To deprive an individual of a public employment or office against his or her will. The term is usually applied to the deprivation of all authority of a sovereign.

In ancient usage, to testify as a WITNESS; to give evidence under oath.

DEPOSITION The TESTIMONY of a PARTY or WITNESS in a civil or criminal proceeding taken before trial, usually in an attorney's office.

Deposition testimony is taken orally, with an attorney asking questions and the DEPONENT (the individual being questioned) answering while a court reporter or tape recorder (or sometimes both) records the testimony. Deposition testimony is generally taken under OATH, and the court reporter and the deponent often sign AFFIDAVITS attesting to the accuracy of the subsequent printed transcript.

Depositions are a DISCOVERY tool. (Discovery is the process of assembling the testimonial and documentary evidence in a case before trial.) Other forms of discovery include INTERROGATORIES (written questions that are provided to a party and require written answers) and requests for production of documents.

Depositions are commonly used in civil litigation (suits for money damages or equitable relief); they are not commonly used in criminal proceedings (actions by a government entity seeking fines or imprisonment). A minority of states provide for depositions in criminal matters under special circumstances, such as to compel statements from an uncooperative witness and a few provide for depositions in criminal matters generally.

Before a deposition takes place, the deponent must be given adequate notice as to its time and place. Five days' notice is usually sufficient, but local rules may vary. Persons who are witnesses but not parties to the lawsuit must also be served with a SUBPOENA (a command to appear and give testimony, backed by the authority of the court).

Depositions commonly take place after the exchange of interrogatories and requests for

Depositions are often recorded by a court reporter on a stenographic machine.

production of documents, because the evidence obtained from the latter often provides foundation for the questions posed to the deponent. Any documents, photographs, or other evidence referred to during the deposition is marked and numbered as exhibits for the deposition, and the court reporter attaches copies of these exhibits to the subsequent deposition TRANSCRIPT. Generally, at the outset of the deposition, the court reporter, who is often also a NOTARY PUBLIC, leads the deponent through an oath that the testimony that will be given will be true and correct.

The examining attorney begins the deposition and may ask the deponent a wide variety of questions. Questions that could not be asked of a witness in court because of doubts about their relevance or concerns about HEARSAY (statements of a third party) are usually allowed in the deposition setting, because they might reasonably lead to ADMISSIBLE statements or evidence. A party who refuses to answer a reasonable question can be subject to a court order and sanctions. However, a party may refuse to answer questions on the basis of PRIVILEGE (a legal right not to testify). For example, statements made to an attorney, psychiatrist, or physician by a client seeking professional services can remain confidential, and a client may assert a privilege against being required to disclose these statements.

After the examining attorney's questions are completed, the attorney representing the adverse party in the litigation is permitted to ask follow-up questions to clarify or emphasize the deponent's testimony. In litigation involving a number of represented parties, any other attorney present may also ask questions.

The court reporter often records the proceedings in a deposition on a stenographic machine, which creates a phonetic and coded paper record as the parties speak. Occasionally, an attorney or witness may ask the court reporter to read back a portion of previous testimony during the deposition.

Most modern stenographic machines also write a text file directly to a computer diskette during the deposition. In the past, arduous manual labor was required to turn the phonetic and coded paper copy into a complete hand-typed transcript. This is now rarely necessary because sophisticated computer programs can create a transcript automatically from the text file on the diskette. When the transcription is complete, copies are provided to the attorneys, and the deponent is given the opportunity to review the testimony and correct any typographic errors.

A sample subpoena requiring witnesses to attend an examination before trial to give evidence by deposition

SUPREME COURT OF THE STATE OF _____
COUNTY OF _____

_____,
                                    Plaintiff,
        -against-   SUBPOENA
_____,   Index No. _____
                                    Defendant.

THE PEOPLE OF THE STATE OF _____

To:

WE COMMAND YOU, that all business and excuses being laid aside, to appear and attend before _____, a notary public, at his office located at _____, City of _____, County of _____, State of _____, on the _____ day of _____, 19__, at _____ o'clock in the _____ noon of that day, and at any adjourned date, to testify and give evidence, as a witness on an examination before trial by deposition upon oral questions in the above entitled action now pending in the Supreme Court, County of _____; and for a failure to attend you will be deemed guilty of a contempt of court, and liable to pay all losses and damages sustained thereby to the party aggrieved and forfeit fifty ($50) dollars in addition thereto.

Attorney for Plaintiff [or Defendant]
P.O. Address
Tel. No.

The deposition, because it is taken with counsel present and under oath, becomes a significant evidentiary document. Based upon the deposition testimony, MOTIONS for SUMMARY JUDGMENT or partial summary judgment as to some claims in the lawsuit may be brought. (Summary judgment allows a judge to find that one party to the lawsuit prevails without trial, if there are no disputed material facts and judgment must be rendered as a MATTER OF LAW.) If motions for summary judgment are denied and the case goes to trial, the deposition can be used to IMPEACH (challenge) a party or witness who gives contradictory testimony on the witness stand.

The advent of sophisticated and low-cost video technology has resulted in increased videotaping of depositions. Both sides must agree to the videotaping, through a signed agreement called a STIPULATION, and in some jurisdictions, the parties must also seek a court order.

A videotaped record of a deposition offers several advantages. First, a videotape shows clearly the facial expressions and posture of the witnesses, which can clarify otherwise ambiguous statements. Second, physical injuries such as burns, scars, or limitations can easily be demonstrated. Third, a videotape may have a greater effect on a jury if portions of the deposition are introduced at trial as evidence. Finally, a videotape can serve as a more effective substitute for a party who cannot testify at trial, like an expert witness from another state or a witness who is too ill to be brought to the courtroom. If a witness dies unexpectedly before trial, a videotaped deposition can be admitted in lieu of live testimony because the deposition was taken under oath and the opposing attorney had the opportunity to cross-examine the witness.

Another advance in technology is the ability to take depositions by telephone. Telephonic depositions are allowed under the federal rules and are acceptable in most states. The procedures for a telephonic deposition are the same as for a regular deposition, although it is preferable (and sometimes required) that the examining attorney state for the record that the deposition is being taken over the telephone. A telephonic deposition can occur with the attorneys and the deponent in three different sites; in any case, federal and state rules stipulate that the judicial district within which the deponent is located is the official site of the deposition.

Another technology used for depositions is videoconferencing, where sound transmitters and receivers are combined with video cameras and monitors, allowing the attorneys and deponents to see each other as a deposition proceeds. Videoconferencing makes the examination of exhibits easier and also helps reduce confusion among the participants that may result from ambiguous or unclear verbal responses.

DEPOSITORY The place where a deposit is placed and kept, e.g., a bank, savings and loan institution, credit union, or trust company. A place where something is deposited or stored as for safekeeping or convenience, e.g., a safety deposit box.

This term should not be confused with *depositary*, which is the person or institution taking responsibility for the deposit, rather than the place itself.

U. S. depositories are banks selected and designated to receive deposits of the public funds (e.g., taxes) of the United States.

DEPOSITS IN COURT The payments of funds or property to an OFFICER OF THE COURT as a precautionary measure during the pendency of litigation.

The amount placed with the court constitutes the acknowledged LIABILITY of a person who is uncertain as to whom he or she is liable. The ascertainment of the court as to who is entitled to the property is binding.

This term also encompasses payment into court pursuant to court order.

DEPRECIATION The gradual decline in the financial value of PROPERTY used to produce INCOME due to its increasing age and eventual obsolescence, which is measured by a formula that takes into account these factors in addition to the cost of the property and its estimated useful life.

Depreciation is a concept used in ACCOUNTING to measure the decline in an ASSET's value spread over the asset's economic life. Depreciation allows for future INVESTMENT that is required to replace used-up assets. In addition, the U.S. INTERNAL REVENUE SERVICE allows a reasonable DEDUCTION for depreciation as a business expense in determining taxable net income. This deduction is used only for property that generates income. For example, a building used for rent income can be depreciated, but a building used as a residence cannot be depreciated.

Depreciation arises from a strong public policy in favor of investment. Income-producing assets such as machines, trucks, tools, and structures have a limited useful life—that is, they wear out and grow obsolete while generating income. In effect, a taxpayer using such assets in business is gradually selling those assets. To encourage continued investment, part of the GROSS INCOME should be seen as a return on a capital expenditure, and not as PROFIT. Accordingly, tax law has developed to separate the return of capital amounts from net income.

Generally, depreciation covers deterioration from use, age, and exposure to the elements. An asset likely to become obsolete, such as a computer system, can also be depreciated. An asset that is damaged or destroyed by fire, accident, or disaster cannot be depreciated. An asset that is used in one year cannot be depreciated; instead, the loss on such an asset may be written off as a business expense.

Several methods are used for depreciating income-producing business assets. The most common and simplest is the straight-line method. STRAIGHT-LINE DEPRECIATION is figured by first taking the original cost of an asset and subtracting the estimated value of the asset at the end of its useful life, to arrive at the depreciable basis. Then, to determine the annual depreciation for the asset, the depreciable basis is divided by the estimated life span of the asset. For example, if a manufacturing machine costs $1,200 and is expected to be worth $200 at the end of its useful life, its depreciable basis is $1,000. If the useful life span of the machine is 10 years, the depreciation each year is $100 ($1,000 divided by 10 years). Thus, $100 can be deducted from the business's taxable net income each year for 10 years.

Accelerated depreciation provides a larger tax write-off for the early years of an asset.

Various methods are used to accelerate depreciation. One method, called declining-balance depreciation, is calculated by deducting a percentage up to two times higher than that recognized by the straight-line method, and applying that percentage to the undepreciated balance at the start of each tax period. For the manufacturing machine example, the business could deduct up to $200 (20 percent of $1,000) in the first year, $160 (20 percent of the balance, $800) the second year, and so on. As soon as the amount of depreciation under the declining-balance method would be less than that under the straight-line method (in our example, $100), the straight-line method is used to finish depreciating the asset.

Another method of accelerating depreciation is the sum-of-the-years method. This is calculated by multiplying an asset's depreciable basis by a particular fraction. The fraction used to determine the deductible amount is figured by adding the number of years of the asset's useful life. For example, for a 10-year useful life span, one would add 1, 2, 3, 4, 5, 6, 7, 8, 9, and 10, to arrive at 55. This is the denominator of the fraction. The numerator is the actual number of useful years for the machine, 10. The fraction is thus 10/55. This fraction is multiplied by the depreciable basis ($1,000) to arrive at the depreciation deduction for the first year. For the second year, the fraction 9/55 is multiplied against the depreciable basis, and so on until the end of the asset's useful life. Sum-of-years is a more gradual form of accelerated depreciation than declining-balance depreciation.

Depreciation is allowed by the government as a reward to those investing in business. In 1981, the Accelerated Cost Recovery System (ACRS) (I.R.C. § 168) was authorized by Congress for use as a tax accounting method to recover capital costs for most tangible depreciable property. ACRS uses accelerated methods applied over predetermined recovery periods shorter than, and unrelated to, the useful life of assets. ACRS covers depreciation for most depreciable property, and more quickly than prior law permitted. Not all property has a predetermined rate of depreciation under ACRS. The Internal Revenue Code indicates which assets are covered by ACRS.

See also INCOME TAX; TAXABLE INCOME.

DEPUTY 📖 A person duly authorized by an officer to serve as his or her substitute by performing some or all of the officer's functions. 📖

A *deputy* SHERIFF is designated to act on behalf of the sheriff in regard to official business.

A *general deputy* or undersheriff, pursuant to an appointment, has authority to execute all of

Depreciation
Corporate Depreciation Claimed to IRS, 1980 to 1992

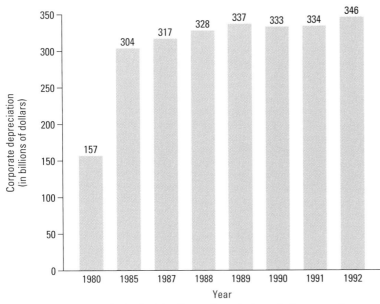

Source: U.S. Internal Revenue Service, *Statistics of Income, Corporation Income Tax Returns,* annual.

the regular duties of the office of sheriff and serves process without any special authority from the sheriff.

A *special deputy*, who is an officer *pro hac vice* (Latin for "for this turn"), is appointed to render a special service. A special deputy acts under a specific, rather than a general, appointment and authority.

See also SERVICE OF PROCESS.

DERIVATIVE ACTION 📖 A lawsuit brought by a shareholder of a CORPORATION on its behalf to enforce or defend a legal right or claim, which the corporation has failed to do. 📖

A derivative action, more popularly known as a STOCKHOLDER'S DERIVATIVE SUIT, is derived from the primary right of the corporation to seek redress of legal grievances through the courts. The procedure to be followed in such an action is governed by the rules of federal CIVIL PROCEDURE and state provisions, where applicable.

DERIVATIVE EVIDENCE 📖 Facts, information, or physical objects that tend to prove an issue in a criminal prosecution but which are excluded from consideration by the trier of fact because they were learned directly from information illegally obtained in violation of the constitutional guarantee against unreasonable SEARCHES AND SEIZURES. 📖

Derivative evidence is INADMISSIBLE as proof because of the application of the FRUIT OF THE POISONOUS TREE doctrine, which treats the original EVIDENCE and any evidence derived from it as tainted because of the illegal way in which it was obtained by agents of the government.

DEROGATION 📖 The partial REPEAL of a law, usually by a subsequent act that in some way diminishes its original intent or scope. 📖

Derogation is distinguishable from ABROGATION, which is the total annulment of a law.

DERSHOWITZ, ALAN MORTON Scholar and constitutional authority Alan Morton Dershowitz is a well-known, controversial, and successful U.S. APPELLATE attorney. A professor at the Harvard School of Law, he has a reputation for taking on the cases of little-loved criminal defendants. His list of clients is a who's who of notoriety, ranging from wealthy socialites to a

pornographic film star and a convicted spy. He has captured attention both in the courtroom and out, as much for his sometimes brilliant legal strategies as for his ubiquitous books, articles, and TV appearances. A staunch defender of FIRST AMENDMENT freedoms, civil and human rights, and Jewish issues, he has earned praise and enmity for his influence on U.S. law.

Dershowitz, born September 1, 1938, in Brooklyn, was raised in the orthodox Jewish area of Boro Park, New York. Dershowitz attended Yeshiva University High School, where a principal advised the unexceptional but talkative student to seek a career "where you use your mouth, not your brains" (Keegan 1992). He apparently ignored that advice, graduating magna cum laude from Brooklyn College and gaining admittance to Yale Law School. As a law student, he quickly distinguished himself: he was named editor of the *Yale Law Journal* in his second year, and his research on the relationship of psychiatry to the law was such that Harvard offered Dershowitz a teaching position upon his graduation. Finishing at the top of his class in 1962, he postponed the Harvard offer to clerk for Chief Judge David L. Bazelon, of the U.S. Court of Appeals. This clerkship was followed by another with Supreme Court justice ARTHUR J. GOLDBERG.

Appointed associate professor at Harvard Law School in 1964, Dershowitz went on to become, three years later, the youngest tenured professor in the school's history at twenty-eight. His specialty, criminal law, did not prevent him from continuing the academic research he had begun at Yale, and he coauthored the standard casebook *Psychoanalysis, Psychiatry, and the Law* (1967). He also began a lifelong immersion in liberal political issues. As protest over the Vietnam War galvanized campuses around the United States, Dershowitz created a course on legal concerns raised by the war, which inspired similar courses at numerous law schools. He worked privately on behalf of several antiwar protesters, including Harvard students facing disciplinary proceedings and the antiwar leader Dr. Benjamin M. Spock. In 1972

BIOGRAPHY

CHIASSON/LIAISON

Alan Morton Dershowitz

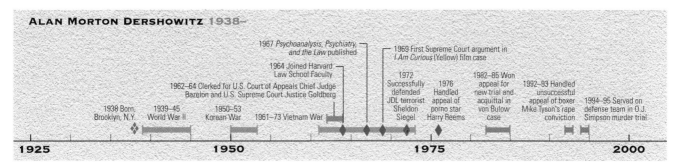

ALAN MORTON DERSHOWITZ 1938–

1938 Born, Brooklyn, N.Y.

1939–45 World War II

1950–53 Korean War

1961–73 Vietnam War

1962–64 Clerked for U.S. Court of Appeals Chief Judge Bazelon and U.S. Supreme Court Justice Goldberg

1964 Joined Harvard Law School Faculty

1967 *Psychoanalysis, Psychiatry, and the Law* published

1969 First Supreme Court argument in *I Am Curious* (Yellow) film case

1972 Successfully defended JDL terrorist Sheldon Siegel

1976 Handled appeal of porno star Harry Reems

1982–85 Won appeal for new trial and acquittal in von Bulow case

1992–93 Handled unsuccessful appeal of boxer Mike Tyson's rape conviction

1994–95 Served on defense team in O.J. Simpson murder trial

1925   1950   1975   2000

he drafted a successful appeal for WILLIAM M. KUNSTLER, a radical lawyer convicted of CONTEMPT of court for his defense of the Chicago Eight antiwar activists at the 1968 Democratic convention.

Free speech concerns animated Dershowitz to fight censorship of PORNOGRAPHY. In his view, "There is simply no justification for government censorship of offensive material of any kind." Even if pornography can be shown to lead to violence against women, Dershowitz opposes any controls on it. His position is that of a classic First Amendment absolutist: fight bad speech with good speech, but do not limit speech.

Dershowitz made his first Supreme Court argument in 1969, attempting to remove a Boston ban on screenings of the internationally acclaimed Swedish film *I Am Curious (Yellow)*. Championed by intellectuals such as Norman Mailer, the sexually explicit film was the first of its kind to be distributed commercially in the United States. Dershowitz successfully argued before a three-judge Court that the First Amendment protected the rights of consenting adults to view whatever they chose in a discreet setting. After the Supreme Court remanded the case, the prosecution was dismissed and the ban was lifted.

In 1976 Dershowitz handled the appeal of Harry Reems, a star in the pornographic film *Deep Throat*. Several years after acting in the film, Reems had been convicted on federal charges of taking part in an ongoing CONSPIRACY to transport it across state lines. Dershowitz won a new trial for Reems, and the Justice Department later dropped the INDICTMENT.

The attorney took his first criminal case in 1972. His defense of Sheldon Seigel, accused of making a bomb used by the terrorist Jewish Defense League (JDL), established a pattern that Dershowitz would follow throughout his career: a commitment to civil liberties and constitutional rights regardless of the notoriety or apparent immorality of his clients. The bomb Seigel was said to have made had exploded in the Manhattan office of arts impresario Sol Hurok, killing a young woman. While associated with the JDL, Seigel had also been a government informer. When the case came to trial, the government denied making a deal protecting him from testifying against his associates. Using secret tape recordings of his client and government agents, Dershowitz destroyed the prosecution's claims. An appellate court ruled against forcing Seigel to testify, and the case against the JDL suspects was dismissed for lack of evidence. Dershowitz later said he cried

upon realizing that he had gotten Seigel acquitted, thinking about the woman killed by the bomb. Yet the case had allowed him to challenge what he saw as systematic unconstitutionality in the government's handling of informers.

Defending other unpopular clients has sometimes earned Dershowitz the criticism of his peers. The attorney nonetheless accepts cases few other lawyers will touch, making him, in the words of *Time Magazine*, the "patron saint of hopeless cases." In 1975 he was widely criticized for agreeing to represent Bernard Bergman, a New York City nursing home operator, on appeal of his conviction for Medicare FRAUD and attempted BRIBERY. The press and the public had vilified Bergman for running a chain of nursing homes in which elderly patients were abused. Dershowitz tried, unsuccessfully, to have Bergman's one-year sentence reduced to four months, arguing that the special prosecutor in the case had violated a PLEA BARGAIN. In 1980 Dershowitz represented two brothers, Ricky Tison and Raymond Tison, who were convicted and sentenced to die for the crime of felony murder. The brothers had helped their father, Gary Tison, escape from prison; the father subsequently took part in a murder. Dershowitz raised the question of whether the brothers could be executed for a murder they did not plan or commit. In 1987 he argued for their lives before the Supreme Court, which remanded the case and ordered a new hearing.

A 1982 appeal for socialite Claus von Bülow catapulted Dershowitz to greater public attention than had any of his previous endeavors. Closely watched by the press, von Bülow's trial seemed the stuff of best-selling fiction. He had been convicted of attempting to murder his wife, heiress Martha (Sunny) Crawford von Bülow by injecting her with insulin—presumably, to lay hands on her millions. On appeal, Dershowitz made multiple arguments for reversal or retrial. He contended that his client had been the victim of an unconstitutional search, that evidence had been withheld from the defense, and that new medical evidence raised doubts about the insulin found in Crawford's blood. The appeals court reversed von Bülow's conviction in April 1984, and at a subsequent trial, with Dershowitz directing the defense strategy, a second jury acquitted him in 1985. The attorney wrote an account of the trial, *Reversal of Fortune* (1986), which later became an Academy Award–winning film.

Throughout the 1980s and early 1990s, Dershowitz seldom escaped public notice for his work on behalf of a string of controversial clients. He represented, among others, Leona

"IN POKER IT IS IMPOSSIBLE TO BLUFF WITH ALL YOUR CARDS SHOWING. IN LAW IT IS DIFFICULT, BUT NOT IMPOSSIBLE."

Helmsley, a hotel magnate convicted of tax evasion; Michael R. Milken, a Wall Street junk-bond financier who pleaded guilty to six felonies; Jonathan Pollard, a U.S. intelligence analyst who pleaded guilty to spying for Israel; and Mike Tyson, a former heavyweight champion who was convicted of rape. Dershowitz lost these appeals, but not for want of trying. His tactics routinely include a vociferous use of the media, on the assumption that judges and juries are influenced by what they see and read. Besides numerous interviews, he also has taken out full-page ads in the *New York Times* on behalf of clients, for example, Milken. But not all Dershowitz's clients are celebrities. He conducts pro bono work for those unable to afford a lawyer, let alone his reputed $400-an-hour fee.

As an appellate lawyer, Dershowitz estimates his chance of losing a client's appeal at 95 percent, saying, "I'm like a brain surgeon brought in after the tumor's been discovered." He cites constitutional concerns as his justification for his choice of clients. Others have accused him of greed and grandstanding. His one-time ally, the late Kunstler, was one such critic, bemoaning what he considered a former idealist's selling out. No stranger to criticism, Dershowitz gives as well as he takes. He frequently addresses audiences, writes articles, gives press conferences, and conducts debates with his critics and those with whom he disagrees. In the mid-1980s, he attacked the Justice Department under President RONALD REAGAN as "dangerous for our constitutional health." A major area of battle for him in the early 1990s was the trend on university and college campuses toward "political correctness," which he views as stifling to free speech and detrimental to education. Denouncing the trend, Dershowitz said, "We are tolerating and teaching intolerance and hypocrisy."

Committed to working on behalf of Jewish rights, Dershowitz traveled to the Soviet Union in 1974 as part of the Soviet Jewry Defense Project. This U.S. group submitted appeals on behalf of fourteen Russian Jews and two non-Jews sentenced to prison terms for conspiracy after their emigration visas were refused. The effort helped to bring about the early release of several prisoners, who immigrated to Israel. Dershowitz also attempted to represent Russian dissident Anatoly Scharansky, but was blocked by Soviet authorities. A tireless foe of anti-Semitism whose office door is decorated with hate mail, Dershowitz argued in his best-selling 1991 book *Chutzpah* that U.S. Jews have too long accepted being second-class citizens. Named for the Yiddish expression for brashness, *Chutzpah* made an impassioned plea for greater pride: "We need not be apologetic or defensive about our power in America." The book won high praise from Nobel laureate Saul Bellow and others, although some Jewish intellectuals regarded it as overzealous.

Dershowitz has received many awards honoring his work on civil and human rights. These include a Guggenheim Fellowship in 1979, a commendation from the New York Criminal Bar Association in 1981, and the William O. Douglas First Amendment Award from the Anti-Defamation League of the B'nai Brith in 1983.

DESCENT Hereditary succession. Succession to the ownership of an ESTATE by INHERITANCE, or by any act of law, as distinguished from *purchase*. Title by descent is the TITLE by which one person, upon the death of another, acquires the real estate of the latter as an HEIR at law. The title by inheritance is in all cases called descent, although by statute law the title is sometimes made to ascend. The division among those legally entitled thereto of the REAL PROPERTY of INTESTATES.

DESCENT AND DISTRIBUTION The area of law that pertains to the transfer of REAL PROPERTY or PERSONAL PROPERTY of a DECEDENT who failed to leave a WILL or make a valid will and the rights and liabilities of HEIRS, NEXT OF KIN, and DISTRIBUTEES who are entitled to a share of the property.

Origin of the Law The passage of property from ancestors to children has been recognized and enforced since biblical times. As a general rule, the law, and not the deceased person, confers the right of SUCCESSION—the passing of TITLE to a decedent's property—and determines who shall take INTESTATE property. In the United States, such law is derived from the CIVIL LAW and English statutes of distributions, rather than from the COMMON LAW, which preferred the eldest male, under the doctrine of PRIMOGENITURE, and males over females. Statutes in every state prescribe the order in which persons succeed to a decedent's property if he or she dies intestate, which means without a lawfully executed will. These statutes provide for an orderly administration by identifying successors to a decedent's, also called an intestate's, ESTATE. They seek to implement the distribution that most intestates would have provided had they made wills, on the theory that most persons prefer that their property pass to their nearest relatives rather than to more remote ones. An order of preference among certain relatives of the deceased is established by the statute. If there are no relatives who can inherit the property, the estate ES-CHEATS, or reverts, to the state.

Persons Entitled The terms *heirs, next of kin,* and *distributees* usually refer to the persons who by OPERATION OF LAW—the application of the established rules of law—inherit or succeed to the property of a person intestate on his or her death. Statutes generally confer rights of inheritance only on blood relatives, adopted children, adoptive parents, and the surviving spouse. *Line of descent* is the order or series of persons who have descended one from the other or all from a common ancestor, placed in a line in the order of their birth showing the connection of all blood relatives. The direct line of descent involves persons who are directly descended from the same ancestor, such as father and son, or grandfather and grandson. Whether an adopted child can be regarded as in the direct line of descent depends upon the law in the particular JURISDICTION. The collateral line of descent involves persons who are descended from a common ancestor, such as brothers who share the same father or cousins who have the same grandfather. Title by descent differs from title by purchase because descent involves the operation of law, while purchase involves the act or agreement of the parties. Usually direct descendants have first preference in the order of succession, followed by ascendants, and finally, COLLATERAL HEIRS. Each generation is called a DEGREE in determining the CONSANGUINITY, or blood relationship, of one or more persons to an intestate. Where the next of kin of the intestate who are entitled to share in the estate are in equal degree to the deceased, such as children, they share equally in the estate. For example, consider a mother who has two daughters, her only living relations, and dies intestate, leaving an estate of $100 thousand. Since the two daughters occupy the same proximity of blood relationship to their mother, they share her estate equally, each inheriting $50 thousand.

ISSUE has been defined as all persons in the line of descent without regard to the degree of nearness or remoteness from the original source.

Law Governing If at the time of an intestate's death, his or her estate is located in the state of his or her domicile or permanent RESI-DENCE, the law of that state will govern its descent and distribution. Local laws that govern the area where the property is located generally determine the descent of real property, such as land, houses, and farms, regardless of the domicile of the deceased owner. The succession to and the disposition and distribution of personal or movable property, wherever situated, are governed by the law of the domicile of the owner or intestate at the time of death, unless a statute in the state where the property is located provides otherwise.

Since the privilege of receiving property by INHERITANCE is not a natural right but a creation of law, the legislature of a state has plenary power, or complete authority, over the descent and distribution of property within the borders of the state subject to restrictions found in constitutions and treaties. The disposition of the property of an intestate is governed by the statutes in force at the time of death.

Property Subject to Descent and Distribution As a general rule, property subject to descent and distribution includes all VESTED rights and interests owned by the deceased at the time of death. However, rights or interests that are personal to the deceased, and not of an inheritable nature, ordinarily are not subject to descent and distribution. Examples are a personal right to use land or a statutory right to CONTEST a will.

If a seller dies prior to the completion of the sale of real property, the LEGAL TITLE to land that the seller contracted to sell vests in the heirs at law on the owner's death, subject to their obligation to convey the land to the purchaser according to the CONTRACT. A few states authorize the distribution of property among different persons according to whether it is real or personal, but this is not the general rule.

Representation, per Stirpes, per Capita Representation is the principle of law by which the children, or their descendants, of an heir to an estate, who dies without leaving a will, have a collective interest in the intestate's share of the property. Taking by representation means taking PER STIRPES. For example, Robert, who only has two daughters, Ellen and Pam, dies intestate, leaving an estate of $200 thousand after the payment of debts and charges. Under a typical statute, Robert's daughters are his distributees, each receiving $100 thousand. However, Ellen predeceases her father and leaves two sons, David and George. Since Ellen is not alive to take her share, there would be a per stirpes division of Robert's estate, which means that Ellen's share of $100 thousand would be divided equally between David and George, and each would receive $50 thousand. Pam's $100 thousand-dollar share of her father's estate remains unaffected. Since they are brothers, the degree of blood relationship between David and George is equal, and therefore, they take PER CAPITA, or equal, parts of Ellen's share. However, they have taken per stirpes shares of Robert's estate. Assume that George also died before his grandfather and left two daughters, Ruth and Janet, but his brother David was still alive. David would take $50 thousand, but Ruth and Janet would equally share $50 thousand—$25 thousand apiece. Pam, who is still alive, would still be entitled to $100 thousand, her share of Robert's estate. The degrees of consanguinity among David and Ruth and Janet are unequal, since David is Robert's grandchild, while Ruth and Janet are his great-grandchildren. David and Ruth and Janet share Ellen's portion of Robert's estate per stirpes. David takes 50 percent, or $50 thousand, whereas Ruth and Janet each take 25 percent, or $25 thousand, because of the unequal degrees of blood relationship to Ellen. David is one generation removed from Ellen, while Ruth and Janet are two generations removed from her. The following chart depicts this example:

Descent and Distribution
Illustration of Representation in a Theoretical Family Line

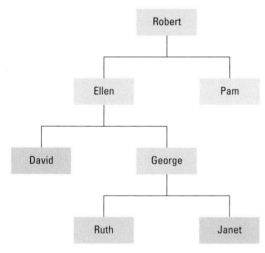

Kindred of the Half Blood The term *kindred of the half blood* refers to persons who share a half blood relationship with the intestate because they have only one parent in common with each other. As a general rule, kindred of the half blood inherit equally with kindred of the whole blood who have the same parents, unless expressly prohibited by statute. For example, A and B shared the same father with C and D but had a different mother. If A dies, leaving no surviving spouse, children, or parents, C and D share equally with B in A's estate, even though C and D were of the half blood in relation to A, since they had only one parent in common. C and D inherit as if they had both the same parents as A and B.

Necessary or Forced Heirs The law of forced heirship gave certain relatives, besides the spouse, an absolute legal right, of which they could not be deprived by will or gift, to inherit a certain portion of the decedent's estate. Ordinarily, a person has no right to prevent another from disposing of his or her property by gift or will to someone else. The law of forced heirship in effect in only Louisiana limits the disposition of a decedent's property if his or her parents or legitimate children or their descendants are alive at his or her death. Such persons are expressly declared by law to be forced heirs, and a decedent cannot deprive them of the portion of an estate reserved to them by law unless there is just cause to DISINHERIT them. Anyone else who received the property can be legally obligated to return it or to make up the portion of which the forced heirs have been deprived out of his or her own property.

Designated Heirs In some jurisdictions, statutes permit a person, the designator, to name another to stand in his or her place as an heir at law in the event of his or her death. Anyone can be a designated heir, even a stranger to the designator. The statute does not grant a designated heir any status until the designation becomes effective on the death of the designator. The designator can revoke the designation until the time of his or her death and then designate another. After the death of the designator, a designated heir has the status of an heir at law, and under the statute, the status of a legitimate child of the designator. For example, H designates his wife W as his heir at law. H and W are childless. H is the only child of F. F dies intestate after H's death. The applicable statute of descent and distribution gives all of F's property to his LINEAL descendants. W will inherit all of F's property since she was H's designated heir at law and is, for inheritance purposes, considered a child of H. She is, therefore, a lineal descendant of F. If the designated heir dies before the designator, his or her heirs generally will not have a right of inheritance in the designator's intestate estate.

Descendants Subject to the rights of the surviving spouse, children have superior inheritance rights compared to those of other blood relatives. In many jurisdictions, the same principle applies to adopted children of the intestate. Once the debts of the estate have been paid and the surviving spouse has taken his or her legal share, the remainder of the estate is apportioned in equal distributive shares, the portions specified by the law of descent and distribution, among the number of children of the decedent. The rights of the decedent's child or children are greater than not only those of the deceased's brothers and sisters, nephews and nieces, and other collateral kindred but also of the deceased's parents.

Posthumous Children A POSTHUMOUS CHILD is one born after the death of its father or mother (as, for example, by Caesarean section). Both at common law and under various state statutes, a posthumous child takes as an heir and a distributee as long as it is born alive after a period of fetal existence that indicates that it was conceived before the death of the intestate father, usually a period of nine months. Some statutes require that a child be born within ten months after the death of the intestate in order to be regarded as a posthumous child. The technique of artificial insemination, through which a woman can be impregnated with frozen sperm months or even years after the death of the father, poses problems for courts interpreting posthumous child statutes.

Children of Successive Marriages On the death of an intestate who had children by different MARRIAGES, all of his or her children take equal shares of the estate once the estate debts have been paid off and the surviving spouse has taken the legal portion. This method of distribution applies unless barred by statute, such as in cases where the property of an intestate was received from a deceased spouse of a former marriage. In that instance, only children of that particular marriage would inherit that property to the exclusion of children of other marriages. In a few states, a slightly different distribution is made of COMMUNITY PROPERTY of the first marriage—one half of that property belonging to the deceased spouse going to the children of that marriage in equal shares, and those children together with the children of the second marriage dividing equally the other half, subject to any rights of the surviving spouse.

Issues of Children Who Predecease Intestate The share that a child who dies before the intestate would have inherited if he or she had survived the intestate parent is inherited by his or her children or descendants by the right of representation in per stirpes shares. Grandchildren have better inheritance rights than brothers and sisters of the intestate and their children. However, they do not inherit unless their parent, the child of the intestate, is dead.

Illegitimate Children At common law, an illegitimate child was a FILIUS NULLIUS (Latin for "child of no one") and had no right to inherit. Only legitimate children and issue could inherit an estate upon the death of an intestate parent.

This is no longer the case as a result of statutes that vary from state to state. As a general rule, an illegitimate child is treated as the child of the mother and can inherit from her and her relatives and they from the child. In some jurisdictions, the illegitimate child is usually not regarded as a child of the father unless legitimated by the subsequent marriage of the parents or acknowledged by the father as his child, such as in AFFILIATION PROCEEDINGS. A legitimated child has the same inheritance rights as any other child of the parent. Many statutes permit a child to inherit from his or her father if the paternity is judicially established before the father's death. In the case of *Trimble v. Gordon*, 430 U.S. 762, 97 S. Ct. 1459, 52 L. Ed. 2d 31 (1977), the Supreme Court of the United States decided that it is unconstitutional for states to deprive an illegitimate child of the right to inherit from his or her father when he dies without leaving a will, especially in cases where paternity is already established in state court proceedings prior to the father's death.

Parents Some statutes permit one or both parents of the intestate to inherit, to some extent, the property of a child leaving no issue or descendants subject to the rights of a surviving spouse. Provisions differ as to whether one or both parents take, whether they take exclusively or share with brothers and sisters, and as to the extent of the share taken. Frequently, if one parent is dead, the surviving parent takes the entire estate, both real and personal, of a deceased child who dies without issue. Some statutes provide that a surviving parent shares with the brothers and sisters.

Stepchildren, Stepparents Ordinarily, a stepparent does not inherit from the estate of a deceased stepchild. Similarly, stepchildren do not inherit from their stepparent unless the terms of a statute grant them this right.

Brothers, Sisters, and Their Descendants

Brothers and Sisters If an intestate dies without a surviving spouse, issue, or parents, the decedent's brothers and sisters and the children of deceased brothers and sisters will inherit the estate. Brothers and sisters inherit when and only when there are no other surviving persons having priority by virtue of statute. Their inheritance rights are subordinate to children and grandchildren and the parents of the intestate in a number of jurisdictions.

Nephews and Nieces Nephews and nieces usually inherit only if their parent is deceased and would have inherited if he or she had survived the intestate.

Grandparents and Remote Ascendants Generally, where paternal and maternal grandparents are next of kin to the decedent, they share equally in the estate of an intestate. Some statutes provide that where the estate descended to the intestate from his or her father, it will go to a paternal grandparent to the exclusion of a maternal grandparent. State statutes vary as to whether the grandparents all inherit, or where there are surviving aunts and uncles, as to whether they are excluded by the grandparents. There is a similar division of authority as to whether great-grandparents share with surviving great-uncles and great-aunts.

Remote Collaterals A collateral heir is one who is not of the direct line of the deceased but comes from a collateral line, such as a brother, a sister, an uncle, an aunt, a nephew, a niece, or a cousin of the deceased. People are related collaterally when they have a common ancestor, such as a parent or grandparent. Where the property in question is within a statute directing the course of descent of property that came to the intestate by GIFT, DEVISE, or DESCENT from an ancestor, as long as they are the nearest heirs, the remote collateral heirs (for example, cousins) who share that common ancestor are entitled to inherit to the exclusion of collateral heirs who do not.

Operation and Effect of a Will Rights under intestacy laws are only taken away by a properly executed will disposing of the testator's entire property. These laws can, however, operate in case of partial intestacy where part of the decedent's property is not disposed of by will.

Surviving Spouse The right of a surviving spouse to share in the estate of a deceased spouse arises automatically from the marital status and not from any contract, CONVEYANCE, or other act of the spouse. Statutes conferring such rights on a surviving spouse make the spouse a statutory heir. Some statutes regulating the rights of inheritance of a surviving spouse treat property acquired by the decedent prior to the marriage differently than that acquired during the course of the marriage. Others relating to the descent of ancestral estates and property acquired by gifts do not, ordinarily, exclude a surviving spouse.

Right of Surviving Wife As a general rule, modern statutes confer rights of inheritance on a widow. At common law, the wife was entitled to DOWER, which was a fixed interest in all the land owned by her husband during the marriage. This interest in the lands of her husband was INCHOATE during his life. She had to survive her husband before she could take possession of her interest in the property. Most states have abolished common-law dower and have replaced it with statutes allowing the surviving widow to take a an ELECTIVE SHARE prescribed by statute, usually one-third or what would have gone to her by intestacy or the provision made in her spouse's will. The extent of and the method for computing the inheritance depends on the terms of the statute applicable to the facts in the particular case. Her rights attach only to property that her husband owned at the time of death. The right of a wife to share in the estate of her husband is qualified by his right to make a valid will. The widow, however, will be given a RIGHT OF ELECTION to choose between the elective share, which is usually her share under the laws of intestacy, or the provision in the will, whichever is larger.

Right of Surviving Husband At common law, a surviving husband had an estate by CURTESY in his wife's real property to which he was absolutely entitled upon her death. Curtesy has been abolished by many jurisdictions. Today, a husband's rights of inheritance are regulated by statute applicable to the facts in the particular case. As a general rule, a widower's rights of inheritance attach only to property that his wife owned and possessed at the time she died.

Rights in Case of Remarriage Unless a statute provides otherwise, a surviving spouse's rights of inheritance are not affected by a later marriage after the death of the decedent. The rights of a survivor of a second or subsequent marriage of the decedent are the same as though he or she were the survivor of the first marriage. In a number of states, the rights of a survivor of a second or subsequent marriage of the deceased or of a surviving spouse who subsequently remarries are, or have been, governed by statutes specifically regulating descent in cases of remarriage.

Waiver or Release of Right A spouse can WAIVE the right of inheritance to the estate of the other spouse by an antenuptial agreement, which is fairly entered into by both parties with knowledge of all the relevant facts, such as the extent of the spouse's wealth. This is frequently done by couples who remarry late in life, in order to protect the inheritance rights of their children by previous marriages. For example, an affluent couple executes an antenuptial agreement by which they both agree to surrender their inheritance rights in each other's estate. This insures the inheritance rights of their children from prior marriages in their respective estates, without having the estate

Pablo Picasso, with Françoise Gilet and their children Claude and Paloma, did not leave a will and so his estate was divided among his heirs according to the laws of descent and distribution.

reduced by the share given to the surviving spouse under the laws of intestacy. To be effective as a bar, the agreement must, in clear terms or by necessary implication, relinquish the surviving spouse's right of inheritance. It must affirmatively appear that neither spouse took advantage of the CONFIDENTIAL RELATION existing between the parties at the time of its execution. See also PREMARITAL AGREEMENT.

Unless there are statutory provisions to the contrary, a husband or wife can waive, release, or be estopped (prevented) from asserting rights of inheritance in the estate of the other by certain acts or conduct on his or her part during marriage. As a general rule, a spouse can waive his or her rights in the estate of the other by an express postnuptial agreement. Such an agreement is effective only if it manifests a clear and unmistakable intention to trade away such rights, and it must be supported by a valid and valuable CONSIDERATION, freely and fairly made, be just and equitable in its provisions, and free from FRAUD and DECEIT. In one case, the assent of a wife to cohabit with her husband only upon his execution of a release of any claim on her property did not constitute sufficient consideration for his agreement, since she was under a legal duty as his wife to live with him.

A separation agreement can provide for the mutual release of the rights of each spouse in the other's property, including an inchoate or potential right of inheritance that will not vest until the death of one spouse. The rights of inheritance in the property of the husband or wife are not to be denied the surviving spouse unless the purpose to exclude him or her is expressed or can be clearly inferred. A property settlement agreement conditioned upon a DIVORCE cannot bar a spouse's statutory share in the other's estate where the divorce was never finalized because of the death of the spouse. A mere agreement between husband and wife in contemplation of divorce, by which specific articles of property are to be held by each separately, is no bar to the rights of the surviving spouse, if no divorce has in fact been granted.

The surviving spouse, however, is not prevented from asserting his or her rights in the estate of the deceased spouse by an agreement entered into as a result of ignorance or MISTAKE as to his or her legal rights.

Forfeiture of Rights As a general rule, a surviving spouse's misconduct, whether criminal or otherwise, does not bar his or her rights to succeed to the deceased person's estate where the statute of descent and distribution confers certain rights on the surviving spouse and makes no exception on account of misconduct.

Abandonment, Adultery, and Nonsupport Unless there are statutes to the contrary, the fact that one spouse abandoned or deserted the other, or even the fact that he or she abandoned the other and lived in ADULTERY, does not bar that spouse's rights of inheritance in the other's estate. However, in a number of jurisdictions express statutory provisions do not permit a surviving wife to succeed to her husband's estate if she has abandoned him or left him to live in adultery. A surviving husband similarly loses his statutory right to inherit from his wife's estate where he abandoned or willfully and maliciously deserted her or neglected or refused to support her. In order to constitute a forfeiture of inheritance rights, such conduct must be deliberate and unjustified and continue for a period of time specified by statute. Mere separation is not necessarily ABANDONMENT or DESERTION if the parties have consented to the separation or there is reasonable and justifiable cause for the action. The fact of one spouse's subsequent meretricious conduct is not abandonment if a separation agreement does not provide for forfeiture of that spouse's right to share in the decedent's estate.

Murder of Spouse There is no uniform rule as to whether a person who MURDERS his or her spouse can succeed to the decedent's estate as the surviving spouse. Some jurisdictions refuse to recognize the murderer as a surviving spouse. In others, a statute that confers certain rights on the surviving spouse does not strip the spouse of that right because he or she caused the death of the intestate spouse by criminal conduct. Different states have enacted statutes that preclude any person who has caused or procured the death of another from inheriting the decedent's property under certain circumstances. An intentional killing will bar an inheritance, but a death that occurs as a result of NEGLIGENCE, accidental means, or INSANITY will not have this effect. For example, where conviction is essential to create a FORFEITURE under the statute, a surviving spouse who is not convicted but is committed to a state hospital for the legally insane is not excluded from the rights of inheritance. A conviction of MANSLAUGHTER might be sufficient to satisfy the statutory requirement of conviction, but it is insufficient if the statute requires actual conviction of murder.

Bigamous Marriage In some jurisdictions, a spouse who commits BIGAMY, marrying while still legally married to another, can be denied any rights of inheritance in the estate of his or her lawful spouse. This is true even if the bigamous marriage had been terminated long before the death of the lawful spouse. In a few jurisdictions, the fact that one who was legally married to the decedent contracted a bigamous marriage does not bar his or her rights of inheritance in the decedent's estate.

Divorce Generally, a person who has been divorced can claim no share in the estate of the former spouse. Under some statutes, a divorce A MENSA ET THORO (Latin for "from bed or board"), which is a legal separation, can abrogate any right of intestate inheritance in the spouse's estate, even though the decedent and spouse remained lawfully married until the death of the decedent.

Rights and Liabilities of Heirs No one is an heir to a living person. Before the death of the ancestor, an expectant heir or distributee has no vested interest but only a mere EXPECTANCY or possibility of inheritance. Such an individual cannot on the basis of his or her prospective right maintain an ACTION during the life of the ancestor to cancel a transfer of property made by the ancestor.

Advancements An ADVANCEMENT is similar to an absolute or irrevocable gift of money or real or personal property. It is made in the present by a parent to a child in anticipation of what the child's intestate share will be when the parent dies. An advancement differs from an ordinary gift in that it reduces only the child's distributive share of the parent's estate by the stated amount, while a gift diminishes the entire estate. The doctrine of advancements is based on the theory that a parent is presumed to intend that all his or her children have equal rights in not only in what may remain at the parent's death but in all property owned by the parent. Statutes of descent and distribution can provide for consideration of advancements made by a deceased during his or her lifetime to achieve equality in the distribution of the estate among the children.

An advancement can also be made by grandparents and, where statutes permit, by spouses and collateral relatives. A parent's gifts to a child cannot be deemed advancements while the donor is alive, since they are significant only in relation to a decedent's estate. Several statutes provide that no gift or grant of realty can be deemed to have been made as an advancement unless expressed in writing by the DONOR or acknowledged in writing by the DONEE. A transfer based on love and affection or a nominal consideration can constitute an advancement, while a transfer for a valuable consideration cannot, since as a gift, an advancement is made without consideration.

Release, Renunciation, or Acceptance of Rights An heir can relinquish his or her rights to an estate by an express WAIVER, RELEASE, or

ESTOPPEL. Generally, the release of an expected share, fairly and freely made to an ancestor in consideration of an advancement or for other valuable consideration, excludes the heir from sharing in the ancestor's estate at the time of death. It is necessary that the person executing the release be competent to contract at the time, that the release not be obtained by means of fraud or UNDUE INFLUENCE, and that the instrument or transaction in question be sufficient to constitute a release or renunciation of rights. In one case, a daughter gave her father a receipt acknowledging payment of money that she accepted as her "partial" share of all real estate left by him. The court held that she was not barred from sharing in the remainder of the real estate left upon her father's death, since the word *partial* indicated that the money received was merely an advancement.

At common law, a person could not renounce an intestate share, but modern statutes permit RENUNCIATION. A renunciation or a waiver sometimes requires the execution and delivery of a formal document. Renunciation is frequently employed by those who would incur an increased tax burden if the gift were to be accepted.

A simple ACCEPTANCE can be either EXPRESS or IMPLIED. A person can be barred from accepting his or her rights to an estate by a lapse of time, as specified by statute. Once a person accepts an intestate share, he or she cannot subsequently renounce the share under most statutes. A person who renounces the succession cannot revoke the renunciation after the other heirs have accepted the property that constitutes his or her share. However, that person can accept his or her share if the other heirs have not yet done so.

Gifts and Conveyances in Fraud of Heirs A person ordinarily has the right to dispose of his or her property as he or she sees fit, so that heirs and distributees cannot attack transfers or distributions made during the decedent's lifetime as being without consideration or in fraud of their rights. For example, a parent during his or her life can distribute property among his or her children any way he or she wants with or without reason, and those adversely affected have no STANDING to challenge the distribution.

One spouse can deprive the other of rights of inheritance given by statute through absolute transfers of property during his or her life. In some jurisdictions, however, transfers made by a spouse for the mere purpose of depriving the other of a distributive share are invalid. Whether a transfer made by a spouse was real or made merely to deprive the other spouse of the statutory share is determined by whether the person actually surrenders complete ownership and possession of the property. For example, a husband's transfer of all his property to a TRUSTEE is VOID and illusory as to the rights of his surviving wife if he reserves to himself the income of the property for life, the power to revoke and modify the TRUST, and a significant amount of control over the management of the trust. There is no intent to part with ownership of his property until his death. Such a trust is a device created to deprive the wife of her distributive share. Advancements or gifts to children, including children by a former marriage, which are reasonable in relation to the amount of property owned and are made in good faith without any intent to DEFRAUD a spouse, afford that spouse no grounds of complaint. GOOD FAITH is shown where the other spouse knew of the advancements. If a spouse gives all or most of his or her property to the children without the other spouse's knowledge, a REBUTTABLE PRESUMPTION of fraud arises that might be explained by the children.

Title of Heirs and Distributees Inheritance rights vest immediately on the death of an intestate, and the heirs are usually determined as of that time. The title to realty ordinarily vests in an intestate's heirs immediately upon his or her death, subject, under varying circumstances, to certain burdens, such as the rights of the surviving spouse or the debts of the intestate. The title obtained by the heirs on the death of their ancestor is subject to funeral expenses, the expenses, debts, or charges of the administration, and the charges for which the real property is liable, such as LIENS and ENCUMBRANCES attached to the land during the lifetime of the intestate.

At common law and under the statutes of most states, the title to personal property of a deceased person does not ordinarily vest in his or her heirs, next of kin, or distributees on his or her death. Their title and rights, therefore, must generally be obtained or enforced by virtue of ADMINISTRATION or distribution. Legal title to personal property is suspended between the time of the intestate's death and the granting of the LETTERS OF ADMINISTRATION. On distribution, the title of the distributees relates back to the date of the intestate's death. While the title to personal property does not immediately vest in the heirs, their interest in the estate does. The heirs have a vested equitable right, title, or estate in the personal property, subject to the rights of CREDITORS and to charges and expenses of the administration. The personal estate of an intestate goes ultimately to those who are next of kin at the time of the intestate's death as opposed to those who are next of kin at the time that the estate is to be distributed. If a person who is entitled as a distributee dies after the death of the intestate and before distribution, his or her share does not go to the other persons entitled as distributees, but instead passes to his or her own heirs.

Debts of Intestate Estate   Heirs and distributees generally receive property of their ancestor subject to his or her DEBTS. The obligation of an heir or distributee to pay an ancestor's debt is based upon his or her possession of the ancestor's property. All property of an intestate ordinarily can be applied to pay his or her debts, but, generally, the personal property must be exhausted first before realty can be used.

Rights and Remedies of Creditors, Heirs, and Distributees   The interest of an heir or distributee in the estate of an ancestor can be taken by his or her creditors for the payment of debts, depending upon the applicable law. Advancements received by an heir or distributee must be deducted first from his or her share before the rights of creditors of the heir or distributee can be enforced against the share.

DESCRIPTIVE WORD INDEX 📖 An alphabetically arranged aid used in legal research to locate cases that have discussed a particular topic. 📖

The descriptive word index contains key words and phrases that lead researchers to the information being sought. To prepare a BRIEF concerning a client who slipped and fell in a supermarket, an attorney might look in the descriptive word index under the heading "slip and fall" to find legal PRECEDENT for the case.

Descriptive word indexes are a part of the DECENNIAL DIGESTS.

DESEGREGATION   See SCHOOL DESEGREGATION.

DESERTION 📖 The act by which a person abandons and forsakes, without justification, a condition of public, social, or family life, renouncing its responsibilities and evading its duties. A willful abandonment of an employment or duty in violation of a legal or moral obligation.

Criminal desertion is a husband's or wife's abandonment or willful failure without just cause to provide for the care, protection, or support of a spouse who is in ill health or necessitous circumstances. 📖

Desertion, which is called ABANDONMENT in some statutes, is a DIVORCE ground in a majority of states. Most statutes mandate that the abandonment continue for a certain period of time before a divorce action may be commenced. The length of this period varies between one and five years; it is most commonly one year. The period of separation must be continuous and uninterrupted. In addition, proof that the departed spouse left without the consent of the other spouse is required in most states.

Ordinarily, proof of desertion is a clear-cut factual matter. Courts generally require EVIDENCE that the departure was voluntary and that the deserted husband or wife in no way provoked or agreed to the abandonment. CONSTRUCTIVE DESERTION occurs when one party makes life so intolerable for his or her spouse that the spouse has no real choice but to leave the marital home. For an individual to have legal justification for departing, it is often required that the spouse act so wrongfully as to constitute grounds for divorce. For example, a wife might leave her husband if she finds that he is guilty of ADULTERY.

In desertion cases, it is not necessary to prove the emotional state of the abandoning spouse, but only the intent to break off matrimonial ties with no animus revertendi, the intention to return.

Mere separation does not constitute desertion if a husband and wife agree that they cannot cohabit harmoniously. Sexual relations between the parties must be totally severed during the period of separation. If two people live apart from one another but meet on a regular basis for sex, this does not constitute desertion. State law dictates whether or not an infrequent meeting for sexual relations amounts to an interruption of the period required for desertion. Some statutes provide that an occasional act of sexual intercourse terminates the period only if the husband and wife are attempting reconciliation.

Unintentional abandonment is not desertion. For example, if a man is missing in action while serving in the armed services, his wife may not obtain a divorce on desertion grounds since her spouse did not intend to leave his family and flee the marital relationship. The COMMON LAW allows an individual to presume that a spouse is dead if the spouse is unexplainably absent for a seven-year period. If the spouse returns at any time, the marriage remains intact under common law.

Laws that embody the ENOCH ARDEN DOCTRINE grant a divorce if evidence establishes that an individual's spouse has vanished and cannot be found through diligent efforts. A particular period of time must elapse. Sometimes, if conditions evidencing death can be exhibited, a divorce may be granted prior to the expiration of the time specified by law.

In some JURISDICTIONS, the law is stringent regarding divorce grounds. In such instances, an Enoch Arden decree might be labeled a DISSOLUTION of the marriage rather than a divorce.

Upon the granting of an Enoch Arden decree, the marriage is terminated regardless of whether or not the absent spouse returns. Generally, the court provides that the plaintiff must show precisely what has been done to locate the missing person. Efforts to find the absent spouse might include inquiries made to friends or relatives to determine if they have had contact with the missing spouse, or checking public records for such documents as a marriage license, death certificate, tax returns, or application for SOCIAL SECURITY in locations where the individual is known to have resided.

Desertion is frequently coupled with NON-SUPPORT, which is a failure to provide monetary resources for those to whom such an obligation is due. Nonsupport is a CRIME in a majority of states but prosecutions are uncommon.

DESK AUDIT 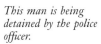 An evaluation of a particular CIVIL SERVICE position to determine whether its duties and responsibilities correspond to its job classification and salary grade.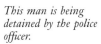

DESTROY 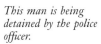 In general, to ruin completely; may include a taking. To ruin the structure, organic existence, or condition of a thing; to demolish; to injure or mutilate beyond possibility of use; to nullify.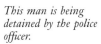

As used in policies of INSURANCE, in LEASES, and in maritime law, and under various statutes, this term is often applied to an act that renders the subject useless for its intended purpose, though it does not literally demolish or annihilate it.

In relation to WILLS, CONTRACTS, and other documents, the term *destroy* does not mean the annihilation of the instrument or its resolution into other forms of matter, but a destruction of its legal efficacy, which may be by cancellation, obliterating, tearing into fragments, and so on.

DETAINER 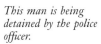 The act (or the juridical fact) of withholding from a lawfully entitled person the possession of land or goods, or the restraint of a person's personal liberty against his or her will; detention. The wrongful keeping of a person's goods is called an UNLAWFUL DETAINER although the original taking may have been lawful.

A request filed by a criminal justice agency with the institution in which a prisoner is incarcerated asking the institution either to hold the prisoner for the agency or to notify the agency when release of the prisoner is imminent.

DETECTIVES Individuals whose business it is to observe and provide information about alleged criminals or to discover matters of secrecy for the protection of the public.

Private detectives are those who are hired by individuals for private protection or to obtain information. A private detective is licensed but is not ordinarily considered to be a public officer. In cases where private detectives perform the duties and exercise the powers of public officers, the constitutional provisions governing such officers can be applied to them.

Public detectives are employed by the general community for the protection of society and, as members of public law enforcement agencies and police departments, are considered PEACE OFFICERS.

The incorporation of private detective companies or associations may be subject to statutory requirements. Detectives are regulated by legislation as well as the rules of the municipality where they are employed. In the absence of contrary statutory provision, private detectives do not have the same powers as public peace officers.

A private detective can be held liable for *rough shadowing*—the open and public surveillance of an individual done in an unreasonable manner that constitutes an invasion of PRIVACY.

DETENTION The act of keeping back, restraining, or withholding, either accidentally or by design, a person or thing.

This man is being detained by the police officer.

RENEE LYNN/PHOTO RESEARCHERS

Detention occurs whenever a police officer accosts an individual and restrains his or her freedom to walk away, or approaches and questions an individual, or stops an individual suspected of being personally involved in criminal activity. Such a detention is not a formal arrest. Physical restraint is not an essential element of detention.

Detention is also an element of the TORT of FALSE IMPRISONMENT.

DETERMINABLE 📖 Liable to come to an end upon the happening of a certain contingency. Susceptible of being determined, found out, definitely decided upon, or settled. 📖

DETERMINATE SENTENCE 📖 A SENTENCE to confinement for a fixed or minimum period that is specified by statute. 📖

Determinate sentencing encompasses SENTENCING guidelines, mandatory minimum sentences, and enhanced sentences for certain crimes. Sentencing guidelines allow judges to consider the individual circumstances of the case when determining a sentence, whereas mandatory minimum and enhanced sentence statutes leave little or no discretion to judges in setting the terms of a sentence.

Determinate sentencing statutes have existed at various times throughout the history of the United States. They became popular in the 1980s when public concern over crime increased dramatically and the public demanded stringent laws to address the crime problem. Operating under the belief that certainty of punishment deters crime, Congress and the states responded by passing laws that dictate specific sentences for certain crimes or for repeat offenders. These laws have been a source of considerable controversy.

Many of the determinate sentencing measures adopted during the 1980s and 1990s were a by-product of the war on drugs. They require strict, harsh, and nonnegotiable sentences for the possession of narcotics. These stringent laws have led to some unintended and inconsistent results. For example, repeat offenders who have information that is useful to the police sometimes receive lighter sentences than do nonviolent first-time offenders in return for their testimony.

Another type of determinate sentence popular in the 1990s is the "three-strikes-and-you're-out" law, which mandates a heavy sentence for anyone convicted of a third FELONY. For example, California Penal Code, section 667, requires a minimum sentence of twenty-five years to life for a third conviction for a serious felony, and doubles the usual sentence imposed for a crime when it is a second offense. The purpose of the law is to incapacitate repeat

offenders and deter others from committing crimes.

Supporters of three-strikes laws maintain that the severity of the third crime is not important. Rather, the pattern of violations indicates a life of lawlessness deserving severe penalty. Critics contend that the punishment is sometimes out of proportion to the crime. They point to the example of Jerry Williams, who was in January 1995 convicted of felony petty theft for stealing a slice of pizza from a group of children in Redondo Beach. Usually, petty THEFT is a MISDEMEANOR; prosecutors were allowed to charge Williams with *felony* petty theft because he had previous felony convictions. His 1995 conviction triggered the three-strikes law and cost him an automatic sentence of twenty-five years to life. A similar case involved Steve Gordon, who turned to petty crime to support his drug habit after he was fired from his job in 1985. Gordon was convicted of stealing $200 from the cash register at a fast-food restaurant and of snatching a purse, and then, in March 1994, of attempting to steal a wallet. This third conviction triggered the mandatory minimum sentence of twenty-five years to life.

Many judges oppose determinate sentencing when it prescribes mandatory minimum terms. A 1994 survey of federal judges conducted by the American Bar Association found that a majority strongly supported repealing most or all mandatory minimum sentences. In March 1994, during a hearing before the House Appropriations Committee on the Supreme Court's budget, Justice ANTHONY M. KENNEDY, of the Supreme Court, called mandatory sentence legislation imprudent, unwise, and potentially unjust. Most judges feel that sentencing guidelines, which prescribe sentences that may be altered in accord with aggravating or MITI-

As a judge establishes the length of this man's sentence he may be guided by determinate sentencing, or sentences determined by law.

GATING CIRCUMSTANCES, are preferable to mandatory minimums.

Some judges have attempted to circumvent determinate sentences, but their efforts have failed. In July 1994, Judge Lawrence Antolini, of the Sonoma County, California, Superior Court, challenged California's three-strikes law by sentencing Jeffrey Missamore, a three-time offender, to PROBATION and drug treatment instead of the twenty-five years to life mandated by the statute. The state petitioned the appellate court to overturn Antolini's probation order. The Superior Court of Sonoma County granted the writ, stating that it is not the role of the judiciary to question the appropriateness of the PUBLIC POLICY decisions embodied in the three-strikes law. The court held, "If people (including judges) feel those provisions . . . lead to unfair results, the law can be changed" (*People v. Superior Court*, 45 Cal. Rptr. 2d 392).

Another divisive issue in the determinate sentencing debate is the disparate effects of new laws concerning cocaine. The penalties for the possession of crack cocaine are substantially higher than those for powder cocaine. Crack is a less expensive form of cocaine that is smoked rather than inhaled. Because crack is less expensive than powder, it is used more widely by young people, poor people, and members of minority groups—who constitute a disproportionate number of those incarcerated on drug charges. Critics have attacked the enhanced and mandatory penalties for possession of crack as discriminatory.

Whether determinate sentences work to deter crime is an open question. Both sides of the debate summon statistical evidence to support their position. Opponents claim that from 1986 to 1991, when determinate sentencing was used extensively, violent crime continued to increase, even as the rate of incarceration rose dramatically. Supporters counter that the FBI's Uniform Crime Index shows a four percent drop in serious crime between 1989 and 1993, suggesting that perhaps stringent sentencing is beginning to affect the crime rate. Supporters also cite statistics indicating that the number of federal drug convictions doubled from 1985 to 1993; opponents counter that most of those convicted were first-time offenders or low-level drug dealers, not the powerful drug kingpins the laws were designed to ensnare.

DETERMINATION 📖 The final resolution or conclusion of a controversy. 📖

In legal use, determination usually implies the conclusion of a dispute or lawsuit by the rendering of a FINAL DECISION. After consideration of the facts, a determination is generally set forth by a court of justice or other type of formal decision maker, such as the head of an administrative agency.

Determination has been used synonymously with ADJUDICATION, AWARD, DECREE, and JUDGMENT. A RULING is a judicial determination concerning matters, such as the admissibility of evidence or a judicial or an administrative interpretation of a statute or regulation.

DETINUE 📖 One of the old common-law FORMS OF ACTION used to recover PERSONAL PROPERTY from a person who refuses to give it up. Also used to collect money DAMAGES for losses caused by the wrongful DETENTION. 📖

Dating back to the twelfth century, detinue is one of the oldest forms of action in COMMON LAW, along with the action of DEBT—a lawsuit for a specific sum of money owed. In detinue a favorable judgment awarded the plaintiff the actual CHATTELS—items of personal property—or their value in money. For example, an action of detinue was available against someone who wrongfully refused to return goods that were held subject to a BAILMENT, such as a deposit for safekeeping or repair. It could be used against an EXECUTOR who refused to turn over a deed for the deceased person's property to the proper heir. Since the plaintiff did not have to show wrongful detention to prove his or her case, the action was appropriate for recovering goods from a thief as well as from someone who first acquired the property lawfully.

There were several drawbacks in an action of detinue. The defendant could prove his or her case by WAGER OF LAW, for example. That meant that the defendant could swear in open court and bring along eleven neighbors who would take an oath that they, in good conscience, believed the defendant was telling the truth. If the plaintiff won the case, the defendant was required only to give up the items in question. This was small comfort when the goods were damaged or spoiled, since there was no remedy at detinue for harm done to the property while it was in the hands of the defendant. By the fifteenth century, plaintiffs were able to use the more satisfactory form of action on the case, and in the sixteenth century a special kind of action on the case, called TROVER, was introduced. After that, these forms were used much more often than detinue to recover personal property.

Today the action of detinue has been almost entirely superseded by statutes that streamline CIVIL PROCEDURE, but the principles underlying the ancient common law form of action are still the foundation of modern actions for the recovery of personal property.

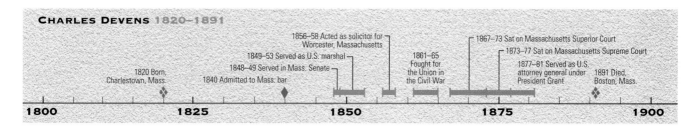

CHARLES DEVENS 1820–1891

1856–58 Acted as solicitor for Worcester, Massachusetts

1849–53 Served as U.S. marshal

1848–49 Served in Mass. Senate

1820 Born, Charlestown, Mass.

1840 Admitted to Mass. bar

1861–65 Fought for the Union in the Civil War

1867–73 Sat on Massachusetts Superior Court

1873–77 Sat on Massachusetts Supreme Court

1877–81 Served as U.S. attorney general under President Grant

1891 Died, Boston, Mass.

1800   1825   1850   1875   1900

DETRIMENT ▯ Any loss or harm to a person or property; relinquishment of a legal right, benefit, or something of value. ▯

Detriment is most frequently applied to CONTRACT formation, since it is an essential element of CONSIDERATION, which is a prerequisite of a legally enforceable contract. To incur detriment means to cement a PROMISE by either refraining from doing something that one has a legal right to do or by doing something that one is not under any legal OBLIGATION to do.

DEVENS, CHARLES Charles Devens was born April 14, 1820, in Charlestown, Massachusetts. He graduated from Harvard University in 1838 and received a doctor of laws degree in 1877. He was admitted to the Massachusetts bar in 1840 and began a career that encompassed military and legal achievements.

He participated in the Massachusetts Senate during 1848 and 1849, followed by service as U. S. marshal from 1849 to 1853. He acted as solicitor for the city of Worcester, Massachusetts, from 1856 to 1858 and then left government service to pursue a military career in 1861.

The Civil War provided Devens with many opportunities to display his military expertise. He fought in the battles of Fredericksburg, Chancellorville, Cold Harbor, and others, earning the rank of major general.

In 1867, he began his judicial career and served as judge of the Massachusetts Superior Court. In 1873, he sat on the bench of the Massachusetts Supreme Court.

He began service to the federal government in 1877 as attorney general, a post he held until 1881.

An army post, Camp Devens, in Ayer, Mas-

Charles Devens

Thomas E. Dewey

sachusetts, was named for Charles Devens in recognition of his military accomplishments.

Devens died January 7, 1891, in Boston.

DEVIANCE ▯ Conspicuous dissimilarity with, or variation from, customarily acceptable behavior. ▯

Deviance implies a lack of compliance to societal norms, such as by engaging in activities that are frowned upon by society and frequently have legal sanctions as well, for example, the illegal use of drugs.

DEVISE ▯ A TESTAMENTARY disposition of land or realty; a gift of REAL PROPERTY by the last WILL and testament of the donor. When used as a noun, it means a testamentary disposition of real or PERSONAL PROPERTY, and when used as a verb, it means to dispose of real or personal property by will.

To contrive; plan; scheme; invent; prepare. ▯

DEWEY DECIMAL SYSTEM ▯ A numerical classification system of books employed by libraries. ▯

The Dewey Decimal System, created by Melvil Dewey, is a reference system that classifies all subjects by number. The numbers in a particular grouping all refer to a designated general topic. For example, the numbers in the 340s concern topics of law. Each new number after the decimal point further subdivides the previous number and the subject it covers.

DEWEY, THOMAS E. Thomas E. Dewey was born March 24, 1902, in Owasso, Michigan. He received a bachelor of arts degree in 1923 from the University of Michigan and a bachelor of laws degree from Columbia University in 1925.

After his admission to the bar in 1925, Dewey established his legal practice before be-

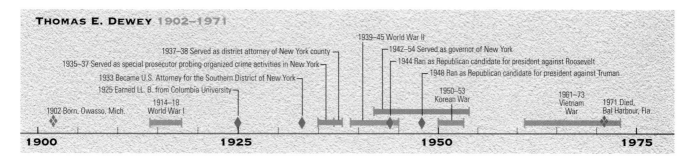

THOMAS E. DEWEY 1902–1971

1939–45 World War II

1937–38 Served as district attorney of New York county

1942–54 Served as governor of New York

1935–37 Served as special prosecutor probing organized crime activities in New York

1944 Ran as Republican candidate for president against Roosevelt

1933 Became U.S. Attorney for the Southern District of New York

1948 Ran as Republican candidate for president against Truman

1925 Earned LL. B. from Columbia University

1950–53 Korean War

1961–73 Vietnam War

1902 Born, Owasso, Mich.

1914–18 World War I

1971 Died, Bal Harbour, Fla.

1900   1925   1950   1975

coming U. S. Attorney for the Southern District of New York in 1933. During the next three years, Dewey achieved prominence for his campaign against crime in New York City, serving as special prosecutor to probe the activities of organized crime from 1935 to 1937 and as district attorney of New York county from 1937 to 1938.

Dewey's public service to the state of New York culminated in his election as governor in 1942; he remained in this post until 1954.

Twice during his years as governor, Dewey unsuccessfully sought election to the U. S. presidency. He was the Republican candidate in 1944 but was defeated by FRANKLIN DELANO ROOSEVELT; he ran again in 1948 but lost by a small percentage of votes to HARRY S. TRUMAN.

As an author, Dewey is famous for several publications, including *Journey to the Far Pacific* (1952), which is a chronicle of his trip to the Far East.

Dewey died March 16, 1971, in Bal Harbour, Florida.

DICKINSON, JOHN   John Dickinson was born November 8, 1732, in Talbot County, Maryland. He was educated at the College of New Jersey (today known as Princeton University), where he earned a doctor of laws degree in 1768. He also pursued legal studies at the Middle Temple, Inn of the Court, England.

After his admission to the Philadelphia bar in 1757, Dickinson established a prestigious legal practice in that city and subsequently entered politics on the state level.

In 1760, Dickinson served in the Assembly of Lower Counties, Delaware, and performed the duties of speaker. Two years later, he participated in the Pennsylvania legislature, representing Philadelphia until 1764, and again, from 1770 to 1776. In 1765, Dickinson wrote a pamphlet titled *The Late Regulations Respecting the British Colonies on the Continent of America Considered*, which protested the passage of two unjust acts of taxation, the STAMP ACT and the Sugar Act, by England. In the same year, he also served at the Stamp Act Congress and drafted a

"IT IS INSEPARABLY ESSENTIAL TO THE FREEDOM OF A PEOPLE THAT NO TAXES BE IMPOSED ON THEM BUT WITH THEIR OWN CONSENT, GIVEN PERSONALLY OR BY THEIR REPRESENTATIVES."

BIOGRAPHY

John Dickinson

series of requests to King George III. Although he opposed many of the policies enforced by England, Dickinson favored conciliatory action over violence.

England passed the unpopular TOWNSHEND ACTS in 1767, which levied TARIFFS on colonial imports of certain items. Dickinson composed another publication in protest, known as "Letters from a Farmer in Pennsylvania"; these letters advocated nonimportation of the taxed materials, rather than a violent reaction to the passage of the act.

Dickinson continued to serve in pre-Revolutionary War activities, including the Committee of Correspondence in 1774 and the Continental Congress from 1774 to 1776 and from 1779 to 1781. He still hoped for reconciliation with England and, as a result of this sentiment, opposed the DECLARATION OF INDEPENDENCE. However, with the outbreak of the Revolutionary War, Dickinson served a tour of military duty.

From 1781 to 1785, Dickinson was a participant in state government activities, acting as administrator of the Supreme Council of Delaware in 1781 and performing the same duty for the Supreme Council of Pennsylvania from 1782 to 1785.

Dickinson was instrumental in the formation of the ARTICLES OF CONFEDERATION, adopted in 1781, by serving as presiding officer of the committee appointed to compose the document and creating the outline that became the foundation of the articles. In 1787, he represented Delaware at the Constitutional Convention and advocated the ratification of the CONSTITUTION through a series of letters published under the name of Fabius.

In addition to his achievements as a statesman, Dickinson also contributed to the field of education as a founder of Dickinson College, located at Carlisle, Pennsylvania.

Dickinson died February 14, 1808, in Wilmington, Delaware.

DICTA   Opinions of a judge that do not embody the resolution or determination of the

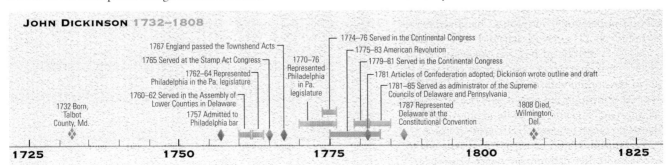

JOHN DICKINSON 1732–1808

1774–76 Served in the Continental Congress
1767 England passed the Townshend Acts
1775–83 American Revolution
1765 Served at the Stamp Act Congress
1770–76 Represented Philadelphia in Pa. legislature
1779–81 Served in the Continental Congress
1762–64 Represented Philadelphia in the Pa. legislature
1781 Articles of Confederation adopted; Dickinson wrote outline and draft
1760–62 Served in the Assembly of Lower Counties in Delaware
1781–85 Served as administrator of the Supreme Councils of Delaware and Pennsylvania
1732 Born, Talbot County, Md.
1757 Admitted to Philadelphia bar
1787 Represented Delaware at the Constitutional Convention
1808 Died, Wilmington, Del.

1725   1750   1775   1800   1825

specific case before the court. Expressions in a court's OPINION that go beyond the facts before the court and therefore are individual views of the author of the opinion and not binding in subsequent cases as legal PRECEDENT. The plural of *dictum*. 📖

DICTUM 📖 [*Latin, A remark.*] A statement, comment, or opinion. An abbreviated version of OBITER DICTUM, "a remark by the way," which is a collateral opinion stated by a judge in the decision of a case concerning legal matters that do not directly involve the facts or affect the outcome of the case, such as a legal principle that is introduced by way of illustration, argument, analogy, or suggestion. 📖

Dictum has no BINDING AUTHORITY and, therefore, cannot be cited as PRECEDENT in subsequent lawsuits. Dictum is the singular form of *dicta*.

DIGEST 📖 A collection or compilation that embodies the chief matter of numerous books, articles, court decisions, and so on, disposed under proper heads or titles, and usually by an alphabetical arrangement, for facility in reference.

An INDEX to reported cases, providing brief statements of court holdings or facts of cases, which is arranged by subject and subdivided by JURISDICTION and courts. 📖

As a legal term, *digest* is to be distinguished from *abridgment*. The latter is a summary of the contents of a single work, in which, as a rule, the original order or sequence of parts is preserved, and in which the principal labor of the compiler is in the matter of consolidation. A digest is wider in its scope, is made up of quotations or paraphrased passages, and has its own system of classification and arrangement. An *index* merely points out the places where particular matters may be found, without purporting to give such matters *in extenso*. A TREATISE or *commentary* is not a compilation, but an original composition, though it may include quotations and excerpts.

DILATORY 📖 Tending to cause a delay in judicial proceedings. 📖

Dilatory tactics are methods by which the rules of procedure are used by a party to a lawsuit in an abusive manner to delay the progress of the proceedings. For example, when numerous MOTIONS brought before a court for postponement are baseless, time is wasted because the court must stop the course of ongoing proceedings to examine whether there is any merit to the motions. The party in whose interests the motion is brought uses this tactic to gain time to enhance his or her position, or to postpone an action by a court as long as possible to minimize the impact of a decree rendered against him or her. A party found to engage in dilatory tactics may be held in CONTEMPT of court.

DILATORY PLEA 📖 In COMMON-LAW-PLEADING, any of several types of defenses that could be asserted against a plaintiff's CAUSE OF ACTION, delaying the time when the court would begin consideration of the actual facts in the case. 📖

Under COMMON LAW, a plaintiff began the lawsuit and drew up a paper reciting the events that supported his or her claim to relief. The defendant was entitled to enter a PLEA responding to the plaintiff's ALLEGATIONS. If the defendant's plea required the court to decide some threshold question not related to the merits of the plaintiff's case, it was called a dilatory plea. For example, a plea to the JURISDICTION challenged the authority of the court to hear the kind of matters described by the plaintiff. A *plea in suspension* presented facts to justify a temporary halt to the proceedings, such as when a guardian was needed for one of the parties. A plea in ABATEMENT objected to the place, manner, or time of the lawsuit; it did not defeat the plaintiff's claim entirely but, if successful, forced the plaintiff to renew the suit in another form, place, or time.

Federal courts and states that follow the pattern of pleading permitted by the rules of federal CIVIL PROCEDURE no longer specifically allow dilatory pleas. The same assertions can be made by MOTION, but the motions may sometimes be called dilatory pleas by persons complaining that they unnecessarily delay proceedings.

DILIGENCE 📖 Vigilant activity; attentiveness; or care, of which there are infinite shades, from the slightest momentary thought to the most vigilant anxiety. Attentive and persistent in doing a thing; steadily applied; active; sedulous; laborious; unremitting; untiring. The attention and care required of a person in a given situation; the opposite of NEGLIGENCE. 📖

There may be a high DEGREE of diligence, a common degree of diligence, and a slight degree of diligence, with their corresponding degrees of negligence. Common or ordinary diligence is that degree of diligence which persons generally exercise in respect to their own concerns; high or great diligence is, of course, extraordinary diligence, or that which very prudent persons take of their own concerns; and low or slight diligence is that which persons of less than common prudence, or indeed of any prudence at all, take of their own concerns.

JOE SOHM/CHROMOSOHM/PHOTO RESEARCHERS

Safe driving in rush hour traffic requires the diligence of each driver.

Special diligence is the skill that a good businessperson exercises in his or her specialty. It is more highly regarded than ordinary diligence or the diligence of a nonspecialist in a given set of circumstances.

DIMINISHED CAPACITY 📖 This doctrine recognizes that although, at the time the offense was committed, an accused was not suffering from a mental disease or defect sufficient to exonerate him or her from all criminal responsibility, the accused's mental capacity may have been diminished by intoxication, trauma, or mental disease so that he or she did not possess the specific mental state or INTENT essential to the particular offense charged. 📖

DIMINUTION 📖 Taking away; reduction; lessening; incompleteness. 📖

The term *diminution* is used in law to signify that a record submitted by an inferior court to a superior court for review is not complete or not fully certified.

Diminution in market value is a rule of DAMAGES, within which the proper measure of damages for permanent injury to REAL PROPERTY is the reduction of MARKET VALUE for any use to which the property might be appropriated. It is a rule providing for the before-and-after value of stolen or damaged property.

DIPLOMATIC AGENTS 📖 Government representatives sent by one country to live and work in another to serve as intermediaries for the two countries. 📖

The concept of diplomatic agents residing in another country has been around since the fifteenth century, but the role of diplomats has evolved with the passage of time. Originally, agents were asked to help work out specific negotiations between countries; now, agents cultivate a relationship between their native country and the host country, serve as an intermediary by relaying each country's positions to the other, try to get the best possible treatment for their home country, and more.

The Vienna Convention on Diplomatic Relations (Apr. 18, 1961, 23 U.S.T. 3227, 500 U.N.T.S. 95) contains the most widely accepted description of the INTERNATIONAL LAW on diplomacy. The convention splits the functions of diplomatic agents into six categories: representing the sending state; protecting the sending state's nationals within the receiving state; negotiating with the receiving state; notifying the sending state of conditions and developments within the receiving state; promoting friendly relations between the two states; and developing economic, cultural, and scientific relations between the two states.

Historically, the nomination of U.S. ambassadors to foreign countries is based on the recommendation of the president and is subject to approval by the Senate. It has also been a U.S. tradition that nominations are often given to acquaintances of the president or to those who have contributed heavily to political campaigns. The United States is the only major country that assigns ambassadorships as political rewards.

Despite legislation passed by Congress in 1980 stating that "contributions to political campaigns should not be a factor in the appointment" of an ambassador (22 U.S.C.A. § 3944), this practice of political spoils continues. Former president GEORGE BUSH nominated six Republicans as U.S. ambassadors in 1989: each was a member of Bush's Team 100, contributors who had given more than $100,000 to the GOP.

The practice did not change when Democrat BILL CLINTON won the president's seat in 1992. According to an Associated Press review, by the end of Clinton's first year in office, he had nominated five $100,000-plus donors as foreign ambassadors. However, Clinton was able to deflect some of the criticism following these appointments by shifting the focus to the qualifications of his appointees. He stressed that his recommendations extended beyond campaign participation and required some real expertise that suited the demands of the appointment. For example, Clinton's pick for ambassador to

APWIDE WORLD PHOTOS

Walter Mondale served as ambassador to Japan from 1993 to 1996.

Japan, Walter F. Mondale, was regarded by the Japanese as a well qualified diplomat who many believed would help steady the U.S.-Japan partnership. And investment banker Nicholas A. Rey was chosen as ambassador to Warsaw on the basis that he spoke fluent Polish and had previously led an effort to stimulate private investments in Poland.

Another topic involving diplomatic agents that has come under scrutiny in the 1990s involves a shift toward commercialism. Promoting exports and assisting U.S. businesses with their foreign dealings has become a top priority for the U.S. embassies. Since Deputy Secretary of State Lawrence Eagleburger took office in 1989, all new foreign service officers and ambassadors have studied commerce as part of their basic training. Eagleburger has emphasized a necessity for diplomats to understand the needs of U.S. businesses and how to help them make the right connections abroad. This transition toward trade diplomacy is not new: diplomats have always tried, in one way or another, to increase U.S. exports. The trend now is for diplomats to help specific companies get specific bids overseas and to help find buyers for U.S. exports.

U.S. ambassadors direct, supervise, and coordinate a body of representatives in the country to which they have been assigned. This body of representatives from the sending government is referred to as a diplomatic mission. Under the Vienna Convention, both the property and the employees of a diplomatic mission are considered inviolable. However, the convention leaves to the receiving state the decision of how

to protect a resident diplomatic agent from assault.

In the United States, specific legislation outlines the penalties that will be imposed if someone attacks a diplomatic officer residing in the United States. The penalties apply to anyone who "assaults, strikes, wounds, imprisons, or offers violence to a foreign official, official guest, or internationally protected person, his official premises, private accommodation, or means of transport or attempts to commit any of the foregoing" (Act of Oct. 24, 1972, P.L. No. 92-539, 18 U.S.C.A. § 112(a)). This statute criminalizes acts or attempts to "intimidate, coerce, threaten or harass a foreign official" (18 U.S.C.A. § 112). This section applies to any conduct outside the District of Columbia, which has somewhat different laws that penalize certain conduct directed at foreign embassies (see *Boos v. Barry*, 485 U.S. 312, 108 S. Ct. 1157, 99 L. Ed. 2d 333 (1988) [striking down part of the D.C. law as violating freedom of speech]).

The United States is among a number of other countries that have also signed two separate conventions intended to protect visiting dignitaries. They are the Organization of American States Convention to Prevent and Punish the Acts of Terrorism Taking the Form of Crimes against Persons and Related Extortion That Are of International Significance, and the United Nations Convention on the Prevention and Punishment of Crimes against Internationally Protected Persons, Including Diplo-

Diplomatic Agents

Civilian Employment in the U.S. State Department, May 1995

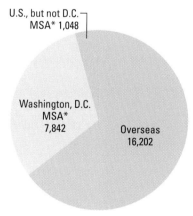

Total number of employees: 25,092

U.S., but not D.C.
MSA* 1,048

Washington, D.C.
MSA*
7,842

Overseas
16,202

*MSA stands for Metropolitan Statistical Area.

Source: Workforce Analysis and Statistics Division, U.S. Office of Personnel Management.

matic Agents. Both conventions require host countries to take measures to prevent terroristic acts, and to make an effort to arrest and punish the offenders should an attack occur.

The Vienna Convention grants special privileges and immunities to diplomats, on the grounds that these are necessary to allow diplomats to perform their duties without outside interference or constraint. Some examples of PRIVILEGES are exemption from customs on goods that diplomats import for their own or their family's use, from property taxes on mission property, from income taxes for pay received for their diplomatic duties, and from military obligations. Diplomatic agents and their families are also immune from civil or criminal prosecution. If a diplomat is accused of committing a crime, specific steps are taken by the State Department, including notifying the diplomat's home country and asking to have the diplomat's IMMUNITY waived so that the case can advance to the U.S. judicial system. Diplomatic agents are also exempt from being a witness in a civil or criminal proceeding, unless their country waives their immunity if the agents feel their testimony is essential to the case. For example, in 1881 Venezuela asked its minister to the United States to testify in the trial of Charles J. Guiteau for the assassination of U.S. president JAMES GARFIELD.

See also AMBASSADORS AND CONSULS; DIPLOMATIC IMMUNITY.

DIPLOMATIC IMMUNITY 📖 A principle of INTERNATIONAL LAW that provides foreign diplomats with protection from legal action in the country in which they work. 📖

Established in large part by the Vienna conventions, diplomatic immunity is granted to individuals depending on their rank and the amount of IMMUNITY they need to carry out their duties without legal harassment. Diplomatic immunity allows foreign representatives to work in host countries without fully understanding all the customs of that country. However, diplomats are still expected to respect and follow the laws and regulations of their host countries; immunity is not a license to commit crimes.

In the United States, several levels of immunity are granted: the higher the rank, the greater the immunity. DIPLOMATIC AGENTS and their immediate families have the most protection, and are immune from criminal prosecution and civil lawsuits. The lowest level of protection is granted to embassy and consular employees, who receive immunity only for acts that are part of their official duties—for example, they cannot be forced to testify in court about the actions of the people they work with. The Diplomatic Relations Act of 1978 [22 U.S.C.A. § 254a et seq.] follows the principles introduced by the Vienna conventions. The United States has had a tendency to be generous when granting diplomatic immunity to visiting diplomats, because a large number of U.S. diplomats work in host countries less protective of individual rights. If the United States were to punish a visiting diplomat without sufficient grounds, U.S. representatives in other countries could receive harsher treatment.

In the United States, if a person with immunity is alleged to have committed a crime or faces a civil lawsuit, the Department of STATE alerts the government that the diplomat works for. The Department of State also asks the home country to WAIVE immunity of the alleged offender so that the complaint can be moved to the courts. If immunity is not waived, prosecution cannot be undertaken. However, the Department of State still has the discretion to ask the diplomat to withdraw from her or his duties in the United States. In addition, the diplomat's visas are often canceled, and the diplomat and her or his family are barred from returning to the United States. Crimes committed by members of a diplomat's family can also result in dismissal.

Abuse of diplomatic immunity was made more visible by media coverage in the early 1990s. The abuse spans a variety of activities, ranging from parking violations to more serious criminal behavior such as domestic abuse and rape. In February 1995 Mayor Rudolph Giuliani of New York City forgave $800,000 in parking tickets accumulated by foreign diplomats. Although no clear reason was given, the action, which was perhaps meant as a show of goodwill, sent a message to visiting diplomats that the U.S. government may be willing to allow diplomats greater leniency than its own private citizens. This example serves as the best example of how some diplomatic debts have either been erased or not collected. However, outstanding debts may not be the worst illustration of how diplomatic immunity can be abused.

Diplomats and their families have also been known to use diplomatic immunity to avoid prosecution for criminal behavior. This is illustrated in a 1983 case where the New York City Police Department suspected a diplomat's son of fifteen different RAPES. The son was allowed to leave the United States without ever being taken to court, because he claimed diplomatic immunity. If diplomatic immunity is used as a shield, the police cannot prosecute, no matter how serious the crime may be.

U.S. citizens and businesses are often at a disadvantage when filing civil claims against a diplomat, especially in cases of unpaid DEBTS, such as rent, ALIMONY, and CHILD SUPPORT. In the summer of 1994 U.S. diplomat Victor Marrero reportedly complained to the United Nations secretariat that foreign diplomats' debts in the United States were $5.3 million. The *New Yorker* later reported that a well-informed source had said the figure had risen "closer to $7 million."

The bulk of diplomatic debt lies in the rental of office space and living quarters. Individual debts can range from a few thousand dollars to $1 million in back rent. A group of diplomats and the office space in which they work are referred to as a *mission*. CREDITORS cannot sue missions individually to collect money they owe. Landlords and creditors have found that the only thing they can do is contact a city agency to see if they can try to get some money back. They cannot enter the offices or apartments of diplomats to evict them because the Foreign Sovereign Immunities Act says that "the property in the United States of a foreign state shall be immune from attachment, arrest and execution" (28 U.S.C.A. § 1609). This has led creditors who are owed money by diplomats to become more cautious about their renters and to change their rental or payment policies. For example, Milford Management, a New York–based company that rents deluxe apartments, is owed more than $20,000 in back rent from diplomats from five different countries. Milford and other creditors have created their own "insurance" policies by refusing to rent to foreign missions unless there is a way of guaranteeing payment, such as collecting money in advance.

The issue of abusing diplomatic immunity in family relations, especially alimony and child support, has become enough of a widespread problem that it prompted discussion at the 1995 United Nations Fourth World Conference on Women, in Beijing. Historically, the United Nations has not gotten involved with family disputes and has refused to garnish the wages of diplomats who owe money for child support, citing SOVEREIGN IMMUNITY. However, this may change. In September 1995, the incumbent head of legal affairs for the United Nations acknowledged there is a moral and legal obligation to take at least a partial responsibility in family disputes. Deadbeat "diplodads" are increasing in numbers in the United Nations:

several men who have left their wives and children are still claiming U.N. dependency, travel, and education allowances for their families even though they are no longer supporting those families. One U.S. woman, Barbara Elzohairy, and her daughter were threatened with eviction from their New Jersey apartment because they did not pay their rent. Their reason? Elzohairy's husband, a U.N. representative from Egypt, refused to pay her $16,000 in court-ordered support. The United Nations tells diplomats they must meet their moral obligations, but there are no consequences if they do not.

DIVORCE is difficult for the spouses of foreign diplomats, as illustrated in the case of *Fernandez v. Fernandez*, 545 A.2d 1036. This case involved a U.S. citizen, Barbara Fernandez, who wanted a divorce from her husband, Antonio Diende Fernandez, a U.N. representative from the Republic of Mozambique. Along with the divorce, Fernandez wanted a monetary settlement and property rights to the home the couple owned in a New York suburb. Her husband asked that the courts dismiss her claim on the grounds that he had diplomatic immunity. Under the trial court's interpretation of the Vienna Convention, a U.S. citizen who marries a foreign diplomat is married until either the diplomat dies or the diplomat's country grants permission for divorce proceedings. The Republic of Mozambique gave the court permission to grant the divorce but would not allow the court to make a decision on Fernandez's property or monetary claims. The case went on to the Connecticut Supreme Court, which dissolved the marriage and allowed Fernandez to claim property rights under article 31 of the Vienna Convention.

Article 31 gives diplomats immunity from all civil cases except for those that involve "private immovable property." The Connecticut Supreme Court interpreted that exception to apply to Fernandez's claim on the home, which was valued at more than $8 million. Article 30 of the Vienna Convention does not allow the "private residence of a diplomatic agent" to be included in a civil suit. However, the Connecticut Supreme Court declined to consider this article as a form of defense for Fernandez's husband. The Vienna Convention specifically does not allow exceptions for spouses to seek monetary compensation in divorce proceedings, so Fernandez was not granted any money by the Connecticut court.

The *Fernandez* decision did not settle all the issues revolving around dissolution of diplomats' marriages, such as whether U.S. courts can grant a divorce without the permission of the diplomat's country. Critics of *Fernandez* say it may cause foreign countries to think twice before granting permission to dissolve marriages, because property claims can then also be brought against the diplomats.

See also AMBASSADORS AND COUNSULS.

DIRECT 📖 As a verb, to point to; guide; order; command; instruct. To advise; suggest; request. As an adjective, immediate; proximate; by the shortest course; without circuity; operating by an immediate connection or relation, instead of operating through an intermediary; the opposite of *indirect*. In the usual or regular course or order, as distinguished from that which diverts, interrupts, or opposes. The opposite of cross, contrary, collateral, or remote. Without any intervening medium, agency, or influence; unconditional. 📖

DIRECTED VERDICT 📖 A procedural device whereby the decision in a case is taken out of the hands of the JURY by the judge. 📖

A VERDICT is generally directed in a jury trial where there is no other possible conclusion because the side with the burden of proof has not offered sufficient evidence to establish a PRIMA FACIE case.

A directed verdict is provided for by federal and state rules of CIVIL PROCEDURE. In a criminal action, an ACQUITTAL may be directed in favor of a defendant, based upon rules of criminal procedure.

DIRECT EVIDENCE 📖 EVIDENCE in the form of TESTIMONY from a WITNESS who actually saw, heard, or touched the subject of questioning. Evidence that, if believed, proves existence of the fact in issue without inference or presumption. That means of proof which tends to show the existence of a fact in question, without the intervention of the proof of any other fact, and which is distinguished from CIRCUMSTANTIAL EVIDENCE, often called *indirect*.

Evidence that directly proves a fact, without an inference or presumption, and which in itself, if true, conclusively establishes that fact. 📖

DIRECT EXAMINATION 📖 The primary questioning of a WITNESS during a trial that is conducted by the side for which that person is acting as a witness. 📖

During the course of a direct examination, the attorney who is conducting the interrogation generally asks specific questions that provide the foundation of the case. After a witness is directly examined, the opposing side conducts a CROSS-EXAMINATION, the purpose of which is to IMPEACH or test the validity of the TESTIMONY.

DIRECTOR 📖 One who supervises, regulates, or controls. 📖

A director is the head of an organization, either elected or appointed, who generally has certain powers and duties relating to management or administration. A corporation's BOARD OF DIRECTORS is composed of a group of people who are elected by the shareholders to make important company policy decisions.

Director has been used synonymously with MANAGER.

DIRECTORY 📖 A provision in a statute, rule of procedure, or the like, that is a mere direction or instruction of no obligatory force and involves no invalidating consequence for its disregard, as opposed to an imperative or mandatory provision, which must be followed. The general rule is that the prescriptions of a statute relating to the performance of a public duty are so far directory that, though neglect of them may be punishable, it does not affect the validity of the acts done under them, as in the case of a statute requiring an officer to prepare and deliver a document to another officer on or before a certain day. 📖

Generally, statutory provisions that do not relate to the essence of a thing to be done, and as to which compliance is a matter of convenience rather than of substance, are *directory*, while provisions that relate to the essence of a thing to be done, that is, matters of substance, are MANDATORY.

DIRECT TAX 📖 A charge levied by the government upon property, which is determined by its financial worth. 📖

A direct tax is usually a PROPERTY tax or AD VALOREM tax, as opposed to an indirect tax imposed upon some right or privilege, such as a FRANCHISE tax.

DISABILITY 📖 The lack of COMPETENT physical and mental faculties; the absence of legal capability to perform an act.

The term *disability* usually signifies an incapacity to exercise all the legal rights ordinarily possessed by an average person. CONVICTS, MINORS, and INCOMPETENTS are regarded to be under a disability. The term is also used in a more restricted sense when it indicates a hindrance to marriage or a deficiency in legal qualifications to hold office.

The impairment of earning capacity; the loss of physical function resulting in diminished efficiency; the inability to work. 📖

In the context of WORKERS' COMPENSATION acts, disability consists of an actual INCAPACITY to perform tasks within the COURSE OF EMPLOYMENT, with resulting wage loss, in addition to physical

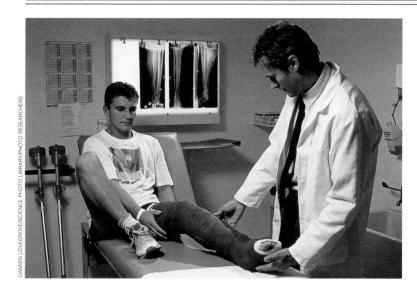

Disability includes the incapacity to perform the job that this patient held before he broke his leg.

impairment that might, or might not, be incapacitating.

Under federal law, the definition of a disability, for SOCIAL SECURITY benefits purposes, requires the existence of a medically ascertainable physical or mental impairment that can be expected to result in death or endures for a stated period, and an inability to engage in any substantial gainful activity due to the impairment.

See also DISABLED PERSONS.

DISABLED PERSONS ▯ Persons who have a physical or mental impairment that substantially limits one or more major life activities. Some laws also include in their definition of disabled persons those people who have a record of or are regarded as having such an impairment. ▯

Approximately 43 million people in the United States are physically or mentally disabled. Like individuals of various races, colors, religions, genders, and national origins, individuals with physical or mental limitations historically have faced DISCRIMINATION in the forms of exclusion from mainstream society; intentional and unintentional segregation; unequal or inferior services, benefits, or activities; and screening criteria that do not correlate with actual ability. Legal commentators have noted that the discrimination against disabled persons differs from other forms of discrimination in that a rational basis for treating members of other excluded groups differently rarely exists, whereas a person's disability may hinder his or her abilities and may provide a rational basis for different treatment. Thus, the mere fact that an individual with a disability is treated differently is insufficient for a finding of illegal discrimination.

Another frequently noted difference between discrimination based on disability and discrimination based on race, color, religion, gender, and national origin is the attitude behind the discrimination. For example, discrimination based on race tends to be rooted in hostility toward a different race. On the other hand, discrimination based on disability is often caused by discomfort and pity, or misguided compassion that materializes as paternalistic and patronizing behavior. Other times, discrimination against disabled persons is the result of "benign neglect" and is "primarily the result of apathetic attitudes rather than affirmative animus" (*Alexander v. Choate*, 469 U.S. 287, 105 S. Ct. 712, 83 L. Ed. 2d 661 [1985]). For example, a restaurant owner who fails to provide a wheelchair ramp to the restaurant's entrance is more likely to be guilty of failing to consider the needs of patrons than of expressing a dislike of wheelchair users.

Whatever its roots, discrimination impedes those with disabilities from obtaining jobs they are qualified to perform, access to some buildings and modes of transportation, and the independence and dignity that nondisabled people take for granted. The U.S. Constitution provides little relief. Courts have held that mentally and physically disabled persons do not fall within a suspect or quasi-suspect class (classes subjected to a history of purposeful unequal treatment or political powerlessness). This means that under the Constitution's Equal Protection Clause, courts review government action affecting disabled people without the heightened or STRICT SCRUTINY afforded suspect or quasi-suspect classes formed by race or religion.

This lack of distinct constitutional protection has resulted in legislative action. Following a concerted lobbying effort by and on behalf of individuals with disabilities, Congress in the late 1960s and early 1970s passed the first federal laws designed to protect disabled persons. Lobbying continued when these laws proved to be inadequate owing to their limited coverage. Then, in 1990, Congress passed the much-heralded Americans with Disabilities Act (ADA) (42 U.S.C.A. §§ 12101–12213), legislation with a much broader application and a fair amount of controversy over the relative cost of its effectiveness.

Rehabilitation Act of 1973 The Rehabilitation Act of 1973 (19 U.S.C.A. §§ 791, 793, 794) prohibits disability discrimination by federal agencies, federal contractors, and other recipients of federal financial assistance. Types

Persons with Disabilities, 1991 to 1992

Covers civilian noninstitutional resident population age 15 and over, as well as members of the armed forces living off post or with their families on post.

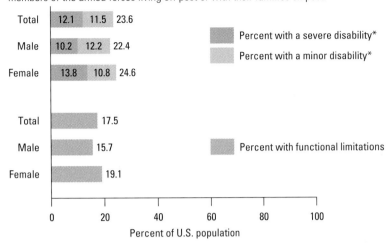

* In general, a disability is considered a reduced ability to perform tasks one would normally do at a given stage in life, thus the presence of disability varies by age.

Source: U.S. Bureau of the Census, *Current Population Reports*, P70-33.

of prohibited discrimination include employment; education; building accessibility; and health, welfare, and social services. Courts have held that private individuals may file ACTIONS under the Rehabilitation Act against federal employers or against recipients of federal financial assistance; the action need not be brought by a government entity. A plaintiff who proves that a federal employer discriminated intentionally in violation of the Rehabilitation Act may receive compensatory and PUNITIVE DAMAGES.

What constitutes a disability under the Rehabilitation Act is often the source of controversy. Blindness, deafness, diabetes, cardiac problems, mobility impairments, and chronic fatigue syndrome have been recognized as physical impairments. The U.S. Supreme Court held that tuberculosis, a contagious disease, is a physical impairment (*School Board v. Arline*, 480 U.S. 273, 107 S. Ct. 1123, 94 L. Ed. 2d 307 [1987]). Numerous courts have followed the logic in *Arline* in holding that individuals who have AIDS or who have tested positive for HIV, the virus that causes AIDS, are physically impaired. Courts have also held that alcoholism, anxiety panic disorder, and posttraumatic stress disorder are impairments under the Rehabilitation Act.

Prior to the enactment of the Americans with Disabilities Act, section 504 of the Rehabilitation Act was the principal federal prohibition of discrimination on the basis of disability. Even with the ADA, the Rehabilitation Act remains an important protection for those with disabilities. The ADA expressly excludes from its coverage protection against discriminatory acts by the federal government, so the Rehabilitation Act provides the only private cause of action for disability discrimination by federal employers and agencies. The Rehabilitation Act also remains an alternative means of remedying discrimination even when a plaintiff concurrently invokes ADA protection.

Individuals with Disabilities Education Act The Individuals with Disabilities Education Act (IDEA) (20 U.S.C.A. §§ 1400–1485) requires states to provide a free, appropriate public education to children who are disabled. Formerly known as the Education of the Handicapped Act or the Education for All Handicapped Children Act, the law was established in 1975 in response to studies showing that more than half of all disabled children were receiving an inappropriate public education, and about one-eighth of those children were simply excluded from public education altogether.

IDEA requires states seeking federal financial assistance for education to develop plans ensuring disabled children a free education that meets their needs. IDEA covers children ages three to twenty-one who have educational disabilities—in other words, mental retardation; hearing, speech, or language impairments; visual impairments; serious emotional disturbances; orthopedic impairments; autism; traumatic brain injuries; and specific learning disabilities—and as a result of such conditions require special education and related services such as transportation to and from school. The act does not, under normal circumstances, cover a child who is nearsighted and needs glasses, or a child who walks with a leg brace; many children with minor disabilities can be educated without special attention.

Each child covered by IDEA is entitled to have an individualized educational program, or IEP, developed jointly by the child's parents and school personnel. The IEP describes the child's abilities and needs, and outlines educational placement and services that will address the listed needs. IDEA contains procedural safeguards designed to ensure that parents can participate in the IEP process and have methods of recourse if they disagree with educators about their child's education.

Finally, IDEA supports the integration of disabled children by requiring that they receive their education in the least restrictive environment. The goal of this requirement is to keep children with disabilities in regular public

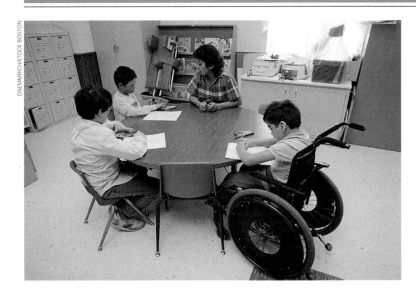

school classrooms to the extent possible. Only when a satisfactory education cannot be achieved in regular classes, even with the use of supplementary aids and services, may a disabled child be removed from regular classes. In many cases, children with disabilities are mainstreamed—placed in a regular educational setting—for part of their school day, and removed to a special needs setting for the other part. Depending on the disability, children may be mainstreamed into certain academic classes or simply during lunch, during study hall, or on the school bus.

States must provide free and appropriate public education to children who are disabled.

Architectural Barriers Act The Architectural Barriers Act (ABA) (42 U.S.C.A. §§ 4151–4157) requires that federally owned, leased, or financed buildings be accessible to disabled persons. Originally enacted in 1968, this law requires each of four federal agencies—the Department of Housing and Urban Development, the Defense Department, the General Services Administration, and the Postal Service—to promulgate design, construction, and alteration standards for buildings within its jurisdiction.

The coverage, and thus the effectiveness, of the ABA is limited. The act encompasses the subway system in Washington, D.C., as well as (1) structures that the federal government constructs or alters; (2) structures that the federal government leases; and (3) structures that depend on federal grants or loans for their design, construction, or alteration. If a federal agency is housed in a building that was constructed by the federal government prior to the ABA's original enactment date in 1968, and that building is not altered, it need not be accessible to disabled individuals under the ABA. Further, when structures covered by the ABA are al-

tered, only the altered portion need be made accessible. Thus, an altered wing of a building may have elevators, wheelchair ramps, and accessible rest rooms, whereas stairs in front of the building's entrance render the building inaccessible to wheelchair users. Perhaps the most obvious shortcoming of the ABA's effectiveness is that it covers only buildings that are owned, leased, or financed by the U.S. government. Even after the ABA's enactment, individuals with disabilities remained challenged by the many inaccessible buildings not covered under it.

Americans with Disabilities Act Despite the efforts of Congress, until 1990, no federal law outlawed most of the disability discrimination by employers, owners of places of public accommodation, and program administrators. In the late 1980s, two-thirds of employable, working-age disabled persons in the United States had a job, and many of those who were employed held a job far below their actual capabilities. In the United States in 1990, more than 8 million persons with disabilities who wanted to work were unable to find jobs and were forced to live on WELFARE and other government subsidies funded by taxpayers.

Disabled individuals faced more obstacles when it came to transportation. Because disabilities often prevent people from driving cars, many with disabilities must rely on buses, trains, and subways. As of 1990, very few public modes of transportation were accessible to those having disabilities. That same year, Congress passed the Americans with Disabilities Act in the hope of alleviating day-to-day problems faced by those with disabilities.

Employment Discrimination and the ADA Titles I and II of the ADA prohibit employers, employment agencies, labor organizations, and joint labor-management committees, in the private sector and in state and local governments, from discriminating on the basis of disability. At the ADA's effective date in July 1992, the act covered private employers with twenty-five or more employees; since July 1994, the act has covered private employers with fifteen or more employees. All state and local government employers are covered, regardless of their number of employees.

The EQUAL EMPLOYMENT OPPORTUNITY COMMISSION (EEOC) is the federal agency charged with overseeing the employment discrimination provisions of the ADA. That agency administers complaints and enforces the ADA. The act also provides that its powers, remedies, and procedures may be invoked by the EEOC, the U.S. attorney general, and any person alleging illegal discrimination pursuant to the ADA or its underlying regulations. Any party seeking redress for ADA-prohibited discrimination must exhaust certain administrative remedies before instituting a lawsuit.

The employment discrimination outlawed by the ADA may take one of several forms explicitly defined by the act: (1) limiting, segregating, or classifying job applicants or employees in a way that adversely affects the status or opportunities of a disabled individual; (2) entering into a contract or business arrangement that has the effect of discriminating against a disabled individual; (3) implementing administrative procedures or criteria that have the effect of discriminating against a disabled individual; (4) denying a disabled person equal jobs or benefits; (5) failing to make reasonable accommodations to allow those with disabilities to perform their job in the workplace; (6) using criteria that screen or tend to screen disabled individuals from the workplace; and (7) administering employment tests for the purpose or partial purpose of measuring a job applicant's disabilities. In determining whether illegal discrimination has occurred under the ADA, it is irrelevant that the employer did not intend to discriminate. But discriminatory actions are permissible if they are job related and necessary for the business, and the required job performance cannot be accomplished with reasonable accommodation.

Reasonable accommodation can be modifications or adjustments to the job application process, to the work environment, or to the manner or circumstances under which the job is performed. The ADA does not require an employer to reasonably accommodate an employee who does not make her or his disability known to the employer, and unless it is obvious, the employer may legally require documented proof of a disability before accommodating it. Some examples of reasonable accommodation are making work areas, and nonwork areas such as lunchrooms and rest rooms, accessible; modifying work schedules; modifying equipment such as computers and desks; and providing interpreters for blind or deaf workers. An accommodation that imposes an undue hardship, causing the employer significant difficulty or expense, is not a reasonable accommodation. An accommodation that fundamentally alters the business is also not reasonable. For example, a nightclub would not be forced to provide bright lighting for a visually impaired employee, because bright lighting would significantly alter the nightclub's business. An employer is not responsible for providing personal items of accommodation such as eyeglasses, leg braces, and prostheses, nor is an employer responsible for accommodating current users of illegal drugs. But the ADA does protect rehabilitated drug users and both rehabilitated and nonrehabilitated alcoholics, provided the employees do not threaten the employer's property or the health and safety of others in the workplace. Whether an accommodation is reasonable is, under the ADA, determined on a case-by-case basis, considering all relevant factors including hardship and cost to the employer.

The ADA does not require employers to accommodate every individual with a disability. Only qualified individuals with disabilities—disabled individuals who can perform, with or without reasonable accommodation, the job's essential functions—are protected from discrimination. Two factors are involved in the determination of whether a disabled individual is qualified. First, the employer must determine whether the individual satisfies the job prerequisites at the time of the hiring decision. This determination should not be based on speculative fears that the employee will not be able to function on the job in the future, or that the employer's INSURANCE premiums will rise. Second, the employer must determine whether the individual can perform the job's essential functions with or without reasonable accommodation. The essential functions of a job are tasks that are fundamental as opposed to marginal. Written job descriptions are frequently considered relevant evidence of essential functions.

To ensure that employers do not consider a person's disability at the time of hiring, the ADA prohibits employers from inquiring about disabilities or conducting medical examinations of prospective employees before hiring them. It

People who use wheelchairs often find it necessary to modify their homes in order to make them accessible.

CRAIG STRONG/GAMMA LIAISON NETWORK

is illegal to ask questions about medical history, prior workers' compensation claims, and overall health before a hiring decision is made. The employer is permitted to inquire about the applicant's abilities as they relate to essential or nonessential job functions—although refusing to hire an applicant because of his or her inability to perform a nonessential job function is prohibited. Upon extending a job offer, the employer may require the prospective worker to submit to a medical examination, provided all prospective workers face the same requirement. In fact, a job offer may be conditioned upon the results of the examination, and the employer may rescind the offer if the examination indicates that the prospective worker would pose a direct threat to health or safety in the workplace, or would not be able to perform the job's essential functions even with reasonable accommodation. The ADA does not consider tests for illegal drugs within its definition of a medical examination; therefore, before extending a job offer, employers may test applicants for illegal drugs—but not prescription drugs or alcohol. An employer may legally test for HIV only after an employment offer has been extended. Even then, the employer may not fire or refuse to hire an individual because of that person's HIV status, unless such discrimination is both related to the job and necessary for the business.

When an employer violates the ADA, the aggrieved party usually is entitled only to equitable relief, such as a court order requiring the construction of wheelchair ramps or the provision of voice-activated computers. Only when the employee shows intentional discrimination may compensatory or punitive damages be awarded. Where the dispute involves the provision of a reasonable accommodation, and the employer made GOOD FAITH efforts to make reasonable accommodation, the court may not award money DAMAGES; it may award only equitable relief. See also EQUITY.

Public Accessibility and the ADA Title II of the ADA requires that state and local government programs and activities be accessible to those with disabilities. Title III of the ADA applies the same requirement to certain private entities that own, lease, or operate places of public accommodation: (1) hotels, motels, and certain other places of lodging; (2) restaurants, bars, and other establishments that serve food or drink; (3) theaters, stadiums, concert halls, and other places of exhibition or entertainment; (4) auditoriums, convention centers, and lecture halls; (5) retail or rental establishments such as grocery stores, bakeries, shopping centers, and

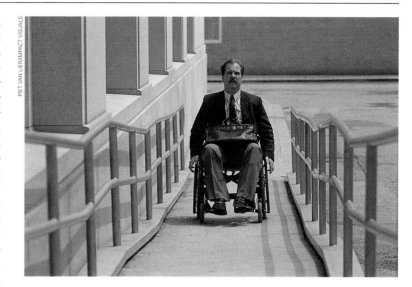

hardware stores; (6) self-service laundries, dry cleaners, banks, hair salons, travel services, shoe repair services, gas stations, law offices, accounting offices, pharmacies, doctors' offices, hospitals, and other service establishments; (7) public transit stations and depots; (8) museums, libraries, and galleries; (9) parks, zoos, and other places of recreation; (10) private schools; (11) day care centers, homeless shelters, food banks, and other social service establishments; and (12) health clubs, gymnasiums, bowling alleys, golf courses, and other places of exercise or recreation. The ADA does not limit its coverage to the size of the public accommodation; if a private entity fits into one of the twelve descriptive categories, it must comply with the ADA accessibility requirements. The ADA does exempt from its coverage some private CLUBS and religious entities.

When a private entity falls within a class of public accommodation, it must provide reasonable modifications in its practices, policies, or procedures, or auxiliary aids and services, for those with disabilities, unless such modifications would fundamentally alter the nature of the entity or would result in an undue burden of significant difficulty or expense. Title III requires only that those with disabilities be given equal opportunities to achieve the same results as nondisabled individuals. For example, a clothing store need not print price tags in braille so long as a salesclerk is available to read the price tags to a blind shopper. Auxiliary aids, such as closed-captioned televisions for hearing impaired hotel guests, are required, but this provision is often flexible. Thus, the owner or operator of a public accommodation may often determine the type of auxiliary aid to assist the disabled individual, provided the chosen aid is effective.

Public places such as this county building must be accessible to employees and others who visit the facility.

Title III also requires the owners and operators of public accommodation in existing facilities to remove structural, architectural, and communication barriers when such removal is "easily accomplishable and able to be carried out without much difficulty and expense" (42 U.S.C.A. § 12181(9)). To determine whether barrier removal is readily achievable, courts look at the nature and cost of the action needed; the number of people employed at the facility and its financial resources; the action's effect on the facility; and the size, nature, type, and financial resources of the covered entity. Under title II, state and local governments must remove barriers unless the removal would cause a fundamental alteration to the program or activity, or cause the government entity an undue financial and administrative burden.

A private individual can enforce the provisions of title III, as can the U.S. attorney general. To enforce the provisions of title II, a private individual can file an administrative complaint with the appropriate federal agency (usually the agency that provides federal funding to the public entity that is the subject of the complaint) or the U.S. Department of Justice, or the individual can file a federal lawsuit.

The ADA and Public Perception   Many individuals with disabilities credit the ADA with helping them overcome the special challenges they face from day to day. From the visually impaired social worker who is able to take his licensing test in braille, to the wheelchair user who is able to park her car just a few yards from her office's entrance, the ADA has helped many disabled people become fully functioning members of society. But the act is not heralded by everyone, particularly when the price of compliance outweighs the legislation's effectiveness. Business owners complain that they have to make their buildings accessible even when those buildings are never used by disabled individuals. Between 1990 and 1995, local governments within Orange County, Florida, spent more than $2 million on architectural changes to make buildings accessible. The city of Winter Park, Florida, spent approximately $35,000 to make a new tennis facility accessible to the disabled, yet the facility's manager reported that only one disabled person used the building in the first year after it opened.

Other critics of the ADA contend that the law is draining administrative and legal resources. In the first three years following the effective date of the ADA's employment provisions, the EEOC reported a 25 percent increase in its workload owing to ADA-related complaints. About 20 percent of those complaints were found to be without merit. By the early 1990s, the act had done little to improve the employment rate for those with disabilities. According to figures by the National Organization on Disability, a private group, as of December 1993, 31 percent of working-age disabled people were employed, whereas in 1986, prior to the ADA's enactment, 33 percent were employed. More recent figures indicate that employment and opportunities for disabled persons are on the rise.

Some legal commentators argue that the act is new and is evolving. As courts interpret the law and Congress fine-tunes it, the ADA's benefits will become clearer. Peter David Blanck, a fellow at the Annenberg Washington Program, has stated that people with disabilities are not the only beneficiaries of the ADA. Businesses have found a new market, and new technology developed to help those with disabilities often helps the nondisabled as well.

See also ACQUIRED IMMUNE DEFICIENCY SYNDROME.

DISAFFIRM ⬛ Repudiate; revoke consent; refuse to support former acts or agreements. ⬛

Disaffirm is commonly applied in situations where an individual has made an agreement and opts to cancel it, which he or she may do by right—such as a MINOR who disaffirms a CONTRACT.

A disaffirmance is a denial or nullification of the existence of something, as opposed to a REVOCATION, which is the breaking of an existing agreement.

DISALLOW ⬛ To exclude; reject; deny the force or validity of. ⬛

The term *disallow* is applied to such things as an insurance company's refusal to pay a claim.

DISARMAMENT See ARMS CONTROL AND DISARMAMENT.

DISASTER RELIEF ⬛ Monies or services made available to individuals and communities that have experienced losses due to disasters such as floods, hurricanes, earthquakes, drought, tornadoes, and riots. ⬛

The term *disaster* has been applied in U.S. law in a broad sense to mean both human-made and natural catastrophes. Human-made catastrophes include civil disturbances such as RIOTS and demonstrations; warfare-related upheavals, including those created by guerrilla activity and terrorism; refugee crises involving the forced movements of people across borders; and many possible accidents, including transportation, mining, pollution, chemical, and nuclear incidents.

Natural disasters may be divided into three categories: meteorological disasters, such as hurricanes, hailstorms, tornadoes, typhoons, snowstorms, droughts, cold spells, and heat waves; topological catastrophes, such as earthquakes, avalanches, landslides, and floods; and biological disasters, including insect swarms and disease epidemics.

A disaster may also be defined in sociological terms as a major disruption of the social pattern of individuals and groups.

Disaster relief efforts are typically an example of FEDERALISM at work, as local, state, and national governments take on varied responsibilities. However, disaster relief has historically been considered a local responsibility, with the federal government providing assistance when local and state relief capacities are exhausted.

Most states have agencies that coordinate disaster relief and planning. A majority of states have statutes that define appropriate procedures for disaster declarations and emergency orders. Such statutes also empower relief agencies to utilize state and local resources, commandeer private property, and arrange for temporary housing during an emergency.

The federal government has played an increasingly influential role in disaster response and preparedness. In fact, as federal disaster assistance grew in the late twentieth century, it became a unique form of aid to states and localities. Often, significant amounts of money are made available to a disaster area for years after the disaster has occurred.

At all levels of government, disaster relief is carried out under the authority of an executive official: a city mayor, a state governor, or the nation's president. In the last instance, federal disaster legislation gives the president wide powers. The president decides what situations may be declared disasters and dictates the extent of federal assistance.

Under the Robert T. Stafford Disaster Relief and Emergency Assistance Act (Stafford Act) (42 U.S.C.A. § 5121 et seq. [1974]), the president may declare a catastrophe either an emergency or a major disaster. This classification is not necessarily indicative of the severity of the event. Instead, the designation determines the extent of federal aid available for the particular calamity. In general, more federal funds are available for major disasters than for emergencies. For the president to declare either an emergency or a major disaster, the governor of the affected state must announce that the catastrophe is of such severity that state resources cannot effectively cope with it.

After a formal declaration has been made at the federal level, all authority for disaster relief operations descends from the president,

through the FEDERAL EMERGENCY MANAGEMENT AGENCY (FEMA), and down to other agencies engaged in relief operations. First established in 1979, FEMA coordinates federal efforts related to natural disaster planning, preparedness, response, and recovery. FEMA funds emergency programs and works closely with state and local governments.

After the president declares an emergency or major disaster, FEMA implements the Federal

Hurricanes, Tropical Storms, and Floods, 1985–1994

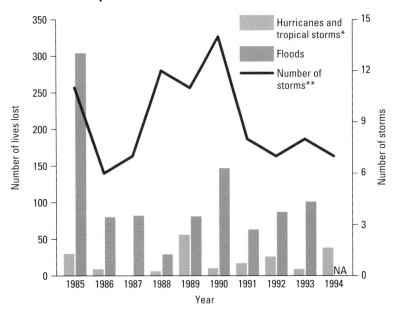

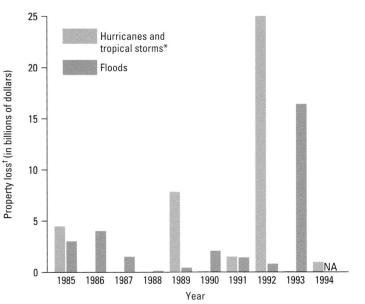

*Tropical storms have maximum sustained winds of 39 to 73 mph; hurricanes have maximum sustained winds of 74 mph or higher.

**Includes North Atlantic tropical storms and hurricanes that reach U.S. coast.

†In 1990 dollars.

Source: U.S. National Oceanic and Atmospheric Administration, *Storm Data*, monthly.

FEMA provides federal assistance to victims of disasters such as earthquakes, sometimes in an effort to prevent future damage.

Response Plan. This plan identifies twelve emergency support functions (ESFs), each of which entails a particular aspect of the relief operation, and assigns specific federal agencies to each function. For example, under the Stafford Act, the Department of DEFENSE (DOD) is the primary agency responsible for ESF 3 (public works and engineering), and ESF 9 (urban search and rescue). The DOD may provide secondary support for all other ESFs.

FEMA administers the President's Disaster Assistance Program, which provides supplemental federal assistance in declared disasters and emergencies. FEMA also operates the Emergency Food and Shelter Program, which provides grants to private, nonprofit organizations for temporary food and shelter for homeless persons. In addition, FEMA controls the Federal Insurance Administration, which oversees the National Flood Insurance Program, a self-supporting program that provides flood insurance to communities that adopt its floodplain management regulations to reduce the effect of future floods.

Although the Stafford Act authorizes the president to call on the DOD to assist state and local governments in times of disaster, the use of the federal armed forces in such situations is limited by law. For example, the Posse Comitatus Act (18 U.S.C.A. § 1385) prohibits the military from performing the duties of civil law enforcement. The DOD has no independent authority to undertake disaster relief operations, though according to the Stafford Act, it may do so for an emergency ten-day period before the president declares an emergency or disaster. In times of civil disturbance such as the 1992 Los Angeles riots, the president may issue a proclamation that permits federal armed forces to take on law enforcement duties in order to put down a civil disturbance (10 U.S.C.A. §§ 331–334).

Congress and state legislatures may also make assistance available in times of disaster. For example, the Disaster Assistance Act of 1988 (7 U.S.C.A. §§ 1421, 1471; 26 U.S.C.A. § 451) made $5 billion available to farmers during a severe drought. Farmers who had lost more than 35 percent of their crops could receive up to $100,000 to cover 65 percent of their losses over an initial threshold. When Hurricane Hugo hit the southeastern coastal states in 1989, Congress approved $1.1 billion in aid only six days later.

Congress has also authorized other agencies to provide disaster assistance. The SMALL BUSINESS ADMINISTRATION's Office of Disaster Assistance supplies loans to businesses that suffer economic losses owing to natural disasters. The AGRICULTURE DEPARTMENT provides emergency loans to eligible farmers and ranchers for losses owing to natural disasters. It may also give farmers cost-sharing assistance as well as the use of land that was previously set aside for conservation purposes. The U.S. government's Agency for International Development makes disaster relief and planning available to foreign countries.

Private organizations, including the Red Cross and the Salvation Army, play a significant role in disaster relief as well. In 1905, Congress officially recognized the Red Cross and its role in responding to significant crises (36 U.S.C.A. § 1), and all subsequent federal disaster laws have renewed this recognition. The Red Cross makes a careful distinction between its humanitarian relief activities, including the provision of food and shelter, and activities that it believes are best handled by government.

Experts on disaster relief have increasingly called for a greater emphasis on prevention as opposed to relief. Plans for improved disaster preparedness often call for a greater use of new technologies, including satellite and radar technologies that would aid in the early detection of potential disasters.

Before 1950, disaster response was characterized by an ad hoc, or case by case, approach. Relief involved a reaction to specific crises with little planning or preparation for future disasters. Then, as now, it was initially activated by local or state officials, and, if necessary, appeals were made to the federal government. Such an approach was often so disorganized that it frustrated effective disaster relief. Federal aid was rarely immediate and instead came some time after a disaster had occurred. Critics often complained that the federal response to disasters was dilatory, insufficient, and inconsistent.

During the 1930s, the expansion of the federal government under the New Deal—including greater federal participation in public works projects—led to a greater federal role in disaster assistance. New Deal agencies such as the Reconstruction Finance Corporation, Federal Emergency Relief Administration, Federal Civilian Works Administration, Works Progress Administration, and Civilian Conservation Corps all participated in disaster control and recovery. The Army Corps of Engineers helped communities to prevent and recover from flood damage, and the Department of Agriculture offered aid to farmers who sustained economic losses in disasters. The 1930s marked the federal government's first use of low-interest loans and outright grants for disaster relief—both features of subsequent disaster laws. During this same decade, Congress considered making the American Red Cross a government agency, but Red Cross officials chose to keep their organization private.

With the passage of the Disaster Relief Act of 1950 (Pub. L. No. 81-875, 64 Stat. 1109), Congress for the first time authorized a coordinated federal response to major disasters. The act, which was repealed in 1970, defined a disaster as "[a]ny flood, drought, fire, hurricane, earthquake, storm, or other catastrophe in any part of the U.S. which in the determination of the President, is or threatens to be of sufficient severity and magnitude to warrant disaster assistance by the Federal government." Significantly, this definition gave the president broad powers to respond to a crisis, powers that are related to the president's role as commander in chief of the nation's military and that have remained in all subsequent federal disaster legislation.

Later laws gradually increased the scope of federal disaster assistance. In the 1950s and 1960s, Congress authorized the provision of temporary shelter, surplus federal supplies, loans, and unemployment assistance for disaster victims. Many of these features were later incorporated into the comprehensive Disaster Relief Act of 1970 (84 Stat. 1744 [42 U.S.C.A. § 4401 et seq.]). This act also offered generous assistance for the reconstruction of public facilities, authorizing 100 percent federal financing for such projects even when reconstruction went beyond damage caused by a particular disaster.

The Stafford Act (Pub. L. No. 93-288, 42 U.S.C.A. § 5121 et seq.) expands still further

the role of the federal government in disaster relief. Under this legislation, the federal government may provide grants to fund a number of additional forms of assistance: the full cost for the reconstruction of certain private, nonprofit facilities and owner-occupied private residential structures; loans to local governments to cover operating expenses; free temporary housing for up to twelve months; the installation of essential utilities; mortgage or rental payments to individuals for up to one year; and food stamps, legal services, and counseling services for low-income citizens. The act also includes an unprecedented authorization of long-range community economic recovery programs for disaster areas. Under these provisions, recovery planning councils develop five-year recovery investment plans, which are eligible to receive up to 90 percent of their funding from the federal government.

In 1979, concerns about overly bureaucratic procedures and a lack of coordination in government efforts to respond to disasters, as well as the need for improved programs for disaster prevention and preparedness, led to the creation of FEMA. A poor federal response to disasters such as Hurricane Hugo and the Loma Prieta earthquake, both occurring in 1989, prompted calls for a greater use of the military in disaster relief. In 1993, amendments to the Stafford Act empowered the president to more readily call on the federal armed forces to assist in disaster relief.

See also REFUGEES.

DISBAR To revoke an attorney's LICENSE to practice law.

In 1949 after an explosion at a Swift & Co. plant in Sioux City, Iowa, plant workers spent the night looking for victims of the blast. The Red Cross provided coffee and food on the site.

APWIDE WORLD PHOTOS

A disbarment proceeding is the investigation into the conduct of a member of the bar in order to determine whether or not that person should be disbarred or disciplined. The state BAR ASSOCIATION normally takes such action based on allegations of a lawyer's unethical conduct. For example, the bar association might initiate an action for disbarment against a lawyer who has revealed information obtained from the PRIVILEGED COMMUNICATION between lawyer and client.

DISCHARGE 📖 To liberate or free; to terminate or extinguish. A discharge is the act or instrument by which a CONTRACT or agreement is ended. A MORTGAGE is discharged if it has been carried out to the full extent originally contemplated or terminated prior to total execution.

Discharge also means to release, as from legal confinement in prison or the military service, or from some legal obligation such as jury duty, or the payment of debts by a person who is bankrupt. The document that indicates that an individual has been legally released from the military service is called a discharge. 📖

The performance of a duty discharges it. An attorney may speak of discharging a legal obligation.

DISCIPLINARY RULES 📖 Precepts, such as the Code of PROFESSIONAL RESPONSIBILITY, that proscribe an ATTORNEY from taking certain actions in the practice of law. 📖

Proceedings can be instituted to DISBAR an attorney who violates the disciplinary rules.

DISCLAIMER 📖 The denial, refusal, or rejection of a right, power, or responsibility. 📖

A disclaimer is a defensive measure, used generally with the purpose of protection from unwanted claims or LIABILITY. A restaurant may disclaim responsibility for loss or damage to a customer's PERSONAL PROPERTY, or a disclaimer clause in a CONTRACT might set forth certain promises and deny all other promises or responsibilities.

A disclaimer of WARRANTY, which is provided for in the UNIFORM COMMERCIAL CODE, limits a warranty in the sale of goods. It may be general or specific in its terms.

DISCONTINUANCE 📖 Cessation; ending; giving up. The discontinuance of a lawsuit, also known as a DISMISSAL or a nonsuit, is the voluntary or involuntary termination of an ACTION. 📖

DISCOVERY 📖 A category of procedural devices employed by a PARTY to a civil or criminal action, prior to trial, to require the adverse party to disclose information that is essential for the preparation of the requesting party's case and that the other party alone knows or possesses. 📖

Civil Procedure Discovery devices used in civil lawsuits are derived from the practice rules of EQUITY, which gave a party the right to compel an adverse party to disclose MATERIAL facts and documents that established a CAUSE OF ACTION. The federal rules of civil procedure have supplanted the traditional equity rules by regulating discovery in federal court proceedings. State laws governing the procedure for civil lawsuits, many of which are based upon the federal rules, have also replaced the equity practices.

Discovery is generally obtained either by the service of an adverse party with a NOTICE to examine prepared by the applicant's attorney or by a court order pursuant to statutory provisions.

Discovery devices narrow the issues of a lawsuit, obtain EVIDENCE not readily accessible to the applicant for use at trial, and ascertain the existence of information that might be introduced as evidence at trial. PUBLIC POLICY considers it desirable to give litigants access to all material facts not protected by PRIVILEGE to facilitate the fair and speedy administration of justice. Discovery procedures promote the SETTLEMENT of a lawsuit prior to trial by providing the parties with opportunities to realistically evaluate the facts before them.

Discovery is CONTINGENT upon a party's reasonable belief that he or she has a good CAUSE OF ACTION or DEFENSE. A court will deny discovery if the party is using it as a FISHING TRIP to ascertain information for the purpose of starting an action or developing a defense. A court is responsible for protecting against the unreasonable investigation into a party's affairs and must deny discovery if it is intended to annoy, embarrass, oppress, or injure the parties or the

This restaurant may disclaim responsibility for injury sustained by a customer while eating next to the street.

RAFAEL MACIA/PHOTO RESEARCHERS

witnesses who will be subject to it. A court will stop discovery when used in BAD FAITH.

Information Discovered Pretrial discovery is used for the disclosure of the identities of persons who know facts relevant to the commencement of an action but not for the disclosure of the identities of additional parties to the case. In a few JURISDICTIONS, however, the identity of the proper party to sue can be obtained through discovery. Discovery pursuant to state and federal procedural rules may require a party to reveal the names and addresses of WITNESSES to be used in the development of the case.

Discovery is not automatically denied if an applicant already knows the matters for which he or she is seeking discovery since one of its purposes is to frame a PLEADING in a lawsuit. On the other hand, discovery is permitted only when the desired information is material to the preparation of the applicant's case or defense. Discovery is denied if the matter is irrelevant or if it comes within the protection of a privilege.

Privileged Information Privileged matters are not a proper subject for discovery. For example, a person cannot be forced to disclose confidential communications regarding matters that come within the ATTORNEY-CLIENT PRIVILEGE. Discovery cannot be obtained to compel a person to reveal information that would violate his or her constitutional guarantee against SELF-INCRIMINATION. However, if a party or witness has been granted IMMUNITY regarding the matters that are the basis of the asserted privilege, that party can be required to disclose such information on pretrial examination.

A person who refuses to comply with discovery on the basis of an asserted privilege must claim the privilege for each particular question at the time of the pretrial examination. An attorney or the court itself cannot claim the privilege for that person. However, a person may WAIVE the privilege and answer the questions put to him or her during discovery.

Objections A party may challenge the validity of a pretrial examination if asserted prior to trial. The merits of such an OBJECTION will be evaluated by the court during the trial when it rules on the admissibility of the evidence. If the questions to be asked during a discovery, such as the identity and location of a particular witness, pose a threat to anyone's life or safety, a party can make a MOTION to a court for a PROTECTIVE ORDER to deny discovery of such information.

Refusal to Respond Failing to appear or answer questions at an examination before trial might result in a CONTEMPT citation, particularly if the person has disobeyed the command of a SUBPOENA to attend. If discovery is pursuant to a court ORDER, the court will require that the party's refusal to answer questions be treated as if the party admitted them in favor of the requesting party. Such an order is called a PRECLUSION ORDER since the uncooperative party is precluded from denying or contradicting the matters admitted due to his or her intentional failure to comply with a discovery order.

Costs A party who makes a motion for a court to order discovery may be required to pay or make provision for payment of COSTS—expenses incurred in obtaining discovery when it is granted. If the party eventually wins the lawsuit, the court may demand that the costs be paid by the adversary in the proceedings.

Types of Discovery Devices Discovery of material information is obtainable by use of depositions, interrogatories, requests for the production and inspection of writings and other materials, requests for admission of facts, and physical examinations.

Depositions A party to a lawsuit may obtain an oral pretrial examination of an adverse party or witness—the DEPONENT—who is under oath to respond truthfully to the questions. This interrogation is known as a DEPOSITION or an examination before trial, commonly called an E.B.T. The notice or order of examination must specify the particular matters to be discovered and the line of questioning is usually restricted to such matters. However, the scope and extent of the examination is within the discretion of the court.

In some jurisdictions, a deponent may bring along documents to refresh his or her memory and facilitate testimony. Such materials can be used only when relevant to the line of questioning to which the deponent is subject and only by the designated deponent.

Interrogatories INTERROGATORIES are specific written questions submitted by a person, pursuant to a discovery order, to an adversary who must respond under oath and in writing. Interrogatories must state questions in a precise manner so as to elicit an answer that is pertinent to the issues being litigated.

Production and Inspection A litigant is generally entitled to the production and inspection of relevant documents in the possession or control of an adversary pursuant to discovery. The applicant must have a reasonable belief that such evidence is necessary to the lawsuit if discovery is to be granted.

Requests for Admissions of Facts A party may ask an adversary to admit any material fact or the authenticity of a document that is to be

JOHN NEUBAUER/PHOTOEDIT

This attorney and her client examine interrogatories that have been submitted to them in the process of discovery.

presented as evidence during the trial. This procedure, called a request for an admission of fact, facilitates the fair and efficient administration of justice by minimizing the time and expense incurred in proving issues that are not in dispute.

Only FACTS, not matters or CONCLUSIONS OF LAW or opinions, can be admitted when there is no disagreement between the parties. The requesting party does not have to make a motion before a court prior to making such a demand but must comply with any statutory requirements. The matters or documents to be admitted must be particularly described and there must be a time limit for a reply. The response should admit or deny the request or explain in detail the reason for refusing to do so—for example, if the request calls for admission of a MATTER OF LAW. Failure to make a response within the specified time results in the matter being admitted, precluding the noncomplying party from challenging its admission during the trial.

Physical Examination A mental or physical examination of a party whose condition is an issue in litigation may be authorized by a court in the exercise of its discretion.

Criminal Procedure Under COMMON LAW, there was no discovery in criminal cases. In federal and many state criminal prosecutions today, only limited discovery is permissible, unlike the full disclosure of information available in CIVIL ACTIONS. Limited discovery prevents the possible intimidation of prosecution witnesses and the increased likelihood of PERJURY that might result from unabridged disclosure. The obligation of the prosecutor to prove the case BEYOND A REASONABLE DOUBT, the possibility of an unconstitutional infringement upon a defendant's right against self-incrimination,

and violations of the attorney-client privilege pursuant to a client's right to COUNSEL also hinder complete discovery. A defendant who requests particular documents from the government may be required to submit items of a similar nature to the government upon its request for discovery. The disclosure of false evidence or the failure of the prosecution to disclose documents that are beneficial to the defense can result in a denial of due process of law.

The federal Jencks Act (18 U.S.C.A. § 3500 [1957]) entitles a defendant to obtain access to prosecution documents necessary to IMPEACH the testimony of a prosecution witness by showing that the witness had made earlier statements that contradict present testimony. Theoretically, the defense cannot receive the statements until the witness has finished testimony on DIRECT EXAMINATION, but, in practice, such statements are usually available before then. The states are not subject to the requirements of the Jencks Act, but many have adopted similar disclosure rules.

DISCRETIONARY TRUST An arrangement whereby property is set aside with directions that it be used for the benefit of another, the BENEFICIARY, and which provides that the TRUSTEE (one appointed or required by law to administer the property) has the right to accumulate, rather than pay out to the beneficiary, the annual income generated by the property or a portion of the property itself.

Depending on the terms of the instrument that creates the TRUST, such income can be accumulated for future distributions to the income beneficiaries or added to the CORPUS, the main body or principal of a trust, for the benefit of the remainderman, one who is entitled to the balance of the ESTATE after a particular estate carved out of it has expired. This is a discretionary trust since the trustee has the latitude or discretion to give or deny the beneficiary some benefits under the trust. The beneficiary cannot compel the trustee to use any of the trust property for the beneficiary's advantage.

In this type of trust the beneficiary has no interest that can be transferred or reached by CREDITORS unless the trustee decides to pay or apply some of the trust property for the benefit of the beneficiary. At that time, the beneficiary's creditors can reach it unless it is protected by a SPENDTHRIFT TRUST clause. An assignee, a person who has received an interest in the trust from the beneficiary by ASSIGNMENT (a transfer of property), can hold the trustee liable for any future payment to the beneficiary by giving notice of the assignment. As an illustration, the

SETTLOR, one who creates a trust, delivers $10 thousand to the trustee in trust for the beneficiary, and the trustee has the discretion to make any and every payment, or no payment at all, to the beneficiary from the corpus or income. Before the trustee has decided to make any payment to the beneficiary, the beneficiary assigns a right to $50 of any payment the trustee elects to make to him or her. The assignee notifies the trustee of the assignment and demands that if the trustee decides to pay the beneficiary any amount up to $50, the trustee must pay the assignee and not the beneficiary. If the trustee decides not to pay the beneficiary, the assignee has no right to payment. If the trustee subsequently decides to pay the beneficiary $50, the trustee will be liable to the assignee for it.

A person can create a discretionary trust for his or her own benefit, but creditors can reach the maximum amount that the trust can apply for or pay to the beneficiary under the trust terms, regardless of whether he or she actually received payment.

DISCRETION IN DECISION MAKING

Discretion is the power or right to make official decisions using reason and judgment to choose from among acceptable alternatives.

Legislatures, the PRESIDENT and the governors of the various states, trial and appellate JUDGES, and ADMINISTRATIVE AGENCIES are among the public officers and offices charged with making discretionary decisions in the discharge of public duties. All discretionary decisions made are subject to some kind of review, and are also subject to reversal or modification if there has been an abuse of discretion.

An ABUSE OF DISCRETION occurs when a decision is not an acceptable alternative. The decision may be unacceptable because it is logically unsound, because it is arbitrary and clearly not supported by the facts at hand, or because it is explicitly prohibited by a statute or rule of law.

Discretion in decision making can be viewed from the perspective of the flexibility and choices granted to the decision maker based on the decision being made. Only the Constitution, through judicial enforcement, can limit discretionary decision making by legislative bodies to pass laws. Great flexibility is granted to the EXECUTIVE BRANCH in the area of foreign relations decision making. Statutes and prior judicial decisions limit the flexibility and discretion of a judge in a court of law. And Congress has granted broad decision-making authority to administrative agencies and their administrators, giving them great flexibility to make decisions within their area of concern.

Legislative Discretion Legislatures have very broad discretion to create and pass laws that prohibit, regulate, and encourage a wide variety of activities. In Article I, Section 8, of the U.S. Constitution, Congress is empowered to "make all Laws which shall be necessary and proper" for carrying out its enumerated powers. Most state legislatures are empowered by similar language from their state CONSTITUTION. An example of a proper exercise of legislative discretion is to make stalking a crime and to make that crime punishable by fines or imprisonment.

The discretion of legislatures is also limited by the U.S. and state constitutions. A state may not pass a statute that allows the police to search any person's residence at any time for any reason, because that statute would clearly violate the U.S. Constitution's FOURTH AMENDMENT protection against unreasonable SEARCHES AND SEIZURES.

Executive Discretion Executive discretion, like that vested in the president by Article II of the U.S. Constitution, is most evident in the area of foreign affairs: the president is the commander in chief of all the military forces and also has the power to make TREATIES with other countries. If Congress is silent on a particular issue—that is, if Congress has not passed a specific statute or resolution concerning that issue—then the president has broad discretion to act. This can be particularly important in the area of foreign policy during war or other military action, when decisions must be made quickly in response to rapidly changing circumstances.

One improper exercise of executive discretion that is almost always reversed by reviewing courts is IMPOUNDMENT, whereby a president places in reserve a sum of money appropriated by Congress for a particular purpose, effectively blocking that appropriation. Courts have routinely held that the president has no implied power to take such action. Implied powers are those held by the president but not granted expressly by statute, regulation, or constitution. The act of impoundment, then, constitutes an abuse of discretion by the executive branch.

Judicial Discretion Judicial discretion is a very broad concept because of the different kinds of decisions made by judges and because of the different limits placed on those decisions. Article III, Section 2, of the U.S. Constitution grants the JUDICIARY broad power, which extends "to all Cases, in Law and Equity, arising under this Constitution, the Laws of the United States, and Treaties made." Judges' decisions must be made based on the "rule of law," which, in the United States, derives not only from statutes passed by Congress but also from the tenets of the Constitution. In addition, COMMON LAW, or judge-made law, provides limits based on the principle of STARE DECISIS, which holds that a court's decision in a particular case must comport with the rules of law as they have been determined by that court or by other, higher-level courts, in previous cases. Legal conclusions that do not fit within the prescribed limits of both statutory and common law may be overturned by a reviewing court if that court determines that the conclusions were an abuse of judicial discretion.

At one time, the sentencing of those convicted of crimes was almost entirely within the discretion of judges. Judges could take into account various mitigating factors (circumstances reducing the degree of blame or fault attributed to the offender) and craft a punishment that most appropriately fit the crime. For example, a first-time petty offender convicted of shoplifting might be sentenced to PAROLE and community service.

Today, however, with the Federal Sentencing Guidelines and with mandatory minimum sentencing legislation, which has been passed in both Congress and the states, judges no longer have the broad latitude to make the SENTENCE fit the crime and the defendant. In some states, first-time offenders are being sent to jail for life for the possession of large amounts of controlled substances. Many federal judges must incarcerate parole violators for minor parole violations because the guidelines specifically direct them to and severely limit their sentencing choices. A judge's failure to abide by the sentencing guidelines in issuing a sentence would constitute an abuse of judicial discretion.

Judges' discretion in decision making has been reduced by federal sentencing guidelines, but they still enjoy some latitude as they make decisions.

SPENCER GRANT/PHOTO RESEARCHERS

B. TAM NOMOTO
JUDGE

Administrative Agency Discretion

Legislative, executive, and judicial discretion in decision making is limited within the structure of the three branches of the U.S. government as established in the Constitution. Each branch is subject to the influence, review, and even rejection of certain decisions. Administrative agencies, granted authority by Congress to administer specific government programs and areas of concern, operate outside of this tripartite system, and many decisions made by administrative agencies are protected from review. For this reason, the administrative branch of both the federal and state governments has often been referred to as the headless fourth branch of government.

The U.S. Constitution does not expressly grant administrative authority. However, Congress may create administrative agencies as an extension of its authority to make laws that are necessary and proper, to help it execute its powers (U.S. Const. art. I). The president may appoint the heads of these agencies under a general grant of authority to appoint "public Ministers and Consuls" and "all other Officers of the United States, whose Appointments are not herein otherwise provided for" (U.S. Const. art. II). The judiciary, under its very broad grant of authority to hear all cases in law and equity, has a right, in some circumstances, to review and overturn administrative decisions (U.S. Const. art. III).

Administrative agencies, like the Social Security Administration, the Equal Employment Opportunity Commission (EEOC), and the Immigration and Naturalization Service, make both rules and adjudicative decisions, which means that they not only promulgate regulations but also decide conflicts dealing with their area of concern.

For example, the Social Security Administration promulgates regulations concerning the provision of income for totally disabled people, and also decides who is or is not disabled. The EEOC promulgates regulations and guidance dealing with SEXUAL HARASSMENT, and also decides whether PROBABLE CAUSE exists to pursue a particular claim of harassment. (Probable cause, which is a reasonable basis to believe the facts alleged, must be established before litigation can commence.) The Immigration and Naturalization Service not only helps to set immigration quotas but also makes individual decisions regarding deportation.

To review an agency decision under the standard of abuse of discretion, courts must follow a three-part analysis. First, courts must look to the legislation passed by Congress that gave the decision-making authority to the particular agency, and determine if the administrator acted within the limits of that authority. Second, courts must determine if a clear error of judgment has occurred. Without clear error, a court cannot substitute its own judgment; if it did so, the court would itself commit an abuse of discretion. Third, courts must determine whether the administrator followed the procedural requirements.

Courts reviewing administrative decisions for abuse of discretion give great deference to the administrator or agency, which not only is an expert in the area of concern but also had access to all the facts that influenced the decision. This "hands-off" approach gives administrative agencies the opportunity to execute the authority granted them by Congress efficiently and effectively.

An administrative decision that is difficult to reverse or challenge is that made by the Board of Immigration Appeals to uphold an immigration judge's decision to deport an ALIEN. Once a deportation decision is made and upheld, the alien can seek to have the attorney general reverse it. Should the attorney general uphold the deportation, a court reviewing this discretionary decision will have limited opportunity to challenge it, because the Board of Immigration Appeals clearly has authority to make the decision in the first place. The alien must show either failure to follow procedure or clear error of judgment on the part of the board. Deportation challenges are common, but successful challenges are rare because the great discretion afforded to the Immigration and Naturalization Service makes an abuse of discretion extremely difficult to prove.

DISCRIMINATION 📖 In constitutional law, the grant by statute of particular privileges to a class arbitrarily designated from a sizable number of persons, where no reasonable distinction exists between the favored and disfavored classes. Federal laws, supplemented by court decisions, prohibit discrimination in such areas as employment, housing, voting rights, education, and access to public facilities. They also proscribe discrimination on the basis of race, age, sex, nationality, disability, or religion. In addition, state and local laws can prohibit discrimination in these areas and in others not covered by federal laws. 📖

In the 1960s, in response to the CIVIL RIGHTS MOVEMENT and an increasing awareness of discrimination against minorities, several pieces of landmark legislation were signed into law. Title

Charges of Discrimination Filed with the EEOC in 1995

Total number of complaints: 87,600

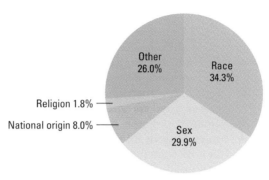

Source: Equal Employment Opportunity Commission.

VII of the CIVIL RIGHTS ACT of 1964 (42 U.S.C.A. § 2000e et seq.), the most comprehensive civil rights legislation in U.S. history, prohibits discrimination on the basis of sex, race, religion, nationality, or color. Title VII was designed to provide for parity in the use and enjoyment of public accommodations, facilities, and education as well as in federally assisted programs and employment. It further allows an injured party to bring suit and obtain DAMAGES from any individual who illegally infringes upon the party's CIVIL RIGHTS. The VOTING RIGHTS ACT OF 1965 (42 U.S.C.A. § 1973 et seq.) prohibits the states and their political subdivisions from imposing voting qualifications or prerequisites to voting or standards, practices, or procedures that deny or curtail the right of citizens to vote, because of race, color, or membership in a language minority group. The Fair Housing Act of 1968 (42 U.S.C.A. § 3601 et seq.) prohibits discrimination based on race, color, religion, sex, and national origin, in connection with the sale or rental of residential housing. In 1988, Congress passed the Fair Housing Amendments Act, which extends the same protections to handicapped people.

Other important federal laws have been aimed at remedying discrimination against other groups, including older U.S. citizens and individuals with disabilities. The Age Discrimination in Employment Act of 1967 (ADEA) (29 U.S.C.A. § 621 et seq.) prohibits employers with twenty or more employees from discriminating because of age against employees over age forty. Industries affecting commerce as well as state and local governments are covered by the ADEA. Disabled individuals received fed-

The Pregnancy Discrimination Act of 1978 prohibits discrimination against employees on the basis of pregnancy and childbirth.

eral protection against discrimination with the passage of the Rehabilitation Act of 1973 (29 U.S.C.A. § 701 et seq.), which prohibits any program activity receiving federal funds from denying access to a handicapped person. In 1990, Congress enacted the Americans with Disabilities Act (ADA) (codified in scattered sections of 42, 29, 47 U.S.C.A.). The ADA was widely hailed as the most significant piece of civil rights legislation since the Civil Rights Act of 1964. It provides even broader protection, prohibiting discrimination against disabled individuals, in employment, public accommodations, transpc·tation, and telecommunications.

Although discrimination on the basis of gender is included in title VII of the Civil Rights Act of 1964, a number of other federal laws also prohibit SEX DISCRIMINATION. The Equal Pay Act of 1963 (29 U.S.C.A. § 206 [d]) amended the FAIR LABOR STANDARDS ACT of 1938 (29 U.S.C.A. §§ 201–219). It prohibits discrimination in terms of different forms of compensation for jobs with equal skill, effort, and responsibility. The Pregnancy Discrimination Act of 1978 (42 U.S.C.A. § 2000e[k]) prohibits discrimination against employees on the basis of pregnancy and childbirth, in employment and benefits. Title IX of the Education Amendments of 1972 (20 U.S.C.A. §§ 1681–1686) prohibits sex discrimination in educational institutions that receive federal funds, including exclusions from noncontact team sports on the basis of sex. In addition, the Equal Credit Opportunity Act (15 U.S.C.A. § 1691 et seq.) prohibits discrimination in the extension of CREDIT, on the basis of sex or marital status.

State and local laws can also protect individuals from discrimination. For example, gays and lesbians, though not yet included under federal civil rights laws, are protected in many cities by local ordinances outlawing discrimination against individuals on the basis of sexual orientation. Minnesota, New Jersey, Rhode Island, Vermont, Wisconsin, and other states have passed such legislation—though some voters have sought to repeal it, with mixed results.

CROSS-REFERENCES

Affirmative Action; Age Discrimination; Colleges and Universities; Disabled Persons; Equal Employment Opportunity Commission; Gay and Lesbian Rights.

DISFRANCHISEMENT The removal of the rights and privileges inherent in an association with some group; the taking away of the rights of a free citizen, especially the right to vote. Sometimes called disenfranchisement.

The relinquishment of a person's right to membership in a CORPORATION is distinguishable from amotion, which is the act of removing an officer from an office without depriving him or her of membership in the corporate body.

In U.S. law, disfranchisement most commonly refers to the removal of the right to vote, which is also called the franchise or SUFFRAGE. Historically, states have passed laws disfranchising poor people, insane people, and criminals. Most conspicuously, the JIM CROW LAWS passed by southern states effectively disfranchised African Americans from the late nineteenth century until well into the twentieth century.

During Reconstruction, following the Civil War, African Americans in the South briefly enjoyed voting privileges nearly equal to those of whites. However, beginning roughly in 1890, legally sanctioned disfranchisement occurred on a huge scale in the South. For example, during the years directly following the Civil War, African Americans made up as much as 44 percent of the registered electorate in Louisiana, but by 1920, they constituted only one percent of the electorate. In Mississippi, almost 70 percent of eligible African Americans were registered to vote in 1867; after 1890, fewer than six percent were qualified to vote. There were similar decreases in the percentages of elected black officials in all southern states.

Although the FIFTEENTH AMENDMENT to the Constitution, passed in 1870, asserts that "[t]he right of citizens of the United States to vote shall not be denied or abridged by the United States or by any State on account of race, color, or previous condition of servitude," southern states established laws and practices that circumvented these provisions. They employed disfranchisement devices such as POLL TAXES, property tests, literacy tests, and all-white primaries to prevent African Americans from voting. On the surface, such laws discriminated on the basis of education and property ownership rather than race, but their practical and intended effect was to block African Americans from the POLLS; legal devices called GRANDFATHER CLAUSES allowed poor and illiterate whites to avoid discriminatory tests on the grounds that they or their ancestors had previously had the franchise. When discriminatory laws were combined with the violence and intimidation directed at potential black voters by white hate groups such as the Ku Klux Klan, the silencing of the African American political voice was almost complete.

Despite Supreme Court rulings striking down such discriminatory measures as early as 1915 (see, e.g., *Guinn v. United States*, 238 U.S. 347, 35 S. Ct. 926, 59 L. Ed. 1340 [1915]), southern states continued to bar African Americans from the voting booth for most of the twentieth century. Only with the passage of the VOTING RIGHTS ACT OF 1965 (42 U.S.C.A. § 1973 et seq.) did twentieth-century African Americans finally reach the polls in significant

Black Elected Officials, by Office, 1970 to 1993

▓ U.S. and State Legislatures*
░ City and County Offices**
▒ Law Enforcement†
▓ Education††

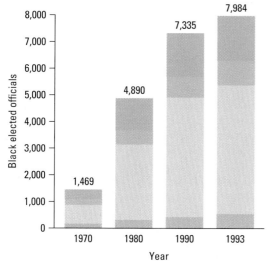

* Includes state administrators.
** Includes county commissioners and council members, mayors, vice mayors, aldermen, alderwomen, regional officials, and other similar positions.
† Includes judges, magistrates, constables, marshals, sheriffs, justices of the peace, and other similar positions.
†† Includes members of state education agencies, college boards, school boards, and similar positions.

Source: Joint Center for Political and Economic Studies, Washington, D.C., *Black Elected Officials: A National Roster*, annual.

numbers in the South. For example, in 1965, only 19 percent of nonwhites were registered to vote in Alabama, seven percent in Mississippi. Only four years later, after passage of the act, the percentages of nonwhite registrants in Alabama and Mississippi had jumped to 57 and 59, respectively.

Other forms of disfranchisement, including the disfranchisement of criminals, have remained controversial. As of the early 1990s, all but three states prohibited imprisoned offenders from voting. Thirty-five states disfranchise offenders on PROBATION or PAROLE, and fourteen disfranchise ex-offenders for life. Because a disproportionate share of convicted criminals are nonwhite, some have argued that such laws constitute a type of racially discriminatory voting barrier that is as pernicious as poll taxes and literacy tests. Many state criminal disfranchisement laws date back to the days of Jim Crow, and such laws were often targeted at offenses for which African Americans were disproportionately convicted. For this reason, some groups have called for the reform or removal of criminal disfranchisement laws.

DISHONOR 📖 To refuse to accept or pay a DRAFT or to pay a PROMISSORY NOTE when duly presented. An instrument is dishonored when a necessary or optional presentment is made and due acceptance or payment is refused, or cannot be obtained within the prescribed time, or in case of bank collections, the instrument is seasonably returned by the midnight deadline; or presentment is excused and the instrument is not duly accepted or paid. Includes the insurer of a LETTER OF CREDIT refusing to pay or accept a draft or demand for payment.

As respects the FLAG, to deface or defile, imputing a lively sense of shaming or an equivalent acquiescent callousness. 📖

DISINHERIT 📖 To cut off from an INHERITANCE. To deprive someone, who would otherwise be an HEIR to property or another right, of his or her right to inherit. 📖

A parent who wishes to disinherit a child may specifically state so in a WILL.

DISINTERESTED 📖 Free from BIAS, PREJUDICE, or partiality. 📖

A *disinterested witness* is one who has no interest in the case at bar, or matter in issue, and is legally COMPETENT to give testimony.

DISMISSAL 📖 A discharge of an individual or corporation from employment. The disposition of a civil or criminal proceeding or a claim or charge made therein by a court order without a trial or prior to its completion which, in effect, is a denial of the relief sought by the commencement of the action. 📖

The legal effect of a dismissal varies depending upon its type. A dismissal, granted by a court that has exercised its discretion in evaluating the particular case before it, operates similarly in civil and criminal actions.

Civil Proceedings Rules embodied in state codes of CIVIL PROCEDURE and the Federal Rules of Civil Procedure govern the granting of dismissals in CIVIL ACTIONS brought in state and federal courts. The primary function of a dismissal is to promote the speedy and efficient administration of justice by removing from the consideration of a court any matters that have been unnecessarily delayed to the disadvantage of the defendant.

Dismissal with Prejudice A dismissal with prejudice is a JUDGMENT rendered in a lawsuit on its MERITS that prevents the PLAINTIFF from bringing the same lawsuit against the same DEFENDANT in the future. It is a harsh remedy that has the effect of canceling the action so that it can never again be commenced. A dismissal with prejudice is RES JUDICATA as to every issue litigated in the action.

The possibility of such a dismissal acts as a deterrent to the use of DILATORY tactics by a plaintiff who wants to prejudice a defendant's case by unreasonably hindering the disposition of the action from the time of the filing of the action to the actual trial of the issues. It is also designed to minimize, if not eliminate, the congestion of court calendars caused by unnecessary delays in pending cases. Because it is regarded as a drastic remedy, courts grant dismissals with prejudice only in the most egregious cases in response to a motion brought by a defendant or by a court SUA SPONTE, or on its own will.

Motion by a defendant A defendant may make a MOTION to a court to dismiss the CAUSE OF ACTION if the plaintiff has failed to appear to prosecute his or her case. A plaintiff is obligated to prosecute the action with due diligence within a reasonable time of commencing the action. If the passage of time hurts the defendant in the preparation of his or her case or if it substantially affects the defendant's rights, then the defendant may seek a dismissal with prejudice. A dismissal will not be granted if the failure to prosecute resulted from unavoidable circumstances, such as the death of the plaintiff, and there is a delay in the appointment of a PERSONAL REPRESENTATIVE to continue the action. When the parties attempt to negotiate a settlement of the controversy, consequent delays in reaching an agreement will not provide a basis for dismissal with prejudice. If, however, a plaintiff delays prosecution based on the mere possibility of a settlement without demonstrating concrete efforts to achieve an agreement, a court may grant a dismissal upon the defendant's motion.

The defendant must be free of any responsibility for delay when he or she seeks a dismissal for failure to prosecute. A lawsuit will not be dismissed if the defendant caused or contributed to the delay, such as if the individual leaves the state to avoid the trial.

Sua sponte power of court A court has inherent power to dismiss an action with prejudice if it is vexatious, brought in BAD FAITH, or when there has been a failure to prosecute it within a reasonable time. If a plaintiff who has commenced an action fails to comply with DISCOVERY devices, a court, which has issued the order of compliance, may *sua sponte* dismiss the case with prejudice.

Dismissal without Prejudice A plaintiff is not subsequently barred from suing the same defendant on the same cause of action when a court grants a dismissal without prejudice of his or her case. Such a dismissal operates to terminate the case. It is not, however, an ultimate disposition of the controversy on the merits, but rather it is usually based upon procedural errors that do not substantially harm the defendant's rights. It effectively treats the matter as if the lawsuit had never been commenced, but it does not relieve a plaintiff of the duty of complying with the STATUTE OF LIMITATIONS, the time limit within which his or her action must be commenced. A dismissal without prejudice is granted in response to a notice of dismissal, stipulations, or a court order.

Notice of dismissal A plaintiff may serve a NOTICE of dismissal upon a defendant only if the defendant has not yet submitted an ANSWER in response to the plaintiff's COMPLAINT. A notice

A judge may order the dismissal of an action or a proceeding before it goes to trial.

STOCK BOSTON

of dismissal preserves the right of the plaintiff to commence a lawsuit at a later date. While not commonly employed, such a notice is useful when exigent circumstances—such as the sudden unavailability of witnesses—warrant the termination of the action. The clerk of the court in which the lawsuit was commenced must receive a copy of the notice of dismissal served upon the defendant to adjust the record of the action accordingly.

Stipulation Once a defendant has served an answer to the plaintiff's complaint, the plaintiff may obtain a dismissal without prejudice by entering a formal agreement, a STIPULATION, with the defendant. The parties agree to the terms of the dismissal, which must be filed with the court clerk and put into effect by the action of the clerk. A dismissal agreed is a court order that enforces the stipulation of the parties. A dismissal by stipulation is a dismissal without prejudice unless the parties otherwise agree and record their agreement in the text of the stipulation.

Court order A plaintiff may make a motion to dismiss his or her action without prejudice if the plaintiff cannot serve a notice of dismissal or obtain a stipulation. A dismissal will not be granted to a plaintiff, however, if it would prejudice the rights of any other individual who has a legal interest in the subject matter of a lawsuit. If a joint tenant fails to agree with his or her co-tenant to dismiss an action against a landlord for breach of the WARRANTY of HABITABILITY without prejudice, then there will not be a dismissal.

Criminal Prosecutions A dismissal in a criminal prosecution is a decision of a court, which has exercised its discretion prior to TRIAL or before a VERDICT is reached, that terminates the proceedings against the defendant. The procedure by which dismissals in state and federal criminal actions are obtained are governed, respectively, by the state and federal rules of CRIMINAL PROCEDURE. In criminal prosecutions, delay often prejudices the defendant's rights because of the greater likelihood that evidence would be lost or memories or events would not be recalled easily. The possibility of dismissal ensures the prompt government prosecution of individuals accused of criminal activity.

The legal effect of a dismissal in a criminal prosecution is dependent upon the type that is granted by the court.

Dismissal with Prejudice A dismissal with prejudice bars the government from prosecuting the accused on the same charge at a later date. The defendant cannot subsequently be reindicted because of the constitutional guarantee against DOUBLE JEOPARDY. A dismissal with prejudice is made in response to a motion to the court by the defendant or by the court *sua sponte*.

Motion by a defendant A defendant may make a motion to the court to have the charges against him or her—whether embodied in an INDICTMENT, INFORMATION, or complaint—dismissed with prejudice because the delay has violated the individual's constitutional right to a SPEEDY TRIAL or there is no sufficient evidence to support the charges. In deciding whether a delay is unreasonable, the court evaluates the extent of the delay, the reasons for it, the prejudice to the defendant, and the defendant's contribution to the delay.

Sua sponte power of court A court with jurisdiction to decide criminal matters can *sua sponte* dismiss a criminal prosecution with prejudice if the facts of the case clearly established that an accused has been deprived of his or her constitutional right to a speedy trial.

Dismissal without Prejudice A dismissal without prejudice that permits the reindictment or retrial of a defendant on the same charge at a subsequent date may be granted by a court acting *sua sponte* or after the prosecuting attorney has made a motion to do so. Only nonconstitutional grounds that do not adversely affect the rights of the defendant, such as the crowding of court calendars, might be sufficient to warrant the dismissal of a criminal action without prejudice.

DISORDERLY CONDUCT A broad term describing conduct that disturbs the peace or endangers the morals, health, or safety of a community.

Unlike the offense of BREACH OF THE PEACE, which originated under COMMON LAW, disorderly conduct is strictly a statutory crime. It is commonly considered a broader term than breach of the peace and, under some statutes, breach of the peace is an element of disorderly conduct.

The elements of disorderly conduct vary from one jurisdiction to another. Most statutes specify the misconduct that constitutes the offense. Acts such as the use of vulgar and OBSCENE language in a public place, VAGRANCY, loitering, causing a crowd to gather in a public place, or annoying passengers on a mode of public transportation have been regarded as disorderly conduct by statute or ordinance. The offense is not committed unless the act complained of clearly falls within the statute.

In most jurisdictions, the decision of whether or not the act complained of is disorderly conduct is made by a judge. Following

This homeless man may be charged with vagrancy or loitering, both elements of disorderly conduct, in order to remove him from a public park.

this determination, a jury decides whether or not the accused is guilty of the offense, provided there is a QUESTION OF FACT to be decided.

The punishment for disorderly conduct is usually fixed by statute. Under most statutes the penalty consists of a fine, imprisonment, or both. Some statutes provide that an accused cannot be imprisoned for disorderly conduct unless he or she has been given an opportunity to pay a fine and has defaulted on the payment.

See also DISTURBANCE OF THE PEACE.

DISORDERLY HOUSE 📖 A place where individuals reside or which they frequent for purposes that pose a threat to public health, morals, convenience, or safety, and that may create a public NUISANCE. A *disorderly house* is an all-inclusive term that may be used to describe such places as a house of PROSTITUTION, an illegal gambling casino, or a site where drugs are constantly bought and sold. It is any place where unlawful practices are habitually carried on by the public. 📖

Various offenses concerning disorderly houses exist at COMMON LAW and under criminal statutes. The maintenance of a disorderly house is considered to be an ongoing offense and, at times, the offense involves a specific type of place, such as a bordello or GAMING house. The offenses are divided into four classes, which encompass keeping or maintaining a disorderly house, letting a house to be used as a disorderly house, frequenting or abiding permanently in a disorderly house, and disguising a disorderly house by displaying a sign of an honest occupation—such as disguising a house of prostitution as a dress shop.

Statutes In most jurisdictions, the maintenance of a disorderly house is an offense and, in order to be valid, each statute must clearly state the nature of the offense. Ordinarily, most

statutes merely define the common-law offense rather than create a new statute. In states with statutes that provide for the punishment of an offense but do not define what a disorderly house is, the common law is examined to determine what the definition should be. In contrast, where the statute embodies a characterization of the house as well as prohibited conduct therein, the statute itself determines what constitutes the offense.

The prohibition against disorderly houses and the offenses they encompass are valid exercises of the POLICE POWER of the state.

Elements The elements of the offense of maintaining a disorderly house depend on statutory provisions that vary from state to state. A place may be named a disorderly house if ALCOHOL is sold on the premises and if the law in that jurisdiction prohibits such sale. Essential to all offenses involving disorderly houses is the character of the house.

House or Other Building or Place The commission of the offense is dependent upon the presence of a house or place of public resort, the physical characteristics of which are immaterial. A disorderly house may be any place, including a room in a building or a steamship, an apartment, a garden, or a space under the grandstand at the racetrack.

The character of the place as a public resort is important. The general rule is that a disorderly house must be a place to which the general public or a segment of the public retreats for immoral purposes without prior invitation. A disorderly house may be used for other purposes that are not prohibited by law in addition to immoral purposes, but this in no way affects its classification as a disorderly house.

Annoyance or Injury to the Public The annoyance to the general public, as opposed to anyone in particular, is an essential element of the definition of a disorderly house. This annoyance or injury is based on the fact that activities being conducted are considered detrimental to public morals, welfare, and safety. They need not disturb the peace and quiet of a neighborhood to be construed as disorderly. A house where drugs are sold quietly or where a bordello is discreetly operated would be considered an endangerment to the public peace.

Persons Liable The LIABILITY of those concerned in offenses in connection with disorderly houses is not based upon their civil or contractual status. Some statutes specify who may be liable and in such cases, only those designated may be prosecuted. Partners, servants, and AGENTS as well as the officers of a

CORPORATION have all been held liable for the operation of disorderly houses and the various offenses committed on the premises.

DISPARAGEMENT In old English law, an injury resulting from the comparison of a person or thing with an individual or thing of inferior quality; to discredit oneself by marriage below one's class. A statement made by one person that casts aspersions on another person's goods, property, or intangible things.

In TORTS, a considerable body of law has come about concerning interference with business or economic relations. The tort of INJURIOUS FALSEHOOD, or disparagement, is concerned with the publication of derogatory information about a person's TITLE to his or her property, to his or her business in general, or anything else made for the purpose of discouraging people from dealing with the individual. Generally, if the aspersions are cast upon the quality of what the person has to sell, or the person's business itself, proof of DAMAGES is essential.

Disparagement of goods is a false or misleading statement by an entrepreneur about a competitor's goods. It is made with the intention of influencing people adversely so they will not buy the goods.

Disparagement of title is a false or MALICIOUS statement made about an individual's title to real or personal property. Such disparagement may result in a pecuniary loss due to impairment of vendibility that the defamatory statements might cause.

See also DEFAMATION.

DISPOSABLE EARNINGS That portion of one's income that a person is free to spend or invest as he or she sees fit, after payment of taxes and other obligations.

Legally mandated DEDUCTIONS are those for the payment of taxes and SOCIAL SECURITY. Any deductions for medical insurance, pension plans, life insurance, or employee savings plans do not qualify and must be included in the disposable earnings. Take-home pay is, therefore, not necessarily synonymous with disposable earnings because of this distinction between the deductions.

The federal CONSUMER CREDIT PROTECTION ACT (15 U.S.C.A. § 1601 et seq. [1968]) establishes a minimum amount of disposable earnings that can be garnished by a debtor's CREDITORS. The lesser figure of 25 percent of a worker's weekly disposable earnings or the amount by which his or her disposable earnings exceed thirty times the maximum hourly wage is subject to GARNISHMENT.

State laws also impose restrictions on the garnishment of debtor's wages.

DISPOSITION Act of disposing; transferring to the care or possession of another. The parting with, alienation of, or giving up of property. The final settlement of a matter and, with reference to decisions announced by a court, a judge's ruling is commonly referred to as disposition, regardless of level of resolution. In criminal procedure, the sentencing or other final settlement of a criminal case. With respect to a mental state, means an attitude, prevailing tendency, or inclination.

DISPOSITIVE FACT Information or EVIDENCE that unqualifiedly brings a conclusion to a legal controversy.

Dispositive facts clearly settle an issue. The fact that the defendant in a PERSONAL INJURY case ran a red light and hit the plaintiff with his or her car settles the question of the defendant's NEGLIGENCE and is, therefore, a dispositive fact.

DISPOSSESSION The wrongful, nonconsensual ouster or removal of a person from his or her property by trick, compulsion, or misuse of the law, whereby the violator obtains actual occupation of the land.

The term encompasses intrusion, disseisin, or DEFORCEMENT.

DISPUTE A conflict or controversy; a conflict of claims or rights; an assertion of a right, claim, or demand on one side, met by contrary claims or allegations on the other. The subject of litigation; the matter for which a suit is brought and upon which issue is joined, and in relation to which jurors are called and witnesses examined.

A *labor dispute* is any disagreement between an employer and his or her employees concerning anything job-related, such as tenure, hours, wages, fringe benefits, and employment conditions.

During a labor dispute at American Airlines these striking employees picketed an airport, encouraging customers to fly on other airlines.

DISQUALIFY 📖 To deprive of eligibility or render unfit; to disable or incapacitate. 📖

To be disqualified is to be stripped of legal CAPACITY. A wife would be disqualified as a juror in her husband's trial for murder due to the nature of their relationship. A person may be disqualified for employment at a certain job because of a physical disability.

DISSENT 📖 An explicit disagreement by one or more judges with the decision of the majority on a case before them. 📖

A dissent is often accompanied by a written dissenting OPINION, and the terms *dissent* and *dissenting opinion* are used interchangeably.

Dissents have several functions. In some cases, they are a simple declaration of disagreement with the majority. In others, they instruct, prod, scold, or otherwise urge the majority to consider the dissenter's point of view.

Dissents carry no precedential weight and are not relied on as authority in subsequent cases. However, attorneys and judges sometimes consult them to understand the dissenter's analysis of the majority opinion. Attorneys and judges may also cite a dissent if they agree with its reasoning and conclusion and seek support for a change in the law.

Although the majority opinion constitutes the judgment of the court, its legal weight can be diminished if a sufficient number of judges dissent. On issues that divide the courts and the country, there can be sharply divergent opinions on what the law is or should be. During the 1990s, for example, one divisive question before the U.S. Supreme Court was whether AFFIRMATIVE ACTION programs to redress the effects of past DISCRIMINATION were constitutional. In *Miller v. Johnson*, 515 U.S. 900, 115 S. Ct. 2475, 132 L. Ed. 2d 762 (1995), the U.S. Supreme Court held that Georgia's congressional redistricting plan, implemented to give minorities a strong voting block, constituted racial GERRYMANDERING and violated the Equal Protection Clause. However, the case was not an unqualified success for those urging the rejection of affirmative action. Five justices joined in the majority block (plurality) in the case, and four justices filed dissents. With such a large minority, the dissents gained significance. Legal analysts monitor close cases such as *Miller* because a shift by one justice would signal a change in the law.

Dissents are a relatively recent phenomenon. Chief Justice JOHN MARSHALL, who served on the Supreme Court from 1801 to 1835, urged unanimity on the Court to demonstrate that its opinions were the last word on an issue. Others believed that individual conscience should dictate a justice's opinions, without regard to unanimity. In its early years, most of the Supreme Court's decisions showed little or no dissent. During the late 19th century and early 20th century, as the Court became firmly established as the law of the land, more dissents appeared. Yet, even those who dissented during this period often recognized the importance of consensus opinions. For instance, Justice OLIVER WENDELL HOLMES, JR., a frequent and famous dissenter, wrote a scathing dissent in *Lochner v. New York*, 198 U.S. 45, 25 S. Ct. 539, 49 L. Ed. 937 (1905), but not before he expressed his reluctance to do so: "I regret sincerely that I am unable to agree with the judgment in this case, and that I think it is my duty to express my dissent" *(Lochner)*.

By the 1960s and 1970s, dissents were an accepted part of the Court's business, perhaps reflecting the fractious political and social climate of those years. One frequent dissenter during the mid–twentieth century was Justice WILLIAM O. DOUGLAS. During his thirty-six years on the Court, from 1939 to 1975, Douglas wrote 524 opinions of the Court, 154 concurring opinions, and an astounding 486 dissenting opinions. In addition, he dissented without opinion in 309 cases.

Justice BENJAMIN N. CARDOZO, of the Supreme Court, defended those who disagree with the majority, writing that the dissenter is "the gladiator making a last stand against the lions." A few justices raised their roles as dissenters to an art form. Justices WILLIAM J. BRENNAN, JR., and THURGOOD MARSHALL displayed particular courage in opposition to the majority. During their long tenure on the Court, Brennan and Marshall were unwavering in their conviction that the death penalty violates the Constitution. By doggedly and relentlessly repeating their dissent, they sought to win

Justice William Brennan, Jr., along with Thurgood Marshall, opposed the majority of the Supreme Court on the issue of capital punishment repeatedly by submitting dissents to majority opinions in many cases.

AP/WIDE WORLD PHOTOS

others to their view that the law on CAPITAL PUNISHMENT should be changed.

Together as well as separately, Brennan and Marshall wrote scores of dissents in death penalty cases. In so doing, they opposed clear precedent that supported the legality of capital punishment. However, both were convinced that they were justified in their continued opposition. Brennan felt that the intrinsic morality of the EIGHTH AMENDMENT superseded any right of individual states to impose capital punishment. He wrote, "It would effectively write the (Cruel and Unusual Punishment) [C]lause out of the Bill of Rights were we to permit legislatures to police themselves by having the last word on the scope of the protection that the clause is intended to secure against their own overreaching." Marshall's opposition was less philosophical and more practical. He repeatedly pointed out that the application of the death penalty was arbitrary and unfair, and affected minorities disproportionately. He felt a responsibility to continue bringing this issue before the public and believed that most people, if sufficiently informed about all its ramifications, would find capital punishment "shocking, unjust, and unacceptable" (*Furman v. Georgia*, 408 U.S. 238, 92 S. Ct. 2726, 33 L. Ed. 2d 346 [1972] [Marshall, J., dissenting]).

Some legal analysts believe that dissents are an important part of the system of checks and balances. Justice CHARLES E. HUGHES—who served on the Court from 1910 to 1916, left the bench to run for president, and then returned to the Court as chief justice from 1930 to 1941—wrote, "A dissent . . . is an appeal to the brooding spirit of the law, to the intelligence of a future day, when a later decision may possibly correct the error into which the dissenting judge believes the court to have been betrayed."

See also COURT OPINION.

DISSOLUTION 📖 Act or process of dissolving; termination; winding up. In this sense it is frequently used in the phrase *dissolution of a partnership.* 📖

The dissolution of a CONTRACT is its RESCISSION by the parties themselves or by a court that nullifies its binding force and reinstates each party to his or her original position prior to the contract.

The dissolution of a CORPORATION is the termination of its existence as a legal entity. This might occur pursuant to a statute, the surrender or expiration of its CHARTER, legal proceedings, or BANKRUPTCY.

In domestic relations law, the term *dissolution* refers to the ending of a marriage through DIVORCE.

The dissolution of a PARTNERSHIP is the end of the relationship that exists among the partners as a result of any partner discontinuing his or her involvement in the partnership, as distinguished from the winding up of the outstanding obligations of the business.

DISSOLVE 📖 To terminate; abrogate; cancel; annul; disintegrate. To release or unloose the binding force of anything. 📖

The dissolution of something is the act of disorganizing or disuniting it, as in marriage, contracts, or corporations.

DISTINGUISH 📖 To set apart as being separate or different; to point out an essential disparity. 📖

To distinguish one case from another case means to show the dissimilarities between the two. It means to prove a case that is cited as applicable to the case currently in dispute is really inapplicable because the two cases are different.

DISTRAIN 📖 To seize the PROPERTY of an individual and retain it until an obligation is performed. The taking of the goods and CHATTELS of a tenant by a LANDLORD in order to satisfy an unpaid debt. 📖

Distrain is a comprehensive term that may be used in reference to any detention of PERSONAL PROPERTY, lawful or unlawful.

Several families were evicted from houses owned by Gallaway Mills in May 1935. If the families owed further debts to the landlord, their personal possessions could be distrained, or seized, in order to satisfy the debt.

UPI/CORBIS-BETTMANN

DISTRESS 📖 The seizure of PERSONAL PROPERTY for the satisfaction of a demand. 📖

The process of distress, sometimes called DISTRAIN, began at COMMON LAW wherein a LANDLORD had the right to confiscate the CHATTELS of a tenant who had defaulted on a rent payment. Today, it is regulated by statute, and is used to mean the taking of property to enforce the performance of some obligation.

A *warrant of distress* is a WRIT that authorizes an officer to seize a person's goods. It is usually used in situations where a landlord has the right to obtain a LIEN on a tenant's goods for nonpayment of rent.

If personal property is seized to enforce the payment of taxes and then publicly sold if the taxes are not subsequently paid, the sale is called a *distress sale*. *Distressed goods* are chattels sold at a distress sale.

DISTRIBUTEE 📖 An HEIR; a person entitled to share in the distribution of an ESTATE. This term is used to denote one of the persons who is entitled, under the statute of distributions, to the personal estate of one who is dead INTESTATE. 📖

DISTRIBUTOR 📖 A wholesaler; an individual, CORPORATION, or PARTNERSHIP buying goods in bulk quantities from a manufacturer at a price close to the cost of manufacturing them and reselling them at a higher price to other dealers, or to various retailers, but not directly to the general public. 📖

DISTRICT 📖 One of the territorial areas into which an entire state or country, county, municipality, or other political subdivision is divided, for judicial, political, electoral, or administrative purposes.

The CIRCUIT or territory within which a person may be compelled to appear. Circuit of authority; province. 📖

A *judicial district* is a designated area of a state over which a court has been empowered to hear lawsuits that arise within it or that involve its inhabitants. A *federal judicial district* is an area of a state in which a federal DISTRICT COURT sits to determine matters involving FEDERAL QUESTIONS or DIVERSITY OF CITIZENSHIP of the parties.

A *congressional district* is a geographical subdivision of a state that elects a representative to CONGRESS.

A *legislative district* is a specific section of a state that elects a representative to the state legislature.

DISTRICT AND PROSECUTING ATTORNEYS 📖 The elected or appointed public officers of each state, county, or other political subdivision who institute criminal proceedings on behalf of the government. 📖

Federal attorneys who represent the United States in prosecuting federal offenses are U.S. attorneys.

A district or prosecuting attorney is the legal representative of the state, county, or municipality, whose primary function resides in instituting criminal proceedings against violators of state or municipal penal laws. The law of the particular JURISDICTION determines whether they are appointed or elected to office and their term of office.

The legislature may, within the restrictions imposed by constitution or statute, prescribe

the qualifications of the prosecuting attorney. He or she may be required to reside in the district or satisfy a particular minimum-age requisite. District attorneys usually must be attorneys-at-law who are licensed to practice in the state and, depending upon the jurisdiction, must have spent a specified number of years practicing law.

The duty of the district attorney is to ensure that offenses committed against the public are rectified pursuant to the commencement of criminal prosecutions. He or she may exercise considerable discretion in ascertaining the manner in which the duty of district attorney should be performed. The prosecuting attorney, however, must be fair and unbiased, and refrain from conduct that would deprive the defendant of any constitutional or statutory right. The legislature may regulate his or her functions within statutory or constitutional limitations.

A district attorney determines when to initiate a particular prosecution and must exercise due diligence in conducting the prosecution. The individual may neither restrain the GRAND JURY from considering charges by asserting that the government will not prosecute nor dismiss a criminal charge pending before it. He or she does, however, maintain control of criminal proceedings in the trial court. Statutes define the duties of the prosecuting attorney with respect to civil litigation.

The respective powers of the district attorney and of the ATTORNEY GENERAL, the principal law officer of the state, are ordinarily disparate. Neither the district attorney nor the attorney general may impinge upon powers reserved exclusively to the other.

A district attorney is immune from LIABILITY for DAMAGES incurred as a result of his or her acts or omissions that occur within the scope of official duties, although the person may be held liable for conduct in excess of such scope.

Statutes prescribe the compensation of prosecuting attorneys.

A prosecuting attorney whose term is regulated by law cannot be removed or suspended from office, other than pursuant to the manner authorized by constitution or statute. The grounds specified by law govern removal. Mere misconduct committed in office, such as habitual intoxication, is usually an insufficient basis for removal. In some jurisdictions, however, conduct that is entirely extraneous to official duties may reveal flaws in personal character that render the individual unfit to hold the office and subject him or her to removal.

Suspension or removal may ensue from official misconduct or neglect of duty, such as the improper refusal to initiate criminal investigations or prosecutions, or inept execution of such proceedings.

Removal may also be justified on the basis of the prosecuting attorney's failure to comply with the constitutional duties of disclosure imposed by *Brady v. Maryland*, 373 U.S. 83, 83 S. Ct. 1194, 10 L. Ed. 2d 215 (1963). The Supreme Court held that "the suppression by the prosecution of evidence favorable to an accused upon request violates due process where the evidence is material either to guilt or to punishment, irrespective of the good faith or bad faith of the prosecution."

Removal of a prosecuting attorney may also be predicated on his or her conferral of positions in the office to friends or relatives regardless of their qualifications.

The removal process must comply with constitutional or statutory requirements. In some jurisdictions, the district attorney may be removed by the court in proceedings commenced by the interested parties or by IMPEACHMENT. The legislature, within constitutional limitations, may designate the nature of the removal proceeding.

Statutes provide for the appointment of assistant district attorneys to render supplementary services to the district attorney. Independent of statute, however, the courts frequently exercise discretionary power to appoint attorneys to assist the prosecuting attorney in criminal cases. Statutes primarily govern the qualifications, salary, tenure, powers, and removal of such attorneys.

SPECIAL PROSECUTORS are attorneys appointed by the government to investigate criminal offenses involving officials of the executive branch, since the government cannot effectively investigate itself.

CROSS-REFERENCES

Criminal Procedure; Due Process of Law; Prosecutor; Selective Prosecution.

DISTRICT COURT 📖 A designation of an

inferior state court that exercises GENERAL JURISDICTION that it has been granted by the constitution or statute which created it. A U.S. judicial tribunal with ORIGINAL JURISDICTION to try CASES OR CONTROVERSIES that fall within its limited JURISDICTION. 📖

A state district might, for example, determine civil actions between state residents based upon CONTRACT violations or tortious conduct that occurred within the state.

Federal district courts are located in places designated by federal law, hearing cases in at least one place in every state. Most federal cases, whether civil actions or criminal prosecutions for violations of federal law, commence in

district court. Cases arising under the Constitution, federal law, or treaty, or cases between citizens of different states, must also involve an interest worth more than $75,000 before the district court can exercise its jurisdiction.

The federal district courts also have original and exclusive jurisdiction of BANKRUPTCY cases, and ADMIRALTY, maritime, and PRIZE cases, which determine rights in ships and cargo captured at sea. State courts are powerless to hear these kinds of controversies.

A party can APPEAL a decision made in district court in the COURT OF APPEAL.

See also FEDERAL COURTS.

DISTRICT OF COLUMBIA "To exercise exclusive Legislation in all Cases whatsoever, over such District (not exceeding ten miles square) as may, by Cession of particular States, and the acceptance of Congress, become the Seat of the Government of the United States" (U.S. Const. art. I, § 8). The U.S. Constitution, with this proclamation, left the legal formation of a national capital up to the U.S. Congress. To this day, the District of Columbia is neither a state nor a territory and remains under congressional JURISDICTION.

History The location of the national capital was born out of a political compromise between the northern and southern states after the United States had achieved its independence. The South feared that the North would have too much influence if the capital were placed in a northern city. The North demanded federal assistance in paying its Revolutionary War debt, something the South was strongly against. ALEXANDER HAMILTON initiated a compromise whereby the federal government would pay off the war debt in return for locating the capital between the states of Maryland and Virginia on the Potomac River.

In 1800 Virginia and Maryland ceded portions of land to the federal government. The citizens living in the new capital were required to give up all the political rights they had enjoyed as inhabitants of Maryland and Virginia. In return, Congress, which had exclusive power over the district, would allow them some form of self-government. In 1802 Congress called for an appointed mayor and an elected council in the district. By 1820 the election of the mayor was also permitted.

This form of representative government lasted in the district until 1874, when Congress abolished the citizens' right to vote for their local officials and established a three-person board of commissioners appointed by the president. For over one hundred years, the residents of the District of Columbia were denied the democratic right to elected local representation.

Although residents of the district had always been required to pay federal INCOME TAX and serve in the military, their right to vote in presidential ELECTIONS had been denied until the 1961 passage of the Twenty-third Amendment to the Constitution. This amendment granted the district a number of votes in the ELECTORAL COLLEGE, not to exceed the number given to the least populous state.

Home Rule In 1967 through an executive order (Exec. Order No. 11379, 32 FR 15625, 1967 WL 7776 [Pres.]), President LYNDON B. JOHNSON did away with the three-member board of commissioners and appointed a mayor and a council for the district. In 1970 the district was given back its nonvoting delegate in Congress. But this still did not satisfy residents who demanded full self-determination. Congress then passed the District Home Rule Act of 1973 (Pub. L. 93-198, Dec. 24, 1973, 87 Stat. 774) and restored to the citizens their right to vote for a local government. For the first time in exactly a hundred years, the residents of the District of Columbia were able to vote for a mayor and a thirteen-member council.

The Constitution granted Congress complete legislative authority over the District of Columbia. Congress alone has the jurisdiction to expand the district's powers over local government affairs. It also has the jurisdiction to

contract those same powers. Congress, through the Home Rule Act, dictated the legislative powers to the district council and the executive powers to the mayor. Advisory neighborhood commissions, which are groups elected by the residents, advise the council on matters of public policy. Congress still retains ultimate legislative authority through its power to veto any of the district's legislation.

Statehood Besides the citizens of U.S. territories, district residents are the only U.S. citizens without full representation in Congress and with federal limitations on their own local government. Advocates of statehood rebel against such restrictions. They argue that because the district's congressional delegate is not allowed to vote, residents are subject to a fundamental democratic wrong, TAXATION without representation. They add that because Congress retains control over the city's purse strings, city officials are powerless in raising more revenue. Federal restrictions on taxation have prevented the district from taxing commuters as have some other U.S. cities, which could have given the district a huge tax windfall.

Opponents of statehood argue that the District of Columbia belongs to all U.S. citizens, and therefore all citizens should have a say in how it is managed. Constitutionally, Congress has complete authority over the district, and to

This 1792 engraving of the design for the District of Columbia by Andrew Ellicott was based on Pierre L'Enfant's manuscript. The plan was adopted as the final design for the Federal City of Washington.

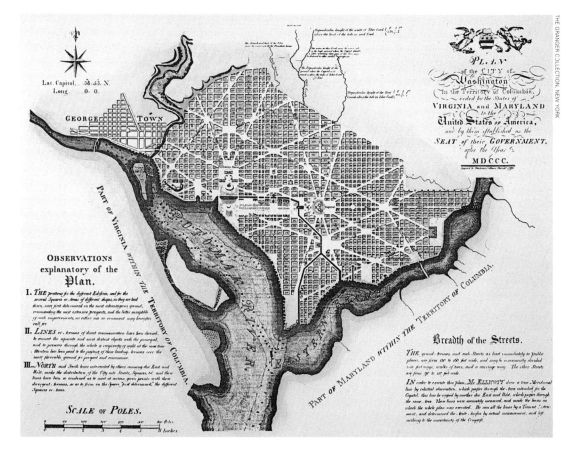

have it otherwise would require a constitutional amendment (supporters dismiss this argument, pointing out that thirty-seven states were allowed into the Union through only a simple majority vote in Congress). If the district were to become an independent state, some opponents argue, the federal government would have to abide by the laws of this new state. Opponents of statehood also maintain that the district's power needs to be checked by Congress because of the district's financial difficulties.

The push toward statehood has become a partisan issue, with the Democratic party generally in favor of it and the Republican party generally opposed. One reason for this division is the political makeup of the city, which is predominantly Democratic. Statehood would add more Democratic members to the House and the Senate. When the Democrats won the White House in 1992, the stage was set for the statehood issue to move forward through the 103d Congress.

On November 21, 1993, the House considered Bill 51, calling for the creation of New Columbia, the nation's fifty-first state. Democrats spoke in favor of statehood, saying it would give D.C. residents the same benefits of citizenship as are enjoyed by other U.S. citizens. Republicans spoke out against it, saying the city was unable to govern itself. Republican sentiments carried the day, defeating the bill by a vote of 277 to 153.

The Courts The courts of the District of Columbia were established by an act of Congress. Originally, FEDERAL COURTS heard controversies that arose in the District of Columbia. Disputes over federal or district law came under the jurisdiction of the federal district courts. Appeals went from the district courts to the Court of Appeals for the District of Columbia Circuit, and then to the U.S. Supreme Court.

Just as the legislative branch of the district government became less dependent on the federal system in the 1970s, so too did the courts. The district court system was completely reorganized under the district of Columbia Court Reform and Criminal Procedure Act of 1970 (Pub. L. 91-358, July 29, 1970, 84 Stat. 473; Pub. L. 99-573, § 17, Oct. 28, 1973, 100 Stat. 3234, 3235). The U.S. District court no longer has jurisdiction over criminal or civil actions occurring under D.C. law. These cases are now heard by the district's new trial court, the Superior Court. The District of Columbia Court of Appeals has jurisdiction to review decisions of the Superior Court.

DISTURBANCE OF PUBLIC MEETINGS
It was a MISDEMEANOR at COMMON LAW to be guilty of conduct that tended to disturb a public

assembly, though the prosecution, in most instances, was required to prove that the disturbance was caused wantonly or willfully. In most jurisdictions there is statutory crime for such conduct and the disturbance need not be so turbulent as to constitute a RIOT.

DISTURBANCE OF THE PEACE An offense constituting a MALICIOUS and willful intrusion upon the peace and quiet of a community or neighborhood.

The crime is usually committed by an offensive or tumultuous act, such as the making of loud or unusual noises, or quarreling in public.

The term is similar in meaning to BREACH OF THE PEACE; however, the latter is generally a broader term, encompassing all violations of public peace and order. It can also be a form of DISORDERLY CONDUCT and is similarly punishable upon conviction by a fine, imprisonment, or both.

DIVERS Several; any number more than two; different.

Divers is a collective term used to group a number of unspecified people, objects, or acts. It is used frequently to describe property, as in divers parcels of land.

DIVERSION A turning aside or altering of the natural course or route of a thing. The term is chiefly applied to the unauthorized change or alteration of a water course to the prejudice of a lower riparian, or to the unauthorized use of funds.

A program for the disposition of a criminal charge without a criminal trial; sometimes called operation de nova, intervention, or deferred prosecution.

The disposition is conditional on the defendant's performing certain tasks or participating in a treatment program. If the conditions are successfully completed, the charge is dismissed. But if the accused does not meet his or her obligations, prosecution may be instituted.

See also RIPARIAN RIGHTS.

DIVERSITY OF CITIZENSHIP A phrase used with reference to the JURISDICTION of the FEDERAL COURTS which, under the U.S. Constitution, Art. III, § 2, extends to cases between CITIZENS of different states designating the condition existing when the party on one side of a lawsuit is a citizen of one state and the party on the other side is a citizen of another state, or between a citizen of a state and an ALIEN. The requisite jurisdictional amount must, in addition, be met.

Diversity of citizenship is one of the factors that will allow a federal DISTRICT COURT to exercise its authority to hear a lawsuit. This authority is called diversity jurisdiction. It means that a case involving questions that must be answered according to state laws may be heard in federal court if the PARTIES on the two sides of the case are from different states. No matter how many parties are involved in a lawsuit, there must be complete diversity in order for the federal court to exercise this type of authority. If a single plaintiff is a citizen of the same state as any defendant, there is no diversity and the case must be pursued in a state court.

Being a citizen of a state is something more than simply owning property or being physically present within the state. Citizenship means that the individual has a RESIDENCE in the state and intends to have that residence as his or her present home. Residence plus this intent makes that place the individual's domicile, and a party can have only one domicile at a time. Citizenship does not mean that the individual must swear that he or she never intends to move, but the residence and the intent to consider it home are essential. Students, prisoners, and service personnel can establish a domicile in a state even though they are living in it involuntarily or temporarily.

CORPORATIONS are citizens of the state in which they are incorporated and also of the state where they maintain their principal place of business. This citizenship in two places has the effect of narrowing the number of cases that qualify for a federal court's diversity jurisdiction because a corporation's citizenship is not diverse from the citizenship of anyone else in either of those two states.

The citizenship of each party must be determined as of the time the lawsuit is commenced. A party's domicile at the time of the events that give rise to the cause of action or a change of domicile during the course of proceedings does not affect the court's jurisdiction. This rule, of course, gives a person contemplating a lawsuit the opportunity to change his or her domicile just before serving legal papers that start an ACTION. This tactic has been challenged on a few occasions on the ground that it violates another federal law that prohibits COLLUSION to create federal jurisdiction. Generally, the courts have ruled that a plaintiff's motives in moving to a new state are not determinative, and the only question is whether in fact the plaintiff's domicile is different from that of the defendants at the time the lawsuit begins.

The right of an individual to take his or her case into a federal court is assured by Article III, § 2 of the U.S. Constitution. This provision extends the federal judicial power to controversies between the citizen of a state and the government of a different state, citizens of a different state, or between a state or its citizens and a foreign government or its citizens. It is put into effect by a statute that limits federal diversity jurisdiction to cases involving a dispute worth more than $10,000. This minimum is intended to keep small cases from clogging the calendars of federal courts. Cases worth less than $10,000 must be brought in a state court even though diversity of the parties' citizenship otherwise would entitle them to be brought in federal court.

The origin and purposes of federal diversity jurisdiction have long been debated. It was created when the Constitution was first adopted, a time when loyalty to one's state was usually stronger than feelings for the United States. It was undoubtedly intended to balance national purposes with the independence of the states. Chief Justice JOHN MARSHALL of the Supreme Court wrote in *Bank of United States v. Deveaux*, 9 U.S. (5 Cranch) 61, 87, 3 L. Ed. 38 (1809):

> However true the fact may be, that the tribunals of the states will administer justice as impartially as those of the nation, . . . it is not less true that the constitution itself either entertains apprehensions on this subject, or views with such indulgence the possible fears and apprehensions of suitors, that it has established national tribunals for the decision of controversies . . . between citizens of different states.

Some scholars believe that the opportunity to take business and commercial disputes into an impartial federal court helped to encourage investment in the developing South and West. People from the industrialized Northeast felt more secure when their financial transactions in other states were not necessarily at the mercy of local prejudices.

Even if diversity jurisdiction did help the economic growth of the United States, many people question whether it continues to be useful. Because these cases require substantial investments of time and energy by the federal judiciary in cases that arise under state law, proposals to curtail or abolish diversity jurisdiction have been introduced repeatedly in Congress since the 1920s. None of the proposals have been adopted, however.

DIVEST ◫ To deprive or take away. ◫

Divest is usually used in reference to the relinquishment of authority, power, PROPERTY, or TITLE. If, for example, an individual is disinherited, he or she is divested of the right to inherit money. Similarly, an individual may be divested of his or her citizenship for TREASON.

Divest is also spelled *devest*.

DIVIDEND 📖 The distribution of current or accumulated earnings to the shareholders of a corporation PRO RATA based on the number of shares owned. Dividends are usually issued in cash. However, they may be issued in the form of STOCK or property. The dividend on preferred shares is generally a fixed amount; however, on common shares the dividend varies depending on such things as the earnings and available cash of the CORPORATION as well as future plans for the acquisition of property and equipment by the corporation. 📖

DIVINE RIGHT OF KINGS 📖 The authority of a monarch to rule a realm by virtue of birth. 📖

The concept of the divine right of kings, as postulated by the patriarchal theory of government, was based upon the laws of God and nature. The king's power to rule was derived from his ancestors who, as monarchs, were appointed to serve by God. Regardless of misconduct, a king or his heir could not be forced to forfeit the right to the obedience of subjects or the right to succeed to the throne. This concept was formulated to dispel any possibility of papal and ecclesiastical claims to supremacy in secular as well as spiritual matters.

DIVORCE 📖 A court decree that terminates a MARRIAGE; also known as marital dissolution. 📖

A divorce decree establishes the new relations between the parties, including their duties and obligations relating to property they own, support responsibilities of either or both of them, and provisions for any children.

When a marriage breaks up, divorce law provides legal solutions for issues that the HUSBAND AND WIFE are unable to resolve through mutual cooperation. Historically, the most important question in a divorce case was whether a divorce should be granted by the court. If a divorce was granted, the resolution of continuing obligations was simple: the wife was awarded custody of any children, and the husband was required to support the wife and children.

Modern divorce laws have inverted the involvement of courts. The issue of whether a divorce should be granted is now generally decided by one or both of the spouses. Contemporary courts are more involved in determining the legal ramifications of the marriage breakup, such as spousal maintenance, CHILD SUPPORT, and CHILD CUSTODY. Other legal issues related to divorce include court JURISDICTION, antenuptial and postnuptial agreements, and the right to obtain a divorce. State laws govern a wide range of divorce issues, but district, county, and family courts are given broad discretion in fixing legal obligations between the parties.

In early civilizations marriage and marriage dissolution were considered private matters. Marriage and divorce were first placed under comprehensive state regulation in Rome during the reign of Augustus (27 B.C.–A.D. 14). As Christianity grew, governments came under religious control and the Catholic Church, the most powerful of the Christian sects, strictly forbade divorce. The only exception to this ban was if one of the parties had not been converted to Christianity before the marriage.

During the 1500s the Protestant Reformation movement in Europe rejected religious control over marriage and helped move the matter of divorce from the church to the state. Divorces were granted by European courts upon a showing of fault, such as ADULTERY, CRUELTY, or DESERTION.

England struggled with the matter of divorce. From 1669 to 1850, only 229 divorces were granted in that country. Marriage and divorce were controlled by the Anglican Church, which, like the Catholic Church, strictly forbade divorce. The Anglican Church allowed separations, but neither spouse was allowed to remarry while the other was still living.

The law of divorce in the American colonies varied according to the religious and social mores of the founding colonists. England insisted that its American colonies refrain from enacting legislation that contradicted the restrictive English laws, and a colonial divorce was not considered final until it had been approved by the English monarch. Despite these deterrents a few northern colonies adopted laws allowing divorce in the 1650s.

Divorce law in the middle and northern colonies was often curious. Under one late-seventeenth-century Pennsylvania law, divorce seemed a mere afterthought: if a married man committed SODOMY or BESTIALITY, his punishment was castration, and "the injured wife shall have a divorce if required." In Connecticut divorce was allowed on the grounds of adultery, desertion, and the husband's failure in his CONJUGAL duties. In the Massachusetts Bay Colony, a woman was allowed to divorce her husband if the husband had committed adultery and another offense. A man could divorce if his wife committed adultery or the "cruel usage of the husband."

After the Revolutionary War, divorce law in the United States continued to develop regionally. The U.S. Constitution was silent as to divorce, leaving the matter to the states for regulation. For the next 150 years, state legislatures passed and maintained laws that granted

A sample finding of fact and conclusions of law, which are part of a judgment and decree of divorce

[Add Special Term Caption]

Present: Hon. _____, Justice. [Add title of cause]

DECISION

Index No. _____

The above entitled action having been duly brought on for a judgment of divorce in favor of the plaintiff and against the defendant by reason of the cruel and inhuman treatment of the plaintiff by the defendant, and the Summons bearing the notation "Action for a Divorce" having been duly personally served upon the defendant within the State of New York, and the plaintiff having duly complied with the Conciliation Proceeding requirements specified in the Domestic Relations Law, and the defendant not having appeared within the Statutory Period prescribed therefor, and his time to do so has fully expired, and the plaintiff having applied to the Court at a Special Term thereof, held in and for the County of _____, for judgment for the relief demanded in the verified complaint, and the plaintiff having appeared before me by _____, Esq., her attorney, on the _____ day of _____, 19___, and having presented her verified complaint and written and oral proof of the service of the Summons upon the defendant, and the testimony having been taken in open court in support of the allegations of the verified complaint, and due deliberation having been had, I decide and find as follows:

FINDING OF FACT

FIRST: That jurisdiction as required by Section 230 of the Domestic Relations Law has been obtained.

SECOND: That plaintiff and defendant were married on _____, 19___, in _____.

THIRD: That there is issue of this marriage, viz., _____, age _____ years.

FOURTH: That on the _____ day of _____, 19___, defendant at premises located at _____ struck the plaintiff in the face with his fist, causing plaintiff to bleed and require medical attention.

FIFTH: That the conduct of the defendant towards the plaintiff has so endangered the physical or mental well-being of the plaintiff as to render it unsafe or improper for the plaintiff to cohabit with the defendant.

CONCLUSIONS OF LAW

FIRST: That the plaintiff, _____, is entitled to a judgment against the defendant, _____, dissolving the marriage relation heretofore existing between the parties hereto, by reason of the cruel and inhuman treatment of the plaintiff by the defendant, as prayed for in the complaint.

SECOND: That the plaintiff be awarded sole custody of the infant issue of the marriage of the parties, hereto, viz., _____, age _____ years. [*If visitation is granted, add provision for visitation here.*]

THIRD: That the defendant pay to the plaintiff for her support and maintenance, the sum of _____ ($_____) Dollars per week and for the support and maintenance of the infant issue of the marriage of the parties hereto, viz., _____, the sum of _____ ($_____) Dollars per week making the total sum of _____ ($_____) Dollars per week by check or money order at the residence of the plaintiff or at such other place as she may designate in writing commencing from the date of the entry of the judgment herein.

I direct that judgment be entered accordingly.

Dated: _____, New York.

_____, 19___.

_____

Justice of the Supreme Court

divorce only on a showing of FAULT on the part of a spouse. This meant that if a divorce was contested, the divorcing spouse was required to establish, before a court, specific grounds for the action. If the court felt that the divorcing spouse had not proved the grounds alleged, the court was free to deny the PETITION for divorce.

The most common traditional grounds for divorce were cruelty, desertion, and adultery. Other grounds included nonsupport or neglect, alcoholism, drug addiction, insanity, criminal conviction, and voluntary separation. Fault-based divorce laws proliferated, but not without protest. In 1901 author James Bryce was moved to remark that U.S. divorce laws were "the largest and the strangest, and perhaps the saddest, body of legislative experiments in the sphere of family law which free, self-governing communities have ever tried."

In 1933 New Mexico became the first state to allow divorce on the ground of incompatibility. This new ground reduced the need for divorcing spouses to show fault. In 1969 California became the first state to completely revise its divorce laws. The California Family Law Act of 1969 provided, in part, that only one of two grounds was necessary to obtain a divorce: IRRECONCILABLE DIFFERENCES that have caused the irremediable breakdown of the marriage, or incurable insanity (Cal. Civ. Code § D. 4, pt. 5 [West], *repealed by* Stat. 1992, ch. 162 [A.B. 2650], § 3 [operative Jan. 1, 1994]). In divorce proceedings TESTIMONY or EVIDENCE of specific acts of misconduct were excluded. The one exception to this rule was where the court was required to award child custody. In such a case, serious misconduct on the part of one parent would be relevant.

California's was the first comprehensive "no-fault" divorce law, and it inspired a nationwide debate over divorce reform. Supporters of no-fault divorce noted that there were numerous problems with fault-based divorce. Fault-based divorce was an odious event that destroyed friendships. It also encouraged spouses to fabricate one of the grounds for divorce required under statute. No-fault divorce, conversely, recognized that a marriage breakdown may not be the result of one spouse's misconduct. No-fault divorce laws avoided much of the acrimony that plagued fault-based divorce laws. They also simplified the divorce process and made it more consistent nationwide, thus obviating the need for desperate couples to cross state lines in search of simpler divorce laws.

In 1970 the National Conference of Commissioners on Uniform State Laws prepared a Uniform Marriage and Divorce Act, which provides for no-fault divorce if a court finds that the marriage is "irretrievably broken" (U.L.A., Uniform Marriage and Divorce Act § 101 et seq.). Such a finding requires little more than the desire of one spouse to end the marriage. Many state legislatures adopted the law, and by the end of the 1970s, nearly every state legislature had enacted laws allowing no-fault divorce, or divorce after a specified period of separation. Some states replaced all traditional grounds

with a single no-fault provision. Other states added the ground of irreconcilable differences to existing statutes; in such states a divorce petitioner remains free to file for divorce under traditional grounds.

Most states allow the filing of a divorce petition at any time, unless the petitioner has not been a resident of the state for a specified period of time. Some states require a waiting period for their residents. The waiting period can range from six weeks to two or three years.

Illinois and South Dakota maintain the strictest divorce laws. In Illinois a marriage may be dissolved without regard to fault where three conditions exist: the parties have lived apart for a continuous period of two years; irreconcilable differences have caused the irretrievable breakdown of the marriage; and efforts at reconciliation would be impracticable and not in the best interests of the family (Ill.Rev. Stat. ch. 750 I.L.C.S. 5/401(a)(2)). In South Dakota irreconcilable differences are a valid ground for divorce, which suggests some measure of fault blindness (S.D. Codified Laws Ann. § 25:4-2). However, irreconcilable differences exist only when the court determines that there are "substantial reasons for not continuing the marriage and which make it appear that the marriage should be dissolved" (§ 25:4-17.1).

In Minnesota the statute covering dissolution of marriage reads like a primer on no-fault divorce. Minnesota Statutes Annotated, section 518.05, defines dissolution as "the termination of the marital relationship between a husband and wife" and concludes that a divorce "shall be

Duration of Marriage and Median Age at Divorce, 1970 to 1990

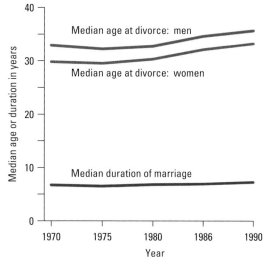

Source: U.S. National Center for Health Statistics of the United States, *Vital Statistics of the United States,* annual.

granted by a county or district court when the court finds there has been an irretrievable breakdown of the marriage relationship." "Irretrievable breakdown" is left undefined in the statute. In Texas the no-fault statute is titled "Insupportability." This law provides that on petition by either party, "a divorce may be decreed without regard to fault if the marriage has become insupportable because of discord or conflict of personalities" that destroys the purpose of marriage and renders reconciliation improbable (Tex. Fam. Code Ann. § 3.01 [West]).

No-fault is not without its detractors. Some critics argue that strict no-fault divorce can provide a cover for serious marital misconduct. By refusing to examine the marital conduct of parties in setting future obligations, some states prevent spouses, usually impoverished wives, from exposing and receiving redress for tortious or criminal conduct. In response to this problem, the vast majority of states have abolished statutes that prevent one spouse from suing the other. However, TORT claims for marital misconduct are often treated with suspicion, and juries are seldom eager to settle marital discord. A marital tort claim is also subject to business judgment: if the case does not appear cost-effective, attorneys may be reluctant to accept it.

Fault has survived in some aspects of divorce proceedings. It was once relevant to a decree of divorce and is relevant to such matters as child custody and property divisions. Under current trends marital misconduct is irrelevant to the divorce itself, but it may be relevant to related matters such as child custody, child support and child visitation rights, spousal maintenance, and property distribution.

Historically, custody of the children of divorcing parents was awarded to the mother. Today, courts exercise their discretion in awarding custody, considering all relevant factors, including marital misconduct, to determine the children's best interests. Many parents are able to reach settlements on custody and visitation through mediation. Joint custody is a popular option among conciliatory spouses. Child custody is, however, a frequent battleground for less-than-conciliatory spouses.

In determining child support obligations, courts generally hold that each parent should contribute in accordance with his or her means. Child support is a mutual duty. However, for preschool children the primary caretaker may not be obligated to obtain employment; in such cases caretaking may be regarded as being in lieu of financial contribution.

All states have enacted some form of the Reciprocal Enforcement of Support Act, a uniform law designed to facilitate the interstate enforcement of support obligations by spouses and parents (U.L.A. Uniform Interstate Family Support Act of 1992). Such statutes prevent a nonsupporting spouse or parent from escaping obligations by moving to a different state. State laws also make nonsupport of a spouse or child a criminal offense, and uniform laws now give states the power to detain and surrender individuals wanted for criminal nonsupport in another state.

Property distribution is frequently contested in modern divorce proceedings. Commonly disputed property includes real estate, personal property, cash savings, stocks, bonds, savings plans, and retirement benefits. The statutes that govern property division vary by state, but they can generally be grouped into two types: equitable distribution and community property. Most states follow the equitable distribution method. Generally, this method provides that courts divide a divorcing couple's assets in a fair and equitable manner given the particular circumstances of the case.

Some equitable distribution states look to the conduct of the parties and permit findings of marital fault to affect property distribution. New Hampshire, Rhode Island, South Carolina, and Vermont have statutes that explicitly include both economic and marital misconduct as factors in the disposition of property. Connecticut, Florida, Maryland, Massachusetts, Missouri, Virginia, and Wyoming all consider marital conduct in property distribution. In Florida and Virginia, only fault relating to economic welfare is relevant in property distribution. Alaska, Kentucky, Minnesota, Montana, and Wisconsin expressly exclude marital misconduct from consideration in the disposition of marital property.

Equitable distribution states generally give the court considerable discretion in which to divide property between the parties. The courts consider not only the joint assets held by the parties, but also separate assets that the parties either brought with them into the marriage or inherited or received as gifts during the marriage. Generally, if the separate property is kept separate during the marriage, and not commingled with joint assets like a joint bank account, then the court will recognize that it belongs separately to the individual spouse and will not divide it along with the marital assets. A minority of states, however, support the idea that all separate property of the parties becomes joint marital property upon marriage.

As for the division of marital assets, equitable distribution states look to the monetary and nonmonetary contributions each spouse made

HENRY HORENSTEIN/THE PICTURE CUBE

to the marriage. If one party made a greater contribution, the court may grant that party a greater share of the joint assets. Some states do not consider a professional degree earned by one spouse during the marriage to be a joint asset, but do acknowledge any financial support contributed by the other spouse and let that be reflected in the property distribution. Other states do consider a professional degree or license to be a joint marital asset and have devised various ways to distribute it or its benefits.

States that follow community property laws provide that nearly all the property acquired during the marriage belongs to the marital "community," such that the husband and wife each have a one-half interest in it upon death or divorce. It is presumed that all property acquired during the marriage by either spouse, including earned income, belongs to the community unless proved otherwise. Exceptions are made for property received as a gift or through inheritance, and for the property each party brought into the marriage. These types of property are considered separate and not part of the community. Upon divorce each party gets his or her own separate property, as well as one-half of the community property. True community property systems exist in Arizona, California, Idaho, Louisiana, Nevada, New Mexico, Texas, and Washington. Other states, such as Wisconsin, have adopted a variation of the community property laws.

ALIMONY, or spousal maintenance, is the financial support that one spouse provides to the other after divorce. It is separate from, and in addition to, the division of marital property. It can be either temporary or permanent. Its use originally arose from the common-law right of a wife to receive support from her husband. Under contemporary law both men and women

Joint custody of children is common for divorced couples who are conciliatory.

are eligible for spousal maintenance. Factors relevant to an order of maintenance include the age and marketable skills of the intended recipient, the length of the marriage, and the income of both spouses.

Maintenance is most often used to provide temporary support to a spouse who was financially dependent on the other during the marriage. Temporary maintenance is designed to provide the necessary support for a spouse until he or she either remarries or becomes self-supporting. Many states allow courts to consider marital fault in determining whether, and how much, maintenance should be granted. These states include Connecticut, Georgia, Hawaii, Iowa, Kansas, Kentucky, Maine, Massachusetts, Missouri, Nebraska, North Carolina, Ohio, Oklahoma, Pennsylvania, Rhode Island, South Carolina, South Dakota, Tennessee, Virginia, West Virginia, and Wisconsin.

Like the entire body of divorce law, the issue of maintenance differs from state to state. If a spouse is found to have caused the breakup of the marriage, Georgia, North Carolina, Virginia, and West Virginia allow a court to refuse maintenance, even if that spouse was financially dependent on the other. North Carolina requires a showing of the supporting spouse's fault before awarding maintenance. Illinois allows fault grounds for divorce but excludes consideration of fault in maintenance and property settlements. Florida offers only no-fault grounds for divorce but admits evidence of adultery in maintenance determinations.

An antenuptial agreement, or premarital agreement, is a contract between persons planning to marry, concerning property rights upon divorce. A postnuptial agreement is a contract entered into by divorcing parties before they reach court. Traditionally, antenuptial agreements were discouraged by state legislatures and courts as being contrary to the public policy in favor of lifetime marriage. An antenuptial agreement is made under the assumption that the marriage may not last forever, which suggests that it facilitates divorce. No state expressly prohibits antenuptial agreements, but, as in any contract case, courts reserve the right to VOID any that it finds UNCONSCIONABLE or to have been made under DURESS.

State statutes that authorize antenuptial and postnuptial agreements usually require that the parties fulfill certain conditions. In Delaware, for example, a man and a woman may execute an antenuptial agreement in the presence of two witnesses at least ten days before their marriage. Such an agreement, if notarized, may be filed as a DEED with the office of the recorder

Divorce law is different in each state and the District of Columbia, but all states have forms of maintenance, child custody, and child support.

in any county of the state (Del. Code Ann. tit. 13, § 301). Both antenuptial and postnuptial contracts concerning REAL ESTATE must be recorded in the registry of deeds where the land is situated (§ 302). See also PREMARITAL AGREEMENT.

Jurisdiction over a divorce case is usually determined by RESIDENCY. That is, a divorcing spouse is required to bring the divorce action in the state where she or he maintains a permanent home. States are obligated to acknowledge a divorce obtained in another state. This rule is from the FULL FAITH AND CREDIT CLAUSE of the U.S. Constitution (art. IV, § 1), which requires states to recognize the valid laws and court orders of other states. However, if the divorce was originally granted by a court with no jurisdictional authority, a state is free to disregard it.

In a divorce proceeding where one spouse is not present (an EX PARTE proceeding), the divorce is given full recognition if the spouse received proper notice and the original divorce FORUM was the bona fide domicile of the divorcing spouse. However, a second state may reject the divorce decree if it finds that the divorce forum was improper.

State courts are not constitutionally required to recognize divorce judgments granted in foreign countries. A U.S. citizen who leaves the country to evade divorce laws will not be protected if the foreign divorce is subsequently challenged. However, where the foreign divorce court had valid jurisdiction over both parties, most U.S. courts will recognize the foreign court's decree.

The only way that an individual may obtain a divorce is through the state. Therefore, under the Due Process Clause of the FOURTEENTH AMENDMENT to the U.S. Constitution, a state must make divorce available to everyone. If a party seeking divorce cannot afford the court

expenses, filing fees, and costs attached to the serving or publication of legal papers, the party may file for divorce free of charge. Most states offer MEDIATION as an alternative to court appearance. Mediation is less expensive and less adversarial than appearing in public court.

In January 1994 the American Bar Association Standing Committee on the Delivery of Legal Services published a report titled *Responding to the Needs of the Self-Represented Divorce Litigant.* In the report the committee recognized that a growing number of persons are divorcing PRO SE, or without the benefit of an attorney. Some of these persons are pro se litigants by choice, but many want the assistance of an attorney and are unable to afford one. In response to this trend, the committee offered several ideas to the state bar associations and state legislatures, including the formation of simplified divorce pleadings and the passage of plainly worded statutes. The committee also endorsed the creation of courthouse day care for children of divorcing spouses, night court divorce sessions, and workshop clinics that give instruction to pro se divorce litigants. Many such programs are currently operating at district, county, and family courts around the United States.

In the United States, divorce law consists of fifty-one different sets of conditions—one for each state and for the District of Columbia. Each state holds dear its power to regulate domestic relations, and peculiar divorce laws abound. Divorce law in most states has nonetheless evolved to recognize the difference between regulating the actual decision to divorce and regulating the practical ramifications of such a decision, such as property distribution, support obligations, and child custody. Most courts ignore marital fault in determining whether to grant a divorce, but many still consider fault in setting future obligations between the parties. To determine the exact nature of the rights and duties related to a divorce, one must consult the relevant statutes for the state in which the divorce is filed.

See also ANNULMENT; FAMILY LAW.

DNA EVIDENCE   Among the many new tools science has provided for the analysis of forensic EVIDENCE is the powerful and controversial analysis of deoxyribonucleic acid, or DNA, the material that makes up the genetic code of all organisms. DNA analysis, also called DNA typing or DNA profiling, examines DNA found in physical evidence such as blood, hair, and semen and determines whether it can be matched to DNA taken from specific individuals. DNA analysis has become a common form of evidence in criminal trials. It is also used in civil litigation, particularly in cases involving the determination of paternity or identity.

History and Process of DNA Analysis DNA, sometimes called the building block or genetic blueprint of life, was first described by the scientists Francis H. C. Crick and James D. Watson in 1953. Crick and Watson identified the double helix structure of DNA, which resembles a twisted ladder, and established the role of DNA as the material that makes up the genetic code of living organisms. The pattern of the compounds that constitute the DNA of an individual life-form determines the development of that life-form. DNA is the same in every cell throughout an individual's body, whether it is a skin cell, sperm cell, or blood cell. With the exception of identical twins, no two individuals have the same DNA blueprint.

DNA analysis was first proposed in 1985 by the English scientist Alec J. Jeffreys. By the late 1980s, it was being performed by law enforcement agencies, including the FEDERAL BUREAU OF INVESTIGATION (FBI), and by commercial laboratories. It consists of comparing selected segments of DNA molecules from different individuals. Because a DNA molecule is made up of billions of segments, only a small proportion of an individual's entire genetic code is analyzed.

In DNA analysis for a criminal investigation, using highly sophisticated scientific equipment, first a DNA molecule from the suspect is disassembled, and selected segments are isolated and measured. Then the suspect's DNA profile is compared with one derived from a sample of physical evidence to see if the two match. If a conclusive nonmatch occurs, the suspect may be eliminated from consideration. If a match occurs, a statistical analysis is performed to determine the probability that the sample of physical evidence came from another person with the same DNA profile as the suspect's. This statistical result is used by juries in determining whether a suspect is guilty or innocent.

Although DNA analysis is sometimes called DNA fingerprinting, this term is a misnomer. Because the entire DNA structure of billions of compounds cannot be evaluated in the same way that an entire fingerprint can, a "match" resulting from DNA typing represents only a statistical likelihood. Thus, the results of DNA typing are not considered absolute proof of identity. A DNA nonmatch is considered conclusive, however, because any variation in DNA structure means that the DNA samples have been drawn from different sources.

An example from the early 1990s illustrates how DNA evidence is used in the criminal justice system. After a Vermont woman was kidnapped and raped in a semitrailer truck, the police identified Randolph Jakobetz, a truck driver, as a suspect in the crime. Police officers searched the trailer hauled by Jakobetz the night of the crime and found hairs matching those of the victim. After arresting Jakobetz, law enforcement officials sent a sample of his blood to the FBI laboratory in Washington, D.C., for DNA analysis and for comparison with DNA taken from semen found in the victim shortly after the crime.

At Jakobetz's trial, an FBI expert testified that the blood and semen samples were a "match," concluding that there was one chance in 300 million that the semen samples could have come from someone other than Jakobetz. Based on this and other strong evidence, Jakobetz was convicted and sentenced to almost thirty years in prison.

Jakobetz appealed the decision, claiming that DNA profiling was unreliable and should not be admitted as evidence. In the first major federal decision on DNA profiling, the Court of Appeals for the Second District upheld the lower court's decision to admit the DNA evidence (*United States v. Jakobetz*, 955 F.2d 786 [2d Cir. 1992]). The U.S. Supreme Court later declined to hear an appeal.

The *Jakobetz* case illustrates how the probabilities generated by DNA analysis can be used

DNA analysis is the comparison of a disassembled DNA molecule from a suspect and one from a piece of physical evidence. A perfect match is unattainable because of the billions of compounds in DNA, but scientists can establish a statistical likelihood of a match.

BILL HORSMAN/STOCK BOSTON

DNA EVIDENCE: BOON OR BOONDOGGLE FOR CRIMINAL JUSTICE?

Since its first use in the late 1980s, DNA typing evidence has been a subject of controversy in the U.S. criminal justice system. Although courts have increasingly allowed DNA analysis to be admitted as evidence, doubts about its use remain. In general, the debate over DNA evidence pits those, such as prosecutors and law enforcement officials, who are eager to use it as a tool to fight crime, against those, particularly defense attorneys, who claim that it is unreliable and will lead to the wrongful conviction of innocent people.

Law enforcement officials and prosecuting attorneys are quick to identify the benefits of DNA typing evidence for the criminal justice system. DNA typing, they argue, is even more useful than fingerprinting, with several advantages over that more traditional tool of investigation. DNA evidence is more readily available in criminal investigations than are legible fingerprints, because body fluids and hair are more likely to be left at the scene of a crime. DNA evidence is also "robust"—that is, it does not decay or disappear over time. The DNA in a piece of physical evidence such as a hair may be examined years after a crime.

Law enforcement officials have confidence in the reliability of DNA analysis performed by commercial and government forensic laboratories. They maintain that innocent people have no need to worry about the use of DNA evidence in the legal system. In fact, they argue, DNA evidence will help to ensure that innocent suspects are not convicted, because the DNA of such suspects will not match that taken from crime-related samples.

Proponents of DNA evidence fear that successful courtroom attacks on its reliability will erode public confidence in its use, giving the state less power to bring criminals to justice. But most remain confident that it will be a permanent part of criminal investigation. Ac-

cording to Eric E. Wright, an assistant attorney general for Maine, "[T]he history of forensic DNA evidence consistently and ever increasingly demonstrates its reliability. It has been subjected to savage scrutiny unlike any forensic science before, and it has survived. Soon the only wonder about DNA evidence will be: What was all the fuss about?"

IN FOCUS

Defense attorneys and others who are skeptical about DNA evidence strongly disagree with many of these claims. While generally accepting the scientific theory behind DNA typing, including its ability to exculpate the innocent suspect, they assert that it is not nearly as reliable in practice as its proponents claim. They argue that DNA evidence may be unreliable for any number of reasons, including contamination owing to improper police procedures, and faulty laboratory work that may produce incorrect results.

Barry C. Scheck is a leading critic of DNA evidence. A professor at the Benjamin N. Cardozo School of Law, a defense attorney in several notable cases involving DNA evidence, and an expert for the defense in the celebrated trial of O. J. Simpson for murder in 1995, Scheck has led the movement for increased scrutiny of DNA evidence. Conceding that "there is no scientific dispute about the validity of the general principles underlying DNA typing," he nevertheless argues that serious problems with DNA evidence remain. He finds particular fault in the work of forensic laboratories, and points to research that has shown that as many as one to four percent of the DNA matches produced by laboratories are in error. Laboratories deny such claims.

Scheck also criticizes the procedures used by laboratories to estimate the likelihood of a DNA match. Because juries consider the probabilities generated by the labs—figures such as one in

300 million or one in 5 million—when assessing the validity of DNA results, it is important to ensure that they are accurate.

DNA critics assert that statistical estimates of a match may be skewed by incorrect assumptions about the genetic variation across a population. In some population subgroups, they claim, individuals may be so genetically similar that a DNA match is more likely to occur when comparing samples drawn from within that subgroup. Examples of such subgroups are geographically isolated populations or tightly knit immigrant or religious communities. Other problems may occur in cases where suspects are closely related to one another. Critics call for more research on population substructures and DNA similarities within them, in order to get a better understanding of statistical properties.

In response to these arguments, proponents of DNA analysis maintain that the importance of frequency calculations has been overrated. They claim that such calculations are, if anything, conservative. Furthermore, they argue that a match itself is more important than a frequency calculation, and that questions of how to calculate frequency should not mean that DNA evidence is inaccurate.

DNA critics call for a number of other procedures to make DNA testing more accurate. They advocate sample splitting, a procedure by which samples of physical evidence are sent to two forensic laboratories in order to better guard against mistaken matches. They also ask that all DNA laboratories be required to undergo proficiency testing through blind trials. Such trials would have laboratories analyze DNA samples without knowing whether the analysis was being done for an actual investigation or for evaluation purposes only. Blind trials would yield error rates for each laboratory that could be given to a jury to help it weigh the significance of DNA evidence. Blind trials would also provide incentives for laboratories to lower their error rates.

Criminal defense lawyers have also called for state-funded access to the services of experts who can evaluate the handling and analysis of DNA evidence. These "counter experts" would give the defense a chance to scrutinize DNA evidence more closely. Defense attorneys also assert the need for access to laboratory records and physical samples for retesting. Providing this access would require the state to preserve samples.

Science may eventually solve many of the problems regarding DNA evidence. In the meantime, debate over its use has already led to changes that will allow courts and juries to better assess the guilt or innocence of criminal suspects.

as devastating evidence against a criminal suspect. Juries have tended to view the statistical results of this analysis as highly incriminating, which has caused many defense attorneys to challenge the validity of the results and many prosecuting attorneys to defend them. At the same time, DNA analysis has also been used by defense attorneys as evidence to reverse the conviction of their clients.

Legal History of DNA Evidence In general, DNA evidence has been increasingly accepted by state and federal courts as ADMISSIBLE evidence. The first state APPELLATE COURT decision to admit DNA evidence was in 1988 (*Andrews v. Florida*, 533 So. 2d 841 [Fla. Dist. Ct. App.]), and the first major FEDERAL COURT decision to admit it occurred in *Jakobetz*. By the mid-1990s, most states allowed DNA test results into evidence.

No court has rejected DNA evidence on the grounds that the underlying scientific theory is invalid. However, some courts have excluded it as evidence because of problems with the possible contamination of samples, questions surrounding the significance of its statistical probabilities, and laboratory errors. Several states have passed laws that recognize DNA evidence as admissible in criminal cases, and others have enacted laws that specifically admit DNA evidence to resolve civil paternity cases.

The admissibility of novel scientific evidence such as DNA profiling is governed by two different judicial tests or standards: the *Frye*, or general acceptance, standard, and the *Daubert*, or relevancy-reliability, standard. The *Frye* test, which comes from the 1923 case *Frye v. United States* 293 F. 1013 (D.C. Cir.), holds that the admissibility of evidence gathered by a specific technique (such as DNA analysis) is determined by whether that technique has been "sufficiently established to have gained general acceptance in the particular field in which it belongs." In *Frye*, the Court of Appeals for the District of Columbia ruled that a lie detector test using a blood pressure reading was not admissible as evidence. By the 1970s, forty-five

states had adopted this common-law standard for the admission of novel scientific evidence.

The U.S. Supreme Court overruled use of the *Frye* test in federal courts in its 1993 decision *Daubert v. Merrell Dow*, 509 U.S. 579, 113 S. Ct. 2786, 125 L. Ed. 2d 469. In *Daubert*, the Court held that the Federal Rules of Evidence, which were created by Congress in 1975, govern the admission of novel scientific evidence in federal courts. It found that *Frye* provides too stringent a test and is incompatible with the federal rules, which allow the admission of all evidence that has "any tendency to make the existence of any fact that is of consequence to the determination of the action more probable or less probable than it would be without the evidence" (rule 401). The Court found that judges have a responsibility to "ensure that any and all scientific testimony or evidence admitted is not only relevant, but reliable."

In general, courts that have used the *Daubert* standard have been more likely to admit DNA evidence, although many JURISDICTIONS that have relied on *Frye* have permitted it as well. Nearly all the cases in which DNA evidence has been ruled inadmissible have been in jurisdictions that have used *Frye*.

States are free to adopt their own standards for the admission of evidence, and have been increasingly adopting the *Daubert* standard. By 1995, the number of states using the *Frye* standard had dropped to twenty-three, while twenty-one had adopted the *Daubert* standard.

See also FORENSIC SCIENCE.

DOCK ⏃ To curtail or diminish, as, for example, to dock a person's wages for lateness or poor work. The cage or enclosed space in a criminal court where prisoners stand when brought in for trial. ⏃

DOCKET ⏃ A written list of judicial proceedings set down for trial in a court.

To enter the dates of judicial proceedings scheduled for trial in a book kept by a court. ⏃

In practice, a docket is a roster that the CLERK of the court prepares, listing the cases pending trial.

An *appearance docket* contains a list of the APPEARANCES in ACTIONS and a brief abstract of the successive steps in each case.

A *judgment docket* is a listing of the JUDGMENTS entered in a particular court that is available to the public for examination. Its purpose is to give official notice of the existence of LIENS or judgments to interested parties.

A *docket fee* is a sum of money charged for the docketing of a case or a judgment or a set amount chargeable as part of the COSTS of the action.

DOCTRINE 📖 A legal rule, tenet, theory, or principle. A political policy. 📖

Examples of common legal doctrines include the clean hands doctrine, the doctrine of FALSE DEMONSTRATION, and the doctrine of MERGER.

The MONROE DOCTRINE, enunciated by President JAMES MONROE on December 2, 1823, was an American policy to consider any aggression by a European country against any western hemisphere country to be a hostile act toward the United States.

DOCTRINE OF EQUALITY OF STATES One of the fundamental rights of a state is equality with all other states. This right is inherent in the concept of a state as a subject of INTERNATIONAL LAW and is given general recognition by long-standing state practice. Precise definition of the principle of equality of states is difficult, however, since many factors affect its application in any particular situation. Thus, it is best to differentiate between *legal equality*, that is, the concept of state equality as it applies to the legal relations that states maintain with each other, and *political equality*, which reflects the relative distribution of economic and military power between states.

In its legal effects the principle of state equality has several important consequences. Probably the most important manifestation of the doctrine is the right of every state to have one vote in matters requiring the consent of states. A natural consequence of this is that the vote of every state, no matter how large or small the state, counts the same as the individual votes of all other states. Legal equality also means that no state can claim JURISDICTION over other states, and as corollary, a state is independent of the political will of all other states. From this also flows the concept of SOVEREIGN IMMUNITY, which prevents one state from being sued in the courts of another state without the consent of the first state. Likewise, equality of states means that no other state can question the legality of official acts of another state, a rule known in U.S. law as the act of state doctrine.

The doctrine of equality of states means one thing in legal effect, but it also must be reflected against the realities imposed by differences in political power. Political equality is in some sense a fiction, because in political terms few states are equals. More powerful states can establish arrangements that less powerful states assent to informally, even though under a strict legal regime, they would not be bound by the agreement.

The differences between legal and political equality are also recognized in the organization of the UNITED NATIONS. Although the Charter of the United Nations expressly recognizes the sovereign equality of states, and the General Assembly formally operates according to that principle, the five permanent members of the Security Council retain express veto power over several important aspects of U.N. functions, such as use of enforcement measures, admission to membership, amendments to the Charter, and election of the Secretary-General. Notwithstanding the fact that nations recognize limits on the principle of state equality in instances where political power is crucial, the principle of legal equality is basic to the operation of international law and a symbolic concept incorporated into the formal structure of most international institutions.

DOCUMENT 📖 A written or printed instrument that conveys information. 📖

The term *document* generally refers to a particular writing or instrument that has a bearing upon specific transactions. A DEED, a marriage LICENSE, and a record of account are all considered to be documents.

When a document is signed and the SIGNATURE is authentic, the law accurately expresses the state of mind of the individual who signed it. A *false document* is one of which a material portion is purported to have been made or authorized by someone who did not do so. It can also be a document that is falsely dated or which has allegedly been made by or on behalf of someone who did not in fact exist.

An ancient document is a writing presumed by the court to be genuine due to its antiquity, because it has been produced from a reliable source where it would be logically found, and because it has been carefully kept. See also ANCIENT WRITING.

A *private document* is any instrument executed by a private citizen. A *public document* is one that is or should legally be readily available for inspection by the public, as a document issued by Congress or a governmental department.

Judicial documents include inquisitions, DEPO-SITIONS, examinations, and AFFIDAVITS.

DOCUMENTARY EVIDENCE 📖 A type of written proof that is offered at a trial to establish the existence or nonexistence of a fact that is in dispute. 📖

Letters, CONTRACTS, DEEDS, LICENSES, CERTIFICATES, tickets, or other writings are documentary evidence.

DOCUMENT OF TITLE 📖 Any written instrument, such as a BILL OF LADING, a WAREHOUSE RECEIPT, or an order for the delivery of goods, that in the usual course of business or financing is considered sufficient proof that the person who possesses it is entitled to receive, hold, and dispose of the instrument and the GOODS that it covers. 📖

A document of title is usually either issued or addressed by a BAILEE—an individual who has custody of the goods of another—to a BAILOR—the person who has entrusted the goods to him or her. Its terms must describe the goods covered by it so that they are identifiable as well as set forth the conditions of the contractual agreement. Possession of a document of title is symbolic of ownership of the goods that are described within it.

Documents of title are an integral part of the business world since they facilitate commercial transactions by serving as SECURITY for loans sought by their possessors and by promoting the free flow of goods without unduly burdening the channels of commerce.

A person who possesses a document of title can legally transfer ownership of the goods covered by it by delivering or endorsing it over to another without physically moving the goods. In such a situation, a document of title is a NEGOTIABLE INSTRUMENT because it transfers legal rights of ownership from one person to another merely by its delivery or endorsement. It is negotiable only if its terms state that the goods are to be delivered to the BEARER, the holder of the document, to the order of the named party, or, where recognized in overseas trade, to a named person or his or her ASSIGNS. The UNIFORM COMMERCIAL CODE and various federal and state regulatory laws define the legal rights and obligations of the parties to a document of title.

DOING BUSINESS 📖 A qualification imposed in state LONG-ARM STATUTES governing the SERVICE OF PROCESS, the method by which a lawsuit is commenced, which requires nonresident CORPORATIONS to engage in commercial transactions within state borders in order to be subject to the PERSONAL JURISDICTION of state courts. 📖

The Due Process Clause of the U.S. Constitution, and similar provisions found in state constitutions, guarantees the fair and orderly administration of justice by the courts by providing that any individual, including corporations, must receive notice of the charges against him or her or it and an opportunity to present a defense prior to the rendition of judgment. This clause has been interpreted by courts to require a state to have some tie or relationship to a defendant before its courts acquire the power to bind the individual personally. Employing this reasoning, state legislatures enacted statutory provisions requiring nonresident or foreign corporations to do or transact business within the state if they are to be amenable to the personal jurisdiction of its courts. Doing business is one kind of MINIMUM CONTACT that brings such a corporation within the JURISDICTION of the court.

The nature and extent of business to be done within a state varies according to the jurisdiction. It must be an exercise of some of the functions for which the enterprise is incorporated and it must be of a sufficient nature to justify an inference that the corporation is present within the state. If so, the corporation is viewed as having received some benefit of the laws of the state and, therefore, should also be liable for its actions therein. In the past, there had to be a substantial tie to the state, such as the operation of an office or the presence of a resident employee. Today, courts consider this requirement fulfilled by a single commercial transaction, if the CAUSE OF ACTION—facts providing a right to a judicial remedy—arises from it. If the cause of action does not, however, a nonresident corporation is not amenable to service of process unless it has a substantial and regular relationship with the state comparable to the residency of an individual, such as having its corporate headquarters in the FORUM state. In cases involving SUBSIDIARY corporations, the intrastate business engaged in by a subsidiary is sufficient to make its parent corporation amenable to process in the state because the parent corporation is deemed to be doing business in the state.

The laws of each state must be consulted to determine whether a foreign corporation is doing business within a state to make it amenable to process therein.

The phrase *doing business* is sometimes used in the assessment of local taxes upon a nonresident corporation in jurisdictions other than the place of its incorporation in which it engages in business.

DOLE, ROBERT JOSEPH Bob Dole overcame childhood poverty and a wartime injury that left him partially paralyzed to become one of the most powerful players in national politics. The Republican majority leader from Kansas often won praise from Republicans and Democrats alike for finding a middle course through difficult issues. His long career in national politics put him at the center of major legislative debates; and whether in budgetary, social, or foreign policy matters, he often bridged party differences. These battles made him not only a skilled negotiator but, by the 1990s, the most powerful leader in his party. His politics were generally characterized by economic conservatism, support for CIVIL RIGHTS, and moderation on social issues. In addition to being a vice presidential candidate in 1976, Dole mounted three presidential campaigns, in 1980, 1988, and 1996.

The values of Dole's working-class family informed his upbringing. He was born on July 22, 1923, in Russell, Kansas, the son of an egg and cream station owner, Doran Ray Dole, and a traveling sewing machine saleswoman, Bina Talbot Dole. An athletic young man, Dole excelled in football, basketball, and track. He worked at several jobs and wanted to be a doctor. At age eighteen, he enrolled in the premed program at the University of Kansas. Drafted two years later, in 1943, he found himself fighting in Italy. World War II had almost ended in April 1945 when a shell hit him on the battlefield, smashing his neck, shoulder, and spine. Doctors thought he would be crippled. But Dole's persistence through three years of operations and therapy brought an amazing recovery. His only permanent disabilities are a lack of control of his right arm and hand, and partial loss of control of his left.

The twenty-five-year-old survivor was transformed. With new earnestness, he finished his undergraduate studies at the University of Arizona and earned a law degree with honors from Washburn University of Topeka.

Law quickly led to politics. Dole served one term in the Kansas Legislature in 1951, and for

MIKE ROEMER/THE GAMMA LIAISON NETWORK

Bob Dole

"THE GOVERNMENT CANNOT DIRECT THE PEOPLE, THE PEOPLE MUST DIRECT THE GOVERNMENT."

the remainder of the decade worked as a PROSECUTOR in his local county. He entered national politics in 1960 with election to the U.S. House of Representatives, where he won reelection every two years through 1968. Dole advocated fiscal conservatism while supporting limited WELFARE spending. He voted against the Great Society programs of President LYNDON B. JOHNSON, but he supported aid to hungry and DISABLED PERSONS and to farmers. He strongly backed civil rights legislation, a position from which he never wavered throughout his career. His model in politics—and the figure who ultimately became his mentor—was RICHARD M. NIXON, a friend since the 1950s. Dole's election to the U.S. Senate in 1968 gave President Nixon a vociferous supporter, and earned Dole the post of Republican National Committee (RNC) chairman in 1971.

The 1970s and 1980s brought Dole prominence in national politics. One reason for this was his marriage in 1975 to Elizabeth Hanford, an accomplished Harvard graduate who later held the posts of secretary of transportation and secretary of labor. Dole's chairmanship of the RNC also brought dividends. In 1976, President GERALD R. FORD chose Dole as his vice presidential running mate in an unsuccessful bid for reelection. The 1976 race whetted Dole's appetite for more, and he mounted his own campaign for president in 1980, losing out to RONALD REAGAN.

In 1984 Dole was elevated to Senate majority leader. Although his function in this role was to deliver party loyalty on votes in the Senate, he also became a strong supporter of president Reagan. During the IRAN-CONTRA scandal Dole took a leading role in damage control. He made public reassurances and traveled the United States to rally support for the president.

Dole made another bid for president after Reagan's departure in 1988. This unsuccessful struggle for the Republican nomination against Vice President GEORGE BUSH revealed what many critics had long seen as a mixed blessing in Dole: his acerbic tongue. This had appeared as an issue as early as 1976, when, while cam-

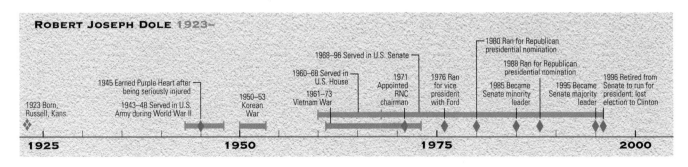

ROBERT JOSEPH DOLE 1923–

1923 Born, Russell, Kans.

1943–48 Served in U.S. Army during World War II

1945 Earned Purple Heart after being seriously injured

1950–53 Korean War

1960–68 Served in U.S. House

1961–73 Vietnam War

1968–96 Served in U.S. Senate

1971 Appointed RNC chairman

1976 Ran for vice president with Ford

1980 Ran for Republican presidential nomination

1985 Became Senate minority leader

1988 Ran for Republican presidential nomination

1995 Became Senate majority leader

1996 Retired from Senate to run for president; lost election to Clinton

1925   1950   1975   2000

paigning as Gerald Ford's running mate, Dole had ridiculed Democratic candidate Jimmy Carter as "Southern Fried McGovern." In 1988, again while campaigning, he lashed out at George Bush on national TV, saying Bush had lied about him. The attack on Bush raised some speculation about whether Dole could control his temper.

In 1996 Dole's third run for the White House was characterized by a rightward shift. Soon after declaring his candidacy, he attacked Hollywood for making movies that "revel in mindless violence and loveless sex." Dole called for making English the nation's official language, returned the campaign contribution of a gay Republican organization (later calling the move a mistake), and quit attending a United Methodist church that conservative critics had denounced as excessively liberal.

More crucially, perhaps, Dole's ideas on economics now resembled those that he had found untenable in President Reagan. The senator who had won bipartisan praise for a 1982 tax compromise now told voters, "We can cut taxes and balance the budget at the same time." And less apparent was his trademark willingness to compromise: throughout late 1995 and early 1996, Dole and House Majority Leader NEWT GINGRICH (R-Ga.) engaged in a budget deadlock with President BILL CLINTON that forced a shutdown of the federal government. He lost the 1996 election to Bill Clinton.

Dole's career stands as a testimony to the necessity of pragmatism and compromise in Washington, D.C. Even with Republican presidents, including Reagan, the most popular president in history, the GOP needed help in Congress with its agenda. Dole's mastery of deal cutting—and occasional firm stifling of opposition—provided it. A man of resolve, rather than image, Dole was a bulwark of Republican party politics for nearly three decades.

DOLE, SANFORD BALLARD Sanford Ballard Dole was a prominent figure in the creation of Hawaii as a republic and its annexation

Sanford Ballard Dole

"THE UPRISING OF A SMALL PEOPLE MAY BE AS INSPIRING AS THE UPRISING OF A GREAT NATION."

to the United States. Dole was born in 1844. His parents were American missionaries assigned to Hawaii, and Dole was raised and educated there. After attending Williams College and his admission to the Massachusetts bar in 1868, he settled in Hawaii and began his law practice.

In 1884 and 1886, he served in the Hawaiian legislature. His first act of dissension against the existing monarchy was as a leader of the Bayonet Revolution in 1887. As a result, the power of the monarchy was reduced and a more equitable constitution was adopted.

Also in 1887, Dole sat on the bench of the Hawaii Supreme Court as an associate justice.

In 1893, Queen Liliuokalani refused to recognize the limitations imposed upon her by the 1887 constitution. An insurrection occurred and the queen was overthrown. Dole left his post as justice to become the leader of the revolutionary provisional government that replaced the monarchy.

The republic of Hawaii was created in 1894, and Dole acted as its president. He began his efforts for the U.S. annexation of Hawaii, but his first attempts were thwarted by President GROVER CLEVELAND, who opposed the deposition of the monarchy. Dole wrote a treatise defending the revolution and its results but to no avail. He was finally able to achieve annexation under the administration of President WILLIAM MCKINLEY in 1898. Dole continued to serve as president throughout these years.

With the annexation of Hawaii completed, Dole became the first governor of the newly formed Territory of Hawaii. He performed these duties from 1900 to 1903.

In 1904, Dole returned to the judiciary and served as justice of the U.S. district court for Hawaii until 1915. He died in Hawaii in 1926.

DOMAIN 📖 The complete and absolute ownership of land. Also the REAL ESTATE so owned. The inherent sovereign power claimed by the legislature of a state, of controlling private property for public uses, is termed the *right of* EMINENT DOMAIN.

National domain is sometimes applied to the

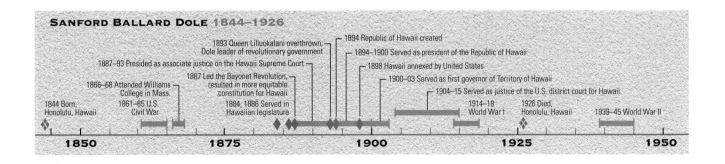

SANFORD BALLARD DOLE 1844–1926

1844 Born, Honolulu, Hawaii

1861–65 U.S. Civil War

1866–68 Attended Williams College in Mass.

1884, 1886 Served in Hawaiian legislature

1887 Led the Bayonet Revolution, resulted in more equitable constitution for Hawaii

1887–93 Presided as associate justice on the Hawaii Supreme Court

1893 Queen Liliuokalani overthrown; Dole leader of revolutionary government

1894 Republic of Hawaii created

1894–1900 Served as president of the Republic of Hawaii

1898 Hawaii annexed by United States

1900–03 Served as first governor of Territory of Hawaii

1904–15 Served as justice of the U.S. district court for Hawaii

1914–18 World War I

1926 Died, Honolulu, Hawaii

1939–45 World War II

1850   1875   1900   1925   1950

aggregate of the property owned directly by a nation. PUBLIC DOMAIN embraces all lands, the TITLE to which is in the United States, including land occupied for the purposes of federal buildings, arsenals, dock-yards, and so on, and land of an agricultural or mineral character not yet granted to private owners.

Sphere of influence. Range of control or rule; realm. 📖

DOMBEC 📖 [*Saxon, Judgment book.*] The name given by the Saxons to the code of laws by which they lived. 📖

Several Saxon kings published dombecs, also spelled dombocs. Dombecs were also known as dome-books or doom-books. The dombec compiled during the ninth-century reign of Alfred the Great was among the most important because it contained the law for the entire kingdom of England, encompassing the principal maxims of COMMON LAW, the penalties for crimes, and the forms of judicial proceedings.

A dombec is not the same as the DOMESDAY BOOK, although the two are often confused.

DOMESDAY BOOK 📖 An ancient record of land ownership in England. 📖

Commissioned by William the Conqueror in the year 1085 and finished in 1086, the book is a superb example of thorough and speedy administration, unequaled by any other project undertaken during the Middle Ages. Minute and accurate surveys of all of England were done for the purpose of compiling information

The Domesday Book was finished in 1086 and contains a remarkably thorough survey of England.

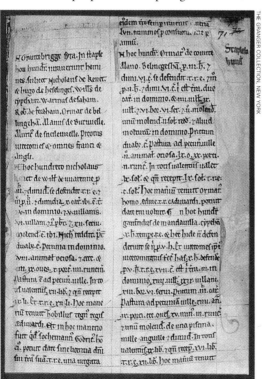

essential for levying taxes and enforcing the land tenure system.

The work was done by five justices in each county who took a census and listed all the feudal landowners, their personal property, and other information. The judges gathered their information by summoning each man and having him give testimony under oath. This is perhaps the earliest use of the INQUEST procedure in England, and it established the right of the king to require citizens to give information, a foundation of the JURY trial.

Domesday was a Saxon word meaning Judgment Day, at the end of time when God will pronounce judgment against all of mankind. The name given to this record may have come from the popular opinion that the inquiry was as thorough as that promised for Judgment Day.

Two volumes of the Domesday Book are still in existence, and they continue to be valuable for historical information about social and economic conditions. They are kept in the Public Record Office in England.

DOMESTIC 📖 Pertaining to the house or home. A person employed by a household to perform various servient duties. Any household servant, such as a maid or butler. Relating to a place of birth, origin, or domicile. 📖

That which is domestic is related to household uses. A *domestic animal* is one that is sufficiently tame to live with a family, such as a dog or cat, or one that can be used to contribute to a family's support, such as a cow, chicken, or horse. When something is *domesticated*, it is converted to domestic use, as in the case of a wild animal that is tamed.

Domestic relations are relationships between various family members, such as a HUSBAND AND WIFE, that are regulated by FAMILY LAW.

A domestic CORPORATION of a particular state is one that has been organized and chartered in that state as opposed to a foreign corporation, which has been incorporated in another state or territory. In tax law, a domestic corporation is one that has originated in any U.S. state or territory.

Domestic products are goods that are manufactured within a particular territory rather than imported from outside that territory.

DOMESTIC VIOLENCE 📖 Any abusive, violent, coercive, forceful, or threatening act or word inflicted by one member of a family or household on another can constitute domestic violence. 📖

Domestic violence, once considered one of the most underreported crimes, became more widely recognized during the 1980s and 1990s. During this time, law enforcement and mental health professionals grappled with the severity, complexity, and prevalence of the problem.

Various individuals and groups have defined domestic violence to include everything from saying unkind or demeaning words, to grabbing a person's arm, to hitting, kicking, choking, or murdering. Domestic violence most often refers to violence between married or cohabiting couples, although it sometimes refers to violence against other members of a household, such as children or elderly relatives. It occurs in every racial, socioeconomic, ethnic, and religious group, although conditions such as poverty, drug or alcohol abuse, and mental illness increase its likelihood. Studies indicate that the incidence of domestic violence among homosexual couples is approximately equivalent to that found among heterosexual couples.

Domestic violence involving married or cohabiting couples received vast media attention during the 1990s. The highly publicized 1995 trial of former professional football player and movie actor O. J. (Orenthal James) Simpson for the murders of his former wife Nicole Brown Simpson and her friend Ronald Lyle Goldman thrust it onto the front pages of newspapers for many months. Simpson was acquitted of the murder charges, but evidence produced at his trial showed that he was arrested in 1989 for spousal BATTERY and that he had threatened to kill his former wife. The disclosure that a prominent sports figure and movie star had abused his wife prompted a national discussion on the causes of domestic violence, its prevalence, and effective means of eliminating it.

Those who have studied domestic violence believe that it usually occurs in a cycle with three general stages. First, the abuser uses words or threats, perhaps humiliation or ridicule. Next, the abuser explodes at some perceived infraction by the other person, and the abuser's rage is manifested in physical violence. Finally, the abuser "cools off," asks forgiveness, and promises the violence will never occur again. At this point, the victim often abandons any attempt to leave the situation or to have charges brought against the abuser, although some prosecutors will go forward with charges even if the victim is unwilling to do so. Typically, the abuser's rage begins to build again after the reconciliation, and the violent cycle is repeated.

In some cases of repeated domestic violence, the victim eventually strikes back and harms or kills the abuser. People who are repeatedly

Victims of Violence

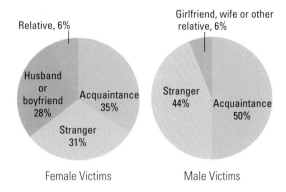

Source: U.S. Department of Justice, Bureau of Justice Statistics, "Violence Against Women: A National Crime Vicitimization Survey Report," Jan. 1994

victimized by spouses or other partners often suffer from low self-esteem, feelings of shame and guilt, and a sense that they are trapped in a situation from which there is no escape. Some who feel they have no outside protection from their batterer may turn to self-protection. During the 1980s, in a number of cases in which a victim of repeated domestic abuse struck back, the battered spouse defense was used to exonerate the victim. However, in order to rely on the battered spouse defense, victims must prove that they genuinely and reasonably believed that they were in immediate danger of death or great bodily injury and that they used only such force as they believed was reasonably necessary to protect themselves. Because this is a very difficult standard to meet, it is estimated that fewer than one-third of victims who invoke the battered spouse defense are acquitted.

Heightened awareness and an increase in reports of domestic violence led to a widespread legal response during the 1980s and 1990s. Once thought to be a problem best handled without legal intervention, domestic abuse is now treated as a criminal offense. Many states and municipalities have instituted measures designed to deal swiftly and harshly with domestic abusers. In addition, governments have attempted to protect the victims of domestic violence from further danger and have launched programs designed to address the root causes of violence. An example is Alexandria, Virginia, which, in 1994, began prosecuting repeat abusers under a Virginia law (Va. St. § 18.2–57.2 Code 1950, § 18.2–57.2) that makes the third conviction for ASSAULT AND BATTERY a FELONY punishable by up to five years in prison. In addition, the city established a shelter for battered women, a victims' task force, and a domestic violence intervention program that includes a mandatory arrest policy and court-ordered counseling. As a result, domestic HOMICIDES in Alexandria declined from 40 percent of all homicides in 1987 to 16 percent in 1988 to 1994. Similar measures have been adopted by other states. States that already had specific laws dealing with domestic violence toughened the penalties during the 1990s. For example, a 1995 amendment to California's domestic abuse law (West's Ann. Cal. Penal Code §§ 14140–14143) revoked a provision that allowed first-time abusers to have their criminal record expunged if they attended counseling.

Public outrage over domestic violence also led to the inclusion of the Violence against Women Act as title IV of the Violent Crime Control and Law Enforcement Act of 1994 (Pub. L. No. 103-322, 108 Stat. 1796 [codified as amended in scattered sections of 18 and 42 U.S.C.A.]). The act authorizes research and education programs for judges and judicial staff to enhance knowledge and awareness of domestic violence and sexual assault. It also provides funding for police training and for shelters, increases penalties for domestic violence and RAPE, and provides for enhanced privacy protections for victims. A controversial portion of the act makes gender-motivated crimes a violation of federal CIVIL RIGHTS law (42 U.S.C.A. § 13981).

Studies on the incidence of domestic violence vary a great deal. In a 1995 survey conducted by Dr. Jeanne McCauley of Johns Hopkins University School of Medicine, one in three women responding to a confidential questionnaire indicated that she had been physically or sexually attacked, half before age eighteen. The National Coalition against Domestic Violence reported in 1993 that 50 percent of all married women will experience some form of violence from their spouse, and that more than one-third are battered repeatedly every year. Figures from the U.S. Department of Justice (DOJ) for 1991 indicate an annual average number of domestic ASSAULTS against women of approximately 700,000. Research conducted during the 1980s and by Murray A. Straus, of the University of New Hampshire, and Richard J. Gelles, of the University of Rhode Island, veterans of twenty-five years of research into family violence, resulted in higher numbers than those reported by the DOJ, but far lower than those reported by Dr. McCauley. Straus and Gelles found that approximately 4 million people each year are victims of all types of domestic assault, ranging from minor threats and thrown objects to severe beatings. This number represents both women and men who report suffering attacks by partners. Straus and Gelles found that men are almost as likely to endure domestic assault as women, although women are far more likely to be injured. Domestic violence activists dispute the notion that men suffer domestic assault at approximately the same rate as women.

See also CHILD ABUSE; FAMILY LAW.

DOMICILIARY ADMINISTRATION

The settlement and distribution of a decedent's ESTATE in the state of his or her permanent RESIDENCE, the place to which the DECEDENT intended to return even though he or she might actually have resided elsewhere.

Domiciliary administration is deemed principal or primary administration and is distinguishable from ANCILLARY ADMINISTRATION, which is the management of a decedent's property in the state where it is situated, which is other than the state in which the decedent permanently resided.

DOMINANT
Prevalent; paramount in force or effect; of primary importance or consideration. That which is dominant possesses rights that prevail over those of others.

In PROPERTY law, the estate to which an EASEMENT, or right of use, is given is called the *dominant tenement* or *estate*, and the one upon which the easement is imposed is called the *servient tenement* or *estate*.

DOMINANT CAUSE
The essential or most direct source of an accident or injury, regardless of when it occurred.

In TORT law, the dominant cause of an injury is the PROXIMATE CAUSE, or the primary or moving cause, without which the injury would not have occurred.

DOMINION
Perfect control in right of ownership. The word implies both TITLE and POSSESSION and appears to require a complete retention of control over DISPOSITION. Title to an article of property, which arises from the power of disposition and the right of claiming it. SOVEREIGNTY; as in the dominion of the seas or over a territory.

In CIVIL LAW, with reference to the title to property that is transferred by a sale of it, dominion is said to be either *proximate* or *remote*, the former being the kind of title vesting in the purchaser when he or she has acquired both the ownership and the possession of the article, the latter describing the nature of the title when he or she has legitimately acquired the ownership of the property but there has been no DELIVERY.

DONATIVE
Relating to the gratuitous transfer of something as in the nature of a GIFT.

A *donative* TRUST is the CONVEYANCE of property in trust set up as a gift from one person to another.

Donative intent is the intent to give something as a gift.

DONEE 📖 The recipient of a GIFT. An individual to whom a power of APPOINTMENT is conveyed. 📖

DONOR 📖 The party conferring a power. One who makes a GIFT. One who creates a TRUST. 📖

DOOM 📖 An archaic term for a court's JUDGMENT. 📖

Today, some criminal sentences still end with the phrase " . . . which is pronounced for doom."

DORMANT 📖 Latent; inactive; silent. That which is dormant is not used, asserted, or enforced. 📖

A *dormant* partner is a member of a PARTNERSHIP who has a financial interest yet is silent, in that he or she takes no control over the business. The partner's identity is secret because the individual is unknown to the public.

DORR, THOMAS WILSON Known for his central role in Rhode Island's 1842 Dorr's Rebellion, Thomas Wilson Dorr fought for changes in the voting laws of his native state. Until the tumultuous 1842 election of Dorr as governor, long-standing laws, based on the state's initial charter from England, had limited voting rights to men who owned at least $134 in land. Dorr helped to initiate a new state constitution that granted more liberal voting rights to white males. Once he was governor, some of Rhode Island's other authorities treated him as a traitor to the aristocracy. However, Dorr's extension of voting rights to a larger section of the populace stands as a cornerstone in the democratization of the United States.

The changes in voting rights that Dorr proposed flew in the face of Rhode Island's staunch political conservatism. Although the example of newer, noncolonial states had changed the way in which some older, seaboard states practiced government, Rhode Island adhered to the charter it had received from the English monarchy in 1663. This document's property requirement for voting excluded more than half of the white

BIOGRAPHY

Thomas Wilson Dorr

males in the state. By 1840 even though only one other state retained a possession-of-property requirement, Rhode Island's leaders claimed that their constitution served as a standard of law and order. The Rhode Island charter, they said, had spared the state from one unwelcome effect of industrialization: political turmoil. Changes in government, however, were inevitable, even in Rhode Island. An increase in industry led to an increase in crime, unemployment, and poverty. Such changes brought a demand for a populist voice in the workings of government.

During this time of change, Dorr emerged as a legal spokesman. Born November 5, 1805, the son of a wealthy Providence merchant, Dorr graduated from Harvard in 1823. He then pursued legal studies, and was admitted to the Rhode Island bar in 1827. In 1834 he participated in the Rhode Island legislature, where he led a campaign to secure extended voting rights. When the movement gained momentum, the Rhode Island Suffrage Association was founded, which Dorr headed in 1840. As support for Dorr grew, he formed the People's party. In 1841 the party organized a convention and drafted a more liberal state constitution, the People's Constitution. It appealed to voteless urban workers by issuing the vote to all white adult males.

To counteract Dorr's movement, the Rhode Island state legislature called for a convention in Newport in November 1841. Conservatives saw this as their chance to derail the newly drafted constitution. Many others, however, supported Dorr's constitution, and two rival positions emerged. In 1842 Dorr's supporters elected him governor of the state. For a while, Rhode Island had to juggle two state governments. Samuel H. King, representing opponents of Dorr's efforts, also served as governor, under the guides of the old charter. Both sides wooed the federal government for recognition. President JOHN TYLER wrote to King and warned him that any attempt to overthrow Dorr's government would result in the presence of federal troops in Rhode Island.

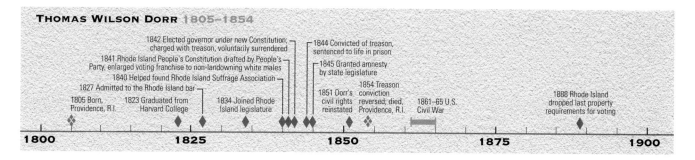

THOMAS WILSON DORR 1805–1854

1842 Elected governor under new Constitution; charged with treason, voluntarily surrendered
1841 Rhode Island People's Constitution drafted by People's Party, enlarged voting franchise to non-landowning white males
1840 Helped found Rhode Island Suffrage Association
1827 Admitted to the Rhode Island bar
1805 Born, Providence, R.I.
1823 Graduated from Harvard College
1834 Joined Rhode Island legislature
1844 Convicted of treason, sentenced to life in prison
1845 Granted amnesty by state legislature
1851 Dorr's civil rights reinstated
1854 Treason conviction reversed; died, Providence, R.I.
1861–65 U.S. Civil War
1888 Rhode Island dropped last property requirements for voting

| 1800 | 1825 | 1850 | 1875 | 1900 |

Dorr sought to establish an entirely new state government in Providence. King declared that Dorr's party had initiated an insurrection. The sides of the dual government clashed, and, under King's authority, many of Dorr's supporters were imprisoned. On May 17, 1842, Dorr countered King's efforts to crush the People's "treason" and attacked the Providence arsenal. But the state MILITIA held back the attack, and Dorr subsequently fled the state. King declared MARTIAL LAW and offered a reward for Dorr's capture.

A compromise came about when the state drafted a new constitution that extended voting rights. When the state adopted the new constitution, Dorr surrendered to authorities. Convicted of TREASON in 1844, Dorr faced a life sentence of solitary confinement and hard labor. Protests followed the severe sentence. One year later, the state legislature granted him AMNESTY and Dorr was set free.

Meanwhile, a suit arose from the competing state governments (*Luther v. Borden*, 48 U.S. (7 How.) 1, 12 L. Ed. 581 [1849]). In response to one of the "POLITICAL QUESTIONS" in the case, the Supreme Court declared that Congress, under Article IV, Section 4, of the Constitution, held the power to ensure a republican state government while simultaneously recognizing the lawful government of that state. The court ruled that the president had the authority to support a lawful state government with federal troops if an armed conflict occurred. The federal courts could not disturb these rights of Congress and the president. As President Tyler had not taken the opportunity to act on his power, the Court was left with much to decide regarding the balance between Rhode Island's new constitution and the federal executive and legislative powers.

The reform movement set forth by Dorr, later known as Dorrism, had helped to solidify a greater trend in U.S. government. As more and more people were granted the right to vote, the United States strayed further and further from the original English monarchical rule. Although the rebellion of Dorr and his followers consisted of only a few skirmishes, its influence extended through a long period of time. For conservatives, Dorrism represented bloody class conflict. For many others, Dorr appeared to be less a traitor than a representative for the common person. In 1851, Dorr's civil rights were reinstated, and in 1854, the verdict against him was reversed. Later that year, on December 27, Dorr died in Providence, in his native Rhode Island.

DOUBLE ENTRY ▥ A BOOKKEEPING system that lists each transaction twice in the ledger. ▥

"THE SERVANTS OF A RIGHTEOUS CAUSE MAY FAIL OR FALL IN THE DEFENSE OF IT. BUT ALL THE TRUTH THAT IT CONTAINS IS INDESTRUCTIBLE."

Double-entry bookkeeping is a method whereby every transaction is shown as both a DEBIT and a CREDIT. This is done through the use of horizontal rows and vertical columns of numbers. The reason for the use of this bookkeeping method is that if the total of horizontal rows and vertical columns is not the same, it is easier to find mistakes than when the records are kept with only a single ENTRY for each item.

DOUBLE INDEMNITY ▥ A term of an INSURANCE policy by which the insurance company promises to pay the insured or the BENEFICIARY twice the amount of coverage if loss occurs due to a particular cause or set of circumstances. ▥

Double indemnity clauses are found most often in life insurance policies. In the case of the accidental death of the insured, the insurance company will pay the beneficiary of the policy twice its face value. Such a provision is usually financed through the payment of higher premiums than those paid for a policy that entitles a beneficiary to recover only the face amount of the policy, regardless of how the insured died.

In cases where the cause of death is unclear, the insurance company need not pay the proceeds until the accidental nature of death is sufficiently established by a PREPONDERANCE OF EVIDENCE. A beneficiary of such a policy may sue an insurance company for breach of contract to enforce his or her right to the proceeds, whenever necessary.

DOUBLE INSURANCE ▥ Duplicate protection provided when two companies deal with the same individual and undertake to INDEMNIFY that person against the same losses. ▥

When an individual has double INSURANCE, he or she has coverage by two different insurance companies upon the identical interest in the identical subject matter. If a HUSBAND AND WIFE have duplicate medical insurance coverage protecting one another, they would thereby have double insurance. An individual can rarely collect on double insurance, however, since this would ordinarily constitute a form of UNJUST ENRICHMENT, and a majority of insurance CONTRACTS contain provisions that prohibit this.

DOUBLE JEOPARDY ▥ A second prosecution for the same offense after ACQUITTAL or CONVICTION or multiple punishments for same offense. The evil sought to be avoided by prohibiting double jeopardy is double trial and double conviction, not necessarily double punishment. ▥

The FIFTH AMENDMENT to the U.S. Constitution provides, "No person shall . . . be subject for the same offence [*sic*] to be twice put in jeopardy of life or limb." This provision, known as the Double Jeopardy Clause, prohibits state and federal governments from prosecuting individuals for the same crime on more than one occasion, or imposing more than one punishment for a single offense. Each of the fifty states offers similar protection through its own constitution, statutes, and COMMON LAW.

Five policy considerations underpin the double jeopardy doctrine: (1) preventing the government from employing its superior resources to wear down and erroneously convict innocent persons; (2) protecting individuals from the financial, emotional, and social consequences of successive prosecutions; (3) preserving the finality and integrity of criminal proceedings, which would be compromised were the state allowed to arbitrarily ignore unsatisfactory outcomes; (4) restricting prosecutorial discretion over the charging process; and (5) eliminating judicial discretion to impose cumulative punishments not authorized by the legislature.

The concept of double jeopardy is one of the oldest in Western civilization. In 355 B.C., Athenian statesman Demosthenes said, "[T]he law forbids the same man to be tried twice on the same issue." The Romans codified this principle in the Digest of JUSTINIAN I in A.D. 533. The principle also survived the Dark Ages (A.D. 400–1066), notwithstanding the deterioration of other Greco-Roman legal traditions, through canon law and the teachings of early Christian writers.

In England, the protection against double jeopardy was considered "a universal maxim of the common law" (*United States v. Wilson*, 420 U.S. 332, 340, 95 S. Ct. 1013, 1020, 43 L. Ed. 2d 232 [1975]) and was embraced by eminent jurists HENRY DE BRACTON (1250), SIR EDWARD COKE (1628), Sir Matthew Hale (1736), and SIR WILLIAM BLACKSTONE (1769). Nonetheless, the English double jeopardy doctrine was extremely narrow. It was afforded only to defendants accused of capital FELONIES, and applied only after conviction or acquittal. It did not apply to cases dismissed prior to final judgment, and was not immune from flagrant abuse by the Crown.

The American colonists, who were intimately familiar with Coke, Blackstone, and the machinations of the Crown, expanded the protection against double jeopardy, making it applicable to all crimes. Yet JAMES MADISON's original draft of the Double Jeopardy Clause was perceived by some as too broad. It provided, "No person shall be subject . . . to more than one punishment or *one trial* for the same offense" (emphasis added) (*United States v. Halper*, 490 U.S. 435, 440, 109 S. Ct. 1892, 1897 104 L. Ed. 2d 487 [1989]). Several House members objected to this wording, arguing it could be misconstrued to prevent defendants from seeking a second trial on APPEAL following conviction. Although the language was later amended by the Senate to address this concern, the final version ratified by the states left other questions for judicial interpretation.

Double jeopardy litigation revolves around four central questions: In what type of legal proceeding does double jeopardy protection apply? When does jeopardy begin, or, in legal parlance, attach? When does jeopardy terminate? What constitutes successive prosecutions or punishments for the same offense? Although courts have answered the second and third questions with some clarity, they continue struggling over the first and last.

Where Jeopardy Applies Only certain types of legal proceedings invoke double jeopardy protection. If a particular proceeding does not place an individual in jeopardy, then subsequent proceedings against the same individual for the same conduct are not prohibited. The Fifth Amendment suggests that the protection against double jeopardy extends only to proceedings threatening "life or limb." Nevertheless, the Supreme Court has established that the right against double jeopardy is not limited to capital crimes or corporal punishment, but extends to all felonies, MISDEMEANORS, and juvenile delinquency ADJUDICATIONS, regardless of the punishments they prescribe.

In *Benton v. Maryland*, 395 U.S. 784, 89 S. Ct. 2056, 23 L. Ed. 2d 707 (1969), the Supreme Court ruled that the federal Double Jeopardy Clause is applicable to both state and federal prosecutions. Prior to this ruling, an individual accused of violating state law could rely only on that particular state's protection against double jeopardy. Some states offered greater protection against double jeopardy than did others. The Supreme Court, relying on the doctrine of incorporation, which makes fundamental principles in the Bill of Rights applicable to the states through the Equal Protection Clause of the FOURTEENTH AMENDMENT, said this was not permissible. The right against double jeopardy is so important, the Court concluded, that it must be equally conferred upon the citizens of every state. Under this decision, no state can provide its residents with less protection against double jeopardy than that offered by the federal Constitution.

The Supreme Court has also held that the right against double jeopardy precludes only subsequent *criminal* proceedings. It does not preclude ordinary civil or administrative proceedings against a person who has already been prosecuted for the same act or omission. Nor is prosecution barred by double jeopardy if it is preceded by a final civil or administrative determination on the same issue.

Courts have drawn the distinction between criminal proceedings on the one hand, and civil or administrative proceedings on the other, based on the different purposes served by each. Criminal proceedings are punitive in nature and serve two primary purposes: deterrence and retribution. Civil proceedings are more remedial; their fundamental purpose is to compensate injured persons for any losses incurred. Because civil and criminal remedies fulfill different objectives, the government may provide both for the same offense.

The multiple legal proceedings brought against O. J. (Orenthal James) Simpson in the death of Nicole Brown Simpson and Ronald Lyle Goldman illustrate these various objectives. The state of California prosecuted Simpson for the murders of his former wife and her friend. Despite Simpson's acquittal in the criminal case, three civil suits were filed against him by the families of the two victims. The criminal proceedings were instituted with the purpose to punish Simpson, incarcerate him, and deter others from similar behavior. The civil suits were intended to make the victims' families whole by compensating them with money damages for the losses they suffered.

The distinctions between criminal and civil proceedings and between punitive and remedial remedies may appear semantic, but they raise real legal issues. Courts have recognized that civil remedies may advance punitive goals. When they do, double jeopardy questions surface. For example, a civil FORFEITURE or civil FINE, though characterized by the legislature as

O. J. Simpson was prosecuted by the state of California in a criminal trial and was later sued by the Brown and Goldman families in civil court to recover damages for their losses.

remedial, becomes punitive when the value of the property seized or the amount of the fine imposed is "overwhelmingly disproportionate" to the loss suffered by society (*Halper*). This principle was exemplified when the Supreme Court prohibited the federal government from seeking a $130,000 civil penalty against a man who had previously been sentenced to prison for the same offense, filing $585 worth of false Medicare claims (*Halper*). The Court concluded that the gross disparity between the fine imposed and the economic loss suffered by society reflected a punitive remedial aim.

Conversely, many courts have ruled that PUNITIVE DAMAGES awarded in civil suits are not sufficiently criminal for double jeopardy purposes when the plaintiff seeking those damages is a private party, not the state. This ruling can best be explained by noting that the Bill of Rights guarantees protection only against government action. It does not create a system of rights and remedies for disputes between private citizens, as does the law of CONTRACTS and TORTS. Courts have not determined whether punitive damages recovered by the government in a civil suit would bar subsequent prosecution.

Nor have courts agreed whether a number of administrative proceedings can be uniformly characterized as punitive or remedial. Cases involving the revocation of professional LICENSES, driving privileges, PROBATION, and PAROLE have divided courts unable to reach accord over the purposes underlying these proceedings.

When Jeopardy Attaches Courts have provided much clearer guidance on the question of when jeopardy begins, or attaches. This question is crucial to answer because any action taken by the government before jeopardy attaches, such as dismissing the INDICTMENT, will not prevent later proceedings against a person for the same offense. Once jeopardy has attached, the full panoply of protection against multiple prosecutions and punishments takes hold.

The Supreme Court has held that jeopardy attaches during a jury trial when the JURY is sworn. In criminal cases tried by a judge without a jury, jeopardy attaches when the first WITNESS is sworn. Jeopardy begins in juvenile delinquency adjudications when the court first hears evidence. If the defendant or juvenile enters a PLEA agreement with the prosecution, jeopardy does not attach until the plea is accepted by the court.

When Jeopardy Terminates Determining when jeopardy terminates is no less important, but a little more complicated. Once jeopardy has terminated, the government cannot hail someone into court for additional proceedings on the same matter without raising double jeopardy questions. If jeopardy does not terminate at the conclusion of one proceeding, it is said to be continuing, and further criminal proceedings are permitted. Jeopardy can terminate in four instances: after acquittal, after dismissal, after a mistrial, and on appeal after conviction.

A jury's VERDICT of acquittal terminates jeopardy, and cannot be overturned on appeal even if it is contrary to overwhelming proof of a defendant's guilt and derived from a trial rife with reversible error. This elemental maxim of double jeopardy jurisprudence entrusts the jury with the power to nullify criminal prosecutions tainted by egregious police, prosecutorial, or judicial misconduct.

A jury can also impliedly acquit a defendant. If a jury has been instructed by the judge on the elements of a particular crime and a lesser included offense, and the jury returns a guilty verdict as to the lesser offense but is silent as to the greater, reprosecution for the greater offense is barred by the Double Jeopardy Clause. For example, a jury that has been instructed as to the crimes of first- and second-degree murder can impliedly acquit the defendant of first-degree murder by returning only a guilty verdict as to murder in the second degree. A not guilty verdict as to the greater offense is inferred from the silence.

A DISMISSAL is granted by the trial court for errors and defects that operate as an absolute barrier to prosecution. It may be entered before a jury has been impaneled, during the trial, or after a conviction. But jeopardy must attach before a dismissal implicates double jeopardy protection.

Once jeopardy attaches, a dismissal granted by the court for insufficient evidence terminates it. Such a dismissal also bars further prosecution, with one exception: the prosecution may appeal a dismissal entered after the jury has returned a guilty verdict. If the APPELLATE COURT reverses the dismissal, the guilty verdict can be reinstated without necessitating a second trial. A dismissal granted for lack of EVIDENCE after a case has been submitted to a jury but before a verdict has been reached may not be appealed by the state.

Reprosecution is permitted, and jeopardy continues, when a case is dismissed by the court on a MOTION by the defendant for reasons other than sufficiency of the evidence. For example, courts may dismiss a case when the defendant's right to a SPEEDY TRIAL has been denied by

prosecutorial pretrial delay. The Supreme Court has held that no double jeopardy interest is triggered when defendants obtain dismissal for reasons unrelated to their guilt or innocence (see *United States v. Scott*, 437 U.S. 82, 98 S. Ct. 2187, 57 L. Ed. 2d 65 [1978]).

A MISTRIAL is granted when it has become impracticable or impossible to finish a case. Courts typically declare a mistrial when jurors fail to reach a unanimous verdict. Like a dismissal, a mistrial declared at the defendant's behest will not terminate jeopardy or bar reprosecution. Nor will a mistrial preclude reprosecution when declared with the defendant's consent. Courts disagree about whether a defendant's mere silence is tantamount to consent.

A different situation is presented when a mistrial is declared over the defendant's OBJECTION. Reprosecution is then allowed only if the mistrial resulted from "manifest necessity," a standard more rigorous than "reasonable necessity," and less exacting than "absolute necessity." A mistrial that could have been reasonably avoided terminates jeopardy, but jeopardy continues if a mistrial was unavoidable.

The manifest necessity standard has been satisfied where mistrials have resulted from defective indictments, disqualified or deadlocked jurors, and procedural irregularities willfully occasioned by the defendant. Manifest necessity is never established for mistrials resulting from prosecutorial or judicial manipulation. In determining manifest necessity, courts balance the defendant's interest in finality against society's interest in a fair and just legal system.

Every defendant has the right to appeal a conviction. If the conviction is REVERSED on appeal for insufficient evidence, the reversal is treated as an acquittal and further prosecution is not permitted. However, the defendant may be reprosecuted when the reversal is not based on a lack of evidence. The grounds for such a reversal include defective SEARCH WARRANTS, unlawful seizure of evidence, and other so-called technicalities. Retrials in these instances are justified by society's interest in punishing guilty people. A defendant's countervailing interests are subordinated when a jury's verdict is overturned for reasons unrelated to guilt or innocence.

The interests of accused individuals are also subordinated when courts permit PROSECUTORS to seek a more severe SENTENCE during the retrial of a defendant whose original conviction was thrown out on appeal. Courts have suggested that defendants who appeal their conviction assume the risk that a harsher sentence will be imposed during reprosecution. However, in most circumstances, courts are not permitted to impose a death sentence on a defendant during a second trial when the jury recommended life in prison during the first. The recommendation of life imprisonment is construed as an acquittal on the issue of capital punishment.

What Constitutes the Same Offense

The final question courts must resolve in double jeopardy litigation is whether successive prosecutions or punishments are for the same offense. Jeopardy may have already attached and terminated in a prior criminal proceeding, but the state may bring further CRIMINAL ACTION against a person so long as it is not for the same offense. Courts have analyzed this question in several ways, depending on whether the state is attempting to reprosecute a defendant or to impose multiple punishments.

At common law, a single episode of criminal behavior produced only one prosecution, no matter how many wrongful acts were committed during that episode. Under current law, a proliferation of overlapping and related offenses may be prosecuted as separate crimes stemming from the same set of circumstances. For example, an individual who has stolen a car to facilitate an abduction resulting in attempted rape could be separately prosecuted and punished for auto theft, kidnapping, and molestation. This development has significantly enlarged prosecutors' discretion over the charging process.

The Supreme Court curbed this discretion in *Blockburger v. United States*, 284 U.S. 299, 52 S. Ct. 180, 76 L. Ed. 306 (1932). The Court said that the government may PROSECUTE an individual for more than one offense stemming from a single course of conduct only when each offense requires proof of a fact that the other offenses do not require. *Blockburger* requires courts to examine the elements of each offense as they are delineated by statute, without regard to the actual evidence that will be introduced at trial. The prosecution has the burden to demonstrate that each offense has at least one mutually exclusive element. If any one offense is subsumed by another, such as a lesser included offense, the two offenses are deemed the same and punishment is allowed for only one.

Blockburger is the exclusive means by which courts determine whether cumulative punishments pass muster under the Double Jeopardy Clause. But several other methods have been used by courts to determine whether successive prosecutions are for the same offense. COLLATERAL ESTOPPEL, which prevents the same parties from relitigating ultimate factual issues previously determined by a valid and final judgment, is one such method. In *Ashe v. Swenson*, 397 U.S. 436, 90 S. Ct. 1189, 25 L. Ed. 2d 469 (1970), the Supreme Court collaterally estopped the government from prosecuting an individual for robbing one of six men at a poker game. Here, a jury had already acquitted the defendant of robbing one of the other players. Although the second prosecution would have been permitted under *Blockburger* because two different victims were involved, it was disallowed because the defendant had already been declared not guilty of essentially the same crime.

The "same-transaction" analysis, which is used by many state courts to bar successive prosecutions, requires the prosecution to join all offenses that were committed during a continuous interval and share a common factual basis and display a single goal or intent. Although Justices WILLIAM J. BRENNAN, JR., WILLIAM O. DOUGLAS, and THURGOOD MARSHALL have endorsed the same-transaction test, no federal court has ever adopted it.

Both state and federal courts have employed the "actual-evidence" test to preclude successive prosecutions for the same offense. Unlike *Blockburger*, which demands that courts examine the statutory elements of proof, the actual-evidence test requires courts to compare the evidence *actually* introduced during the first trial with the evidence *sought to be* introduced by the prosecution at the second. The offenses are characterized as the same when the evidence necessary to support a conviction for one offense would be sufficient to support a conviction for the other.

Los Angeles police officer Stacey Koon was acquitted of criminal charges in the beating of motorist Rodney King but was found guilty of violating King's civil rights in a federal case.

AP/WIDE WORLD PHOTOS

Under the "same-conduct" analysis, the government is forbidden to prosecute an individual twice for the same criminal behavior, regardless of the actual evidence introduced during trial or the stautory elements of the offense. In *Grady v. Corbin*, 495 U.S. 508, 110 S. Ct. 2084, 109 L. Ed. 2d 548 (1990), the Supreme Court applied this analysis to prevent someone's being prosecuted for vehicular homicide resulting from drunk driving, when he had earlier been convicted of driving while under the influence of alcohol. The second prosecution would have been permitted had the state been able to prove the driver's NEGLIGENCE without proof of his intoxication. Although *Grady* was abandoned by the Supreme Court three years later, the same-conduct analysis is still used by state courts interpreting their own constitutions and statutes.

The "dual-sovereignty" doctrine received national attention in the early 1990s when two Los Angeles police officers were convicted in FEDERAL COURT for violating the CIVIL RIGHTS of RODNEY KING during a brutal, videotaped beating, even though they had previously been acquitted in state court for excessive use of force (*United States v. Koon*, 833 F. Supp. 769, convictions affirmed 34 F. 3d 1416, rehearing denied 45 F. 3d 1303). Although many observers believed that the officers had been tried twice for the same offense, the convictions were upheld on appeal over double jeopardy objections. Under the dual-sovereignty doctrine, the appellate court ruled, a defendant who violates the laws of two sovereigns, even if by a single act, has committed two distinct offenses, punishable by both authorities.

The dual-sovereignty doctrine is designed to vindicate the interest each sovereign claims in promoting peace and dignity within its forum, and permits both state and federal governments to prosecute someone for the same behavior after either has already done so. A defendant may also be prosecuted successively by two states for the same act or omission. But successive prosecutions by a state and one of its political subdivisions, such as a county, city, or village, are not permitted, because these entities are deemed one sovereign.

DOUBLE TAXATION AGREEMENTS

Double TAXATION occurs when the same transaction or INCOME source is subject to two or more taxing authorities. This can occur within a single country, when independent governmental units have the power to tax a single transaction or source of income, or may result when different sovereign states impose separate taxes, in which case it is called international double

taxation. The source of the double taxation problem is that taxing JURISDICTIONS do not follow a common principle of taxation. One taxing jurisdiction may tax income at its source, while others will tax income based on the RESIDENCE or nationality of the recipient. Indeed, a jurisdiction may use all three of these basic approaches in imposing taxes.

The consequence of double taxation is to tax certain activities at a higher rate than similar activity located solely within a taxing jurisdiction. This leads to unnecessary relocation of economic activity in order to lower the incidence of taxation, or other, more objectionable forms of TAX AVOIDANCE. Businesses especially have had the most trouble with double taxation, but individuals may also find it uneconomic to work abroad if all of their income is subject to taxation by two authorities, regardless of the origin of the income.

The problems presented by double taxation have long been recognized, and with the growing integration of domestic economies into a world economy, countries have undertaken several measures to reduce the problem of double taxation. An individual country can offer tax credits for foreign taxes paid or outright exemptions from taxation of foreign-source income.

Treaties have also been negotiated between states to address the double taxation problem. One of the most important of these agreements was the International Tax Convention concluded by the United States and the United Kingdom in 1946. It has served as a model for several other tax conventions. Under the tax convention between the United States and the United Kingdom, for example, exemptions from taxes, credits for taxes paid, and reduction or equalization of overall tax rates are all utilized to reduce double taxation. Within the

International companies are often taxed by both their home country and the other countries within which they do business. Double taxation agreements provide tax exemptions or tax credits to alleviate this problem.

United States, many states have worked to prevent the incidence of taxation from reaching uneconomic levels on income derived from multistate sources.

DOUBT 📖 To question or hold questionable. Uncertainty of mind; the absence of a settled opinion or conviction; the attitude of mind toward the acceptance of or belief in a proposition, theory, or statement, in which the judgment is not at rest but inclines alternately to either side. 📖

Proof BEYOND A REASONABLE DOUBT is not beyond all possible or imaginary doubt, but such PROOF as precludes every REASONABLE hypothesis except that which it tends to support. It is proof *to a moral certainty*, that is, such proof as satisfies the judgment and consciences of the JURY, as reasonable people and applying their reason to the evidence before them, that the crime charged has been committed by the defendant, and so satisfies them as to leave no other reasonable conclusion possible.

A REASONABLE DOUBT is such a doubt as would cause a reasonable and prudent person in the graver and more important affairs of life to pause and hesitate to act upon the truth of the matter charged. It does not mean a mere possible doubt, because everything relating to human affairs, and depending on moral evidence, is open to some possible or imaginary doubt.

DOUGLAS, STEPHEN ARNOLD Stephen Arnold Douglas achieved prominence as a U.S. senator and as the originator of the policy known as Popular Sovereignty. He was born on April 23, 1813, in Brandon, Vermont. He pursued legal studies and was admitted to the Illinois bar in 1834.

In 1843 Douglas entered the legislative branch of the federal government as a member of the U.S. House of Representatives. Four years later, he was elected to the U. S. Senate and served until 1861.

During his lengthy tenure as senator from Illinois, Douglas became an outspoken leader in the SLAVERY controversy, and his many debates and innovative policies earned him the name "Little Giant." He was presiding officer of the

"THERE CAN BE BUT TWO GREAT POLITICAL PARTIES IN THIS COUNTRY."

BIOGRAPHY

LIBRARY OF CONGRESS

Stephen Arnold Douglas

Committee on Territories, a forum for the discussion of whether slavery should be allowed in the new territories.

Douglas was instrumental in the formulation of the bills which constituted that section of the COMPROMISE OF 1850 that allowed the residents of Utah and New Mexico to decide whether or not their states would institute slavery. This freedom of choice became known as the policy of Popular Sovereignty. Four years later, Douglas again attempted to apply this policy to the slavery issue involved in the admission of Kansas and Nebraska to the Union. The plan was not successful, however, for the proslavery and antislavery forces in Kansas clashed in a violent action. Two separate governments were established, the Lecompton, or proslavery, faction and the abolitionist faction. Douglas vehemently opposed the Lecompton Constitution, and criticized President JAMES BUCHANAN'S support of such a measure. After much violence and debate, Kansas was admitted as a free state. See also KANSAS-NEBRASKA ACT.

ABRAHAM LINCOLN and Douglas were opponents in the Illinois senatorial election of 1858, and they met seven times throughout their campaign to debate the issues. These arguments were the famous Lincoln-Douglas debates, and several of Douglas's responses won him disfavor with southern Democrats. Although he won the senatorial election, this faction was responsible for Douglas's removal from the Committee on Territories.

In 1860 Douglas fared better with the Democrats, and his Popular Sovereignty policy was incorporated into the national program. He was chosen as the Democratic candidate for the presidential election. The southern Democrats still refused to accept him and supported their own candidate, John C. Breckinridge. Both Douglas and Breckenridge lost the election to the Republican candidate, Abraham Lincoln.

At the outbreak of the Civil War, Douglas staunchly supported the newly elected Lincoln. Adept at public speaking, Douglas's last contribution to government was a tour of the Northwest to encourage support of the Union, during

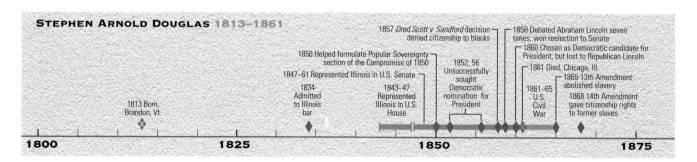

STEPHEN ARNOLD DOUGLAS 1813–1861

1813 Born, Brandon, Vt.

1834 Admitted to Illinois bar

1843–47 Represented Illinois in U.S. House

1847–61 Represented Illinois in U.S. Senate

1850 Helped formulate Popular Sovereignty section of the Compromise of 1850

1852, 56 Unsuccessfully sought Democratic nomination for President

1857 *Dred Scott v. Sandford* decision denied citizenship to blacks

1858 Debated Abraham Lincoln seven times; won reelection to Senate

1860 Chosen as Democratic candidate for President, but lost to Republican Lincoln

1861 Died, Chicago, Ill.

1861–65 U.S. Civil War

1865 13th Amendment abolished slavery

1868 14th Amendment gave citizenship rights to former slaves

1800   1825   1850   1875

which he contracted a fatal case of typhoid fever. Douglas died June 3, 1861, in Chicago, Illinois.

DOUGLAS, WILLIAM ORVILLE William Orville Douglas, a legal educator, New Deal reformer, environmental advocate, and prolific author, was an outspoken and controversial associate justice to the Supreme Court in the twentieth century. For thirty-six and one-half years, under six presidents and five chief justices, Douglas's opinions—including an unequaled 531 dissents—touched and shaped the momentous constitutional questions and crises of the Depression, World War II, the COLD WAR, the Korean War, the CIVIL RIGHTS MOVEMENT, the VIETNAM WAR, the rise of the welfare state, and the fall of RICHARD M. NIXON.

Asserting that the purpose of the Constitution was to "keep the government off the backs of the people," Douglas became a champion of civil liberties on the High Court in seminal cases interpreting FREEDOM OF SPEECH, the right to PRIVACY, PORNOGRAPHY, TREASON, the rights of the ACCUSED, the limits of the military, the limits of Congress, and even the limits of the president of the United States. As an outspoken New Deal reformer and a popular libertarian, he was courted by the Democratic party for high political office, and likewise excoriated by leading Republicans who three times tried to IMPEACH him. A man of enormous energy, he did not confine his public views to opinions from the Supreme Court alone, but wrote over thirty books on a variety of legal and social topics. As an engaging storyteller, vigorous outdoorsman, and blunt social critic, he was irresistible to the liberal press, under whose influence he was named Father of the Year in 1950. At his death in 1980, he was lionized as an outstanding protector of U.S. freedoms.

Since his death, however, historians have criticized both his public career and his private life. From his position on the Supreme Court, he twice flirted with a place on the presidential ticket—with FRANKLIN D. ROOSEVELT in 1944 and with HARRY S. TRUMAN in 1948—despite the clear opposition of his Court colleagues. He

BIOGRAPHY

William Orville Douglas

wrote his opinions faster, and with less scholarship or collegial cooperation, than any of his fellow justices. His lifelong stream of books, bearing the cover commendation Associate Justice of the Supreme Court, showed a similar haste to regard primarily his own views as he exhorted the nation impatiently on foreign policy, anthropology, religion, history, law, economics, and the environment. Unprecedented for a Supreme Court justice, he advocated public issues in extralegal activities around the world, creating difficulties for both the Court and the government. He claimed that J. EDGAR HOOVER had bugged the inner conference room of the Supreme Court Building and had had Federal Bureau of Investigation (FBI) agents plant marijuana on his mountain retreat property in Goose Prairie, Washington; when no evidence of these activities was ever found, he refused to recant. When a stroke at age seventy-five left him paralyzed in a wheelchair, wracked with pain, and periodically incoherent, he nonetheless refused to resign his seat in the High Court until forced to do so through the extraordinary efforts of his colleagues. And even then he insisted on lingering in his judicial office for months, demanding attention as though he were still on the Court.

This brilliant and complex man was born October 16, 1898, in Maine, Minnesota. He grew up in small towns of rural Minnesota, California, and Washington as his family moved in search of a climate that would preserve the frail health of his father, a hardworking Presbyterian minister of Scottish pioneer ancestry. Douglas's father died in Washington when the boy was five, leaving the family with only a meager inheritance, which a local attorney immediately squandered on a foolish investment. Douglas's widowed mother, Julia Bickford Fiske Douglas, had saved just enough to buy a house for the family in Yakima, across the street from the elementary school, where she raised Douglas and his two siblings on the virtues of hard work and high ambition as preparation for success in life. All three of the children achieved success in school and in professional life, but

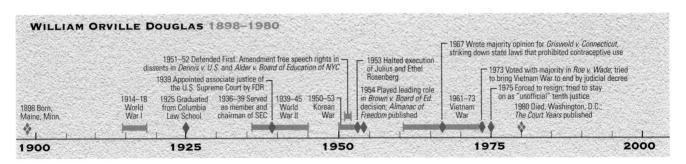

WILLIAM ORVILLE DOUGLAS 1898–1980

1898 Born, Maine, Minn.

1914–18 World War I

1925 Graduated from Columbia Law School

1936–39 Served as member and chairman of SEC

1939 Appointed associate justice of the U.S. Supreme Court by FDR

1939–45 World War II

1950–53 Korean War

1951–52 Defended First Amendment free speech rights in dissents in *Dennis v. U.S.* and *Alder v. Board of Education of NYC*

1953 Halted execution of Julius and Ethel Rosenberg

1954 Played leading role in *Brown v. Board of Ed.* decision; *Almanac of Freedom* published

1961–73 Vietnam War

1967 Wrote majority opinion for *Griswold v. Connecticut*, striking down state laws that prohibited contraceptive use

1973 Voted with majority in *Roe v. Wade*; tried to bring Vietnam War to end by judicial decree

1975 Forced to resign; tried to stay on as "unofficial" tenth justice

1980 Died, Washington, D.C.; *The Court Years* published

1900 1925 1950 1975 2000

Douglas was brilliant: valedictorian of his high school class, Phi Beta Kappa at Whitman College, and second in his class and on law review at Columbia Law School.

Polio had stricken Douglas when he was an infant, and the local doctor had advised the family that he would never fully recover the use of his legs and would probably be dead by age forty. His mother, who favored her firstborn with the name Treasure, went to work massaging the muscles of his legs vigorously in two-hour shifts around the clock for months, telling him that he would recover to run again "like the wind," the way she had as a girl. He not only recovered the use of his legs but, as an adolescent, put himself on a merciless discipline of hiking miles a day in the mountains under full pack, to strengthen his legs to the point of outstanding endurance, determined that no one would ever call him puny.

In 1920 he graduated from Whitman College, in Walla Walla, Washington, and returned home for two years to teach English, Latin, and public speaking in Yakima High School. He pursued a Rhodes Scholarship unsuccessfully, and then decided to hitch by rail across the country to enter Columbia Law School, although he did not yet possess the money for tuition. While in law school, in 1924, he married Mildred Riddle, with whom he had his only two children, Millie Douglas and William O. Douglas, Jr. The marriage ended in divorce twenty-nine years later.

After graduating from Columbia Law in 1925, he practiced in a Wall Street firm for one year before joining the faculty at Columbia and a year later at Yale, where he specialized in corporate law and finance, writing respected casebooks and gaining recognition as an expert in the field. Desperate for a cure to continuous headaches and stomach pains that had plagued him since Wall Street, he briefly undertook psychoanalysis at Yale.

Following the stock market crash of 1929, he did original and painstaking work with the help of sociologist Dorothy S. Thomas, interviewing failed businesses in bankruptcy court to determine the causes of their loss. He was asked to head a study committee of the SECURITIES AND EXCHANGE COMMISSION (SEC) in 1934. In 1936 he became a member of the SEC, and in 1937 he was appointed chairman with the mandate from Franklin D. Roosevelt to reform practices of the stock exchange that had led to the great crash.

In 1939 Roosevelt had Douglas, then chairman of the SEC, hailed off a golf course to meet immediately with him at the White House. "I have a new job for you," the president said in the Oval Office. "It's a job you'll detest." Pausing dramatically to light up a cigarette, the president continued, "I am sending your name to the Senate as Louis Brandeis' successor." Douglas was stunned. At forty, he was about to become the second-youngest Supreme Court justice in history.

Douglas was sworn in on April 17, 1939, and quickly helped constitute a new majority on the Court that supported Roosevelt's New Deal laws regulating the economy. Within two years he had opposed the Court's leading personality, FELIX FRANKFURTER, and its reigning philosophy of defending civil liberties from the BILL OF RIGHTS in cases involving religious freedom and the rights of the accused. It was the beginning of a two-decade battle with Frankfurter and his philosophy of judicial restraint. This conflict did not end amicably, but it helped transform Douglas into a champion of civil liberties. After World War II, Douglas joined forces frequently with Justice HUGO L. BLACK and later Justice WILLIAM J. BRENNAN, JR., in applying the Bill of Rights to protect individual liberties.

In 1951, when fears of COMMUNISM exacerbated by the public ravings of Senator JOSEPH R. MCCARTHY overtook the nation, Douglas's dissent in *Dennis v. United States*, 341 U.S. 494, 71 S. Ct. 857, 95 L. Ed. 1137 (1951), defended the First Amendment free speech rights of Eugene Dennis and ten other members of the American Communist party who admitted teaching the works of KARL MARX, Friedrich Engels, VLADIMIR LENIN, and JOSEPH STALIN. Douglas argued that despite current fears of Communist influence in U.S. society, their speech alone presented no "clear and present danger" to the nation. Similarly, in dissent, he defended the FIRST AMENDMENT rights of several New York schoolteachers who challenged the state's Feinberg law (Educ. Law N.Y.S. 3022) giving authorities the right to compile a list of subversive organizations to which a teacher could not belong. Douglas wrote that teachers need the guarantee of free expression more than anyone and that the Feinberg Law "turn[ed] the school system into a spying project" (*Alder v. Board of Education of City of New York*, 342 U.S. 485, 72 S. Ct. 380, 96 L. Ed. 517 [1952]).

During this same period, he vigorously opposed the expanding use of government WIRE TAPPING enabled by the 1929 *Olmstead* decision, *Olmstead v. United States*, 277 U.S. 438, 48 S. Ct. 564, 72 L. Ed. 944 (1928). Writing for the public in his book *Almanac of Freedom* (1954), Douglas declared that "wire tapping, wherever used, has a black record. The invasion of pri-

"THE FIFTH AMENDMENT IS AN OLD FRIEND AND A GOOD FRIEND . . . ONE OF THE GREAT LANDMARKS IN MAN'S STRUGGLE TO BE FREE OF TYRANNY, TO BE DECENT AND CIVILIZED."

vacy is ominous. It is dragnet in character, recording everything that is said, by the innocent as well as by the guilty. . . . wire tapping is a blight on the civil liberties of the citizen."

In 1953 Douglas single-handedly halted the execution of Julius Rosenberg and Ethel Rosenberg, the defendants in the most sensational spy trial of the cold war (*Rosenberg v. United States*, 346 U.S. 273, 73 S. Ct. 1173, 97 L. Ed. 1607 [1953]). After voting four times not to hear the case, he finally ordered a stay at the last possible minute, and then headed off on vacation. Unable to reach Douglas en route, the other justices called a special session to vacate the stay, and the Rosenbergs were executed. His colleagues accused him of grandstanding. His enemies in Congress accused him of treason, and he survived three IMPEACHMENT attempts led by GERALD R. FORD. Ford, eager to be rid of Douglas, declared that "an impeachable offense is whatever a majority of the House of Representatives considers it to be at a given moment in history." But Douglas was not a traitor but an adamant civil libertarian, unwilling to let the heavy hand of the government crush any individual's rights.

During the tenure of Chief Justice EARL WARREN (1953–69), Douglas found more frequent majorities for his activist philosophy. He took a leading role in reaching a majority for the 1954 *Brown* decision (*Brown v. Board of Education of Topeka, Kansas*, 347 U.S. 483, 74 S. Ct. 686, 98 L. Ed. 873 [1954]) desegregating public schools, telling his colleagues simply that "a state can't classify by color in education." He argued in dissent in several cases that the Bill of Rights was applicable to the states through the Due Process Clause of the FOURTEENTH AMENDMENT, an argument the Court finally accepted in *Mapp v. Ohio*, 367 U.S. 643, 81 S. Ct. 1684, 6 L. Ed. 2d 1081 (1961), which held the Fourth Amendment provision prohibiting unreasonable SEARCHES AND SEIZURES applicable to the states. He supported each of the Warren Court's major decisions extending the rights of criminal suspects, including the right to counsel, in *Gideon v. Wainwright*, 372 U.S. 335, 83 S. Ct. 792, 9 L. Ed. 2d 799 (1963), and the right to know your constitutional rights before being interrogated, in *Miranda v. Arizona*, 384 U.S. 436, 86 S. Ct. 1602, 16 L. Ed. 2d 694 (1966).

In 1965 Douglas wrote for the majority in *Griswold v. Connecticut*, 381 U.S. 479, 85 S. Ct. 1678, 14 L. Ed. 2d 510, striking down a state law that prohibited the use of contraceptives. In the opinion, he argued that, taken together, the First, Fourth, Fifth, and Ninth Amendments created a constitutional right to PRIVACY. This

may have been Douglas's most influential single opinion on the Court. He argued that the government did not belong in the bedroom, which was one of the "zones of privacy" protected by "penumbras" emanating from the specific guarantees in the Bill of Rights. Criticism of the *Griswold* opinion was fierce. But based on this right to privacy, a majority of the Court, Douglas concurring, would vote for a woman's right to have an ABORTION in *Roe v. Wade*, 410 U.S. 113, 93 S. Ct. 705, 35 L. Ed. 2d 147 (1973).

Douglas made no secret of his long-standing dislike for Nixon and the Vietnam War. In the fall of 1967, he dissented from the Court's decision not to review several cases that might have raised the issue of the legality of the Vietnam War. On August 4, 1973, in a solitary performance reminiscent of the Rosenberg stay of execution, acting from the Yakima courthouse near his summer vacation home, Douglas reinstated a lower-court order to stop the Nixon administration's bombing of Cambodia and, in effect, bring the Vietnam War to a halt by judicial decision. Douglas wrote that only Congress could declare war, and Congress had not done so. Six hours later, eight members of the Court reversed him by the telephone polling of Justice THURGOOD MARSHALL.

In his most personal relationships, Douglas was a tyrant. He sternly demanded the back-breaking sixteen-hour days and six-day weeks from his law clerks that he loved to put in himself (when a clerk asked for time off to get married, he granted him twenty-four hours), but never allowed them significant responsibilities for his opinions. One clerk said, "It was a master/slave relationship" (Simon 1980). He married four times while serving on the Supreme Court, to successively younger women: after Riddle, Mercedes Davidson (1953), whom he met in Washington, D.C.; Joan Martin (1962), a twenty-three-year-old college student who had written her senior thesis in praise of him; and Catherine Heffermin (1965), a twenty-one-year-old college student whom he met while she was working as a waitress. Most of his wives found him distant, demanding, and faithless. The 860 pages of his two-volume autobiography (*The Court Years*, 1980) are filled with revenge upon his personal and political enemies, but contain less than a page for his wife of twenty-nine years, Riddle. He was so inept and cold as a father that his two children fled him. As his son put it, "[F]ather was scary."

Felled by a stroke in 1974, he became confined to a wheelchair pushed by an aide, wracked by constant pain, glazed by medication, and increasingly incoherent. But he would not resign. He tried to return to the Court in 1975, refusing all advice to the contrary. His presence was embarrassing to the Court and impossible to sustain. He officially resigned on November 12, 1975, but tried to hang on to an unofficial role as the Court's tenth justice. When even his clerks would not support his fantasy, he prepared a statement of farewell to be read for him to the justices while he sat in his wheelchair. His farewell compared the relationship he had shared with his Court colleagues to the slow warm growth of friendships on a camping trip in the wilderness. His colleagues wept.

Douglas died on January 18, 1980, in Washington, D.C.

The view of the High Court as a somber gathering of old people in black robes pondering the weighty truths of the Constitution was shattered by Douglas. His irrepressible personality, extralegal activities, popular book writing, and serial marriages brought unprecedented color and controversy to the Court. A libertarian by disposition and principle, he would not easily allow the government to abridge the liberties of others, nor would he conform to the traditional role of Supreme Court justice.

CROSS-REFERENCES

Brown v. Board of Education of Topeka, Kansas; Dennis v. United States; Gideon v. Wainwright; Griswold v. Connecticut; Olmstead v. United States; Roe v. Wade; Rosenberg, Julius and Ethel.

DOUGLASS, FREDERICK
A very influential African American leader of the nineteenth century, Frederick Douglass used his exceptional skills as an orator, writer, journalist, and politician to fight for the ABOLITION of SLAVERY and an end to racial DISCRIMINATION. He helped shape the climate of public opinion that led to the ratification of the Thirteenth, Fourteenth, and Fifteenth Amendments to the Constitution, which were created in large measure to protect, respectively, the freedom, citizenship, and voting rights of ex-slaves. His *Narrative of the Life of Frederick Douglass* (1845) is a classic account

BIOGRAPHY

Frederick Douglass

SCHOMBURG CENTER FOR RESEARCH IN BLACK CULTURE

of the dehumanizing effects of slavery for slave and slaveholder alike.

Douglass was born Frederick Augustus Washington Bailey in 1817 or 1818, on a Talbot County, Maryland, plantation. His mother was a black slave and his father most likely her white owner. Douglass was separated from his mother at an early age, and at seven years was sent to Baltimore to work for a family. He later regarded this change from the plantation to the city as a great stroke of fortune because in Baltimore, he was able to begin to educate himself. His master's wife taught him the alphabet, and Douglass, under the tutelage of young boys on the streets and docks, proceeded to teach himself how to read and write. Even when he was very young, his limited reading convinced him of the evils of slavery and the need to seek his freedom.

But Douglass continued to suffer under slavery. At times during the 1830s, he was sent back to the plantation to endure its scourges, including beatings and whippings. He briefly attempted to teach fellow slaves to read and write, but his efforts were quickly put to an end by whites.

In 1838, living again in Baltimore and caulking ships, Douglass escaped north and won his freedom. He married a free African American woman, Anna Murray, and settled in New Bedford, Massachusetts. Now a fugitive slave, he changed his name to Frederick Douglass in order to avoid capture. Douglass quickly became a respected member of the African American community in New Bedford. However, he was disappointed to find that racism was prevalent in the North as well as in the South.

Shortly after his arrival in the North, Douglass became an avid reader of the *Liberator*, a newspaper published by a leading abolitionist, William Lloyd Garrison. He became involved in abolitionist campaigns and soon earned a reputation as an eloquent speaker for the cause. In 1841, he met Garrison and was recruited to speak for the Massachusetts Anti-Slavery Society. Throughout his life, he would travel all

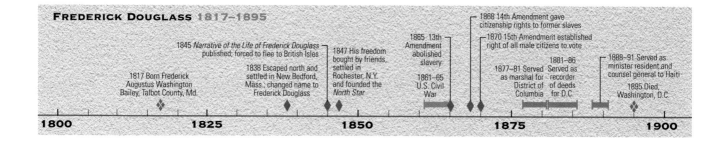

FREDERICK DOUGLASS 1817–1895

1817 Born Frederick Augustus Washington Bailey, Talbot County, Md.

1838 Escaped north and settled in New Bedford, Mass.; changed name to Frederick Douglass

1845 *Narrative of the Life of Frederick Douglass* published; forced to flee to British Isles

1847 His freedom bought by friends, settled in Rochester, N.Y. and founded the *North Star*

1861–65 U.S. Civil War

1865 13th Amendment abolished slavery

1868 14th Amendment gave citizenship rights to former slaves

1870 15th Amendment established right of all male citizens to vote

1877–81 Served as marshal for District of Columbia

1881–86 Served as recorder of deeds for D.C.

1888–91 Served as minister resident and counsel general to Haiti

1895 Died, Washington, D.C.

1800   1825   1850   1875   1900

over the United States on speaking engagements, becoming a famous and sought-after orator.

In part to refute those who did not believe that someone as eloquent as he had once been a slave, Douglass published *Narrative of the Life of Frederick Douglass* in 1845. The book became a best-seller and made Douglass into a celebrity. It also made known his status as a fugitive slave, and he was forced to flee to the British Isles for safety in 1845. During his travels, he was greatly impressed by the relative lack of racism in Ireland, England, and Scotland. English friends purchased his legal freedom in 1846, paying his old master $711.66.

Upon his return to the States in 1847, Douglass settled in Rochester, New York, and founded his own abolitionist newspaper, the *North Star.* In its pages, he published African American writers and focused on African American achievements. He also wrote highly influential editorials for the paper. Douglass published a series of newspapers, including *Frederick Douglass' Weekly,* until 1863.

Douglass continued to lecture widely and became sympathetic to other reformist causes of the day, including the temperance, peace, and feminist movements. By the 1850s and 1860s, he increasingly came to doubt that slavery could be ended by peaceful means. He became friends with the militant abolitionist John Brown, although he did not join Brown in his ill-fated 1859 military campaign against slavery at Harpers Ferry, Virginia.

During the Civil War (1861–65), Douglass fought hard to make the abolition of slavery a Union goal, and he also lobbied for the enlistment of African Americans into the Union armed forces. In public speeches and even in private meetings with President ABRAHAM LINCOLN, Douglass made his case forcefully. Aided by rising sentiment against slavery in the North, both of Douglass's goals became a reality. Lincoln's 1863 EMANCIPATION PROCLAMATION sent a strong signal that the North would seek the abolition of slavery in the South, and in 1865, the THIRTEENTH AMENDMENT to the Constitution formally ended the institution of slavery in the United States. By the end of the war, nearly two hundred thousand African Americans had enlisted in the Union armed forces. Douglass personally helped enlist men for the Fifty-fourth and Fifty-fifth Massachusetts Colored Regiments and served as a leading advocate for the equal treatment of African Americans in the military.

After the Thirteenth Amendment had been ratified in 1865, some abolitionists pronounced their work over. Douglass argued that much more remained to be done, and he continued to struggle for the rights of African Americans. He called for voting rights for African Americans, the repeal of racially discriminatory laws, and the redistribution of land in the South. Although disappointed that land redistribution was never achieved, he was encouraged by the passage of the FOURTEENTH (1868) and FIFTEENTH (1870) AMENDMENTS, which, respectively, protected against the infringement of constitutional rights by the states and established the right of all citizens to vote.

Although these constitutional amendments appeared to guarantee the CIVIL RIGHTS of African Americans, the actual laws and practices of states and localities continued to discriminate against blacks. African Americans were also harassed by violence from private groups. The Ku Klux Klan waged a campaign of terror against African Americans who sought to exercise their civil rights, and white lynch mobs killed hundreds of black men each year. Douglass spoke out against these forms of terrorism and called for federal laws against lynching.

Douglass was a loyal spokesman for the Republican party and vigorously campaigned for its candidates. His support helped gain hundreds of thousands of black votes for Republicans. As a result of such work, several Republican presidents rewarded him with political offices. In 1871, President ULYSSES S. GRANT named him assistant secretary to the Santo Domingo Commission. Later, Republican presidents appointed him marshal (1877–81) and recorder of deeds (1881–86) for the District of Columbia. In 1888, President BENJAMIN HARRISON appointed Douglass minister resident and consul general to Haiti, the first free black republic in the Western Hemisphere. He resigned the position in 1891, over policy differences with the Harrison administration. Although such positions did not afford Douglass great political power in themselves, they provided a comfortable living as well as some recognition for his significant contributions to the public life of the country.

Douglass was also the first African American ever nominated for the vice presidency. He declined the nomination, which came from the little known Equal Rights party in 1872.

To the end of his life, Douglass continued to lecture and write for the cause of freedom. He died on February 20, 1895, in Washington, D.C., after attending a meeting of the National Council of Women.

"NO MAN CAN PUT A CHAIN ABOUT THE ANKLE OF HIS FELLOW MAN WITHOUT AT LAST FINDING THE OTHER END FASTENED ABOUT HIS OWN NECK."

DOWER 📖 The provision that the law makes for a widow out of the lands or TENEMENTS of her husband, for her support and the nurture of her children. A species of LIFE ESTATE that a woman is, by law, entitled to claim on the death of her husband, in the lands and tenements of which he was seised in FEE during the MARRIAGE, and which her issue, if any, might by possibility have inherited. The life estate to which every married woman is entitled on the death of her husband, INTESTATE, or, in case she dissents from his WILL, one-third in value of all lands of which her husband was beneficially seized in law or in fact, at any time during COVERTURE. 📖

The REAL PROPERTY must be inheritable by the wife's offspring in order for her to claim dower. Even if, however, their marriage produces no offspring, the wife is entitled to dower as long as any such progeny of her husband would qualify as his HEIRS at the time of his death.

Prior to the death of the husband, the interest of the wife is called an INCHOATE right of dower, in the sense that it is a claim that is not a present interest but one that might ripen into a legally enforceable right if not prohibited or DIVESTED. It is frequently stated that an inchoate right of dower is a mere EXPECTANCY and not an ESTATE. The law governing dower rights is the law in existence at the time of the husband's death and not the law existing at the time of the marriage.

The courts, however, protect the inchoate right of dower from a FRAUDULENT CONVEYANCE—a transfer of property made to DEFRAUD, delay, or hinder a CREDITOR, or in this case, the wife, or to place such property beyond the creditor's reach—by the husband in contemplation of, or subsequent to, the marriage. Protection is also available against the claims of creditors if the claims arose after the marriage. The posting of SECURITY can be required to protect the interest if oil, gas, or other substances are removed from the land, which thereby results in a DEPRECIATION—a reduction of worth—with respect to the value of the estate. Decisions supporting a contrary view take the position that a wife cannot interfere with her husband's complete enjoyment of the land during his lifetime.

A wife can relinquish her inchoate right of dower by an antenuptial agreement—which is a contract entered into by the prospective spouses prior to the marriage that resolves issues of support, division of property, and distribution of wealth in the event of death, separation, or divorce—or by a RELEASE, that is, the relinquishment of a right, claim, or privilege. See also PREMARITAL AGREEMENT.

The claim of dower is based upon proof of a legally recognized marriage, as distinguished from a GOOD FAITH marriage or a DE FACTO marriage—one in which the parties live together as husband and wife but that is invalid for certain reasons, such as defects in form. A VOIDABLE marriage, one that is VALID when entered into and which remains valid until either party obtains a lawful court order dissolving the marital relationship, suffices for this purpose if it is not rendered VOID—of no legal force or binding effect—before the right to the dower arises.

Most states have varied the dower provisions. The fraction of the estate has frequently been increased from one-third to one-half. The property affected has been expanded from realty only to both realty and PERSONALTY. The time of ownership has sometimes been changed from "owned during marriage" to "owned at death." The type of interest given to the surviving spouse has been expanded from a life estate to outright ownership of property.

In many states, a widow is entitled to a statutory share in her husband's estate. This is often called an ELECTIVE SHARE because the surviving spouse can choose to accept the provisions made for her in the decedent's WILL or

Dower is the provision the law makes for a widow in the distribution of her husband's estate.

UPI/CORBIS-BETTMANN

accept the share of the property specified by law of DESCENT AND DISTRIBUTION or the particular law governing the elective share. In many JURISDICTIONS, dower has been abolished and replaced by the elective share. In others, statutes expressly provide that a spouse choose among the elective share, the dower, or the provisions of the will.

Common law prescribes that an absolute DIVORCE will bar a claim of dower. A legal separation— sometimes labeled a divorce from bed and board, A MENSA ET THORO—does not end the marital relationship. Unless there is an express statute, such a divorce will not defeat a claim of dower. This is also true with respect to an INTERLOCUTORY decree of divorce, an interim or temporary court order.

In some states, statutes provide that dower can be denied upon proof of particular types of misconduct, such as ADULTERY, which is voluntary sexual intercourse of a married person with a person other than his or her spouse. Statutes in several states preserve dower if a divorce or legal separation is obtained due to the fault of the other spouse.

In many states, statutes provide that a murderer is not entitled to property rights in the estate of the victim upon the principle that a person must not be allowed to profit from personal wrong. Following this theory, a CONSTRUCTIVE TRUST will be declared in favor of the heirs or devisees of the deceased spouse.

DOWN PAYMENT 📖 A percentage of the total purchase price of an item that is proffered when the item is bought on credit. 📖

In an INSTALLMENT sales agreement, a buyer is required to pay part of the total price, usually in cash, and later pays the balance through a number of regularly scheduled payments.

A down payment is sometimes known as EARNEST MONEY, or a sum of money that a buyer pays upon entering a CONTRACT to indicate a GOOD FAITH intention as well as an ability to pay the balance.

DRACONIAN LAWS 📖 A code of laws prepared by Draco, the celebrated lawgiver of Athens. 📖

These laws were exceedingly severe, and the term is now sometimes applied to any laws of unusual harshness.

DRAFT 📖 A written order by the first party, called the DRAWER, instructing a second party, called the DRAWEE (such as a bank), to pay money to a third party, called the PAYEE. An order to pay a sum certain in money, signed by a drawer, payable ON DEMAND or at a definite time, to order or BEARER.

A tentative, provisional, or preparatory writing out of any document (as a will, contract, lease, and so on) for purposes of discussion and

Sample sight and time drafts

$\$$_____   [*City, State*] _____, 19_____

At sight (*or* on presentation; *or* on demand) pay to the order of _____ (*or* to bearer) _____ dollars at _____.

To _____
     Name of Drawee   Signature of Drawer

_____ Bank
For Customer's Use

$\$$_____   [*City, State*] _____, 19_____

On _____ Pay to the order of the _____ Bank _____ dollars, with exchange and collection charges.

Value received and charged to the account of

To _____

correction, which is afterward to be prepared in its final form.

Compulsory CONSCRIPTION of persons into military service.

Also, a small arbitrary deduction or allowance made to a merchant or importer, in the case of goods sold by weight or taxable by weight, to cover possible loss of weight in handling or from differences in scales. ▥

A draft that is payable on demand is called a SIGHT DRAFT because the drawee must comply with its terms of payment when it is presented, in his or her sight or presence, by the payee. In contrast, a TIME DRAFT is one that is payable only on the date specified on its face or thereafter.

A draft may be payable to a designated payee or to the bearer—the person who has possession of the draft at the time it is presented to the drawee for payment—pursuant to the drawer's directions.

A draft is sometimes synonymous with a BILL OF EXCHANGE, COMMERCIAL PAPER, or NEGOTIABLE INSTRUMENT.

DRAFTER ▥ The person who draws or frames a legal document such as a WILL, PLEADING, CONVEYANCE, or CONTRACT. One who writes an original legislative bill for the U.S. Senate or House of Representatives is called the drafter of that bill. ▥

DRAIN ▥ A trench or ditch to convey water from wet land; a channel through which water may flow off. The word has no technical legal meaning. Any hollow space in the ground, natural or artificial, where water is collected and passes off, is a ditch or drain.

Also, sometimes, the EASEMENT or SERVITUDE (acquired by GRANT or PRESCRIPTION) that consists of the right to drain water through another's land. ▥

A number of states have *drainage statutes* in order to protect the welfare of the public. Such statutes provide for the construction of drains in areas that are swampy, marshy, or overflowed past their natural boundaries. Also contained in drainage statutes are provisions that regulate the creation and organization of *drainage districts*. The state legislature has the discretion to decide which lands will be included within a particular drainage district. For example, such a district might include territory of a city or village or property in two or more counties.

The specific plan for the construction of a drain is within the discretion of local authorities as modified by limitations or restrictions set forth by state drainage statutes. Only land that will be benefited through drainage improvements should properly be included within a drainage district.

The Army Corps of Engineers built this drain to control water that was overflowing from a nearby river.

In certain instances, LIABILITY has been extended to drainage districts that have failed to maintain existing drains. In order to remedy this situation, in some cases, landowners are given a certain portion of a drain to clean out and maintain in proper repair. Regardless of whether or not a landowner is specifically given the responsibility for maintenance, a landowner may only close or obstruct a drain with his or her neighbors' consent. If the land of an individual is injured because a public drain is being obstructed by a neighbor, then the person can bring suit for the damage resulting therefrom.

Subject to limitations imposed by the U.S. Constitution, a state legislature has the power to authorize drainage districts to prescribe SPECIAL ASSESSMENTS to cover the cost of drainage improvements. Generally, only those lands included within a particular district are subject to such assessment. In certain states, school lands are exempted from assessments that drainage districts levy. Assessment review boards frequently entertain objections to drainage assessments; however, if no such board exists, assessments are subject to judicial reviews in the courts. A property owner can, therefore, go to court to challenge what he or she believes to be an unjust drainage assessment against his or her land.

DRAMSHOP ACTS ▥ Statutes, also called civil liability acts, that impose civil LIABILITY upon one who sells intoxicating liquors when a third party has been injured as a result of the purchaser's INTOXICATION and such sale has either caused or contributed to the state of intoxication. 📖

A dramshop is any type of drinking establishment where liquor is sold for consumption on the premises, such as a bar, a saloon, or, in some cases, a restaurant. Under dramshop acts, the seller of liquor can be sued by an individual who is injured by an intoxicated person. Such acts protect the injured third party not only against PERSONAL INJURIES and property damages resulting directly from the actions of the intoxicated individual (such as those resulting from drunken driving or ASSAULT AND BATTERY) but also against the loss of family support owing to such injuries. Generally, the person who became intoxicated cannot sue the seller if she or he is injured, nor can any active participant in the drinking.

The dramshop laws are based on the principle that anyone who profits from the sale of alcoholic beverages should be held liable for any resulting damages. For a seller to be held liable, it is unnecessary to show that he or she is negligent, provided it is proved that the seller sold liquor to a habitual drunkard or a person who was already drunk, which is generally illegal in itself.

Dramshop acts originated in the TEMPERANCE MOVEMENT of the mid-1800s. In Illinois, for example, the first such law was passed in 1872 and amended in subsequent decades. By the 1990s, more than forty states had either dramshop acts or court rulings that made a commercial server or seller of ALCOHOL liable if an intoxicated customer caused an accident or injury upon leaving the server's or seller's establishment (e.g., the Iowa Alcoholic Beverage Control Act [Iowa Code Ann. § 123.92 (West)]). Typical modern statutes include limitations on awards, specifications regarding the commercial defendant's type and degree of liability, and a STATUTE OF LIMITATIONS.

By the late 1980s, dramshop statutes and court rulings had caused a dramatic increase in lawsuits involving liquor liability, with a corresponding increase in damage awards to victims. As a result, liquor liability insurance became increasingly expensive and difficult to obtain.

To guard against costly dramshop suits, liquor vendors have taken a variety of steps to prevent negligent behavior: eliminating "happy hours," reducing late-night operation, offering free Breathalyzer tests, instituting designated-driver programs, and training servers on how to deal with intoxicated patrons. Several states

Dramshop Acts
Alcohol-related Traffic Fatalities, 1985 to 1993*

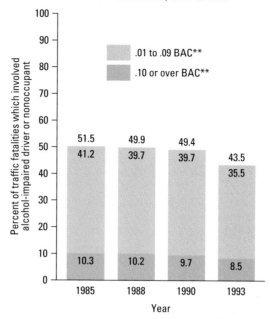

* Based on data from the Fatal Accident Reporting System (FARS). FARS data are gathered on motor vehicle accidents that occur on roadways customarily open to the public, resulting in the death of a person within thirty days of the accident.

** BAC stands for blood alcohol concentration. The BAC level applies to accidents in which the driver *or* nonoccupant was intoxicated.

Source: National Traffic Safety Administration, *Fatal Accident Reporting System,* annual.

have made precautions such as these mandatory. Some, such as Oklahoma, have banned happy hours (see 37 Okla. Stat. Ann. § 537 [West]); others have required server training. Many insurance companies either require such preventive measures or offer incentives for their use.

Many states have extended dramshop liability to corporate or individual social hosts who provide alcoholic beverages without charge. This new source of liability has produced an extraordinary number of lawsuits. Accordingly, individuals wishing to host a social or business function in one of these states would now be required to take many of the same precautions commercial establishments do, including obtaining liquor liability insurance, or else they would have to hold their gathering at an insured bar or hotel.

DRAW 📖 To aim a firearm, or deadly weapon, at a particular target.

To prepare a written BILL OF EXCHANGE, COMMERCIAL PAPER, DRAFT, or NEGOTIABLE INSTRUMENT and place one's SIGNATURE on it, creating a legal obligation under its terms. To write a document, such as a DEED, COMPLAINT, or PETITION, including the essential information necessary to make it legally effective upon its execution by the designated parties.

To lawfully remove money from an account held in a bank, treasury, or other depository. 📖

DRAWEE 📖 A person or BANK that is ordered by its depositor, a DRAWER, to withdraw money from an account to pay a designated sum to a person according to the terms of a CHECK or a DRAFT. 📖

See also COMMERCIAL PAPER.

DRAWER 📖 A person who orders a BANK to withdraw money from an account to pay a designated person a specific sum according to the term of a BILL, a CHECK, or a DRAFT. An individual who writes and signs a COMMERCIAL PAPER, thereby becoming obligated under its terms. 📖

DRED SCOTT v. SANDFORD In *Dred Scott v. Sandford*, 60 U.S. (19 How.) 393, 15 L. Ed. 691 (1857), the U.S. Supreme Court faced the divisive issue of SLAVERY. Chief Justice ROGER B. TANEY, a former slaveholder, authored the Court's opinion, holding that the U.S. Constitution permitted the unrestricted ownership of black slaves by white U.S. CITIZENS. In a stunning 7–2 decision, the Court declared that slaves and emancipated blacks could not be full U.S. citizens. Any attempt by Congress to limit the spread of slavery in U.S. territories was held to be a direct violation of slaveowners' DUE PROCESS rights.

Chief Justice Taney's opinion fueled the nineteenth-century abolitionist movement and helped push the United States toward civil war. Although Taney was an accomplished jurist who served as chief justice for twenty-nine years, his record was permanently tarnished by what many considered to be his flawed reasoning in *Dred Scott*.

African slavery was introduced in the American colonies in 1619. As the new country grew, slavery spread throughout the South, where cheap labor was needed for harvesting large cotton and tobacco crops. During the early nineteenth century, opponents of slavery began to organize in the North.

Abolitionists wanted to restrict slavery to the Southern states; their ultimate goal was to outlaw black servitude throughout the United States. As new territories from the Louisiana Purchase applied for U.S. statehood, the issue became a sticking point. Most Southerners supported the spread of slavery, viewing it as a necessary condition for their social, political, and economic survival. Most Northerners favored the containment and eventual eradication of slavery. Although political moderates called

for voters in each new territory to resolve the slavery issue, a national consensus on this point was never reached.

The 1820 MISSOURI COMPROMISE was an attempt by the U.S. Congress to balance the competing viewpoints. Congress passed a law designating as free states any new states located north of a line drawn across the Louisiana Purchase. New states south of the line would be slave states. In other words, slavery was outlawed north of Missouri's border and west to the Rocky Mountains. After the passage of the Missouri Compromise, two new states were admitted: Missouri, where slavery was permitted, and Maine, where it was forbidden.

The Missouri Compromise did not improve the bitter rivalry between pro-slavery and anti-slavery forces. The controversial *Dred Scott* opinion further exacerbated regional tensions.

Dred Scott was a slave owned by Dr. John Emerson, a U.S. Army officer. In 1834, Scott moved with Emerson from Missouri, a slave state, to Illinois, a state in which slavery was prohibited by statute. Scott and Emerson also lived in Northern U.S. territories that later became the free states of Minnesota and Wisconsin. In 1838, Scott and his family returned to Missouri with Emerson.

When Emerson died, Scott sued Emerson's widow in Missouri state court, seeking freedom for himself and his family. Scott's 1846 lawsuit claimed that his prior residence in a free state and free territories entitled him to liberty and back wages since 1834.

Scott won his case in the lower court. Emerson's widow appealed to the state supreme court, which sided with her. Then, she married Calvin Clifford Chafee, a prominent Massachusetts abolitionist and member of Congress. The new Mrs. Chafee switched to the abolitionist camp and agreed to seek a federal ruling against slavery on Scott's behalf.

Scott was sold in a sham transaction to Mrs. Chafee's brother, John F. A. Sandford, an abolitionist from New York. Sandford agreed to participate in the *Dred Scott* case as a personal protest against slavery.

Scott filed a lawsuit against his new owner in federal court. A federal court was able to hear the case because of diversity of JURISDICTION, which entitles litigants from two different states (in this case, Missouri and New York) to pursue claims in federal court.

Like the state lawsuit, the federal case claimed that Scott was no longer a slave, owing to his previous residence in a free state and free territory. The federal court ruled against Scott,

Dred Scott sued for his freedom in 1857, claiming that his residence with his owner in a free state and free territories entitled him to liberty. The Supreme Court ruled against Scott, sparking outrage among abolitionists. The U.S. Civil War began in 1861.

who then brought his case before the U.S. Supreme Court in a WRIT of error—an order from an appeals court requiring a trial court to send records to the U.S. Supreme Court for review.

The Supreme Court conducted a four-day hearing. Chief Justice Taney delivered what he hoped would be the definitive statement on slavery in the United States. Taney, a respected Maryland lawyer and former U.S. attorney general, had succeeded the legendary John Marshall as chief justice. He used *Dred Scott* as a national forum on constitutional rights and race.

Chief Justice Taney's colleague Associate Justice SAMUEL NELSON urged the Court to reach a narrow decision based on the facts in *Dred Scott*. Because Scott's original action was brought in a Missouri court, Nelson believed simply that state law should prevail in the case. Under Missouri law, a slave's status was not affected by a temporary change in residence.

Chief Justice Taney did not want Scott defeated in a narrow holding. Instead, he wrote a sweeping defense of slavery, emphasizing the slaveowners' constitutional rights and privileges. Taney observed that under the Due Process Clause of the FIFTH AMENDMENT of the U.S. Constitution, no person can be deprived of property without legal proceedings. By outlawing slavery in certain U.S. territories, the Missouri Compromise stripped slaveowners of their constitutional right to own PROPERTY, or "articles of merchandise," as Taney referred to slaves. Taney found the Missouri Compromise unconstitutional. (Actually, the Missouri Com-

promise had been repealed by Congress in 1854, but Taney's ruling nevertheless worried abolitionists, who feared that Taney's findings could be applied to any federal legislation that restricted slavery.) Thus, the *Dred Scott* decision not only sanctioned slavery but encouraged its spread throughout all U.S. territories.

Taney's opinion also declared that black slaves and their descendants could not become U.S. citizens. Because blacks were ineligible for citizenship, they could not sue in federal court. Taney claimed that the architects of the U.S. Constitution did not intend for blacks to have constitutionally protected rights and immunities. The Founding Fathers had regarded blacks as socially and politically unfit. Taney observed that even if Scott were free, he could not appear before federal court, because of his race. However, Taney determined that Scott was not free, because his brief residence in a free state did not divest him of slave status.

President JAMES BUCHANAN hoped that the Supreme Court's unequivocal ruling in *Dred Scott* would dispose of the slavery issue once and for all. The opinion had the opposite effect. Outrage among abolitionists and fence-sitters was deep. The nascent Republican party benefited from *Dred Scott*, as new members joined in the wake of the pro-slavery ruling. The Republican party denounced the *Dred Scott* decision, calling for measures to restrict slavery. Presidential candidate ABRAHAM LINCOLN used the case as a campaign issue and pledged to overturn the Court's ruling against Scott. Lincoln won the presidential election in 1860, and in 1861, the Civil War began.

After the unfortunate ruling, Scott was freed by Sandford and worked as a porter in a St. Louis hotel. He died of tuberculosis in 1858 or 1859.

Sandford was institutionalized for mental illness, a condition his friends traced to his public involvement in the *Dred Scott* fiasco.

The Supreme Court's reputation suffered greatly owing to its poor handling of the slavery issue. Newspaper editors and politicians lambasted the Court for its colossal misstep. Historians single out Taney's *Dred Scott* decision as one of the lowest points in U.S. jurisprudence.

DRIVING UNDER THE INFLUENCE (DUI)
See DWI.

DROIT 📖 [*French, Justice, right, law.*] A term denoting the abstract concept of law or a RIGHT. 📖

Droit is as variable a phrase as the English *right* or the Latin *jus*. It signifies the entire body of law or a right in terms of a duty or obligation.

DRUGGIST ▥ An individual who, as a regular course of business, mixes, compounds, dispenses, and sells medicines and similar health aids. ▥

The term *druggist* may be used interchangeably with pharmacist.

Ordinarily, druggists must be registered under the Food, Drug, and Cosmetic Act (21 U.S.C.A. § 301 et seq. [1938]). Federal drug abuse laws make provisions for the special registration of any individual who handles controlled substances.

Regulation As a public health measure, states have the power to regulate the preparation and dispensing of drugs. They can proscribe the sale of certain substances without a prescription and specifically designate who is permitted to deal in prescription drugs. Statutes govern the procedures that must be observed when drugs are handled, as well as the steps that must be taken for the inspection of drugstores and pharmacy records by agents of the state.

States can properly mandate that pharmacists be licensed, provided the necessary qualifications are not unreasonable. For example, although it would be reasonable for a state to require that pharmacists earn college degrees, it would be unreasonable to require them to be natural-born citizens of the United States. State legislatures have the authority to prohibit any type of improper competition that would tend to lower the service standards.

Druggists must be licensed and registered because they handle controlled substances.

JEFF GREENBURG/PHOTOEDIT

Education and License A druggist must ordinarily be a graduate of an accredited pharmacy school and be of sound moral character. In some instances, he or she might be required to pass a written qualifying examination. An individual who conforms to all the requisite qualifications cannot be refused a LICENSE arbitrarily.

An individual who is licensed in one state does not have the authority to dispense drugs in other states, except where one state consents to recognize a license that has been issued in another state. A license might have to be periodically renewed and can be revoked or suspended for misconduct, such as the selling of an unlabeled drug, the unauthorized substitution of a cheaper for a more expensive drug, or the sale of prescription drugs to an individual who does not have a valid prescription.

Any state board decision to grant, revoke, or suspend a license is a proper subject for court review. A judge has the power to modify the decision of the board in the event that it is either arbitrary or unsupported by EVIDENCE.

Any business or individual engaged in handling drugs has a legal obligation to exercise proper care.

A druggist does not have the duty to fill every prescription that is presented, and he or she is not permitted to fill a prescription that appears to be a sham. A druggist who refuses to fill a prescription must return such prescription to the customer. The pharmacist is not permitted to retain it, for example, merely because money is owed by the customer.

Pharmacists are required to maintain written records of the drugs they sell and must allow the proper state officials to inspect such records. It is not ordinarily unlawful for a pharmacist to fill a prescription on the direction of a doctor who telephones it in, even if the doctor does not subsequently send a written authorization. The pharmacist, however, is required to make a written record at the time the prescription is filled.

Although a pharmacist is not required to know everything possible about drugs, he or she is required to be as skilled as most others in the profession. Additionally, a pharmacist owes customers a high degree of care in the service given to them, and they may properly make the assumption that the drugs that they are sold are suitable for the use that he or she recommends. Customers can rely upon any specific claims that the pharmacist makes for the drugs.

Liability for Injuries A druggist who has failed to comply with the legal responsibilities of the profession can be subject to a legal action by a consumer. LIABILITY is extended to a licensed pharmacist for his or her own NEGLIGENCE as well as the negligence of employees who work for him or her. The pharmacist is not ordinarily held liable for injuries sustained due to medicines sold by him or her in their original packages.

Drugstores A state can require that a drugstore be registered, and some mandate that the individual who runs the store be a licensed pharmacist. Regardless of whether or not this is a requirement, only a licensed pharmacist is permitted to dispense drugs. In addition, depending on individual state statute, some types of drugs can be sold only by a pharmacist.

Certain types of drugs have been designated patent medicines and household remedies, such as hydrogen peroxide, zinc oxide, camphor olive oil, aspirin, isopropyl alcohol, and essence of peppermint, and they may or may not be sold exclusively by pharmacists. Foods ordinarily do not fall under the category of drugs to be sold only by pharmacists regardless of health claims that are made for them. Vitamins are regarded as medicines in some instances and as food in others. Ordinarily, all of these items may be sold without a pharmacy license.

A physician does not have any special right to own or operate a drugstore. A person should not, however, be denied a license merely because he or she is also a medical doctor. Laws governing pharmacy do not generally interfere with the right of a physician to sell drugs to his or her patients. The physician cannot, however, make it a regular practice to fill prescriptions that other physicians send.

CROSS-REFERENCES
Drugs and Narcotics; Health Care; Physicians and Surgeons.

DRUGS AND NARCOTICS

Drugs are articles intended for use in the diagnosis, cure, mitigation, treatment, or prevention of disease in humans or animals, and any articles other than food intended to affect the mental or body function of humans or animals. *Narcotics* are any drugs that dull the senses and commonly become addictive after prolonged use.

In the scientific community, drugs are defined as substances that can affect a human's or animal's biological and neurological states. They may be organic, such as the chemical tetrahydrocannabinol (THC), which occurs naturally in marijuana; or synthetic, such as amphetamines or sedatives, which are manufactured in laboratories. Drugs can be swallowed, injected with a needle, applied to the skin, taken as a suppository, or smoked. Scientists catego-

rize drugs according to their effects. Among their categories are analgesics, which kill pain, and psychoactive drugs, which alter the mind or behavior. Some psychoactive substances produce psychological highs or lows according to whether they are stimulants or depressants, respectively. Others, called hallucinogens, produce psychedelic states of consciousness; lysergic acid diethylamide (LSD) and mescaline are examples of such drugs. Marijuana is placed in its own category.

U.S. law categorizes these substances differently. Commonly, federal and state statutes distinguish drugs from narcotics. Drugs are substances designed for use in and on the body for the diagnosis, cure, treatment, or prevention of disease. These substances are regulated by the FOOD AND DRUG ADMINISTRATION (FDA). Drugs have been defined to include such things as herb tonics, cold salves, laxatives, weight reduction aids, vitamins, and even blood. Narcotics are defined by statute as substances that either stimulate or dull an individual's senses, and that ordinarily become habit-forming (addictive) when used over time. The regulation of narcotics falls into two areas. Legal narcotics are regulated by the FDA and are generally available only with a physician's prescription. The production, possession, and sale of illegal narcotics—commonly called controlled substances—are banned by statute.

Drug Laws Authority to regulate drug use rests foremost with the federal government, derived from its power to regulate interstate commerce. States are free to legislate so long as their laws remain consistent with federal law. Most states have adopted federal models for their own drug legislation.

Current law has two main objectives. First, it regulates the manufacture, sale, and use of legal drugs such as aspirin, sleeping pills, and antidepressants. Second, it prohibits and punishes the manufacture, possession, and sale of illegal drugs from marijuana to heroin, as well as some dangerous legal drugs.

The distinction between legal and illegal drugs is a twentieth-century phenomenon. During the nineteenth century, there was very little control over drugs. The federal government regulated the smallpox vaccine in 1813 (2 Stat. 806) and established some controls through the Imported Drugs Act of 1848 (9 Stat. 237, *repealed by* Tariff Act of 1922 [42 Stat. 858, 989]). But addictive substances such as opium and cocaine were legal; in fact, the latter remained a minor ingredient in Coca-Cola soft drinks until 1903. Heroin, discovered in 1888, was prescribed for treating other addictions.

California began restricting opium in 1875, but widespread criminalization of the substance would wait for decades.

States began a widespread movement toward control of legal and illegal drugs at the turn of the twentieth century. The federal government joined this process with the PURE FOOD AND DRUG ACT OF 1906 (34 Stat. 768, 1906, ch. 3915, §§ 1–13, *repealed by* Federal Food, Drug, and Cosmetics Act of 1938), which primarily sought to protect consumers from "misbranded or poisonous" drugs, medicines, and alcohol. Establishing federal JURISDICTION over the domestic manufacture and sale of drugs, it also regulated foreign imports.

Nevertheless, when Congress passed the Harrison Act of 1914 (Pub. L. No. 223, 38 Stat. 785), which imposed a tax on opium and cocaine, it stopped short of declaring either drug illegal. Most efforts to restrict drug use focused on ALCOHOL, demonized by the temperance movement, whose Prohibition crusade culminated in the passage of the EIGHTEENTH AMENDMENT and the VOLSTEAD ACT of 1920 (41 Stat. 305), which made alcohol illegal. Alcohol remained illegal until the repeal of Prohibition in 1933.

Despite numerous amendments, flaws in the Pure Food and Drug Act spurred Congress to replace it. In 1938 federal lawmakers enacted the Federal Food, Drug, and Cosmetics Act (FFDC) (21 U.S.C.A. § 301 et seq.), which established the Food and Drug Administration (FDA) as the federal agency charged to enforce the law. The FFDC exerted broad control over the domestic commercial drug market. Over the next two decades, states and the federal government continued to criminalize nonmedicinal and recreational drugs, and by midcentury the division between legal and illegal drugs was firmly in place. In 1970 Congress passed the Comprehensive Drug Abuse Prevention and Control Act (21 U.S.C.A. § 801 et seq.), which continues to be the primary source of federal law on controlled substances.

Both over-the-counter and prescription drugs are tightly regulated under the FFDC. This act and the Kefauver-Harris Drug Amendments of 1962 (Pub. L. No. 87-781, 76 Stat. 781) give the FDA a broad mandate. The agency protects consumers from the potential hazards of dangerous drugs, misleading labels, and FRAUD. The FDA sets standards of safety and quality, and its enforcement duties include the research, inspection, and licensing of drugs for manufacture and sale. Because the law requires that drugs not be adulterated, the FDA ascertains that they conform to legal standards of strength, quality, and purity. It also classifies which drugs are to be dispensed only by a physician's prescription. Finally, new drugs can be placed on the market only after being approved by the FDA. Traditionally a slow process, FDA approval was speeded up significantly for some drugs in the 1980s and 1990s, largely in response to the AIDS epidemic.

To control the use of dangerous drugs, federal law and most state statutes use a classification system outlined by the Uniform Controlled Substances Act, based on the federal Comprehensive Drug Abuse Prevention and Control Act. This system includes both illegal and dangerous legal drugs. It uses five groups, called schedules, to organize drugs according to their potential for medical use, harm, or abuse, and it imposes a series of controls and penalties for each schedule.

Heroin, hallucinogens, and marijuana are placed on schedule I, since they are thought to have a high potential for harm and no medical use. Other types of opiates and cocaine are on schedule II. Most depressants and stimulants are on schedule III. Some mild tranquilizers are on schedule IV. Schedule V is for drugs, like cough syrup mixtures containing some codeine, that are considered medically useful and less dangerous but can cause limited physical and psychological dependence. Under the law, drugs may be rescheduled as new evidence of their uses or risks becomes apparent, and the attorney general has the authority to put new drugs on the schedules at any time.

Penalties are established according to the severity of the crime. POSSESSION of a controlled substance is the most simple crime involving drugs, possession with intent to sell is more serious, and selling or trafficking incurs the greatest penalties. The exact penalty for a particular offense depends on numerous factors, including the type of drug, its amount, and the convicted party's previous criminal record. Penalties range from small monetary fines, to life imprisonment and even greater punishments. Under a general expansion of federal offenses that can invoke CAPITAL PUNISHMENT, the 1994 crime bill imposed the death penalty for major drug trafficking (Pub. L. No. 103-322, 108 Stat. 1796). Generally, the highest price paid by drug offenders is prison time for trafficking. According to 1993 statistics from the Department of Justice, the average federal sentence for selling powder cocaine was 79 months; the average for trafficking in crack cocaine was 141 months.

Between the mid-1980s and early 1990s, lawmakers enacted the harshest drug laws in U.S. history. The impetus for these laws came from the so-called war on drugs, a broad federal and state public policy push initiated under President RONALD REAGAN that received widespread public support. Among its many initiatives was the creation of the cabinet-level office of the national director of drug control policy, known as the drug czar, to coordinate national and international antidrug efforts.

The war on drugs also created a patchwork of antidrug laws. These included the Anti–Drug Abuse Act of 1986 (Pub. L. No. 99-570, 100 Stat. 3207), which toughened penalties for drug violations involving cocaine, especially its smokable derivative, crack. The law imposed mandatory minimum sentences, even for first-time offenders. For sentencing purposes, it established a ratio that regards one gram of crack as equivalent to one hundred grams of powder cocaine. While greatly increasing the number of drug offenders in prisons, the law has provoked considerable controversy over its effect on minorities. The Anti–Drug Abuse Act of 1988 (Pub. L. No. 100-690, 102 Stat. 4181) further increased federal jurisdiction over drug crime. For the first time, it became a federal crime to possess even a minimal amount of a controlled substance. Penalties were added for crimes involving MINORS, pregnant women, and the sale of drugs within one hundred feet of public and private schools. States toughened their laws, too. Michigan, for example, imposed life imprisonment without parole for cocaine trafficking (Mich. Comp. Laws Ann. § 333.7403(2)(a)(i)).

Drug Policy and Law Enforcement

The enforcement of U.S. drug laws involves the use of substantial federal and state resources to educate, interdict, and prosecute. Estimates of the total annual cost of drug enforcement ranged from $20 billion to $30 billion in the 1990s. The federal government directs drug enforcement policy through the national director of drug control policy. Policy implementation involves both federal and state agencies, including the Justice Department, the Drug Enforcement Administration (DEA), the Federal Bureau of Investigation (FBI), the State Department, branches of the armed services and the U.S. Coast Guard, and local police departments. Drug enforcement is primarily a national effort, yet because drugs enter the United States from other countries, it also has international ramifications.

The war on drugs may be traced back to the 1960s when illicit drugs became popular. The accompanying increase in drug use led to comprehensive antidrug legislation under President RICHARD M. NIXON, whose administration intro-

Drugs and Narcotics

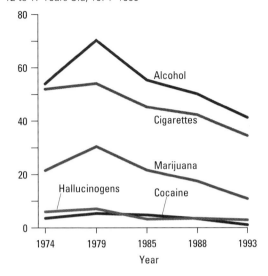

Selected Drugs Ever Used by Minors 12 to 17 Years Old, 1974–1993

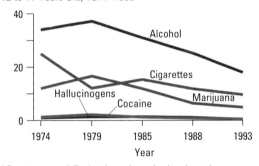

Selected Drugs Currently Used by Minors 12 to 17 Years Old, 1974–1993*

*_Current users_ are defined as those who used a given drug at least once within the month prior to the study.

Source: U.S. Substance Abuse and Mental Health Services Administration, _National Household Survey on Drug Abuse,_ annual.

duced the metaphor of war for the drive to enforce drug laws. In the 1980s, under President Reagan, the campaign took its present form. The Reagan administration's public relations campaign, based on the slogan Just Say No, was bolstered by stricter state and federal drug laws. Federal spending to enforce drug laws rose from $37 million in 1969 to $1.06 billion in 1983. Over the next decade, it increased to approximately $30 billion, including the full cost of federal, state, and local law enforcement efforts, along with costs incurred by the judiciary and prison and health care systems.

Enforcement efforts are shared between federal and state governments. Joint federal-state task forces investigate illegal drug sales for two key reasons. First, states have declared an interest in eradicating the illegal sale and use of controlled substances through the enactment of

CRACK COCAINE AND THE WAR ON DRUGS

In the war on drugs in the United States, race is a critical issue. Although statistics indicate that African Americans account for only 12 percent of all illegal drug use, they make up 44 percent of all drug arrests. This racial disparity has drawn the attention of policy makers, politicians, and the courts. Many observers attribute much of it to the severe penalties imposed for offenses involving crack cocaine, which lead to the arrest and conviction of primarily black defendants.

Smokable cocaine, or crack, originated in the 1980s in U.S. inner cities. Because crack costs much less than powder cocaine, it quickly became the choice of poor drug users. In response to the resulting increased use of crack, Congress passed the Anti–Drug Abuse Act of 1986 (Pub. L. No. 99-570, 100 Stat. 3207 [codified as amended in scattered sections of 21 U.S.C.A. §§ 801–970]).

The 1986 law regards one gram of crack as equivalent to one hundred grams of powder cocaine. The U.S. Sentencing Commission adopted this ratio when it revised the Sentencing Guidelines that same year. In 1988 the Anti–Drug Abuse Act was amended to establish new mandatory minimum sentences. The amendment's sponsor, Representative E. Clay Shaw, Jr. (R-Fla.), said of the tougher sentences: "Crack is an extraordinarily dangerous drug so we must take extraordinary steps to combat it."

Under federal law the offense of selling five grams of crack, for example, is punishable by a mandatory minimum sentence of five years. To receive the same sentence for trafficking in powder cocaine, an offender would have to sell five hundred grams. Thus, small-time crack dealers can receive longer prison terms than cocaine wholesalers. In addition, mandatory minimum sentences for crack offenses mean that plea bargaining for a reduced sentence is not available. First-time offenses involving crack or powder cocaine are also differentiated. First-time offenders convicted in powder cocaine cases often receive parole and drug treatment; most first-time offenders in crack cases receive jail sentences.

By the early 1990s, the effect of these harsher laws on African Americans was evident. In a survey of 1992 sentencing data, the U.S. Sentencing Commission found that 92.6 percent of offenders sentenced for crack offenses were black, whereas 4.7 percent were white. With regard to cocaine offenses in general, 78 percent of offenders were black, and 6 percent were white.

The Department of Justice's Bureau of Justice Statistics concluded in 1993 that blacks are jailed longer than whites for drug offenses. The bureau explained that "the main reasons that African Americans' sentences are longer than whites' . . . was that 83 percent of all Federal offenders convicted of trafficking in crack cocaine in guideline cases were black, and the average sentence imposed for crack trafficking was twice as long as for trafficking in powdered cocaine."

Some critics believe that the racial disparities in sentencing are a result of intentional discrimination. They argue that race has long been an issue in drug enforcement laws, from concerns about Chinese laborers and opium at the turn of the twentieth century, to fears about blacks and cocaine in the early 1900s that produced headlines such as "Negro Cocaine 'Fiends' Are a New Southern Menace." Other critics take the suggestion of conspiracy further, arguing that the comparatively heavy drug use (as well as violence) in the black community is a result of deliberate attempts by whites to foster black self-destruction.

Not all critics believe that the racial disparities created by the war on drugs are intentional. At least one state court has struck down enhanced penalties for crack offenses as a violation of equal protection under the state constitution (*State v. Russell*, 477 N.W.2d 886 [Minn. 1991]). In that case the court said that state law treated black crack offenders and white powder cocaine offenders unfairly although that result may have been unintentional.

On the federal level, several convicted crack offenders have argued that the discrepancy between sentences for crack and powder cocaine violates equal protection or due process, but nearly every appellate court has rejected this argument. In May 1996 the U.S. Supreme Court held that statistics showing that most crack defendants are black do not in themselves support the claim of selective prosecution. Instead, the Court ruled, the burden is on defendants to prove that "similarly situated defendants of other races could have been prosecuted, but were not" (*United States v. Armstrong*, ____U.S.____, 116 S. Ct. 1480, 134 L. Ed. 2d 687).

Lawmakers have also rejected the assertion that racial discrepancies are unjust. In April 1995 the U.S. Sentencing Commission proposed abandoning the current guidelines. Determining that the penalties were too harsh, the seven-member commission voted 4–3 to equalize penalties for crack and powder cocaine. Although most black members of Congress supported changing the Sentencing Guidelines conservatives argued that crack sentencing had nothing to do with race and that revising the guidelines would allow serious offenders to serve little or no time. The current penalties remained intact.

As long as the war on drugs remains a priority for domestic policy, prosecution and incarceration for drug crimes will continue on a large scale. The challenge facing legislators, attorneys, and the courts is how to make a system that reduces the effects of drug use on our society, while avoiding excessive punishment of particular societal groups.

See also Due Process of Law; Equal Protection; Selective Prosecution; Sentencing Guidelines.

IN FOCUS

severe antidrug laws, but they lack the necessary resources. Second, in return for their participation, state law enforcement agencies are eligible for federal funds that are crucial to their operation. Besides helping meet administrative expenses, these funds are used by local undercover police officers to buy drugs so they can arrest dealers.

As a result of these shared operations, PROSECUTORS have broad discretion in pursuing drug offenses. They can charge defendants under federal law, state law, or sometimes both. The U.S. Constitution's protection against DOUBLE JEOPARDY (being tried twice for the same crime) does not apply when separate jurisdictions bring charges, and the dual-sovereignty doctrine allows successive federal and state prosecutions; however, many states prohibit prosecution in their courts if the conduct has already been the subject of a federal prosecution. Prosecutors consider several factors when deciding where to bring charges: the relative severity of state and federal drug laws, the existence of minimum mandatory SENTENCING guidelines in federal court, and the comparative leniency of federal rules regarding wiretaps and informants. Although federal law generally is tougher because of its mandatory minimum sentences, nearly every state has enacted laws requiring mandatory prison time for certain drug offenses.

Prosecutors also take into account the kind of drug involved. Under federal sentencing guidelines, crack cocaine is treated much more harshly than powder cocaine. Prosecutors can also seek civil fines and civil FORFEITURE of property.

In addition to domestic efforts to police drug sales, international efforts are part of the war on drugs. These efforts include interdiction by federal law enforcement agents at the U.S. border to prevent drugs from entering the country. The federal government has also posted DEA agents in other countries, such as Bolivia and Colombia, as part of a broader campaign to prevent the flow of drugs into the United States. Throughout the 1980s and 1990s, the United States applied diplomatic pressure to the governments of Bolivia and Colombia to persuade them to end drug production in their countries. To continue receiving U.S. aid and government-backed loans, foreign nations have had to cooperate with the antidrug initiatives of Washington, D.C. In March 1996 President BILL CLINTON cut off such aid to Colombia for lack of cooperation.

The courts have played a significant role in the war on drugs. Broadly speaking, under the FOURTH AMENDMENT, they have expanded the power of the police to conduct SEARCHES AND SEIZURES. In a series of decisions in the 1980s and 1990s, the U.S. Supreme Court ruled that police officers had the power to conduct warrantless searches of bus passengers, car interiors, mobile homes, fenced private property and barns, luggage, and trash cans. In *Minnesota v. Dickerson*, 508 U.S. 366, 113 S. Ct. 2130, 124 L. Ed. 2d 334 (1993), the Court held that no WARRANT was needed to seize narcotics that are recognizable by "plain feel" while an officer is frisking a suspect for concealed weapons.

In contrast, the Court restricted the power of state and federal governments to use civil fines and civil forfeiture of property as penalties in drug cases. In a 1989 case that had a substantial bearing on prosecutorial initiative in drug enforcement, the Court held that the government could not recover both a criminal fine and a civil penalty in separate proceedings (*United States v. Halper*, 490 U.S. 435, 109 S. Ct. 1892, 104 L. Ed. 2d 487). In 1993 the Court curtailed civil forfeiture laws by ruling that CONFISCATION of property is subject to the EIGHTH AMENDMENT's protections against excessive fines (*Austin v. United States*, 509 U.S. 602, 113 S. Ct. 2801, 125 L. Ed. 2d 488).

CROSS-REFERENCES

Criminal Law; Criminal Procedure; Education Law; Employment Law; Privacy; Schools and School Districts; Sports Law.

DRUNKARD One who habitually engages in the overindulgence of ALCOHOL.

In order for an individual to be labeled a drunkard, drunkenness must be habitual or must recur on a constant basis. A person who regularly drinks heavily but is sometimes not under the influence of alcohol would be considered a drunkard, whereas a person who occasionally gets drunk would not. The test is the question of whether or not excessive drinking has become a frequent behavior pattern for a particular person.

DRUNKENNESS The state of an individual whose mind is affected by the consumption of ALCOHOL.

Drunkenness is a consequence of drinking intoxicating liquors to such an extent as to alter the normal condition of an individual and significantly reduce his capacity for rational action and conduct. It can be asserted as a DEFENSE in civil and criminal actions in which the state of mind of the defendant is an essential element to be established in order to obtain legal relief.

DUAL NATIONALITY 📖 An equal claim, simultaneously possessed by two nations, to the allegiance of an individual. 📖

This term is frequently perceived as synonymous with dual citizenship, but the latter term encompasses the concept of state and federal citizenship enjoyed by persons who are born or naturalized in the United States.

Under INTERNATIONAL LAW, the determination of citizenship when dual nationality is involved is governed by TREATY, an agreement between two or more nations.

A person who possesses dual citizenship generally has the right to "elect," or to choose, the citizenship of one nation over that of another, within the applicable age limit or specified time period. A person could be a U.S. CITIZEN because of his or her birth in the United States and a citizen of a foreign country because his or her immigrant parents returned with their child to their native land. Foreign law could deem the child to be a citizen of the parents' native land, but it cannot DIVEST the child of U.S. citizenship.

Under federal law, a native-born or naturalized U.S. citizen relinquishes his or her U.S. citizenship if the individual procures naturalization in a foreign state through a personal application, or pursuant to an application filed in his or her behalf by a parent, GUARDIAN, or duly authorized AGENT, or through the naturalization of a parent having legal custody. An exception, however, provides that the individual will not lose his or her U.S. citizenship as the consequence of the naturalization of a parent or parents while he or she is under twenty-one years of age, or as the result of a naturalization obtained on his or her behalf while under twenty-one years of age by a parent, guardian, or authorized agent, unless the individual fails to enter the United States to establish a permanent RESIDENCE prior to the twenty-fifth birthday.

The treaty between the United States and the foreign nation determines whether the individual may maintain the dual citizenship if he or she elects to retain the U.S. citizenship, or

A person who is born in the United States to parents who are not U.S. citizens and whose parents subsequently return to their home country has dual nationality.

may lose his or her foreign citizenship and remain only a U.S. citizen.

BIOGRAPHY

W. E. B. Du Bois

DU BOIS, WILLIAM EDWARD BURGHARDT W. E. B. Du Bois was an African American intellectual, sociologist, poet, and activist whose fierce commitment to racial equality was the seminal force behind important sociopolitical reforms in the twentieth-century United States.

Although Du Bois may not have the same name recognition as FREDERICK DOUGLASS or MARTIN LUTHER KING, JR., he is regarded by most historians as an influential leader. King himself praised Du Bois as an intellectual giant whose "singular greatness lay in his quest for truth about his own people." Reflecting on Du Bois's legacy, playwright Lorraine Hansberry noted that "his ideas have influenced a multitude who do not even know his name."

Born February 23, 1868, in Great Barrington, Massachusetts, during the Reconstruction period following the U.S. Civil War, Du Bois was of African, French, and Dutch descent. His tremendous potential was apparent to his fellow townspeople, who raised money in the local churches to send him to Tennessee's Fisk University, a predominantly African American school. Du Bois earned a bachelor of arts degree from Fisk in 1888. He then attended Harvard University, where his professors included George Santayana and William James. An outstanding student, Du Bois received three degrees from Harvard: a bachelor's in 1890, a master's in 1891, and a doctor's in 1895.

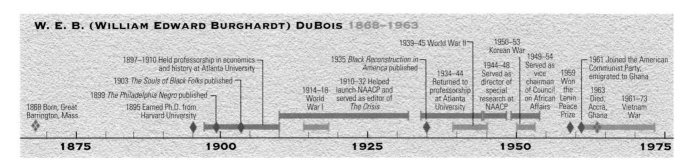

W. E. B. (WILLIAM EDWARD BURGHARDT) DUBOIS 1868–1963

1868 Born, Great Barrington, Mass.
1895 Earned Ph.D. from Harvard University
1899 *The Philadelphia Negro* published
1903 *The Souls of Black Folks* published
1897–1910 Held professorship in economics and history at Atlanta University
1914–18 World War I
1910–32 Helped launch NAACP and served as editor of *The Crisis*
1935 *Black Reconstruction in America* published
1934–44 Returned to professorship at Atlanta University
1939–45 World War II
1944–48 Served as director of special research at NAACP
1949–54 Served as vice chairman of Council on African Affairs
1950–53 Korean War
1959 Won the Lenin Peace Prize
1961 Joined the American Communist Party; emigrated to Ghana
1963 Died, Accra, Ghana
1961–73 Vietnam War

1875　1900　1925　1950　1975

Du Bois traveled extensively in Europe during the early 1890s and did postdoctoral work at the University of Berlin, in Germany. It was there that he pledged his life and career to the social and political advancement of African Americans. When Du Bois returned to the United States, he accepted his first teaching position at Ohio's Wilberforce University. He later taught at the University of Pennsylvania and at Atlanta University.

Du Bois made his mark as an accomplished sociologist and historian, publishing groundbreaking studies on African American culture. In *The Philadelphia Negro* (1899), he interviewed five thousand people to document the social institutions, health, crime patterns, family relationships, and education of African Americans in northern urban areas. In his 1903 book *The Souls of Black Folk*, he published a beautifully written collection of essays on the political history and cultural conditions of African Americans.

Although his success in academe was well recognized, Du Bois chose to cut a bolder swath as a passionate social activist. He became a symbol of principled social protest on behalf of African Americans. Du Bois combined his scholarly endeavors with the profound outrage he felt over racial injustice and the South's discriminatory JIM CROW LAWS. He used his position as a respected intellectual to decry the unequal treatment of African Americans and to push for fundamental change. According to King, Du Bois knew it was not enough to be angry. The task was to organize people so that the anger became a transforming power. As a result, King said, "It was never possible to know where the scholar Du Bois ended and the organizer Du Bois began. The two qualities in him were a single unified force."

Du Bois was a contemporary of Booker T. Washington, the head of Alabama's famed Tuskegee Institute and the undisputed leader of the African American community at the turn of the twentieth century. A former slave, Washington was a powerful figure who favored the gradual acquisition of CIVIL RIGHTS for African Americans. He believed that the best route for African Americans was agricultural or industrial education, not college. Although Du Bois agreed with some of Washington's ideas, he eventually lost patience with the slow pace and agenda of Washington's program.

To Du Bois, Washington's Tuskegee Machine was much too accommodating to the white power structure. Du Bois favored a more militant approach to achieving full social and political justice for African Americans. Because of Du Bois's talent as a writer, he became an effective spokesperson for the opponents of Washington's gradualism. He became the unambiguous voice of indignation and activism for African Americans. Du Bois insisted on the immediate rights of all people of color to vote; to obtain a decent education, including college; and to enjoy basic civil liberties.

His beliefs led to the creation of the Niagara movement in 1905. This organization was formed by like-minded African Americans to protest Washington's compromising approach to the so-called Negro problem. Du Bois preached power through achievement, self-sufficiency, racial solidarity, and cultural pride. He came up with a plan called the Talented Tenth, whereby a select group of African Americans would be groomed for leadership in the struggle for equal rights. The Niagara movement lasted until 1910 when Du Bois became involved in a new national organization.

In 1910, Du Bois helped launch the biracial NATIONAL ASSOCIATION FOR THE ADVANCEMENT OF COLORED PEOPLE (NAACP). He became the group's director of research and the editor of the NAACP publication *The Crisis*. Du Bois's work on *The Crisis* provided a wide audience for his views on racial equality and African American achievement. His writings influenced scores of African Americans who eventually made their demands for full citizenship heard in the nation's legislatures and courtrooms. Du Bois was a guiding force in the NAACP until 1934 when his interest in COMMUNISM led him to leave the organization.

On September 9, 1963, the NAACP Board of Directors recognized Du Bois's contributions to the CIVIL RIGHTS MOVEMENT in the following resolution: "It was Dr. Du Bois who was primarily responsible for guiding the Negro away from accommodation to racial segregation to militant opposition to any system which degraded black people by imposing upon them a restricted status separate and apart from their fellow citizens."

Du Bois was also a proponent of Pan-Africanism, a movement devoted to the political, social, and economic empowerment of people of color throughout the world. Later, he became active in trade unionism, women's rights, and the international peace movement. Never one to shy away from controversy, Du Bois also embraced socialism and communism at a time when they were especially unpopular in the United States. He joined the American Communist party in 1961, after winning the Lenin Peace Prize in 1959 from the former Soviet Union.

"THE COST OF LIBERTY

IS LESS THAN THE

PRICE OF REPRESSION."

Du Bois became increasingly disenchanted with the United States, and emigrated to Ghana in 1961. He was a citizen of that country at the time of his death in 1963.

Du Bois's influence on U.S. law was indirect but powerful. He spoke out eloquently against injustice and inspired generations of African Americans to work for racial equality. With twenty-one books to his credit and a zeal for organizing social protest, he helped plant the seeds for the civil rights and black power movements in the United States during the 1950s and 1960s. His unswerving commitment to equal rights helped bring about changes in the laws governing education, voting, housing, and public accommodations for racial minorities.

In 1900, Du Bois wrote *Credo*, a statement of his beliefs and his desire for social change. The poet in him was revealed when he wrote,

> I believe in Liberty for all men: the space to stretch their arms and their souls, the right to breathe and the right to vote, the freedom to choose their friends, enjoy the sunshine, and ride on the railroads, uncursed by color; thinking, dreaming, working as they will in a kingdom of beauty and love.

DUCES TECUM ▥ [*Latin, Bring with you.*] Commonly called a SUBPOENA DUCES TECUM, a type of legal WRIT requiring one who has been summoned to appear in court to bring some specified item with him or her for use or examination by the court. ▥

A person served with a *subpoena duces tecum* might be required to present documents, such as business records or other pieces of physical EVIDENCE, for the inspection of the court.

DUE ▥ Just; proper; regular; lawful; sufficient; reasonable, as in the phrases *due care, due process of law, due notice.*

Owing; payable; justly owed. That which one contracts to pay or perform to another; that which law or justice requires to be paid or done. Owed, or owing, as distinguished from payable. A DEBT is often said to be *due* from a person where he or she is the party owing it, or primarily bound to pay, whether the time for payment has or has not arrived. The same thing is true of the phrase *due and owing.* ▥

The term *due* is essentially contextual in nature and has various legal applications, all of which involve the sufficiency or reasonableness of an action or obligation.

Due care is the use of the requisite amount of caution needed in a particular set of circum-

stances based upon what a reasonably prudent person would do under similar circumstances. Exercising due care while driving might mean obeying traffic regulations.

Due consideration is the proper weight or significance given to a matter or a factor as circumstances mandate. It may also have application in sufficiency of CONSIDERATION in the law of CONTRACTS.

DUE DATE ▥ The particular day on or before which something must be done to comply with law or contractual obligation. ▥

DUELING ▥ The fighting of two persons, one against the other, at an appointed time and place, due to an earlier quarrel. If death results, the crime is MURDER. It differs from an AFFRAY in this, that the latter occurs on a sudden quarrel, while the former is always the result of design. ▥

In dueling, the use of guns, swords (rapiers), or other harmful weapons resolves quarrels through trial by combat. Duels used to occur commonly between opposing individuals seeking restitution or satisfaction outside the court system. In early U.S. history, some members of law enforcement attempted to treat dueling as a crime, but the practice went mostly unpunished. However, with the results of one duel especially—between AARON BURR and ALEXANDER HAMILTON—the practice lost prestige in the northern states. Along with growing public sentiment against dueling, new laws in the mid-1800s finally treated the form of confrontation as outright or attempted HOMICIDE. In states that have not incorporated dueling into their homicide statutes, dueling is now a crime punishable by a fine or imprisonment, or both. It is also an offense in some states merely to give or accept a challenge to engage in a duel.

Around the time of the Revolutionary War, dueling occurred in every state of the nation—in some areas, regularly—for even relatively slight offenses, such as insults, or to resolve gambling disputes. Few laws prohibited this tradition inherited from the Old World, which continued to evolve, even in Europe. Although no binding set of rules governed the proceedings of a duel in the United States—largely, no doubt, because dueling was outside the law—U.S. citizens adopted the European rules from their ancestors.

U.S. citizens based their dueling codes on the Code Duello of Ireland. This Irish code of 1777 contained twenty-six commandments covering all aspects of a duel. It included ways to avert a duel, such as the manner in which to apologize when one had committed a duel-provoking offense. If a duel could not be avoided, the scenario was a familiar one: usually, opponents would stand back-to-back, then pace a set number of steps away from each other, turn, and shoot. The Code Duello declared, "The aggressor must either beg pardon in expressed terms . . . or fire on until a severe hit is received by one party or the other." In the United States, less strict variations of the Code Duello allowed the contest to end without bodily injury, providing for some form of public mockery for the contestant who sought to end the duel.

Sometimes, U.S. politicians made dueling a sensational event. Critics, such as THOMAS JEFFERSON and THOMAS PAINE, wanted to make the practice punishable by law with the death penalty. But others insisted on resorting to duels in order to uphold their political reputation.

Perhaps the most famous duel in U.S. history was fought in 1804 between the Federalist leader Alexander Hamilton and New England politician Aaron Burr. The two had confronted and spoken harshly to each other for several years, beginning in 1791. Hamilton became furious with Burr during Burr's unsuccessful campaign for a New York senate seat in 1792. He claimed that Burr had used dirty politics, and ridiculed Burr as "unprincipled and dangerous," casting him as a power-hungry "embryo Caesar." When Burr aspired to become president in the 1800 election, Hamilton voted for Thomas Jefferson—an opponent of his own Federalist party—just for the principle of voting against Burr. Burr settled for the vice presidency, and held a grudge for Hamilton's disparaging treatment.

After serving as vice president, Burr challenged Hamilton to a duel. Hamilton knew that Burr was a much better sharpshooter than himself, but because of unwritten codes of honor that pressured him not to back out of a duel, he accepted Burr's challenge. On July 11, the two and their seconds (seconds who would take the place of their principal if he could not show) met at the predetermined site of Weehawken, New Jersey, overlooking the Hudson River. (Though both men lived in New York, New Jersey had fewer legal restrictions on dueling than did New York.) Major Nathaniel Pendleton, one of Hamilton's friends, recited the accepted rules of dueling before the firing of shots. After both parties said they were ready for the duel, by declaring themselves present, their final confrontation began. When Pendleton shouted, "Fire," Burr pulled his trigger first. The bullet hit Hamilton in his side and pierced his liver. Burr was unharmed. About thirty-six hours later, Hamilton died from his wound.

Even though Burr had killed an elder and respected political leader, neither New Jersey nor New York issued a warrant for his arrest. New York, ignoring the case of murder, pressed MISDEMEANOR charges for breaking the state's minor restrictions on duels. New Jersey charged Burr with murder, but the case never went to trial. The only punishment Burr received was a public outcry against him. Attempting to hide himself from Hamilton's supporters, Burr spent the rest of his life in seclusion and poverty.

Some, especially those in the North who were upset with the loss of Hamilton, began to cast the practice of dueling as barbaric and absurd. Drastic legislation in Pennsylvania and several New England states, including New

LIBRARY OF CONGRESS

The results of the duel between Alexander Hamilton and Aaron Burr—perhaps the most famous U.S. duel—caused dueling to lose favor in the United States.

York, followed. Farther west, the new state of Illinois, in 1819, hung a man for killing a neighbor in a rifle duel at the range of twenty-five paces. Most states, however, still did not have laws against dueling.

Dueling continued, especially in the South, where notions of individual honor remained deep. In 1838, Governor John Lyde Wilson, of South Carolina, wrote the first official U.S. adaptation of the Irish Code Duello. As an innovation on the Irish code, Wilson's Code Duello formalized the U.S. principle that required satisfaction to follow a confrontation: if a person challenged to a duel, or that person's second, refused to raise arms, public insults would follow, such as postings on walls declaring the individual a coward, a poltroon, a puppy, or worse. Although Wilson did not proclaim enthusiastic support of duels, he did believe that in certain instances, they were necessary and proper; dueling, he felt, served as a logical recourse for any individual seeking satisfaction in a case where the law could not provide it. Wilson's sixteen-page pamphlet remained popular and was reprinted until 1858.

After a fatal duel between two legislators, Jonathan Cilley and William J. Graves, Congress passed an anti-dueling law. HENRY CLAY, of Kentucky, an opponent of duels, made his support of the bill known by explaining, "When public opinion is renovated and chastened by reason, religion and humanity, the practice of dueling will be discountenanced." The bill banned dueling in the District of Columbia beginning on February 20, 1839. In the next decades, various states followed Congress's lead. Members of the clergy and concerned politicians continued to give impassioned speeches further criticizing the "peculiar practice."

Although dueling persisted into the early 1800s, and reached its height during that period, by the middle of the century it had largely disappeared. Historians attribute the decline to an increase in the number of laws banning it, and in the penalties for dueling. These laws reflected a change in attitude toward the practice, which came to be viewed as barbarous, rather than honorable. The Code Duello's unyielding, Old World conception of honor was discredited by younger generations. Outlawed and outmoded, dueling remains an interesting chapter in the history of dispute resolution in the United States.

DUE NOTICE ▥ Information that must be given or made available to a particular person or to the public within a legally mandated period of time so that its recipient will have the opportunity to respond to a situation or to ALLEGATIONS that affect the individual's or public's legal rights or duties. ▥

Due notice is not a fixed period of time in every instance but varies from case to case, depending upon the facts and the applicable statutory requirements. In some situations, it might be a specified time; in others, it might be considered a reasonable time, thereby presenting a QUESTION OF FACT in a lawsuit to determine if TIMELY notice has been given.

DUE PROCESS OF LAW ▥ A fundamental, constitutional guarantee that all legal proceedings will be fair and that one will be given notice of the proceedings and an opportunity to be heard before the government acts to take away one's life, liberty, or property. Also, a constitutional guarantee that a law shall not be unreasonable, arbitrary, or capricious. ▥

The constitutional guarantee of due process of law, found in the Fifth and Fourteenth Amendments to the U.S. Constitution, prohibits all levels of government from arbitrarily or unfairly depriving individuals of their basic constitutional rights to life, liberty, and property. The Due Process Clause of the FIFTH AMENDMENT, ratified in 1791, asserts that no person shall "be deprived of life, liberty, or property, without due process of law." This amendment restricts the powers of the federal government and applies only to actions by the federal government. The Due Process Clause of the FOURTEENTH AMENDMENT, ratified in 1868, declares, "[N]or shall any State deprive any person of life, liberty, or property, without due process of law" (§ 1). This clause limits the powers of the states rather than those of the federal government.

The Due Process Clause of the Fourteenth Amendment has also been interpreted by the Supreme Court in the twentieth century to incorporate protections of the BILL OF RIGHTS, so that those protections apply to the states as well as to the federal government. Thus, the Due Process Clause serves as the means whereby the Bill of Rights has become binding on state governments as well as the federal government.

The concept of due process originated in English COMMON LAW. The rule that individuals shall not be deprived of life, liberty, or property without notice and an opportunity to defend themselves predates written constitutions and was widely accepted in England. The MAGNA CHARTA, an agreement signed in 1215 that defined the rights of English subjects against the king, is an early example of a constitutional guarantee of due process. That document includes a clause that declares, "No free man shall be seized, or imprisoned . . . except by the lawful judgment of his peers, or by the law of the land" (ch. 39). This concept of the law of the land was later transformed into the phrase "due process of law." By the 1600s, Great Britain's American colonies were using the phrase "due process of law" in their statutes.

The application of constitutional due process is traditionally divided into the two categories of substantive due process and procedural due process. These categories are derived from a distinction made between two types of law. SUBSTANTIVE LAW creates, defines, and regulates rights, whereas PROCEDURAL LAW enforces those rights or seeks redress for their violation. Thus, in the United States, substantive due process is concerned with such issues as FREEDOM OF SPEECH and PRIVACY, whereas procedural due process is concerned with provisions such as the right to adequate notice of a lawsuit, the right to be present during testimony, and the right to an attorney.

Substantive Due Process The modern notion of substantive due process emerged in decisions of the U.S. Supreme Court during the late nineteenth century. In the 1897 case of *Allgeyer v. Louisiana*, 165 U.S. 578, 17 S. Ct. 427, 41 L. Ed. 832, the Supreme Court for the first time used the substantive due process framework to strike down a state statute. Before that time, the Court had generally used the COMMERCE CLAUSE or Contracts Clause of the Constitution to invalidate state legislation. The *Allgeyer* case concerned a Louisiana law that made it illegal to enter into certain CONTRACTS with insurance firms in other states. The Court found that the law unfairly abridged a right to enter into lawful contracts guaranteed by the Due Process Clause of the Fourteenth Amendment.

The next forty years after *Allgeyer* were the heyday of what has been called the freedom-of-contract version of substantive due process. During these years, the Court often used the Due Process Clause of the Fourteenth Amendment to void state regulation of private industry, particularly regarding terms of employment such as maximum working hours or minimum wages. In one famous case from this era, *Lochner v. New York*, 198 U.S. 45, 25 S. Ct. 539, 49 L. Ed. 937 (1905), the Court struck down a New York law (N.Y. Laws 1897, chap. 415, art. 8, § 110) prohibiting employers from allowing workers in bakeries to be on the job more than ten hours a day and sixty hours a week. The Court found that the law was not a valid exercise of the state's police power. The Court argued that it could find no connection between the number of hours worked and the quality of the baked goods, thus the law was arbitrary.

In *Allgeyer* and *Lochner*, and other cases like them, the Court did not find that state legislatures had failed to enact their laws using the proper procedures—which would present an issue of procedural due process. Instead, it found that the laws themselves violated certain economic freedoms. Those economic freedoms inhered in the Due Process Clause, specifically its protection of liberty and what the Court described as freedom or liberty of contract.

This freedom meant that individuals had the right to purchase or sell labor or products without unreasonable interference by the government.

This interpretation of the Due Process Clause put the Court in direct opposition to many of the reforms and regulations passed by state legislatures during the Progressive Era of the early twentieth century. Justices opposed to the Court's position in such cases, including OLIVER WENDELL HOLMES, JR., and JOHN M. HARLAN, saw such rulings as unwarranted judicial activism in support of a particular free-market ideology. See also JUDICIAL REVIEW.

During the 1930s, the Court used the doctrine of substantive due process to strike down federal legislation as well, particularly legislation associated with President FRANKLIN D. ROOSEVELT's New Deal. After a 1937 court-packing scheme in which Roosevelt attempted to overcome Court opposition to his programs by appointing additional justices, the Court changed its position on substantive due process and began to uphold New Deal legislation. Now, a majority on the Court, including Chief Justice CHARLES E. HUGHES and Justice BENJAMIN N. CARDOZO, abandoned the freedom-of-contract version of substantive due process.

Chief Justice Hughes, in his opinion for *West Coast Hotel Co. v. Parrish*, 300 U.S. 379, 57 S. Ct. 578, 81 L. Ed. 703 (1937), which upheld a

The 1897 case of Allgeyer v. Louisiana *was the first time the Supreme Court used the Due Process Clause of the Fourteenth Amendment to the Constitution to strike down a state statute.*

Washington State minimum wage law, argued that the Constitution nowhere mentioned a freedom of contract. He questioned not the doctrine of substantive due process itself, but the freedom-of-contract ideology that had dominated its interpretation for decades. The state, he argued, had the right to promote the health and welfare of its citizens through passing appropriate and reasonable laws.

Even before the Court abandoned the freedom of contract approach to substantive due process, it began to explore using the Due Process Clause of the Fourteenth Amendment to reevaluate state laws and actions affecting civil freedoms protected by the Bill of Rights. Since the 1833 case of *Barron ex rel. Tiernan v. Mayor of Baltimore*, 32 U.S. (7 Pet.) 243, 8 L. Ed. 672, the Supreme Court had interpreted the Bill of Rights as applying only to the federal government. Beginning in the 1920s, however, the Court began to apply the Bill of Rights to the states through the incorporation of those rights into the Due Process Clause of the Fourteenth Amendment. In *Gitlow v. New York*, 268 U.S. 652, 45 S. Ct. 625, 69 L. Ed. 1138 (1925), the Court ruled that the liberty guarantee of the Fourteenth Amendment's Due Process Clause protects FIRST AMENDMENT free speech from state action. In *Near v. Minnesota*, 283 U.S. 697, 51 S. Ct. 625, 75 L. Ed. 1357 (1931), the Court found that FREEDOM OF THE PRESS was also protected from state action by the Due Process Clause, and it ruled the same with regard to freedom of RELIGION in *Cantwell v.*

This 1935 cartoon by Clifford Berryman pokes fun at the large number of new agencies created during Franklin Roosevelt's administration to heal the ailing United States.

Connecticut, 310 U.S. 296, 60 S. Ct. 900, 84 L. Ed. 1213 (1940).

Because incorporation has proceeded gradually, with some elements of the Bill of Rights still unincorporated, it has also been called selective incorporation. Nevertheless, during the twentieth century, most of the provisions of the Bill of Rights were incorporated by the Due Process Clause of the Fourteenth Amendment, thereby protecting individuals from arbitrary actions by state as well as federal governments. See also INCORPORATION DOCTRINE.

By the 1960s, the Court had extended its interpretation of substantive due process to include rights and freedoms that are not specifically mentioned in the Constitution but that, according to the Court, extend or derive from existing rights. These rights and freedoms include the FREEDOMS OF ASSOCIATION and nonassociation, which have been inferred from the First Amendment's freedom-of-speech provision, and the right to privacy. The right to privacy, which has been derived from the First, Fourth, and Ninth Amendments, has been an especially controversial aspect of substantive due process. First established in *Griswold v. Connecticut*, 381 U.S. 479, 85 S. Ct. 1678, 14 L. Ed. 2d 510 (1965), it was later used by the Court to protect a woman's decision to have an ABORTION free from state interference, in the first trimester of pregnancy (*Roe v. Wade*, 410 U.S. 113, 93 S. Ct. 705, 35 L. Ed. 2d 147 [1973]).

Procedural Due Process The phrase "procedural due process" refers to the aspects of the Due Process Clause that apply to the procedure of arresting and trying persons accused of crimes and to any other government action that deprives an individual of life, liberty, or property. Procedural due process limits the exercise of power by the state and federal governments, by requiring that they follow certain procedures in criminal and civil matters. In cases where an individual has claimed a violation of due process rights, the courts must determine whether a citizen is being deprived of "life, liberty, or property," and what procedural protections are "due" that individual.

The Bill of Rights contains provisions that are central to procedural due process. These protections give a person a number of rights and freedoms in criminal proceedings, including freedom from unreasonable SEARCHES AND SEIZURES; freedom from DOUBLE JEOPARDY, or being tried more than once for the same crime; freedom from SELF-INCRIMINATION, or testifying against oneself; the right to a speedy and public trial by an impartial JURY; the right to be told of the crime being charged; the right to cross-

THE GRANGER COLLECTION, NEW YORK

examine witnesses; the right to be represented by an attorney; freedom from CRUEL AND UN-USUAL PUNISHMENT; and the right to demand that the state prove any charges BEYOND A REASONABLE DOUBT. In a series of Supreme Court cases during the twentieth century, all these rights were applied to the states. In one such case, *Gideon v. Wainwright*, 372 U.S. 335, 83 S. Ct. 792, 9 L. Ed. 2d 799 (1963), the Supreme Court ruled that the Due Process Clause of the Fourteenth Amendment incorporates the SIXTH AMENDMENT right to have an attorney in "all criminal prosecutions," including prosecutions by a state. The case proved to be a watershed in establishing rights to legal COUNSEL for poor people.

Procedural due process also protects individuals from government actions in the civil as opposed to criminal sphere. These protections have been extended to include not only land and personal property, but also entitlements, including government-provided benefits, licenses, and positions. Thus, for example, the Court has ruled that the federal government must hold hearings before terminating WELFARE benefits (*Goldberg v. Kelly*, 397 U.S. 254, 90 S. Ct. 1011, 25 L. Ed. 2d 287 [1970]). Court decisions regarding procedural due process have exerted a great deal of influence over government procedures in prisons, schools, Social Security, civil suits, and public employment.

CROSS-REFERENCES

Criminal Procedure; *Gideon v. Wainwright*; *Gitlow v. New York*; *Griswold v. Connecticut*; Labor Law; *Lochner v. New York*; Right to Counsel; *Roe v. Wade*.

DULLES, JOHN FOSTER John Foster Dulles served as U.S. secretary of state from 1953 to 1959. A prominent New York City attorney, Dulles participated in international affairs for much of his legal career. His term as secretary of state occurred during the height of the cold war and was marked by his strong anti-Communist policies and rhetoric.

Dulles was born in Washington, D.C., on February 25, 1888, at the home of his maternal grandfather, John W. Foster, secretary of state

"THE ABILITY TO GET TO THE VERGE OF WAR WITHOUT GETTING INTO THE WAR IS THE NECESSARY ART . . . IF YOU ARE SCARED TO GO TO THE BRINK, YOU ARE LOST."

BIOGRAPHY

John Foster Dulles

under President BENJAMIN HARRISON. Dulles was raised in Watertown, New York, where his father, the Reverend Allen M. Dulles, served as a Presbyterian minister. Known as Foster, the young Dulles was a precocious student, graduating from high school at age fifteen and attending Princeton University at age sixteen. He graduated in 1908 and then entered George Washington University Law School. Again, he worked quickly, and graduated in two years.

Through the efforts of his well-connected grandfather, Dulles joined the New York City law firm of Sullivan and Cromwell, which has been called the greatest corporate law firm of the early twentieth century. In 1919 family friend and international financier Bernard M. Baruch invited Dulles to be his aide at the Paris Peace Conference. This conference, which was convened to negotiate the terms of peace to end World War I, stimulated Dulles's interest in international politics and diplomacy.

In the 1920s Dulles quickly moved ahead at Sullivan and Cromwell. In 1926, at the age of only thirty-eight, Dulles was made head of the firm. Representing many of the largest U.S. corporations, Dulles became a very wealthy man. As his stature rose, he became a prominent figure in the Republican party. A confidant of New York governor THOMAS E. DEWEY, Dulles was promised the position of secretary of state if Dewey was elected president in 1948, but Dewey was unsuccessful and Dulles lost that opportunity.

Dulles was an active participant in the effort to reshape foreign relations after World War II. He helped form the UNITED NATIONS and was a U.S. member to the General Assembly from 1945 to 1949. He performed the duties of U.S. ambassador-at-large and was the chief author of the 1951 Japanese peace treaty. He also negotiated the Australian, New Zealand, Philippine, and Japanese security treaties in 1950 and 1951.

In 1949 he filled a vacancy in the Senate created by the death of Senator ROBERT WAGNER, of New York, but was unsuccessful in his attempt the same year to win election to a six-year term. Dulles's political fortunes im-

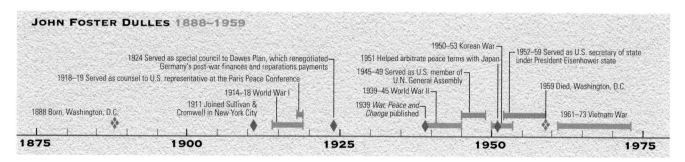

JOHN FOSTER DULLES 1888–1959

1924 Served as special council to Dawes Plan, which renegotiated Germany's post-war finances and reparations payments

1918–19 Served as counsel to U.S. representative at the Paris Peace Conference

1914–18 World War I

1911 Joined Sullivan & Cromwell in New York City

1888 Born, Washington, D.C.

1939 *War, Peace and Change* published

1939–45 World War II

1945–49 Served as U.S. member of U.N. General Assembly

1951 Helped arbitrate peace terms with Japan

1950–53 Korean War

1952–59 Served as U.S. secretary of state under President Eisenhower state

1959 Died, Washington, D.C.

1961–73 Vietnam War

1875   1900   1925   1950   1975

proved when he aligned himself with the 1952 presidential candidacy of DWIGHT D. EISENHOWER. He helped Eisenhower defeat conservative senator Robert Taft, of Ohio, at the nominating convention and was rewarded with his long-desired appointment as head of the STATE DEPARTMENT.

As secretary of state, Dulles exhibited a rigid opposition to COMMUNISM. He advocated going to the brink of war to achieve results—a position that led to the coinage of the term *brinkmanship* to describe his foreign policy.

Dulles is also remembered for his doctrine of "massive retaliation," which warned the Soviet Union that the United States would react instantaneously with nuclear weapons to even the smallest provocation. Dulles believed that such a policy would discourage aggressive acts, though many allies were concerned that it would turn small wars into much larger and much more destructive ones.

Dulles died May 24, 1959, in Washington, D.C.

See also COLD WAR.

DUMMY Sham; make-believe; pretended; imitation. Person who serves in place of another, or who serves until the proper person is named or available to take his place (e.g., dummy corporate directors; dummy owners of real estate).

DURESS Unlawful pressure exerted upon a person to coerce that person to perform an act that he or she ordinarily would not perform.

Duress also encompasses the same harm, threats, or restraint exercised upon the affected individual's spouse, child, or parent.

Duress is distinguishable from UNDUE INFLUENCE, a concept employed in the law of WILLS, in that the latter term involves a wrongdoer who is a FIDUCIARY, one who occupies a position of trust and confidence in regard to the TESTATOR, the creator of the will.

Duress also exists where a person is coerced by the wrongful conduct or threat of another to enter into a CONTRACT under circumstances that deprive the individual of his or her volition.

As a defense to a CIVIL ACTION, the federal Rules of Civil Procedure require that duress be pleaded affirmatively.

Except with respect to HOMICIDE, a person who is compelled to commit a crime by an unlawful threat from another person to injure him, her, or a third person, will generally not be held responsible for its commission.

See also THREATS.

DURHAM RULE A principle of CRIMINAL LAW used to determine the validity of the INSAN-ITY DEFENSE asserted by an ACCUSED, that he or she was insane at the time of committing a crime and therefore should not be held legally responsible for the action.

The *Durham* rule was created in 1954 by Judge David L. Bazelon, of the U.S. Court of Appeals for the District of Columbia, in *Durham v. United States*, 214 F.2d 862. The rule, as stated in the court's decision, held that "an accused is not criminally responsible if his unlawful act was the product of mental disease." It required a jury's determination that the accused was suffering from a mental disease and that there was a causal relationship between the disease and the act. Because of difficulties in its implementation, the *Durham* rule was rejected by the same court in the 1972 case *United States v. Brawner*, 471 F.2d 969 (en banc).

The *Durham* rule replaced a nineteenth-century test of criminal responsibility called the M'NAGHTEN RULE. The *M'Naghten* rule, or "right-wrong" test, required the ACQUITTAL of defendants who could not distinguish right from wrong. This rule was supplemented by the "irresistible impulse" test, added in the District of Columbia in 1929, which allowed a jury to inquire as to whether the accused suffered from a "diseased mental condition" that did not allow him or her to resist an "insane impulse."

By the mid–twentieth century, these early legal tests of insanity came under increasing criticism. Critics of the *M'Naghten* rule, for example, charged that it was outdated and did not take into consideration the broad range of mental disorders that had been identified by modern science. Commentators also claimed that these earlier rules did not allow expert witnesses to communicate fully the findings of modern psychology and psychiatry to a JURY.

The *Durham* rule sought to overcome these problems. It attempted to create a simple and open-ended insanity test that would, Judge Bazelon later wrote, "open up the courtroom to all the information and analysis available to the scientific community about the wellsprings of human behavior." Bazelon hoped that the new rule would allow experts to bring to the jury and the public new insights into "the physiological and cultural, as well as individual psychological, factors contributing to criminal behavior." Bazelon intended it to be not a precise test but rather a loose concept comparable to the legal definition of NEGLIGENCE. Thus, he compared the term *fault* in the negligence context to the term *responsibility* in the *Durham* context. The meaning of such terms, he argued, would have to be determined by a jury in light of the facts relevant to each case.

Implementation of the *Durham* rule ran into serious difficulties. The rule did not elicit the detailed courtroom discussion of mental illness and criminal behavior that Judge Bazelon and others had hoped for. Instead, just as expert witnesses had before been asked the yes-or-no question, Was the accused capable of distinguishing right from wrong? experts were now asked the simple yes-or-no question, Was the accused's act a product of mental disease or defect? The *Durham* rule, therefore, perpetuated the dominant role of expert TESTIMONY in determining criminal responsibility, a task that many critics felt was best left to a jury.

As a result of such difficulties, the District of Columbia Circuit unanimously rejected the *Durham* rule in the 1972 *Brawner* case. The court replaced it with a standard developed by the American Law Institute: "A person is not responsible for criminal conduct if at the time of such conduct as a result of mental disease or defect he lacks substantial capacity to appreciate the wrongfulness of his conduct or to conform his conduct to the requirements of the law" (Model Penal Code § 4.01[1]).

This new test has been described as a more subtle and less restrictive version of the pre-*Durham* right-wrong and irresistible impulse tests. In coming to its conclusion, however, the court in *Brawner* emphasized that no particular formulation of words provides an easy solution to the difficult problems involved in assessing the sanity of a person accused of committing a criminal act. Instead, the court asserted that criminal responsibility in such trials is best assessed by a properly informed jury that is not overly dominated by expert testimony. To help juries make such assessments, the court required experts to explain the underlying reasons for their opinions rather than giving yes-or-no answers to simplistic questions.

DUTY A legal OBLIGATION that entails mandatory conduct or performance. With respect to the laws relating to CUSTOMS DUTIES, a tax owed to the government for the import or export of goods.

A FIDUCIARY, such as an EXECUTOR or TRUSTEE, who occupies a position of confidence in relation to a third person, owes such person a duty to render services, provide care, or perform certain acts on his or her behalf.

In the context of NEGLIGENCE cases, a person has a duty to comport himself or herself in a particular manner with respect to another person.

DUTY OF TONNAGE A fee that encompasses all taxes and CUSTOMS DUTIES, regardless of their name or form, imposed upon a vessel as an instrument of commerce for entering, remaining in, or exiting from a port.

Conceptually, a duty of tonnage is assessed for the privilege of transacting business in a port.

DUVALL, GABRIEL Gabriel Duvall was born December 6, 1752. He was admitted to the Maryland bar in 1778. Duvall served in the militia before beginning his government career in 1783, serving on the Maryland Governor's Council from 1783 to 1784, and in the Maryland House of Delegates from 1787 to 1794.

From 1794 to 1796, Duvall acted as a representative from Maryland to the U.S. House of Representatives. He returned to Maryland as chief justice of the Maryland General Court in 1796 and remained on the bench until 1802. Duvall then returned to federal service, and from 1802 to 1811 served as first comptroller of the U.S. Treasury under President THOMAS JEFFERSON.

Duvall was appointed to the Supreme Court by President James Madison to replace Samuel Chase. He served on the Court from 1811 to 1835, mainly writing minor opinions on commercial law and maritime law. Though he tended to vote with chief justice John Marshall, Duvall was a strong opponent of slavery. He wrote a memorable dissent in *Mima Queen and Child v. Hepburn*, 11 U.S. 290 (1813), a case argued for the plaintiffs by Francis Scott Key. The majority disallowed hearsay evidence to prove a purported slave was free. Duvall opined that hearsay should be admitted to prove freedom whenever the facts are so old that living testimony cannot be procured.

Duvall died on March 6, 1844.

BIOGRAPHY

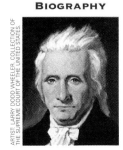

Gabriel Duvall

"IT WILL BE UNIVERSALLY ADMITTED THAT THE RIGHT TO FREEDOM IS MORE IMPORTANT THAN THE RIGHT OF PROPERTY."

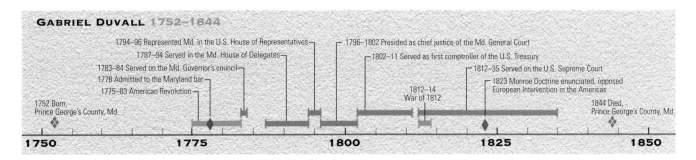

GABRIEL DUVALL 1752–1844

1794–96 Represented Md. in the U.S. House of Representatives
1787–94 Served in the Md. House of Delegates
1783–84 Served on the Md. Governor's council
1778 Admitted to the Maryland bar
1775–83 American Revolution
1752 Born, Prince George's County, Md.

1796–1802 Presided as chief justice of the Md. General Court
1802–11 Served as first comptroller of the U.S. Treasury
1812–35 Served on the U.S. Supreme Court
1823 Monroe Doctrine enunciated, opposed European intervention in the Americas
1812–14 War of 1812
1844 Died, Prince George's County, Md.

1750   1775   1800   1825   1850

DWI An abbreviation for *driving while intoxicated,* which is an offense committed by an individual who operates a motor vehicle while under the influence of ALCOHOL or DRUGS AND NARCOTICS.

An abbreviation for *died without* ISSUE, which commonly appears in genealogical tables.

A showing of complete intoxication is not necessary for a charge of driving while intoxicated. State laws indicate levels of blood-alcohol content at which an individual is deemed to be under the influence of alcohol.

DWORKIN, ANDREA Andrea Dworkin is a radical feminist writer concerned with illuminating and clarifying sexual and social values, who seeks to create a world in which men have no dominion over women. Famous for making pointed statements such as "I am a feminist . . . not the fun kind," Dworkin is considered an extremist by most people familiar with her work, including many of her fellow feminists. She has zealously advocated the CENSORSHIP of all PORNOGRAPHY, which, she says, degrades women, discriminates against them as a class, and incites men to sexual violence. She has also argued that men use sex to oppress women, and therefore *all* sexual intercourse between heterosexuals is detrimental to women. With Professor CATHARINE MACKINNON, of the University of Michigan Law School, Dworkin has championed antipornography ORDINANCES for several cities in the United States. The two also helped author the Violence against Women Act (S. 11, 103d Cong., 1st Sess. [1993]), a federal law signed by President BILL CLINTON as part of a larger crime bill in September 1994, which makes sex-based violence a CIVIL RIGHTS violation and allows victims to sue for compensatory and PUNITIVE DAMAGES and attorney's fees (42 U.S.C.A. § 13981 [Supp. V 1993]). The MacKinnon-Dworkin definition of pornography was unanimously affirmed by the Canadian Supreme Court in *Butler v. The Queen* (1 S.C.R. 452) in February 1992, making the shipment and sale of pornographic materials in Canada more difficult for that country's booksellers. MacKinnon and Dworkin define pornography

BIOGRAPHY

Andrea Dworkin

"WOMAN IS NOT BORN: SHE IS MADE. IN HER MAKING, HER HUMANITY IS DESTROYED. SHE BECOMES SYMBOL OF THIS, SYMBOL OF THAT: MOTHER OF EARTH, SLUT OF THE UNIVERSE; BUT SHE NEVER BECOMES HERSELF BECAUSE IT IS FORBIDDEN FOR HER TO DO SO."

as any material whose "dominant characteristic is the undue exploitation of sex or of sex and any one or more of the following subjects, namely crime, horror, cruelty and violence."

Dworkin was born September 26, 1946, in Camden, New Jersey, the daughter of Harry Spiegel and Sylvia Spiegel. She has devoted much of her adult life to fighting what she sees as the most visible signs of men's need to control and do violence to women: pornography, PROSTITUTION, INCEST, DOMESTIC VIOLENCE, SEXUAL HARASSMENT, stalking, and RAPE.

Although much has been written about Dworkin, little of the coverage has dealt with her early life. However, Dworkin's admittedly autobiographical novel *Mercy* (1991) may provide insight into some of the events that helped to shape this controversial feminist crusader: the book chronicles the sexual victimization—including molestation and rape—faced by the protagonist, "Andrea," as a child, a rebellious teenager, and a young woman.

Dworkin was drawn toward the law after graduating from high school in 1964, but she did not pursue a legal career because she believed law schools at the time were run by people who didn't think women should be there. She joined the embryonic anti–Vietnam War movement; graduated from Bennington College, of Vermont; and spent the late 1960s living overseas. While in Amsterdam, she married a political radical, who beat her repeatedly.

Having been a waitress, receptionist, secretary, typist, salesperson, and factory worker, Dworkin fully embarked on a career as a radical feminist after her marriage ended and she returned to the United States in 1972. In the 1970s, she began speaking and writing about the politics of sexuality and her affinity for women. Her early books include *Woman Hating: A Radical Look at Sexuality* (1974) and a compilation of essays called *Our Blood: Prophecies and Discourses on Sexual Politics* (1976), which called for an abandonment of women's quest for sexual equality in favor of more radical solutions necessary to achieve a complete social realignment of the sexes. During the time she

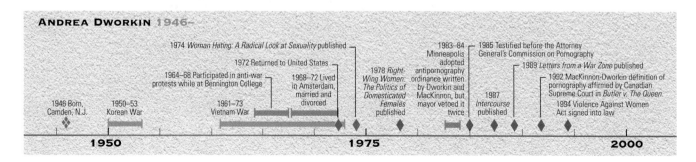

was publishing these, Dworkin gained notoriety for her assertions that all sex is rape and all sexually explicit materials are evidence of rape.

After the 1991 Anita Hill–CLARENCE THOMAS hearings, Dworkin wrote an introduction to a book called *Sexual Harassment: Women Speak Out* (Sumrall and Taylor, eds., 1993), in which she shared some of her experiences with sexual harassment.

Dworkin met MacKinnon, a graduate of Yale Law School and also an avid feminist, in 1977. They began giving speeches and lobbying together for antipornography ordinances. In the fall of 1983, they attracted attention when they teamed up to teach a course on pornography at the University of Minnesota Law School, the first class of its kind. As a result of the course, several members of the city council in Minneapolis asked the pair to write an antipornography ordinance for the city. In the resulting ordinance, Dworkin and MacKinnon defined pornography as "the graphic sexually explicit subordination of women, whether in picture or in words." The law would have allowed female rape victims to sue producers and distributors of erotic materials for damages if their attacker claimed that pornography made him do it, even if no criminal charges were filed. Following two days of explosive public hearings on the issue, the city council adopted the ordinance in late 1983, only to have the mayor VETO it. In 1984 a new Minneapolis city council again adopted the same ordinance, and the mayor again vetoed it. A Dworkin-MacKinnon supporter in Minneapolis reportedly doused herself with gasoline and set herself ablaze amidst the controversy.

Dworkin and MacKinnon subsequently proposed the same type of ordinance in Indianapolis, but after booksellers and readers challenged its constitutionality, the U.S. Court of Appeals for the Seventh Circuit ruled that the ordinance discriminated on the grounds of free speech (*American Booksellers Ass'n v. Hudnut*, 771 F.2d 323 [1985]). In the late 1980s, Dworkin again coauthored a similar ordinance, this time for Bellingham, Washington. Although voters in Bellingham endorsed the concept by ballot in November 1988, the AMERICAN CIVIL LIBERTIES UNION (ACLU) persuaded a federal judge to invalidate the ordinance in February 1989 on First Amendment FREEDOM-OF-THE-PRESS grounds. In the early 1990s, Dworkin and MacKinnon introduced yet another similar initiative in Cambridge, Massachusetts, which was opposed by the ACLU and ultimately struck down.

In addition to leading antiporn legislative efforts in several states Dworkin also looked for change at a national level. In 1985 she testified before Attorney General EDWIN MEESE III's Commission on Pornography—established at President RONALD REAGAN's behest to assess pornography's social effects—about the causal link between pornography and violence against women.

As part of her evidence that pornography provides a "blueprint for male domination over women," she cited serial killer Ted Bundy's admission, on the eve of his execution, that pornography had made him kill women. The resulting bill, officially called the Pornography Victims' Compensation Act (S. 1521, 102d Cong., 2d Sess.) but nicknamed the Bundy Bill, would have allowed victims of sex crimes to sue producers and distributors of sexual material if the victims could prove that the material incited the crimes. The bill did not pass in Congress. Dworkin went on to consult with Senator Joseph R. Biden, Jr. (D-Del.), who in 1990 sponsored a related bill (S. 2754, 101st Cong., 1st Sess.). A version of this bill was ultimately incorporated into President Clinton's crime bill and passed as the Violence Against Women Act (108 Stat. 1902 to 1955).

See also WOMEN'S RIGHTS.

DYER ACT 📖 A name given to a federal law that makes it a crime to transport stolen motor vehicles across state borders in interstate or foreign commerce. 📖

The Dyer Act, also called the National Motor Vehicle Theft Act (18 U.S.C.A. § 2311 et seq.), was enacted in 1919 to impede the interstate trafficking of stolen vehicles by organized thieves.

There are three elements that must be established BEYOND A REASONABLE DOUBT if an accused is to be convicted of the offense: (1) a vehicle is stolen, (2) the defendant knows that the vehicle is stolen, and (3) the defendant transports the vehicle in interstate or foreign commerce. A person who AIDS AND ABETS in the commission of this offense is equally culpable as a principal who has actually committed the crime.

The punishment for conviction under the Dyer Act is an unspecified fine, imprisonment of no longer than ten years, or both.

DYING DECLARATION 📖 A statement by a person who is conscious and knows that death is imminent concerning what he or she believes to be the cause or circumstances of death that can be introduced into EVIDENCE during a TRIAL in certain cases. 📖

A dying declaration is considered credible and trustworthy evidence based upon the general belief that most people who know that they are about to die do not lie. As a result, it is an exception to the HEARSAY rule, which prohibits the use of a statement made by someone other than the person who repeats it while testifying during a trial, because of its inherent untrustworthiness. If the person who made the dying declaration had the slightest hope of recovery, no matter how unreasonable, the statement is not ADMISSIBLE into evidence. A person who makes a dying declaration must, however, be COMPETENT at the time he or she makes a statement, otherwise, it is inadmissible.

A dying declaration is usually introduced by the prosecution, but can be used on behalf of the accused.

As a general rule, courts refuse to admit dying declarations in civil cases, even those for WRONGFUL DEATH, or in criminal actions for crimes other than the HOMICIDE of the DECEDENT.

State and federal rules of evidence govern the use of dying declarations in their respective proceedings.

EARL WARREN LEGAL TRAINING PRO-GRAM The Earl Warren Legal Training Program was begun in 1972 for the purpose of increasing the number of black attorneys in the United States. The program provides financial aid on the basis of need to qualified law students for the three full years of law school. Emphasis is placed on scholarships for applicants who wish to enroll in law schools in the South. The program seeks to retain professional and personal relations with minority lawyers and holds training institutes for young and experienced minority lawyers. Begun as a special project of the NAACP Legal Defense and Education Fund, the program is now a separate corporation.

EARNED INCOME Sources of money derived from the labor, professional service, or entrepreneurship of an individual taxpayer as opposed to funds generated by investments, dividends, and interest.

Wages, salaries, and fees are types of earned income that, if below a statutorily determined amount, entitle a taxpayer to a reduction of INCOME TAX liability.

EARNEST MONEY A sum of money paid by a buyer at the time of entering a CONTRACT to indicate the intention and ability of the buyer to carry out the contract. Normally such earnest money is applied against the purchase price. Often the contract provides for FORFEITURE of this sum if the buyer DEFAULTS. A deposit of part payment of purchase price on sale to be consummated in future.

EASEMENT A right of use over the PROPERTY of another. Traditionally the permitted kinds of uses were limited, the most important being RIGHTS OF WAY and rights concerning flowing waters. The easement was normally for the benefit of adjoining lands, no matter who the owner was (an easement appurtenant), rather than for the benefit of a specific individual (easement in gross).

Easements frequently arise among owners of adjoining parcels of land. Common examples of easements include the right of a property owner who has no street front to use a particular segment of a neighbor's land to gain access to the road, as well as the right of a MUNICIPAL CORPORATION to run a sewer line across a strip of an owner's land, which is frequently called a right of way.

Easements can be conveyed from one individual to another by WILL, DEED, or CONTRACT, which must comply with the STATUTE OF FRAUDS and can be inherited pursuant to the laws of DESCENT AND DISTRIBUTION.

An easement is a nonpossessory interest in another's land that entitles the holder only to the right to use such land in the specified manner. It is distinguishable from a PROFIT A PRENDRE that is the right to enter another's land and remove the soil itself or a product thereof, such as CROPS or timber.

An *easement appurtenant* attaches to the land permanently and benefits its owner. In order for it to exist, there must be two pieces of land owned by different individuals. One piece, the *dominant* ESTATE or TENEMENT, is the land that is benefited by the easement. The other piece, known as the *servient estate* or *tenement*, is the land that has the burden of the easement. An easement appurtenant is a COVENANT running with the land since it is incapable of a separate

C. J. ALLEN/STOCK BOSTON

and independent existence from the land to which it is annexed. A common example would be where one landowner—A—is the owner of land that is separated from a road by land owned by B. If B sells A a right of way across his or her land, it is a right that is appurtenant to A's land and can only be used in connection thereof.

An easement *in gross* is not appurtenant to any estate in land. It arises when a servient piece of land exists without a dominant piece being affected. This type of easement is ordinarily personal to the holder and does not run with the land. For example, if A has a number of trees on his or her property and B contracts with A to enter A's land to remove timber, B has both an easement in gross and a profit. At COMMON LAW, an easement in gross could not be assigned; however, most courts currently allow certain types of easements in gross to be transferred.

Easements are categorized as being either *affirmative* or *negative*. An *affirmative easement* entitles the holder to do something on another individual's land, whereas a *negative easement* DIVESTS an owner of the right to do something on the property. For example, the owner of land might enter into an agreement with the owner of an adjoining piece of land not to build a high structure that would obstruct the light and air that go onto the adjoining owner's land. This easement of light and air deprives the property owner who gives it up from enjoying ownership rights in the land to the fullest possible extent and is labeled a negative easement.

There are various ways in which easements are created. An *express easement* is clearly stated in a contract, deed, or will. An easement by *implication* occurs when the owner of a piece of land divides such land into smaller pieces and

Easements include rights of way, which may be used by a municipal corporation or a public utility company to run pipes through an individual's land.

BIOGRAPHY

Dorman Bridgman Eaton

sells a smaller piece to another person, retaining a right to enter such piece of land. For example, a seller divides his or her property and sells half to a purchaser. The piece that the purchaser buys has a sewer pipe beneath it that serves both pieces of property. The seller has an implied easement to use the sewer pipe that runs under the purchaser's land.

An *easement by prescription* arises through an individual's use of land as opposed to the possession thereof. An easement of this nature will be recognized in these instances: (1) the easement is adverse or contrary to the interests, and absent the permission, of the landowner; (2) it is open and notorious; (3) it is continuous and uninterrupted; and (4) it exists for the period of time prescribed by state statute. If for a period of time beyond the prescribed statutory period A creates and openly uses a right of way across B's land without B's permission then an easement by PRESCRIPTION is created.

An easement can either be terminated through the expiration of its term as determined upon its creation or by one of several events occurring subsequent to creation. Events that can extinguish an easement include these: (1) the same individual becoming the owner of the dominant as well as the servient estate when an appurtenant easement existed; (2) the owner of an easement in gross obtaining ownership of the servient estate; (3) the owner of the dominant tenement executing a deed or will releasing the easement in favor of the owner of the servient tenement; and (4) the abandonment of an easement.

EATON, DORMAN BRIDGMAN   Dorman Bridgman Eaton was born June 27, 1823, in Hardwick, Vermont. He was a successful lawyer who achieved prominence for his work in the establishment of the U.S. Civil Service Commission.

After receiving a doctor of laws degree from the University of Vermont in 1848, Eaton attended Harvard Law School in 1850 and was admitted to the New York bar, practicing law there until 1870.

Eaton was a staunch believer in a merit system as opposed to a spoils system in the acquisition of local or national government employment. In 1873, he became the chairperson of the U.S. Civil Service Commission, an organization that embodied the ideas of the MERIT SYSTEM. He served until 1875, when funding for the commission ceased, and he subsequently went to England to examine the structure of the English Civil Service Commission. In 1883, he formulated the Pendleton Act (5 U.S.C.A. § 1101 et seq. [1883]), which provided

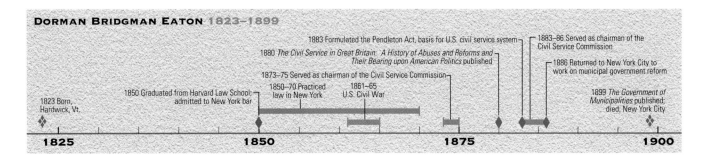

DORMAN BRIDGMAN EATON 1823–1899

1823 Born, Hardwick, Vt.

1850 Graduated from Harvard Law School; admitted to New York bar

1850–70 Practiced law in New York

1861–65 U.S. Civil War

1873–75 Served as chairman of the Civil Service Commission

1880 *The Civil Service in Great Britain: A History of Abuses and Reforms and Their Bearing upon American Politics* published

1883 Formulated the Pendleton Act, basis for U.S. civil service system

1883–86 Served as chairman of the Civil Service Commission

1886 Returned to New York City to work on municipal government reform

1899 *The Government of Municipalities* published; died, New York City

1825   1850   1875   1900

for the foundation of the permanent Civil Service Commission. He performed the duties of chairperson of this new commission from 1883 to 1886. Eaton died December 23, 1899, in New York City.

In 1880, Eaton wrote the publication *The Civil Service in Great Britain: A History of Abuses and Reforms and their Bearing upon American Politics.*

ECCLESIASTICAL COURTS In England, the collective classification of particular courts that exercised jurisdiction primarily over spiritual matters. A system of courts, held by authority granted by the sovereign, that assumed jurisdiction over matters concerning the ritual and religion of the established church, and over the rights, obligations, and discipline of the clergy.

EDELMAN, MARIAN WRIGHT During her career, Marian Wright Edelman has appeared in Mississippi jail cells, Capitol Hill offices, and TV talk shows, with the same objective: to help poor or disenfranchised U.S. citizens. Best known as the founder and president of the CHILDREN'S DEFENSE FUND (CDF), Edelman is a lawyer, lobbyist, author, and mentor to First Lady HILLARY RODHAM CLINTON. Edelman began her career as a civil rights attorney in the Deep South during the 1960s. While working on voter registration campaigns—and keeping demonstrators out of jail—Edelman vowed to do something about the plight of the United States' children. Improving children's lives seemed like a logical

BIOGRAPHY

Marian Wright Edelman

starting point for improving all of society. By the mid-1990s, Edelman's influence extended from day care centers to the Oval Office as she helped shape the future for the United States' youngest citizens.

Edelman was born June 6, 1939, in Bennettsville, a small, segregated town in South Carolina. Her father, Arthur Jerome Wright, was a Baptist minister, and her mother, Maggie Leola Wright, was the director of the Wright Home for the Aged. Named after singer Marian Anderson, Edelman recalls a childhood of hard work and high expectations. She was an outstanding student whose parents instilled in her a strong sense of purpose and social awareness. Edelman's parents extolled the virtues of self-reliance and personal initiative, and lived their own counsel when they established the Wright Home, the first African American residence for elderly people in South Carolina. Edelman's parents founded the nursing home because they saw a need and felt obliged to fill it. Given the example set by them, it is no surprise that Edelman chose a life of self-directed social activism.

After high school, Edelman attended well-respected Spelman College, in Atlanta. Edelman planned a career in the foreign service and took preparatory courses at the Sorbonne, in Paris, and at the University of Geneva, in Switzerland. After spending a summer in Moscow, Edelman returned to the United States for her senior year at Spelman. Before long, she was caught up in the emerging CIVIL RIGHTS

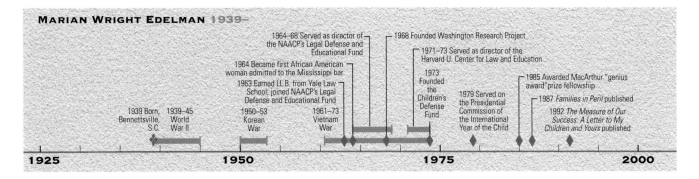

MARIAN WRIGHT EDELMAN 1939–

1939 Born, Bennettsville, S.C.

1939–45 World War II

1950–53 Korean War

1961–73 Vietnam War

1963 Earned LL.B. from Yale Law School; joined NAACP's Legal Defense and Educational Fund

1964 Became first African American woman admitted to the Mississippi bar

1964–68 Served as director of the NAACP's Legal Defense and Educational Fund

1968 Founded Washington Research Project

1971–73 Served as director of the Harvard U. Center for Law and Education

1973 Founded the Children's Defense Fund

1979 Served on the Presidential Commission of the International Year of the Child

1985 Awarded MacArthur "genius award" prize fellowship

1987 *Families in Peril* published

1992 *The Measure of Our Success: A Letter to My Children and Yours* published

1925   1950   1975   2000

movement. After a campus visit by MARTIN LUTHER KING, JR., and considerable soul-searching, Edelman dropped her plans for the foreign service and joined other African Americans in the struggle for equal rights.

To make herself more valuable to the movement, Edelman decided to attend law school. After earning a degree from Yale University Law School in 1963, she became counsel for the Legal Defense and Educational Fund of the NATIONAL ASSOCIATION FOR THE ADVANCEMENT OF COLORED PEOPLE (NAACP). In New York, Edelman received NAACP training in civil rights law for one year. She moved to Jackson, Mississippi, in 1964 and became the first African American woman ever admitted to the Mississippi bar. (At the time, Mississippi had a grand total of three African American lawyers.)

Edelman's first assignment was the Mississippi Summer Project. This was an African American voter registration drive conducted by volunteers and college students from the North. Edelman also served as the attorney for the Child Development Group of Mississippi, where one of her proudest accomplishments was helping to reinstate federal funding for Head Start, a successful program that encourages the intellectual and social development of poor, at-risk children.

When Senator ROBERT F. KENNEDY toured Mississippi in 1967, Edelman showed him the wretched poverty endured by thousands of African American children. Many credit her with opening Kennedy's eyes to the reality of hunger in the United States.

In 1968, Edelman married Peter B. Edelman, a Harvard-trained lawyer who was Senator Kennedy's legislative assistant. The couple moved to Washington, D.C., where eventually they had three sons. Edelman hoped a move to the nation's capital would enable her to focus national attention on the poverty she witnessed in Mississippi.

Edelman's first job in Washington, D.C., was as congressional and federal agency liaison for the 1968 Poor People's Campaign. Also during 1968, Edelman founded the Washington Research Project, an advocacy and research group that lobbied Congress for an expansion in Head Start services. In 1971, Edelman and her family moved to Boston for her to complete a two-year stint as director of the Center for Law and Education at Harvard University. Her husband served as vice president of the University of Massachusetts at the same time. Upon their return to Washington, D.C., in 1973, Edelman created an offshoot of her Washing-

ton Research Project, which she called the Children's Defense Fund.

Edelman's CDF began as a small, nonprofit organization interested in children's issues and funded entirely by private foundation grants. In CDF's early days, Hillary Rodham Clinton worked as a staff attorney and later became a member of the CDF board of directors. In 1995, with a staff of one hundred and a budget of $10.5 million, CDF had grown considerably in size and stature but remained committed to its original goal: providing hope and social change for the poor, neglected, and abused children in the United States. CDF conducts research, drafts legislation, lobbies, and provides educational support on issues affecting children. It has buttonholed elected officials on issues including childhood diseases and immunizations, homelessness, CHILD ABUSE, education, and foster care. Edelman lobbied for a national CHILD CARE bill, increases in Medicaid spending, and, of course, additional spending for her cherished Head Start programs.

Edelman's productivity and stamina are legendary. In addition to lobbying, she gives an average of fifty speeches a year and has made frequent appearances on popular talk shows. She has received over forty-five honorary degrees. In 1992, Edelman wrote *The Measure of Our Success: A Letter to My Children and Yours.* The slim volume on parenting and the unmet needs of U.S. children sold one-quarter of a million copies and appeared on the best-seller list.

Edelman cites some sobering statistics to explain why she continues to crusade for CHILDREN'S RIGHTS. In 1992, thirteen million children lived in poverty in the United States; one in two African American children were poor; and almost 30 percent of children were not covered by health insurance. Until these statistics improve, Edelman will likely remain the nation's foremost champion of children.

EDICT 📖 A DECREE or law of major import promulgated by a king, queen, or other sovereign of a government. 📖

An edict can be distinguished from a public PROCLAMATION in that an edict puts a new statute into effect whereas a public proclamation is no more than a declaration of a law prior to its actual enactment.

Under ROMAN LAW, an edict had different meanings. It was usually a MANDATE published under the authority of a ruler that commanded the observance of various rules or injunctions. Sometimes, however, an edict was a citation to appear before a judge.

"WE MUST NOT, IN TRYING TO THINK ABOUT HOW WE CAN MAKE A BIG DIFFERENCE, IGNORE THE SMALL DAILY DIFFERENCES WE MAKE WHICH, OVER TIME, ADD UP TO BIG DIFFERENCES THAT WE OFTEN CANNOT FORESEE."

EDUCATION DEPARTMENT Created in 1980, the U.S. Department of Education (DOE) is the cabinet-level agency that establishes policy for, administers, and coordinates most federal assistance to education. It is directed by the secretary of education, who assists the president of the United States by executing policies and implementing laws enacted by Congress.

The DOE has six major responsibilities: (1) providing national leadership and building partnerships to address critical issues in U.S. education; (2) serving as a national clearinghouse of ideas on schools and teaching; (3) helping families pay for college; (4) helping local communities and schools meet the most pressing needs of their students; (5) preparing students for employment in a changing economy; and (6) ensuring nondiscrimination by recipients of federal education funds.

Although the current DOE has existed for only a short time, its history dates back to 1867, when President ANDREW JOHNSON signed legislation creating the first education department as a non-cabinet-level, autonomous agency. Within one year, the department was demoted to an office because Congress feared that the department would exercise too much control over local schools. Since the Constitution did not specifically mention education, Congress made clear its intention that the secretary of education and other officials be prohibited from exercising direction, supervision, or control over the curriculum, instructional programs, administration, or personnel of any educational institution. Such matters are the responsibility of states, localities, and private institutions.

Over the next several decades the office remained small, operating under different titles and housed in various government agencies, including the U.S. Department of the Interior and the former U.S. Department of Health, Education, and Welfare (now the U.S. Department of Health and Human Services).

Beginning in 1950 political and social changes resulted in greatly expanded federal aid to education. The Soviet Union's successful launch of the satellite Sputnik in 1957 resulted in an increase in aid for improved education in the sciences. President LYNDON B. JOHNSON's War on Poverty in the 1960s involved many programs to improve education for poor people. In the 1970s these programs were expanded to include members of racial minorities, women, individuals with disabilities, and non-English-speaking students.

In October 1979 Congress passed the Department of Education Organization Act (93 Stat. 668 [20 U.S.C.A. § 3508]), which established the current Department of Education. Since that time, the DOE has continued to expand its duties by taking an active role in education reform. In 1983 the DOE published *A Nation at Risk*, a report that described the deficiencies of U.S. schools, stating that mediocrity, not excellence, was the norm in public education. This led to the development in 1990 of a long-range plan to reform U.S. education by the year 2000.

Called America 2000: An Educational Strategy, the plan has eight goals: (1) all children will start school ready to learn by participating in preschool programs; (2) the high-school graduation rate will increase to at least 90 percent; (3) all students will leave grades 4, 8, and 12 having demonstrated competency in English, mathematics, science, foreign languages, civics and government, economics, art, history, and geography; (4) teachers will have opportunities to acquire the knowledge and skills needed for preparing students for the twenty-first century; (5) students will be first in the world in mathematics and science achievement; (6) every adult will be literate and will possess the knowledge and skills necessary to compete in a global economy; (7) every school will be free of drugs, violence, and the unauthorized presence of firearms and alcohol; and (8) every school will promote partnerships to increase parental involvement in the social, emotional, and academic growth of children.

In the 1860s, federal education had a budget of $15,000 and 4 employees to handle education fact-finding. By 1965, the Office of Education employed 2,113 employees and had a budget of $1.5 billion. In 1995, the DOE administered about $33 billion, or about 2 percent of all federal spending, and had 4,900 employees, making it the smallest cabinet agency.

The DOE's elementary and secondary education programs annually serve fifteen thousand local school districts and almost 50 million students attending more than eighty-four thousand public schools and twenty-four thousand private schools. Approximately 7 million postsecondary students receive grant, loan, and work-study assistance. From 1975 to 1995, approximately 40 million students attended college on student financial aid programs. An additional 4 million adults received assistance each year to attend literacy classes and upgrade their skills to further their employment goals.

Although the nation spends about $500 billion a year on education for elementary to postsecondary education, the federal government contributes only eight percent of that amount. Federal funding helps about one out of two students pay for their postsecondary education, and about four out of five disadvantaged elementary and secondary school students receive special assistance in learning the basics.

Structure The organizational structure of the DOE is made up of the offices of a number of administrative officials, including a secretary, deputy secretary, and under secretary; seven program offices; and seven staff offices. Reporting directly to the secretary are the deputy secretary, under secretary, general counsel, inspector general, and public affairs director. All other staff offices and program offices are under the jurisdiction of the deputy secretary.

Offices of the Secretary The secretary of education advises the president of the United States on federal education plans, policies, and programs. The secretary directs department officials in carrying out these programs and activities and serves as the chief spokesperson for public affairs, promoting public understanding of the DOE's goals, objectives, and programs.

The secretary also performs certain federal responsibilities for four federally aided corporations. The American Printing House for the Blind in Louisville, Kentucky, distributes braille books, talking books, and other educational aids without cost to educational institutions for blind people. Gallaudet University, in Washington, D.C., provides a liberal arts education for deaf persons. Howard University, also in Washington, D.C., is a comprehensive university that offers instruction in seventeen schools and colleges, and was established primarily to support African American students. The National Technical Institute for the Deaf, a division of the Rochester Institute of Technology, located in Rochester, New York, provides educational programs that focus on careers and are geared toward helping hearing-impaired individuals obtain marketable skills in a society that increasingly relies on technology.

The deputy secretary serves as the principal policy adviser to the secretary on all major program and management issues and is responsible for the department's internal management and daily operations. The deputy oversees the Executive Management Committee and the Reinvention Coordination Council, coordinates federal-state relations, and serves as acting secretary in the secretary's absence.

The under secretary advises the secretary on matters relating to program plans and budget. Through the Planning and Evaluation Service and the Budget Service, this officer directs, coordinates, and recommends policy and administers analytical studies on the economic, social, and institutional effect of existing and proposed policies, legislative proposals, and program operations.

Program Offices

Bilingual Education and Minority Languages Affairs The Office of Bilingual Education and Minority Languages Affairs funds programs designed to help persons with limited English proficiency participate effectively in classrooms and work environments in which English is the primary language. This is accomplished through fourteen grant programs and one formula grant program as well as through contracts for research and evaluation, technical assistance, and clearinghouse activities.

Civil Rights The Civil Rights Office enforces federal statutes that prohibit DISCRIMINATION based on race, color, national origin, sex, age, or handicapping condition in education programs receiving federal financial assistance. CIVIL RIGHTS laws extend to a wide range of educational institutions, including every school district, college, and university as well as proprietary schools, libraries, museums, and correctional facilities.

Educational Research and Improvement The primary function of the Office of Educational Research and Improvement is to gather, analyze, and make available to the public statistical and other types of information about the condition of U.S. education. This is accomplished through the dissemination of information and research findings about successful education practices, student achievements, and nationally significant model projects. The office also supports a wide range of research and development activities and promotes the use of technology in education.

Elementary and Secondary Education The Office of Elementary and Secondary Education formulates policy for, directs, and coordinates activities relating to preschool, elementary, and secondary education. Grants and contracts are awarded to state educational agencies, local school districts, postsecondary schools, and nonprofit organizations for compensatory, migrant, and Indian programs; drug-free programs; other school improvement programs; and impact aid, which compensates school districts for the loss of property taxes for students who live on federally owned property such as military bases or Indian reservations.

Postsecondary Education The Postsecondary Education Office formulates policy and

Education Department

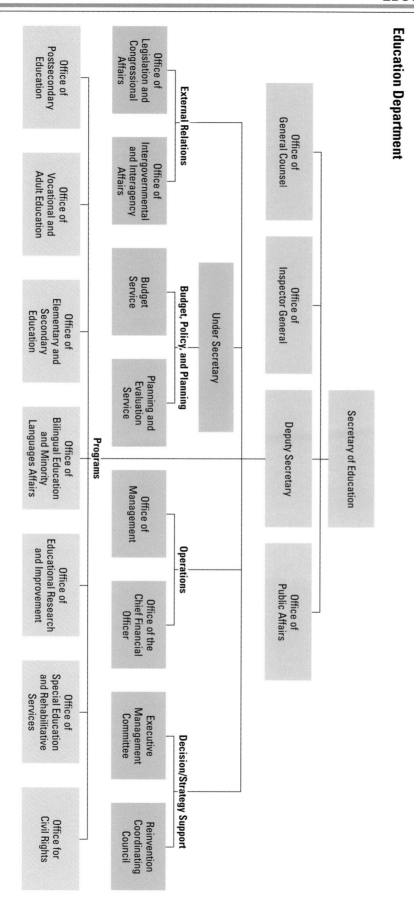

*The Education
Department's Office
of Educational
Research and
Improvement studies
new educational
practices and
promotes the use of
technology in
classrooms.*

directs and coordinates programs for assistance to postsecondary institutions and to students who need financial assistance to attend college or a vocational training center. Financial aid is awarded in the form of grants, loans, and jobs. In addition, this office provides support for institutional development, student services, housing and facilities, veterans' affairs, cooperative education, international and graduate education, colleges for African Americans, foreign language and area studies, and innovative teaching methods and practices.

Special Educational and Rehabilitation Services The Office of Special Educational and Rehabilitation Services supports programs that help educate children with special needs, provides for the rehabilitation of youths and adults with disabilities, and supports research to improve the life of individuals with disabilities regardless of age. Programs include support for the training of teachers and other professional personnel; grants for research; financial aid to help states initiate, expand, and improve their resources; and media services and captioned films for hearing-impaired individuals.

Vocational and Adult Education Grant, contract, and technical assistance programs for vocational-technical education and adult education and literacy are administered through the Office of Vocational and Adult Education. This office also works with the Department of Labor in administering the School-to-Work Opportunities Initiative, which helps states and localities design and build innovative systems to prepare youths for college and careers.

Staff Offices

Assistant Secretary for Management The assistant secretary for management provides the deputy secretary with advice and guidance on administrative management and is responsible

for activities involving personnel, training, grants and procurement management, management evaluation, automated data processing, and other support functions.

Chief Financial Officer The chief financial officer manages grants and contract services and oversees financial management, financial control and accounting, and program analysis.

Assistant Secretary of Intergovernmental and Interagency Affairs The assistant secretary of intergovernmental and interagency affairs acts as a liaison to state and local governments and other federal agencies and oversees the DOE's ten regional offices.

Inspector General The inspector general audits and investigates programs and operations to promote their efficiency and effectiveness and to detect and prevent fraud, waste, and abuse. This officer seeks to recover misused federal funds through courts and administrative procedures and, in cooperation with the Department of Justice, prosecutes wrongdoers.

General Counsel As the chief legal adviser to the secretary and other department officials, the general counsel directs, coordinates, and recommends policy for activities involving the preparation of legal documents and department rules and regulations, including proposed or pending legislation.

Public Affairs Director The public affairs director, who reports directly to the secretary, develops and coordinates public affairs policy and serves as the chief public information officer.

Assistant Secretary for Legislation and Congressional Affairs The assistant secretary for legislation and congressional affairs serves as the principal adviser to the deputy secretary on the DOE's legislative program and congressional relations.

CROSS-REFERENCES

Colleges and Universities; School Desegregation; Schools and School Districts.

EDUCATION LAW ◫ The body of state and federal constitutional provisions; local, state, and federal statutes; court opinions; and government regulations that provide the legal framework for educational institutions. ◫

The laws that control public education can be divided into two categories: those written exclusively for schools and those pertaining to society in general. Federal statutes regarding the education of children with disabilities are an example of the former, and title VII (Civil Rights Act of 1964, § 701 et seq., as amended, 42 U.S.C.A. § 2000e et seq.), a federal statute that covers employment in schools and elsewhere, is an example of the latter. Much of the litigation, legislation, and debate in education law has centered around nine main issues: student speech and expression; searches of students; the separation of church and state; racial segregation; the education of disabled children; employment law; employee sexual harassment and abuse of students; instructional programming; and the financing of public education.

History   Throughout the United States' history, government, in one form or another, has expressed an interest in education. Indeed, this interest predates the American Revolution by more than a hundred years. In 1647, the General Court of the Colony of Massachusetts Bay passed the Old Deluder Satan Act. Section 2 of that act provided that "when any town increased to one hundred families or households a grammar school would be established with a master capable of preparing young people for university level study." The Massachusetts Bay Colony was not unique in its concern for education: other colonies also gave unrestricted aid through land grants and appropriations of money. Both forms of support were adopted later by the Continental Congress and the Congress of the United States.

The first measure enacted by the federal government in support of education came when the Continental Congress passed the Ordinance of 1785, which disposed of lands in the Western Territory and reserved section 16 of each congressional township for the support of schools. Two years later the same Congress passed the NORTHWEST ORDINANCE, which represents the first policy statement by Congress with respect to education. Its third article recognizes knowledge as essential to good government and the public welfare and encourages happiness of mankind, schools, and the means of education.

These early acts by the colonies, and support from the federal Congress, forged a partnership in public education that continues to this day. This partnership has thrived despite the absence of any explicit reference to education in the Constitution. The legal authority for the intrusion of the federal government into education is based on an interpretation given to the GENERAL WELFARE Clause of the Constitution, which reads, "The Congress shall have Power To lay and collect Taxes, Duties, Imposts and Excises to pay the Debts and provide for the common Defence and general Welfare of the United States" (art. I, § 8).

The TENTH AMENDMENT to the Constitution provides the basis in legal theory for making education a function of the states. It reads, "The powers not delegated to the United States by the Constitution, nor prohibited by it to the States, are reserved to the States respectively, or to the people." Although this amendment does not specifically direct the states to assume the responsibility for providing education, its effect has been no less. Each state constitution provides for the establishment of a statewide school system. Some state constitutions define in detail the structure for organizing and maintaining a system of public education; others merely ac-

The provision of an education to each child is a function of the states, not the federal government. This 1933 Tennessee schoolroom sometimes held as many as forty students.

TENNESSEE VALLEY AUTHORITY

cept that responsibility and delegate authority for its implementation to the state legislature. Both the U.S. Supreme Court and the state courts have consistently ruled that education is a function of the states.

Student Speech and the First Amendment In the mid–twentieth century, the Supreme Court began to recognize that children do not give up their constitutional rights as a condition of attending public school. The Court acknowledged that the public school is an appropriate setting in which to instill a respect for these rights. Freedom of expression is perhaps the most preciously shielded of individual liberties, and the Court has noted that it must receive "scrupulous protection" in schools "if we are not to strangle the free mind at its source and teach youth to discount important principles of our government as mere platitudes" (*West Virginia Board of Education v. Barnette*, 319 U.S. 624, 63 S. Ct. 1178, 87 L. Ed. 1628 [1943]).

The Court also has recognized that schools function as a "marketplace of ideas" and that the "robust exchange of ideas is a special concern of the First Amendment" (*Keyishian v. Board of Regents*, 385 U.S. 589, 87 S. Ct. 675, 17 L. Ed. 2d 629 [1967]).

The right to free expression can nevertheless be restricted. As Justice OLIVER WENDELL HOLMES, JR., noted, freedom of speech does not allow an individual to yell "Fire!" in a crowded theater when there is no fire (*Schenck v. United States*, 249 U.S. 47, 39 S. Ct. 247, 63 L. Ed. 470 [1919]). A determination that specific conduct communicates an idea does not ensure constitutional protection. The judiciary has recognized that defamatory, obscene, and inflammatory expression may fall outside the protections of the FIRST AMENDMENT. Moreover, the Supreme Court has acknowledged that "the con-

stitutional rights of students in public school are not automatically coextensive with the rights of adults in other settings" (*Bethel School Dist. 403 v. Fraser*, 478 U.S. 675, 106 S. Ct. 3159, 32 Ed. Law Rep. 1243 [1986]). Accordingly, students' rights to free expression may be restricted by policies that are reasonably designed to take into account the special circumstances of the educational environment.

It was not until 1969 that the Supreme Court specifically addressed the scope of students' freedom of expression in public schools. Its landmark decision in this area, *Tinker v. Des Moines Independent Community School District*, 393 U.S. 503, 89 S. Ct. 733, 21 L. Ed. 2d 731, often is referred to as the Magna Charta of students' rights. *Tinker* arose from an incident in which students were suspended for wearing black armbands to protest the Vietnam War. Concluding that school authorities suspended the students for expression that was not accompanied by any disorder or disturbance, the Supreme Court ruled that "undifferentiated fear or apprehension of disturbance is not enough to overcome the right to freedom of expression."

For almost two decades lower courts interpreted the *Tinker* mandate broadly, applying it to controversies involving a range of expressive activities by students, both school sponsored and non–school sponsored. Although *Tinker* has not been overturned, the Supreme Court limited the application of its principle in the late 1980s and early 1990s, beginning with the 1986 decision of *Bethel School Dist. 403 v. Fraser*. In *Fraser*, the Court upheld disciplinary action taken against a student for using a sexual metaphor in a nominating speech during a student government assembly. The Court recognized that the inculcation of fundamental values of civility is an important objective of public schools and that a school board has the authority to determine what manner of speech is inappropriate in classes and assemblies.

Two years after *Fraser*, the Supreme Court affirmed the right of a school principal to delete two pages from the school newspaper because of the content of articles on divorce and teenage pregnancy (*Hazelwood v. Kuhlmeier*, 484 U.S. 260, 108 S. Ct. 562, 98 L. Ed. 2d 592 [1988]). The Court acknowledged school authorities' broad discretion to ensure that expression appearing to bear the school's imprimatur is consistent with educational objectives. Further, the Court expansively interpreted the category of student expression subject to CENSORSHIP as that occurring in school publications and in all school-sponsored activities. In both *Hazelwood* and *Fraser*, the Court indicated that school

The freedom of expression of students in public schools has been defined by court cases from the late 1960s to the present.

ROBERT FINKE/THE PICTURE CUBE

authorities could determine for themselves what expression is consistent with their school's objectives.

Although many questions remain unanswered concerning the application of the First Amendment guarantee of free speech in the unique forum of the public school, the law does seem to be settled in the following areas:

- School officials can discipline students when their speech or expression materially and substantially disrupts the educational environment (*Bethel School Dist. 403 v. Fraser*).
- School administrators can reasonably regulate the content and distribution of printed material at school (*Hazelwood School Dist. v. Kuhlmeier*).
- The Equal Access Act (Pub. L. 98-377, Title VIII, Aug. 11, 1984, 98 Stat. 1302 [20 U.S.C.A. § 4071 et seq.]) requires a school to permit religious student groups to meet during noninstructional time if the school permits other noncurriculum groups to meet in the same or a similar manner (*Board of Education v. Mergens*, 496 U.S. 226, 110 S. Ct. 2356, 60 Ed. Law Rep. 320 [1990]).
- School officials have far more control and flexibility in selecting and rejecting curriculum materials than deciding similarly about library books and magazines (*Board of Education v. Pico*, 457 U.S. 853, 102 S. Ct. 2799, 4 Ed. Law Rep. 1013 [1982]).
- School officials can make judgments on the appropriateness of student speech in school, based on the content of the speech, when that speech is vulgar or otherwise offensive in nature (*Bethel School Dist. 403 v. Fraser*).
- School officials can reasonably regulate student speech and expression when its exercise either intrudes on the rights of others or is in some way inconsistent with the school's overall curricular mission (see *Fraser*).

Searches of Students and Lockers

The FOURTH AMENDMENT to the U.S. Constitution provides that "the right of the people to be secure in their persons, houses, papers, and effects, against unreasonable searches and seizures, shall not be violated, and no Warrants shall issue, but upon probable cause." This provision is made applicable to the states through the DUE PROCESS Clause of the FOURTEENTH AMENDMENT. To what extent is it applicable to searches of minor students by public school officials?

The Supreme Court has stated that the BILL OF RIGHTS (the first ten amendments to the Constitution) is applicable to children, even in a classroom setting. To paraphrase the Court in *Tinker*, students do not shed their rights at the schoolhouse gates. Does the *Tinker* ruling suggest that the Fourth Amendment protection from unreasonable searches extends to public schools? Must a principal obtain a WARRANT before searching students or their lockers? Are principals to be held to the "PROBABLE-CAUSE" standard that is generally required by the Fourth Amendment? These are important questions because evidence of wrongdoing that is obtained in an illegal search is generally INADMISSIBLE—that is, must be excluded from consideration—at trial. The issue of admissibility of evidence is especially critical when school officials are searching for drugs, alcohol, and weapons.

These questions were addressed by the Supreme Court in 1985, in *New Jersey v. T. L. O.*, 469 U.S. 325, 105 S. Ct. 733, 83 L. Ed. 2d 720. The case involved a fourteen-year-old girl, T. L. O., and a female companion, whom a teacher observed smoking in the girls' rest room in violation of school rules. T. L. O. denied smoking on that occasion and claimed she did not smoke at all. The assistant principal opened T. L. O.'s purse and found a pack of cigarettes. While searching the purse, he also discovered evidence of marijuana possession, use, and sale. He then called the police. T. L. O. subsequently admitted her involvement in selling marijuana to other students, but she sought to have the evidence excluded in criminal court on the ground that the search violated her rights under the New Jersey Constitution and the Fourth Amendment to the U.S. Constitution.

This issue was litigated at three levels in the New Jersey courts and finally decided by the U.S. Supreme Court. The Court held that a warrant was not needed for the assistant principal to search T. L. O. and that the reduced standard of "reasonable suspicion" governs school searches. The Court established a two-pronged test of reasonableness: (1) the search must be justified at its inception, and (2) as conducted, the search must be reasonably related in scope to the circumstances. The Court weighed T. L. O.'s interest in PRIVACY against the school's need to obtain evidence of violations of school rules and of the law. The result tipped the scale in favor of broad school discretion in searching for contraband in the pockets and purses of students and in their lockers.

State and federal courts have expanded the scope of *T. L. O.* since it was decided in 1985. The reasonable suspicion standard has survived student challenges in searches of lockers, desks, and cars in school parking lots.

A 1995 ruling by the Supreme Court continued the erosion of students' Fourth Amendment rights that began with the *T. L. O.* decision. In *Vernonia School District 471 v. Acton*, 515 U.S. 646, 115 S. Ct. 2386, 132 L. Ed. 2d 564, the Supreme Court rejected a constitutional challenge to a public school district's random urinalysis testing program for students participating in interscholastic athletics. In examining the "nature of the privacy interest" at stake, the Court explained that in general, public school children have diminished privacy interests because they require constant supervision and control. Athletes' privacy interests are further diminished, the Court said, because they regularly undergo physical exams and routinely experience conditions of "communal undress" in locker rooms. Further, the Court said that the district's random testing program was minimally intrusive because it required urine collection under conditions virtually identical to those students confront in public school rest rooms. Finally, the Court found several goals of the school district sufficiently compelling to justify random testing: deterring drug use in schoolchildren, maintaining the functioning of the schools, and protecting athletes from drug-related injury. The Court's ruling will enable school systems following the procedures approved in *Vernonia* to test student athletes randomly for drugs. It remains unclear, however, whether school districts may conduct drug testing of students who are not involved in athletics.

Will the scope of *Vernonia* expand in the years ahead, as has that of *T. L. O.?* If drug problems continue in schools, courts will likely determine that the Fourth Amendment rights of students may be restricted further. Additional limitations on those rights may include random sampling of all students for evidence of drug use.

Separation of Church and State The First Amendment provides that "Congress shall make no law respecting an establishment of religion, or prohibiting the free exercise thereof." The First Amendment has been incorporated into the Fourteenth Amendment and applies to the states and their subdivisions. The first provision is called the Establishment Clause; the second, the Free Exercise Clause. Thus, the guarantee of religious freedom has a double aspect. The Establishment Clause prohibits laws requiring that anyone accept any belief or creed or the practice of any form of worship. The courts have relied on the Establishment Clause to nullify numerous practices in public schools, such as offering school-prescribed prayers in classrooms and at commencement exercises, posting the Ten Commandments in classrooms, requiring Bible

reading, displaying religious symbols, observing moments of silence, studying Scientific Creationism, and distributing Bibles.

The Free Exercise Clause safeguards the freedom to engage in a chosen form of RELIGION. Again, practices in the public schools have produced a host of litigation on this clause of the First Amendment. Parents with strong religious convictions have brought numerous suits alleging that a part of the science, health, or reading curriculum included content contrary to the family's religious convictions and values, thus restricting the family's right to engage in its chosen religion.

Likewise, a series of state and federal statutes has been challenged on separation-of-church-and-state grounds. The courts have ruled that the following practices do not violate the First Amendment religion clauses:

- Transportation of students to private, sectarian schools at public expense
- Public purchase of secular textbooks for use in religious schools
- Use of school facilities by religious organizations pursuant to policies that allow nonreligious groups to use such facilities
- Release of students from public schools to attend religious instruction classes
- Provision of a signer at public expense for a deaf student in a religious school
- Permission for student-organized religious clubs to meet on school property during the noninstructional part of the day

Practices that have been prohibited by the courts include these:

- Sending public school teachers into private, sectarian schools to provide remedial instruction
- Providing a publicly funded salary supplement to teachers in religious schools

Racial Segregation The Supreme Court's 1954 ruling in *Brown v. Board of Education*, 349 U.S. 294, 75 S. Ct. 753, 99 L. Ed. 1083, held unconstitutional the deliberate segregation of schools by law on account of race. *Brown* overruled the 1896 case of *Plessy v. Ferguson*, 163 U.S. 537, 16 S. Ct. 1138, in which the Court had recognized as valid separation of black and white school children. The principles enunciated in *Brown* provided the foundation for new federal laws expanding access to education and other public services to previously unserved populations, such as disabled students and adults.

In *Brown*, four separate cases—from Delaware, Kansas, South Carolina, and Virginia—were consolidated for argument before the Supreme Court. The Court framed the issue before it as being whether "segregation of children in public schools solely on the basis of race, even though the physical facilities and other tangible factors may be equal, deprives the children of the minority group of equal educational opportunity." The Court answered in the affirmative, holding that the Fourteenth Amendment's EQUAL PROTECTION Clause forbids state-imposed segregation of races in public schools, and stating, "In the field of public education the doctrine of 'separate but equal' has no place. Separate educational facilities are inherently unequal."

The Court further stated, "Such an opportunity [education] . . . is a right which must be made available to all on equal terms"—not a privilege that is granted to some and denied others. This statement of public policy opened the public schools to minorities and to other populations previously denied access. For example, advocates for better access to schools for disabled students seized upon this language to press Congress into passing the Education for All Handicapped Children Act (EAHCA) in 1975 (Pub. L. 94-142, Nov. 29, 1975, 89 Stat. 773 [20 U.S.C.A. §§ 1232, 1400 et seq.]).

Numerous lawsuits have alleged violation of *Brown* since 1954. Although the efforts to desegregate the schools have not been uniformly successful, de jure segregation in public schools— the evil addressed specifically in *Brown*—does not exist today. However, the goal of creating an integrated public school system has not been achieved. Most minority children still attend schools where they are the majority of students, or where their numbers are disproportionately high compared to the area population. The location of public housing, middle-class flight from central cities, economic deprivation of minorities, and a host of other variables have frustrated legislative and judicial efforts to fully integrate public schools.

Education of Children with Disabilities The Individuals with Disabilities Education Act (IDEA) (20 U.S.C.A. §§ 1400 et seq.)—formerly the EAHCA—was passed by Congress in 1975 to address the failure of state education systems to meet the educational needs of children with disabilities. Congress's enactment of IDEA was in part a response to two well-publicized federal court cases: *Mills v. Board of Education*, 348 F. Supp. 866 (D.D.C. 1972), and *Pennsylvania Ass'n of Retarded Children v. Commonwealth of Pennsylvania*, 343 F. Supp. 279 (E.D. Pa. 1972). The courts in both cases found that children with disabilities were denied access to public schools because of their disabilities. For example, school laws in Pennsylvania and in the nation's capital permitted

Children with Disabilities by Age and Educational Environment, 1991

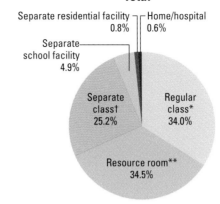

Total

- Separate residential facility 0.8%
- Home/hospital 0.6%
- Separate school facility 4.9%
- Separate class† 25.2%
- Regular class* 34.0%
- Resource room** 34.5%

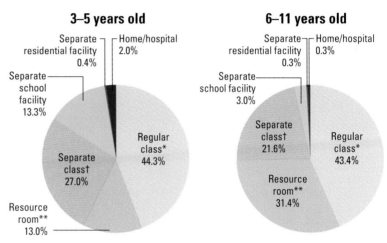

3–5 years old

- Separate residential facility 0.4%
- Home/hospital 2.0%
- Separate school facility 13.3%
- Regular class* 44.3%
- Separate class† 27.0%
- Resource room** 13.0%

6–11 years old

- Separate residential facility 0.3%
- Home/hospital 0.3%
- Separate school facility 3.0%
- Separate class† 21.6%
- Regular class* 43.4%
- Resource room** 31.4%

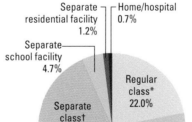

12–17 years old

- Separate residential facility 1.2%
- Home/hospital 0.7%
- Separate school facility 4.7%
- Regular class* 22.0%
- Separate class† 28.7%
- Resource room** 42.7%

18–21 years old

- Separate residential facility 3.0%
- Home/hospital 1.1%
- Separate school facility 13.1%
- Regular class* 17.1%
- Separate class† 30.7%
- Resource room** 35.0%

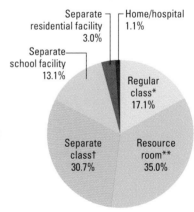

* Receives special education and related services less than 21 percent of the school day.
**Receives services between 21 and 60 percent of the school day.
†Receives services for more than 60 percent of the school day.

Source: U.S. Department of Education, Office of Special Education Programs, Data Analysis Systems (DANS).

schools to deny entry to children whose IQ was below seventy (one hundred being classified as normal intelligence), until such children reached the age of eight. Once admitted to

In order to qualify for matching IDEA funds, states must provide free appropriate public education to disabled children who qualify for IDEA coverage.

school, many of these children were expelled because they could not learn how to read.

IDEA defines the types of disabilities covered and limits coverage to children who are educationally disabled. The act provides for matching funds to states with federally approved plans. To qualify for those funds, a state plan must ensure a free appropriate public education (FAPE) for all qualifying children, and guarantee access to a complex due process procedure for a parent or guardian who wishes to challenge a child's FAPE.

IDEA differs from most legal provisions for public education in one important aspect: the parent of a disabled child has been elevated to an equal partner with school officials in shaping an educational experience for the child, whereas the parent of a child without disabilities is expected by law to be a rather passive participant in the public education that is provided by the teachers and school officials. This empowerment of parents of children with disabilities has generated countless and endless legal challenges of school officials' decisions and practices. Each case is decided on narrow factual grounds, with little generalizability.

Employment Law The myriad federal and state laws and regulations that control public employment in general apply with equal force to public school employment. In addition, all states have statutes that control the school board–employee relationship. These state laws

pertain to contracts, tenure, certification, retirement, and other matters of special interest to teachers. Despite the similarities of the issues covered in state statutes, there is very little reciprocity between states, making generalizations across state lines almost meaningless.

In contrast, federal statutes pertaining to public employment are enforceable throughout the nation. For example, title VII makes it "an unlawful employment practice" to discriminate against any individual with respect to "compensation, terms, conditions, or privileges of employment" because of race, color, religion, sex, or national origin (42 U.S.C.A. § 2000e-2(a)(1)). In 1986, the Supreme Court decided a case concerning SEXUAL HARASSMENT and the interpretation of title VII. In *Meritor Savings Bank v. Vinson*, 477 U.S. 57, 106 S. Ct. 2399, 91 L. Ed. 2d 49, the defendant, Meritor Savings Bank, argued that the discrimination prohibited by the statute concerned economic loss and not "purely psychological" aspects of the workplace environment. Because the female employee who filed the lawsuit suffered no economic loss, the employer argued that she had no grounds for a lawsuit under title VII. The Supreme Court disagreed. After ruling that title VII protection is not limited to economic discrimination, the Court quoted with approval an appeals court opinion that said, "One can readily envision environments so heavily polluted with discrimination as to destroy completely the emotional and psychological stability of employees."

The principles enunciated in *Meritor* were refined by the Supreme Court's 1992 ruling in *Harris v. Forklift Systems*, 510 U.S. 17, 114 S. Ct. 367, 126 L. Ed. 2d 295. The Court in *Harris* was asked to set a standard of review in cases alleging the newly discovered "hostile environment" theory of sexual harassment. Justice SANDRA DAY O'CONNOR, writing for the majority, explained that simply uttering an "epithet which engenders offensive feelings in an employee" does not sufficiently affect the conditions of employment to implicate title VII. The Court was equally clear in rejecting the employer's argument that title VII requires a showing that the harassment "seriously affects the plaintiff's well-being." Rather, O'Connor wrote, the statute is violated when the workplace environment "would reasonably be perceived and is perceived as hostile and abusive." Further, the Court stated that four circumstances (in addition to psychological harm) should be considered: "[t]he frequency of the conduct; its severity; whether it is physically threatening or humiliating, or a mere offensive utterance; and whether it unreasonably interferes with an employee's work performance." Continuing, O'Connor said that the appropriate standard was that of a "reasonable victim," thus departing from the traditional "reasonable person" standard that is typically applied in cases involving alleged acts of commission or omission that result in an injury or damage to an individual's body, reputation, or property.

Employee Sexual Harassment and Abuse of Students Two federal statutes, title IX of the Education Amendments of 1972 (§§ 901–909, as amended, 20 U.S.C.A. §§ 1681–1688) and Section 1983 of the CIVIL RIGHTS ACT of 1964 (42 U.S.C.A. § 1983), provide students with potentially powerful tools of redress for and protection against sexual harassment and abuse perpetrated by school employees. Title IX provides, "No person in the United States shall, on the basis of sex, be excluded from participation in, be denied the benefits of, or be subjected to discrimination under any education program or activity receiving Federal financial assistance." Section 1983 prohibits the deprivation of federal constitutional and statutory rights "under color of state law."

The most notable court ruling on the application of title IX is the Supreme Court's 1992 decision in *Franklin v. Gwinnett County Public Schools*, 503 U.S. 60, 112 S. Ct. 1028, 117 L. Ed. 2d 208. In this landmark case, the Court held that a female high school student who had been subjected to sexual abuse by her teacher could receive money damages under title IX. The Court implicitly accepted as "sexual harassment" the type of behavior that existed in *Franklin*, which involved coercive sexual activity between a male high school teacher–coach and a female student. Accordingly, sexual harassment, in all its forms, is SEX DISCRIMINATION prohibited by title IX. As defined by the Office of Civil Rights, "[s]exual harassment consists of verbal or physical conduct of a sexual nature, imposed on the basis of sex, by an employee or agent . . . that denies, limits, provides different, or conditions the provision of aid, benefits, or services or treatment protected under Title IX."

Under section 1983 (42 U.S.C.A. § 1983), the violation of a student's liberty right to bodily security by a school district or an employer implicates the substantive due process rights of the student under the Fourteenth Amendment. However, in order to demonstrate liability, the plaintiff must show that the school had notice of a pattern of unconstitutional conduct. This is a difficult standard to meet. For example, a handful of complaints received by various school officials that a bus driver had kissed or fondled several handicapped children was insufficient to support a section 1983 claim (*Jane Doe A v. Special School Dist. of St. Louis County*, 908 F.2d 642, 60 Ed. Law Rep. 20 [8th Cir. 1990]).

Litigation involving claims of sexual abuse by teachers is expanding rapidly. The courts are creating new legal avenues of redress, and students are becoming more willing to confront their abusers. Further, some state courts have waived statutory time limits on the filing of claims in cases involving sexual abuse of MINORS, permitting lawsuits many years after an alleged abuse.

Instructional Programming Contemporary debate on the school curriculum by advocates of a return to the basics, multicultural studies, and a range of educational approaches continues to attract public attention as those advocates press their claims in courts and legislative chambers. With some notable exceptions, courts generally give state legislative and local administrative authorities wide latitude to tailor curriculums to keep abreast of ever-expanding concepts of education. In every state, local districts must offer a curriculum that the state prescribes. Because the federal Constitution has delegated the responsibility for public education to the several states, the power of the state legislature over public schools is said to be plenary, limited only by the state constitution and some provisions in the federal Constitution. Accordingly, the local school board selects its curriculum offerings on the basis of the extent of authority delegated by the state. Most state legislatures have chosen to prescribe a small number of course offerings in all public schools in the state, and delegate to local school authorities the balance of authority to control the curriculum. The curricular choices of local school boards may not satisfy some constituents and taxpayers, but displeasure alone will not persuade a court to substitute its judgment for that of a school board. Critics of the local choices pertaining to school curriculum, textbooks, library holdings, and teaching methods generally must take their complaints to the local school board and state legislature for remedy.

Financing of Public Education Public schools in the United States are financed through a system of fiscal FEDERALISM—that is, the funds used for their operation have been appropriated on the federal, state, and local levels. Nationally, from the mid-1970s to the mid-1990s, the combined federal and state support for public education accounted for slightly less than 50 percent of all operating expenses,

Local Funding of Public Elementary and Secondary Schools, by State, 1995–96

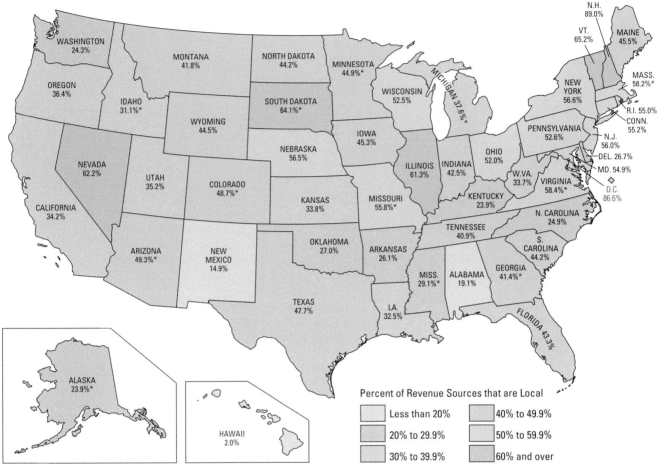

Percent of Revenue Sources that are Local

Less than 20%	40% to 49.9%
20% to 29.9%	50% to 59.9%
30% to 39.9%	60% and over

* Includes NEA estimate.

Source: National Education Association.

with the federal treasury providing less than 10 percent of the total cost of public education. Therefore, approximately one-half of the money required by school districts has been provided by local sources, primarily local property taxes. States have constructed myriad property classifications and state aid distribution formulas in attempts to equalize educational opportunities for students in property-rich and poor school districts. Further, most states provide special funding for school transportation, for the education of students with disabilities, and for other high-cost services and programs.

As state creations, school boards can only exercise the fiscal powers delegated to them by the state, so they depend heavily on both direct state subsidies and legislative authorization to levy school district taxes. The states' options to limit and allocate direct state assistance to different classes of school districts, to fix the sources and limits of school district revenues, and even to transfer school district funds place

the ultimate control of school finance in state legislatures and not in local school boards. Financially stressed school districts and citizen groups have, therefore, resorted to constitutional challenges to overturn state laws that they deem to be unduly restrictive or unfair. These challenges have not fared well under the federal Constitution and have met with mixed success under state constitutions.

The Supreme Court, in *San Antonio Independent School District v. Rodriguez*, 411 U.S. 1, 93 S. Ct. 1278, 36 L. Ed. 2d 16 (1993), upheld the use of local property tax systems to support public schools, against the claim that such systems violate the Fourteenth Amendment equal protection rights of children in impoverished areas. The Court further declared that public education is not a fundamental constitutional interest.

Following *Rodriguez*, litigation has proceeded in about one-half of the states, under the equal protection and education clauses of state constitutions. The state constitutional challenges do not have a uniform thrust. The themes of equality (equal protection) and quality (efficient public education) may, depending on the wording and construction of each state's constitution, lead toward different policies and results. Despite adverse court rulings, the school finance litigation has inspired a trend of legislative reform in many states. The new laws are calculated to balance educational opportunities for all children, regardless of the wealth of their school districts or the income of their parents.

Conclusion The history of education law is marked by a series of landmark court opinions and legislative acts that, with some exceptions, express the PUBLIC POLICY preference for universality in public education. The major exception is the Supreme Court's 1896 "separate-but-equal" ruling in *Plessy v. Ferguson.* From the early days of the Old Deluder Satan Act to the present, the trend has been toward inclusion, not exclusion. Examples of significant expansions of this concept of universality are the enactment of compulsory attendance laws in all fifty states in the twentieth century; the *Brown* decision in 1954; and the 1975 enactment of the EAHCA, now IDEA.

CROSS-REFERENCES

Abington School District v. Schempp; Brown v. Board of Education of Topeka, Kansas; Colleges and Universities; Disabled Persons; Drugs and Narcotics; Education Department; *Engel v. Vitale;* Flag; Freedom of Speech; In Loco Parentis; School Desegregation; School Prayer; Schools and School Districts; Searches and Seizures.

EEOC An abbreviation for EQUAL EMPLOYMENT OPPORTUNITY COMMISSION.

EFFECT As a verb, to do; to produce; to make; to bring to pass; to execute; enforce; accomplish. As a noun, that which is produced by an agent or cause; result; outcome; consequence. The result that an instrument between parties will produce in their relative rights, or which a statute will produce upon the existing law, as discovered from the language used, the forms employed, or other materials for construing it. The operation of a law, of an agreement, or an act. The phrases *take effect, be in force,* and *go into operation,* are used interchangeably.

In the plural, a person's effects are the REAL and PERSONAL PROPERTY of someone who has died or who makes a WILL.

EFFECTIVE RATE Another name for ANNUAL PERCENTAGE RATE that refers to the amount of yearly interest to be charged by a lender on the money borrowed by a debtor.

In federal INCOME TAX law, the actual tax rate that an individual taxpayer pays based upon his or her TAXABLE INCOME.

Federal income tax laws increase the rate of TAXATION as a taxpayer reaches certain marginal income levels. For example, taxpayers might pay a tax rate of 20 percent on the first $10,000 of taxable income. Thereafter, any increase in income up to an additional $5,000 might be taxable at a rate of 22 percent on that $5,000. The effective rate of tax is computed by dividing the total amount of tax paid by the total of the person's taxable income, adding the tax paid on the person's first $10,000 at a 20 percent rate to the tax paid on the next $5,000 that is at a 22 percent rate. The effective rate is not an average of the tax rates imposed since the average does not take into account the differences in the marginal income levels. A taxpayer's effective tax rate is, however, more than the person's bottom marginal rate but less than his or her top marginal rate.

EFFICIENT CAUSE That which actually precipitates an accident or injury.

The term *efficient cause* is frequently used interchangeably with PROXIMATE CAUSE—the immediate act in the production of a particular effect—or the cause that sets the others in operation.

E.G. An abbreviation for *exempli gratia* [*Latin, for the sake of an example*].

The phrase *e.g.* is frequently used in law books in lieu of the phrase "for example."

EIGHTEENTH AMENDMENT The Eighteenth Amendment to the U.S. Constitution reads:

Section 1. After one year from the ratification of this article the manufacture, sale, or transportation of intoxicating liquors within, the importation thereof into, or the exportation thereof from the United States and all territory subject to the jurisdiction

This local referendum measured support for Prohibition in the early twentieth century. The Eighteenth Amendment outlawed the manufacture, sale, and transportation of alcohol. It was repealed in 1933.

CULVER PICTURES

thereof for beverage purposes is hereby prohibited.

Section 2. The Congress and the several States shall have concurrent power to enforce this article by appropriate legislation.

Section 3. This article shall be inoperative unless it shall have been ratified as an amendment to the Constitution by the legislatures of the several States as provided in the Constitution, within seven years from the date of the submission hereof to the States by the Congress.

The Eighteenth Amendment was passed in 1919 and subsequently repealed in 1933.

The VOLSTEAD ACT (41 Stat. 305 [1919]) was enacted pursuant to the Eighteenth Amendment to provide for enforcement of its prohibition. The 1933 ratification of the TWENTY-FIRST AMENDMENT in 1933 resulted in the repeal of the Eighteenth Amendment and the Volstead Act.

See also ALCOHOL.

EIGHTH AMENDMENT The Eighth Amendment to the U.S. Constitution reads:

Excessive bail shall not be required, nor excessive fines imposed, nor cruel and unusual punishments inflicted.

The Eighth Amendment to the U.S. Constitution, ratified in 1791, has three provisions. The Cruel and Unusual Punishments Clause restricts the severity of punishments that state and federal governments may impose upon persons who have been convicted of a criminal offense. The Excessive Fines Clause limits the amount state and federal governments can fine a person for a particular crime. The Excessive Bail Clause restricts judicial discretion in setting BAIL for the release of persons accused of a criminal activity during the period following their arrest but preceding their trial.

Courts are given wide latitude under the Excessive Fines Clause of the Eighth Amendment. FINES imposed by a trial court judge or magistrate will not be overturned on APPEAL unless the judge or magistrate abused her or his discretion in assessing them (*United States v. Hyppolite*, 65 F.3d 1151 [4th Cir. 1995]). Under the "abuse-of-discretion" standard, APPELLATE COURTS may overturn a fine that is ARBITRARY, capricious, or "so grossly excessive as to amount to a deprivation of property without due process of law" (*Water-Pierce Oil Co. v. Texas*, 212 U.S. 86, 111, 29 S. Ct. 220, 227, 53 L. Ed. 417 [1909]). Fines are rarely overturned on appeal for any of these reasons.

Trial court judges are given less latitude under the Excessive Bail Clause. Bail is the amount of money, property, or BOND a defendant must pledge to the court as security for his or her appearance at trial. If the defendant meets bail, or is able to pay the amount set by the court, the defendant is entitled to receive the pledged amount back at the conclusion of the criminal proceedings. If the defendant fails to appear as scheduled during the prosecution, the defendant FORFEITS the amount pledged, and still faces further criminal penalties if convicted of the offense or offenses charged.

When fixing the amount of bail for a particular defendant, the court takes into consideration several factors: (1) the seriousness of the offense; (2) the weight of evidence against the ACCUSED; (3) the nature and extent of any ties, such as family or employment, the accused may have to the community where she or he will be prosecuted; (4) the accused's ability to pay a given amount; and (5) the likelihood that the accused will flee the JURISDICTION if released.

In applying these factors, courts usually attempt to set bail for a REASONABLE amount. Setting bail for an unreasonable amount would unnecessarily restrict the freedom of a person who has been only accused of wrongdoing, is presumed innocent until proved otherwise, and is entitled to earn a living and support a family like the rest of society. At the same time, courts are aware that bail needs to be set sufficiently high to ensure that the defendant will return for trial. Defendants are less likely to flee the jurisdiction when they would forfeit large amounts of money as a result. Courts are also aware that they must protect communities from the harm presented by particularly dangerous defendants. In this regard, the Supreme Court has permitted lower-court judges to deny bail for defendants who would create abnormally dangerous risks to the community if released.

Appellate courts usually defer to lower court decisions when a criminal penalty is challenged under the Excessive Fines and Excessive Bail Clauses of the Eighth Amendment. They give much closer scrutiny to criminal penalties challenged under the Cruel and Unusual Punishments Clause. Both state and federal governments are prohibited from inflicting CRUEL AND UNUSUAL PUNISHMENTS on a defendant no matter how heinous the crime committed. The prohibition against cruel and unusual punishment by states derives from the doctrine of INCORPORATION, through which selective liberties contained in the BILL OF RIGHTS have been applied to the states by the Supreme Court's interpretation of the Due Process and Equal Protection Clauses of the FOURTEENTH AMENDMENT.

The Eighth Amendment requires that every punishment imposed by the government be commensurate with the offense committed by the defendant. Punishments that are disproportionately harsh will be overturned on appeal. Examples of punishments overturned for being unreasonable are two Georgia statutes that prescribed the death penalty for rape and kidnapping (see *Coker v. Georgia*, 433 U.S. 584, 97 S. Ct. 2861, 53 L. Ed. 2d 982 [1977]; *Eberheart v. Georgia*, 433 U.S. 917, 97 S. Ct. 2994, 53 L. Ed. 2d 1104 [1977]).

The Supreme Court has also ruled that criminal SENTENCES that are inhuman, outrageous, or shocking to the social conscience are cruel and unusual. Although the Court has never provided meaningful definitions for these characteristics, the pertinent cases speak for themselves. For example, the Georgia Supreme Court explained that the Eighth Amendment was intended to prohibit barbarous punishments such as castration, burning at the stake, and quartering (*Whitten v. Georgia*, 47 Ga. 297 [1872]). Similarly, the U.S. Supreme Court said the Cruel and Unusual Punishments Clause prohibits crucifixion, breaking on the wheel, and other punishments that involve a lingering death (*In re Kemmler*, 136 U.S. 436, 10 S. Ct. 930, 34 L. Ed. 519 [1890]). The Supreme Court also invalidated an Oklahoma law (57 O.S. 1941 §§ 173, 174, 176–181, 195) that compelled the government to sterilize "feeble-minded" or "habitual" criminals in an effort to prevent them from reproducing and passing on their deficient characteristics (*Skinner v. Oklahoma*, 316 U.S. 535, 62 S. Ct. 1110, 86 L. Ed. 1655 [1942]). Significantly, however, fifteen years earlier the Supreme Court had let stand a Virginia law (1924 Va. Acts C. 394) that authorized the sterilization of mentally retarded individuals institutionalized at state facilities for the "feeble-minded" (*Buck v. Bell*, 274 U.S. 200, 47 S. Ct. 584, 71 L. Ed. 1000 [1927]).

A constitutional standard that allows judges to strike down legislation they find shocking but let stand other legislation they find less disturbing, inherently possesses a subjective and malleable quality. A punishment that seems outrageous to one judge on a particular day may seem sensible to a different judge on the same day or to the same judge on a different day. For example, in *Hudson v. McMillian*, 503 U.S. 1, 112 S. Ct. 995, 117 L. Ed. 2d 156 (1992), the Supreme Court reviewed a case where a prisoner was handcuffed by two Louisiana correc-

CORBIS-BETTMANN

tions officers and beaten to the point where his teeth were loosened and his dental plate was cracked. Seven Supreme Court justices ruled that this prisoner had suffered cruel and unusual punishment under the Eighth Amendment. Two justices, ANTONIN SCALIA and CLARENCE THOMAS, disagreed.

Another amorphous measure by which the constitutionality of criminal sentences is reviewed allows the Supreme Court to invalidate punishments that are contrary to "the evolving standards of decency that mark a maturing society" (*Trop v. Dulles*, 356 U.S. 86, 78 S. Ct. 590, 2 L. Ed. 2d 630 [1958]). Under the *Trop* test, the Supreme Court must determine whether a particular punishment is offensive to society at large, not just shocking or outrageous to a particular justice. In determining which criminal sentences are offensive to society, the Supreme Court will survey state legislation to

The Eighth Amendment prohibits the use of cruel and unusual punishments such as forcing this woman to walk across white-hot plowshares to prove her innocence. Corporal punishments like this were used in England and in colonial America.

calculate whether they are authorized by a majority of jurisdictions. If most states authorize a particular punishment, the Court will not invalidate that punishment, since it is not contrary to "evolving standards of decency."

Applying this test, the Supreme Court ruled that the death penalty may be imposed upon sixteen-year-old U.S. citizens who have been convicted of murder, because a national consensus, as reflected by state legislation, supported CAPITAL PUNISHMENT for juveniles of that age (*Stanford v. Kentucky*, 492 U.S. 361, 109 S. Ct. 2969, 106 L. Ed. 2d 306 [1989]). Under the same reasoning, the Supreme Court permitted the state of Texas to execute a mentally retarded person who had been convicted of murder, despite claims that the defendant's handicap minimized his moral culpability (*Penry v. Lynaugh*, 492 U.S. 302, 109 S. Ct. 2934, 106 L. Ed. 2d 256 [1989]).

Another test employed by the Supreme Court to evaluate the constitutionality of particular punishments is somewhat less pliable but still controversial. Popularly known as the originalist approach, this test permits the Supreme Court to invalidate punishments that the Framers of the Eighth Amendment "originally" intended to remove from legislative fiat. In attempting to ascertain which punishments the Framers disapproved of, the Supreme Court has developed a simplistic formula: If a particular punishment was prohibited by the states at the time they ratified the Eighth Amendment in 1791, then that particular punishment is necessarily cruel and unusual; if a particular punishment was permitted by most states, or at least some states, in 1791, then the Framers did not intend to remove that punishment from the legislative arena.

The Eighth Amendment requires that punishments be commensurate with the offense committed by the defendant.

The narrow originalist formula has been criticized on a number of grounds. Some critics argue that merely because a state representative voted to ratify the Eighth Amendment does not mean that the representative believed that all the punishments authorized by the government comported with the Cruel and Unusual Punishments Clause. The representative may not have considered whether a particular punishment was in any way cruel or unusual as he cast his vote for RATIFICATION. Conversely, the representative may have cast his vote for ratification primarily because he believed that a certain punishment would be deemed cruel and unusual under the Eighth Amendment. No documentary evidence from the state ratification proceedings reflects which punishments particular representatives found permissible or impermissible under the Eighth Amendment.

Nor is there much evidence indicating that the Framers intended their understanding of the Constitution to be binding on subsequent generations. JAMES MADISON, who was the primary architect of the Bill of Rights, believed that the thoughts and intentions of the Framers should have no influence on courts interpreting the provisions of the Constitution. "As a guide in expounding and applying the provisions of the Constitutions," Madison wrote, "the debates and incidental decisions of the [Constitutional] Convention can have no authoritative character." For this reason, Madison refused to publish his *Notes of the Debates in the Federal Convention* during his lifetime.

Another criticism of the narrow originalist approach emanates from the language of the Eighth Amendment itself. Proponents of this viewpoint observe that the Eighth Amendment is written in very abstract language. It prohibits "excessive" bail and "excessive" fines, and does not set forth any specific amount judges may use as a yardstick when setting bail or imposing fines. Although it prohibits Cruel and Unusual Punishments, it does not enumerate which criminal penalties should be abolished.

The Framers could have drafted the Eighth Amendment to explicitly outlaw certain barbaric punishments. They were obviously familiar with how to draft constitutional provisions with such specificity. For example, Article I, Section 9, of the Constitution provides that "[n]o Bill of Attainder or ex post facto Law shall be passed." No clearer or more precise language could have been used in this provision. The Framers could have employed similar concrete language for the Eighth Amendment, some critics reason, but did not choose to do so.

Although there is not enough evidence to determine conclusively the appropriate manner in which the Framers expected or hoped the Constitution would be interpreted, the origins of the Eighth Amendment are fairly clear. The notion that the severity of a punishment should bear some relationship to the severity of the criminal offense is one of the oldest in Anglo-Saxon law. In 1215, the MAGNA CHARTA, the ancient charter of English liberties, provided, "A free man shall not be [fined] for a small offense unless according to the measure of the offense, and for a great offense he shall be [fined] according to the greatness of the offense" (ch. 20).

By the seventeenth century, England had extended this principle to punishments that called for INCARCERATION. In one case, the King's Court ruled that "imprisonment ought always to be according to the quality of the offence" (*Hodges v. Humkin*, 2 Bulst. 139, 80 Eng. Rep. 1015 [K.B. 1615] [Croke, J.]). In 1689, the principle of proportionality was incorporated into the English Bill of Rights, which used language that the Framers of the U.S. Constitution later borrowed for the Eighth Amendment: "[E]xcessive bail ought not to be required, nor excessive fines imposed, or cruel and unusual punishments inflicted." Nine states adopted similar provisions for their own constitution after the American Revolution.

The concerns underlying the Eighth Amendment were voiced in two state ratification conventions. In Massachusetts, one representative expressed "horror" that Congress could "determine what kind of punishments shall be inflicted on persons convicted of crimes" and that nothing restrained Congress "from inventing the most cruel and unheard-of punishments" that would make "racks" and "gibbets" look comparatively "mild" (as quoted in *Furman v. Georgia*, 408 U.S. 238, 92 S. Ct. 2726, 33 L. Ed. 2d 346 [1972]). In Virginia, PATRICK HENRY was worried that Congress might legalize torture as a method of coercing CONFESSIONS from criminal defendants, and that the government should be prevented from employing such "cruel and barbarous" tactics (as quoted in *Furman*).

The concerns expressed by these representatives were legitimate in light of the punishments authorized by many states at the time the Eighth Amendment was ratified. These punishments ranged from whipping, branding, and pillory to various methods of mutilation, including the slitting of nostrils and removal of body parts. The death penalty was also prevalent. If James Madison or the other Framers intended to preserve these forms of punishment, they kept their intention to themselves.

CROSS-REFERENCES

Criminal Law; Criminal Procedure; Due Process of Law; Equal Protection; Original Intent; Prisoners' Rights.

BIOGRAPHY

Dwight David Eisenhower

EISENHOWER, DWIGHT DAVID Dwight David Eisenhower achieved prominence in military and political careers and as the thirty-fourth president of the United States.

Eisenhower was born October 14, 1890, in Denison, Texas. A graduate of West Point Military Academy in 1915, he served during World War I as officer in charge of Camp Colt, which was located at Gettysburg, Pennsylvania, and which served as the center of training for the U.S. Army Tank Division.

From 1922 to 1924, Eisenhower was assigned to a post in the Panama Canal Zone. Five years later, he served as an administrator in the Assistant Secretary of War Office and acted in this capacity until 1933. In 1935, he was stationed in the Philippine Islands, and, for the next five years, he displayed his exceptional military expertise. As a result of his achievements, Eisenhower—promoted to general—became chief of operations in Washington, D.C., in 1942.

Throughout the years of World War II, Eisenhower continued to demonstrate his military proficiency. In 1942, he was in charge of the battle operations in Europe. He subse-

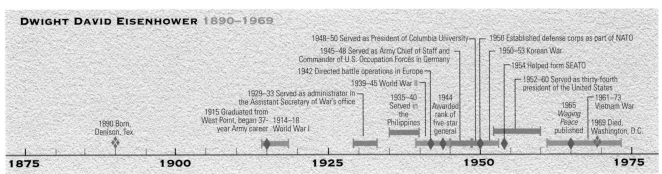

quently directed the U.S. maneuvers in North Africa and, in 1943, commanded the Allied armies there. Later that year, he supervised the victorious attacks on Sicily and the mainland of Italy. As a result of these successes, he was transferred to England to serve as supreme commander of the Allied Expeditionary Force. He was instrumental in coordinating the armed services of the Allies and in directing the use of land, sea, and air battle units in the war maneuvers in Europe.

In 1944, Eisenhower was awarded the prestigious rank of five-star general. He was assigned to Germany the following year, and, subsequently, became Army chief of staff.

Eisenhower resigned as chief of staff in 1948 and entered the education field, serving as president of Columbia University. Two years later, he returned to the military and established a defense corps as part of the NORTH ATLANTIC TREATY ORGANIZATION, which was composed of countries determined to prevent Soviet aggression.

In 1952, Eisenhower officially ended his association with the military and began a brilliant political career. As a Republican, he campaigned for the office of U.S. president against Democrat ADLAI STEVENSON; he was victorious, primarily because of his impressive military achievements and his pledge to end the war in Korea. As president, Eisenhower was instrumental in the achievement of peace in Korea in 1953. His main concern was the growing threat of the spread of COMMUNISM, and he adopted a policy—similar to that of predecessor HARRY S. TRUMAN—to keep communism in check. As part of this program, the United States formed defense treaties with South Korea and Formosa, now Taiwan; South Vietnam received military assistance; and, in 1954, the SOUTHEAST ASIA TREATY ORGANIZATION (SEATO) was created to prevent the spread of communism in Far Eastern countries.

Despite Eisenhower's intent to stop the growth of communism, he sought to reach a harmonious relationship with the Soviets, as was evidenced by his speeches at the 1955 Geneva Summit Conference. Participants included Eisenhower, Nikolai Bulganin, and Chairman Nikita Krushchev from the Soviet Union, Anthony Eden from Great Britain, and Edgar Faure from France. No agreements were reached, but foreign relations were strengthened.

In 1956, Eisenhower again defeated Adlai Stevenson for the presidency. During this administration he became a proponent of the CIVIL RIGHTS MOVEMENT and ordered the federal militia to Little Rock, Arkansas, in 1957 to ensure the enforcement of desegregation of schools; in addition, he was responsible for CIVIL RIGHTS legislation.

Eisenhower's second administration was again hampered by global tensions, and he issued the Eisenhower Doctrine in response to these pressures. This program, drafted in 1957, provided that any country in the Middle East requiring military and economic assistance to counteract the threat of communism would receive it upon request. In 1958, the doctrine was put to its first test in Lebanon when the U.S. Marine Corps was dispatched to that country.

World tensions continued through the latter years of his second term, and in 1960, Eisenhower was criticized publicly by Soviet leader Krushchev for condoning espionage flights over Soviet territory. A year later, Eisenhower severed relations with Cuba after Communist leader Fidel Castro assumed Cuban leadership.

In addition to his presidential and military achievements, Eisenhower wrote three noteworthy publications: *Crusade in Europe* (1948), a chronicle of the defeat of Germany in World War II by the Allies; *Mandate for Change* (1963), an account of his years as president; and *Waging Peace* (1965). Eisenhower died March 28, 1969, in Washington, D.C.

CROSS-REFERENCES

Dulles, John Foster; President; School Desegregation; Warren Court.

EJECTMENT One of the old FORMS OF ACTION for recovery of the POSSESSION of REAL PROPERTY.

Originally the ownership of land in England could be passed to another only by delivering the actual possession of the land. The present owner passed TITLE to another by picking up a clod of dirt on the land and handing it to the other person in front of others from the community. This ceremonial act from ancient times was called LIVERY OF SEISIN, or delivery of possession. Instead of a clod, a twig or a key could be handed over as a symbol of ownership, but only later was it permissible to deliver the symbol of ownership anywhere but on the land itself. As time passed and writing became more common, a written DEED could symbolize the delivery of ownership. The purpose of the ceremony was to make the acquiring of land a public act generally known in the community, so that disputes were less likely to arise.

Everyone in old England was tied to the land. The feudal land tenement system determined social, economic, political, and legal rights. The stability of the system was founded on the security of each person's right to possess or own a parcel of land. For this reason the first kinds of lawsuits were those allowing the assertion of rights in land. By the end of the thirteenth century, the action of TRESPASS was allowed against one who intruded on property possessed by the plaintiff. The action of ejectment branched off from this as another action for the relief of one whose possession had been disturbed. By it, the plaintiff might claim that he or she had been in possession of a certain parcel of land and that the land had been taken by the defendant. The plaintiff could do this by obtaining from the clerk of the court a WRIT of entry—a command from the king telling the defendant to let the plaintiff go back on the land taken by the defendant or to appear in court to answer the charge. The defendant could then appear and deny that the plaintiff had been dispossessed or show that as the defendant, he or she had a prior and better right to hold the land. A trial was held to settle the issue. If it were found that the defendant had wrongfully withheld possession of the property from the plaintiff, he or she could be made to pay an amercement, or fine. This fine became a precedent for the later practice of awarding money DAMAGES to the successful plaintiff in addition to restoring possession of the land.

Originally, the action of ejectment was intended to protect the rights of a TENANT who leased the land. Ultimately, it came to be the principal method for determining the ownership of real property. When the question of title to land became the issue, it was essential to describe the property as carefully as it would be described in a deed to a purchaser. This led to enforcement of very strict technicalities by the court, and the action of ejectment became less attractive to plaintiffs because of the chance that the case would be lost on a point of procedure. The old action of ejectment does not exist today, but every state has a statute that outlines a modern procedure for recovering the possession of real property. Modern ejectment actions still are somewhat slow and expensive. They are most often used by LANDLORDS trying to recover possession of their premises from stubborn tenants. States generally have another law that permits the efficient ousting of a tenant by SUMMARY PROCEEDINGS, but a landlord can pursue the simpler procedure only when the tenant has broken the LEASE in certain specified ways. The details of ejectment and summary proceedings to dispossess vary greatly from state to state.

ELDER LAW 📖 A relatively new specialty devoted to the legal issues of senior citizens, including ESTATE planning, health care, planning for incapacity or mental incompetence, the receipt of benefits, and employment discrimination. 📖

The genesis of elder law can be found in the convergence of several profound social developments. One phenomenon is a rapid increase in the elderly population. According to the U.S. Census Bureau, 12 percent of the population in the United States was over the age of sixty-five in 1985; and that percentage is expected to rise to 20 percent by the year 2050. Another phenomenon is that generally, older U.S. citizens today are more wealthy and better educated than ever before. These two circumstances have led to a rise in the collective political clout of older U.S. citizens. This newfound political strength has coincided with a trend toward cutting the government benefits and entitlements on which many elderly U.S. citizens depend. At the same time, health care costs have skyrocketed. As a result of this confluence, more and more elderly U.S. citizens are seeking legal assistance to protect their financial interests.

Another phenomenon behind the elder law specialization is that older people in the United States are subjected to AGE DISCRIMINATION by a populace obsessed with youth and afraid of aging. Ageism stigmatizes the process of growing old and leads to abuse and neglect of seniors. It also leads to DISCRIMINATION against elderly workers by employers who perceive them as less productive than younger workers. These same older workers often receive higher pay because of their years with the company. For these reasons, employers often try to replace older workers with younger workers, who may produce more and work for less compensation. Elder law addresses these and other special legal problems of the elderly.

A primary issue for older people is planning for final medical care. Many people, especially seniors, write a living WILL. This is a document that gives individuals advance control over their final medical situation. Through a living will, a person may direct the termination of life support in the event of terminal illness, permanent unconsciousness, or brain death.

A senior may wish to place HEALTH CARE decision making in the hands of a trusted third party, with an advance health care directive. All states allow this directive for property management, but not all states allow it for health management. The legislative trend favors the allowance of advance health care directives through a durable POWER OF ATTORNEY. This is a legal document in which a senior appoints a trusted third party to make major health care decisions in case of mental INCAPACITY.

Without a durable power of attorney, a GUARDIAN will be appointed, in the event of mental incapacity, to make health care decisions. A conservator will be appointed to manage property. The appointment of a guardian and a conservator is accomplished by a judicial proceeding. This proceeding is involuntary, and the court is free to appoint whoever will act in the best interests of the person who is mentally incompetent. A court appointee may or may not be a friend or relative, so the durable power of attorney is a more effective way to ensure that a person's health care wishes will be followed in case of sudden mental incapacity.

Seniors must also prepare for the possibility of living in a nursing home. Nursing homes are regulated by the Nursing Home Reform Act (NHRA) (42 U.S.C.A. § 1396r), enacted as part of the Omnibus Budget Reconciliation Act of 1987. The NHRA covers a host of requirements for the licensing of nursing homes. It also contains a list of the rights of nursing home residents. These rights include PRIVACY, confidentiality, and freedom from abuse and restraints.

Many seniors are forced to move into nursing homes to convalesce from surgery or to receive long-term custodial care. Without adequate planning, the financial consequences can be devastating. Nursing homes are very expensive, ranging in cost from $2,000 to $6,000 a month. Most seniors are unable to make such payments and must rely on the federal government programs Medicare and Medicaid for support.

Medicare (42 U.S.C.A. § 1395 et seq.) is authorized by the U.S. Congress to provide for the acute health care of senior citizens. Any person who is age sixty-five or older and is eligible for SOCIAL SECURITY benefits is entitled to Medicare coverage. Medicaid (42 U.S.C.A. § 1396 et seq.) pays for the medical expenses of low-income individuals who are aged, blind, or disabled.

Medicare is more available than Medicaid, but it generally provides less coverage. For example, Medicare covers nursing home care for only a short period of time, whereas Medicaid provides extended nursing home care but requires that a senior be impoverished to qualify. In other words, seniors with property and income have to deplete their own resources before qualifying for Medicaid's coverage of long-term health maintenance. Seniors who need custodial care but do not qualify for Medicaid often buy private long-term care INSURANCE. This type of insurance pays for nursing home care and home health care and is governed by state statutes.

The issues surrounding Medicare and Medicaid are complex, amorphous, and political. The coverage under these programs is subject to numerous exceptions and caveats, and many people, politicians and otherwise, dispute the wisdom of public funding of health care for seniors. Medicare and Medicaid exist only so long as Congress maintains the statutes that enable them, and the statutes can be changed to increase or decrease eligibility and coverage.

After retirement, seniors rely on a variety of benefits for financial support. One common source is Old-Age Survivors and Disability Insurance (42 U.S.C.A. § 401 et seq.), a part of the Social Security program. Social Security provides lifetime monthly payments after age sixty-five, derived from payroll taxes collected from employees and employers. The amount of the applicant's monthly payment is based on her or his earnings history.

Eligibility for Social Security benefits is determined by a measure called quarters of coverage. Generally, this means that the applicant must have earned a specified minimum amount of wages within a three-month period at least forty times. Anyone over age sixty-five who has earned ten years, or forty quarters, of coverage qualifies for Social Security. Social Security also

Old-Age, Survivors, and Disability Insurance (OASDI) Benefits and Beneficiaries, May 1996

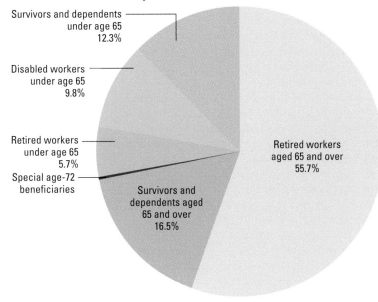

Survivors and dependents under age 65 12.3%

Disabled workers under age 65 9.8%

Retired workers under age 65 5.7%

Special age-72 beneficiaries

Retired workers aged 65 and over 55.7%

Survivors and dependents aged 65 and over 16.5%

Source: U.S. Department of Health and Human Services, Social Security Administration.

provides benefits for surviving spouses and children under age eighteen, and disability benefits for those unable to work until an expected retirement age.

Monthly Social Security benefits will be adjusted up or down if a senior postpones retirement or retires early, respectively. Wages earned after retirement and above a certain amount will lower monthly Social Security benefits, and benefits may be taxed by the federal government if a recipient gains income from another source. A dispute over qualification or payments must be heard by the Social Security Administration before it can go to court.

Many seniors receive income from other sources. Military personnel wounded in action qualify for veterans' benefits. The amounts of these benefits vary with the severity of the disability. Veterans' benefits are also available to parents, children, and spouses of deceased veterans. The Veterans Benefits Administration processes claims and oversees the disbursal of veterans' benefits. Appeals must proceed through administrative hearings and reviews before they can be heard in court.

About half of all seniors receive benefits from pension plans. A PENSION is compensation paid by an employer to an employee upon retirement. Pensions are not a general public benefit paid by the government, and thus, pension disputes are not required to pass through any administrative hearings and instead go directly to court. Unionized companies, large employers, and the government typically provide pensions for their workers. The Pension Benefit Guaranty Corporation, a federal agency authorized by the U.S. Congress, provides insurance to workers whose employers are unable to redeem pension plans.

Supplemental Security Income (SSI) is a federal program created to provide cash payments to aged, blind, or disabled persons living below the poverty line. A senior with no income and no Social Security payments can benefit from SSI. Any senior who qualifies for SSI automatically qualifies for Medicaid. A denial-of-benefits or denial-of-payment dispute must be heard by the Social Security Administration before it can be heard in court.

Elder law is also concerned with protecting working seniors. The primary piece of legislation in this area is the Age Discrimination in Employment Act (ADEA) (29 U.S.C.A. §§ 621–634 [1988 & Supp. V 1993]). Originally enacted by Congress in 1967, the ADEA protects workers age forty and over from discrimination in hiring, firing, compensation, and conditions of employment. The purpose of the

ADEA is to promote the employment of older persons, prohibit arbitrary age discrimination in employment, and encourage solutions to the problems associated with aging workers.

Not all workers over age forty are protected by the ADEA. Workers in a business with fewer than twenty employees are not protected. And executives and policy makers are excluded if they have nonforfeitable retirement benefits of at least $44,000 a year.

To establish a case of discrimination in hiring, generally, a senior must (1) be age forty or over; (2) apply for and be qualified for a job for which the employer was seeking applicants; (3) be rejected for the job; and (4) show that the position remained open after the rejection, and that the employer sought applicants with similar qualifications or filled the position with a younger person possessing comparable qualifications. In case of discharge, a senior worker must gather information showing that the reason for the discharge was old age. A senior may also use statistics to try to prove a pattern of discrimination in hiring or firing.

A clause in the ADEA allows employers to defend an age discrimination suit by showing that the refusal to hire or the discharge was based on "reasonable factors other than age" (29 U.S.C.A. § 623(f)(1)). This means that an employer may discharge an elderly worker for lack of production, even if age is contributing to the lack of production. Employers may facially (with obvious intent) discriminate based on age if youth is a "bona fide occupational qualification reasonably necessary to the normal operations of the particular business" (29 U.S.C.A. § 623(f)). This defense is effective where a position calls for physically strenuous activity or involves public safety, such as that of airplane pilot, air traffic controller, or bus driver.

Working seniors, such as this ninety-year-old Texas woman, are protected by the Age Discrimination in Employment Act.

The U.S. Supreme Court has noted that older people do not constitute a discrete and insular group. Instead, they form a fluid group of which everyone with a normal life span will be a member. According to the Supreme Court, this means that seniors, as a group, do not need "extraordinary protection from the majoritarian process" (*Massachusetts Board of Retirement v. Murgia*, 427 U.S. 307, 96 S. Ct. 2562, 49 L. Ed 2d 520 [1976]). Because aging necessarily involves some physical and mental deterioration, age discrimination in employment receives less judicial scrutiny than do racial and sex discrimination.

Many state bar associations have formed elder law sections. These sections comprise attorneys who volunteer time to keep seniors abreast of changes in the law that affect them as a group. The challenge for the law is to find and enforce the rights of older citizens, being ever mindful that the human frailties that make elder law necessary await us all.

See also DEATH AND DYING.

ELECTION CAMPAIGN FINANCING

Election campaigns for public office are expensive. Candidates need funding for support staff, advertising, traveling, and public appearances. Unless they are independently wealthy, most must finance their campaign with contributions from individuals and from businesses and other organizations. Today state and federal laws set limits on campaign contributions, create contribution disclosure requirements, and impose record-keeping requirements for candidates seeking elective office.

Before 1974 most election campaigns were financed by CORPORATIONS and small groups of wealthy donors. In 1972, for example, insurance executive W. Clement Stone contributed approximately $2.8 million directly to the reelection campaign committee of President RICHARD M. NIXON. Such contributions raised concerns of undue influence on the selection of available candidates and on subsequent legislation. Many in Congress felt the need to limit the influence of money in political campaigns in order to regain the confidence of the public in the wake of the WATERGATE scandal, a series of events that ultimately led to charges of abuse of power and obstruction of justice involving Nixon's campaign activities.

In 1974 Congress made radical changes to the Federal Election Campaign Act of 1971 (FECA) (2 U.S.C.A. §§ 431–456 [1996]). In its amended form, FECA limited contributions to individual candidates and political parties, personal spending by candidates, overall campaign spending for federal office, and independent spending by groups not directly associated with a candidate's campaign. The act also created on federal tax forms a checkoff box that allowed taxpayers to contribute a dollar to a presidential campaign fund, and it devised a formula for payments from the fund.

James L. Buckley, who was running for the U.S. Senate from New York, and other candidates for federal office challenged FECA in federal court. In 1976 the Supreme Court struck down the act's spending limits in *Buckley v. Valeo*, 424 U.S. 1, 96 S. Ct. 612, 46 L. Ed. 2d 659 (1976). According to the High Court, setting mandatory limits on the amount of money a candidate may spend in a campaign violated the FIRST AMENDMENT. However, the Court upheld the act's disclosure requirements, private contribution limits, and provision for the public funding of qualified presidential candidates (the tax form checkoff).

The remains of FECA are still operative. In addition, most states have enacted statutes, or changed their existing statutes, to place limits on contributions and to create record-keeping and disclosure requirements.

Private Funding of Federal Election Campaigns FECA illustrates the way election campaign finance laws work. FECA requires that candidates for federal office form a campaign committee and a campaign fund, and disclose campaign contributions to the FEDERAL ELECTION COMMISSION. A candidate is subject to these requirements if the candidate or an authorized agent of the candidate has received campaign contributions totaling more than $5,000 or has made campaign expenditures totaling more than $5,000. Most campaigns for federal office cost more than $5,000, so most candidates are subject to the financial reporting requirements set by the act.

FECA places dollar limits on campaign contributions. No person may contribute more than $1,000 a year to a candidate's campaign committee. No person may contribute more than $20,000 in one calendar year to a candidate through the candidate's national political committee, and no more than $5,000 may be contributed to other political committees (§ 441a(2)(3)). The act also places special limits on contributions by national banks, corporations, labor organizations, and government contractors (§§ 441b, 441c).

A person may contribute unlimited sums of money to the state and national committees of a political party, but only if those sums are for the benefit of the party in general. If a contribution

Candidates for federal office must form a campaign committee and a campaign fund and disclose campaign contributions to the Federal Election Commission if they have received or spent more than $5,000. The donation of funds to buy posters and other promotional materials is excluded from the definition of a contribution.

is intended to fund a candidate's campaign directly, the contribution will be subject to the limits set by the act.

FECA makes several exceptions to the limits on contributions made directly to a candidate's campaign committee. It excludes from the definition of *contribution* assistance such as the donation of REAL PROPERTY, of services, and of funds to buy promotional materials like bumper stickers, handbills, and posters (§ 431(8)(B)).

The act also creates a limited exception to limits for contributions to state and national committees of a political party. Under § 441a(d)(1)(2), the national committee of a political party may contribute to its presidential candidate an amount equal to two cents multiplied by the number of people of voting age in the United States. The national and state committees of a political party may contribute to a Senate candidate an amount equal to two cents multiplied by the number of people of voting age in the candidate's home state, or at least $20,000. A House of Representatives candidate may receive $10,000 from the national and state committees of her or his political party.

Critics argue that FECA strengthens the domination of the two major political parties. By limiting an individual's direct contributions to a candidate, the act prevents minor parties from amassing enough funds to gain ground on the two major parties. The Democratic and Republican parties can survive such limitations because they have large numbers of contribu-

tors. According to some critics, they have large numbers of contributors because they have the power to give political favors. Minor parties, by definition, begin their mission with fewer supporters, and have no political favors to give. With contribution limits on their few supporters, minor parties have few opportunities to mount serious challenges to the major party candidates.

Other critics of FECA focus on the reporting and bookkeeping responsibilities required by the act and the sheer complexity of the law. Minor parties, with their meager funds, find it difficult to manage the detailed records and reporting requirements, and to pay for the legal assistance needed to comply with the law. By comparison, major parties possess enough experience and support staff to surmount the demands of the act.

"Soft" money is another concern for critics of FECA. In the context of political campaigns, soft money is cash given to a political party, not directly to a candidate. There is no limit to the amount a person or organization may give to a political party. Political parties may use the contributions they receive to benefit themselves generally; they may not use those contributions to benefit one particular candidate. There are, however, effective detours around this roadblock. For example, a party may run a television commercial that criticizes the opponent of a particular candidate. The money spent by the party on such a commercial will not be listed as a direct contribution to the party's candidate if the commercial does not mention the party's own candidate. Major party candidates, with this kind of help from the national and state committees of their party, benefit from this practice more frequently than do minor party candidates.

Defenders of FECA note that the major parties are subjected to the same requirements as the minor parties. They also point out that nothing in the act prevents the large numbers of people who contribute to the major parties from switching and contributing to minor parties.

Public Funding of Presidential Campaigns Some presidential candidates may receive federal tax dollars to fund their campaigns. Federal funding for presidential campaigns comes in three forms: general-election grants given to individual candidates, matching funds given to nominated candidates for primary campaigns, and funding provided to parties for their nominating conventions.

Under the Presidential Election Campaign Fund Act (Fund Act) (26 U.S.C.A. §§ 9001–9013), presidential candidates must meet certain standards to obtain federal tax money for their campaign. The Fund Act distinguishes between major party candidates and minor party candidates. For purposes of the act, a major party is defined as any political party that received at least 25 percent of the popular vote in the previous presidential election. A minor party is defined as a political party that received less than 25 percent but more than five percent of the popular vote in the previous presidential election.

Under the Fund Act, a presidential candidate from a major party is entitled to a general-election grant of $20 million plus cost-of-living

expenses. In 1996 this amount totaled over $60 million each for President BILL CLINTON and Republican party nominee BOB DOLE.

Minor party presidential candidates can receive a general-election grant only if their party had a candidate on the ballot in at least ten states in the previous presidential election and that candidate won at least five percent of the popular vote. If a minor party candidate qualifies, the election grant is equal to the total amount of the general-election grants received by the major party candidates in the previous presidential election, multiplied by the percentage of popular votes received by the minor party candidate divided by the percentage of popular votes received by the two major party candidates. To illustrate, assume that each of the two major party candidates received $50 million under the act in the previous election. The minor party candidate received five percent of the popular vote, and the major party candidates together received 95 percent of the popular vote. The minor party candidate will receive $1 for every $19 received by the major party candidates, or about $5.3 million.

Presidential candidates do not receive general-election grants until after the election.

Some presidential candidates may qualify for additional taxpayer funding for their campaigns. Under 26 U.S.C.A. §§ 9031–9042, the Federal Election Commission may authorize funds to presidential candidates who participated in their party primaries. Under the act, the presidential campaign fund matches every contribution of $250 or less that was given to the candidate during the primaries. To qualify for these matching funds, a presidential candidate must receive at least $5,000 in contributions from contributors in at least twenty different states. Only contributions of $250 or less may be counted in reaching the $5,000 threshold.

Under the matching-funds provision, no candidate may spend more than a specified amount in each state's primary election campaign. If a presidential candidate is eligible for matching funds and decides to claim them, the candidate may spend no more than $50,000 of his or her own money on the campaign. Candidates must keep specific records and submit them to the commission for audit. No distinction is made between major and minor parties in determining whether a candidate qualifies for federal matching funds.

Finally, under § 9008, a political party may receive taxpayer funds to pay for its political convention. Major parties are entitled to $4 million of public funds for their convention. A minor party is entitled to the same amount that

In the 1996 presidential election Bill Clinton received a grant of more than $60 million to fund his campaign under the Presidential Election Campaign Fund Act.

its candidate received under the Fund Act. For the vast majority of minor political parties, this amount is zero, because most minor party presidential candidates receive less than five percent of the popular vote.

Like private funding, public funding for presidential campaigns is criticized as being biased toward the two major parties. Under the Fund Act, major party candidates and their parties receive more money than do minor party candidates and their parties. With more money, major party candidates can spend more on support staff, advertising, traveling, and personal appearances. By creating these advantages, the federal funding scheme, according to the critics, ensures the continued success of the two major parties in presidential campaigns and the continued failure of minor party candidates.

Generally, advocates of the funding scheme for presidential candidates concede that it favors the two major parties. However, they insist that it should not be expensive for popular candidates to run for president, and that public funding is necessary to ensure that it is not. Defenders note further that the funding scheme does not restrict access to ballots, and does not prevent people from voting for the candidate of their choice.

Finally, according to defenders of the funding scheme, any claim that the scheme is responsible for the inability of minor parties to win presidential elections is speculative. As the Supreme Court stated in *Buckley*, "[T]he inability, if any, of minor-party candidates to wage effective campaigns will derive not from lack of public funding but from their inability to raise private contributions."

CROSS-REFERENCES

Democratic Party; Elections; Independent Parties; Republican Party.

ELECTION OF REMEDIES

The liberty of choosing (or the act of choosing) one out of several means afforded by law for the redress of an injury, or one out of several available forms of action. An *election of remedies* arises when one having two coexistent but inconsistent remedies chooses to exercise one, in which event she or he loses the right to thereafter exercise the other. Doctrine provides that if two or more remedies exist that are repugnant and inconsistent with one another, a party will be bound if he or she has chosen one of them.

The doctrine of the election of remedies was developed to prevent a plaintiff from a double recovery for a loss, making the person pursue only one REMEDY in an ACTION. Although its application is not restricted to any particular CAUSE OF ACTION, it is most commonly employed in CONTRACT cases involving FRAUD, which is a MISREPRESENTATION of a material fact that is intended to deceive a person who relies on it. A plaintiff can sue for either DAMAGES, thereby acknowledging the contract and recovering the difference between the contract price and the actual value of the subject of the contract, or RESCISSION—annulment—of the contract and the return of what has been paid under its provisions, restoring the plaintiff to the position he or she would occupy had the contract never been made. If a plaintiff sought both damages and rescission, the person would be asking a court to acknowledge and enforce the existence of a contract while simultaneously requesting its unmaking—two inconsistent demands. The granting of both remedies would result in the plaintiff recovering the difference between the contract price and actual value as well as what was paid to the defendant. The person would, therefore, earn a profit by the defendant's wrongful conduct against him or her, since the person would have more than he or she had when entering the contract.

Once a plaintiff elects a remedy, he or she precludes the pursuit of other inconsistent methods of relief. Not all JURISDICTIONS require a plaintiff to elect remedies, and many have abolished this requirement because of its sometimes harsh effects. In the jurisdictions that retain the election of remedies, a plaintiff usually must choose a remedy early in the action. Since an election can be made by conduct, a plaintiff who does not take affirmative steps in designating a remedy is often deemed to have done so by inactivity. For example, a court may preclude a plaintiff from rescission if there has been an unreasonable lapse of time from the time of injury until the time of the commencement of the action. The only remedy available to the person in such a situation is to seek damages.

Although a revocation would not adversely affect the rights of a defendant, a plaintiff cannot revoke an election and seek another means of relief. In some jurisdictions, an election does not compensate a plaintiff for all his or her losses. A plaintiff who elects to rescind a contract—as opposed to suing for damages for its breach—might not recover any expenses incurred in the transaction that were not paid to the defendant. Such expenses would be considered damages, a remedy from which the plaintiff is precluded by his or her election of the remedy of rescission.

ELECTIONS 📖 The processes of voting to decide a public question or to select one person from a designated group to perform certain obligations in a government, corporation, or society. 📖

Elections are commonly understood as the processes of voting for public office or PUBLIC POLICY, but they are also used to choose leaders and settle policy questions in private organizations, such as CORPORATIONS, LABOR UNIONS, and religious groups. They also take place within specific government bodies. For example, the U.S. HOUSE OF REPRESENTATIVES and state LEGISLATURES elect their own leader, who is called the Speaker of the House.

In elections, a candidate is a person who is selected by others as a contestant. A ballot is anything that a voter uses to express his or her choice, such as a paper and pen or a lever on a machine. A poll is the place where a voter casts his or her ballot.

For government policy and leadership, a general election is commonly understood as a process of voting that regularly occurs at specified intervals. For national elections, Congress has designated the first Tuesday after the first Monday in November as election day. A special election is held under special circumstances. For example, if an elected official dies or resigns from office during her or his term, a special election may be held before the next scheduled general election for the office.

The free election of government leaders is a relatively recent practice. Until the eighteenth century, leaders gained political power through insurrection and birthright. Political thought changed dramatically in eighteenth-century Europe, where industrial progress inspired the reconsideration of individual rights and government. The notion that government leaders should be chosen by the governed was an important product of that movement.

The United States held its first presidential election on February 4, 1789. In that election, GEORGE WASHINGTON was chosen U.S. president by a small, unanimous vote of electors. Since its infancy, the United States has held elections to decide who will assume public offices, such as the offices of the president and vice president, U.S. senators and representatives, and state and local legislators. Individual states have also held elections for a wide range of other government officials, such as judges, attorneys general, district attorneys, public school officials, and police chiefs.

Elections for public offices are governed by federal and state laws. Article I of the U.S. Constitution requires that a congressional election be held every two years and that senators be elected every six years. Article II states that a president and a vice president shall be elected for a four-year term. In 1951, the states ratified Amendment 22, which provides that no person may serve as president more than twice.

For the federal oversight of national elections for public office, Congress created the FEDERAL ELECTION COMMISSION (FEC) with 1974 amendments to the Federal Election Campaign Act of 1971 (2 U.S.C.A. § 431 et seq.). The FEC provides for the public financing of presidential elections. It also tracks and reveals the amounts and sources of money used by candidates for national office and their political committees. The FEC enforces the limits on financial contributions to, and expenditures of, those candidates and committees. To receive FEC funding, political committees must register with the FEC.

States regulate many aspects of government elections, including eligibility requirements for candidates, eligibility requirements for voters, and the date on which state and local elections are held. U.S. citizens have the right to form and operate political parties, but that right can be regulated by the state legislature. For example, a candidate may not be placed on an election ballot unless he or she has registered with the state election board. Many states maintain stringent requirements for would-be candidates, such as sponsorship by a certain number of voters on a petition. A monetary deposit may also be required. Such a deposit may be forfeited if the candidate fails to garner a certain proportion of the vote in the election.

No state may abridge voting guarantees of the U.S. Constitution. Under the Constitution's TWENTY-FOURTH AMENDMENT, for example, no state may make the payment of a POLL

U.S. citizens vote in local, state, and federal elections at their local polls. The voter is often asked to verify his or her address and sign in.

WESLEY BOCXE/PHOTO RESEARCHERS

TAX or other tax a requirement for voting privileges. Under the FIFTEENTH AMENDMENT, states may not deny the right to vote based on "race, color, or previous condition of servitude." The NINETEENTH AMENDMENT prevents states from denying or abridging the right to vote based on sex.

In the early 1990s, fifteen states passed legislation that limited the tenure of U.S. senators and representatives. In 1995, these "term-limit" measures were declared unconstitutional by the U.S. Supreme Court. In *United States Term Limits v. Thornton*, 514 U.S. 779, 115 S. Ct. 1842, 131 L. Ed. 2d 881 (1995), the state of Arkansas had amended its constitution to preclude persons who had served a certain number of terms in the U.S. CONGRESS from placing their name in future U.S. Congress elections. Arkansas cited Article I, Section 4, Clause 1, of the U.S. Constitution for support. This clause allows that "[t]he Times, Places and Manner of holding Elections for Senators and Representatives, shall be prescribed in each State by the Legislature thereof." Arkansas further argued that its amendment merely restricted ballot access and was not an outright disqualification of congressional incumbents.

The Court disagreed with Arkansas. In a 5–4 opinion, the Court rejected the constitutionality of any term-limits legislation. According to the majority, the only qualifications for U.S. congressional office were contained in two constitutional clauses. Article I, Section 2, Clause 2, of the federal Constitution provides that a representative should be at least twenty-five years of age, a citizen of the United States for at least seven years, and a resident of the represented state at the time of the election. Article I, Section 3, Clause 3, states that a senator should be at least thirty years of age, a citizen of the United States for at least nine years, and an inhabitant of the represented state when elected. These provisions, according to the Court, were designed to be the only qualifications for U.S. congressional office, and any additional qualifications are unconstitutional.

Although the Constitution prohibits term limits for the U.S. Congress, it does not prevent states from setting term limits for their own state legislature.

Administration of Government Elections Voters register with a PRECINCT, which is a local voting district. Registration must be accomplished in the manner prescribed by state statute. The voting location may be any structure authorized by the state to serve as such. All states allow ABSENTEE VOTING for persons who cannot be present in their precinct on election

day. Voting is secret, whether by absentee ballot or at the POLLS.

Election officials are charged with the supervision of voting. In some states, voters indicate their preferences by pulling a lever in a voting machine; in other states, they use a paper and pen. At the end of the voting day, election officials count, or canvass, the results and report them to city or county officials or to the state board of elections. The complete results are filed with the secretary of state or some other designated state government official. The candidate with the most votes is then declared the winner of the election. This is called a direct election because the winner is determined by a straight count of the popular vote.

The election of a president and vice president is an indirect election. That is, the winner is determined not by a popular vote but by an electoral vote. Each state has a certain number of ELECTORS, which is equal to the total number of senators and representatives to which the state is entitled in Congress. In theory, an elector may vote for whomever she or he wants, but in practice, electors vote for the winner of the popular vote in their state.

Primaries and Conventions A political party is entitled to nominate candidates for public office, subject to regulation by Congress and state legislatures. The nominating process is accomplished through a system of primaries, caucuses, and nominating conventions. The process varies from state to state, but generally, primaries and caucuses produce delegates who later cast votes at a nominating convention held several weeks or months before election day. Nominating conventions are held by political parties at the local, state, and national levels to officially choose candidates for public office in the upcoming elections.

Voter registration and participation usually increase in years that have a presidential election, but qualified individuals may register to vote at any time.

A primary is a preliminary election held by a political party before the actual election to determine a party's candidates. A primary may be open or closed. An open primary is one in which all registered voters may participate. The number of delegates a candidate receives is then based on the candidate's performance. In some states, the winner of the popular vote wins all the delegates available to the state at the nominating convention. In other states, candidates receive a portion of delegates based on their respective showings.

In a closed primary, only voters who have declared their allegiance to the party may vote. Closed primaries may be indirect or direct. In an indirect closed primary, party voters only elect delegates who later vote for the party's candidates at a nominating convention. In a direct closed primary, party voters actually decide who will be the party's candidates, and then choose delegates only to communicate that decision at the nominating convention.

In some states, political parties use a *caucus* system instead of a primary system to determine which candidates to support. A caucus is a local meeting of registered party members. The manner in which delegates are chosen at these caucuses varies widely from state to state. In some states, each party member who shows up at the caucus is entitled to one vote for each office. The caucus then produces an allotment of delegates based on the popular vote in the caucus, and these delegates later represent the caucus in the county, legislative district, state, and national conventions. In other states, those who attend the caucus vote for delegates who pledge their support for certain candidates. These delegates then represent the caucus at the party's nominating conventions.

At a convention, delegates vote to determine who will emerge as the party's candidate. Usually, if no candidate wins a majority of the delegates on the first round, delegates are free to vote for a different candidate than the one they originally chose to support. More often than not, candidates have garnered sufficient delegates in the primaries and caucuses before the nominating convention to win the nomination. Where nominations are locked up prior to the convention, the convention becomes a perfunctory celebration of the party policies, and an advertising vehicle for the nominated candidates.

Conflicts over nomination procedures often arise within a political party. In 1991, the Freedom Republicans, a group representing minority members of the Republican party, launched an attack on the party's allocation of delegates between the states. Since 1916, the Republican party had employed a bonus delegate system as a method to determine delegate representation at its national convention for nominating presidential candidates. Under this system, each state received a number of delegates equal to three times its ELECTORAL COLLEGE vote. States that elected Republican presidents, senators, representatives, and governors then received an additional allotment of delegates. The bonus delegate system gave certain Republican-dominated states a greater say in choosing the party's presidential candidate.

According to the Freedom Republicans, the bonus delegate system reduced the representation of minority interests within the party because minority members often came from Democrat-dominated states. The largely rural, Republican-dominated western states contained small minority populations, so minorities were poorly represented in the Republican delegate system. The Freedom Republicans sued the FEC under title VI of the CIVIL RIGHTS ACT of 1964 (42 U.S.C.A. § 2000d) in an attempt to stop FEC funding of the Republican National Convention.

The U.S. District Court for the District of Columbia ordered the FEC to create and enforce regulations governing the selection of delegates to the publicly funded national nominating conventions of political parties. On appeal by the FEC, the U.S. Circuit Court of Appeals for the District of Columbia vacated the order. The appeals court held that the connection between the FEC funding and the Republican delegate scheme was insufficient to hold the FEC accountable for the delegate scheme. According to the court, it was also unlikely that the Republican party would change its delegate scheme if funding were withheld (*Freedom Republicans, Inc. v. Federal Election Com'n*, 13 F. 3d 412 [D.C. Cir. 1994]).

Initiatives and Referendums The voting results on important questions of public policy are commonly known as REFERENDUMS or propositions. These results decide whether a policy becomes law or whether a state constitution will be revised or amended. An INITIATIVE is the initiation of legislative or constitutional changes through the filing of formal petitions. If an initiative is supported by a certain percentage of the population, it may be included on an election ballot for public approval. Referendums and initiatives allow for the development of legislation independent of formal legislative processes. Not all state constitutions provide for referendums and initiatives.

Campaigns A campaign is the time preceding an election that a candidate uses for promotion. Election campaigns for public of-

Elections

Percent of Voting-Age Population Reporting They
Registered and Voted, 1980 to 1994

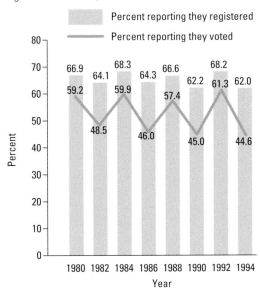

Percent Reporting They Voted in 1992, by Age

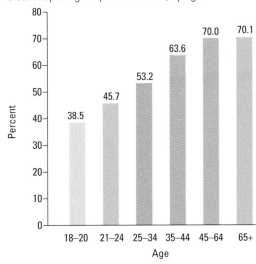

Source: U.S. Bureau of the Census, *Current Population Reports.*

fices in the United States have evolved into complex, expensive affairs. Candidates rely on a variety of support, from financial contributions to marketing and campaign specialists. Elections for national office require large sums of money for advertising and travel. Local elections also favor candidates who are well financed. Historically, the money needed for successful campaigns has come from major political parties, such as the Republican and Democratic parties.

Criminal Aspects The U.S. Congress and state legislatures prohibit a wide variety of conduct in connection with elections. It is criminal conduct, for example, for a candidate to promise an appointment to public office in return

for campaign contributions (18 U.S.C.A. § 599). Numerous laws prohibit the coercion of voters, including the solicitation of votes in exchange for money, interference with voting rights by armed forces personnel and other government employees, and the intimidation of voters.

The enforcement of criminal laws can face the odd challenge on election day. In *State v. Stewart*, 869 S.W.2d 86 (Mo. App. W.D. 1993), Robbin Stewart was stopped for speeding as he returned from voting in a primary election. Stewart argued that the case against him should have been dismissed because article VIII, section 4, of the Missouri Constitution provided that voters should be "privileged from arrest while going to, attending and returning from elections, except in case of treason, felony or breach of the peace."

The Missouri Court of Appeals for the Western District rejected Stewart's argument. The appeals court noted that in the past, the Missouri Committee on Suffrage and Elections had entertained the idea that the clause cited by Stewart should apply to primary elections as well as general elections, and that the committee had refused to adopt the expansion. In a footnote, the court advised that the U.S. Supreme Court had construed the phrase "treason, felony or breach of the peace" as including all criminal offenses (*Williamson v. U.S.*, 207 U.S. 425, 28 S. Ct. 163, 52 L. Ed. 278 [1908]). Such a reading would seem to nullify the objective of Missouri's constitutional clause. Nevertheless, the existence of such an election-day privilege is a testament to the importance of free elections in the United States.

CROSS-REFERENCES

Election Campaign Financing; Gerrymander; Voting Rights Act of 1965.

ELECTIVE SHARE 📖 Statutory provision that a surviving spouse may choose between taking that which is provided in the WILL of the deceased spouse or taking a statutorily prescribed share of the ESTATE. Such election may be presented if the will leaves the spouse less than he or she would otherwise receive by statute. This election may also be taken if the spouse seeks to set aside a will that contains a provision to the effect that an attempt to contest the will defeats the rights of one to take under the will. 📖

ELECTOR 📖 A voter who has fulfilled the qualifications imposed by law; a constituent; a selector of a public officer; a person who has the right to cast a ballot for the approval or rejection of a political proposal or question, such as the issuance of BONDS by a state or municipality to finance public works projects.

A member of the ELECTORAL COLLEGE—an association of voters elected by the populace of each state and the District of Columbia—which convenes every four years to select the president and vice president of the United States. 📖

ELECTORAL COLLEGE 📖 Nominated persons, known as ELECTORS, from the states and the District of Columbia, who meet every four years in their home state or district and cast ballots to choose the PRESIDENT and VICE PRESIDENT of the United States. 📖

In the popular election, the American people actually vote for electors, not the candidates themselves. The candidate receiving the majority of votes from electors takes office. Although the Constitution allows the electors to vote for any candidate, they usually vote for the candidate of the political party that nominated them. In a limited number of instances, the structure of the electoral college has led to unusual election results.

The republican basis of the electoral college stems from the Constitution. When the founders of the United States set out to secure a system of political representation, many among them feared mob rule. ELECTIONS based on representative blocks of votes would implement checks within the system. The founders took into consideration that large numbers of regional candidates could appeal to the interests of various select groups, and thus the populace could be divided widely, and disturbances in the succession of power could ensue. The founders surmised that Congress should have the power to settle issues not resolved in a popular election, and created the electoral college. As a contributor to this system, ALEXANDER HAMILTON said that it made sure "the office of President will seldom fall to the lot of any man who is not in eminent degree endowed with the requisite qualifications." Rogue politicians, riding any waves of popular sentiments, would need to meet a higher approval before their election. The electoral college thus ensured an orderly transfer of power, especially in the two-party system that the United States developed.

Electors receive their appointments from a wide and various informal circuit of possible electoral candidates during election times and are nominated in many states according to the guideline of individual state legislatures. The procedures for nominating electors, whether at party conventions, primary elections, or party organizational meetings, differ throughout the United States. The terms of electors are generally not set by statute, and in some states parties adopt their own criteria for selecting the college's members. However, the Constitution provides that "no Senator or Representative, or Person holding an Office of Trust or Profit under the United States, shall be appointed an Elector" (U.S. Const. art. II, § 1, cl. 2).

In most states, only the names of the presidential and vice presidential candidates—not the names of the electors—appear on election ballots. The party that gains the most popular votes in a state receives one electoral vote for each of its electors. In each state, each party nominates the same number of electors as there are representatives and senators for that state in Congress.

On the first Monday after the second Wednesday in December following the popular election, the electors from each state's victorious party cast their ballots. The structure of the electoral college was established in Article II, Section 1, of the U.S. Constitution. Under the original provision, each elector of the college cast two votes for president, and the candidate receiving the second-highest number of votes assumed the vice presidency. In 1804, the TWELFTH AMENDMENT modified the original plan to separate the votes cast for the president and the vice president. The electors may choose to vote for another candidate—as West Virginia's electors did in the 1916 race between CHARLES EVANS HUGHES and WOODROW WILSON. However, this occurs only rarely, and even less often does it sway the results of an election. As the electoral system is designed, generally, all the electoral votes from each state go to the winner of the state's popular vote. Only Maine does not use the winner-take-all system. Maine uses the district plan (discussed later in this article).

The electors then sign, seal, and certify lists of their ballots. These lists go to Washington, D.C., where the president of the Senate, in the presence of the Senate and the House of Representatives, opens them. The votes are counted. If the electors fail to cast a majority vote, the House of Representatives chooses the U.S. president and vice president by ballot. In 1824 John Quincy Adams was chosen president by the House. Although the recipient of the majority of the electoral votes is determined by the college, Congress retains the power of verifying the results and makes official the election of president and vice president.

The workings of the electoral college have not gone unchallenged. The controversial presidential election of 1876 pitted Republican RUTHERFORD B. HAYES, a former governor of Ohio, against Democrat SAMUEL J. TILDEN, a former governor of New York. Reacting against the Reconstruction measures of Republicans in

Electoral College

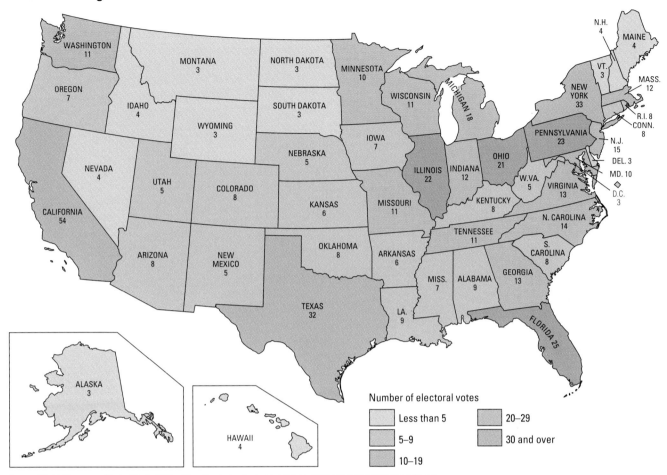

Number of electoral votes

- Less than 5
- 5–9
- 10–19
- 20–29
- 30 and over

Source: *World Almanac and Book of Facts, 1997 edition.* The electoral vote apportionment is based on the 1990 census figures.

the South, Tilden received strong support from Southern Democrats. When the election returns came in on November 7, 1876, Tilden had clearly received the majority of the popular votes. However, Republicans determined that if they challenged the outcome of the voting in key areas of Florida, Louisiana, and South Carolina, Hayes could win. The Republicans sought victory at all costs and went all out to claim the electoral votes from those states as their own.

The Republicans waged a publicity campaign through the national press, suppressing the tallies of the popular vote. Republican election committees dubiously managed to demonstrate that several key counties contained discrepancies in population figures, voter registration, and ballots cast. Democrats, for obvious reasons, contested the Republicans' tactics. The parties agreed to let an electoral commission, appointed by Congress, determine the winner of the disputed electoral votes. The commission consisted of fifteen members from the Supreme Court, the House, and the Senate. In the end, a Republican justice, JOSEPH P. BRADLEY, swayed the outcome of the commission's findings. With less than forty-eight hours before Tilden's scheduled inauguration, the commission announced that Hayes had won the necessary electoral votes. On March 3, 1877, Hayes was inaugurated.

The results of the election posed issues for both proponents and critics. Defenders of the electoral system claimed that the problems surrounding the 1876 election had less to do with the college than with political corruption. They maintained that the election could have resulted in a greater debacle if the constitutional structure of the college had not finally settled the contested issues. Critics countered that direct elections would fit the wishes of the people better than did what looked like oligarchic manipulations of the college.

In following years, critics added more ammunition to their attack with the election race between BENJAMIN HARRISON and GROVER

CLEVELAND in 1888. With an unusual demographic breakdown of ballots, Harrison became president with the majority of electoral votes but with fewer popular votes than Cleveland. Throughout the next century, many wondered how such confused elections could take place.

Proposed alternatives to the current electoral college system generally fall into three categories. In the first, the candidate with the most popular votes in a state would automatically receive those electoral votes. This system would eliminate independent voting among electors. In the second proposed alternative, a proportionality scheme, the breakdown of popular votes would correlate directly with the breakdown of electoral votes. This plan would abandon the winner-take-all structure of the college. In the third alternative, the district plan used in Maine, individual congressional districts would be treated as representative of a single electoral vote, and the two electoral votes that each state receives for its two senators would go to the winner of the majority of the districts. To some advocates, there also exists a fourth option: abolishing the electoral college altogether and letting a direct vote of the people determine who wins the offices of president and vice president.

Despite two controversial elections and occasional calls for change, the electoral system has more or less secured an extended series of peaceable transfers of power in the United States. Absent drastic changes in the political landscape, its role in selecting the U.S. president and vice president seems secure.

ELECTRICITY Electricity was discovered by BENJAMIN FRANKLIN in 1752. The electric generator was invented by Michael Faraday in 1831. Thomas Edison's invention of the electric lightbulb in 1879 sparked the demand for electric power that continues to this day, and initiated the need for legislative and regulatory controls on the electric-power-generating industry.

History By the end of the nineteenth century, the United States had completed its transition from using wood as a major ENERGY source to using coal, and the next transition from coal to oil and natural gas was just beginning. By the early twentieth century, both homes and businesses increased their demand for electric power, and electric utilities obtained long-term franchises from municipalities.

In 1920, the Federal Power Act (16 U.S.C.A. §§ 791a–828c) was passed in response to increased competition between electric utilities and to a lack of consistent service to rural areas. The Federal Power Act gave the Federal Power

Commission the authority to license hydroelectric plants. Later, President FRANKLIN D. ROOSEVELT encouraged Congress to create part II of the act, which gave the Federal Power Commission the power to regulate the transmission of electric energy (16 U.S.C.A. §§ 824–824m). This legislation was necessary to guard against potential abuses of the utility companies' monopolistic structure and to ensure adequate and consistent service nationwide.

As more and larger electric generating plants were constructed and as more electric power lines were strung, legislators believed that through economies of scale, electric utility monopolies could actually offer lower costs to consumers than could competition between smaller utilities. Because of the capital-intensive nature of providing electric power, and the sunken costs of building plants and stringing lines, it is more cost-effective to spread these costs over the large and consistent customer base provided by a MONOPOLY.

Structure of the Industry Modern electric utilities have three major organizational components: generation (power plants), transmission (high-voltage bulk power between utilities), and distribution (low-voltage power to ultimate consumers). Modern electric utilities not only produce the power they need for their consumers but also pool and coordinate excess electricity with other utilities.

In 1995, a total of thirty-five hundred electric utilities around the United States had the ability to produce over 640 million megawatts of electrical energy. Pooling and coordination of electrical energy take place through high-voltage wires that are maintained and referred to as the national grid; high-voltage wires are used because they allow transmission at a lower current, which generates less heat and results in less energy loss. At regional distribution centers closer to the ultimate consumers, the electrical energy is transformed into the low-voltage, higher-current electricity delivered to homes and businesses.

Major electric utilities produce electric power by burning coal, harnessing the hydroelectric energy produced by dams, and initiating and maintaining nuclear fission. Smaller, independent power producers use hydroelectric energy in addition to wood energy, geothermal energy, and biomass, which are all forms of renewable energy. Nuclear electric generating plants were constructed after the passage of the Atomic Energy Act (42 U.S.C.A. § 2011), which removed the government's monopoly over NUCLEAR POWER, in 1946, and the Price-Anderson Act (42 U.S.C.A. § 2210), which allowed for private ownership of uranium, in 1957. Commercial nuclear energy expanded in the 1960s and the early 1970s, and most consumers welcomed what was thought to be a safe and inexpensive source of energy. From the late 1970s to the 1990s, the dangers of nuclear energy and the expense of environmental contamination and lack of safe waste storage contributed to the end of nuclear power plant construction. No U.S. nuclear power plants have been ordered since 1978. Coal and hydroelectric energy continue to be the principal sources of commercial electric power.

Modern Legislation and Regulation of the Industry The generation, transmission, and distribution of electric power are heavily regulated. At the federal level, the transmission of electric power between utilities is governed by the Public Utilities Regulatory Policies Act (PURPA) (Pub. L. No. 95-617 [codified in various sections of U.S.C.A. tits. 15, 16]). In PURPA, Congress gave the Federal Energy Regulatory Commission jurisdiction over energy transmission. PURPA requires that independent power producers (IPPs) be allowed to interconnect with the distribution and transmission grids of major electric utilities. In addition, PURPA protects these IPPs from paying burdensome rates for purchasing backup power from these utilities, and sets the rate at which the utilities can purchase power from these IPPs at the major utilities' "avoided cost" (market cost minus the production costs "avoided" by purchasing from another utility) of producing the power.

The primary regulation of the generation, distribution, and transmission of electric power occurs at the state level through various state PUBLIC UTILITY commissions. Because the production of electric energy is connected with a PUBLIC INTEREST, states have a vested interest in overseeing it and working to guarantee that electricity will be produced in a safe, efficient, and expedient manner. In exchange for a monopoly in a particular geographic region, an electric utility must agree to supply electricity continuously and has a duty to avert unreasonable risks to its consumers. Electric utility companies must provide electricity at applicable lawful rates, and must file rate schedules with the public service commissions. Sometimes these rates are challenged, and administrative hearings are held to allow the utilities to petition for rate increases. Electricity rates must be high enough to cover the cost of production and must allow a fair return on the current value of capital investment. Rates that would allow significantly more than a fair

Electricity

U.S. Electric Utilities Sales, Revenue, and Customers, 1992

Sales

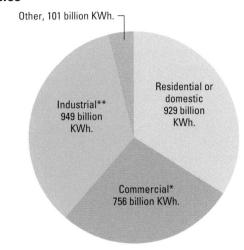

Other, 101 billion KWh.

Industrial** 949 billion KWh.

Residential or domestic 929 billion KWh.

Commercial* 756 billion KWh.

Revenue

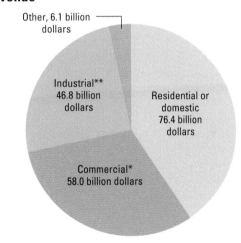

Other, 6.1 billion dollars

Industrial** 46.8 billion dollars

Residential or domestic 76.4 billion dollars

Commercial* 58.0 billion dollars

Total Customers

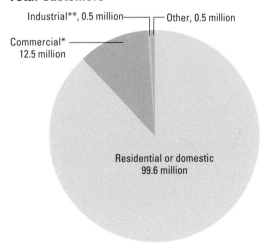

Industrial**, 0.5 million   Other, 0.5 million

Commercial* 12.5 million

Residential or domestic 99.6 million

*Small light and power.
**Large light and power.

Source: Edison Electric Institute, Washington, D.C., *Statistical Yearbook of the Electric Utility Industry*, annual.

return may be struck down as unreasonably high.

Dangers and Liabilities Electricity, especially at high voltages or high currents, is a dangerous commodity. Faulty wiring, power lines that are close to trees and buildings, and inadequate warning signs and fences around transformer stations and over buried electrical cables can subject an individual to electric shock or even electrocution. Because of the ultrahazardous nature of providing electric power, states have many statutes and regulations in place to protect the public from electric shock.

Other dangers from electricity include stray voltage and electromagnetic field radiation. Stray voltage affects farm animals, especially dairy cattle. On dairy farms, it occurs when cattle drink from electric feeding troughs or are attached to electric milking machines, and small electric shocks pass through the cattle, through their hooves, and into the ground. Repeated shocks can inhibit or destroy the milk-producing capability of dairy cattle. Liability for stray voltage on farms can be attributed to public utilities when wiring is faulty or negligently connected to a farmer's equipment. Some juries have awarded thousands of dollars to farmers whose cattle have been damaged by this phenomenon.

Electromagnetic fields are created whenever current moves through power lines. The strength of these fields drops off exponentially as the distance from the power lines increases. Individuals whose homes or businesses are close to power wires must live and work in these fields. Some individuals who live or work near high-voltage power lines have developed brain cancer and leukemia, and blame their condition on the constant exposure to electromagnetic field radiation. Studies have shown a correlation between electromagnetic fields and cancer, but many of the studies have been challenged as methodologically flawed. By the mid-1990s, no conclusive scientific evidence proved an epidemiological relationship between cancer and the electromagnetic fields produced by high-voltage power lines.

ELECTRONIC FRONTIER FOUNDATION

The Electronic Frontier Foundation (EFF) is a nonprofit organization that seeks to increase the understanding of civil liberties and other legal issues in cyberspace, or what it calls the electronic frontier. Concerned with preserving the principles embodied in the U.S. Constitution and Bill of Rights, the EFF defends the rights of computer users, network users, and members of the on-line community.

Widely recognized for its expertise in legal matters related to computer networks and electronic media, the EFF has become a leading resource for those seeking to better understand the complex issues associated with new communications technology. As part of its civil liberties mission, the EFF seeks to ensure that the creators of electronic communications have the same political freedoms as the creators of newspapers, books, journals, and other traditional media.

The EFF was founded on July 10, 1990, by Mitchell D. Kapor, the founder of Lotus Development Corporation and ON Technology, and John Perry Barlow, a writer and lyricist. Kapor and Barlow formed the organization after becoming alarmed by what they saw as misguided and unconstitutional actions by state and federal law enforcement officials against individual computer users. Initial funding for the EFF came from Kapor; Steve Wozniak, cofounder of Apple Computer; and other computer and technology entrepreneurs.

Among the EFF's first efforts were the defense of several hackers, or computer enthusiasts, in cases against the government. The EFF has continued to sponsor lawsuits when it feels that individuals' on-line civil liberties have been violated. The EFF also submits advisory reports, called amicus curiae briefs, to courts and arranges for the charitable donation of attorneys' services for individuals who cannot afford their own legal counsel.

As part of its effort to promote laws that better accommodate new technology, the EFF monitors legislation and lobbies for changes in the law. It also creates and distributes legal analyses to companies, utilities, governments, and other organizations, and it maintains a free telephone hot line for use by those in the on-line community who have questions regarding their legal rights. The EFF runs a speakers' bureau, which disseminates the organization's views to law enforcement organizations, attorneys' associations, universities, and other groups.

The EFF promotes improved intellectual property laws, including PATENT and COPYRIGHT laws, for electronic media. It also encourages the creation of policies that will promote the distribution of electronic information by public and private providers. The EFF sponsors summits and working groups that bring together people from business, government, education, and nonprofit organizations.

Specific proposals advanced by the EFF include a "common carriage" approach to free speech on electronic networks. Under a common carriage scheme, network providers must carry all speech, regardless of its content, but are not liable for the actions of users. The EFF has called for an electronic-freedom-of-information act to allow broader public access to information, and it has set forth specific proposals that promote wider access to computer networks such as the Internet.

The EFF publishes the *EFFector Online,* an electronic bulletin; the *EFFector,* a hard copy newsletter; and various pamphlets and books. It maintains several communications forums on the Internet, including a World Wide Web site, and news group forums on Usenet and on private on-line systems.

See also COMPUTER CRIME; E-MAIL; FREEDOM OF SPEECH.

ELECTRONIC SURVEILLANCE 📖 Observing or listening to persons, places, or activities—usually in a secretive or inobtrusive manner—with the aid of electronic devices such as cameras, microphones, tape recorders, or wire taps. Its objective when used in law enforcement is to gather EVIDENCE of a crime or to accumulate intelligence about suspected criminal activity. CORPORATIONS use electronic surveillance to maintain the security of their buildings and grounds or to gather information about competitors. 📖

Electronic surveillance permeates almost every aspect of life in the United States. The president, Congress, judiciary, military, and law enforcement all use some form of this technology in the public sector. In the private sector, business competitors, convenience stores, shopping centers, apartment buildings, parking facilities, hospitals, banks, employers, and spouses have employed various methods of electronic eavesdropping. Litigation has even arisen from covert surveillance of rest rooms.

Three types of electronic surveillance are most prevalent: WIRE TAPPING, bugging, and videotaping. Wire tapping intercepts telephone calls and telegraph messages by physically penetrating the wire circuitry. Someone must actually "tap" into telephone or telegraph wires to accomplish this type of surveillance. Bugging is accomplished without the aid of telephone wires, usually by placing a small microphone or other listening device in one location to transmit conversations to a nearby receiver and recorder. Video surveillance is performed by conspicuous or hidden cameras that transmit and record visual images that may be watched simultaneously or reviewed later on tape.

Electronic eavesdropping serves several purposes: (1) enhancement of security for persons and property; (2) detection and prevention of criminal, wrongful, or impermissible activity; and (3) protection or appropriation of valuable, useful, scandalous, embarrassing, and discrediting information. The law attempts to strike a

APWIDE WORLD PHOTOS

Wiretapped conversations between John Gotti and his associates were used against Gotti in court in 1991.

balance between the need for electronic surveillance and the PRIVACY interests of those affected.

Constitutional Law The FOURTH AMENDMENT to the U.S. Constitution protects the "right of the people to be secure in their persons, houses, papers, and effects, against unreasonable searches and seizures." It further provides that "no Warrants shall issue, but upon probable cause, supported by Oath or affirmation, and particularly describing the place to be searched, and the persons or things to be seized."

Electronic surveillance did not exist in 1789, when this amendment was written, and was probably not contemplated by the Founding Fathers. But the colonists were familiar with unbridled methods of law enforcement. British officials conducted warrantless SEARCHES AND SEIZURES, and made arrests based on mere suspicion. Even when a search was made pursuant to a WARRANT, the warrant was often general in nature, vesting British officials with absolute discretion to determine the scope and duration of the search.

The Fourth Amendment was carefully drafted in response to this colonial experience. It provides two basic protections. First, it prohibits government officials, or persons acting under COLOR OF LAW, from performing unreasonable searches and seizures. Second, it forbids magistrates to issue warrants that are not supported by PROBABLE CAUSE or that fail to specify the persons, places, and things subject to search

Some limousines and taxi cabs are equipped with video recording equipment for the safety of the driver and passengers.

and seizure. The Supreme Court has held that searches performed without a warrant are presumptively unreasonable. When a search is presumptively unreasonable, evidence seized by the police during the search will not be ADMISSIBLE against the defendant at trial unless the prosecution demonstrates that the evidence seized falls within an exception to the warrant requirement such as the "good faith" exception.

The Supreme Court first considered the Fourth Amendment implications of electronic surveillance in *Olmstead v. United States*, 277 U.S. 438, 48 S. Ct. 564, 72 L. Ed. 944 (1928). In *Olmstead*, federal agents intercepted incriminating conversations by tapping the telephone wires outside the defendant's home without a warrant or his consent. In a 5–4 decision, the Court ruled that electronic eavesdropping involves neither a search nor a seizure, within the meaning of the Fourth Amendment. The Court reasoned that no search took place in *Olmstead* because the government intercepted the conversations without entering the defendant's home or office and thus without examining any "place." No seizure occurred because the intercepted conversations were not the sort of tangible "things" the Court believed were protected by the Fourth Amendment. In a prescient dissent, Justice LOUIS D. BRANDEIS argued that nonconsensual, warrantless eavesdropping offends Fourth Amendment privacy interests without regard to manner or place of surveillance.

The Supreme Court whittled away at the *Olmstead* holding for the next forty years, finally overruling it in *Katz v. United States*, 389 U.S. 347, 88 S. Ct. 507, 19 L. Ed. 2d 576 (1967). In *Katz*, the police attached a listening device to the outside of a public telephone booth where the defendant was later recorded making incul-

patory statements. The Court declared this type of warrantless surveillance unconstitutional. The Court emphasized that the Fourth Amendment protects persons, not places, and held that the amendment's protections extend to any place where an individual maintains a reasonable expectation of privacy. The Court determined that in *Katz*, the defendant maintained a reasonable expectation of privacy in both the particular conversation he had and the public telephone booth where it took place. *Katz* made government electronic surveillance, and legislation authorizing it, subject to the strictures of the Fourth Amendment.

Legislation One year after *Katz*, Congress enacted the Omnibus Crime Control and Safe Streets Act of 1968 (Pub. L. 90-351, June 19, 1968, 82 Stat. 197; Pub. L. 90-462, § 1, Aug. 8, 1968, 82 Stat. 638; Pub. L. 90-618, Title III, Oct. 22, 1968, 82 Stat. 1236). Title III of the act governs the interception of wire and oral communications in both the public and private sectors. Electronic surveillance is used in the public sector as a tool of criminal investigation by law enforcement, and in the private sector as a means to obtain or protect valuable or discrediting information. Many of the fifty states have enacted legislation similar to title III.

Public Sector Title III outlines detailed procedures the federal government must follow before conducting electronic surveillance. Pursuant to authorization by the attorney general, or a specially designated assistant, federal law enforcement agents must make a sworn written application to a federal judge specifically describing the location where the communications will be intercepted, the reasons for the interception, the duration of the surveillance, and the identity of any persons whose conversations will be monitored. The application must also explain whether less intrusive investigative techniques have been tried. Electronic surveillance may not be used as a first step in criminal investigation when less intrusive means are likely to succeed without creating a significant danger to law enforcement personnel or the public.

A federal judge must then review the surveillance application to ensure that it satisfies each of the statutory requirements and establishes probable cause. The surveillance must be executed as soon as practicable, terminate after fulfillment of its objective, and in no event last longer than thirty days without further judicial approval. Federal agents must also take steps to minimize the interception of communications not relevant to the investigation. Evidence obtained in violation of title III or of the Fourth Amendment is generally not admissible in court, and may give rise to civil and criminal penalties.

Courts have interpreted title III to cover information intercepted from satellite unscrambling devices, cellular telephones, and pagers. However, title III does not cover information intercepted from pen registers, which record the telephone numbers of outgoing calls, or caller identification, which displays the telephone numbers of incoming calls, because neither intercepts conversations of any sort. Although title III does not regulate photographic interception, some federal courts have used it as a guide when reviewing the constitutionality of video surveillance.

The procedural requirements of title III are not without exception. Where there are exigent circumstances involving conspiratorial activities that threaten national security, title III permits federal law enforcement agents to conduct electronic surveillance for up to forty-eight hours before seeking judicial approval. At one time, many observers believed that title III also sanctions warrantless electronic surveillance by the executive branch for national security purposes. In 1972, the Supreme Court ruled to the contrary, holding that presidential surveillance of domestic organizations suspected of national security breaches during the Nixon administration had to comply with the Fourth Amendment's warrant requirement (*United States v. United States District Court for Eastern District of Michigan, Southern Division*, 407 U.S. 297, 92 S. Ct. 2125, 32 L. Ed. 2d 752).

Congress attempted to clarify the murky area of covert presidential surveillance by passing the Foreign Intelligence Surveillance Act of 1978 (FISA), Pub. L. 95-511, Oct. 25, 1978, 92 Stat. 1783. FISA regulates the federal government's surveillance of foreign officials, emissaries, and agents within the United States, but has no application to such surveillance abroad. Similar to title III, FISA sets forth specific application procedures that a federal judge must review for probable cause before any form of eavesdropping may commence. Unlike title III, FISA has been interpreted to govern video surveillance as well.

Private Sector Electronic surveillance is most common in two areas of the private sector: employment and domestic relations. In addition to legislation in many of the fifty states, title III governs these areas as well. It prohibits any person from intentionally using or disclosing information knowingly intercepted by electronic surveillance, without the consent of the interested parties. The INTENT element may be satisfied if the person knew or had reason to know that the information intercepted or disclosed was acquired by electronic surveillance; it is not satisfied if the person inadvertently intercepted or disclosed such information.

Sixty-eight percent of all reported wiretapping involves DIVORCE cases and custody battles. Spouses, attempting to obtain embarrassing or discrediting information against each other, have planted video recording and listening devices throughout the marital home. Spousal surveillance most commonly involves telephone taps and bedroom bugs, but has also included videotaping of activities as innocuous as grocery shopping and moviegoing. The fruits of interspousal electronic eavesdropping have been offered in court to reveal extramarital affairs, illegal drug use, and other criminal or deviant activity.

If interspousal surveillance is the most pervasive form of electronic eavesdropping, employer surveillance is the fastest growing. Employers videotape employee movement throughout the workplace, search employee computer files, and monitor employee phone calls. Reasons for such surveillance range from deterring theft and evaluating performance to protecting TRADE SECRETS.

The advent of electronic mail (E-mail) has provided employers with a new playground for mechanical snooping. By the year 2000, 40 million people are expected to send 60 billion pieces of E-mail correspondence annually. As with telephone calls, employees may send personal messages while they are at work. Although Congress considered the surveillance of workplace E-mail when it broadened title III's protections in 1986, no federal court has confronted the issue. However, courts have permitted employers to eavesdrop surreptitiously on employee phone calls for legitimate and significant business purposes, and courts may also apply this rationale to employer surveillance of E-mail.

Common Law State COMMON LAW provides a third avenue of legal protection against electronic surveillance. Throughout the twentieth century, common law has increasingly recognized a sphere of private activity beyond public consumption. The sometimes amorphous right to privacy consists of three discrete interests: secrecy, seclusion, and autonomy. The right to secrecy prevents nonconsensual public disclosure of valuable, confidential, embarrassing, or discrediting information. The right to seclusion creates a realm of personal solitude upon which society may not trammel. The right to autonomy represents the freedom to determine one's own fate unfettered by polemical publicity.

Common law protects these distinct privacy interests by imposing civil LIABILITY upon any one who publicizes private facts; besmirches someone's reputation; profits from another's name, likeness, or ideas; or otherwise intrudes upon an individual's private affairs. Common-law protection of privacy interests is broader than title III because it is not limited to wiretapping and bugging but extends to photographic and video surveillance as well. Thus, video surveillance of rest rooms, locker rooms, and dressing rooms may give rise to a claim for invasion of privacy under common law but not under title III.

At the same time, common law is narrower than title III because liability is only established by proof that the published information was sufficiently private to cause outrage, mental suffering, shame, or humiliation in a person of ordinary sensibilities. Title III creates liability for any nonconsensual, intentional disclosure of electronically intercepted information, thus establishing a much lower threshold. For example, a newspaper would not be liable under the common-law invasion-of-privacy doctrine for accurately reporting that someone had engaged in criminal conduct. However, the nonconsensual, electronic interception of such information would give rise to liability under title III.

CROSS-REFERENCES

Criminal Law; Criminal Procedure; Exclusionary Rule; Search Warrant

ELEMENT 📖 A material factor; a basic component. 📖

The term is used to mean one of several parts that unite to form a whole, as in elements of a CRIMINAL ACTION or CIVIL ACTION. In the TORT of ASSAULT AND BATTERY, an essential element of the offense would be unwanted physical contact. An element of the crime of RAPE is lack of consent on the part of the victim.

ELEVENTH AMENDMENT The Eleventh Amendment to the U.S. Constitution reads:

> The Judicial power of the United States shall not be construed to extend to any suit in law or equity, commenced or prosecuted against one of the United States by Citizens of another State, or by Citizens or Subjects of any Foreign State.

The text of the Eleventh Amendment limits the power of FEDERAL COURTS to hear lawsuits against state governments brought by the citizens of another state or the citizens of a foreign country. The Supreme Court has also interpreted the Eleventh Amendment to bar federal courts from hearing lawsuits instituted by citizens of the state being sued, and lawsuits initiated by the governments of foreign countries. For example, the state of New York could invoke the Eleventh Amendment to protect itself from being sued in federal court by its own residents, residents of another state, residents of a foreign country, or the government of a foreign country.

The Eleventh Amendment is rooted in the concept of FEDERALISM, under which the U.S. Constitution carefully enumerates the powers of Congress to govern at the national level, while safeguarding the power of states to govern locally. By limiting the power of federal courts to hear lawsuits brought against state governments, the Eleventh Amendment attempts to strike a balance between the SOVEREIGNTY shared by the state and federal governments.

"The object and purpose of the Eleventh Amendment [is] to prevent the indignity of subjecting a state to the coercive process of [federal] judicial tribunals at the instance of private parties" (*Ex parte Ayers*, 123 U.S. 443, 8 S. Ct. 164, 31 L. Ed. 216 [1887]). The Eleventh Amendment highlights an understanding that the state governments, while ratifying the federal Constitution to form a union, "maintain certain attributes of sovereignty, including sovereign immunity" from being sued in federal court (*Hans v. Louisiana*, 134 U.S. 1, 10 S. Ct. 504, 33 L. Ed. 842 [1890]).

However, the Eleventh Amendment does not bar all lawsuits brought against state governments in federal court. Four major exceptions have been recognized by the Supreme Court. First, the Eleventh Amendment does not apply to lawsuits brought against a state's political subdivisions. Accordingly, counties, cities, and municipalities may be sued in federal court without regard to the strictures of the Eleventh Amendment.

The second exception to the Eleventh Amendment permits a state government to WAIVE its constitutional protections by consenting to a lawsuit against it in federal court. For example, Minnesota could waive its Eleventh Amendment protections by agreeing to allow a federal court to hear a lawsuit brought against it.

The third exception permits Congress to abrogate a state's IMMUNITY from being sued in federal court by enacting legislation pursuant to its enforcement powers under the Equal Protection and Due Process Clauses of the FOUR-

TEENTH AMENDMENT (*Fitzpatrick v. Bitzer,* 427 U.S. 445, 96 S. Ct. 2666, 49 L. Ed. 2d 614 [1976]). Congressional intent to abrogate a state's Eleventh Amendment immunity must be "unmistakably clear" (*Atascadero State Hospital v. Scanlon,* 473 U.S. 234, 105 S. Ct. 3142, 87 L. Ed. 2d 171 [1985]). Evidence of this intent may be found in the legislative floor debates that precede a congressional enactment (*Quern v. Jordan,* 440 U.S. 332, 99 S. Ct. 1139, 59 L. Ed. 2d 358 [1979]). See also LEGISLATIVE HISTORY.

In 1996, the Supreme Court ruled that Congress may not abrogate a state's SOVEREIGN IMMUNITY from being sued in federal court pursuant to its regulatory powers under the Indian Commerce Clause contained in Article I, Section 8, of the Constitution (*Seminole Tribe v. Florida,* __U.S.__, 116 S. Ct. 1114, 134 L. Ed. 2d 252 [1996]). *Seminole* overruled *Pennsylvania v. Union Gas Co.,* 491 U.S. 1, 109 S. Ct. 2273, 105 L. Ed. 2d 1 (1989), which held that Congress may abrogate a state's immunity under the Interstate Commerce Clause, which adjoins the Indian Commerce Clause in Article I.

Although *Seminole* involved the Indian Gaming Regulatory Act (18 U.S.C.A. §§ 1166 to 1168, 25 U.S.C.A. § 2701 et seq.), which governs certain gambling activities of Native American tribes, the Court's decision calls into question the continuing power of federal courts to hear lawsuits against state governments seeking to enforce environmental statutes, bankruptcy laws, intellectual property legislation, and scores of other business regulations that have been enacted pursuant to congressional power under the COMMERCE CLAUSE. See also GAMING.

The Comprehensive Environmental Response, Compensation, and Liability Act (CERCLA) (42 U.S.C.A. § 9601 et seq.) is one federal law passed pursuant to congressional power under the Commerce Clause. This act makes states liable in federal court for costs incurred from cleaning up hazardous waste sites. (See *Pennsylvania v. Union Gas Co.,* 491 U.S. 1, 109 S. Ct. 2273, 105 L. Ed. 2d 1 [1989]). The Court's decision in *Seminole* could affect thousands of lawsuits filed each year under this statute alone.

The final exception to the Eleventh Amendment permits citizens of any state to seek an INJUNCTION against state officials in federal court to "end a continuing violation of federal law" (*Green v. Mansour,* 474 U.S. 64, 106 S. Ct. 423, 88 L. Ed. 2d 371 [1985]; *Ex parte Young,* 209 U.S. 123, 28 S. Ct. 441, 52 L. Ed. 714 [1908]). For example, residents of Ohio are permitted to bring a lawsuit in federal court seeking to compel the state's governor to construct housing in compliance with the Americans with Disabilities Act (42 U.S.C.A. § 12101 et seq.), a federal statute designed to protect the rights of handicapped U.S. citizens (see *Martin v. Voinovich,* 840 F. Supp. 1175 S.D. Ohio [1993]). However, such a lawsuit would be barred by the Eleventh Amendment if the remedy sought were not injunctive relief but money DAMAGES to be paid out of the state's treasury.

The Supreme Court has distinguished permissible lawsuits seeking prospective equitable relief, such as the injunctive remedy sought by the Ohio residents, from impermissible lawsuits seeking money damages for past actions: "[F]ederal court[s] may award an injunction that governs [a state] official's future conduct, but not one that awards retroactive monetary relief" (*Pennhurst State School & Hospital v. Halderman,* 465 U.S. 89, 104 S. Ct. 900, 79 L. Ed. 2d 67 [1984]). The distinction between prospective injunctive relief and retroactive money damages can be traced back to the Framers' original understanding of the Eleventh Amendment. See also EQUITY.

Ratified in 1795, the Eleventh Amendment was drafted to overrule the Supreme Court's decision in *Chisholm v. Georgia,* 2 U.S. (2 Dall.) 419, 1 L. Ed. 440 (1793), which held that a citizen of one state may sue the government of another state in the U.S. Supreme Court. *Chisholm* created a maelstrom across the United States. At the close of the American Revolution, each state was greatly indebted to foreign CREDITORS for financial and other assistance received during the war. Congressional representatives feared that *Chisholm* would permit these foreign creditors to ask federal courts to force the fiscally troubled state treasuries to bear the burden of these DEBTS.

Representatives also expressed concern that British Loyalists who had been dispossessed of their homes and personal belongings by the colonies during the Revolution could now sue the state governments to recover their property. JOHN JAY, the chief justice of the Supreme Court, exacerbated these concerns by advocating the full restoration of Loyalist property. A defiant Georgia House of Representatives passed a resolution providing that any person who attempted to collect a Revolutionary War debt or recover property pursuant to *Chisholm* "shall be declared guilty of a felony and ... suffer death without benefit of clergy, by being hanged."

Two days after *Chisholm* was handed down by the Supreme Court, an anonymous senator submitted to Congress a proposal that later became the Eleventh Amendment to the Constitution. From its inception, the Eleventh Amendment has fueled heated discussions among judges and lawyers about the appropriate manner in which it should be interpreted.

Federal courts derive their power to hear lawsuits from Article III of the Constitution. Section 2 of Article III specifies particular "Cases" and "Controversies" that can be decided by the federal judiciary. These cases and controversies fall into two general categories: those identified by their subject matter and those identified by their parties.

Federal courts have JURISDICTION to hear cases whose subject matter "aris[es] under" the U.S. Constitution, an EXECUTIVE ORDER promulgated by the president, a federal law enacted by Congress, or a TREATY between the United States and another country (U.S. Const. art III, § 2). Such cases are said to present FEDERAL QUESTIONS because they involve legal issues based on one of these species of federal law. For example, cases involving free speech claims under the First Amendment or discrimination claims under the Civil Rights Act of 1871 (42 U.S.C.A. § 1983) present federal questions, and confer upon federal courts the SUBJECT MATTER JURISDICTION to resolve them.

Federal courts also have jurisdiction to hear cases based on the PARTIES involved in the lawsuit. Under what is sometimes called party-based jurisdiction, federal judges have the power to decide cases affecting "Ambassadors" and "other public Ministers and Consuls." The federal judiciary may also entertain disputes "between two or more States," "between Citizens of different states," or *"between a State and Citizens of another State"* (U.S. Const. art. III, § 2). The italicized clause contemplates federal jurisdiction extending to cases between state governments and citizens of other states, and provided the basis for the Supreme Court's decision in *Chisholm.* See also AMBASSADORS AND CONSULS.

Although the Eleventh Amendment was clearly adopted in response to the Supreme Court's interpretation of Article III in *Chisholm,* it has not been applied in a clear or uniform manner by the courts. Four alternative theories of interpretation have been advanced by lawyers and judges.

The first theory of interpretation, espoused by Justice THURGOOD MARSHALL, insists that the Eleventh Amendment protects states from being sued in federal court without their consent. It "had been widely understood prior to ratification of the Constitution," Marshall said, "that the provision in Art[icle] III, Section 2 . . .

would not provide a mechanism for making states unwilling defendants in federal court" (*Department of Public Health & Welfare v. Department of Public Health & Welfare,* 411 U.S. 279, 93 S. Ct. 1614, 36 L. Ed. 2d 251 [1973]). Marshall believed that the Eleventh Amendment did not change this original understanding of federal jurisdiction. For Marshall, then, the meaning of the Eleventh Amendment was simple: A state could not be sued in federal court under any circumstances in which the state did not consent.

According to the second theory of interpretation, the Eleventh Amendment applies only to party-based jurisdiction and not to subject matter jurisdiction. This theory, advanced by Justice WILLIAM J. BRENNAN, JR., permits federal courts to hear lawsuits against states that present federal questions, such as those "arising under" the Constitution, but bars federal judges from deciding cases in which the plaintiff lives in a different state than the one being sued. Adherents of this theory point out that *Chisholm,* the Supreme Court decision that was overruled by the Eleventh Amendment, involved party-based jurisdiction and was not subject matter jurisdiction.

The third theory of interpretation relies on the text of the Eleventh Amendment itself. Again, the language of the Eleventh Amendment suggests that federal courts may hear only two types of lawsuits against state governments: those brought by citizens of another state and those brought by citizens of another country. Under this theory, federal courts can entertain lawsuits seeking to vindicate a federal constitutional or statutory right only if the plaintiff lives in a different state from the one he or she is suing, or is the citizen of a foreign country. If the plaintiff resides in the state he or she is suing, only a state court may hear the case.

The fourth theory of interpretation also focuses on the language of the Eleventh Amendment, but in a different way. This theory stresses that the Eleventh Amendment explicitly limits the "Judicial power of the United States" but makes no mention of federal legislative power (U.S. Const. art. III, § 2). In this light, the Eleventh Amendment explicitly restricts the power of federal judges to hear cases against state governments, and implicitly permits Congress to abrogate a state's sovereign immunity from being sued in federal court. This theory permits citizens of any state, including the state being sued, to file a lawsuit against a state government in federal court to enforce a legal right delineated by congressional legislation. Many advocates of this theory argue that Con-

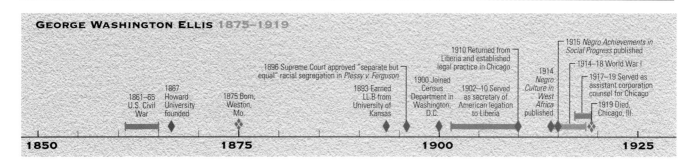

GEORGE WASHINGTON ELLIS 1875–1919

1861–65 U.S. Civil War

1867 Howard University founded

1875 Born, Weston, Mo.

1896 Supreme Court approved "separate but equal" racial segregation in *Plessy v. Ferguson*

1893 Earned LL.B from University of Kansas

1900 Joined Census Department in Washington, D.C.

1902–10 Served as secretary of American legation to Liberia

1910 Returned from Liberia and established legal practice in Chicago

1914 *Negro Culture in West Africa* published

1915 *Negro Achievements in Social Progress* published

1914–18 World War I

1917–19 Served as assistant corporation counsel for Chicago

1919 Died, Chicago, Ill.

1850 — 1875 — 1900 — 1925

gress's authority to enact such legislation derives from any of its constitutionally enumerated powers, and not just its powers under the Fourteenth Amendment as the Supreme Court concluded in *Seminole*.

The diversity of these theories demonstrates the complexity of Eleventh Amendment jurisprudence, as does the Supreme Court's decision in *Seminole*, which overruled a case less than eight years old. Yet, most adherents to these various theories would agree on one point: There is an advantage, however slight, to filing a lawsuit in federal court rather than state court. A federal court is more likely to render an impartial VERDICT than is a judge or juror who resides in the state being sued. For this reason, plaintiffs, and the lawyers representing them, will continue to sue state governments in federal court and argue vociferously for the most narrow interpretation of the Eleventh Amendment's sovereign immunity.

ELLIS, GEORGE WASHINGTON

George Washington Ellis was born May 4, 1875, in Weston, Missouri. He earned a bachelor of laws degree from the University of Kansas in 1893, attended Howard University in Washington, D.C., for two years where he studied psychology and philosophy, and graduated from Gunton's Institute of Economics and Sociology in New York in 1900.

After practicing law for several years, Ellis worked in the Census Department in Washington in 1900. He served as secretary of the American legation to the Republic of Liberia for eight years beginning in 1902.

In 1910, Ellis returned from Liberia and

BIOGRAPHY

Oliver Ellsworth

established a legal practice in Chicago, earning a reputation as a prestigious counselor. From 1917 to 1919, he served as assistant corporation counsel for Chicago.

Ellis's interest in Africa continued throughout his life, and his experiences in Liberia influenced his career as a writer and lecturer. He investigated the social structure and folklore history of that nation and presented speeches concerning Africa and the question of race. He was an editor of the *Journal of Race Development*, and authored several publications, including *Negro Culture in West Africa* (1914); *Negro Achievements in Social Progress* (1915); and *The Leopard's Claw* (1917).

Ellis died November 26, 1919, in Chicago, Illinois.

ELLSWORTH, OLIVER

Oliver Ellsworth served as the third chief justice of the U.S. Supreme Court. Though his tenure on the Court was undistinguished, Ellsworth played an important part in shaping the political and legal structure of the United States as a representative at the Constitutional Convention and as a U.S. senator.

Ellsworth was born April 29, 1745, in Windsor, Connecticut, into a prosperous and distinguished family. He attended Yale College (now Yale University), then transferred to Princeton, where he graduated in 1766. Ellsworth entertained thoughts of becoming a minister but decided to enter the legal profession. He was admitted to the Connecticut bar in 1771 and was quickly recognized as an able attorney.

Politics soon attracted Ellsworth. A proponent of American independence, he served in

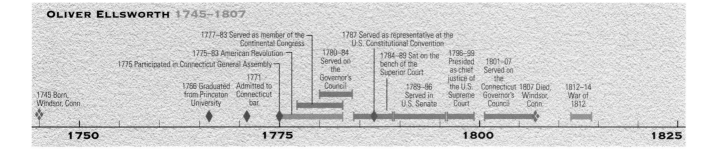

OLIVER ELLSWORTH 1745–1807

1745 Born, Windsor, Conn.

1766 Graduated from Princeton University

1771 Admitted to Connecticut bar

1775 Participated in Connecticut General Assembly

1775–83 American Revolution

1777–83 Served as member of the Continental Congress

1780–84 Served on the Governor's Council

1787 Served as representative at the U.S. Constitutional Convention

1784–89 Sat on the bench of the Superior Court

1789–96 Served in U.S. Senate

1796–99 Presided as chief justice of the U.S. Supreme Court

1801–07 Served on the Connecticut Governor's Council

1807 Died, Windsor, Conn.

1812–14 War of 1812

1750 — 1775 — 1800 — 1825

the Connecticut General Assembly in 1775. From 1777 to 1783 he was a member of the Continental Congress and from 1780 to 1784 he sat on the Connecticut Governor's Council. Ellsworth also served as a trial judge during this period.

Ellsworth advocated a strong national government and aligned himself with the Federalist party. When the Constitutional Convention convened in 1787, Ellsworth served as a representative from Connecticut. During the writing of the Constitution Ellsworth contributed the phrase "United States." More important, Ellsworth and Roger Sherman convinced the convention to adopt their Connecticut Compromise (sometimes called the Great Compromise), which resolved the nature of the federal legislature.

The convention had been divided over this issue. Edmund Randolph offered the Virginia Plan, which was supported by the more populated states. This plan provided for a bicameral (two-chambered) legislature with representation based on each state's population. William Paterson of New Jersey put forward his New Jersey Plan, which was favored by the smaller states. This plan called for equal representation for each state, regardless of population. Ellsworth and Sherman proposed a compromise: the legislature would be bicameral, with the lower house based on proportional representation and the upper house based on equal representation, and all revenue bills would originate in the lower house. The Connecticut Compromise was approved July 16, 1787. The structure proposed in the compromise has proved to be an important check and balance, giving smaller states equality in the upper house, called the Senate.

Ellsworth learned firsthand about the Senate as he served in that institution from 1789 to 1796. He was the leader of the Federalists in the Senate and drafted the conference report that recommended the adoption of the amendments to the Constitution that became known as the Bill of Rights. He also helped write the Judiciary Act of 1789 (1 Stat. 73). The Judiciary Act implemented the vague language of Article III of the Constitution by organizing the federal court system into the Supreme Court, circuit courts of appeal, and district courts. The basic structure of the federal courts has remained substantially the same since 1789.

President George Washington appointed Ellsworth chief justice of the Supreme Court in 1796. Once on the Court, Ellsworth proved generally ineffective. Because of illness and the

undertaking of diplomatic assignments, he had little time or energy to devote to Court business.

Ellsworth resigned in 1799 following an arduous trip to France. President John Adams had sent him there to negotiate a trade agreement with Napoléon. The trip aggravated his illness.

Ellsworth did not abandon public life. He sat on the Connecticut Governor's Council for a second time, serving from 1801 to 1807. In 1807 he was appointed chief justice of Connecticut. He died on November 26 of that year, in Windsor, before taking his seat.

E-MAIL As part of the revolution in high-tech communications, electronic mail, or E-mail, has soared in popularity since appearing in the mid-1980s. Over 40 million U.S. residents now regularly "E-mail" each other by computer. Faster and cheaper than traditional mail, this correspondence is commonly sent over office networks, through national services such as CompuServe Incorporated and MCI Mail, and across the global computer network known as the Internet. It is, however, less secure than traditional mail, even though federal law protects E-mail from unauthorized tampering and interception. Under the Electronic Communications Privacy Act of 1986 (ECPA) (Pub. L. No. 99-508, Oct. 21, 1986, 100 Stat. 1848), third parties are forbidden to read private E-mail. However, a loophole in the ECPA that allows employers to read their workers' E-mail has proved especially controversial. This has provoked several lawsuits and produced legislative and extralegal proposals to increase E-mail privacy.

Congress meant to increase PRIVACY by passing the ECPA. Lawmakers took note of increasingly popular communications devices that were readily susceptible to eavesdropping—

"INSTITUTIONS WITHOUT RESPECT, LAWS VIOLATED WITH IMPUNITY, ARE, TO A REPUBLIC, THE SYMPTOMS AND SEEDS OF DEATH."

Many people have computers at home and at work and they may use E-mail in both places. Under the Electronic Communications Privacy Act, E-mail has nearly the same protection as traditional mail does.

cellular telephones, pagers, satellite dishes, and E-mail. The law updated existing federal criminal codes in order to qualify these emerging technologies for constitutional protection under the FOURTH AMENDMENT. In the case of E-mail, Congress gave it most of the protection already accorded by law to traditional mail. Just as postal employees cannot divulge information about private mail to third parties, neither can E-mail services. The law provides criminal and civil penalties for violators: In cases of third-party interception, it establishes fines of up to $5,000 and prison sentences of up to six months. In cases of industrial espionage—where privacy is invaded for purposes of commercial advantage, malicious destruction, or private commercial gain—it establishes fines of up to $250,000 and prison sentences of up to one year. As with traditional mail, law enforcement agencies can seize E-mail as EVIDENCE in criminal investigations, and litigants can SUBPOENA it in civil lawsuits.

To protect against disclosure of private or sensitive information, some attorneys advise employers and employees to exercise caution with E-mail, since it can be subpoenaed. Some experts have advised users to delete their E-mail regularly, and even to avoid saving it in the first place. Still others advocate the use of encryption software, which scrambles messages and makes them unreadable without a digital password.

EMANCIPATION The act or process by which a person is liberated from the authority and control of another person.

The term is primarily employed in regard to the release of a MINOR by his or her parents, which entails a complete relinquishment of the right to the care, CUSTODY, and earnings of such child, and a repudiation of parental obligations. The emancipation may be express—pursuant to a voluntary agreement between parent and child—or implied from conduct that denotes consent. It may be absolute or conditional, total or partial. A partial emancipation disengages a child for only a portion of the period of minority, or from only a particular aspect of the parent's rights or duties.

There is no determinate age when a child becomes emancipated; it usually, but not automatically, occurs upon the attainment of the AGE OF MAJORITY.

See also PARENT AND CHILD.

EMANCIPATION PROCLAMATION A Civil War–era declaration, formally issued on January 1, 1863, by President ABRAHAM LINCOLN, that freed all slaves in territories still under Confederate control.

The Emancipation Proclamation is often mistakenly praised as the legal instrument that ended SLAVERY—actually, the THIRTEENTH AMENDMENT to the Constitution, ratified in December 1865, outlawed slavery. But the proclamation is justifiably celebrated as a significant step toward the goal of ending slavery and making African Americans equal citizens of the United States. Coming as it did in the midst of the Civil War (1861–65), the proclamation announced to the Confederacy and the world that the ABOLITION of slavery had become an important goal of the North in its fight against the rebellious states of the South. The document also marked a shift in Lincoln's mind toward support for emancipation. Just before signing the final document in 1863, Lincoln said, "I never, in my life, felt more certain that I was doing right than I do in signing this paper."

In the text of the proclamation—which is almost entirely the work of Lincoln himself—Lincoln characterizes his order as "an act of justice, warranted by the Constitution upon military necessity." These words capture the essential character of Lincoln's work in the document. On the one hand, he perceived the proclamation as a kind of military tactic that would aid the Union in its difficult struggle against the Confederacy. As such, it was an extraordinary measure that carried the force of law under the powers granted by the Constitution to the president as commander in chief of the U.S. military forces. But on the other hand, Lincoln saw the proclamation as "an act of justice" that announced the intention of the North to free the slaves. In this respect, it became an important statement of the intent to abolish slavery in the United States once and for all, as well as a vital symbol of human freedom to later generations.

Lincoln had not always regarded emancipation as a goal of the Civil War. In fact, he actively resisted emancipation efforts early in the war, as when he voided earlier emancipation proclamations issued by the Union generals John C. Frémont and David Hunter in their military districts. Lincoln also failed to enforce provisions passed by Congress in 1861 and 1862 that called for the confiscation and emancipation of slaves owned by persons supporting the rebellion.

However, antislavery sentiment in the North grew in intensity during the course of the Civil War. By the summer of 1862, with the Union faring poorly in the conflict, Lincoln had begun to formulate the ideas he would eventually express in the proclamation. In particular, he reasoned that emancipation would work to the

This engraving depicts the first reading of the Emancipation Proclamation before Abraham Lincoln's cabinet in 1862. Standing left to right are Chase, Smith, and Blair; seated left to right are Stanton, Lincoln, Welles, Seward, and Bates.

military advantage of the North by creating a labor shortage for the Confederacy and providing additional troops for the Union. While Lincoln was increasingly sympathetic to abolitionists who wished to end slavery, he was reluctant to proclaim emancipation on a wider scale, out of fear that it would alienate the border slave states of Kentucky, Maryland, and Missouri, which had remained part of the Union. Already stung by military setbacks, Lincoln did not want to do anything to jeopardize the ultimate goal of victory in the war. Even if he had wished to proclaim emancipation on a wider scale, such an act probably would not have been constitutionally legitimate for the presidency.

Lincoln's cabinet was nervous about the effect of issuing the proclamation, and it advised him to wait until the Union had won a major victory before releasing it. As a result, the president announced the preliminary proclamation on September 22, 1862, five days after the Union victory at the Battle of Antietam. In language that would be retained in the final version of the proclamation, this preliminary order declared that on January 1, 1863, all the slaves in the parts of the country still in rebellion "shall be . . . thenceforward and forever, free." It also pledged that "the executive government of the United States, including the military . . . will recognize and maintain the freedom" of ex-slaves. But this preliminary proclamation also contained language that was

not included in the final document. For example, it recommended that slave owners who had remained loyal to the Union be compensated for the loss of their slaves.

The final version of the proclamation specified the regions still held by the Confederacy in which emancipation would apply: all parts of Arkansas, Texas, Mississippi, Alabama, Florida, Georgia, South Carolina, and North Carolina, and parts of Louisiana and Virginia. It also asked that freed slaves "abstain from all violence" and announced that those "of suitable condition will be received into the armed service of the United States." This last provision led to a significant practical effect of the proclamation: by 1865, over 190,000 African Americans had joined the U.S. armed services in the fight against the Confederacy.

News and copies of the proclamation quickly spread through the country, causing many people, especially African Americans, to celebrate. At one gathering, the African American abolitionist FREDERICK DOUGLASS made a speech in which he pronounced the proclamation the first step on the part of the nation in its departure from the servitude of the ages. In following years, many African Americans would continue to celebrate the anniversary of the signing of the proclamation.

However, many abolitionists were disappointed with the limited nature of the proclamation. They called for complete and immediate emancipation throughout the entire country, and they criticized the proclamation as the product of military necessity rather than moral idealism.

Although the practical effects of the proclamation were quite limited, it did serve as an important symbol that the North now intended not only to preserve the Union but also to abolish the practice of slavery. For Lincoln, the proclamation marked an important step in his eventual support of complete emancipation. Later, he would propose that the Republican party include in its 1864 platform a plank calling for the abolition of slavery by constitutional amendment, and he would sign the Thirteenth Amendment in early 1865.

The copy of the proclamation that Lincoln wrote by hand and signed on January 1, 1863, was destroyed in a fire in 1871. Early drafts and copies of the original, including the official government copy derived from Lincoln's own, are held at the National Archives, in Washington, D.C.

EMBARGO 📖 A proclamation or order of government, usually issued in time of war or threatened hostilities, prohibiting the departure of ships or goods from some or all ports until further order. Government order prohibiting commercial trade with individuals or businesses of other specified nations. Legal prohibition on commerce.

The temporary or permanent sequestration of the property of individuals for the purposes of a government, e.g., to obtain vessels for the transport of troops, the owners being reimbursed for this forced service. 📖

EMBARGO ACT 📖 A legislative measure enacted by Congress in 1807 at the behest of President THOMAS JEFFERSON that banned trade between U.S. ports and foreign nations. 📖

The Embargo Act was intended to use economic pressure to compel England and France to remove restrictions on commercial trading with neutral nations that they imposed in their warfare with each other. Napoleon decreed under his Continental system that no ally of France or any neutral nation could trade with Great Britain, in order to destroy the English economy. In retaliation, England caused a BLOCKADE of the northern European coastline, affecting nations that had remained neutral in the dispute between France and England. These vindictive measures hurt neutral American traders, prompting Congress to take action to safeguard the economic interests of the United States. The first enactment was the Nonimportation Act of 1806 (2 Stat. 379), which prohibited the import of designated En-

glish goods to stop the harsh treatment of American ships caught running the blockade. The Embargo Act of 1807 (2 Stat. 451) superseded this enactment and expanded the prohibition against international trade to all nations. A later amendment in 1809 (2 Stat. 506) extended the ban from American ports to inland waters and overland transactions, thereby stopping trade with Canada, and mandated strict enforcement of its provisions.

The American public opposed the act, particularly those segments dependent upon international trade for their livelihoods. This opposition eventually led to the enactment of the Non-Intercourse Act (2 Stat. 528 [1809]), which superseded the stringent provisions of the Embargo Act. Under that act, only trade with England and France was proscribed, but the measure was ineffectual.

Subsequently, in 1810, Nathaniel Macon proposed a measure, called Macon's Bill No. 2, which Congress enacted despite solid Federalist opposition, that empowered the president to resume commerce with the warring nation that lifts its restrictions on neutral trade.

EMBEZZLEMENT 📖 The fraudulent CONVERSION of another's property by a person who is in a position of trust, such as an AGENT or employee. 📖

Embezzlement is distinguished from swindling in that swindling involves wrongfully obtaining property by a false pretense, such as a lie or trick, at the time the property is transferred, which induces the victim to transfer to the wrongdoer TITLE to the property.

Nature There was no crime of embezzlement under the COMMON LAW. It is a statutory crime that evolved from LARCENY. Whereas lar-

Cartoonist Alexander Anderson named the embargo on trade with England "Ograbme," a snapping turtle that hurt U.S. businesses who relied on international trade.

ceny requires a felonious trespassory taking of property at the outset, embezzlement is a wrongful appropriation subsequent to an originally lawful taking. Embezzlement is, therefore, a modification of larceny designed to cover certain fraudulent acts that do not come within its scope. Although they are mutually exclusive crimes, they do overlap slightly under statutes in some states.

Embezzlement was created by the English legislature, which designated specific persons who might be liable for the offense. These were essentially persons entrusted with another's property, such as agents, attorneys, bankers, and corporate officers.

The English definition of the offense is followed in the United States today. Statutes do not usually list the persons who might be liable but, instead, generally describe the offender as a person entrusted with, or in possession of, another's property.

Property The type of property that must be converted is governed by statute. Generally, property is defined as including money, goods, CHATTELS, or anything of value. Intangible PERSONAL PROPERTY; COMMERCIAL PAPER, such as CHECKS, PROMISSORY NOTES, BONDS, or STOCKS; and written documents, such as DEEDS or CONTRACTS, may also be the subject of embezzlement.

Under some statutes, property consists of anything that can be the subject of larceny. In other states, however, the property requirement for embezzlement is broader. For example, the statute might punish the conversion of both real and personal property.

In some states, the embezzlement of public property or public funds is a separate offense. The offense is characterized by the manner in which the money is received. A court clerk who receives BAIL money is a recipient of public money and the person can be liable if such money is wrongfully converted by him or her.

The property subject to embezzlement must have some VALUE, even though value is not an element of the offense. Although a check without a required endorsement does not have value, the fact that the endorsement can be forged gives it sufficient value to make it a subject of embezzlement.

Elements Statutes governing the offense vary widely throughout the states. To determine exactly what elements comprise the offense, it is necessary to examine the particular statute applicable.

Elements common to embezzlement are (1) the property must belong to a person other than the accused, such as an employer or PRINCIPAL; (2) the property must be converted subsequent

If an employee converts property or money that has been entrusted to his or her employer by another, it is embezzlement.

to the defendant's original and lawful possession of it; (3) the defendant must be in a position of trust, so that the property is held by him or her pursuant to some FIDUCIARY duty; and (4) the defendant must have an intent to DEFRAUD the owner at the time of the conversion.

Ownership The principal or employer must be the owner of the property embezzled by an agent or employee at the time the offense is committed. Under many statutes, the ownership requirement is expressed as the property of another. It is sufficient if any person, other than the defendant, owns the property and it does not matter who has title to it or that it is owned by more than one person.

JURISDICTIONS differ on the question of whether a person can embezzle funds belonging to a spouse. In states that retain the spousal privilege, a person can be prevented from testifying to a crime against a spouse and, therefore, spousal embezzlement will not be prosecuted.

Unless a statute provides otherwise, co-owners of property, such as joint tenants or tenants in common, cannot be guilty of the offense with respect to the property that is jointly owned. A co-owner who wrongfully transfers jointly owned property converts his or her own property as opposed to that of another and, therefore, there is no conversion. If a person has any interest in property held jointly with another, the person cannot be convicted of the offense relating to that property. For example, a co-owner of an automobile cannot be guilty of embezzling it if both owners have an equal right to possession. A number of states, however, have statutes punishing embezzlement by co-owners, such as partners who wrongfully convey partnership assets. See also JOINT TENANCY; TENANCY IN COMMON.

In most states, an agent authorized to collect money for his or her principal and to keep a certain amount as commission is guilty of embezzlement if he or she wrongfully transfers the entire sum collected.

Possession or Custody of Property Pos-session is the essential element for distinguishing between embezzlement and larceny. While larceny requires that the thief take the property out of the victim's possession, the person must lawfully possess the property at the time that it is converted for embezzlement.

It is not necessary for the defendant to have physical or exclusive possession. It is sufficient if the person has CONSTRUCTIVE possession—a form of possession that is not actual but that gives the holder power to exercise control over the property either directly or through another person. Alternatively, mere CUSTODY is insufficient for embezzlement. If a master puts a servant in charge of property for purposes of guarding or caring for it, the master is considered to have constructive possession of such property while the servant has mere custody. A servant who wrongfully converts property over which he or she has custody may be guilty of larceny, but not embezzlement.

The fact that an accused person lawfully receives property at different times will not negate an embezzlement charge provided all other elements of the offense are met.

Trust Relationship Since the offense is aimed at punishing persons who convert property for their own use when possession is lawfully acquired, prosecution is limited to instances where the parties are in a fiduciary, or trust, relationship.

Generally, a DEBTOR and a CREDITOR, or an agent and a broker, do not have a fiduciary relationship sufficient for the offense. There must be some further indication that one person has a duty to care for and exert some control over the other's property. The most common type of trust relationships are those existing among corporate officers, partners, and employers and their employees.

Conversion of Property Conversion is an act that interferes with an owner's right of possession to his or her property.

For purposes of embezzlement, conversion involves an unauthorized assumption of the right of ownership over another's property. It may, for example, occur when a person is entrusted with property for one purpose and uses it for another purpose without the consent of the owner. Generally, any type of conversion that occurs after a person obtains lawful possession of property is sufficient.

Although a failure to return property is evidence of conversion, it does not necessarily constitute embezzlement—absent proof of criminal intent. On the other hand, if a statute imposes an absolute duty to return property, the failure to do so is embezzlement provided all other elements are met.

In certain circumstances, a demand is required before a person can claim that his or her property has been converted. Usually, no demand is required if it would be futile, such as when an accused has fled the jurisdiction with the property. If, however, there is no definite time specified for the return of the property, a demand might be necessary. The demand is merely a request that the wrongdoer return the property. The request does not have to be formal, and there is no requirement that the word *demand* be used.

When an agent is given authority to sell property, and thereafter converts the proceeds of the sale, he or she is guilty of embezzlement of the proceeds, as distinguished from the property sold. A person with authority to cash a check but who converts the cash is, likewise, guilty of embezzlement of the cash and not of the check. The person, might, however, be guilty of embezzling the check if at the time of cashing it, the person has a fraudulent intent to convert it.

Intent In a majority of jurisdictions, a fraudulent intent to deprive the owner of his or her property is necessary for embezzlement. It is characterized as an intent to willfully and corruptly use or misapply another's property for purposes other than those for which the

Embezzlement

Persons arrested for embezzlement by age, 1993

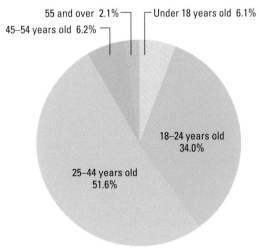

55 and over 2.1%
45–54 years old 6.2%
Under 18 years old 6.1%
18–24 years old 34.0%
25–44 years old 51.6%

Source: U.S. Federal Bureau of Investigation, *Crime in the United States*, annual.

property is held. The defendant's motive is not relevant to the intent element.

Although it is not essential that the intent exist at the time possession is first taken, it must be formed at the time the property is converted. The offense is not committed if there is an intent to return the specific property taken within a reasonable period of time. If, however, there is a fraudulent intent at the time the property is converted, a subsequently formed intent to return the property will not excuse the crime. An offer to restore the property will not bar a prosecution for embezzlement. Some courts have held, however, that an offer of restoration can be considered on the question of intent.

A person who believes that the property to be transferred is his or hers is considered to act pursuant to a claim of right. The possibility that the belief is mistaken, or unreasonable, is not important. If one has a GOOD FAITH belief that one has a right to withhold property or devote it to one's own use, the conversion cannot be fraudulent, and there is no embezzlement.

The validity of a claim of right is a question of fact determined from CIRCUMSTANTIAL EVIDENCE. It is not sufficient if the person merely states he or she acted honestly. If circumstances evince that there was a willful and knowingly wrongful taking, a claim of right defense will not succeed.

Persons Liable One or more persons may be guilty of embezzlement. If there is a CONSPIRACY to embezzle, parties to the agreement are liable as principals. A person who AIDS AND ABETS in the conversion can also be guilty of the offense.

Punishment Since the offense is defined differently in several jurisdictions, the punishment for embezzlement can vary. Generally, the penalty is a fine, imprisonment, or both.

Some states distinguish between grand embezzlement and petit embezzlement on the basis of the value of the property stolen. The former involves property of a greater value and is punishable as a FELONY, while the latter involves property of a lesser value and is punishable as a MISDEMEANOR.

EMBLEMENTS 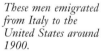 CROPS annually produced by the labor of a tenant. Corn, wheat, rye, potatoes, garden vegetables, and other crops that are produced annually, not spontaneously, but by labor and industry. The doctrine of emblements denotes the right of a TENANT to take and carry away, after the tenancy has ended, such annual products of the land as have resulted from the tenant's care and labor.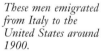

EMBRACERY The crime of attempting to influence a JURY corruptly to one side or the

other by promises, persuasions, entreaties, entertainments, and the like. The person guilty of it is called an *embraceor.* This is both a state and federal crime, and is commonly included under the offense of OBSTRUCTING JUSTICE.

In order for the offense of embracery to be committed, it is essential that the accused individual have an improper intent. If an individual makes statements that would be likely to influence the VERDICT of a juror while the individual is unaware that such juror is present, such conduct is not embracery.

It is not generally a prerequisite for the juror to have been impaneled and sworn, provided the person's name has been drawn and published as a juror or grand juror.

The intent to influence a juror must be coupled with an ATTEMPT to use improper influence, which can be through word or conduct and is the only overt act necessary. The juror can either be approached personally by the individual or through an AGENT. Words intended to influence a juror need not be spoken to the person directly but can be communicated in a manner designed to be overheard by the juror and PREJUDICE his or her decision.

A PARTY to the ACTION, an individual undergoing GRAND JURY investigation, a WITNESS, or an individual who has no connection with the proceeding can be charged with embracery.

Since the crime of embracery itself only constitutes an attempt, there is no such crime as the *attempt to commit embracery.* It is, however, a crime to solicit another to commit embracery.

Embracery is punishable by a fine, imprisonment, or both, depending upon statute.

EMIGRATION The act of moving from one country to another with intention not to return. It is to be distinguished from EXPATRIA-

These men emigrated from Italy to the United States around 1900.

TION, which means the abandonment of one's country and renunciation of one's citizenship in it, while emigration denotes merely the removal of person and property to another country. Expatriation is usually the consequence of emigration. *Emigration* is also sometimes used in reference to the removal from one section to another of the same country. ▥

EMINENT DOMAIN ▥ The power to take private PROPERTY for public use by a state, municipality, or private person or CORPORATION authorized to exercise functions of public character, following the payment of JUST COMPENSATION to the owner of that property. ▥

Federal, state, and local governments may take private property through their power of eminent domain or may regulate it by exercising their POLICE POWER. The Fifth Amendment to the U.S. Constitution requires the government to provide just compensation to the owner of the private property to be taken. A variety of PROPERTY RIGHTS are subject to eminent domain, such as air, water, and land rights. The government takes private property through CONDEMNATION proceedings. Throughout these proceedings, the property owner has the right of DUE PROCESS.

Eminent domain is a challenging area for the courts, which have struggled with the question of whether the regulation of property, rather than its acquisition, is a taking requiring just compensation. In addition, private property owners have begun to initiate action against the government in a proceeding called inverse condemnation.

History The concept of eminent domain is not new. It has existed since biblical times, when King Ahab of Samaria offered Naboth compensation for Naboth's vineyard. In 1789, France officially recognized a property owner's right to compensation for taken property, in the French Declaration of the Rights of Man and of the Citizen, which reads, "Property being an inviolable and sacred right no one can be deprived of it, unless the public necessity plainly demands it, and upon condition of a just and previous indemnity."

Shortly after the French declaration, the United States acknowledged eminent domain in the FIFTH AMENDMENT to the Constitution, which states, ". . . nor shall private property be taken for public use, without just compensation."

The Fifth Amendment grants the federal government the right to exercise its power of eminent domain, and the Due Process Clause of the FOURTEENTH AMENDMENT makes the federal guarantee of just compensation applicable to the states. State governments derive the power to initiate condemnation proceedings from their state constitutions, except North Carolina, which gains its power through statute. The constitutional and statutory provisions require federal, state, and local governments and subdivisions of government to pay an owner for property taken for public use at the time the property is taken.

Eminent domain was created to authorize the government or the condemning authority, called the condemnor, to conduct a compulsory sale of property for the common welfare, such as health or safety. Just compensation is required to ease the financial burden incurred by the property owner for the benefit of the public.

Elements of Eminent Domain To exercise the power of eminent domain, the government must prove that the four elements set forth in the Fifth Amendment are present: (1) private property (2) must be taken (3) for public use (4) and with just compensation. These elements have been interpreted broadly.

Private Property The first element requires that the property taken be private. Private property includes land as well as FIXTURES, LEASES, OPTIONS, STOCKS, and other items. The rifle that was used to kill President JOHN F. KENNEDY was considered private property in an eminent domain proceeding.

Taking The second element refers to the taking of physical property, or a portion thereof, as well as the taking of property by reducing its VALUE. Property value may be reduced because of noise, accessibility problems, or other agents. Dirt, timber, or rock appropriated from an individual's land for the construction of a highway is taken property for which the owner is entitled to compensation. In general, compensation must be paid when a restriction on the use of property is so extensive that it is tantamount to CONFISCATION of the property.

Some property rights routinely receive constitutional protection, such as WATER RIGHTS. For example, if land is changed from waterfront to inland property by the construction of a highway on the shoreline, the owners of the affected property are to be compensated for their loss of use of the waterfront.

Another property right that is often litigated and routinely protected is the right to the reasonable and ordinary use of the space above privately owned land. Specifically, aircraft flights over private property that significantly interfere with the property owner's use may amount to a taking. The flights will not be deemed a taking unless they are so low and so frequent as to create a direct and immediate interference with the owner's use and enjoyment of the property.

The flight of aircraft over private property can constitute a taking if it interferes with the property owner's use and enjoyment of the property.

Actions by the government that courts do not consider takings include the publication of plans or the plotting, locating, or laying out of public improvements, including streets, highways, and other public works, even though the publicity generated by such actions may hinder a sale of the land.

The courts have traditionally not recognized the REGULATION of property by the government as a taking. Regulating property restricts the property owner's use and may infringe on the owner's rights. To implement a regulation, the state exercises its police power and is able to control the use of the property. Although the courts recognized a regulation as a taking in 1922, they have been inconsistent in their later rulings on this issue. In *Pennsylvania Coal Co. v. Mahon*, 260 U.S. 393, 43 S. Ct. 158, 67 L. Ed. 322 (1922), the Supreme Court ruled that coal mining under an owner's property was not a taking, despite a subsidence, or settling, of the property's surface. In 1987, the Supreme Court stated that regulations that are excessive require compensation under the Fifth Amendment (*First English Evangelical Lutheran Church of Glendale v. County of Los Angeles*, 482 U.S. 304, 107 S. Ct. 2378, 96 L. Ed. 2d 250 [1987]). More recently, the Court determined that regulations that strip property of value or that do not substantially advance legitimate state interests are takings for which compensation is required (*Nollan v. California Coastal Commission*, 483 U.S. 825, 107 S. Ct. 3141, 97 L. Ed. 2d 677 [1987]).

Public Use The third element, public use, requires that the property taken be used to benefit the public instead of specific individuals. Whether a particular use is considered public is ordinarily a question to be determined by the courts. However, if the legislature has made a declaration about a specific public use, the courts will defer to legislative intent (*Hawaii Housing Authority v. Midkiff*, 467 U.S. 229, 104 S. Ct. 2321, 81 L. Ed. 2d 186 [1984]). Further, "[t]he legislature may determine what private property is needed for public purpose . . . but when the taking has been ordered, then the question of compensation is judicial" (*Monongahela Navigation Co. v. United States*, 148 U.S. 312, 13 S. Ct. 622, 37 L. Ed. 463 [1893]).

To determine whether property has been taken for public use, the courts first determined whether the property was to be used by a broad segment of the general public. The definition of public use was later broadened to include anything that benefited the public, such as trade centers, municipal civic centers, and airport expansions. The Supreme Court continued to expand the definition of public use to include aesthetic considerations. In *Berman v. Parker*, 348 U.S. 26, 75 S. Ct. 98, 99 L. Ed. 27 (1954), the Court ruled that slums could be cleared in order to make a city more attractive. The Court in *Berman* stated further that it is within legislative power to determine whether a property can be condemned solely to beautify a community.

State courts have also expanded the definition of public use. The Michigan Supreme Court even allowed property to be condemned for the private use of the General Motors Company, under the theory that the public would benefit from the economic revitalization a new plant would bring to the community (*Poletown Neighborhood Council v. City of Detroit*, 410 Mich. 616, 304 N.W.2d 455 [1981]).

Just Compensation The last element set forth in the Fifth Amendment mandates that the amount of compensation awarded when property is seized or damaged through condemnation must be fair to the public as well as to the property owner (*Searl v. School District No. 2 of Lake County*, 133 U.S. 553, 10 S. Ct. 374, 33 L. Ed. 740 [1890]). Because no precise formula for determining it exists, just compensation is the subject of frequent litigation.

The courts tend to emphasize the rights of the property owner in eminent domain proceedings. The owner usually has not initiated the action but has been brought into the litigation because her or his property is needed for public use. The owner must participate in the proceedings, which can impose an emotional and financial burden.

The measure of DAMAGES is often the FAIR MARKET VALUE of the property harmed or taken for public use. The market value is commonly defined as the price that could have reasonably resulted from negotiations between an owner who was willing to sell and a purchaser who desired to buy. The value of REAL PROPERTY is assessed based on the uses to which it can reasonably be put. Elements for consideration include the history and general character of the area, the adaptability of the land for future buildings, and the use intended for the property after its taking. Generally, the best use of the land is considered to be its use at the time it was condemned, even though the condemnor may not intend to use the land in the same manner as the owner. Crops, grass, trees, minerals, rental income, and all other items that fairly enter into the question of value are taken into consideration when determining just compensation. The amount of compensation should be measured by the owner's loss rather than the condemnor's gain, and the owner should be placed in as good a financial position as he or she would have been in had the property not been taken (*Monongahela*). The compensation should be paid in cash, and the amount is determined as of the date TITLE vests in the condemnor. Interest is paid on the award until the date of payment.

Condemnation Proceedings Condemnation proceedings vary according to individual state and federal laws. In general, the proceedings should be conducted as quickly as possible. A proceeding does not require court involvement if the condemnor and landowner enter into a CONTRACT for the taking of the property for a public use. A SEIZURE pursuant to such a contract is as effective as if it were done through formal condemnation proceedings.

Condemnation usually consists of two phases: proceedings that relate to the right of the condemnor to take the property, and proceedings to set the amount of compensation to be paid for the property taken. The commencement of the proceedings does not curtail ordinary use of the condemned property by the owner as long as the use does not substantially change the condition of the property or its value.

States require special procedures for certain cases categorized by either the purpose for which the property is sought or the character of the party seeking to take it. For example, a special procedure is required when property is to be taken for a street, highway, park, drain, levee, sewer, canal, or waterway. In a procedure called a quick taking, the condemnor is permitted to take immediate POSSESSION and use of the property, and the owner must receive cash compensation in advance of the proceeding.

The owner has the right to due process during condemnation proceedings. The owner must be notified in a timely manner and given reasonable opportunity to be heard on the issues of whether the use for which the property is expropriated is public and whether the compensation is just. Due process mandates that the landowner receive an opportunity to present EVIDENCE and to confront or cross-examine WITNESSES. The owner has an automatic right to APPEAL.

RAFAEL MACIA/PHOTO RESEARCHERS

In order to exercise the power of eminent domain, the government must prove that the land taken will be for public use, such as a highway.

Due process does not require a JURY trial in condemnation proceedings, although various state constitutions and statutes provide for assessment by a jury. Absent contrary state provisions, a court has the discretionary power to grant or refuse a MOTION for view of the premises by a jury. A condemnation judgment or order must be recorded.

Inverse Condemnation An increase in environmental problems has resulted in a new type of eminent domain proceeding, called inverse condemnation. In this proceeding, the property owner, rather than the condemnor, initiates the action. The owner alleges that the government has acquired an interest in her or his property without giving compensation, such as when the government floods a farmer's field or pollutes a stream crossing private land. An inverse condemnation proceeding is often brought by a property owner when it appears that the taker of the property does not intend to bring eminent domain proceedings.

EMOLUMENT The profit arising from office, employment, or labor; that which is received as a compensation for services, or which is annexed to the possession of office as salary, fees, and PERQUISITES. Any perquisite, advantage, profit, or gain arising from the possession of an office.

EMPLOYEE RETIREMENT INCOME SECURITY ACT The name of federal legislation, popularly abbreviated as ERISA (29 U.S.C.A. § 1001 et seq. [1974]), which regulates the financing, vesting, and administration of PENSION plans for workers in private business and industry.

The 1974 enactment of ERISA by Congress was intended to preserve and protect the rights of employees to their pensions upon retirement by establishing statutory requirements that govern such matters.

EMPLOYERS' LIABILITY ACTS State and federal laws that define or restrict the grounds under, and the extent to, which the owner of a business who hires workers can be held liable for DAMAGES arising from injuries to such workers that occur during the course of the work.

Statutes such as the Federal Employers' Liability Act (10 U.S.C.A. § 51 et seq. [1908]) and WORKERS' COMPENSATION laws abrogate the principle of COMMON LAW that an employer is not liable to employees who have been injured by the fault or NEGLIGENCE of a fellow worker during the COURSE OF EMPLOYMENT.

EMPLOYMENT AT WILL A common-law rule that an employment CONTRACT of indefinite duration can be terminated by either the employer or the employee at any time for any reason; also known as terminable at will.

Traditionally, U.S. employers have possessed the right to discharge their employees at will for any reason, be it good or bad. The "at-will" category encompasses all employees who are not protected by express employment contracts that state that they may be fired only for GOOD CAUSE. "Good cause" requirements are typically a part of COLLECTIVE BARGAINING AGREEMENTS negotiated by employee unions; nonunion workers rarely have this form of protection.

Today, the United States is the only major industrial power that maintains a general employment-at-will rule. Canada, France, Germany, Great Britain, Italy, Japan, and Sweden all have statutory provisions that require employers to show good cause before discharging employees.

Beginning in the 1980s, employment at will came under challenge in the United States. Employees have grown increasingly dissatisfied with the rule for a variety of reasons. For one thing, a decline in the number of self-employed individuals—due, in part, to a continuing decline in the number of farmers—means that most U.S. citizens work for someone else. For another, a typical worker who is discharged loses more today than in the past in terms of PENSION, INSURANCE, and other benefits.

As a result, a greater number of discharged workers have brought suits alleging wrongful discharge from employment. By the 1980s, as concepts of job security expanded, employees had become increasingly successful in such suits. In 1987, California juries ruled in favor of the employees in over two-thirds of such cases and granted an average award of $1.5 million. In some successful cases, the courts have created exceptions to the employment-at-will practice. Thus far, these exceptions have fallen into three broad categories: (1) breach of contract by the employer, (2) breach of an implied covenant of good faith and fair dealing, and (3) violation of public policy by the employer. Employers and legislatures have responded in a variety of ways.

Breach of Contract Approximately half of the states have allowed exceptions to employment at will on the basis of an express or implied promise by the employer. Typically, a wrongful discharge action alleging the breach of an employer's promise is based on a statement by the employer that expressly or implicitly promises employees a degree of job security. Ordinarily, such statements are found in employee handbooks or in policy memorandums given to employees when they are hired. Some courts have interpreted such statements as unilateral contracts in which the employer promises not to discharge the employees except for just cause and in accordance with certain procedures (*Duldulao v. Saint Mary of Nazareth Hospital Center*, 115 Ill. 2d 482, 106 Ill. Dec. 8, 505 N.E.2d 314 [Ill. 1987]). Courts have been more reluctant to find exceptions to the employment-at-will practice in cases that involve an oral promise of long-term employment.

Breach of an Implied Covenant of Good Faith and Fair Dealing In wrongful dismissal cases based on an implied COVENANT of GOOD FAITH and fair dealing, the discharged employee typically contends that the employer has indicated in various ways that the employee has job security and will be treated fairly. For example, long time employees who have consistently received favorable evaluations might claim that their length of service and positive performance reviews were signs that their job would be secure as long as they performed satisfactorily.

Courts that have recognized good-faith-and-fair-dealing exceptions have found either covenants implied in fact or covenants implied in law. Covenants implied in fact have been found in "objective manifestations," including repeated promotions and pay increases, that might reasonably give an employee cause to believe that he or she has job security and will be treated fairly (*Dare v. Montana Petroleum Marketing*, 687 P.2d 1015 [Mont. 1984]; *Kerr v. Gibson's Products Co.*, 733 P.2d 1292 [Mont. 1987]).

A few JURISDICTIONS have recognized implied-in-law covenants of good faith and fair dealing. California courts have ruled that every employment contract carries with it an implied covenant that neither party will impede the other from receiving the benefits of the agreement. In deciding whether such a covenant is to be inferred, a court looks at such factors as whether the company properly followed its stated personnel policies, the length of the person's employment, any job security assurances that may have been made, a presence or lack of prior criticism of performance, and basic notions of fairness.

In *Khanna v. Microdata Corp.*, 170 Cal. App. 3d 250, 215 Cal. Rptr. 860 (1985), for example, a California court of appeals ruled that a company violated an implied covenant when it fired a leading salesman who had brought suit against the company for unpaid commissions. The court found that a breach of an implied-in-law covenant is established whenever an employer

engages in a bad-faith action outside of a contract and attempts to frustrate an employee's enjoyment of her or his contract rights.

Violation of Public Policy Several PUBLIC POLICY exceptions to the employment-at-will practice have been recognized by courts in some jurisdictions. In public policy cases, the employee alleges that he or she has been discharged in violation of a policy found in a statutory right of the employee, statutes containing penalties, constitutional provisions, and judicial opinions. Courts have generally been more willing to recognize a public policy exception when the policy in question has a statutory basis than when it does not.

Courts in many jurisdictions have been willing to recognize public policy exceptions for employees who were discharged because they asserted a statutory right. For example, in *Firestone Textile Co. Division, Firestone Tire & Rubber Co. v. Meadows*, 666 S.W.2d 730 (1983), the Supreme Court of Kentucky ruled that an employer could not discharge an employee simply because he had filed a WORKERS' COMPENSATION claim.

A public policy exception to employment at will has also been found in cases where an employee was fired for refusing to violate a statute. Wrongful discharge has been found in instances where employees were dismissed for refusing to dispose of waste in a place where doing so is prohibited by federal law, for refusing to commit PERJURY, and for giving TESTIMONY in compliance with a court order.

Courts have much less frequently been willing to recognize exceptions to employment at will owing to constitutional provisions. Nevertheless, in *Novosel v. Nationwide Insurance Co.*, 721 F.2d 894 (3d Cir. 1983), a federal appeals court made a public policy exception for an

A French employee may not be dismissed from a job unless his or her employer has shown good cause to do so.

employee who was dismissed for refusing to join a company's LOBBYING effort because he privately opposed the company's stance on the issue. The court found that the free speech provisions of the Pennsylvania Constitution and the U.S. Constitution's First Amendment protected the employee's refusal. In *Borse v. Piece Goods Shop*, 963 F.2d 611 (1992), a federal circuit court of appeals ruled that Pennsylvania law may protect at-will employees from being fired for refusing to take part in drug-testing programs if the employees' PRIVACY is unreasonably invaded.

The Response by Employers and Legislatures Legal guidelines relating to the status of employment at will are still developing or remain unclear in many states. The evolving judgments of legislatures and courts on this issue reflect a continuing debate over how to protect wrongfully discharged at-will employees while allowing employers the freedom to make personnel decisions.

The rising number of wrongful dismissal suits has alarmed many employers. Faced with the threat of high legal fees, court costs, and huge potential damage awards in such cases, more companies have begun to add express employment-at-will clauses to employment contracts. Many employers have deleted potentially troublesome statements from their handbooks and instructed recruiters to make no promises about just cause or the term of employment. Companies are also turning more frequently to severance pay settlements, in which discharged employees receive a reasonably generous compensation package in exchange for waiving all future claims based on the employment or its termination.

U.S. employers have the right to discharge employees at will for any reason under the common-law rule of employment at will.

The decline of the power of employee unions and COLLECTIVE BARGAINING has provided many employers with the freedom to insert the new contract clauses. In many instances, companies are concerned more with losing expensive termination lawsuits than with inciting union action or public BOYCOTTS.

Whereas employers claim they are simply reasserting their rights under the traditional at-will doctrine, employee advocates believe that many companies may be attempting to cheat workers out of the job security gains they have achieved through several decades of wrongful dismissal lawsuits. They propose legislation that would protect at-will employees from unjust discharge and provide for arbitrators to handle disputes. This solution, they suggest, would be fair to employees and employers alike. Such legislation would protect at-will employees, not just those who fall under the exceptions and who can afford to pursue a lawsuit that may take years to complete. Businesses would benefit not only because employee morale might improve, but also because relief could be limited to back pay and reinstatement rather than possibly including punitive and COMPENSATORY DAMAGES.

Some state legislatures have enacted legislation that struggles to balance the rights of the employee and the employer. In 1987, Montana passed the Montana Wrongful Discharge from Employment Act (Mont. Code Ann. § 39-2-901). This law limits the rights of employees claiming wrongful discharge, by restating the principle that at-will employees may be dismissed for "any reason considered sufficient by the terminating party." However, a discharge could be considered wrongful even under this principle if it was in retaliation for the employee's refusal to violate public policy, if it was not for good cause, or if the employer violated the express provisions of the employer's own personnel policy.

The Montana statute limits the remedies of a discharged employee who sues the former employer. The employee may be awarded lost wages and fringe benefits but only for a period not to exceed four years, and PUNITIVE DAMAGES may be sought only when there is clear and convincing evidence that the employer engaged in actual FRAUD or MALICE in the wrongful discharge. In addition, any earnings that were or could have been accrued following the discharge must be deducted from the amount awarded in lost wages. The Montana Supreme Court upheld the constitutionality of the act in *Meech v. Hillhaven West*, 776 P.2d 488 (1989).

See also EMPLOYMENT LAW.

EMPLOYMENT LAW 📖 The body of law that governs the employer-employee relation-

GREENLAR/THE IMAGE WORKS

In the late nineteenth century the rise of industrialization led to the mass production of capital and consumer goods. The employees in this factory were hired under the concept of liberty of contract, but by the 1930s workers' right to collective bargaining was recognized.

ship, including individual employment contracts, the application of TORT and CONTRACT doctrines, and a large group of statutory regulation on issues such as the right to organize and negotiate COLLECTIVE BARGAINING AGREEMENTS, protection from DISCRIMINATION, wages and hours, and health and safety. 📖

In the modern world, employment is the means by which goods and services are provided. Beyond establishing an economic relationship between employer and employee, work provides a powerful structure for organizing social and cultural life. The employment relationship is more than the exchange of labor for money. In U.S. society, self-worth, dignity, satisfaction, and accomplishment are achieved primarily by one's employment responsibilities, performance, and rewards. The development of employment law demonstrates the importance of work. Since the 1930s, employees have acquired more legal rights as federal and state governments have enacted laws that give them the power and authority to unionize, to engage in collective bargaining, and to be protected from discrimination based on race, gender, or disability.

History English COMMON LAW, and subsequently early U.S. law, defined the relationship between an employer and an employee as that of MASTER AND SERVANT. The master-and-servant relationship arose only when the tasks performed by the servant were under the direction and control of the master and were subject to the master's knowledge and consent.

With the rise of industrialization and mass production in the 1800s, the U.S. economic structure changed dramatically. Employers needed masses of employees to run the equipment that produced capital and consumer goods. By the end of the nineteenth century, the U.S. economy was attracting millions of immigrants. In addition, migration from country to city accelerated.

Nineteenth-century employment law was based on the concept of liberty of contract: a worker had the freedom to bargain with an employer for terms of employment. This concept was challenged when workers organized into unions and engaged employers in COLLECTIVE BARGAINING. The U.S. legal and economic systems at the time were opposed to the idea of collective bargaining. Union organizers noted the inequality of bargaining power between a prospective employee and an employer.

Judges were hostile to attempts by state governments to regulate the hours and wages of employees. In *Lochner v. New York*, 198 U.S. 45, 25 S. Ct. 539, 49 L. Ed. 937 (1905), the U.S. Supreme Court, on a 5–4 vote, struck down a New York state law (N. Y. Laws 1897, chap. 415, art. 8, § 110) that specified a maximum sixty-hour week for bakery employees. The Court ruled that the law was a "meddlesome interference" with business, concluding that the regulation of work hours was an unjustified infringement on "the right to labor, and with the right of free contract on the part of the individual, either as employer or employee."

The U.S. labor movement's persistent attempts to break free of the liberty-of-contract doctrine ultimately led to major changes in employment law. The New Deal era of the 1930s brought federal recognition of the right of workers to organize themselves as unions and collectively bargain with management. The passage of the WAGNER ACT, also known as the National Labor Relations Act of 1935 (29 U.S.C.A. § 151 et seq.), established these rights and also proscribed unfair labor practices (actions taken by employers that interfere with the union rights of employees). The act also established the NATIONAL LABOR RELATIONS BOARD, a federal administrative agency, to administer and enforce its provisions.

Since the 1950s, the federal government has led the way in providing employees more rights concerning the employment relationship.

Physical Safety Both federal and state statutes regulate workplace hazards to avoid or minimize employee injury and disease. These laws deal with problems such as dangerous machinery, hazardous materials, and noise. A more recent trend has been the banning of smoking in the workplace. All of these laws place the burden on employers to maintain a safe and healthy workplace.

The federal government's main tool in workplace safety is the OCCUPATIONAL SAFETY AND HEALTH ACT of 1970 (OSHA) (29 U.S.C.A. §§ 651–678 [1988]). OSHA attempts to balance the employee's need for a safe and healthy working environment against the employer's desire to function without undue government interference. OSHA issues occupational safety and health standards, and employers must meet these standards or face civil and, in rare occurrences, criminal penalties.

When an employee is injured on the job, the employee may file a compensation claim with the state WORKERS' COMPENSATION system. Prior to World War I, an injured employee had to sue his or her employer in state court, alleging a tort violation. This rarely proved successful, as employees were reluctant to testify about work conditions and risk the possible loss of their job. Without witnesses, an employee had little chance of recovery. In addition, employers were protected by legal defenses to NEGLIGENCE that usually allowed them to escape LIABILITY.

Dissatisfaction with this situation led the states to enact workers' compensation laws, which set up an administrative process for compensating employees for work-related injuries. These systems provide compensation while a worker is physically unable to work (temporary disability), provide retraining if the employee can no longer perform the same job, and provide compensation indefinitely if the worker has been severely injured (total disability). Medical benefits are paid for treatment of work-related injuries. Depending on the state, employers fund this system by making state-regulated contributions to a workers' compensation insurance fund, paying INSURANCE premiums to a private insurance company, or assuming the risk through self-insurance.

Discrimination Since the 1960s, employment law has changed most radically in the protection it gives employees against discrimination in the workplace. Although the federal government banned racial discrimination in the making of contracts in the Civil Rights Acts of 1870 and 1871 (42 U.S.C.A. §§ 1981, 1983), the federal courts narrowly construed the provisions to prevent their being used in the employment context. Not until the 1970s did federal courts allow those provisions to be applied to complaints of discrimination by individual employees (*McDonald v. Santa Fe Trail Transportation Co.*, 427 U.S. 273, 96 S. Ct. 2574, 49 L. Ed. 2d 493 [1976]).

Employment Law

Civilian Labor Force Participation Rates, 1970 to 1994

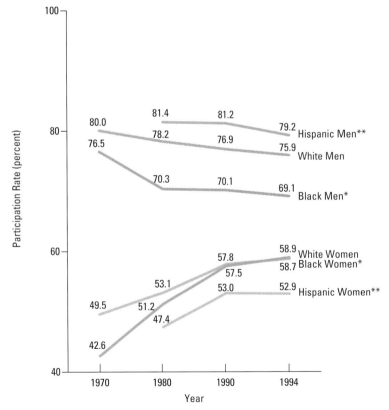

* For 1970, Black and other races.
** Persons of Hispanic origin may be of any race. Statistics for Hispanic men and women were not available for 1970.

Source: U.S. Bureau of Labor Statistics, Bulletin 2307, *Employment and Earnings*, monthly, January issues; *Monthly Labor Review*.

Federal legislation in the 1960s provided employees more avenues to challenge alleged discrimination. The 1963 Equal Pay Act (29 U.S.C.A. § 216 (d)) requires employers to pay men and women equal wages for equal work. The CIVIL RIGHTS ACT of 1964 (42 U.S.C.A. § 2000e et seq.) contains broad prohibitions against discrimination on the basis of race, color, religion, national origin, or sex. Discrimination against persons ages forty and over was banned in 1967 by the Age Discrimination in Employment Act (29 U.S.C.A. § 621 et seq.).

Major amendments to the general civil rights acts were passed in 1972, extending coverage to federal and state employees; in 1978, clarifying the protection of pregnant women; and in 1991, overruling a series of decisions by the Supreme Court that had restricted the reach of antidiscrimination statutes.

In 1990, Congress enacted the Americans with Disabilities Act (ADA) (42 U.S.C.A. § 12101 et seq.), forbidding discrimination against qualified individuals with disabilities and requiring reasonable efforts to accommodate persons with disabilities in some situations.

With the growth of federal antidiscrimination statutes, many states have passed laws banning employment discrimination. A number of cities have also enacted their own programs. Some states and cities deal with issues not covered by the federal statutes, such as discrimination on the basis of sexual orientation.

Termination of Employment   Historically, employment law has limited an employee's right to challenge an employer's unfair, adverse, or damaging practices. The law has generally denied any redress to an employee who is arbitrarily treated, unless the employee is represented by a union or has rights under a written employment contract. Absent these two conditions, or a statutory provision, the general rule has been that an employee or an employer can terminate the employment relationship at any time, for any or no reason, with or without notice. This rule forms the core of the "at-will" employment doctrine.

The at-will doctrine was articulated and refined by U.S. state courts in the 1800s. It provided employers with the flexibility to control the workplace by terminating employees as economic demand slackened. For employees, it provided a simple way of leaving a job if a better employment prospect became available or if working conditions were intolerable.

The at-will employment doctrine has been modified by courts and legislatures. A public policy exception recognizes that an employee should not be terminated because the employee refused to act in an unlawful manner, attempted to perform a duty prescribed by statute, exercised a legal right, or reported unlawful or improper employer conduct ("whistleblowing").

At-will employees may be protected even if no written contract exists. Many state courts now recognize employee rights that are contained in personnel policies or employee handbooks. As businesses grow larger, formal rules and procedures are needed to streamline administrative issues. A handbook or employment policy manual usually contains rules of expected employee behavior, disciplinary or termination procedures that apply if the rules are violated, and compensation and benefit information. An employer must follow the rules for firing an employee that are set out in the handbook or manual, or risk a lawsuit for wrongful termination.

If an employer terminates an employee, the employer must be prepared to show "good cause" for the firing. With the many statutes that forbid discrimination in the workplace, the employer has the burden of showing a nondiscriminatory reason. Good cause can include inadequate job performance, job-related misconduct, certain types of off-the-job conduct, and business needs.

Privacy and Reputation   When an individual seeks employment some PRIVACY rights are surrendered. To become employed, the individual will be asked to disclose personal information and may be required to submit to continuing evaluation. Current or prospective employees may be asked to submit to a physical examination, a polygraph examination, a psychological evaluation, a test for illegal drugs, or a test for HIV. Employers have the right to search lockers or frisk employees even if no reasonable suspicion of theft exists. The modern workplace can be checked by an employer through the monitoring of phone lines and personal computers.

Courts and legislatures have expressed increasing concern about the improper use of information that employers collect on employees. Employers who distribute information more widely than necessary, reveal confidential medical or personal information about an employee, or intrude on an employee's personal, off-work behavior risk lawsuits for invasion of privacy.

The issue of DEFAMATION also affects employment law. Defamation is subdivided into the torts of LIBEL, which involves a writing, and slander, which concerns speech. Liability for defamation may be imposed if an employer

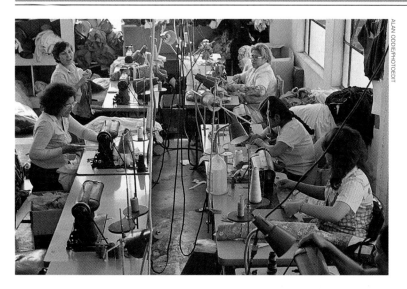

The Fair Labor Standards Act imposes minimum wage standards and overtime standards on employers. Employees who work more than eight hours a day are paid time and a half for overtime hours.

makes a statement about an employee that is false and hurts the reputation of the employee. Employers have been successfully sued for defamation for communicating unfavorable job recommendations about a former employee. As a result, employers are reluctant to give more than basic employment history when asked for a job reference. Also, twenty-five states have enacted "good faith" job reference laws, which protect employers who divulge employee job performance information to a prospective employer.

Wage and Hour Regulations The FAIR LABOR STANDARDS ACT (FLSA) (29 U.S.C.A. § 201 et seq.) imposes minimum wage standards and overtime standards on most employers. The minimum hourly wage is a means of ensuring that a full-time worker can maintain a minimum standard of living; overtime standards mandate that an employer pay employees at least time and a half for working more than eight hours a day. The FLSA does not preempt states or localities from setting a higher minimum wage. An employer operating in a state or locality with a higher minimum wage than that set by the FLSA must abide by the higher standard.

Pensions and Other Employee Benefits The federal government regulates em-

ployee benefit plans under the EMPLOYEE RETIREMENT INCOME SECURITY ACT (ERISA), 29 U.S.C.A. § 1001 et seq., passed in 1974. Title I of the act (29 U.S.C.A. § 1011 et seq.) provides rules with respect to participation, vesting and funding of benefits plans, fiduciary responsibility, reporting and disclosure, and administration and enforcement. Title II contains tax law provisions as amendments to the Internal Revenue Code of 1954 (26 U.S.C.A. § 401 et seq.). Title III deals with jurisdiction, administration, and enforcement (29 U.S.C.A. § 1201 et seq.). Title IV creates the Pension Benefit Guaranty Corporation and establishes a system of employee plan termination insurance (29 U.S.C.A. § 1301 et seq.).

ERISA does not require an employer to provide employee benefit plans. However, if an employer sets up a qualified plan (one that meets ERISA's standards), the employer can take a tax deduction for the employer's contribution. The employer can also deduct the full amount of an employee group health plan that meets tax code standards.

The Family and Medical Leave Act of 1993 (FAMLA) (29 U.S.C.A. § 2601 et seq.) establishes the right of employees to take unpaid leave for family reasons. FAMLA applies to employers of fifty or more. It entitles an employee to take up to twelve weeks of leave during a twelve-month period because of the birth of a child to the employee, the placement of a child with the employee for adoption or foster care, the serious health condition of a family member of the employee, or the employee's own serious health condition.

CROSS-REFERENCES

Age Discrimination; Civil Rights; Disabled Persons; E-Mail; Employment at Will; Gay and Lesbian Rights; Labor Law; Labor Union; *Lochner v. New York;* Pension; Sex Discrimination; Sexual Harassment; Whistle-Blowing.

ENABLING CLAUSE The section of a constitution or statute that provides government officials with the power to put the constitution or statute into force and effect.

Clause 2 of the Nineteenth Amendment is an example of an enabling clause

_____ **AMENDMENT XIX [1920]**

[1] The right of citizens of the United States to vote shall not be denied or abridged by the United States or by any State on account of sex.

[2] Congress shall have power to enforce this article by appropriate legislation.

An example of an enabling statute

ARTICLE 2. GENERAL POWERS AND DUTIES
A. GENERAL PROVISIONS

26:3-31. Enumeration of Specific powers and duties

The local board of health shall have power to pass, alter or amend ordinances and make rules and regulations in regard to the public health within its jurisdiction, for the following purposes:

[Portions omitted for purpose of illustration.]

To act as the agent for a landlord in the engaging of repairmen and the ordering of any parts necessary to restore to operating condition the furnace, boiler or other equipment essential to the proper heating of any residential unit rented by said landlord, provided, however, that at least 24 hours have elapsed since the tenant has lodged a complaint with the local board of health, prior to which a bona fide attempt has been made by the tenant to notify the landlord of the failure of the heating equipment, and the landlord has failed to take appropriate action, and the outside air temperature is less than 55° F.

Any person who supplies material or services in accordance with this section shall bill the landlord directly and by filing a notice approved by the local board of health, with the county clerk, shall have a lien on the premises where the materials were used or services supplied.

Seven of the amendments to the U.S. Constitution contain clauses that give CONGRESS the power to enforce their provisions by appropriate legislation.

ENABLING STATUTE 📖 A law that gives new or extended authority or powers, generally to a public official or to a CORPORATION. 📖

Samples of an enabling clause and an enabling statute appear at left and above.

ENACT 📖 To establish by law; to perform or effect; to decree. 📖

Enact, sometimes used synonymously with ADOPT, is generally applied to legislative rather than executive action.

EN BANC 📖 [*Latin, French. In the bench.*] Full bench. Refers to a session where the entire membership of the court will participate in the decision rather than the regular quorum. In other countries, it is common for a court to have more members than are usually necessary to hear an appeal. In the United States, the Circuit Courts of Appeal usually sit in panels of judges but for important cases may expand the bench to a larger number, when the judges are said to be sitting *en banc*. Similarly, only one of the judges of the U.S. Tax Court will typically hear and decide on a tax controversy. However, when the issues involved are unusually novel or of wide impact, the case will be heard and decided by the full court sitting *en banc*. 📖

ENCROACHMENT 📖 An illegal intrusion in a HIGHWAY or navigable river, with or without obstruction. An encroachment upon a street or highway is a FIXTURE, such as a wall or fence, which illegally intrudes into or invades the highway or encloses a portion of it, diminishing its width or area, but without closing it to public travel. 📖

In the law of EASEMENTS, where the owner of an easement alters the dominant TENEMENT so as to impose an additional restriction or burden on the servient tenement, he or she is said to commit an *encroachment*.

ENCUMBER 📖 To burden property by way of a charge that must be removed before ownership is free and clear. 📖

Property subject to an ENCUMBRANCE may have a LIEN or MORTGAGE imposed upon it.

ENCUMBRANCE 📖 A burden, obstruction, or impediment on PROPERTY that lessens its value or makes it less marketable. An encumbrance (also spelled incumbrance) is any right or interest that exists in someone other than the owner of an ESTATE and that restricts or impairs the transfer of the estate or lowers its value. This might include an EASEMENT, a LIEN, a MORTGAGE, a MECHANIC'S LIEN, or accrued and unpaid taxes. 📖

ENDANGERED SPECIES ACT The federal Endangered Species Act of 1973 (ESA) (16 U.S.C.A. §§ 1531 et seq.) was enacted to protect animal and plant species from extinction by preserving the ecosystems on which they survive and by providing programs for their conservation.

The act classifies species as either endangered or threatened. It defines an endangered species as one "in danger of extinction throughout all or a significant portion of its range" (§ 1532). A threatened species is one that is "likely to become an endangered species within the foreseeable future throughout all or a significant portion of its range" (§ 1532). A current detailed listing of endangered and threatened animal and plant species is provided in the Code of Federal Regulations (see 50 C.F.R. §§ 17.11–.12). As of March 1996, the code listed approximately one thousand endangered and threatened species.

The ESA is administered by two agencies: the National Marine Fisheries Service, which designates marine fish and certain marine mammals, and the U.S. Fish and Wildlife Service, which has jurisdiction over all other wildlife. These agencies may list a species at their own initiative, or any interested person may submit a petition to have a species considered for listing. In either case, the act requires that the decision of whether to include a species must be based solely on the "best scientific and commercial data available," following a review of the status of the species that takes into account any conservation efforts being made to protect the species (§ 1533 (b)(1)(A)).

If an emergency poses a significant risk to the well-being of a species of fish, wildlife, or plant, the secretary of the interior may bypass standard listing procedures and issue regulations that take effect immediately upon publication in the *Federal Register*. Emergency regulations remain in force for 240 days. To issue an emergency regulation, the secretary must publish detailed reasons why the regulation is nec-

In 1995 wildlife officials and others watched as a wolf was released into the wild in central Idaho. The transfer of wolves from Canada to Idaho and Wyoming was done in hopes of eventually removing wolves from the endangered species list.

essary and notify the appropriate state agency in each state where the species is found (§ 1533 (b)(7)).

Critical Habitat The ESA requires that at the same time the decision is made to list a species, the secretary of the interior must develop a recovery plan for the species and, with certain exceptions, designate the species's critical habitat. Critical habitat consists of "the specific areas within the geographical area occupied by the species, at the time it is listed . . . on which are found those physical or biological features (I) essential to the conservation of the species and (II) which may require special management considerations or protection." Critical habitat must be designated on the basis of the best scientific data available and after taking into consideration the economic impact of the designation. An area may be excluded from designation if the benefits of the exclusion outweigh the benefits of the designation, unless the failure to designate will result in the extinction of the species (§ 1533 (b)(2)).

The issue of the economic impact of designating critical habitat was addressed in *Bennett v. Plenert*, 63 F.3d 915 (9th Cir. 1995). In *Plenert*, Oregon ranchers and irrigation districts sued regulators under the ESA over a proposal to change water flow at reservoirs in Oregon and California in order to protect the habitat of two endangered species, the Lost River sucker and the shortnose sucker. They claimed that the proposal did not take economic impact into consideration before designating critical habitat. The district court dismissed the suit. The U.S. Court of Appeals for the Ninth Circuit affirmed the dismissal, holding that because the ranchers and irrigation districts had no interest in preserving the fish under the ESA, they were not within the "zone of interest" protected by the act. As a result, said the court, they lacked standing (a legally protectible interest) to bring a citizen suit. In March 1996, the U.S. Supreme Court agreed to hear the case.

Taking Once a fish or wildlife species is listed as endangered or threatened under the ESA, the act prohibits anyone from taking the species; plants are protected under separate provisions of the act. To take a species means to "harass, harm, pursue, hunt, shoot, wound, kill, trap, capture, or collect, or to attempt to engage in any such conduct" (§ 1532 (19)).

The federal courts have disagreed whether the term *harm* in the ESA's definition of taking includes the detrimental modification of a species's habitat. For example, the U.S. Courts of Appeals for the Fifth and Ninth Circuits had interpreted the taking prohibition to include

Endangered and Threatened Wildlife and Plant Species, 1994

Wildlife or Plant	Mammals	Birds	Reptiles	Amphibians	Fishes	Snails	Clams	Crustaceans	Insects	Arachnids	Plants
				Endangered Species							
Total	307	228	79	14	78	15	53	14	23	4	416
U.S. only	36	58	8	6	62	14	50	14	16	4	404
U.S. and Foreign	19	17	6	——	5	——	1	——	3	——	11
Foreign only	252	153	65	8	11	1	2	——	4	——	1
				Threatened Species							
Total	31	16	33	5	36	7	6	3	9	——	90
U.S. only	6	8	15	4	30	7	6	3	9	——	76
U.S. and Foreign	3	8	4	1	6	——	——	——	——	——	12
Foreign only	22	——	14	——	——	——	——	——	——	——	2

SOURCE: U.S. Fish and Wildlife Service, *Endangered Species Technical Bulletin,* quarterly.

habitat modification (*Palila v. Hawaii Department of Land & Natural Resources*, 639 F.2d 495 [9th Cir. 1981]; *Sierra Club v. Yeutter,* 926 F.2d 429 [5th Cir. 1991]). But the U.S. Court of Appeals for the District of Columbia Circuit, in *Sweet Home Chapter of Communities for a Great Oregon v. Babbitt,* 17 F.3d 1463 (1994), invalidated regulations that included habitat modification within the definition of taking. On appeal of the *Sweet Home* decision, the U.S. Supreme Court resolved this split, holding that habitat destruction that "actually kills or injures" an endangered or threatened species constitutes a violation of the ESA (*Sweet Home,* 515 U.S. 687, 115 S. Ct. 2407, 132 L. Ed. 2d 597).

Violations of the ESA can result in criminal penalties of up to one year in prison and $50,000 in fines. Civil penalties of up to $25,000 for each violation may also be imposed. Private citizens may bring actions against other individuals or government entities for violations of the ESA.

The ESA allows certain exceptions to prohibited activities. For example, the secretary of the interior may issue a permit for a taking of a listed species that is "incidental" to an otherwise lawful activity. The applicant must prepare a conservation plan specifying the probable impact of the taking and the steps the applicant will take to minimize the impact. In the early 1990s, the Department of the INTERIOR relied on this exception when it began negotiating voluntary habitat conservation agreements with timber companies in the Pacific Northwest. Under these agreements, the landowners can set aside habitat for endangered or threatened species and, in return, avoid prosecution for the incidental taking of a species by accidental killing or other harm. By October 1995, the agency had begun negotiating more than forty such plans, covering 5.4 million acres, in Washington and Oregon. For example, Murray Pacific Corporation, a timber company in

Tacoma, Washington, negotiated an agreement to set aside 10 percent of its fifty-four-thousand-acre tree farm and provide buffers to protect spotted owls, salmon, and other species. Plum Creek Timber Company, the second-largest private landowner in the Northwest, developed a far-reaching plan to set aside up to 170,000 acres of habitat that will help protect an estimated 284 species of wildlife, including grizzly bears, gray wolves, moles, fishers, and several different kinds of frogs, fish, and birds.

Experimental Populations In 1982, the ESA was amended to allow the reintroduction of experimental populations of threatened or endangered species into their historic ranges without requiring compliance with many of the act's restrictions (§ 1539 (j)). Currently designated experimental populations are listed in the Code of Federal Regulations (see 50 C.F.R. §§ 17.81–.82). As of March 1996, nine species were designated as experimental populations, including the red wolf and the gray wolf. The experimental population designation relaxed existing ESA regulations by allowing reintroduced species to be managed or controlled; for example, ranchers could kill reintroduced wolves that threatened livestock.

In January 1995, the federal government began a program to restore an experimental population of gray wolves to Yellowstone National Park and central Idaho. The program projected the transfer of 90 to 150 Canadian gray wolves into Yellowstone National Park and central Idaho over three to five years. From January to March 1995, 29 gray wolves from Canada were released into Wyoming and Idaho. The goal of the wolf recovery program was to remove wolves from the endangered species list by 2002.

The release of the experimental population of gray wolves was controversial and created conflict between environmentalists and livestock ranchers. In 1994, just prior to the release, a farm group sued to stop it (*Wyoming Farm Bureau Federation v. Babbitt*, No. 94-CV-286-D [D. Wyo. Nov. 25, 1994]). The following year, an environmental group sued to remove the experimental population designation and allow the wolves to be released under full ESA protection (*National Audubon Society v. Babbitt*, No. CIV95-0305-S-HLR [D. Idaho Jan. 5, 1995]). The two lawsuits were consolidated for hearing in the U.S. District Court for the District of Wyoming.

Proposed Reform In April 1995, Congress, intent on rewriting the ESA to loosen restrictions on private landowners, imposed a moratorium on all new-species listings and critical habitat designations. The moratorium, passed as a rider to the Emergency Supplemental Appropriations and Rescissions for the Department of Defense to Preserve and Enhance Military Readiness Act of 1995 (Pub. L. No. 104-6, 109 Stat. 73), prohibited Secretary of the Interior Bruce Babbitt from spending funds to identify and list any additional endangered or threatened species.

The 1995 freeze created a backlog of nearly 250 plants and animals awaiting decision on protected status under the ESA. In April 1996, as part of an agreement on federal spending for the current fiscal year, Congress agreed to waive the moratorium. In May 1996, the Clinton administration began resolving the backlog, focusing first on species facing immediate extinction, then on species that biologists determine would be most likely to recover if given full protection under the law. The administration said it would also consider making moderate changes to the act, including adding requirements for independent scientific review of decisions to list species and for increased state and local input into decisions about listings and habitat protection, and adding provisions to make habitat plans less restrictive for private landowners.

See also ENVIRONMENTAL LAW.

ENDORSE See INDORSE.

ENDOWMENT 📖 A transfer, generally as a gift, of money or property to an institution for a particular purpose. The bestowal of money as a permanent fund, the income of which is to be used for the benefit of a CHARITY, COLLEGE, or other institution. 📖

A classic example of an endowment is money collected in a fund by a college. The college invests the endowment so that a regular amount of income is earned for the school. Typically, the monies for the endowment are derived from donations by alumni of the college.

Often, an endowment is designed to support

The bestowal of money to an endowment for a college or university is often designed to fund a particular activity or building project.

RICHARD PASLEY/STOCK BOSTON

a particular activity, such as the construction of a new wing by a hospital. Each donor sets up an endowment fund sufficiently large to earn income to pay the expenses of one room or a different part of the wing, such as a library.

The Uniform Management of Institutional Funds Act (7A U.L.A. 233 [West Supp. 1992]), which was first created in 1972 and has since been adopted as law in many states, regulates spending and investment decisions related to such endowments.

The term *endowment* is also used to describe the act of putting aside the amount of property that a wife is lawfully due to inherit from her spouse. At COMMON LAW, a woman was "endowed at the church door," upon marriage, when she acquired her DOWER right—the right to use one-third of her husband's land upon his death for the remainder of her life.

ENERGY Laws and regulations concerning the production and distribution of energy have existed for over one hundred years in the United States. Energy law became recognized as a specialty following the energy crises of the 1970s. It focuses on the production, distribution, conservation, and development of energy resources like coal, oil, natural gas, NUCLEAR POWER, and hydroelectric power.

In 1876, the U.S. Supreme Court, in *Munn v. Illinois*, 94 U.S. (Otto) 113, 24 L. Ed. 77, held that "natural monopolies" could be regulated by the government. *Munn* concerned grain elevators but stood more generally for the principle that the public must be allowed to control private property committed to a use in which the public has an interest. This legal recognition of natural MONOPOLIES provides the basis for much of the legal and regulatory control the government exercises over utility companies.

The regulation of energy in the late 1800s was on a local and regional level, and was primarily market driven. The transition from using wood as a primary source of energy to using coal was almost complete, and a second transition from coal to natural gas and oil was beginning.

In 1900, Standard Oil Company controlled 90 percent of the oil market; within a few years, ANTITRUST litigation had reduced its market share to 64 percent. Aside from antitrust enforcement, the federal government was content to let the market control the energy industry. Oil, coal, and natural gas found their greatest structural impediment in the "bottleneck" of distribution—pipelines for oil and natural gas, and railways for coal. The dominant model of energy policy that emerged from this period and existed unchanged until the 1970s was one of support for conventional resources and regulation of industries whose natural monopolies required some government oversight to ensure that their public purpose served a PUBLIC INTEREST.

On October 17, 1973, the Organization of Petroleum Exporting Countries (OPEC) announced an EMBARGO of oil exports to all countries, including the United States, that were supporting Israel in the Yom Kippur War. Only approximately 10 percent of the United States' oil imports were affected, but the perception of a major oil shortage motivated the next three presidential administrations to exert a strong federal influence over energy.

President RICHARD M. NIXON created the Federal Energy Office (Exec. Order No. 11,930, 41 Fed. Reg. 32, 399) and appointed an "energy czar" to oversee oil supplies. President GERALD R. FORD's administration saw the passage of the Strategic Petroleum Reserve (42 U.S.C.A. § 6234) and the promulgation of minimum efficiency regulations for automobiles. In 1977, JIMMY CARTER's administration created the Department of Energy (42 U.S.C.A. § 7101), which was the framework for the coordination, administration, and execution of a comprehensive national energy program.

The goal of a comprehensive national energy program was achieved with the passage of the National Energy Act of 1978, which consisted of five distinct pieces of legislation. The National Energy Conservation Policy Act (42 U.S.C.A. § 8201 et seq.) set standards and provided financing for conservation in buildings. The Powerplant and Industrial Fuel Use Act (42 U.S.C.A. § 8301 et seq.) encouraged the transition from oil and gas to coal in boilers. The Public Utilities Regulatory Policies Act (15

U.S.C.A. § 2601) granted Congress authority over the interstate transmission of electric power. The Natural Gas Policy Act (15 U.S.C.A. § 3301) unified the gas market and promoted the deregulation of the natural gas industry. The Energy Tax Act (26 U.S.C.A. § 1 et seq.) approved tax credits to promote conservation.

The administration of RONALD REAGAN set policies that marked a significant change in the national energy policy, away from the Carter administration's centralized, governmentally regulated energy plan, which set ambitious goals for market stabilization and energy conservation through government intervention. The Reagan administration favored a more market-driven approach to achieve these goals. Although unsuccessful in its goal to abolish the Department of Energy, the Reagan administration was able to deregulate the natural gas industry through administrative initiatives (under the Federal Energy Regulatory Commission) and the Wellhead Decontrol Act of 1989 (15 U.S.C.A. § 3301).

The administration of GEORGE BUSH also favored a market-driven approach to the regulation of energy, but the Persian Gulf War against Iraq in 1991 required Congress to respond to volatile conditions in the oil-exporting Middle East. The National Energy Policy Act of 1992 (42 U.S.C.A. § 13201) addressed issues such as competition among electric power generators and tax credits for wind and biomass energy production systems.

The National Energy Policy Plan, issued in 1995 during BILL CLINTON's administration, continued the market-focused approach of the

Energy law concerns the production, distribution, and development of energy resources. In the 1990s renewable resources such as wind and solar power gained support.

JIM CORWIN/PHOTO RESEARCHERS

Reagan and Bush administrations. Citing as its primary goal a "sustainable energy policy," the plan states that the "administration's energy policy supports and reinforces the dominant role of the private sector" in achieving this goal.

The mid-1990s focus of market-driven, private sector regulation of energy development, conservation, and distribution may have to change in the years ahead. The energy needs of industrialized nations are intensifying, and the developing countries of the world are increasing their energy demands at a rate of 4.5 percent a year. Oil demand in Asia alone grew 50 percent from 1985 to 1995.

Energy policies in the future are likely to include emphasis on the development of more efficient, sustainable sources of energy. Many countries are already exploring the energy potential of biomass, wind, hydroelectric, and solar power.

CROSS-REFERENCES

Electricity; Energy Department; Environmental Law; Mine and Mineral Law; Public Utilities.

ENERGY DEPARTMENT The Department of Energy (DOE) is an executive agency of the federal government. Its many duties include the administration of federal ENERGY policies and functions, research and development of energy technology, marketing of federally produced power, promotion of energy conservation, oversight of the nuclear weapons program, regulation of energy production and consumption, and collection and analysis of energy-related data.

The DOE was created in 1977 under the Department of Energy Organization Act (42 U.S.C.A. § 7131). The act brought together all major federal energy responsibilities into one cabinet-level department. The DOE divides itself into three major programs, or divisions: energy programs, weapons / waste clean-up programs, and science and technology programs. It also oversees five power administrations and includes the Federal Energy Regulatory Commission. Many of the department's research, development, testing, and production activities are performed by contractors who operate government-owned facilities.

Office of the Secretary The secretary of the DOE provides overall leadership for the department, decides major energy policy, advises the president on energy issues, and acts as the principal spokesperson for the department. The deputy secretary oversees the department's energy programs, and the under secretary has responsibility for the weapons / waste clean up programs and science and technology programs.

Energy Programs The DOE energy programs consist of five offices: Energy Efficiency and Renewable Energy, Fossil Energy, Nuclear Energy, the Energy Information Administration, and Civilian Radioactive Waste Management.

The Office of Energy Efficiency and Renewable Energy directs efforts to increase the production and utilization of renewable power sources such as solar, biomass, wind, geothermal, and alcohol fuels. It also works to improve the energy efficiency of transportation, buildings, and industrial systems. The office supports research and development related to these areas. In addition, it provides financial assistance for state energy planning, weatherizes housing for poor and disadvantaged people, and implements energy conservation measures by government and public institutions.

The Office of Fossil Energy supports research and development programs related to the fossil fuels: coal, petroleum, and gas. It conducts and funds long-term, high-risk research to help the private sector commercialize advanced concepts in fossil fuel energy. The assistant secretary for fossil energy also manages the Clean Coal Technology Program, Strategic Petroleum Reserve, Naval Petroleum and Oil Shale Reserves, and Liquefied Gaseous Fuels Spill Test Facility.

The Office of Nuclear Energy oversees the department's research and development in nuclear fission technology, including nuclear reactor development. This office manages the Remedial Action Program, which performs decontamination work at DOE surplus sites. The office also coordinates efforts to prevent the proliferation of nuclear technology and evaluates new and potential advances in nuclear technology.

The Energy Information Administration collects, processes, and publishes data related to energy production, demand, consumption, distribution, technology, and resource reserves. In addition, the administration helps government and nongovernment users understand energy trends.

The Office of Civilian Radioactive Waste Management manages the Nuclear Waste Fund and other federal programs related to the storage and disposal of high-level radioactive waste and spent nuclear fuel.

Weapons/Waste Clean Up Programs The weapons / waste clean up programs include the Offices of Defense Programs, Environmental Restoration and Waste Management, and Intelligence and National Security.

The Office of Defense Programs directs U.S. nuclear weapons research, development,

Energy Department

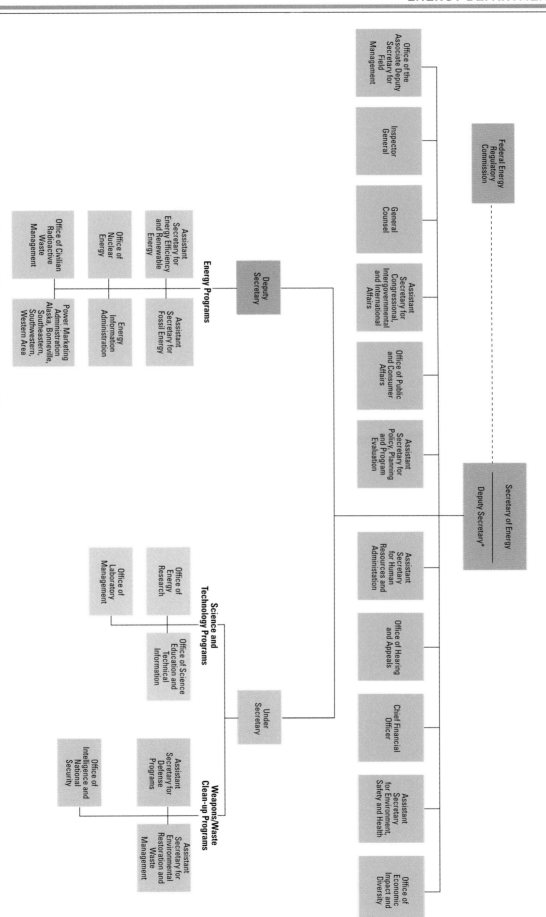

*Deputy Secretary oversees energy program and serves as Chief Operating Officer of the Department within the Office of the Secretary.

The Office of Energy Efficiency and Renewable Energy supports research into energy sources such as burning used tires for energy.

testing, production, and surveillance; manages defense nuclear waste and by-products; and coordinates research in inertial confinement nuclear fusion.

The Office of Environmental Restoration and Waste Management assesses and cleans up the waste sites of inactive nuclear weapons and of other weapons and related matériel.

The Office of Intelligence and National Security meets the intelligence information requirements of the DOE and makes departmental expertise and information available to the intelligence community. The office secures classified information and manages the department's policies relating to arms control, nuclear nonproliferation, and export controls.

Science and Technology Programs

The science and technology programs include the Offices of Energy Research, Science Education and Technical Information, and Laboratory Management.

The Office of Energy Research advises the secretary on DOE energy research and development programs. It manages the basic energy sciences, high-energy physics, and fusion energy research programs. It also administers grants to university and industry researchers.

The Office of Science Education and Technical Information develops and implements DOE policy for science education programs at secondary and postsecondary schools; manages the collection and dissemination of department research and development activities; and represents the United States in international organizations such as the International Atomic Energy Agency and the International Energy Agency.

The Office of Laboratory Management administers DOE laboratories and formulates laboratory research programs and policies.

Power Administrations

The DOE oversees five power administrations that market and transmit electric power produced at federal hydroelectric projects: the Bonneville Power Administration, in the Pacific Northwest; the Alaska Power Administration; the Southeastern Power Administration, serving West Virginia, Virginia, North Carolina, South Carolina, Georgia, Florida, Alabama, Mississippi, Tennessee, and Kentucky; the Southwestern Power Administration, in Arkansas, Kansas, Louisiana, Missouri, Oklahoma, and Texas; and the Western Area Power Administration, serving fifteen midwestern and western states.

Federal Energy Regulatory Commission

The DOE also includes the Federal Energy Regulatory Commission, an independent commission made up of five members. The commission took over many of the functions of the former Federal Power Commission, including the setting of rates and charges for the sale of natural gas and ELECTRICITY. The commission also establishes rates for the transportation of oil by pipeline.

ENFEOFFMENT 📖 Complete surrender and transfer of all land ownership rights from one person to another. In old English law, an enfeoffment was a transfer of PROPERTY by which the new owner was given both the right to sell the land and the right to pass it on to HEIRS, evidenced by *livery of seisin*, a ceremony for transferring the possession of REAL PROPERTY from one individual to another. 📖

Enfeoffment is also know as FEOFFMENT.

ENFRANCHISEMENT 📖 The act of making free (as from SLAVERY); giving a franchise or freedom to; investiture with privileges or capacities of freedom, or municipal or political liberty. Conferring the privilege of voting upon classes of persons who have not previously possessed such. 📖

ENGAGE 📖 To become involved with, do, or take part in something. 📖

To be engaged in something, such as a type of employment, implies a continuity of action. It is used in reference to an occupation or anything in which an individual habitually participates.

A person can also be engaged to do a particular activity by contract or other agreement.

When two people become engaged to marry, they are bound together by an agreement or promise to marry one another.

ENGAGEMENT 📖 A binding, pledging, or coming together. A mutual pact, CONTRACT, or agreement. 📖

An *engagement to marry* is a BILATERAL CONTRACT between two people whereby they mutually promise to marry one another. Formerly, a breach of the engagement to marry was a CAUSE OF ACTION in several jurisdictions, but this is not true today.

An *engagement letter* is a clear delineation of an agreement that covers a particular project or employment. An ATTORNEY can require a CLIENT to sign such a letter to indicate that the person has been employed to perform specifically designated tasks.

ENGEL v. VITALE In 1962, the Supreme Court struck down a state-sponsored prayer in New York public schools, in *Engel v. Vitale*, 370 U.S. 421, 82 S. Ct. 1261, 8 L. Ed. 2d 601, the first in a line of decisions banning school prayer. In finding a twenty-two-word voluntary prayer unconstitutional, the Court opened a Pandora's box. For the next three decades, public anger brought many calls for a CONSTITUTIONAL AMENDMENT to restore what *Engel* took away. On the other hand, the ruling was a landmark victory for church-state separationists who marked it as the beginning of a new era in FIRST AMENDMENT doctrine.

The origins of the case lay in a controversial education project in the early 1950s, started by the New York Board of Regents, a bipartisan citizen commission appointed by the New York State Legislature to oversee state schools. The regents set out to recommend a plan for "moral education," the most controversial part of which included prayer. Religious leaders naturally differed over the wording of a proposed prayer intended to be recited by students each morning, but in 1951, a compromise resulted in what they hoped would be an inoffensive solution. Included as part of the regents' *Statement on Moral and Spiritual Training in the Schools*, the prayer went "Almighty God, we acknowledge our dependence upon Thee, and we Beg Thy blessings upon us, our parents, our teachers and our country."

Going out of their way to avoid trouble, the regents made the prayer entirely optional. Both local school boards and parents could decide if it would be used. Nevertheless, its authors had not written it only to try their hand at prayer making. "We believe," they wrote, "that this Statement will be subscribed to by all men and women of good will, and we call upon all of them to aid in giving life to our program." But fearing religious and legal controversy, New York school districts shunned the prayer. They had good reason: not only was the state quite ethnically and religiously diverse, but also religious instruction in public schools had been declared unconstitutional by the U.S. Supreme Court in 1948 (*McCollum v. Board of Education*,

333 U.S. 203, 68 S. Ct. 461, 92 L. Ed. 549). Most school districts followed the lead of New York City and ignored the prayer. Only about 10 percent of them were using it by the late 1950s.

In 1958, the prayer provoked a lawsuit (*Engel*). Five parents of students in the small suburb of New Hyde Park, Long Island, brought suit to stop its use in their schools. Two parents were Jewish, the third was Unitarian, the fourth was a member of the Ethical Culture Society, and the fifth was a self-professed atheist. They believed that the school system was coercing their children into saying the regents' prayer, even though individually, their children could be excused from participating. The difficulty of granting children the permission to step out of the room during recitation of the prayer had, they argued, made the prayer effectively compulsory. Furthermore, voluntary or not, they said, the prayer violated the Establishment Clause of the First Amendment ("Congress shall make no law respecting an establishment of religion"). The parents received substantial help in their suit from the AMERICAN CIVIL LIBERTIES UNION (ACLU), which had been advocating strict separation of church and state for many years.

At first, the lawsuit failed. The plaintiffs asked the New York State Supreme Court—acting as a trial court—to stop use of the prayer. It refused. Justice Bernard S. Meyer found the prayer clearly religious, but not a violation of the First Amendment. Instead, he ordered school districts to set up safeguards against "embarrassments and pressures" upon children who did not wish to participate. The New York Appellate Division upheld the decision. So did the state's Court of Appeals, by a vote of 5–2. It said the nation's founders had designed the Establishment Clause to prohibit adopting an official RELIGION or favoring a particular religion. "They could not have meant to prohibit mere professions of belief in God," the court held, "for if that were so, they themselves in many ways were violating the rule when and after they adopted it."

After agreeing to review the case, the U.S. Supreme Court heard oral arguments on April 3, 1962. Attorney William J. Butler made the following case for the plaintiffs: all state support to religion violates the First Amendment, and the prayer constituted the "teaching of religion in a public institution" and should therefore be banned. Several powerful groups joined the plaintiffs by filing friend-of-the-court briefs. These included the ACLU; the American Jewish Committee, joined by the Anti-Defamation

League of B'nai B'rith; the Synagogue Council of America, joined by the National Community Relations Advisory Council; and the American Ethical Union. These organizations took different positions. The American Ethical Union saw the prayer as "governmental preference for theism in violation of the First and Fourteenth Amendments." The Synagogue Council argued that any school prayer was unconstitutional— even if voluntary—because it constituted "state aid to religion."

The school board defended the prayer on several grounds. It cited the second part of the First Amendment's religious guarantees, the Free Exercise Clause ("or prohibiting the free exercise thereof"). The prayer was an example of free exercise, Attorney Bertram B. Daiker argued, that fell far short of establishing a religion because it was optional, not compul-

In 1940 the schoolday in this New Mexico school opened with a prayer. Engel v. Vitale was the first of many decisions banning school prayer.

sory. Daiker also found authority in the nation's traditions, calling the prayer "fully in accord with the tradition and heritage that has been handed down to us." Like the plaintiffs, the school board had powerful friends in court. Briefs supporting the prayer came from nineteen state attorneys general who also saw religious and national tradition under attack. The attorneys general said the nation's founders "would be profoundly shocked" by the lawsuit.

On June 25, 1962, the groundbreaking decision was delivered. By a 7–1 majority, the Supreme Court found the prayer unconstitutional (the ninth justice, BYRON R. WHITE, did not participate). Justice HUGO L. BLACK's majority opinion called the prayer "wholly inconsistent" with the Establishment Clause. A considerable series of PRECEDENTS existed from 1940 on for the ruling, but Black did not cite it. Instead, he recalled the bitter history of church-

state conflict in England and colonial America, noting that by the time the Constitution was written, "there was a widespread awareness among many Americans of the dangers of a union of church and state." The First Amendment was added to prevent that union, which "tends to destroy government and to degrade religion." Black scorned the school board's claim that the regents' prayer was harmless. Neither its brevity nor its voluntary nature nor its nondenominational status could protect it from the Constitution. "[O]ne of the greatest dangers to the freedom of the individual to worship in his own way [lies] in the government's placing its official stamp of approval upon one particular kind of prayer or one particular form of religious services," wrote Black.

Critics would immediately blast the *Engel* decision. In a move that seemed to anticipate this response, Black wrote,

> It has been argued that to apply the Constitution in such a way as to prohibit state laws respecting an establishment of religious services in public schools is to indicate a hostility toward religion or toward prayer. Nothing, of course, could be more wrong. . . . It is neither sacrilegious nor antireligious to say that each separate government in this country should stay out of the business of writing or sanctioning official prayers and leave that purely religious function to the people themselves and to those the people choose to look to for religious guidance.

The Court's message to government was simple: stay out of the prayer business, and leave it to religious leaders.

In a sole dissent, Justice POTTER STEWART argued that the majority had overstated the meaning of the Establishment Clause: it prevented only the creation of official religions. "I cannot see how an 'official religion' is established by letting those who want to say a prayer say it," he wrote, and his view was prophetic. For the next thirty years, advocates of school prayer could not see how, either. By 1985, when the school prayer ban reached a new level in *Wallace v. Jaffree*, 472 U.S. 38, 105 S. Ct. 2479, 86 L. Ed. 2d 29, Justice WILLIAM H. REHNQUIST argued similarly in his dissent to the majority ruling banning a so-called moment of silence in the classroom.

Engel was only the first ban against prayer in public schools; a year later, the Court returned to the issue in *Abington School District v. Schempp*, 374 U.S. 203, 83 S. Ct. 1560, 10 L. Ed. 2d 844, with even more far-reaching results. The immediate effect was the end of the regents' prayer. In a much broader sense, by sounding the death knell for a traditional practice, *Engel* created an uproar of protest that continues today.

CROSS-REFERENCES

Abington School District v. Schempp; School Prayer; Schools and School Districts.

ENGLISH LAW 📖 The system of law that has developed in England from approximately 1066 to the present. 📖

The body of English law includes legislation, COMMON LAW, and a host of other legal norms established by Parliament, the Crown, and the judiciary. It is the fountain from which flowed nearly every facet of U.S. law during the eighteenth and nineteenth centuries.

Many of the concepts embodied in the U.S. Constitution—such as the separation and delegation of powers between three branches of government and the creation of an elective national assembly representing the will of the people—trace their roots to English law. Fundamental legal procedures applied in the U.S. civil and criminal justice systems also originated in England. The jury system, for example, slowly matured into its modern form over several hundred years of English history. The antecedents of many substantive areas of U.S. law, including the ubiquitous system of state and federal taxation, may be found in English history as well.

The story of English constitutional law prior to the American Revolution, which is inextricably intertwined with the development of English law as a whole during this period, can be told in three parts: the centralization of power in the monarchy, the creation of Parliament as a limitation on the absolute power asserted by the monarchy, and the struggle for supremacy between Parliament and the monarchy. In large part, the American Revolution resulted from Parliament's failure to check the monarchy's sovereignty and establish itself as the supreme lawmaking body representing the people of England and its colonies.

When William, duke of Normandy, also known as William the Conqueror, vanquished England in 1066, there was no English law as the Americans of 1776 came to know it. No national or federal legal machinery had yet been contemplated. Law was a loose collection of decentralized customs, traditions, and rules followed by the Anglians and Saxons, among others. Criminal cases were indistinguishable from civil cases, and both secular and spiritual disputes were resolved at the local level by community courts. Trials in the modern sense did

not exist, nor did juries. Guilt and innocence were determined by compurgation and ordeal.

Compurgation was a ritualistic procedure in which accused persons might clear themselves of an alleged wrongdoing by taking a sworn oath denying the claim made against them, and corroborating the denial by the sworn oaths of twelve other persons, usually neighbors or relatives. If an accused person failed to provide the requisite number of COMPURGATORS, he or she lost. The number of compurgators was the same as the number of jurors later impaneled to hear criminal cases under the common law. In the United States, the SIXTH AMENDMENT to the Constitution required that all criminal trials be prosecuted before twelve jurors—until 1970, when the Supreme Court ruled that six-person juries were permissible (*Williams v. Florida*, 399 U.S. 78, 90 S. Ct. 1893, 26 L. Ed. 2d 446).

Trial by ORDEAL was a superstitious procedure administered by clerics who subjected accused persons to physical torment in hopes of uncovering divine signs of guilt or innocence. The most common forms of ordeal involved boiling or freezing waters and hot irons. In the ordeal of freezing water, accused persons were thrown into a pool to see if they would sink or float. If they sank, the cleric believed they were innocent, because the water would presumably reject someone with an impure soul. Of course, persons who sank to the bottom and drowned during this ordeal were both exonerated of their alleged misbehavior, and dead.

Battle was another form of primitive trial that was thought to involve divine intervention on behalf of the righteous party. The combatants were armed with long staffs and leather shields, and fought savagely until one party cried, "Craven," or died.

Trial by battle, though in many ways as barbaric as trial by ordeal, foreshadowed modern trials in several ways. The combatants fought in an adversarial arena before robed judges who presided over the battle. The accused person was required to put on a defense, quite literally in the physical sense, against an opponent who was trying to prove the veracity of her or his claims. Some parties to a battle, particularly women, children, and older individuals, were entitled to hire stronger, more able champions to fight on their behalf. This last practice sheds light on the more recent phrase *hired guns*, which is sometimes used to describe U.S. trial attorneys.

William the Conqueror understood the importance of revenue, and that is where he began building the English empire. In 1086, William initiated the Domesday Survey, which sought to determine the amount and value of property held in England, for the purpose of assessing taxes against the owners. The Domesday Survey was conducted by eight panels of royal commissioners who traveled to every county in the country, where they collected information through sworn INQUESTS. Although the survey began as a method of recording REAL PROPERTY held in the kingdom, one contemporary Saxon chronicler moaned "that there was not a single hide . . . nor . . . ox, cow or swine" omitted (Trevelyan 1982). The Court of Exchequer served as auditor, accountant, and tax collector for William, and provided a venue to settle disputes between the Crown and taxpayers, becoming the earliest department of state. See also DOMESDAY BOOK.

William's system for revenue collection began a process that gradually replaced the community courts of justice with a legal system that emanated from a central location, the king's castle in Westminster. One symbol of powerful centralized government in the United States is the Internal Revenue Service. For many U.S. citizens, paying taxes is a necessary evil. Taxes are necessary to keep the government, and its justice system, afloat. At the same time, they take away individuals' money.

HENRY II (1154–89) further strengthened the central government by enlarging the power and jurisdiction of the royal system of justice. During his reign, any crime that breached the ruler's peace was tried before a royal court sitting in Westminster, or by royal itinerant justices who traveled to localities throughout England to hear disputes. Heretofore, the royal court heard only cases that directly threatened the monarch's physical or economic interests. Most other complaints, except for those heard by the Catholic Church, were leveled by private individuals, who were also responsible for proving their accusations. By increasing the sphere of what the government considered public wrongs, Henry II laid the groundwork for the United States' modern criminal justice system, where attorneys for the federal, state, and local governments are invested with the authority to prosecute persons accused of criminal wrongdoing. See also BECKET, SAINT THOMAS.

Henry II also laid the groundwork for the common-law method of deciding cases, whereby judges make decisions in accordance with other decisions they have rendered in similar matters. The royal system of justice was governed by a single set of legal rules and principles, which was applied evenhandedly to litigants presenting claims to the monarch's justices. This system superseded one that applied the often inconsistent customary laws of neighboring communities of different ethnic backgrounds. Because the monarch's law was applied in a uniform manner, it became "common" to every shire in the land. This "common-law" system of adjudication was adopted by the American colonies and continues to be applied in nearly all of the fifty states of the Union.

In addition to becoming more prevalent, the royal system of justice was becoming more popular. Its popularity stemmed from the rational legal procedures and reliable modes of evidence developed by the King's Court, which slowly supplanted their superstitious, ritualistic, and dangerous predecessors, compurgation, ordeal, and battle. One new rational procedure was trial by JURY, which Henry II made available in land disputes between laypersons and the clergy. The juries comprised twelve sworn men who possessed some knowledge of the property dispute, and were asked to announce a verdict to the royal justices based on this knowledge. The trial-by-jury system employed by Henry II, though only an embryonic form, reflected society's growing understanding that verdicts based on personal knowledge of a dispute were more reliable than verdicts based on ordeals of freezing water and contests of brawn and agility.

Henry II also made the law more impersonal and less vindictive. In 1166, the Assize of Clarendon prohibited the prosecution of anyone who had not first been accused by a "presenting jury" of twelve to sixteen men from the community in which the crime occurred. The presenting jury foreshadowed the modern GRAND JURY as an accusatory body that identified persons for prosecution but made no determination as to guilt or innocence. The presenting jury was seen as a more neutral and detached alternative to the system it replaced, which required the alleged victims, some of whom were waging a personal vendetta against the accused person, to identify alleged criminals for prosecution. See also CLARENDON, CONSTITUTIONS OF.

The WRIT *de odio et atia* provided additional safeguards for defendants wrongfully accused of criminal activity, by permitting the defendant to appeal legal issues to the King's Court in cases where the complainant was proceeding out of spite or hatred. This writ of appeal was an early precursor to the modern appellate system in the United States, which similarly permits parties to APPEAL legal issues they believe did not receive appropriate consideration at the trial level.

The presenting jury and writ of appeal underpin two beliefs that have been crucial to the development of the English and U.S. systems of justice. The first is the belief that a wrongfully accused person is no less a victim than is the target of civil or criminal malfeasance. The second is the belief that the legal system must provide an impartial forum for seeking the truth in disputed legal claims. These two beliefs paved the way for an assortment of procedural and evidentiary protections that have evolved to protect innocent persons from being unjustly convicted in criminal cases, and to keep prejudices from biasing judges and jurors in civil cases.

However, the English monarchy did not centralize its power without cost. Frequently, English rulers abused their enlarged power to such an extent that they met with popular resistance. One of the earliest such confrontations occurred in 1215, and produced the first great charter of constitutional liberties, the MAGNA CHARTA. The Magna Charta can best be understood as a peace treaty between three rival jurisdictions of political and legal power: the Crown, the church, and the barons.

In the thirteenth century, the king's system of justice competed for influence with ecclesiastical and manorial courts. The ECCLESIASTICAL COURTS were run by the Catholic Church, with the pope presiding as the spiritual head in Rome. Manorial courts were run by barons, who were powerful men holding large parcels of land from the king, known as MANORS. Each baron, as lord of his manor, retained jurisdiction over most legal matters arising among his tenants, also called vassals, who agreed to work on the land in exchange for shelter and security. The jurisdictions of the Crown, the church, and the barons overlapped and each depended on the others for support.

The tyranny of King John (1199–1216) alienated the church and the barons, converting them into adversaries of the Crown. John was excommunicated by the pope, church services and sacraments were suspended in England, and the barons renounced homage to the Crown. Spearheaded by Stephen Langton, archbishop of Canterbury, the barons confronted King John on the battlefield at Runnymede, where they won recognition for certain fundamental liberties contained in the sixty-three clauses that make up the Magna Charta.

The Magna Charta granted the church freedom from royal interference except in a limited number of circumstances, establishing in nascent form the separation of church and state. The Great Charter required that all fines bear some relationship to the seriousness of the

In 1215 King John approved the Magna Charta, which guaranteed fundamental liberties to the church and to individuals.

offense for which they were imposed, establishing the principle of proportionality between punishment and crime, which the U.S. Supreme Court still applies under the Cruel and Unusual Punishment Clause of the Eighth Amendment to the U.S. Constitution.

Most important the Magna Charta prohibited any "free man" from being "imprisoned, or disseised, . . . or exiled, . . . except by the lawful judgment of his peers, or by the law of the land" (ch. 39). The phrase "law of the land" was later equated with "due process" in the American colonies and received constitutional recognition in the Fifth and Fourteenth Amendments to the U.S. Constitution. The Supreme Court has described DUE PROCESS as the "most comprehensive of liberties" guaranteed in the Constitution (*Rochin v. California*, 342 U.S. 165, 72 S. Ct. 205, 96 L. Ed. 183 [1952]), and has relied on the Due Process Clause of the FOURTEENTH AMENDMENT to make most of the freedoms contained in the Bill of Rights applicable to the states.

Fifty years after Magna Charta, Parliament was created to serve as an additional check on the arbitrary power of the monarchy. In 1265, Parliament was a very small body, consisting of two knights from each shire, two citizens from each city, and two burgesses from each borough. By the fourteenth century, Parliament was being summoned to advise the monarch, vote on financial matters, and supervise the excesses of local officials. Representatives for the barons, later known collectively as the

DR. BONHAM'S CASE

Dr. *Bonham's Case*, 8 Co. Rep. 114 (Court of Common Pleas [1610]), stands for the principle that legislation passed by the English Parliament is subordinate to the common-law decisions made by trial and appellate court judges, and any statute that is contrary to "common right and reason" must be declared void (Thorne 1938).

The decision in this case, which was written by Sir Edward Coke sitting as chief justice for the Court of Common Pleas in England, spawned the concept of judicial review under which courts of law, as the primary oracles of the common law in the British and U.S. systems of justice, are authorized to invalidate laws enacted by the executive and legislative branches of government. The power of judicial review, which was first recognized by the U.S. Supreme Court in *Marbury v. Madison*, 5 U.S. (1 Cranch) 137, 2 L. Ed. 60, is invoked by courts every day across the United States but has since been rendered obsolete in England.

Bonham's Case arose from a dispute regarding the unlicensed practice of medicine. Dr. Thomas Bonham had received a degree in physic medicine from the University of Cambridge. In 1606, Bonham was discovered practicing such medicine in London without a license, and was summoned to appear before the censors at the London College of Physicians, who maintained jurisdiction in that city over the practice of medicine.

Bonham was examined by the college censors in a number of areas regarding his professional practice, and provided answers "less aptly and insufficiently in the art of physic" (Stoner 1992, 49). As a result, Bonham was determined unfit to practice medicine in this field, and was ordered to desist from such practice in London. When Bonham was later discovered flouting this order, he was arrested and placed in the custody of the censors.

Bonham refused to undergo further examination. As a graduate of Cambridge, he asserted that the London College of Physicians had no jurisdiction over him and thus possessed no authority to arrest or fine him. Promising to continue his practice of physic medicine if released, Bonham was immediately jailed.

The case came before the Court of Common Pleas when Bonham claimed that his continued detention by the college amounted to false imprisonment. As a defense, the college relied on its statute of incorporation, which authorized it to regulate all physicians in London and to punish practitioners not licensed by the college. The statute also entitled the college to one-half of all the fines imposed by it.

The Honorable Justice Coke, also a Cambridge graduate, sided with his fellow alumnus. After singing the praises of their alma mater, Coke argued that because the college censors were entitled to receive a portion of the fine they imposed on Bonham, the statute made them prosecutor, plaintiff, and judge in the dispute: "The censors cannot be judges, ministers and parties; judges . . . give sentence or judgment; ministers . . . make summons; and parties . . . have moiety [half] of the forfeiture, because no person may be a judge in his own cause . . . and one cannot be judge and attorney for any of the parties." Coke suggested that the impartiality of a judge is compromised when the judge is also the plaintiff who will benefit financially from any fines imposed on the defendant, or the prosecutor who is the advocate responsible for seeking such fines. Although the parliamentary statute in question clearly contemplated that London College would wear all three of these hats, Coke observed,

[I]t appears in our books, that in many cases, the common law will

controul Acts of Parliament, and sometimes adjudge them to be utterly void: for when an Act of Parliament is against common right and reason, or repugnant, or impossible to be performed, the common law will controul it, and adjudge such Act to be void.

Coke placed the judiciary in the middle of what was becoming a titanic struggle for power between Parliament and the ruler of England. Until the seventeenth century, the English monarchy enjoyed nearly absolute power over all political and legal matters that concerned the country as a whole. Despite the growing popularity and importance of Parliament during the fifteenth and sixteenth centuries, the monarchy's autocratic power, which King James I (1603–25) asserted was divine in origin, included the prerogative to enact laws without parliamentary consent.

By the close of the seventeenth century, however, the pendulum of power had swung in favor of Parliament. The Glorious Revolution of 1688 subordinated the power of the English Crown and judiciary to parliamentary sovereignty. In 1765, English jurist Sir William Blackstone described "the power of Parliament" to make laws in England as "absolute," "despotic," and "without control."

The American Revolution, which began eleven years after Blackstone's pronouncement of Parliament's unfettered power, was commenced in response to the coercive legislation passed in the colonies by what had become a despotic Parliament. Thomas Jefferson, James Madison, and their contemporaries believed that a legislative despot was no better than a monarchical despot. In 1787, the U.S. Constitution established the judiciary as a check on the legislative and executive branches of government, a check that was foreshadowed by Coke's opinion in *Bonham's Case*.

James I was cognizant of the dangers *Bonham's Case* presented to his claims of divine royal prerogative. The king understood that the "common law," which *Bonham's Case* said controlled acts of Parliament, was really just a decision made by a court of law, or, more particularly, by a judge or panel of judges. James also understood that if the judiciary were allowed to assert the power to review acts of Parliament, it was only a short step away from passing judgment on actions taken by the Crown.

Accordingly, King James removed Coke from the Court of Common Pleas in 1613, appointing him chief justice of the King's Bench. This constituted a promotion in name only, since Coke was now under closer scrutiny by the Crown.

Much to the Crown's chagrin, Coke's replacement on the Court of Common Pleas, Sir Henry Hobart, expanded the concept of judicial review intimated by *Bonham's Case*. In *Day v. Savadge*, Hob. 84 (K.B. 1614), Hobart declared that "an act of parliament made against natural equity, as to make a man judge in his own cause, is void in itself" (as quoted in *American General Insurance Co. v. FTC*, 589 F.2d 462 [9th Cir. 1979]). Where did the new chief justice derive the court's power to invalidate the laws of Parliament? Hobart said, "[B]y that liberty and authority that judges have over laws, especially . . . statute laws, according to reason and best convenience, to mould them to the truest and best use" (*Sheffield v. Ratcliff*, Hob. (K.B. 1615), as quoted in Plucknett 1926, 50).

Exasperated by such further attempts to limit his prerogative, James I dismissed Coke from the King's Bench, and ordered him to "correct" his decision in *Bonham's Case*, which had subsequently been published in England's case law reporter known as *The Reports*. Coke refused to accede to the king's demands.

The importance of Coke's opinion in *Bonham's Case* is sometimes downplayed by some scholars who point to England's later recognition of Parliament as the country's supreme sovereign entity. However, this criticism overlooks the indelible imprint left by *Bonham's Case* on U.S. law.

The American colonists were intimately familiar with the writings of Lord Coke. Coke's *Reports* first came to America on the *Mayflower*, and the Massachusetts General Court ordered two complete sets from England in 1647. Coke's opinion in *Bonham's Case* was among his most popular writings.

In *Paxton's Case of the Writ of Assistance*, Quincy 51 (Mass. 1761), colonist James Otis challenged Massachusetts's authority to issue writs of assistance, general search warrants that empowered local sheriffs to enter private homes and businesses to seize smuggled goods. Otis told the colonial court that he objected to such writs, which were created by a parliamentary act in 1662, because they violated the principle of *Bonham's Case*: "As to acts of parliament, an act against the Constitution is void. An act against natural equity is void; and if an act of parliament should be made in the very words of this petition, it would be void. The Executive Courts must pass such acts into disuse."

John Adams, who was in the Boston courtroom where Otis made his argument for the colonial application of *Bonham's Case*, later exclaimed, "Then and there the child Independence was born." Adams might also have exclaimed that the seeds of judicial review had been planted in the American colonies by Otis, who was unequivocally assigning to "Executive Courts" the responsibility of invalidating parliamentary legislation that violated constitutional precepts.

Four years later, the colonies again relied on the principle of *Bonham's Case*, this time in their opposition to the Stamp Act, a parliamentary statute that taxed everything from newspapers to playing cards. Thomas Hutchinson, lieutenant governor of Massachusetts, encouraged the "friends of liberty" and opponents of the Stamp Act to "take advantage of the maxim they find in Lord Coke that an act of parliament against Magna Carta or the peculiar rights of Englishmen is *ipso facto void*."

In 1786, the Superior Court of Rhode Island relied on *Bonham's Case* to strike down a statute that denied the right to trial by jury for certain crimes,

because "Lord Coke" held that such statutes were "repugnant and impossible" (*Trevett v. Weeden* [Newport Super. Ct. Judicature], as quoted in Plucknett 1926, 66).

The U.S. acceptance of the legal principles enunciated in *Bonham's Case* culminated in 1803 when the U.S. Supreme Court handed down its decision in *Marbury*, which established the power of judicial review by authorizing federal judges to invalidate unconstitutional laws enacted by the coordinate branches of government. Nowhere in *Marbury* does the Supreme Court cite *Bonham's Case* or expressly quote Lord Coke. But the influence of both Coke and his opinion cannot be missed.

Chief Justice John Marshall, writing for a unanimous Court, began his opinion in *Marbury* with two premises: the "constitution controls any legislative act repugnant to it," and "an act of the legislature repugnant to the constitution is void." Congress cannot be entrusted to determine the constitutionality of legislation passed by the House and Senate, Marshall implied, for the same reason the London College censors could not be allowed to judge their own cause.

"To what purpose are the powers [of Congress] limited" by the federal Constitution, Marshall asked, "if these limits may, at any time, be passed by those intended to be restrained?" In a passage that harkens back to Chief Justice Hobart's opinion in *Sheffield v. Ratcliff*, Marshall concluded that only the judicial branch of government can be entrusted with such an overreaching power: "It is emphatically the duty of the judicial department to say what the law is. Those who apply the rule to particular cases, must of necessity expound and interpret the rule. If two laws conflict with each other, the court must decide on the operation of each."

Although Chief Justice Marshall's opinion in *Marbury* extended to the United States the principles of judicial review first intimated in *Bonham's Case*, judges, lawyers, and laypersons still debate the legitimacy of allowing unelected (appointed) judges to invalidate legislation enacted by representative institutions in a democratic country.

House of Lords, wielded more power than did representatives for the commoners, later known collectively as the House of Commons, who were summoned merely to assent to royal will.

It was not long, however, before the Commons realized that its approval carried a measure of authority. In 1309, the Commons granted a subsidy to King Edward II (1307–27) on condition that he redress its grievances. During the reign of Edward III (1327–77), Parliament asserted three claims that would be echoed with minor variation in the American colonies: taxes assessed without approval from both houses of Parliament were void, legislation passed by only one house of Parliament lacked legal effect, and the Commons reserved the right to investigate and remedy any abuses by the royal administration. A century later, during the reign of Henry VIII (1509–47), the Commons asserted the power of the purse, arguing that all money bills must originate in its house.

These claims, although fairly innocuous when originally asserted by the Commons, were interpreted by subsequent Parliaments to mean that no one could rule without the consent of Parliament, and royal officials who abused their power, including the ruler, could be impeached and removed from office. When the English civil war known as the War of the Roses (1455–85) substantially depleted the ranks of the barons, the voice of the Commons grew louder as the representatives of the commoners were left to fend almost for themselves against a monarchical power that, culminating in the reign of James I (1603–25), claimed to be divine in origin and absolute in nature.

The struggles between Parliament and the crown for authority over England in the seventeenth century were a prelude to the struggles between Parliament and the colonists for control over the American colonies in the eighteenth century. The monarchy maintained that its power to govern England derived directly from God and thus overrode any earthly power, including that of Parliament and common law. Parliament, on the other hand, maintained that "the people, under God, were the source of all just power, and that Parliament represented the people."

Parliament and the monarchy waged battle on three fronts: military, political, and legal. The military struggle for power began in 1642 when England again erupted into civil war. The political battles constituted a series of muscle-flexing exercises conducted by Parliament and the monarchy. The Commons impeached several of the king's top advisers and demanded redress of the grievances it summarized in the 1628 Petition of Right. The monarchy, in

In 1649 Charles I was tried, convicted, and executed for subverting Parliament.

turn, dismissed Parliament on a number of occasions, and attempted to govern without requesting revenue from the Commons.

These political struggles came to a crescendo when King Charles I (1625–49) and Thomas Wentworth, the commander of the king's largest army, were tried, convicted, and executed for subverting Parliament and the rule of law. The INDICTMENT against the king reads much like the DECLARATION OF INDEPENDENCE:

> Whereas it is notorious, That Charles Stuart, the now king of England, not content with those many encroachments which his predecessors had made upon the people in their rights and freedoms, hath had a wicked design totally to subvert the ancient and fundamental laws and liberties of this nation, and in their place to introduce an arbitrary and tyrannical government; and that besides all other evil ways and means to bring this design to pass, he hath prosecuted with fire and sword, levied and maintained a cruel war in the land against the parliament and kingdom, whereby the country hath been miserably wasted, the public treasure exhausted, trade decayed, thousands of people murdered, and infinite other mischiefs committed.

During the sentencing phase of the trial, the president of the High Court of Justice instructed the king, in language that resonates through the U.S. Constitution, "[T]he Law is your Superior," and the only thing superior to the law is the "Parent or Author of Law, [which] is the people of England."

In 1689, Parliament achieved victory in its constitutional struggle with the monarchy when William and Mary (1689–1702) agreed to govern England as king and queen subject to a bill of rights. This English Bill of Rights, a forerunner to the U.S. Bill of Rights, which was submitted to Congress exactly one hundred years later, declares that the monarchy's "pretended power of suspending of laws or the execution of laws by regal authority without consent of Parliament is illegal." It also guarantees the right of each English subject to "petition the king" for redress of grievances, and acknowledges Parliament's role in "amending, strengthening, and preserving . . . the laws" of the country.

Although the English Bill of Rights ended England's seventeenth-century constitutional struggle between Parliament and the monarchy, America's eighteenth-century constitutional struggle with these two branches of government had not yet begun. By 1765, the pendulum of power had swung fully toward Parliament, prompting eminent English jurist SIR WILLIAM BLACKSTONE to write that "[s]o long as the English constitution lasts . . . the power of Parliament" is "absolute," "despotic," and "without control." Because England had no written constitution that constrained the legislative power of Parliament, "every act of Parliament was in a sense part of the [English] constitution, and all law . . . was thus constitutional."

The American colonists soon discovered that a legislative despot was just as tyrannical as a monarchical despot. The U.S. Constitution put an end to the notion of absolute power resting with any one sovereign, by separating the powers of government into three branches—executive, legislative, and judicial—and carefully delegating the powers of each. Although these safeguards against government-run-amok were the product of the violent American Revolution, they allowed for the tranquil and uneventful integration of many ordinary English legal principles into the U.S. system of justice, including early bankruptcy and welfare laws during the nineteenth century.

ENGLISH-ONLY LAWS 📖 Laws that seek to establish English as the official language of the United States. 📖

The movement to make English the official language of the United States gained momentum at both the state and federal levels in the mid-1990s. In 1995 alone, more than five bills designating English as the official language of the United States were introduced in the U.S.

Congress. In September 1995, Representative John T. Doolittle (R-Cal.) proposed an amendment to the U.S. Constitution that would establish English as the official language of the United States (H.R.J. Res. 109, 104th Cong., 1st Sess., 141 Cong. Rec. H9670-04 [1995]). The proposed amendment states, in part,

> The English language shall be the official language of the United States. As the official language, the English language shall be used for all public acts including every order, resolution, vote or election, and for all records and judicial proceedings of the Government of the United States and the governments of the several States.

Related legislation considered in the U.S. House of Representatives included the National Language Act of 1995 (H.R. 1005, 104th Cong., 1st Sess., 141 Cong. Rec. H1967-04 [1995]), introduced by Representative Peter T. King (R-N.Y.), and the Declaration of Official Language Act of 1995 (H.R. 739, 104th Cong., 1st Sess., 141 Cong. Rec. H889-02 [1995]), introduced by Representative Toby Roth (R-Wis.). Roth's bill would abolish section 203 of the VOTING RIGHTS ACT OF 1965 (42 U.S.C.A. § 1973aa-1a), which requires bilingual ballots, and the federal Bilingual Education Office, which is funded through the Bilingual Education Act of 1968 (20 U.S.C.A. §§ 3281 et seq. [1988]). English-only advocates favor the elimination of these programs, arguing that earlier immigrants to the United States learned English without such government help.

In the U.S. Senate, Senator Richard C. Shelby (R-Ala.) introduced the Language of Government Act of 1995 (S. 356, 104th Cong., 1st Sess., 141 Cong. Rec. S2124-04 [1995]). This legislation states, in part,

> [I]n order to preserve unity in diversity, and to prevent division along linguistic lines, the United States should maintain a language common to all people; . . . the purpose of this Act is to help immigrants better assimilate and take full advantage of economic and occupational opportunities in the United States; . . . by learning the English language, immigrants will be empowered with the language skills and literacy necessary to become responsible citizens and productive workers in the United States.

By the end of 1995, more than twenty states had passed their own laws declaring English to be the official state language. Most state English-only laws have been established since the mid-1980s, although Louisiana's was enacted in 1812. Many of the laws are largely symbolic and lack an enforcement mechanism. For example, the California measure, CA Const. art. 3, § 6 (West), a state constitutional amendment approved in 1986, simply states,

> The Legislature and officials of the State of California shall take all steps necessary to insure that the role of English as the common language of the State of California is preserved and enhanced. The Legislature shall make no law which diminishes or ignores the role of English as the common language of the State of California.

Not all citizens support an English-only policy. For example, in a 1995 poll conducted by the University of Texas Office of Survey Research of 1,010 adult Texans, 45 percent said they felt classes in public schools should be conducted only in English, and 53 percent thought teaching classes in English and Spanish was appropriate. When asked if an English-only state law was a good idea, 44 percent agreed and 49 percent did not.

Advocates of English-only legislation argue that having one official language will serve as a unifying force in the United States. They point to the findings of the 1990 census that 32 million U.S. citizens live in a non-English-speaking household and that of these, 14 million persons do not speak English very well. In a 1995 Labor Day address to the American Legion Convention in Indianapolis, printed in 141 Cong. Rec. E 1703-01 (1995), U.S. Republican presidential candidate and Senate Majority Leader Bob Dole, of Kansas, echoed this unification theme, stating,

> [I]f we are to return this country to greatness, we must do more than restore America's defenses. We must return as a people to the original concept of what it means to be American. . . . For example, English must be recognized as America's official language. . . . Lacking the centuries-old, primal bonds of other nations, we have used our language, our history and our code of values to make the American experiment work. . . . These are the forces that have held us together—allowing us to . . . absorb untold millions of immigrants while coming the closest any country ever has to the classless, upwardly mobile society of our ideals.

Members of U.S. English, an advocacy group founded in 1983, claim that English should be the primary, but not exclusive, language of government. They believe that all official documents and proceedings should be in English, but would make exceptions for the use of other languages in such places as hospitals, emergency rooms, police stations, and tourist sites. Actually, a 1995 study of government print communications, conducted by the General Accounting Office, found that only a small percentage were in a language other than English. The study, requested by advocates of English as the official language of the govern-

Maria-Kelley Yniguez, an employee of the Arizona Department of Administration, encounters many Spanish-speaking and bilingual claimants. But she stopped speaking Spanish on the job after Arizona passed an English-only law, and she later sued the state.

ARIZONA REPUBLIC, NOVEMBER 11, 1988

ment, examined titles released by the Government Printing Office and an agency of the U.S. Commerce Department over a five-year period. Of approximately 400,000 titles examined, only 265, or less than 0.06 percent, were in a foreign language. The study excluded foreign language communications issued by the State and Defense Departments, which most English-only advocates consider to be a legitimate use of languages other than English.

Critics say English-only laws are a hostile reaction to the ongoing influx of immigrants to the United States. In a September 1995 address to the Congressional Hispanic Caucus, President BILL CLINTON attacked the English-only movement, stating,

> Of course English is the language of the United States. . . . That is not the issue. The issue is whether children who come here, while they are learning English, should also be able to learn other things. The issue is whether American citizens who work hard and pay taxes and who haven't been able to master English yet should be able to vote like other citizens.

In May 1995, Governor Parris N. Glendening, of Maryland, vetoed a bill passed by the state legislature that would have made English the official language of state government. He said the legislation's anti-immigrant sentiment would divide the state's citizens. In Arizona, critics of a constitutional provision making English the official language sued the state, the governor, and other state officials to stop its enforcement. In *Yniguez v. Arizonans for Official English*, 69 F.3d 920 (1995), the U.S. Court of Appeals for the Ninth Circuit upheld a lower court's ruling that the provision, which bars state and local employees from using any language other than English in performing official duties, violates free speech rights and is unconstitutionally overbroad.

The case began in October 1987, when an organization called Arizonans for Official English began a petition drive to amend the Arizona Constitution to prohibit the government's use of languages other than English. The drive resulted in the 1988 passage of article XXVIII of the Arizona Constitution, titled English as the Official Language. Article XXVIII provides that English is the official language of the state of Arizona, and that the state and its political subdivisions—including all government officials and employees performing government business—must act only in English.

When the article was passed, Maria-Kelley Yniguez, a Latino, was employed by the Ari-

zona Department of Administration, where she handled medical malpractice claims. She was bilingual in Spanish and English, and communicated in Spanish with Spanish-speaking claimants and in a combination of English and Spanish with bilingual claimants. Because state employees who fail to obey the Arizona Constitution are subject to employment sanctions, Yniguez stopped speaking Spanish on the job immediately upon passage of article XXVIII, because she feared she would be disciplined. In November 1988, Yniguez filed an action against the state of Arizona and various state officials, including the governor and the attorney general, in federal district court. Yniguez sought an injunction against state enforcement of article XXVIII and a declaration that the provision violated the FIRST and FOURTEENTH AMENDMENTS to the U.S. Constitution, as well as federal CIVIL RIGHTS laws. The district court interpreted the provision as barring state officers and employees from using any language other than English in performing their official duties, except with certain limited exceptions, and ruled that it infringed on constitutionally protected speech in violation of the First Amendment.

In December 1995, following the Ninth Circuit's affirmance of the lower court's decision, the defendants petitioned the U.S. Supreme Court to review the decision (*Arizonans for Official English v. Arizona*, __ U.S.__, 116 S. Ct. 1316, 134 L. Ed. 2d 469 [1995]).

ENGROSS 📖 To print a final copy of a document. In archaic criminal law, engrossment was the process of forcing higher the price of a good by buying it up and creating a MONOPOLY. 📖

Engrossment was used in ancient law where the method of drawing up a written DEED or CONTRACT involved working out a rough draft and then having the final terms of the instrument copied legibly onto parchment paper. Today the term denotes modern forms of copying, including engraving or any other such form of printing that will provide a legible final copy.

Engrossment is also used to describe a step in the enactment of STATUTES. During the legislative process, a bill may be debated, read, altered, or amended until it is ultimately passed in a final form. The process of engrossing is the printing of an act in its final form and its enrollment.

ENGROSSED BILL 📖 A legislative proposal that has been prepared in a final form for its submission to a vote of the law-making body after it has undergone discussion and been approved by the appropriate committees. 📖

ENHANCEMENT 📖 Increase in value; improvement. 📖

Enhancement is generally used to mean an increase in the MARKET VALUE of PROPERTY that is the result of an improvement.

The enhancement of a criminal penalty means the increase of punishment, such as by increasing a jail sentence. This type of enhancement might be affected when the criminal's motive is found to be particularly depraved.

ENJOIN 📖 To direct, require, command, or admonish. 📖

Enjoin connotes a degree of urgency, as when a court enjoins one party in a lawsuit by

An example of an engrossed bill from the U.S. House of Representatives

98TH CONGRESS
1ST SESSION
H. J. Res. 175

JOINT RESOLUTION

To authorize and request the President to proclaim May 1983 as "National Amateur Baseball Month."

Whereas the game of baseball having originated in the United States of America; and

Whereas the game of baseball having engendered exceptional interest among the people of this Nation, both as a participant and as a spectator sport, to the extent that it has long been acknowledged as "The National Pastime"; and

Whereas some nineteen million amateur players annually participate in the game of baseball in the United States; and

Whereas many more millions of Americans are spectators each year at amateur baseball games involving players of virtually every age; and

Whereas the game of baseball, while providing wholesome recreational competition, teaches the desirable goals of sportsmanship and teamwork so necessary in developing good citizenship; and

Whereas amateur baseball organizations in the United States have taken the lead in a worldwide effort to obtain recognition of the importance of baseball by the Olympic movement to the extent that the 1984 Olympic games in Los Angeles will include baseball; and

Whereas amateur baseball is made possible by the contributions of time, effort, and financial support of countless millions of individuals from a wide range of business, industrial, fraternal, civic, religious, and service organizations of the United States; and

Whereas it is appropriate to honor and to pay tribute to all those associated on the amateur level with the "game of baseball": Now, therefore, be it

1   *Resolved by the Senate and House of Representatives*

2 *of the United States of America in Congress assembled,*

3 That the month of May 1983, be designated "National Ama-

4 teur Baseball Month," and that the President is authorized

5 and requested to issue a proclamation calling on all Govern-

6 ment agencies and upon all the people of the United States to

7 observe such month with appropriate programs, ceremonies,

1 and activities, so as to testify to the great and significant

2 value of amateur baseball to the American way of life.

Passed the House of Representatives March 21, 1983.

Attest:

Clerk.

ordering the person to do, or refrain from doing, something to prevent permanent loss to the other party or parties. This type of order is known as an INJUNCTION.

ENJOYMENT ◫ The exercise of a right; the possession and fruition of a right or privilege. Comfort, consolation, contentment, ease, happiness, pleasure, and satisfaction. Such includes the beneficial use, interest, and purpose to which property may be put, and implies right to profits and income therefrom. ◫

ENOCH ARDEN DOCTRINE ◫ The legal principles involved when a person leaves his or her spouse under such circumstances and for such a period of time as to make the other spouse believe that the first spouse is dead, with the result that the remaining spouse marries another, only to discover later the return of the first spouse. Generally, in most states, it is safer for the remaining spouse to secure a DIVORCE before marrying again. ◫

The Enoch Arden doctrine is named from the title of the famous poem of Alfred, Lord Tennyson, which recounted the story of a sailor who after being shipwrecked for ten years returned home to discover that his wife remarried. The sailor, however, refused to disrupt the remarriage. Jurisdictions recognized the need to deal with Enoch Arden MARRIAGES since, traditionally, a person can lawfully be married to only one spouse at a time. In an Enoch Arden situation, the spouse who has remarried does so based upon the GOOD FAITH belief that the absent spouse is dead. Nevertheless, he or she could be legally charged with, and prosecuted for, BIGAMY. Under both canon and COMMON LAW, the remarriage was regarded as void AB INITIO and any children born of it were considered illegitimate. In some jurisdictions, the spouse who remarried could also be sued by the new spouse for ANNULMENT or divorce on the ground of bigamy. These harsh results led state courts and legislatures to resolve such cases.

Many jurisdictions passed statutes based upon one enacted in 1603 during the reign of King James I of England, which barred the conviction of a spouse on bigamy charges if he or she remarried seven years after the absent spouse disappeared without any knowledge that the absent spouse was alive. Such statutes transformed the probability of the DEATH of the absent spouse into a legal certainty. States subsequently liberalized the original statute by permitting remarriage after a five-year period as opposed to a seven-year period.

Such statutes do not, however, endow the remarriage with legal status if the absent spouse is alive. Additional legislation was necessary to provide a means for legal recognition of the remarriage. A spouse who plans to remarry can commence an action for divorce based upon DESERTION, if he or she can establish that the absent spouse intended not to resume their marital relationship and willingly left home without justification for the requisite time period.

The facts of many Enoch Arden cases do not establish desertion, however. Legislatures have taken a variety of approaches to solve this difficulty. Some statutes provide for the judicial DISSOLUTION of a marriage, provided a spouse has been absent for five consecutive years without any knowledge that he or she is alive, the spouse who commences the dissolution proceeding believes that the absent spouse is dead, and a diligent search was undertaken but there was no evidence that the absent spouse is alive. A spouse must obtain a dissolution of the marriage by the court before he or she can legally remarry or else the remarriage will be VOID as a bigamous marriage. Statutes usually require the spouse who initiates the proceedings to place a notice for a specified time in a newspaper judicially regarded as most likely to give notice to the absent spouse. Such SERVICE OF PROCESS by publication satisfies the constitutional requirements of DUE PROCESS OF LAW in regard to the dissolution of the marriage, but it does not necessarily affect property or other rights.

Another statutory approach involves a court inquiry made when the spouse planning to remarry applies for a marriage license. The absent spouse receives notice by publication, and the outcome of the proceeding is a court finding of the death of the absentee, provided a diligent search was conducted. Although such a procedure recognizes the common-law presumption of death after seven years' unexplained absence, it permits a finding of death where the absence has been for a shorter time. Once the court makes a finding that the absent spouse is dead, the appropriate agency can issue a marriage license to the applicant and the remarriage is and remains valid, even if the absent spouse returns.

Other jurisdictions dispense with the requirement of legal proceedings and recognize the validity of a remarriage when the spouse is absent and there is no knowledge that he or she is alive for a statutory time period. A few states modify this general rule by either refusing to treat the remarriage as valid if the absent spouse and his or her survivor agreed to separate or if the survivor has not made reasonable inquiries to locate the missing person.

ENROLLED BILL ▥ The final copy of a BILL or JOINT RESOLUTION that has passed both houses of a legislature and is ready for signature. In legislative practice, a bill that has been duly introduced, finally passed by both houses, signed by the proper officers of each, approved by the governor (or president), and filed by the secretary of state. ▥

Under the enrolled bill rule, once an election for the adoption of a STATUTE is held, the

An example of an enrolled bill from the U.S. House of Representatives

H. J. Res. 175

NINETY-EIGHTH CONGRESS OF THE UNITED STATES OF AMERICA

AT THE FIRST SESSION

Begun and held at the City of Washington on Monday, the third day of January, one thousand nine hundred and eighty-three

Joint Resolution

To authorize and request the President to proclaim May 1983 as "National Amateur Baseball Month."

Whereas the game of baseball having originated in the United States of America; and

Whereas the game of baseball having engendered exceptional interest among the people of this Nation, both as a participant and as a spectator sport, to the extent that it has long been acknowledged as "The National Pastime"; and

Whereas some nineteen million amateur players annually participate in the game of baseball in the United States; and

Whereas many more millions of Americans are spectators each year at amateur baseball games involving players of virtually every age; and

Whereas the game of baseball, while providing wholesome recreational competition, teaches the desirable goals of sportsmanship and teamwork so necessary in developing good citizenship; and

Whereas amateur baseball organizations in the United States have taken the lead in a worldwide effort to obtain recognition of the importance of baseball by the Olympic movement to the extent that the 1984 Olympic games in Los Angeles will include baseball; and

Whereas amateur baseball is made possible by the contributions of time, effort, and financial support of countless millions of individuals from a wide range of business, industrial, fraternal, civic, religious, and service organizations of the United States; and

Whereas it is appropriate to honor and to pay tribute to all those associated on the amateur level with the "game of baseball": Now, therefore, be it

Resolved by the Senate and House of Representatives of the United States of America in Congress assembled, That the month of May 1983, be designated "National Amateur Baseball Month," and that

H.J. Res. 175–2

the President is authorized and requested to issue a proclamation calling on all Government agencies and upon all the people of the United States to observe such month with appropriate programs, ceremonies, and activities, so as to testify to the great and significant value of amateur baseball to the American way of life.

Speaker of the House of Representatives.

Vice President of the United States and President of the Senate.

procedural method by which the measure was placed on the ballot cannot be challenged with a lawsuit since judicial inquiry into legislative procedure is barred as an intrusion into the internal affairs of the lawmaking body. In addition, this rule enhances the stability of statutory enactments. Citizens can reasonably rely on the legality of filed enactments. As a result, an enrolled bill is the most authoritative source of statutory law in a jurisdiction.

ENTAIL 📖 To abridge, settle, or limit succession to REAL PROPERTY. An ESTATE whose succession is limited to certain people rather than being passed to all HEIRS. 📖

In real property, a FEE TAIL is the CONVEYANCE of land subject to certain limitations or restrictions, namely, that it may only descend to certain specified heirs.

ENTER 📖 To form a constituent part; to become a part or partaker; to penetrate; share or mix with, as tin *enters* into the composition of pewter. To go or come into a place or condition; to make or effect an entrance; to cause to go into or be received into.

In the law of REAL PROPERTY, to go upon land for the purpose of taking POSSESSION of it. In strict usage, the entering is preliminary to the taking possession but in common parlance the entry is now merged in the taking possession.

To place anything before a court, or upon or among the records, in a formal and regular manner, and usually in writing as in to *enter an appearance*, or to *enter a judgment*. In this sense the word is nearly equivalent to setting down formally in writing, in either a full or abridged form. 📖

ENTERTAINMENT LAW 📖 The areas of law governing professionals and businesses in the entertainment industry, particularly CONTRACTS and INTELLECTUAL PROPERTY; more particularly, certain legal traditions and aspects of these areas of law that are unique to the entertainment industry. 📖

The entertainment industry includes the fields of theater, film, fine art, dance, opera, music, literary publishing, TELEVISION, and radio. These fields share a common mission of selling or otherwise profiting from creative works or services provided by writers, songwriters, musicians, and other artists.

Contracts The entertainment industry exists in a state of economic uncertainty. Entertainment companies continually form, merge, re-form, and dissolve. Furthermore, consumer tastes in artistic products can change quickly, thrusting certain artists or artistic movements to the heights of popularity and reducing others to obscurity. Because of this instability, the

entertainment industry relies on complex contracts, which usually are drafted to protect entertainment companies against economic risk.

Personal Service Agreements The PERSONAL SERVICE agreement is a primary legal instrument in the entertainment industry. This agreement is negotiated between an artist and a company that manufactures, promotes, and distributes the artist's goods or services. The agreement often binds the artist to produce for one company for a certain period of time. Personal service agreements are often governed by statutes, and are often the subject of litigation because they restrict the rights of artists to perform or create for any entity except the company with whom they have contracted.

Artists generally do not have the resources necessary to manufacture, market, and distribute their goods or services. Instead, they must find an appropriate entertainment company to do so. Entertainment producers (e.g., book publishers, record companies, movie studios, and theaters) often invest large amounts of time and money in promoting and selling artists' talents or products to consumers. Most artists will fail to earn a profit for their producer. A few, however, will earn enormous sums. To ensure that artists who generate a profit will remain with the company, producers use personal service agreements to bind artists for a certain time, during which the producers at-

Most artists, such as jazz performer Miles Davis, do not have the resources to produce, manufacture, market, and distribute their own works. They make contracts with entertainment companies to promote and sell their work to consumers.

tempt to recover their investment in the artists, make a profit, and cover losses from less successful artists.

In some entertainment industries, personal service agreements are structured using OPTIONS. Options give a producer the right to extend an agreement for several time periods. For example, a record company may contract with a musician to provide one album during the first year of the agreement, with an option to extend the contract. After one year, if the record company feels it would be economically wise to release a second album by the musician, the record company may exercise its option and require the musician to provide the second album. Under option contracts such as this, producers can keep artists on their roster for many years, or as long as the artists are profitable.

Some option contracts can be disastrous for the artist. Musicians sometimes sign an option agreement without a provision that they can break the agreement if the record company fails to release their products. Many recording artists have been held in professional limbo by record companies that refuse to release their music and also refuse to allow them to record for another company. This practice, known as shelving, is used by some record companies to prevent economically risky artists from becoming valuable assets to other record companies.

Other entertainment industries use short-term personal service agreements rather than option agreements. For example, film studios often contract with actors, directors, screenwriters, and other creative artists on a one-film basis. Short-term agreements allow studios to avoid paying guaranteed fees to artists whose market might dissipate overnight. In the early days of the film industry, studios bound stars to long-term agreements. That system changed in the 1940s when certain stars demanded fees that were higher than studios were willing to pay. Those stars then demanded, and received, one-film contracts for their services, which became the standard. The television industry, on the other hand, still uses long-term agreements for its talent in many areas.

Litigation over personal service agreements is common in the entertainment industry. Often an artist who is relatively unknown is willing to enter into an agreement that drastically favors the company with which she or he is signing. Once the artist achieves success and sees the profits the company is making from her or his services, the artist may demand higher fees or ROYALTIES, or to be released from the contract. Conflicts such as this often end up in court, where the company will often demand that the court order that the artist not perform for anyone else while the contract is in dispute. Whether the contract will be enforced and the artist required to perform under the agreement is usually determined by whether the contract meets certain legal requirements based on the state laws that govern it.

Contract for Rights   Another primary contract in the entertainment industry is the contract for rights. This contract often involves a transfer of COPYRIGHT ownership or a LICENSE to use certain creative property (e.g., a song or photo).

Many times, a contract for rights is combined with a personal service agreement. The agreement will often state that any work created by the artist during the term of the agreement is considered a work for hire. The company with whom the artist has contracted often receives automatic ownership of the copyright to a work for hire. For a work for hire to exist, the artist must either be an employee of the company or create the work pursuant to a valid written agreement—and even then the work must fall within a few specific categories defined by copyright law.

A license is a contract through which the artist or copyright holder grants certain rights to another party. For instance, a novelist might grant a license to a film studio to create a screenplay based on a novel. A license specifies the fee or royalty to be paid to the artist, the exact scope of use of the copyrighted material, and the time period for which the company may use the material, as well as any other conditions the parties agree to attach to the license.

Unique Aspects of Entertainment Industry Contracts

Complex Royalty and Payment Provisions Because entertainment companies often risk large losses, the contracts they use often contain clauses that artists may consider unnecessarily complex or one-sided. For example, film studios often base payments to talent in part on net profits. The calculations necessary to determine net profits, as defined in a typical contract, can be mystifying to those representing the talent. A screenwriter or an actor who receives bonuses or royalties on net profits might be paid little or nothing on a film that has earned hundreds of millions of dollars but is still showing a loss according to the net profits calculation. Net profits clauses have resulted in several high-profile lawsuits, and in 1996, they became the focus of a potential ANTITRUST action against the major film studios.

Record companies also use complex contractual formulas to determine royalty payments to their artists. Companies typically offer seem-

Clint Eastwood accepted an Oscar for best director for the movie Unforgiven, *in which he also acted. Highly successful artists such as Eastwood can command large royalty payments.*

ingly large royalty percentages to artists. Various clauses in the recording agreements then are used to reduce the royalty percentages, reduce the number of units on which royalties are paid, and delay payment for many months. Although a few small record companies have made some effort to simplify the structure of recording agreements, the major record companies and their smaller affiliates have uniformly fought to maintain the more complex, formula-based agreements.

Advances Many entertainment contracts are structured with advances. Advances are payments made to an artist before any actual income is received by the company manufacturing or delivering the artist's products or services. For example, an author might receive an advance of $50,000 when the author's manuscript is approved by the publisher. This advance is normally nonrefundable, even if the publisher never earns money from the publication of the author's work. However, the publisher will keep any royalties that would have been payable to the author, until the author's ADVANCE and other expenses have been recouped by the publisher.

Contracts with Minors Contract law in many states requires that specific steps be taken in or clauses added to a contract with a MINOR, to ensure that the contract is valid. Often, companies will require that the minor's parents execute a valid RELEASE, under which the parents guarantee the services of the child and agree to

be held liable for DAMAGES if the child fails to perform under the terms of the contract.

Contracts with Intermediaries Successful artists are surrounded by many individuals responsible for enhancing and protecting their career. Unknown artists use the services of such intermediaries to help them become known to more powerful figures in the entertainment industry. Intermediaries have various names and functions, but all serve to promote an artist's visibility and success in the industry. For this service, they generally take a percentage of an artist's earnings or a portion of the artist's PROPERTY RIGHTS in the artist's creations.

Agents AGENTS are individuals who procure employment and other opportunities for artists. In film production, agents find actors roles or pitch screenwriters' works to studios, producers, and actors. In music production, agents procure live engagements for musicians. In book publishing, agents attempt to secure publishing agreements for authors. For their services, agents often receive between five and 25 percent of an artist's revenues that are obtained through the agents' efforts. Agents nearly always require an artist to use only their services, while they usually serve many artists. Agents are strictly regulated in some states, especially states with large and successful entertainment enterprises. Agents have become powerful figures in the entertainment industry.

Personal Managers Personal managers are individuals who guide various aspects of an artist's career. In the early stages of an artist's career, the manager might act as agent, publicist, contract negotiator, and emotional counselor. As an artist gains in stature and income, the personal manager's primary task is to choose and direct specialists to handle various aspects of the artist's career. For these services, personal managers often receive 10 to 20 percent of an artist's income from all sources.

Attorneys ATTORNEYS in the entertainment industry perform many standard legal functions such as conducting litigation, giving business advice, protecting intellectual property, and negotiating contracts. Entertainment attorneys also serve as industry intermediaries, promoting their clients in order to procure contracts for the artists' products and services. For these services, entertainment attorneys are paid either an hourly fee or a percentage of an artist's income.

Entertainment attorneys often face difficult CONFLICTS OF INTEREST. For example, an attorney who has represented a record company is often pursued by a recording artist to shop the artist's material to that company. The artist knows that the company will often trust the attorney's

The Fiduciary Duty of Entertainment Attorneys: *Joel v. Grubman*

An attorney has a duty to act solely in the client's best interests, to disclose any potential conflict of interest, and to withdraw if a conflict would impair the attorney's ability to represent the client. In 1992 pop singer Billy Joel sued his former attorney Allen J. Grubman and Grubman's law firm for $90 million, claiming that Grubman had committed fraud and breach of contract. The suit alleged that while representing Joel throughout the 1980s, Grubman had defrauded the singer out of millions of dollars by negotiating secret deals with Joel's manager, Francis Weber, and by allowing Weber to control the law firm's representation, often in direct conflict with Joel's best interests. Joel claimed that if the firm had notified him of Weber's actions, Joel could have prevented millions of dollars in losses to his manager. The singer claimed that the law firm was concerned primarily with enhancing its own

reputation by keeping him on its client roster, and did not want to risk losing Joel as a client by angering Weber.

Joel also alleged that Grubman failed to disclose that the law firm represented Joel's label, Sony Music, and that such representation was an inherent conflict of interest that biased Grubman's judgment during contract negotiations.

The law firm claimed that it had done nothing illegal or unethical in its representation of Joel, and stated that it was hired by Joel only to negotiate contracts, not to monitor the business ventures of Joel's manager. Furthermore, the firm claimed that Joel had earned millions of dollars as a result of his recording contract, proof that its advice to him during negotiations with the label were not affected by the firm's relationship with Sony.

The case sent shock waves through the entertainment industry, where it is not uncommon for attorneys to represent both sides of a contract negotiation, or at least have ongoing client relationships with both sides, and it is also not uncommon for an attorney to respect the decisions of an artist's manager even though the attorney's client is the artist. Joel and Grubman settled the case without disclosing the terms of settlement.

See also Attorney Misconduct; Conflict of Interest.

opinion of the artist's marketability, which gives the artist a better chance of obtaining a recording contract. The attorney, however, is often privy to confidential information about the record company, or still represents the company in related negotiations. Attorneys and artists have been involved in several high-profile disputes because of such conflicts of interest.

Intellectual Property   The entertainment industry's primary product is intellectual property, protected by copyrights and TRADE-MARKS. A majority of the terms in entertainment contracts deal with the ownership and use of this property.

Songs, plays, films, works of fine art, books, and even some choreographed works are copyrightable. The contractual terms that define the ownership and use of these works are often negotiated for months, with both the artist and the entertainment company vying for as much control of the intellectual property as possible.

U.S. copyright law contains provisions specifically directed at the entertainment industry. For example, the songwriter—or the copyright holder, if the songwriter has transferred the

song's copyright or created the song as a work for hire—decides who can first record a song for publication. However, once the song has been recorded and published, the copyright holder may no longer limit who may record the song. If a song's copyright owner has previously granted permission to someone to record a song or if the songwriter has recorded and commercially released a recording of the song, the copyright holder is required by copyright law to grant a license to anyone else who wants to record that song. This is called a compulsory license. A licensee who records a song under a compulsory license is required to follow strict statutory guidelines for notification of its use and reporting sales and royalties to the copyright holder. The fee for a compulsory license is set by Congress at a few cents per recording manufactured, and is adjusted for inflation every few years.

A separate copyright exists in each legally recorded version of a song. Therefore, when a musician records a song after receiving the appropriate license from the owner of the song's copyright, that musician owns a separate copyright in the recorded version of the song. Normally, recording contracts require that a musician record songs—even songs otherwise owned by the musician—as works for hire. The copyrights to such recordings, called the masters, automatically become the property of the record company.

Copyright law also directly addresses the unique needs of dance, theater, and other performing arts. A creator of choreography can claim a copyright for that choreography once it has been fixed in a tangible form, such as on a video recording. The choreography can then be used only with the permission of the copyright holder.

A key aspect of copyright law as applied to the entertainment industry is that of derivative works. A copyright holder initially controls who may create a work based on the artist's original work. For instance, a film studio may create a screenplay based on a novel only with the novelist's, or other copyright holder's, written permission. This control is critical to authors and screenwriters, whose works can be adapted to several other media—films and sequels, television series and movies, audiotapes, toys, games, T-shirts, and so forth. An author can forgo millions of dollars of potential income simply by allowing a publisher to own and control the rights to create and license any such derivative works based on the author's work.

Entertainment company names, band names, performers' pseudonyms, and, more rarely, performers' legal names, can be protected under U.S. trademark laws. Like other businesses, entertainment entities have an interest in preventing others from using names so similar to theirs as to cause confusion among consumers as to exactly who is delivering certain products or services. Therefore, many entertainment entities register their names with the U.S. Trademark Office and claim exclusive right to use their names. In most cases, such names will be registered as service marks, rather than product marks. For instance, bands who register their band name as a trademark typically will register for performance of entertainment services. Once an entity receives a registration from the U.S. Trademark Office, no other entity may use the name, or a confusingly similar name, to provide services similar to those provided by the registrant.

Use and ownership of trademarks by members of a band or other entertainment company can be a source of great controversy when the entity dissolves. If prior to dissolution the owners or members of the entity have not agreed who may use the trademark after dissolution, lengthy legal battles can result as different members or factions try to use, and prevent the other members from using, the trademark.

Personal Rights   A successful artist's name and image can become valuable commodities. Use of the artist's name and likeness by another party can impinge on rights held by the artist. The legitimacy of such uses is often unclear and is based on several areas of law that overlap and sometimes contradict one another, such as right to PRIVACY, right to publicity, UNFAIR COMPETITION, DEFAMATION, and FIRST AMENDMENT law.

See also ART LAW.

ENTICE   To wrongfully solicit, persuade, procure, allure, attract, draw by blandishment, coax, or seduce. To lure, induce, tempt, incite, or persuade a person to do a thing. Enticement of a child is inviting, persuading, or attempting to persuade a child to enter any vehicle, build-

BOB DAEMMRICH/STOCK BOSTON

ing, room, or secluded place with intent to commit an unlawful sexual act upon or with the person of said child.

ENTIRETY   The whole, in contradistinction to a MOIETY or part only. When land is conveyed to husband and wife, they do not take by moieties, but both are seised of the *entirety*. PARCENERS, on the other hand, have not an *entirety* of interest, but each is properly entitled to the whole of a distinct moiety.

The word is also used to designate that which the law considers as one whole, and not capable of being divided into parts. Thus, a judgment, it is held, is an *entirety*, and, if VOID as to one of the two defendants, cannot be VALID as to the other. Also, if a CONTRACT is an *entirety*, no part of the CONSIDERATION is due until the whole has been performed.

Enticement includes inviting or attempting to persuade a child to enter a vehicle with the intent of committing an unlawful sexual act with that child.

ENTITLEMENT 📖 An individual's right to receive a value or benefit provided by law. 📖

Commonly recognized entitlements are benefits, such as those provided by SOCIAL SECURITY or WORKERS' COMPENSATION.

ENTITY 📖 A real being; existence. An organization or being that possesses separate existence for tax purposes. Examples would be CORPORATIONS, PARTNERSHIPS, ESTATES, and TRUSTS. The accounting entity for which accounting statements are prepared may not be the same as the entity defined by law.

Entity includes corporation and foreign corporation; not-for-profit corporation; profit and not-for-profit unincorporated association; business trust, estate, partnership, trust, and two or more persons having a joint or common economic interest; and state, U.S., and foreign governments.

An existence apart, such as a corporation in relation to its stockholders.

Entity includes person, estate, trust, governmental unit. 📖

ENTRAPMENT 📖 The act of government agents or officials that induces a person to commit a crime he or she is not previously disposed to commit. 📖

Entrapment is a DEFENSE to criminal charges when it is established that the agent or official originated the idea of the crime and induced the accused to engage in it. If the crime was promoted by a private person who has no connection to the government, it is not entrapment. A person induced by a friend to sell drugs has no legal excuse when police are informed that the person has agreed to make the sale.

The rationale underlying the defense is to deter law enforcement officers from engaging in reprehensible conduct by inducing persons not disposed to commit crimes to engage in criminal activity. In their efforts to obtain evidence and combat crime, however, officers are permitted to use some deception. For example, an officer may pretend to be a drug addict in order to apprehend a person suspected of selling drugs. On the other hand, an officer cannot use chicanery or FRAUD to lure a person to commit a crime the person is not previously willing to commit. Generally, the defense is not available if the officer merely created an opportunity for the commission of the crime by a person already planning or willing to commit it.

The defense of entrapment frequently arises when crimes are committed against willing victims. It is likely to be asserted to counter such charges as illegal sales of liquor or narcotics, bribery, sex offenses, and gambling. Persons who commit these types of crimes are most easily apprehended when officers disguise themselves as willing victims.

Most states require a defendant who raises the defense of entrapment to prove he or she did not have a previous INTENT to commit the crime. Courts determine whether a defendant had a predisposition to commit a crime by examining the person's behavior prior to the commission of the crime and by inquiring into the person's past criminal record if one exists. Usually, a predisposition is found if a defendant was previously involved in criminal conduct similar to the crime with which he or she is charged.

When an officer supplies an accused with a tool or a means necessary to commit the crime, the defense is not automatically established. Although this factor may be considered as evidence of entrapment, it is not conclusive. The more important determination is whether the official planted the criminal idea in the mind of the accused or whether the idea was already there.

Entrapment is not a constitutionally required defense, and, consequently, not all states are bound to provide it as a defense in their criminal codes. Some states have excluded it as a defense, reasoning that anyone who can be talked into a criminal act cannot be free from guilt.

ENTRY 📖 The act of making or entering a record; a setting down in writing of particulars; or that which is entered; an item. Generally synonymous with *recording*.

Passage leading into a house or other building or to a room; a vestibule.

The act of a merchant, trader, or other business-person in recording in his or her account books the facts and circumstances of a sale, loan, or other transaction. The books in which such memoranda are first (or originally) inscribed are called *books of original entry*, and are PRIMA FACIE evidence for certain purposes.

In COPYRIGHT law, depositing with the register of copyrights the printed title of a book, pamphlet, and so on, for the purpose of securing copyright on the same.

In immigration law, any coming of an ALIEN into the United States, from a foreign part or place or from an outlying possession, whether voluntary or otherwise.

In CRIMINAL LAW, entry is the unlawful making of one's way into a dwelling or other house for the purpose of committing a crime therein. In cases of BURGLARY, the least entry with the whole or any part of the body, hand, or foot, or with any instrument or weapon, introduced for the purpose of committing a FELONY, is sufficient to complete the offense.

In customs law, the entry of imported goods at the custom house consists in submitting them to the inspection of the revenue officers, together with a statement or description of such goods, and the original invoices of the same, for the purpose of estimating the duties to be paid thereon.

In REAL PROPERTY law, the right or authority to assert one's possessory interest or ownership in a piece of land by going onto the land. 📖

ENTRY OF JUDGMENT 📖 Formally recording the result of a lawsuit that is based upon the determination by the court of the facts and applicable law, and that makes the result effective for purposes of bringing an action to enforce it or to commence an APPEAL. 📖

Entering JUDGMENT is a significant action because it establishes permanent evidence of the rendition by the court of a judgment. Under some statutes and court rules, judgment is entered when it is filed with the appropriate official; under others, it must actually be noted in the judgment book or civil DOCKET.

The entry of a judgment is not the same as the rendition of a judgment. Rendition is a judicial act by a court in pronouncing the sentence of law based upon the facts in controversy. Entry occurs after the rendition of judgment and is a ministerial act that consists of recording the ultimate conclusion reached by the court in the action and providing concrete evidence of the judicially imposed consequences. It serves as a memorial of the action.

ENUMERATED 📖 This term is often used in law as equivalent to *mentioned specifically, designated,* or *expressly named or granted;* as in speaking of *enumerated* governmental powers, items of property, or articles in a tariff schedule. 📖

ENVIRONMENTAL LAW 📖 An amalgam of state and federal statutes, regulations, and common-law principles covering air pollution, water pollution, hazardous waste, the wilderness, and endangered wildlife. 📖

Almost every aspect of life in the United States is touched by environmental law. Drinking water must meet state and federal quality standards before it may be consumed by the public. Car manufacturers must comply with emissions standards to protect air quality. State and federal regulations govern the manufacture, storage, transportation, and disposal of the hazardous chemicals used to make deodorants, hair sprays, perfumes, makeup, fertilizers, herbicides, pesticides, detergents, cleansers, batter-

ies, and myriad other common goods and products.

Common Law Under the common law, environmental litigation revolves around six doctrines: nuisance, trespass, negligence, strict liability, prior appropriation, and riparian rights.

Nuisance Modern environmental law traces its roots back to the common-law TORT of nuisance. A NUISANCE is created when an owner or occupier of land unreasonably uses that land in a way that substantially interferes with the rights of others in the area. A nuisance is sometimes referred to as the right thing in the wrong place, like a pig in a parlor instead of the barnyard.

Nuisances can be public or private. A public nuisance interferes with a right or interest common to the general public, such as the public's interest in healthful drinking water. A private nuisance interferes with a right or interest of a private individual, such as a homeowner's right to the QUIET ENJOYMENT of her land.

The primary practical difference between the two types of nuisance is that a government department, such as a state or federal environmental agency, traditionally brings suit to ENJOIN a public nuisance, whereas only private citizens and organizations may sue to stop a private nuisance. The two concepts can also overlap. A nuisance that interferes with a private use of property can simultaneously interfere with a public interest. For example, factory smoke that diminishes the value of neighboring property is a private nuisance, and it is at the same time a public nuisance if it also endangers surrounding wildlife.

Courts engage in a balancing test to determine whether a particular activity amounts to a

Smoke from this paper factory may constitute a private nuisance to neighboring property.

public or private nuisance. A particular activity is declared a nuisance when its usefulness is outweighed by its harmfulness. The harmfulness of an activity is measured by the character and severity of the harm imposed, the social value of the jeopardized interest, the appropriateness of protecting the interest in a particular locality, and the burden to the community or individual in avoiding the harm. An activity's usefulness is measured by the activity's social utility, its suitability to a particular community, and the practicality or expense of preventing the harm it inflicts. Because there is no exact or universally agreed-upon value for each of the competing interests, it is often difficult for judges to apply the balancing test in a consistent fashion.

Gravity of the injury Although courts apply the balancing test for nuisance actions on a case-by-case basis, judges generally follow certain principles. The injury in question must be real and appreciable; the law does not concern itself with trifles. An occasional whiff of smoke, a temporary muddying of a well, a modest intrusion by roots or branches, and intermittent odors of sauces and stews will not rise to the level of a nuisance.

Courts also consider whether the alleged nuisance is of a continuing nature or has produced permanent or long-lasting effects. Nuisance law may excuse an isolated invasion of drifting pesticides, a single overflow of a sewer outlet, or a debris-burning incident lasting only a few days, and some courts have held that recurrence is a necessary prerequisite to a nuisance determination. For example, one court denied a prison inmate's nuisance claim that he was poisoned by pesticide delousing, because it occurred on only one occasion. In such cases, plaintiffs may have a viable claim for trespass or negligence (discussed later in this article) but not for nuisance.

In suits over pollution, courts also consider which party arrived first in the particular community, the polluter or the landowner alleging harm. The law has permitted polluters to escape LIABILITY by proving that a landowner alleging harm moved next to a preexisting nuisance with knowledge of its harmful activities. The rationale for this defense is that the landowner who "comes to the nuisance" generally pays less for the property because the nuisance has reduced its value. If such a landowner were then permitted to remove the nuisance, a windfall would inure to her or his benefit. Increasingly, however, courts place less weight on priority of arrival when evaluating a nuisance claim.

Nuisance claims have traditionally been evaluated from an objective point of view. If an "average" or "normal" person in the relevant community would be offended or annoyed by a certain intrusion, then the intrusion is considered real and appreciable. The idiosyncrasies of a hypersensitive plaintiff are generally discounted. Persons with extreme personal tastes and aesthetic sensitivity are usually denied relief under this objective standard. Persons with abnormal physical vulnerabilities, such as those with heart conditions, breathing problems, and tender eardrums, are usually denied relief as well.

In recent years, however, nuisance law has offered greater protection to society's vulnerable members. People are not necessarily abnormal, courts have held, merely because they enjoy spending time outdoors, sleeping with the windows open, or cultivating crops near smoke-billowing smelters. These activities are increasingly viewed as normal activities deserving protection. Many courts are also becoming more sympathetic to plaintiffs with preexisting health conditions or genetic frailties.

Two cases illustrate this trend. In the first, *Lunda v. Matthews*, 46 Or. App. 701, 613 P.2d 63, a cement plant was held liable for emitting debris, dust, and fumes that encompassed a landowner's house and aggravated his bronchitis and emphysema. The court reached this determination despite arguments that the landowner's illness made him more vulnerable to debris and dust than would be persons of ordinary health. The court also held that the cement plant could not escape liability merely because it was complying with state pollution standards.

In the second case, *Kellogg v. Village of Viola*, 67 Wis. 2d 345, 227 N. W. 2d 55, a landowner was permitted to recover for the loss of mink kittens who were eaten by their skittish mother after being frightened by noises and odors from a nearby dump. The court was not persuaded that the mink were abnormally squeamish or that the landowner was primarily responsible for their death because he had chosen to move next to the dump with full knowledge of its activities.

Aesthetic nuisances are another area where courts have produced inconsistent results. On June 25, 1927, a Pennsylvania court wrote that "[i]n this age, persons living in a community or neighborhood must subject their personal comfort to the necessities of carrying on trade or business," and when an "individual is affected only in his tastes, his personal comfort, or pleasure, or preferences, these he must surrender for the comfort and preferences of the many" (*Pennsylvania Co. for Insurance on Lives & Granting Annuities v. Sun Co.*, 290 Pa. 404, 138 A. 909, 55 A.L.R. 873).

This attitude was expressed more recently when a federal court denied the U.S. government's request that the court enjoin (prohibit) the construction of high-rise office buildings on the Virginia side of the Potomac River—even though the buildings would blight the Washington Monument, Lincoln Memorial, and other national landmarks (*United States v. County Board*, 487 F. Supp. 137 [E.D. Va. 1979]). These cases reflect judges' reluctance to hold themselves out as standard-bearers for good taste.

Yet aesthetic nuisances are still recognized by courts as viable claims when the extent of the injury is more serious. Judges distinguish between minor vibrations and bone-shaking tremors, normal barnyard smells and sickening stenches, and puffs of dust and blizzards of topsoil. An activity that overcomes extreme defensive measures taken by neighboring properties will be declared a nuisance. Nocturnal noises interfering with sleep can also sound the death knell for a particular activity, especially when there is evidence of widespread community dissatisfaction and not just a single complaint.

Utility of the activity An environmental injury will not be declared a nuisance unless it outweighs the utility of the activity. Determining the weight of a particular harm is often difficult for courts. Judges are human, and humans disagree on just about everything, including nuisance law. The easiest type of case for a judge involves an injury inflicted solely for the purpose of causing harm. A fence constructed with the intent to obstruct a neighbor's view will always be declared a nuisance. No socially redeemable value is assigned to animus and hostility.

Most cases, however, do not involve a nuisance created by adverse motivations. For instance, polluters usually produce useful products integral to a local economy, and the market value of an injured property is rarely greater than the business investments made by the polluter. But dollar figures are not always of paramount importance to judges.

Two leading cases illustrate the different results reached by courts in weighting utility. In the first, *Madison v. Ducktown Sulfur, Copper, & Iron Co.*, 113 Tenn. 331, 83 S.W. 658 (1904), the court denied a landowner's requested relief, stating,

In order to protect by injunction several small tracts of land, aggregating in value less than $1,000, we are asked to destroy other property worth nearly $2,000,000, and wreck two great mining and manufacturing enterprises. . . . The result would be practically a confiscation of the [polluter's] property . . . for the benefit of the [landowner]—an appropriation without compensation.

Courts balance the economic benefit of a plant against the environmental harm to the community when deciding if the plant is a nuisance.

In the second case, *Hulbert v. California*, 161 Cal. 239, 118 P. 928 (1911), the court granted the landowner's request for an INJUNCTION, over the polluter's claim of greater hardship, saying, "If the smaller interest must always yield to the larger, all small property rights, and all small and less important enterprises . . . would sooner or later be absorbed by the large and more powerful few."

Some environmentalists maintain that the law must protect the environment at any cost, whereas extreme advocates of the free market believe that business must be allowed to expand unhindered by governmental regulation. Certain results reached by particular judges may appear unreasonable to both extremes, but courts have attempted to strike a moderate balance over the long run.

Technology has often provided the means to moderation. Requiring businesses to shut down and relocate, or homeowners to endure a nuisance or move, are remedies not favored by the law. Courts avoid such remedies by exerting pressure on companies to develop technologies to make their operation safer for the environment. For example, one court ordered a smelting business to install specific arsenic control measures to abate a nuisance, instead of closing down the business as requested by the landowner (*American Smelting & Refining Co. v. Godfrey*, 158 F. 225 [8th Cir. 1907]).

Many nuisances can be remedied without state-of-the-art technology. For example, airports have been forbidden to authorize low-level flights over certain residences, and farmers have been ordered to confine foul odors to particular buildings. Other nuisances can only be abated by the best available technology. Sometimes, however, it is economically impractical or prohibitively expensive for a polluter to use such technology.

Courts disagree about what should be done when a polluter can do nothing short of ceasing operations to lessen an injury. Many courts deny injunctive relief if the polluter is already using the most modern pollution control methods available. Some courts grant an injunction ordering the polluter to shut down when state-of-the-art controls hold no further promise of relief. Other courts award DAMAGES for a nuisance that occurs despite the use of the best available technology.

Trespass and Negligence Nuisance actions deal primarily with continuing or repetitive injuries. TRESPASS and NEGLIGENCE actions provide relief even when an injury results from a single event. A polluter who spills oil, dumps chemicals, or otherwise contaminates neighbor-

Water laden with phosphate flowing off a sugar cane field into a canal may be held to be a nuisance if it is continual or trespass or negligence if it happens on only one occasion.

ing property on one occasion might avoid liability under nuisance law but not under negligence or trespass law.

Trespass involves an intentional interference with the PROPERTY interest of an owner or occupier of land. Negligence occurs when a defendant fails to exercise the amount of care that would be exercised by a reasonably prudent person under the circumstances. Whereas trespass requires the injury to result from deliberate misconduct, negligence results from the accidental and inadvertent.

Under nuisance law, liability is based on an unreasonable and substantial interference with the legal interests of a landowner's property. Conversely, trespass is proved by evidence of any tangible invasion of a landowner's property, however slight. Similarly, pollution resulting from negligence need not produce a substantial injury in order for a landowner to recover. However, a landowner who suffers only minor injuries from the negligence or trespass of a polluter will receive only NOMINAL DAMAGES.

Strict Liability The doctrine of STRICT LIABILITY for abnormally dangerous activities provides a fourth remedy for those suffering environmental harm. To recover under this doctrine, the landowner must demonstrate that a condition or activity qualifies as abnormally dangerous and was in fact the cause of the environmental injury. Many common activities have been decreed abnormally dangerous, including collecting large quantities of water in hydraulic power mains, storing gas in large amounts, and transmitting high-powered electricity under city streets.

Courts sometimes struggle in determining when something rises to the level of abnormally dangerous, and liability generally also attaches for extraordinary, abnormal, exceptional, and nonnatural activities or conditions. Examples of such activities are oil well drilling, crop dusting, pile driving, and blasting.

Prior Appropriation and Riparian Rights A riparian proprietor is the owner of land abutting a stream of water or river and, as such, has a qualified right in the soil to divert the stream as permitted by law. Generally, a riparian owner has the right to all the useful purposes to which a stream passing through the land may be put. Specifically, the rights of riparian owners have been divided into two discrete categories.

The first category is known as prior appropriation. Under the principles of prior appropriation, the law provides that whoever first appropriates stream water for a beneficial purpose acquires a VESTED right to the continued diversion and use of that water against all claimants who might later do the same. Courts often describe prior appropriation as the principle "first in time is first in right."

Prior appropriation places downstream owners at a distinct disadvantage because it permits upstream owners to completely divert or contaminate stream water so long as they do so for a beneficial purpose. Early cases suggested that no beneficial purpose was served when water was diverted for reasons other than commerce or profit, such as for mere personal pleasure. Today, however, courts permit riparian owners to appropriate water for almost any aesthetic, recreational, preservational, or pollution control purpose.

Prior appropriation principles are followed in many western states where water is scarce, and efficient and economic uses for streams and rivers are necessary. In the eastern states, the doctrine of RIPARIAN RIGHTS is followed. This doctrine has two strains. The first provides that each riparian owner has an absolute right to the flow of stream water uninterrupted by any unnatural (i.e., human) causes. The second strain provides that each riparian proprietor has a right to any REASONABLE use of the stream water passing through his or her land, and is protected from unreasonable uses upstream. This doctrine does not encourage the economically efficient use of water, as does the doctrine of prior appropriation—but water is not scarce in the eastern states where riparian rights theory is applied. See also WATER RIGHTS.

Statutory Law Much of the early environmental legislation at the federal level was drafted in response to the shortcomings of the COMMON LAW, and the inadequate and inconsistent protection of the environment by the states. The common law was slow to respond to changes in technology, and often provided inadequate or antiquated remedies. By nature, common-law doctrines were developed only in response to lawsuits filed between the disputing parties. The initial disagreements were often protracted in nature, and litigation was usually the last resort. As a result, by the time a lawsuit was filed, a particular environmental hazard may have become so pervasive or problematic that no common-law remedy could adequately address it.

Even when an appropriate common-law remedy was available, many state courts refused to enjoin larger businesses from polluting, out of concern that the polluters might harm the local economy by laying off employees or increasing prices. Although some states enacted pollution control statutes, many did not. The states that did enact such statutes varied in the level of protection provided and in the quality of enforcement. Thus, an activity might be deemed impermissible under the environmental legislation of one state, but permissible under the legislation of another. Federal air, water, and soil pollution standards and national wilderness and wildlife preservation regulations were drafted largely in response to these problems.

The NATIONAL ENVIRONMENTAL POLICY ACT (NEPA), 42 U.S.C.A. §§ 4321 et seq., is the fulcrum for these federal pollution and preservation regulations. NEPA, passed in 1969, requires the federal government to give environmental issues priority when planning major projects. It was created to establish councils and agencies that, in cooperation with state and local governments and public and private interest groups, would use all practicable means to monitor and protect the environment.

The Council on Environmental Quality (CEQ) and the ENVIRONMENTAL PROTECTION AGENCY (EPA) were both created under the auspices of NEPA. The CEQ prepares an annual report that discloses the quality and condition of the country's environment, evaluates federal programs that may affect the environment, and recommends specific policies to foster environmental protection and improvement. The EPA administers these policies and most federal environmental statutes. Each of the fifty states has drafted environmental regulations similar to those written on the federal level, and the state and federal regulations work together to address the various environmental issues.

Air Pollution Air pollutants are divided into five main classes: carbon monoxide, particulates, sulfur oxide, nitrogen oxide, and hydrocarbons. Carbon monoxide is a colorless,

CHROMOSOHM/JOE SOHM/PHOTO RESEARCHERS

Air pollution from factories is regulated by Title I of the Clean Air Act.

odorless, and poisonous gas produced by the burning of carbon in many fuels. Motor vehicles are one source of this pollutant.

Particulates are solid or liquid particles produced largely by stationary fuel combustion and industrial processes.

Sulfur oxides are acrid, corrosive, and poisonous gases produced by burning fuel containing sulfur. Electrical utilities and industrial plants are their principal sources.

Nitrogen oxides are produced when fuel is burned at very high temperatures, as is the case with stationary combustion plants and motor vehicles. Once emitted into the air, nitrogen oxides can be chemically converted into sulfates and nitrates, which may return to earth as components of precipitation, known as acid rain.

Hydrocarbons, which are produced by cars, motorboats, and power plants, form smog when combined with nitrogen oxides in the atmosphere under the influence of sunlight.

Each of these pollutants is a threat to human health. Acute cases of air pollution have caused marked increases in illness and death, especially among older people and among those with respiratory and cardiac conditions. Such pollutants also contribute to the health problems of society's less vulnerable members, increasing the incidence of emphysema and bronchitis among the general population. For instance, smokers living in polluted cities are more likely to contract lung cancer than are smokers in rural areas.

Federal regulation of air pollution is controlled primarily by the Clean Air Act (CAA)

and its amendments. Air pollution is broadly defined by the act to mean any air pollution agents or combination of agents. The act directs the EPA to establish the National Ambient Air Quality Standards (NAAQS) for air pollutants that endanger public health or welfare. The EPA may consider not the economic or technological feasibility of attaining NAAQS, but only whether the standards are set at levels necessary to protect the public.

States are not divested of the authority to regulate air pollution under the CAA. They retain "primary responsibility for assuring air quality" within their boundaries. Yet, following the promulgation of NAAQS, each state must submit for EPA approval a state implementation plan (SIP) designed to develop and maintain the air quality standards within its jurisdiction. SIPs that are found lacking may be amended by the EPA. States are also required to comply with the minimum national thresholds created by the CAA. These national thresholds permit state governments and their subdivisions to enact more stringent air pollution regulations than those enacted by the federal government, but not less stringent ones.

The CAA has three titles. Title I governs stationary sources of air pollution, including all buildings, structures, facilities, and installations emitting air pollutants. Title II governs mobile sources of air pollution, such as AUTOMOBILES, trucks, and aircraft. Both titles prescribe the amount of pollution that may be emitted into the air without violating the act.

Title III outlines procedures for the enforcement of the act through legal or administrative proceedings. State and federal governments may enforce the act, as may private individuals in so-called citizen suits. The CAA provides a variety of administrative, equitable (nonmonetary), civil, and criminal penalties, ranging from informal measures such as violation notices to more formal measures such as injunctive relief (a court order to perform or refrain from performing a particular act), money damages, and fines.

International attention has focused on three particular forms of air pollution: acid rain, global climate changes, and ozone depletion. Acid rain is created when sulfur from fossil fuels is emitted into the air and converted into a pollutant through oxidation, later mixing with rain or snow and returning to the earth as a component of precipitation. Although the CAA has commissioned a number of federally sponsored studies on the subject, scientists still disagree on the severity of the problems presented by acid rain.

WILL MCINTYRE/PHOTO RESEARCHERS

Scientists also disagree about whether air pollution can influence the global climate. Some scientific studies conclude that air pollution has caused the average temperature on earth to increase during the last twenty-five years or so, resulting in a condition called global warming; some conclude that the average temperature has decreased, resulting in global cooling. Other studies indicate that the global climate remains unaffected by air pollution and will continue to do so. Because of the discord in the scientific community, the CAA has commissioned federally sponsored studies to investigate the relationship between air pollution, acid rain, and the global climate.

The CAA has also commissioned federally sponsored studies regarding the relationship between air pollution and the destruction of the ozone layer. The ozone layer shields the earth from the harmful effects of the sun's radiation, and may be depleted by the release of chloro-fluorocarbons (CFCs) into the atmosphere. CFCs serve as a coolant for refrigerators and air conditioners, as a foaming agent for insulation, as a solvent for computer chips, and as a propellant for aerosol products. The CAA bans nonessential uses of CFCs, but leaves room for judicial interpretation as to what the phrase *nonessential uses* might mean.

Noise pollution is another form of air pollution regulated by the federal government. The rumbling sounds of eighteen-wheelers on the highway, 747s in the air, and jackhammers in the street are all familiar to the modern era. The Noise Control Act of 1972 (NCA) (42 U.S.C.A. § 4901 et seq.) was created to eliminate or reduce such noises when they pose problems to public health and welfare. Under the NCA, the EPA conducts studies on industrial areas with excessive noise, and establishes noise emissions standards. Airports, airplanes, railroads, trains, and trucks have all been required to reduce noise levels through the devel-

This North Carolina forest has been damaged by acid rain, caused when sulfur from fossil fuels is emitted into the air and then mixes with rain or snow and returns to the ground.

opment of quieter motors, engines, and equipment. Any citizen may bring legal action to enforce the provisions of the NCA, but the EPA retains the right to intervene. Remedies include injunctive relief, fines, and criminal penalties.

In the late 1980s and early 1990s, the regulation of air pollution moved indoors. Studies conducted during the late 1980s and early 1990s have shown that people are exposed to higher concentrations of air pollution for longer periods of time inside buildings than outdoors. One prevalent source of indoor air pollution is cigarettes. Many states restrict or prohibit smoking in a variety of public places, including indoor stadiums, restaurants, theaters, grocery stores, buses, trains, and airplanes. The federal government, through the Occupational Safety and Health Act (OSHA), 29 U.S.C.A. § 651 et seq., protects employees from "occupational diseases caused by breathing air contaminated with harmful dusts, fogs, fumes, mists, gases, smokes, sprays, or vapors." See also TOBACCO.

Water Pollution Like clean air, healthy water is indispensable to human existence. Humans depend on water for drinking, cooking, swimming, fishing, and farming. Discharges of organic wastes, heated water, nutrients, sediments, toxic chemicals, and other hazardous substances can all make water unfit for human use. Organic wastes, produced by animals and humans, decompose through the use of oxygen. If a body of water spends too much oxygen during the decomposition of organic wastes within it, certain types of fish will not survive. Aquatic life can also be harmed by the discharge of heated water into lakes and streams, because the increased temperatures accelerate biological and chemical processes that reduce the water's ability to retain oxygen.

The release of nutrients and sediments, such as detergents and fertilizers, can also harm bodies of water. Eutrophication, the natural

DAVE SCHAEFER/THE PICTURE CUBE

Industry is one of three sources of water pollution. Municipal activity and agriculture also present problems.

process by which lakes evolve into swamps and eventually dry land over the course of thousands of years, is accelerated by the discharge of nutrients that make lakes more biologically productive. Discharges of toxic chemicals, heavy metals, and other hazardous material can render both the water and its aquatic life unsafe for human consumption. The three major sources of these types of water pollution are industry, municipal activity, and agriculture.

Federal regulation of water pollution begins with the Federal Water Pollution Control Act (FWPCA) (Pub. L. 87-88, July 20, 1961, 75 Stat. 204, 33 U.S.C.A. §§ 1151 et seq.; 43 U.S.C.A. § 3906). The FWPCA was designed to make waters "fishable and swimmable" and to eliminate the discharge of pollutants into navigable waters. The act delineates water quality standards, requiring many water polluters to implement the best practicable control technology or the best available technology economically achievable. Pursuant to the FWPCA, the EPA is required to maintain a list of toxic substances and to establish separate limitations for each of them based on public health rather than technological or economic feasibility. Although the primary responsibility for the enforcement of the act was left with the states, the federal government and private citizens are also authorized to pursue remedies.

In 1977, the FWPCA was amended by the Clean Water Act (CWA) (Pub. L. No. 95-217,

Dec. 27, 1977, 91 Stat. 1566, 33 U.S.C.A. §§ 1251 et seq.). Under the CWA, conventional water pollutants, such as oil, grease, and fecal coliform bacteria, are to be measured by the best conventional pollutant control technology. The CWA requires the EPA to weigh "the reasonableness of the . . . costs of attaining a reduction in [pollution and the] benefits derived." No cost-benefit analysis was permitted for toxic substances and nonconventional pollutants such as ammonia, chlorides, and nitrates. Civil and criminal penalties, including fines of up to $25,000 a day, are authorized under the CWA.

Oil spills and ocean dumping present two troubling problems for clean-water advocates in the international arena. Section 311 of the FWPCA announces that "it is the policy of the United States that there should be no discharges of oil or hazardous substances into or upon the navigable waters of the United States [or] adjoining shorelines." The same section later prohibits the discharge of any harmful quantity of a hazardous substance into any navigable waters of the United States.

In accordance with this provision, the EPA, on behalf of the president of the United States, has determined that discharges of harmful quantities of oil include, with some minor exceptions, any discharge that discolors or leaves a film on the water or adjoining shorelines. Since the discharge of even a few gallons of oil can leave a film, this provision is tantamount to a no-discharge policy.

It also represents a strict liability standard. There is no escape from liability for a harmful discharge of oil that results from negligence, even if the accident could not have been prevented. By contrast, previous federal legislation prohibited only oil spills that were knowingly discharged. Courts have broadly interpreted the CWA to cover oil discharged by trucks, pipelines, vessels, drilling platforms, and both onshore and offshore facilities. A civil penalty of not more than $5,000 is prescribed for each offense, and some penalty must be imposed for every violation regardless of its severity.

Accompanying the civil penalty scheme are cleanup provisions. These include (1) preparation and publication of a national contingency plan for the removal of hazardous substances and the prevention of spills; (2) authorization for the United States to take summary action (including the removal or destruction of a vessel) whenever a marine disaster creates a substantial threat to the nation's environment, including threats to fish, wildlife, shorelines, and beaches; (3) authorization for the U.S. attorney general, under the direction of the president, to abate any "imminent or substantial" marine disaster through legal action; and (4) imposition of costs for cleanup upon the owner or operator.

The Marine Protection, Research, and Sanctuaries Act of 1972 (MPRSA), popularly known as the Ocean Dumping Act, is the second piece of federal legislation drafted in response to these two international water pollution problems. The MPRSA has three titles. Title I establishes a permit program, administered by the EPA, for dumping materials into and transporting them through ocean waters. Title II creates a research program, under the auspices of the secretary of commerce, to determine ways in which ocean dumping can be reduced or eliminated. Under title III, the secretary of commerce may designate certain parts of ocean water as marine sanctuaries to preserve and restore recreational, ecological, or aesthetic interests.

The MPRSA flatly prohibits any dumping of radiological, chemical, or biological warfare agents into ocean waters. The Coast Guard is responsible for surveillance under the act. Violators face civil penalties of up to $50,000 for each violation. Criminal penalties and injunctive relief may also be pursued by the government. Private citizens harmed by ocean dumping may seek relief as well.

Permits for ocean dumping may be granted in certain circumstances. Both the administrator of the EPA and the secretary of the Army have the power to dispense permits, but the administrator may veto permits issued by the secretary. The considerations in evaluating permit requests include the need for dumping material into ocean waters, other possible methods of disposal, and the appropriateness of the chosen dumping location. Generally, permits are granted when ocean dumping will not "unreasonably degrade or endanger human health, welfare, amenities or the marine environment, ecological systems or economic potentialities."

Toxic and Hazardous Substances   The federal government uses various forms of legislation to regulate the manufacture, storage, disposal, sale, and discharge of hazardous substances, which include toxic substances.

Pesticide regulation   The sale and distribution of pesticides in the United States are governed by the Federal Insecticide, Fungicide, and Rodenticide Act (FIFRA) (Pub. L. No. 100-532, Oct. 25, 1988, 102 Stat. 2654, 7 U.S.C.A. §§ 136 et seq.). Under the FIFRA, no pesticide may be introduced into the stream of commerce without approval by the administra-

The Exxon Valdez oil spill in Alaska required extensive cleanup of the nearby shoreline and islands.

tor of the EPA. If the administrator finds that a pesticide will "cause unreasonable adverse effects on the environment," the pesticide will not receive approval. An unreasonable adverse effect on the environment is defined as "any unreasonable risk to [humans] or the environment, taking into account the economic, social, and environmental costs and benefits of the use of any pesticide."

Once a pesticide is approved by and registered with the EPA, registration may be suspended by the administrator upon proof that continued use would "likely result in unreasonable adverse effects on the environment." Before suspension, the registrant is entitled to an expedited administrative hearing during which the danger and usefulness of the pesticide are measured. In emergency circumstances, the administrator may suspend registration prior to a hearing on the merits.

Chemical manufacturing regulation   The manufacture of chemicals is regulated on the federal level by the Toxic Substance Control Act (TSCA) (15 U.S.C.A. 2601 et seq.). The TSCA is underpinned by three policy considerations. First, industry has the primary responsibility for ascertaining the environmental effects of the chemicals it is manufacturing. Second, the government should have the authority to prevent unreasonable risks of injury to the environment, especially imminent risks. Third, the government should not exercise this authority in a manner that places unreasonable economic barriers to technological innovation. As with most of the statutory law in the environmental arena, the relative weights given to each value are balanced against each other.

The central provisions of the TSCA are sections 4, 5, and 6. Section 4 empowers the EPA to adopt rules requiring a manufacturer to test each substance that may "present an unreasonable risk" to the environment, "enter the environment in substantial quantities," or present a likelihood of "substantial human exposure." Section 5 requires manufacturers to give the EPA notice before producing new chemical substances. New chemicals covered by section 4 must then be tested. New chemicals not covered by section 4 but listed by the EPA as potentially hazardous are evaluated at a hearing provided under section 6.

Resource Conservation and Recovery Act The Resource Conservation and Recovery Act (RCRA), Pub. L. No. 94-580, Oct. 21, 1976, 90 Stat. 2795, 42 U.S.C.A. § 6901 et seq., was passed in 1976 as a response to a growing public awareness of problems relating to the disposal of hazardous waste. In 1981 the EPA estimated that 290 million tons of hazardous waste were produced in the United States annually, 90 percent of which would have been improperly disposed of before the RCRA became law. The chemical, petroleum, and metal industries were the nation's leading generators of hazardous waste during this period. In 1983 government studies indicated that as many as fifty thousand inactive disposal sites contained hazardous waste, with as many as twenty-five hundred posing a serious threat to groundwater and to public drinking supplies.

Hazardous waste was traditionally disposed of on the land of the generator. Occasionally, the generator would transport the waste to an

The Environmental Protection Agency has the authority to inspect disposal sites and regulate the management of hazardous waste.

off-site disposal area. During the twenty-year active life of a disposal site, ownership and operation frequently changed hands. Very few records were kept at the disposal sites, leaving many subsequent owners and operators without any indication of their prior use.

The RCRA attempted to answer these problems by providing "cradle-to-grave" regulation of hazardous materials. The RCRA requires the EPA to promulgate criteria for identifying hazardous waste in light of a substance's toxicity, persistence, degradability, corrosiveness, flammability, and potential for accumulation in organic tissues. Standards are prescribed for the generators and transporters of hazardous materials as well as for storage and disposal sites.

Generators and transporters are subject to record-keeping, reporting, and labeling requirements, with transporters also being subject to the strictures of the Hazardous Materials Transportation Act. Sites for underground storage tanks containing petroleum products, pesticides, and other hazardous products are governed by RCRA provisions that enable the detection, correction, and prevention of leaks. Disposal sites are regulated by a permit system in which the EPA is given broad powers to inspect a site, issue compliance orders, institute CIVIL ACTIONS against violators, and seek injunctive relief. Criminal penalties may also be imposed for violation of the permit system.

In 1984, Congress amended the RCRA, shifting the focus of hazardous waste management from safe land disposal to treatment alternatives. Under the 1984 amendments, land disposal is now the last alternative, and is permitted only when the waste is pretreated to meet standards issued by the EPA, or when the EPA determines "to a reasonable degree of certainty that there will be no migration of hazardous constituents from the disposal unit . . . for as long as the wastes remain hazardous."

When land disposal is deemed permissible, new landfills must use double liners and groundwater monitoring systems, unless the EPA finds that an alternative design or operating practice would be equally effective in preventing the migration of hazardous waste. In addition to providing for EPA regulation and enforcement actions, the RCRA authorizes private citizens to institute legal proceedings against violators of its provisions.

Comprehensive Environmental Response, Compensation, and Liability Act The Comprehensive Environmental Response, Compensation, and Liability Act (CERCLA), also known as the Superfund, was passed in 1980 to clean up hazardous waste disposal sites (42 U.S.C.A. §§ 9601 et seq.). The act consists of four elements. First, CERCLA establishes a system for gathering information to enable federal and state governments to characterize chemical dump sites and develop priorities for response actions. The administrator of the EPA is required to issue regulations designating which chemicals would be hazardous to the public if released into the environment. The owners and operators of hazardous waste storage, treatment, and disposal sites are required to notify the EPA of the amount and types of hazardous substances on-site, and of any known, suspected, or likely releases into the environment. Based on this information, the EPA develops a national priorities list (NPL), which ranks the nation's hazardous waste sites in order of importance.

Second, CERCLA establishes federal authority to respond when hazardous waste has been discharged into the environment. The president is authorized to provide removal and remedial actions consistent with a national contingency plan (NCP), which establishes procedures for cleaning up such discharges. Removal actions are short-term responses to emergencies, whereas remedial actions are intended to offer long-term solutions. The federal government's response actions at sites appearing on the NPL are limited to cases in which the responsible parties cannot be found or fail to take the necessary actions.

Third, CERCLA creates a class of persons who are potentially responsible parties (PRPs), who will be held liable for cleanup and restitution costs. The act provides that all generators and transporters of hazardous materials, and every owner and operator of a disposal or treatment facility, shall be liable for all removal and remedial costs incurred by the state and federal government not inconsistent with the NCP, as well as any other necessary response costs such as consulting fees or attorney fees in certain situations. In each case, CERCLA imposes strict liability upon the responsible party, independent of traditional notions of culpability such as intent and recklessness.

Fourth, the act creates the multi-billion-dollar Hazardous Substance Trust Fund to pay for removal and remedial actions. Money for the fund is raised through federal appropriation and through taxes paid by some disposal site owners and operators. The fund cannot be used to remedy environmental injuries from hazardous waste that "occurred wholly before the enactment of this Act." Private claims may be made against the fund only if the PRPs cannot be found or are insolvent.

The stickiest legal questions arise when courts assign liability for cleanup. For example,

lending institutions regularly foreclose, take title, and resell property without any knowledge or indication that the property was previously used as a hazardous waste site. Such institutions clearly fall within CERCLA's definition of a landowner, yet they assume no traditional responsibilities of land ownership.

Early CERCLA cases imposed liability upon lending institutions in these circumstances, even when the costs of cleanup exceeded the value of the property (see *United States v. Maryland Bank & Trust Co.*, 632 F. Supp. 573 [D. Md. 1986]). Although Congress later amended CERCLA to protect such "innocent landowners," courts still impose liability if the lending institution "had reason to know" of the hazardous waste disposal or failed to make "all appropriate inquiry" into the previous ownership before acquiring the property.

Liability under CERCLA is JOINT AND SEVERAL LIABILITY, which means that once it is established among a group of defendants, any one of the defendants can be held responsible for the entire cost of cleanup. Although defendants are permitted to offer evidence that they are responsible for only part of an environmental injury, the commingling of chemicals at dump sites makes such a defense difficult to prove. Defendants may also seek reimbursement from codefendants who were primarily responsible for a hazardous discharge, but this relief proves futile when a responsible codefendant has disappeared or filed bankruptcy. Thus, wealthy landowners are often left paying the costs of the CERCLA cleanup.

Preservation of Wilderness and Wildlife
NEPA requires the government to "fulfill the responsibilities of each generation as trustee for succeeding generations" to ensure "safe, healthful, productive and aesthetically pleasing surroundings" and protect "important aspects" of the "national heritage."

These cattle are grazing next to a Superfund toxic waste site in Louisiana.

The federal government has three land preservation categories: the National Park System, the National Wilderness Preservation System, and the National Wildlife Refuge. National parks include forested areas, recreational areas, and places of historical importance. Wilderness preserves are not intended for use, and are primarily found in Alaska and the Florida Keys. A wildlife refuge is a sanctuary for fish and game. Federal legislation protects each of these three areas from spoliation, degradation, and misuse.

In addition to establishing sanctuaries and refuges for wilderness and wildlife, Congress has passed the ENDANGERED SPECIES ACT, 16 U.S.C.A. §§ 1531 et seq., which charges the Department of the INTERIOR with the protection of animals teetering on the brink of extinction. The U.S. Supreme Court has interpreted this act very broadly, as reflected by the snail darter case (*Tennessee Valley Authority v. Hill*, 437 U.S. 153, 98 S. Ct. 2279, 57 L. Ed. 2d 117 [1978]).

The snail darter, a plain-looking, three-inch-long fish, was an endangered species inhabiting the rivers of Tennessee when the Tennessee Valley Authority began the construction of a $100 million dam that would have destroyed its habitat. After noting that Congress deemed all species to have incalculable value and finding that the Endangered Species Act "admit[ted] of no exception[s]," the Supreme Court held that the dam could not be completed.

ENVIRONMENTAL PROTECTION AGENCY

The purpose of the Environmental Protection Agency (EPA) is to protect and enhance our environment today and for future generations to the fullest extent possible under the laws enacted by Congress. The mission of the agency is to control and abate pollution in the areas of air, water, solid waste, noise, radiation, and toxic substances. The mandate of the EPA is to mount an integrated, coordinated attack on environmental pollution in cooperation with state and local governments.

The Environmental Protection Agency was established in the EXECUTIVE BRANCH as an independent agency pursuant to Reorganization Plan No. 3 of 1970, effective December 2, 1970.

The Environmental Protection Agency was created to permit coordinated and effective governmental action on behalf of the environment. The EPA endeavors to abate and control pollution systematically, by proper integration of a variety of research, monitoring, standard setting, and enforcement activities. As a complement to its other activities, the EPA coordinates and supports research and antipollution activities by state and local governments, private and public groups, individuals, and educational institutions. The EPA also reinforces efforts among other federal agencies with respect to the impact of their operations on the environment, and it is specifically charged with publishing its determinations when those hold that a proposal is unsatisfactory from the standpoint of public health or welfare or environmental quality. In all, the EPA is designed to serve as the advocate of the public for a livable environment.

Air, Noise, and Radiation Programs The air activities of the agency include development of national programs, technical policies, and regulations for air pollution control; development of national standards for air quality; emission standards for new stationary sources and emission standards for hazardous pollutants; technical direction, support, and evaluation of regional air activities; and provision of training in the field of air pollution control. Related activities include study, identification, and regulation of noise sources and control methods; technical assistance to states and agencies having radiation protection programs; and a national surveillance and inspection program for measuring radiation levels in the environment.

Water and Waste Management Programs The water quality activities of the EPA represent a coordinated effort to restore the waters of the nation. The functions of this program include development of national programs, technical policies, and regulations for water pollution control and water supply; water quality standards and effluent guidelines development; technical direction, support, and evaluation of regional water activities; development of programs for technical assistance and technology transfer; and provision of training in the field of water quality.

Solid Waste Emergency Response Programs The Office of Solid Waste and Emergency Response provides policy, guidance, and direction for the agency's solid waste and emergency response programs. The functions of these programs include development of program policy; development of hazardous waste standards and regulations; enforcement of applicable laws and regulations; guidelines and standards for land disposal of hazardous wastes; analyses on the recovery of useful energy from solid waste; and provision of technical assistance in the development, management, and operation of waste management activities.

Legal and Enforcement Counsel The Office of the Assistant Administrator for En-

The Environmental Protection Agency is concerned with situations where solvents and oils are passing from a site into the groundwater.

forcement has the following functions: (1) provide policy direction to enforcement activities in air, water, toxic substances, hazardous and solid waste management, radiation, and noise control programs; (2) plan and coordinate enforcement conferences, public hearings, and other legal proceedings; and (3) engage in other activities related to enforcement of standards to protect the environment of the nation.

Pesticides and Toxic Substances Programs The Office of Assistant Administrator for Toxic Substances is responsible for development of national strategies for the control of toxic substances; criteria for assessing chemical substances, standards for test protocols for chemicals, rules and procedures for industry reporting, and regulations for the control of substances deemed to be hazardous to man or the environment; and evaluation and assessment of the impact of new chemicals and chemicals with new uses to determine the hazard and, if needed, develop appropriate restrictions. It also coordinates with the activities of other agencies under the Toxic Substances Control Act (15 U.S.C. 2601 et seq. [1976]) for the assessment and control of toxic substances. Additional activities include control and regulation of pesticides and reduction in their use to ensure human safety and protection of environmental quality; establishment of tolerance levels for pesticides that occur in or on food; monitoring of pesticide residue levels in food, hu-

mans, and nontarget fish and wildlife and their environments; and investigation of pesticide accidents.

Research and Development The Office of the Assistant Administrator for Research and Development is responsible for a national research program in pursuit of technological controls of all forms of pollution. It directly supervises the research activities of the national laboratories of the EPA and gives technical policy direction to those laboratories that support the program responsibilities of the regional offices of the EPA. Close coordination of the various research programs is designed to yield a synthesis of knowledge from the biological, physical, and social sciences that can be interpreted in terms of total human and environmental needs. General functions include management of selected demonstration programs; planning for agency environmental quality monitoring programs, coordination of agency monitoring efforts with those of other federal agencies, the states, and other public bodies; and dissemination of agency research, development, and demonstration results.

See also ENVIRONMENTAL LAW.

EPA An abbreviation for ENVIRONMENTAL PROTECTION AGENCY.

EQUAL EMPLOYMENT OPPORTUNITY COMMISSION The Equal Employment Opportunity Commission (EEOC) is the federal agency charged with eliminating DISCRIMINATION based on race, color, religion, sex, national origin, disability, or age, in all terms and conditions of employment. The EEOC investigates alleged discrimination through its fifty field offices, makes determinations based on gathered evidence, attempts CONCILIATION when discrimination has taken place, and files lawsuits. The EEOC also oversees compliance and enforcement activities relating to equal employment opportunity among federal employees and applicants, including discrimination against individuals with disabilities.

The EEOC was created by title VII of the CIVIL RIGHTS ACT of 1964 (42 U.S.C.A. § 2000e-4). Title VII was amended by the Equal Employment Opportunity Act of 1972 (Pub. L. No. 92-261, Mar. 24, 1972, 86 Stat. 103), the Pregnancy Discrimination Act of 1978 (Pub. L. No. 95-555, Oct. 31, 1978, 92 Stat. 2076 [42 U.S.C.A. § 2000e(K)]), and the Civil Rights Act of 1991 (Pub. L. No. 102-166, Nov. 21, 1991, 105 Stat. 1071). On July 1, 1979, responsibility for enforcement of the Equal Pay Act of 1963 and the Age Discrimination in Employment Act of 1967, in private industry as well as state and local governments, was transferred from the Department of Labor to the EEOC. The Equal Pay Act prohibits gender-based pay differences for substantially equal work requiring equal skill and responsibility; the Age Discrimination Act prohibits employment discrimination against workers or applicants forty years of age or older. Title I of the Americans with Disabilities Act of 1990 (ADA) (42 U.S.C.A. §§ 12101 et seq.) has been enforced by the EEOC since July 1992. Title I governs private employers, state and local governments, employment agencies, labor organizations, and joint labor-management committees. The ADA prohibits employment discrimination against qualified individuals with disabilities and requires that employers make reasonable accommodations for these individuals.

Complaints under Title VII of the Civil Rights Act of 1964 Title VII of the Civil Rights Act of 1964 prohibits employment discrimination based on race, color, religion, sex, or national origin, by private employers, state and local governments, educational institutions with fifteen or more employees, the federal government, private and public employment agencies, labor organizations, and joint labor-management committees for apprenticeship and training. Charges of title VII violations outside the federal sector must be filed with the EEOC within 180 days of the alleged violation, or in states with fair employment practices agencies, within 300 days. The EEOC is responsible for notifying the persons charged, within 10 days after receiving a charge. Before investigation, charges must be deferred for 60 days to state or local fair employment practices agencies in localities with a fair employment practices law covering the alleged discrimination. If the agency has been operating less than one year, the charges must be deferred for 120 days.

Under work-sharing agreements between the EEOC and state and local fair employment practices agencies, the EEOC routinely assumes authority over certain charges of discrimination and proceeds with its investigation. If there is reasonable cause to believe that a charge is true, the district, area, or local office uses informal conciliation conferences to try to remedy the unlawful practices. If an acceptable agreement cannot be reached, the case is submitted to the EEOC for possible litigation. If litigation is approved, the EEOC brings suit in federal district court.

Under title VII, the attorney general brings suit when a state or local government or politi-

As this man searches for a job he is protected from discrimination based on his age by the Age Discrimination in Employment Act of 1967.

cal subdivision is involved. If litigation is not approved or if a finding of no reasonable cause is made, the charging party is allowed to sue within 90 days in federal district court. The EEOC may intervene in such actions if the case is of general public interest.

Complaints under the Americans with Disabilities Act of 1990 The Americans with Disabilities Act of 1990 incorporates the remedies and procedures contained in title VII of the Civil Rights Act of 1964. Employment discrimination charges based on disability may be filed at any of the EEOC's field offices. The EEOC investigates and attempts to conciliate the charges using the same procedures as for charges filed under title VII. The litigation procedures under title VII also apply to charges filed under the ADA.

Complaints under the Age Discrimination in Employment Act of 1967 and Equal Pay Act of 1963 The Age Discrimination in Employment Act of 1967 and Equal Pay Act of 1963 cover most employees and job applicants in private industry and in the federal, state, and local governments. An AGE DISCRIMINATION charge must be filed with the EEOC within 180 days of the alleged violation, or where the action took place in a state that has an age discrimination law and an authority administering that law, within 300 days of the violation or 30 days after receiving the notice of termination of state proceedings, whichever is earlier. A lawsuit must be filed within two years of the alleged discriminatory act, or within three years in cases of a willful violation of the law.

Under the Civil Rights Act of 1991, a lawsuit must be filed within 90 days of the plaintiff's receipt of a notice of final action. The EEOC first attempts to end the alleged unlawful practice through informal conciliation. If conciliation fails, the EEOC may sue. Individuals may sue on their own behalf 90 days after filing a charge with the EEOC and the appropriate state agency. If the EEOC takes legal action, an individual covered by the lawsuit may not file a private action.

A lawsuit under the Equal Pay Act of 1963 may be filed by the EEOC or by the complainant. There are no prerequisites to bringing a private action under this law. Wages may be recovered for a period of up to two years prior to the filing of a suit, except in a case of willful violation, for which three years' back pay may be recovered. The name of the individual filing the complaint may be kept confidential at the administrative level.

Complaints against the Federal Government Federal employees or job applicants who want to file complaints of job discrimination based on race, color, national origin, sex, religion, age, or physical or mental disability must first consult an equal employment opportunity counselor with the employees' or applicants' agency within 45 days of the alleged discriminatory action. If the complaint cannot be resolved informally, the person may file a formal complaint within 15 days of receiving a notice of the right to file a complaint. An accepted complaint is investigated by the agency, and the complainant has a right to a hearing before an EEOC administrative judge before the agency issues its final decision. An individual who wishes to file a complaint under the Equal Pay Act of 1963 must follow these procedures. An individual may also elect to file suit under the Equal Pay Act of 1963 without prior resort to the agency or to the EEOC.

A complaint under the Age Discrimination in Employment Act of 1967, against a federal agency or department, must be filed with the head of the agency, director of equal employment opportunity, head of an EEOC field installation, or other designated official. Federal employees may bypass the administrative complaint process and file a CIVIL ACTION directly in a federal district court, by first notifying the EEOC within 180 days of the alleged discriminatory act and then waiting 30 calendar days before filing suit. A federal employee may appeal a decision of an agency, an arbitrator, or the Federal Labor Relations Authority, with the EEOC's Office of Federal Operations, at any time up to 30 calendar days after receiving the agency notice of final decision. A petition for review of a MERIT SYSTEMS PROTECTION BOARD decision may be filed within 30 days of the date that the board decision becomes final. A request for reconsideration of any EEOC decision must be made in writing within 30 days of receiving the decision.

Other Activities The EEOC publishes data on the employment status of women and members of minority groups. Through six employment surveys covering private employers, apprenticeship programs, labor unions, state and local governments, elementary and secondary schools, and colleges and universities, the EEOC tabulates data on employees' ethnic, racial, and gender makeup. The EEOC distributes this information to various federal agencies and makes it available for public use.

Eliminating a large backlog of discrimination charges has been a continuing problem for the EEOC. The EEOC receives over 90,000 new charges each year. At the end of the second quarter of fiscal 1995, EEOC had received over 45,000 new charges for the year, a 7.3 percent increase over the same period in fiscal 1994. As of December 1995, the agency had managed to reduce its pending inventory of charges from an all-time high of 120,000 in mid-1995 to 98,000.

CROSS-REFERENCES

Affirmative Action; Civil Rights; Disabled Persons; Employment Law; Sex Discrimination.

EQUAL PROTECTION 📖 The constitutional guarantee that no person or class of persons shall be denied the same protection of the laws that is enjoyed by other persons or other classes in like circumstances in their lives, liberty, property, and pursuit of happiness. 📖

> We hold these truths to be self-evident, that all men are created equal, that they are endowed by their Creator with certain unalienable Rights, that among these are Life, Liberty and the pursuit of Happiness. (Declaration of Independence)

The concept of equal protection and equality in the United States is as old as the country itself. In 1776, THOMAS JEFFERSON and the American colonists boldly announced the "self-evident" truth of human equality. Yet the meaning of equality was neither obvious nor clearly defined. The "peculiar institution" of SLAVERY was intricately woven into America's economic, social, and political fabric. Many Americans owned slaves, and most, including Jefferson himself, believed in the inferiority of the black race. JAMES MADISON and the other Founding Fathers drafted a national constitution that protected the slave trade and recognized the rights of slave owners. Article I, Section 2, of the Constitution counted a slave as only three-fifths of a person for the purposes of representation in Congress.

Slave codes permitted slave masters to buy, sell, and lease blacks like personal property. Slaves owed their masters an unqualified duty of obedience. Slave owners, on the other hand, were free to do as they pleased, short of murdering their slaves. Only community mores, common sense, and individual conscience restrained slave owners. Very few laws protected slaves from abusive or maniacal masters, and those that did were seldom enforced. In 1857, the U.S. Supreme Court placed its stamp of approval on the institution of slavery, holding that slaves were not "citizens" within the meaning of the Constitution, but only "property" lacking any constitutional protection whatsoever (*Dred Scott v. Sandford*, 60 U.S., 15 L. Ed. 691 [19 How.] 393).

From the United States' inception, then, a gulf has separated the Jeffersonian ideal of human equality from the reality of racial inequality under the law. The tension separating the aspirations of the DECLARATION OF INDEPENDENCE from the barbarism of slavery ultimately erupted in the Civil War (1861–65). The victory won by the North in the War between the States ended the institution of slavery in the United States and commenced the struggle for CIVIL RIGHTS that continues to this day. This struggle began with the ratification of the Thirteenth (1865), Fourteenth (1868), and Fifteenth (1870) Amendments during the aftermath of the Civil War.

The THIRTEENTH AMENDMENT abolished slavery and involuntary servitude, except when imposed as punishment for a crime. The FIFTEENTH AMENDMENT did not expressly grant black citizens the right to vote, but prohibited state and federal governments from denying this right based on "race, color, or previous condition of servitude." Each amendment gave Congress the power to enforce its provisions with "appropriate legislation."

Although both of these amendments were important, the FOURTEENTH AMENDMENT has had the greatest influence on the development of civil rights in the United States. Section 1 of the Fourteenth Amendment provides,

All persons born or naturalized in the United States, and subject to the jurisdiction thereof, are citizens of the United States and of the State wherein they reside. No State shall make or enforce any law which shall abridge the privileges or immunities of citizens of the United States; nor shall any State deprive any person of life, liberty, or property, without due process of

In 1857 the U.S. Supreme Court held in Dred Scott v. Sandford *that slaves were not citizens within the meaning of the Constitution. This contradiction to the concept of equal protection led to the U.S. Civil War and the civil rights movement of the 1960s.*

law; nor deny to any person within its jurisdiction the equal protection of the laws.

The first clause emasculated the *Dred Scott* decision by bestowing national citizenship upon all blacks born or naturalized in the United States, making them eligible for federal protection of their civil rights. The Privileges and Immunities Clause, once believed a potential source for civil rights, was narrowly interpreted by the Supreme Court in 1873 and has since remained dormant (*Slaughter-House* cases, 83 U.S., 21 L. Ed. 394 [16 Wall.] 36).

The Equal Protection Clause was also narrowly interpreted by the Supreme Court in the nineteenth century, but became the centerpiece of the CIVIL RIGHTS MOVEMENT after World War II (1939–45). It spawned desegregation, integration, and AFFIRMATIVE ACTION and promoted equal treatment and concern for the races under state law. It also provided the country with a starting point for a meaningful dialogue regarding the problems of inequality and discrimination. This dialogue has manifested itself in U.S. constitutional, statutory, and COMMON LAW.

Constitutional Law

Inequalities during Reconstruction   The RATIFICATION of the Fourteenth Amendment occurred during a period in U.S. history known as the Reconstruction. In this era, the South was placed under military occupation by the North, and African Americans realized some short-term benefits. Ku Klux Klan violence was temporarily curbed. Black Codes, passed by southern states after the Civil War to replace slavery with a segregated system based on social caste, were dismantled. Blacks were elected to state and federal office. Some achieved prominent status in legal circles, including one African American who obtained a seat on the South Carolina Supreme Court.

But Reconstruction was not a substitute for civil rights, and the improvements realized by African Americans proved evanescent. By 1880 the North's passion for equality atrophied, as did its interest in the fate of African Americans. In the vacuum left by the North's withdrawal, southern racism flourished and Klan terrorism burgeoned. Labor codes were passed relegating blacks to virtual serfdom. These codes made it illegal for anyone to lure blacks away from their job for any reason, including better working conditions and wages. Some codes provided criminal penalties for African Americans who quit their job, even when no debt was owed to their employer.

Advancements made during Reconstruction were further eroded when the Supreme Court invalidated the Civil Rights Act of 1875 (*Civil Rights* cases, 109 U.S. 3, 3 S. Ct. 18, 27 L. Ed. 835 [1883]). This act proclaimed "the equality of all men before the law" and promised to "mete out equal and exact justice" to persons of every "race, color, or persuasion" in public or private accommodations alike. In striking down the law, the Supreme Court said that when

> a man has emerged from slavery, and by the aid of beneficent legislation has shaken off the inseparable concomitants of that state, there must be some stage in the progress of his elevation when he takes the rank of a mere citizen, and ceases to be a special favorite of the law.

The Court was not persuaded that this act was the type of "appropriate legislation" contemplated by the Fourteenth Amendment.

The Rise and Fall of Separate but Equal

The Supreme Court's laissez-faire attitude toward racial inequality was also reflected in the area of segregation. As Reconstruction collapsed, southern states gradually passed statutes formally segregating the races in every facet of society. Public schools, restaurants, rest rooms, railroads, real property, prisons, and voting facilities were all segregated by race. The Supreme Court placed its imprimatur on these forms of racial apartheid in the landmark decision *Plessy v. Ferguson*, 163 U.S. 537, 16 S. Ct. 1138, 41 L. Ed. 256 (1896).

Homer Plessy, who was seven-eighths Caucasian and one-eighth African, was prohibited from traveling on a railway coach for whites, under a Louisiana statute requiring "equal but separate accommodations" for black and white passengers. The Supreme Court, in an 8–1 decision, said this statute did not violate the Equal Protection Clause of the Fourteenth Amendment: "The object of the Amendment was undoubtedly to enforce the absolute equality of the two races before the law, but ... it could not have been intended to abolish distinctions based upon color, or to enforce ... a commingling of the two races upon terms unsatisfactory to either." The Fourteenth Amendment, the Court concluded, was "powerless to eradicate racial instincts or to abolish distinctions based on physical differences."

Following *Plessy*, the "SEPARATE-BUT-EQUAL" doctrine remained the lodestar of Fourteenth Amendment jurisprudence for over half a century. Legally prescribed segregation was upheld by the Court in a litany of public places, including public schools. As Adolf Hitler rose to

The 1896 decision in Plessy v. Ferguson *validated the concept of "separate but equal" by holding that denying African Americans access to certain accommodations did not violate the Equal Protection Clause of the Constitution.*

power in Germany during the 1930s, however, many U.S. citizens began to reconsider their notions of equality. Nazi policies of Aryan superiority, racial purity, ethnic cleansing, and extermination made many U.S. citizens view segregation in a darker light. The juxtaposition of the Allied powers fighting totalitarianism in World War II and the citizenry practicing racial discrimination in the United States seemed hypocritical to many, especially when segregated African American troops were sacrificing their lives on the battlefield.

A series of Supreme Court decisions began to limit the scope of the separate-but-equal doctrine. The first hint of the Court's changing perspective came in the footnote of an otherwise forgettable case, *United States v. Carolene Products*, 304 U.S. 144, 58 S. Ct. 778, 82 L. Ed. 1234 (1938). In *Carolene Products*, the Court upheld a federal statute regulating commerce, applying a PRESUMPTION of constitutionality to legislation in this area. However, in footnote 4, the Court cautioned that this presumption may not apply to legislation "directed at national . . . or racial minorities . . . [where] prejudice against discrete and insular minorities may be a special condition, which tends to seriously curtail the operation of those political processes ordinarily to be relied upon to protect minorities, and which may call for a correspondingly more searching judicial scrutiny."

The Court employed a "more searching judicial scrutiny" in *Missouri ex rel. Gaines v. Canada*, 305 U.S. 337, 59 S. Ct. 232, 83 L. Ed. 208 (1938). This case involved a black applicant who was denied admission to the University of Missouri Law School solely because of his color. The state of Missouri, which had no law school for blacks, attempted to fulfill its separate-but-equal obligations by offering to pay for the black applicant's tuition at a comparable out-of-state law school. The Supreme Court held that this arrangement violated the applicant's Fourteenth Amendment rights. The Court ruled that Missouri was required to provide African American law students with equal educational opportunities within its own borders, and could not shirk this responsibility by relying on educational opportunities offered in neighboring states.

When states did offer black students a separate legal education, the Supreme Court closely examined the quality of the educational opportunities afforded to each race in the segregated schools. In *Sweatt v. Painter*, 339 U.S. 629, 70 S. Ct. 848, 94 L. Ed. 1114 (1950), the Court ruled that the segregated facilities offered to black

and white law students in Texas were not substantially equal. The Court determined that the faculty, library, and courses offered at the African American law school were patently inferior and denied the black students equal protection of the laws.

On the same day *Sweatt* was decided, the Court invalidated Oklahoma's attempt to segregate graduate students of different races within a single educational facility (*McLaurin v. Oklahoma State Regents*, 339 U.S. 637, 70 S. Ct. 851, 94 L. Ed. 1149 [1950]). Black law students at the University of Oklahoma were required to attend class in an anteroom designated for "colored only," study on the mezzanine of the library, and eat in the cafeteria at a different time than white students. The Court struck down these arrangements, determining that segregation impaired the students' "ability to study, engage in discussions, exchange views . . . and in general, learn [the] profession." According to the Court, the Fourteenth Amendment required the integration of black and white graduate students.

Brown v. Board of Education *Plessy, Carolene Products*, and so forth, foreshadowed the watershed equal protection decision handed down by the U.S. Supreme Court in 1954, *Brown v. Board of Education*, 347 U.S. 483, 74 S. Ct. 686, 98 L. Ed. 873. *Brown* reviewed four consolidated cases in which local governments segregated public schools by race. In each case, black students were denied admission on an integrated basis. The question before the Court was not whether the segregated educational facilities were of a similar quality. Instead, the question was whether, under any circumstances, segregated educational opportunities could ever be equal, or substantially equal, in nature. In a resounding unanimous opinion, the Court said that separate-but-equal education is "inherently unequal" and "has no place" in the field of public education.

Citing *Sweatt* and *McLaurin*, the Court reiterated that students' ability to learn is stunted without exposure to the viewpoints of different races. The Court also underscored the sociological and psychological harm segregation inflicts on minority children, finding that segregation "is usually interpreted as denoting the inferiority of the Negro group." The Court added, "Segregation with the sanction of law . . . has a tendency to [retard] the educational and mental development of Negro children and deprive them of some of the benefits they would receive in a racial[ly] integrated school system."

When the *Brown* decision was announced, observers realized that the rationale applied by the Court had far-reaching consequences. If segregation in public schools denoted the inferiority of African Americans, so did segregation elsewhere in society. If integration enhanced educational opportunities for U.S. citizens of every race, then perhaps integration could spur economic growth and social development. Observers also realized that if segregation in public schools violated the Equal Protection Clause, then all forms of government-imposed segregation were vulnerable to constitutional attack.

Modern Equal Protection Jurisprudence
Over the next forty years, the Supreme Court demonstrated that the principles enunciated in *Brown* were not limited to racial segregation and DISCRIMINATION. In addition to striking down most legislative classifications based on race, the Court closely examined classifications based on length of state residency, U.S. citizenship, and gender. The Court looked carefully at

legislation denying benefits to children born out of wedlock. Government classifications denying any group a fundamental right were also reviewed with judicial skepticism.

The Supreme Court has recognized that nearly all legislation classifies on the basis of some criteria, bestowing benefits or imposing burdens on one group and denying them to another. For example, the government offers veterans, indigent people, and elderly people free or low-cost medical services that are not available to the rest of society. Progressive tax rates impose higher rates of taxation on the wealthy. Few such classifications are perfectly drawn by the legislature.

Most classifications are either overinclusive or underinclusive. An overinclusive classification contains all persons who are similarly situated and also persons who should not be included. Legislation that is intended to protect poor and fragile elderly people but actually extends to all senior citizens is overinclusive. An

Educational Attainment, by Blacks and Whites, 1960 to 1994

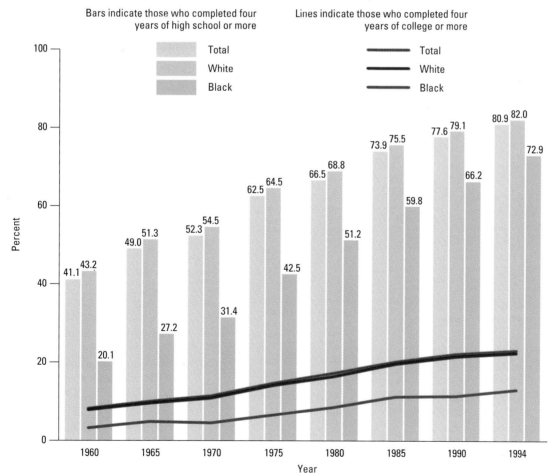

Source: U.S. Bureau of the Census, *Current Population Reports.*

underinclusive classification excludes some similarly situated persons from the intended legislative benefit or detriment. Legislation that is designed to eliminate fraud in government but actually excludes executive branch employees from its regulatory grasp is underinclusive. Some classifications can be both underinclusive and overinclusive.

The Supreme Court has developed a three-tiered approach to examine all such legislative classifications. Under the first tier of scrutiny, known as STRICT SCRUTINY, the Court will strike down any legislative classification that is not necessary to fulfill a compelling or overriding government objective. Strict scrutiny is applied to legislation involving SUSPECT CLASSIFICATIONS and fundamental rights. A suspect classification is directed at the type of "discrete and insular minorities" referenced in the *Carolene Products* footnote. A fundamental right is a right that is expressly or implicitly enumerated in the U.S. Constitution, such as freedom of speech or assembly. Most legislation reviewed by the Supreme Court under the strict scrutiny standard has been invalidated, because very few classifications are necessary to support a compelling government objective.

The second tier of scrutiny used by the Court to review legislative classifications is known as heightened, or intermediate, scrutiny. Legislation will not survive heightened scrutiny unless the government can demonstrate that the classification is substantially related to an important societal interest. Gender classifications are examined under this middle level of review, as are classifications that burden extramarital children.

The third tier of scrutiny involves the least amount of judicial scrutiny and is known as the rational relationship test. The Supreme Court will approve legislation under this standard so long as the classification is reasonably related to a legitimate government interest. The rational relationship test permits the legislature to employ any classification that is conceivably or arguably related to a government interest that does not infringe upon a specific constitutional right. An overwhelming majority of social and economic laws are reviewed and upheld by courts using this minimal level of scrutiny.

Classifications Based on Race Applying strict scrutiny, the Supreme Court has consistently struck down legislative classifications based on race. Relying on the *Brown* decision, the Court struck down a series of state laws segregating parks, playgrounds, golf courses, bathhouses, beaches, and public transportation. Because the Fourteenth Amendment protects

In 1962 demonstrators attempted to stage a sit-in at a restaurant that was refusing service to African Americans.

against only government discrimination, discrimination by private individuals or businesses is not proscribed under the Equal Protection Clause unless the government is significantly involved in the private activity. Although the Equal Protection Clause does not offer protection against discriminatory laws promulgated by the president, Congress, or federal ADMINISTRATIVE AGENCIES, the Supreme Court has interpreted the Due Process Clause of the Fifth Amendment to provide such protection (*Bolling v. Sharpe*, 347 U.S. 497, 74 S. Ct. 693, 98 L. Ed. 884 [1954]).

The equal protection guarantee extends not only to laws that obviously discriminate on their face as did the laws that intentionally segregated races in public schools, but also to government action having a discriminatory purpose, effect, or application. Governmental activity with a discriminatory purpose, also known as purposeful discrimination, may occur when a prosecutor exercises a peremptory challenge (the right to exclude a juror without assigning a reason or legal cause) to exclude a member of a minority race from a JURY (*Batson v. Kentucky*, 476 U.S. 79, 106 S. Ct. 1712, 90 L. Ed. 2d 69 [1986]). If the prosecutor is unable to articulate a reason for striking the juror that is unrelated to race, the peremptory challenge will be nullified by the court.

The discriminatory impact of a race-neutral classification may also doom legislation under the Fourteenth Amendment. For example, following the demise of Reconstruction, many former Confederate states enacted legislation requiring residents to pass literacy tests before they could register to vote, but exempted persons who had been qualified to vote at an earlier time when blacks were disenfranchised slaves (i.e., Caucasians). This "GRANDFATHER CLAUSE" exemption was struck down by the Supreme Court because of its discriminatory impact on African Americans. The Court also struck down other voting restrictions, including "white primaries," which excluded African Americans from participating in a state's electoral process for selecting delegates to a political party convention.

A law can be neutral on its face or in purpose, but still be applied in a discriminatory manner. In *Yick Wo v. Hopkins*, 118 U.S. 356, 6 S. Ct. 1064, 30 L. Ed. 220 (1886), the Supreme Court struck down a San Francisco ordinance banning the operation of hand laundries in wooden buildings, because local officials were closing down only laundries owned by persons of Asian descent. White owners of such institutions were permitted to keep their businesses open.

Proof of discriminatory purpose, effect, or application can be difficult. Courts will search the LEGISLATIVE HISTORY of a particular classification for discriminatory origins. Courts also consider specific discriminatory actions taken by state officials in the past. Statistical evidence is relevant as well, but insufficient to establish discrimination by itself (*McCleskey v. Kemp*, 481 U.S. 279, 107 S. Ct. 1756, 95 L. Ed. 2d 262 [1987]).

McCleskey involved a black man who was convicted and sentenced to death for killing a white police officer. On appeal, attorneys for the defendant relied on a sophisticated statistical analysis indicating that blacks were significantly more likely to receive the death penalty for killing a white person than were whites convicted of killing a black person. In a 5–4 decision, the Supreme Court said this evidence was not enough to demonstrate that the defendant had been denied equal protection. The majority held that the defendant could have prevailed under the Fourteenth Amendment only if he had shown a discriminatory purpose on the part of the Georgia legislature when it enacted the death penalty legislation, or on the part of the jurors in his trial when they imposed the death sentence. See also CAPITAL PUNISHMENT.

Racial Classifications Surviving Judicial Scrutiny Classifications based on race usually sound the death knell for the legislation containing them, with two notable exceptions. The first involves the internment of Americans with Japanese ancestry during World War II, and the second comes in the area of affirmative action.

Japanese American internment Pursuant to concurrent presidential, congressional, and military action, over one hundred thousand

The internment of Japanese Americans during World War II, challenged in Korematsu v. United States, *is the only case where a law including a classification based on race survived the strict scrutiny standard.*

Japanese Americans were confined to "relocation camps" throughout the United States during World War I. Despite Justice HUGO L. BLACK'S assertion that all race-based legal classifications are "immediately suspect" and subject to the "most rigid scrutiny," the Supreme Court ruled in *United States v. Korematsu*, 323 U.S. 214, 65 S. Ct. 193, 89 L. Ed. 194 (1944), that the internment did not violate the Equal Protection Clause. Deferring to the combined war powers of the president and Congress, the Court said relocation of these U.S. citizens was a "military urgency" in the war against Japan, justified by concern over domestic espionage, sabotage, and subversion. Justices OWEN J. ROBERTS, FRANK MURPHY, and ROBERT H. JACKSON dissented, arguing that no evidence of disloyalty had been produced against any of the interned Japanese Americans. *Korematsu* stands as the only case in which the Supreme Court has upheld a racial classification under the strict scrutiny standard.

Affirmative action Affirmative action, sometimes called benign discrimination because it is considered less harmful than other forms of discrimination, is represented by government programs created to remedy past discrimination against blacks, women, and members of other protected groups. These programs include special considerations given to minorities competing against the rest of society for jobs, promotions, and admission to colleges and universities. Opponents of affirmative action characterize it as reverse discrimination because it often excludes individuals with ostensibly superior credentials, solely on account of their race or gender.

The Supreme Court has vacillated over what level of scrutiny applies to affirmative action programs. In *Regents of University of California v. Bakke*, 438 U.S. 265, 98 S. Ct. 2733, 57 L. Ed. 2d 750 (1978), in which there was no majority opinion, four justices applied heightened scrutiny in holding that a university may consider racial criteria as part of a competitive admission process, so long as it does not use fixed quotas. But in *Richmond v. J. A. Croson Co.*, 488 U.S. 469 109 S. Ct. 706, 102 L. Ed. 2d 854 (1989), five justices applied strict scrutiny to invalidate an affirmative action program intended to increase the number of minority-owned businesses awarded city construction contracts.

It appears that a majority of justices now favor application of strict scrutiny to cases involving benign discrimination (not obvious or intentional). When the more stringent level of scrutiny has been applied in these cases, the Court has held that a general legislative desire to correct past injustices was not sufficiently compelling to warrant a racial preference for minorities. Instead, the Court has ruled, benign racial preferences will be tolerated under the Fourteenth Amendment only when the government can demonstrate that they are narrowly tailored to correct specific discriminatory practices by the government itself or by some private sector entity within its jurisdiction.

Classifications Based on Gender The Supreme Court has established that gender classifications are subject to intermediate scrutiny. The seminal case in this area is *Craig v. Boren*, 429 U.S. 190, 97 S. Ct. 451, 50 L. Ed. 2d 397 (1976), which involved an Oklahoma law permitting females between the ages of eighteen and twenty to purchase 3.2 percent beer, but restricting males from purchasing such beer until they reached age twenty-one. The state defended the statute by introducing traffic statistics that suggested that men were more likely than women to be arrested for drunk driving before age twenty-one. The Court agreed that enhanced traffic safety was an "important" government interest, but disagreed that the gender line drawn by the state would "substantially" serve this interest.

Alienage, State Residency, and Legitimacy Classifications The Supreme Court has held that legislation discriminating against ALIENS who are properly within the United States is considered suspect, and will be upheld only if the classification is necessary to serve a compelling government interest. In at least one alienage case, however, the Court has applied only heightened scrutiny to invalidate a state law preventing undocumented children from enrolling in the Texas public school system (*Plyler v. Doe*, 457 U.S. 202, 102 S. Ct. 2382, 72 L. Ed. 2d 786 [1982]). The Court continues to call classifications based on alienage suspect, but may not always apply the most rigorous scrutiny to such legislation.

State laws that condition government benefits on length of state RESIDENCY have also been deemed suspect by the Supreme Court. In *Shapiro v. Thompson*, 394 U.S. 618, 89 S. Ct. 1322, 22 L. Ed. 2d 600 (1969), the Court ruled that legislation denying government benefits to persons residing in a state for less than a year violated the Equal Protection Clause. Although states may restrict WELFARE, educational, and other government benefits to bona fide residents, the Court wrote, they may not restrict the dispensation of government benefits in a way that would unduly burden the right to interstate travel, or deprive interstate travelers of the right to be treated as equal to other state residents. Since *Shapiro*, the Supreme Court has occasionally applied more moderate scrutiny to legislation burdening interstate travelers, prompting critics to assail the Court for its inconsistent application of the three-tiered analysis.

State laws that discriminate against children born out of wedlock are subject to heightened scrutiny. State legislation has been struck down for denying illegitimate children INHERITANCE rights, welfare benefits, and CHILD SUPPORT when such rights were offered to legitimate children. Although ILLEGITIMACY is not a suspect classification subject to strict scrutiny, courts do provide meaningful review of such statutes. The Supreme Court is sensitive to penalizing children for their extramarital status when the children themselves are not responsible for that status.

Classifications Involving Sexual Preference In *Romer v. Evans*, ___ U.S. ___, 116 S. Ct. 1620, L. Ed. 2d (1996), the U.S. Supreme Court reviewed a Colorado state constitutional amendment that prohibited any branch of the state or local governments from taking action designed to protect the status of persons based on their "homosexual, lesbian or bisexual orientation." The immediate effect of the amendment, known popularly as "Amendment 2," was to repeal all existing statutes, regulations, ordinances, and governmental policies that barred discrimination based on sexual preference. Under Amendment 2, state officials and private entities would have been permitted to discriminate against gays and lesbians in a number of areas, including insurance, employment, housing, and welfare services.

The state of Colorado defended Amendment 2 by arguing that it did nothing more than place homosexuals on a level playing field with all other state residents. The amendment, Colorado submitted, simply denied gays and lesbians any "special rights." The Supreme Court dis-

DONNA BINDER/IMPACT VISUALS

In Romer v. Evans *the Supreme Court reviewed a Colorado state constitutional amendment that prohibited the government from protecting the status of persons based on their homosexuality. The Court found the amendment denied equal protection to gays and lesbians and struck it down.*

agreed, holding that Amendment 2 violated the Equal Protection Clause because it "identifies persons by a single trait and then denies them protection across the board," which is something "unprecedented in our Jurisprudence."

Writing for a six-person majority, Justice ANTHONY KENNEDY explained that "Equal Protection of the laws is not achieved through indiscriminate imposition of inequalities." The associate justice said that "[r]espect for this principle" demonstrates "why laws singling out a certain class of citizens for disfavored legal status or general hardships are rare." Amendment 2 is unconstitutional, Kennedy concluded, because any law that generally makes it "more difficult for one group of citizens than all others to seek aid from the government is itself a denial of equal protection of the laws in the most literal sense."

Classifications Involving Fundamental Rights A fundamental right is a right expressly or implicitly enumerated by the U.S. Constitution. In *Palko v. Connecticut*, 302 U.S. 319, 58 S. Ct. 149, 82 L. Ed. 288 (1937), Justice BENJAMIN N. CARDOZO wrote that these freedoms represent "the very essence of a scheme of ordered liberty . . . principles so rooted in the traditions and conscience of our people as to be ranked as fundamental." During the nation's first century, freedom of contract and various property rights were deemed fundamental. In the twentieth century, more personal liberties have been recognized as such. These freedoms include most of those explicitly contained in the BILL OF RIGHTS, such as FREEDOM OF SPEECH, freedom of RELIGION, freedom of assembly, right to counsel, right against unreasonable SEARCH AND SEIZURE, right against SELF-INCRIMINATION, right against DOUBLE JEOPARDY, right to a jury trial, and right to be free from CRUEL AND UNUSUAL PUNISHMENT. They also include freedoms specifically mentioned elsewhere in the Constitution, such as the right to vote. In the late twentieth century, the Supreme Court began to find that fundamental rights embodied freedoms that were not

expressly enumerated by the Constitution but that may be fairly inferred by one of its provisions, such as the rights to personal autonomy and PRIVACY.

Relying on the doctrine of INCORPORATION, the Supreme Court has made these fundamental constitutional principles applicable to the states through the Due Process and Equal Protection Clauses of the Fourteenth Amendment. The Court has concluded, in a series of decisions, that these freedoms are so important to the preservation of liberty that they must be equally conferred upon the citizens of every state. No state may provide its residents with less protection of these fundamental rights than is offered under the federal Constitution. The Fourteenth Amendment thus guarantees state citizens equal protection of the laws, by creating a minimum federal threshold of essential freedoms each state must recognize.

In *Gideon v. Wainright*, 372 U.S. 335, 83 S. Ct. 792, 9 L. Ed. 2d 799 (1963), Clarence Earl Gideon was charged with entering a poolroom with the intent to commit a MISDEMEANOR. Before trial, Gideon, an indigent, asked the judge to appoint an attorney to represent him because he could not afford one. The court denied Gideon's request, and a jury later convicted him. Gideon's request for a court-appointed counsel in a misdemeanor case would have been denied in many states at that time. The Supreme Court held that all states must thereafter provide court-appointed counsel at every critical stage of a criminal proceeding, whether the proceeding concerned a misdemeanor, FELONY, or capital offense. The right to counsel is too fundamental for any state to ignore.

The year after *Gideon* was decided, the Supreme Court handed down another groundbreaking decision in the area of fundamental rights. *Reynolds v. Sims*, 377 U.S. 533, 84 S. Ct. 1362, 12 L. Ed. 2d 506 (1964), involved the dilution of voting rights through legislative APPORTIONMENT in Alabama. Legislative apportionment refers to the manner in which a state, county, or municipality is divided for purposes of determining legislative representation. Some states are divided into voting precincts, whereas others are divided into wards or districts.

In *Reynolds*, the voting subdivisions were so unevenly apportioned that a distinct minority of Alabama voters were electing a majority of the state legislators. As a result, voters in less populated electoral subdivisions had more voting power than did voters in more populated electoral subdivisions. The Supreme Court struck down this arrangement under the Fourteenth Amendment, holding that every voter has a fundamental right to cast a ballot of equal weight. The Court had earlier applied this ONE-PERSON, ONE-VOTE principle to federal congressional districts, requiring that all such districts be as nearly equal in population as practicable (*Wesberry v. Sanders*, 376 U.S. 1, 84 S. Ct. 526, 11 L. Ed. 2d 481 [1964]).

In addition to the Fourteenth Amendment of the U.S. Constitution, most state constitutions provide equal protection guarantees and enumerate certain fundamental rights. In many of the states with these constitutions, courts also employ a three-tiered analysis similar to that developed by the U.S. Supreme Court. State courts can interpret their own constitution to provide more, but not less, protection than that offered under the federal Equal Protection Clause.

Legislation The Fourteenth Amendment authorizes Congress to enact "appropriate legislation" to enforce the Equal Protection Clause. The COMMERCE CLAUSE provides Congress with the authority to enact legislation that affects interstate commerce, an even broader power. Pursuant to these clauses, Congress has enacted major pieces of legislation that have extended protection against discrimination beyond that contained in the Constitution.

The Civil Rights Act of 1871 (42 U.S.C.A. § 1983 et seq.) was one early piece of such legislation. Section 1983 of the act, passed when Ku Klux Klan violence was widespread, created a federal remedy, namely money DAMAGES, for individuals whose constitutional rights had been violated by state officials. Although this statute has been influential and frequently litigated, no relief will be granted under it unless "STATE ACTION" can be demonstrated.

State action means a discriminatory act committed by a government official or agent. Such action may be taken by a legislative, executive, judicial, or administrative body, or some other person or entity acting under "COLOR OF LAW." Section 1983 does not apply to wholly private or nongovernment conduct. If action is taken by a private individual cloaked with some measure of state authority, courts will find state action if one of four tests is satisfied: (1) public function test—state action is found where the government has delegated its traditional responsibilities, such as police protection, to a private party or agency; (2) nexus test—state action is found where there is a sufficiently close connection between the government and a private actor, such as where the state owns or leases property on which private discrimination occurs; (3) state compulsion test—state action is

found where the government coerces or significantly encourages private conduct, such as where federal regulations require private railways to conduct urinalysis after accidents; (4) joint action test—state action is found where the government is a willful participant in discrimination by a private actor.

Other congressional legislation prohibits discrimination in the private sector. Title VII of the 1964 Civil Rights Act prohibits employers from hiring or firing employees on the basis of race, color, sex, or national origin (42 U.S.C.A. § 2000e-2 et seq.). Federal courts have interpreted title VII to prohibit hostile work environments involving SEXUAL HARASSMENT, even when the perpetrator and victim are the same gender. The Age Discrimination in Employment Act (29 U.S.C.A. § 623 et seq.) extends title VII's protections to employment decisions based on age and is applicable to persons between the ages of forty and seventy. Under both statutes, employers may defend their actions by demonstrating nondiscriminatory reasons for a particular decision, such as the dishonesty or incompetency of a discharged employee.

The Americans with Disabilities Act (ADA) (42 U.S.C.A. § 1211 et seq.) prohibits discrimination against "qualified individuals" based on a "physical or mental impairment that substantially limits one or more" of an individual's "major life activities." Title I of the ADA applies to employers, and requires them to make "reasonable accommodations" for disabled employees who are otherwise qualified to perform a job, unless such accommodations would cause undue hardship to the business. Such accommodations can include making existing facilities more accessible, permitting part-time or modified work schedules, and reassigning jobs.

Title II applies to public entities, including any department, agency, or other instrumentality of a state or local government. The ADA does not apply to the federal government, but other legislation does protect disabled federal employees. Title III of the ADA governs public accommodations such as restaurants, theaters, museums, stores, day care centers, and hospitals. The word *disability* includes terminal illnesses and prevents health care facilities from failing to treat patients diagnosed with AIDS or HIV.

Many state statutes also promote equal protection by prohibiting discrimination. Legislation from several states combines many of the federal protections under a single category of human rights law. Depending on the particular JURISDICTION and issue at stake, state human

rights legislation, and the court decisions interpreting it, may provide broader protection than that offered under similar federal laws.

The Common Law The notion of equal protection or equal treatment is rooted in the Anglo-Saxon common law. When HENRY II ascended the throne in 1154, England was divided into political subdivisions consisting of villages, hundreds, shires, and towns. The king, feudal lords, and local assemblies all wielded power to some extent. But there were no effective national executive, legislative, or judicial institutions that could administer laws in a uniform and organized manner. Henry II changed this condition by creating a royal common law, which his officials disseminated throughout the kingdom. Thus, the king's law was made "common" to citizens of the entire realm.

The idea of equality under the law is also rooted in the rule of law, and in the principle that no one is above the law, including the king and the members of Parliament. This principle found expression in Bonham's case, 8 Co. 107a, 77 Eng. Rep. 638 (K.B. 1608), where eminent English jurist SIR EDWARD COKE wrote that "the common law will . . . controul Acts of Parliament, and sometimes adjudge them to be utterly void: for when an Act of Parliament is against common right and reason, or repugnant, or impossible to be performed, the common law will controul it, and adjudge such Act to be void."

In 1761, JAMES OTIS, an American colonist, relied on Coke in the *Writs of Assistance Case,* where he said that any act of Parliament "against the constitution is void" and that it was the duty of the courts to "pass such acts into disuse" because they contravened "the reason of

The Americans with Disabilities Act prohibits discrimination in hiring and requires employers to make reasonable accommodations for disabled employees.

the common law." In a recent application of this principle, President RICHARD M. NIXON lost his battle with the rule of law when the Supreme Court forced him to surrender the infamous Watergate tapes against his assertion of EXECUTIVE PRIVILEGE (*United States v. Nixon,* 418 U.S. 683, 94 S. Ct. 3090, 41 L. Ed. 2d 1039 [1974]).

Courts have also relied on the concept of equal treatment in explaining the common doctrine of STARE DECISIS. When a court has laid down a principle of law in one case, stare decisis requires the court to apply that principle to future cases involving a similar set of facts. Some commentators have suggested that stare decisis serves two policy considerations: continuity and predictability in the law. But this doctrine also promotes equal treatment, federal courts have reasoned, by permitting all similarly situated litigants to obtain the same results under the law.

The American Revolution was sparked by the idea of equality. In 1776, the colonists declared themselves independent of the British Empire, in which the government often acted as if it were above the law. Jefferson and the other revolutionaries announced their steadfast adherence to the rule of law and the idea of human equality. But the idea of equality has always been ambiguous and controversial. U.S. citizens still disagree about whether the Equal Protection Clause of the Fourteenth Amendment guarantees equality of condition, equality of result, or equality of treatment and concern under the law. This disagreement manifests itself in state and federal courthouses and the halls of Congress.

CROSS-REFERENCES

Acquired Immune Deficiency Syndrome; Age Discrimination; *Baker v. Carr; Brown v. Board of Education of Topeka, Kansas;* Civil Rights Acts; Civil Rights Cases; Disabled Persons; *Dred Scott v. Sandford;* English Law *In Focus:* Dr. Bonham's Case; Gay and Lesbian Rights; *Gideon v. Wainwright;* Japanese American Evacuation Cases; Jim Crow Laws; *Korematsu v. United States;* Ku Klux Klan Act; Marshall, Thurgood; *Plessy v. Ferguson; Regents of University of California v. Bakke; Reynolds v. Sims;* Right to Counsel; School Desegregation; *Slaughter-House* Cases; *United States v. Nixon;* Voting Rights Act of 1965; Warren, Earl; *Writs of Assistance* Case.

EQUAL RIGHTS AMENDMENT 📖 A proposed addition to the U.S. Constitution that read, "Equality of rights under the law shall not be denied or abridged by the United States or by any State on account of sex," and that failed to receive ratification by the required number of states. 📖

The Equal Rights Amendment (ERA) was the most highly publicized and debated CONSTITUTIONAL AMENDMENT before the United States for most of the 1970s and early 1980s. First submitted by Congress to the states for RATIFICATION on March 22, 1972, it failed to be ratified by its final deadline of June 30, 1982. If ratified, the ERA would have become the Twenty-seventh Amendment to the Constitution.

The ERA was written by Alice Paul, of the National Woman's party, and was first introduced in Congress in 1923. However, no action on the amendment was taken until the National Organization for Women, which was founded in 1966, revived interest in it.

When the amendment was first submitted to the states in 1972, Congress prescribed a deadline of seven years for ratification. Because an amendment must be ratified by the legislatures or conventions of three-fourths of the states, the ERA required approval by thirty-eight states.

Advocates of the ERA intended it to give women constitutional protection beyond the Equal Protection Clauses of the FIFTH and FOURTEENTH AMENDMENTS. They believed that the ERA would compensate for inadequate statutory protections for women and sluggish judicial enforcement of existing laws. According to a report that accompanied passage of the ERA resolution in the House, the ERA was necessary because "our legal system currently contains the vestiges of a variety of ancient common law principles which discriminate unfairly against women" (H.R. Rep. No. 92-359, 92d Cong. [1971]). These vestigial principles, the report argued, gave preferential treatment to husbands over wives, created a double stan-

Hazel Hunkins Hallinan, a supporter of the suffragists, who won the right to vote in 1920, marched in support of the Equal Rights Amendment in 1977.

dard by giving men greater freedom than women to depart from moral standards, and used "obsolete and irrational notions of chivalry" that "regard women in a patronizing or condescending light."

The ERA encountered significant opposition, particularly in southern states. Opponents of the amendment held that certain inequalities between men and women are the result of biology and that some legislation and state policies must necessarily take this fact into account. Some also contended that the ERA would undermine the social institutions of marriage and family. Others argued that women already had sufficient constitutional protections and that the ERA was made unnecessary by recent liberal Supreme Court decisions, including *Frontiero v. Richardson*, 411 U.S. 677, 93 S. Ct. 1764, 36 L. Ed. 2d 583 (1973), which struck down a federal law that gave preferential treatment to married males over married females in securing salary supplements while in the ARMED SERVICES.

Frontiero also serves as an example of the way in which the ERA influenced the Supreme Court. In a concurring opinion, Justice LEWIS F. POWELL, JR., cited the pending ERA ratification as a reason to delay gender-related constitutional interpretation. He favored waiting for the results of the ERA's ratification process so that the political process might guide the Court's constitutional interpretation.

By 1973, less than two years after its submission to the states, thirty states had ratified the ERA, and the success of the measure seemed likely. However, only five more states ratified the measure by the end of the seven-year deadline, leaving it three states short in its bid to become law. In June 1979, Congress extended the ratification deadline to June 30, 1982. During the extension, ERA supporters organized economic boycotts of states that failed to ratify the amendment. Despite all these efforts, and even though public opinion polls indicated that a majority of U.S. citizens supported the measure, no more states ratified the ERA.

Supporters of the ERA reintroduced the amendment in Congress yet again on July 14, 1982. The House of Representatives voted down the proposal on November 15, 1983.

See also EQUAL PROTECTION; WOMEN'S RIGHTS.

EQUITY 📖 The pursuit of fairness. The money value of PROPERTY in excess of CLAIMS, LIENS, or MORTGAGES on the property. In the U.S. legal system, a body of law that seeks to achieve fairness on an individual basis. 📖

Equity is contrary to the notion that law is simply the strict, formal interpretation of statutes and PRECEDENT (similar previous case decisions). According to the formalist approach, the individual fairness of results is less important than the adherence to predictability.

Historically, the English and U.S. legal systems have honored formalism before equity. Indeed, the subordination of equity is systemic. Equity issues and cases are considered exceptions to the rule of formalism. Equity decisions cannot be decided by a JURY and are left to the sound discretion of a JUDGE. Equity decisions do not even merit the description legal; instead, they are called equitable.

Equity in U.S. law can be traced to England, where it began as a response to the rigid procedures of England's law courts. Through the thirteenth and fourteenth centuries, the judges in England's courts developed the COMMON LAW, a system of accepting and deciding cases based on principles of law shaped and developed in preceding cases. PLEADING became quite intricate, and only certain CAUSES OF ACTION qualified for legal redress. Aggrieved citizens found valid COMPLAINTS dismissed on technicalities. If a complaint was not dismissed, relief was often denied based on little more than the lack of a controlling statute or precedent.

Frustrated plaintiffs turned to the king, who referred these extraordinary requests for relief to a royal court called the CHANCERY. The Chancery was headed by a CHANCELLOR who possessed the power to settle disputes and order relief according to his conscience. The decisions of a chancellor were made without regard for the common law, and they became the basis for the law of equity.

Equity and the common law represented opposing values in the English legal system. The common law was the creation of a judiciary independent from the Crown. Common-law courts believed in the strict interpretation of statutes and precedential cases. Whereas the common law provided results based on years of judicial wisdom, equity produced results based on the whim of the king's chancellor. Common-law judges considered equity ARBITRARY and a royal encroachment on the power of an independent judiciary. Renowned seventeenth-century judge JOHN SELDEN called equity "a roguish thing" and noted that results in equity cases might well depend on the size of a chancellor's foot.

Despite this kind of opposition, equity assumed a permanent place in the English legal system. The powers of the Chancery became more defined; equity cases came to be understood as only claims for which monetary relief was inadequate. By the end of the seventeenth

century, the chancellor's opinions became consistent enough to be written up in a law reporter.

Because of its association with the king, equity was viewed with suspicion in the American colonies. Nonetheless, colonial legislatures understood the wisdom of allowing judges to fashion remedies in cases that were not covered by settled common law or statutes. The Framers of the U.S. Constitution recognized the providence of equity by writing in Article III, Section 2, Clause 1, that the "judicial Power shall extend to all Cases, in Law and Equity." All states eventually allowed for the judicial exercise of equity, and many states created special courts of equity, which maintained procedures distinct from those of courts of law.

In 1938, the Federal Rules of Civil Procedure established one system for processing both law and equity cases. Soon after, most states abolished the procedural distinctions between law and equity cases. In FEDERAL COURTS and most state courts, all civil cases now proceed in the same fashion, regardless of whether they involve legal or equitable redress.

The most important remaining distinction between law and equity is the right to a jury trial in a civil case. Where the plaintiff seeks a remedy of money DAMAGES, the plaintiff is entitled to a jury trial, provided the amount sought exceeds an amount specified by statute. Where the plaintiff seeks a remedy that is something other than money, the plaintiff is not entitled to a jury trial. Instead, the case is decided by one judge. If a plaintiff asks for both equitable and monetary relief, a jury will be allowed to decide the claims that ask for monetary relief, and a judge will decide the equity claims. Judges are guided by precedent in equity cases, but in the spirit of equity, they have

When a plaintiff seeks both monetary and equitable relief for damages, a jury hears the claims asking for monetary relief and a judge decides the equity claims.

broad discretion and can rule contrary to apparent precedent.

Delaware and Mississippi are among the few jurisdictions that still separate law and equity cases. In Delaware, equity cases are heard in a separate court of equity, which is presided over by the chancellor of Delaware. In the words of Chancellor William T. Quillen, this preserves "a touch of royalty" for Delaware's judiciary.

In any court, equity or otherwise, a case or issue may be referred to as equitable. This generally means that the relief requested by the plaintiff is not a money award. Whether to grant equitable relief is left to the discretion of the judge. By contrast, other CIVIL ACTIONS theoretically entitle a plaintiff to a prescribed remedy (usually money damages) from either a judge or a jury if, based on the evidence, the defendant is unable to defeat the plaintiff's case.

Equitable Relief Equitable relief comes in many forms. It may be a RESTRAINING ORDER or an INJUNCTION, which are court orders directing a party to do or not do something. An ACCOUNTING may be requested by a plaintiff who seeks to know how his or her money is being handled. A TRUST or CONSTRUCTIVE TRUST can be ordered by a judge to place the care and management of property with one person for the benefit of another. A PARTITION is an order dividing property held between two or more persons. *Declaratory relief* is granted when a judge declares the rights of certain parties. The effect of a DECLARATORY JUDGMENT is to set future obligations between the parties.

Under the remedy of SPECIFIC PERFORMANCE, a judge may order one party to perform a specific act. This type of relief is often used to resolve contractual disputes involving unique property. For example, the purchaser of a house may not wish to obtain money damages if the seller breaks a CONTRACT for sale of the house. This may be so because a house is considered unique and thus the damage is irreparable—that is, it cannot be fully redressed by mere money damages. If the court agrees that money damages would be inadequate redress for the buyer, the judge may order a completion of the sale to the buyer, instead of money damages, for the seller's breach of contract.

Equitable contract remedies offer a judge an array of choices. RESCISSION discharges all parties to a contract from the obligations of the contract. The remedy of rescission restores the parties to the positions they held before the formation of the contract. RESTITUTION is an order directing one party to give back something she or he should not be allowed to keep. These two remedies may be sought together. For example, if a buyer purchases an antique piano on credit and later discovers it is a fake, the buyer may sue for rescission and restitution. Under such a dual remedy, the buyer would return the piano to the seller, and the seller would return any payments made by the buyer.

REFORMATION is an equitable way to remedy a contractual mistake. Suppose, for example, that a buyer agrees to order 5,000 units of a product but mistakenly signs a contract ordering the shipment of 50,000 units. If the seller refuses to provide fewer than 50,000 units and demands payment for 50,000, the buyer may sue the seller for reformation of the contract. In such a case, the court may change the terms of the contract to reflect the amount of product actually agreed upon.

Equitable relief has long been considered an extraordinary remedy, an exception to the general rule of money damages. Modern courts still invoke the rule that equitable relief is available only where money damages are inappropriate; in practice, however, courts rarely insist on monetary relief when equitable relief is requested by a plaintiff.

Equitable Defenses The doctrine of *clean hands* holds that the plaintiff in an equity claim should be innocent of any wrongdoing or risk dismissal of the case. LACHES proposes that a plaintiff should not "sleep on his or her rights"—that is, if the plaintiff knows of the defendant's harmful actions but delays in bringing suit, and the delay works against the rights of the defendant, the plaintiff risks DISMISSAL of the case. Under modern law, such defenses are available in any civil case. They are nevertheless considered equitable because they invoke notions of fairness; are not provided in statutes; and are decided only by a judge, not by a jury.

Other Equitable Doctrines Many of the equitable doctrines listed here are codified in statutes. This does not make the issues they concern "legal" as opposed to "equitable." Such issues, whether codified by statute or not, are left to the discretion of a judge, who makes a decision based on principles of fairness.

Equitable Adoption Equitable adoption is the ADOPTION of a child that has not been formally completed but that the law treats as final for some purposes. Generally, a child cannot be adopted without the fulfillment of certain procedures. However, it is sometimes fair and in the best interests of the child to imply that an adoption has taken place. If an adult has performed parental duties and has intended to adopt the child but has failed to fulfill formal adoption procedures, a court may order that for some purposes, the child should be considered part of the adult's family. The most common purpose of an equitable adoption is to give a

child the right to INHERIT from the ESTATE of an equitably adoptive parent.

Equitable Conversion Equitable conversion completes a land SALE when the death of a seller occurs between the signing of the sale agreement and the date of the actual sale. In such a case, a judge will convert the TITLE to the purchaser. This is in fulfillment of the time-honored maxim that "Equity looks upon that as done which ought to have been done."

Equitable Distribution Equitable distribution can describe a fair allotment of anything. In the law, *equitable distribution* is a term of art that describes a method used to divide the property of a husband and wife upon DIVORCE. Under this method, the needs and contributions of each spouse are considered when property is divided between them. This differs from the process used under the COMMUNITY PROPERTY method, where all marital property is simply divided in half.

Equitable Estoppel Under the doctrine of equitable ESTOPPEL, a person is prevented, or estopped, from claiming a legal right, out of fairness to the opposing party. For example, suppose that a person willfully withholds information in order to avoid defending a lawsuit. If the withheld information causes the lawsuit to be brought later than the STATUTE OF LIMITATIONS requires, the person may be estopped from asserting a statute-of-limitations defense.

Equitable Lien A lien is an interest in property given to a CREDITOR to secure the SATISFACTION of a DEBT. An equitable lien may arise from a written contract if the contract shows an intention to charge a party's property with a debt or obligation. An equitable lien may also be declared by a judge in order to fairly secure the rights of a party to a contract.

Equitable Recoupment Equitable RECOUPMENT prevents a plaintiff from collecting the full

An equitable adoption is treated as final even if it has not been formally completed.

amount of a debt if she or he is holding something that belongs to the defendant debtor. It is usually invoked only as a defense to mitigate the amount a defendant owes to a plaintiff. For example, if a taxpayer has failed to claim a tax refund within the time period prescribed by the statute of limitations, the taxpayer may regain, or recoup, the amount of the refund in defending against a future tax claim brought by the government.

Equitable Servitude An equitable servitude is a restriction on the use of land or a building that can be continually enforced. When a land buyer is aware of an agreement that restricts the use of the land, the buyer may be held to the terms of the restriction, regardless of whether it was written in the DEED.

Equity in Property Equity in property is the value of REAL ESTATE above all liens or claims against it. It is used to describe partial ownership. For example, suppose the FAIR MARKET VALUE of a home is $80,000. If the homeowner has a mortgage and owes $50,000 on the mortgage, the equity amount is $30,000. The recognition of equity in property allows a property owner to borrow against a portion of the property value, even though the owner cannot claim complete and final ownership.

Equity of Redemption Equity of REDEMPTION is the right of a homeowner with a mortgage (a mortgagor) to reclaim the property after it has been forfeited. Redemption can be accomplished by paying the entire amount of the debt, interest, and court costs of the foreclosing lender. With equity of redemption, a mortgagor has a specified period of time after DEFAULT and before FORECLOSURE, in which to reclaim the property.

Equity Financing When a CORPORATION raises capital by selling STOCK, the financing is called equity financing because the corporation is offering stockholders a partial interest in its ownership. By contrast, debt financing raises capital by issuing BONDS or borrowing money, neither of which conveys an ownership in the corporation. An equity security is an equitable ownership interest in a corporation, such as that accompanying common and preferred shares of stock.

See also DISCRETION IN DECISION MAKING.

EQUITY OF REDEMPTION 📖 The right of a mortgagor, that is, a borrower who obtains a loan secured by a pledge of his or her REAL PROPERTY, to prevent FORECLOSURE proceedings by paying the amount due on the loan, a MORTGAGE, plus interest and other expenses after having failed to pay within the time and according to the terms specified therein. 📖

This right is based upon the equitable principle that it is only fair that a borrower have a final opportunity to keep his or her property even if he or she has failed to make payments on the mortgage, since the property is to be sold in foreclosure proceedings.

The equity of redemption must be exercised by a mortgagor within a certain time after having defaulted on an obligation. It exists only from the time of DEFAULT to the time that foreclosure proceedings are commenced.

ERGO 📖 *Latin, therefore; hence; because.* 📖

ERIE RAILROAD CO. v. TOMPKINS A 1938 landmark decision by the Supreme Court, *Erie Railroad Co. v. Tompkins*, 304 U.S. 64, 58 S. Ct. 817, 82 L. Ed. 1188, that held that in an action in a FEDERAL COURT, except as to matters governed by the U.S. Constitution and acts of Congress, the law to be applied in any case is the law of the state in which the federal court is situated.

Harry J. Tompkins was walking on a footpath alongside railroad tracks on land owned by the Erie Railroad Company when he was struck and injured by a passing train. He claimed that his injuries resulted from the NEGLIGENCE of the railroad in operating the train.

Tompkins wanted to sue the railroad and recover monetary DAMAGES for his injuries. He was a citizen of Pennsylvania, and the Erie Railroad Company was a New York corporation. He instituted an action in federal court, which was empowered, by virtue of its diversity JURISDICTION, to hear the case because the plaintiff and the defendant were citizens of different states.

The issue before the court was what law to apply in deciding the case. The court would have applied a federal statute to decide whether Tompkins was entitled to damages, but none existed. The court would have applied a state statute since there was no federal statute, but Pennsylvania did not have one.

The highest court of Pennsylvania had established a rule to be followed in state courts whenever a case like this occurred. The Pennsylvania rule was that people who use pathways along railroad RIGHT-OF-WAYS, not railroad crossings, are TRESPASSERS to whom railroads were not to be held liable unless the trespassers were intentionally injured by the reckless and WANTON acts of the railroads.

The trial judge refused to apply the Pennsylvania rule. He found that *Swift v. Tyson*, 41 U.S. (16 Pet.) 1, 10 L. Ed. 865 (1842), which held that there was a body of federal COMMON LAW to be applied in such cases, gave federal judges the right to ignore state rules that were not enacted as statutes by their state legislatures. He held

that it was more important for all federal courts to follow a uniform rule, rather than for each federal court to apply local state rules when there was no statute to resolve the case. He allowed a jury to decide whether the railroad company was negligent, and the jury returned a VERDICT of $30,000 for Tompkins.

The Supreme Court reversed the decision and struck down the rule that allowed federal judges to ignore state court decisions in diversity cases. Although this rule had been followed since *Swift v. Tyson* was decided in 1842, the Supreme Court ruled that it was inequitable. According to the old rule, Tompkins could obtain monetary damages if he sued in federal court, but not if he initiated his lawsuit a few blocks away in the Pennsylvania state court. If the plaintiff and defendant were citizens of different states, the plaintiff could take advantage of the right to sue in federal court. There the plaintiff might win, even if he or she had been trespassing on railroad property. If the plaintiff and defendant were both citizens of Pennsylvania, the plaintiff could not sue in federal court. Pennsylvania courts would all be bound to follow the rule that prevented recoveries for those who used paths alongside railroad tracks. The Supreme Court held that it was unjust for the plaintiff's chances of winning to depend on the fact that the railroad was a Pennsylvania corporation.

The new rule of *Erie Railroad Co. v. Tompkins* provided that federal courts do not have the power to formulate their own RULES OF LAW. The federal courts must apply appropriate federal statutes in diversity cases. When there is no federal law to resolve the question in a lawsuit, they must follow the law of the state that is involved. That includes state statutes and controlling decisions made by the highest court of that state.

As a result of this case, the decisions of federal courts are truly uniform only when a question of federal law is involved. Otherwise, the states are free to develop their own law and have it applied to state questions that come into federal court because the parties are from different states.

CROSS-REFERENCES
Diversity of Citizenship; *Swift v. Tyson.*

ERRATUM 📖 [*Latin, Error.*] The term used in the Latin formula for the assignment of MISTAKES made in a case. 📖

After reviewing a case, if a judge decides that there was no error, he or she indicates so by replying, "*In nollo est erratum,*" which means, "no error was committed." The plural is errata.

ERROR 📖 A MISTAKE in a court proceeding concerning a matter of law or fact, which might provide a ground for a review of the judgment rendered in the proceeding. 📖

See also APPEAL.

ERVIN, SAMUEL JAMES, JR. Samuel J. Ervin, Jr., had a long career in law and politics including twenty years in the U.S. Senate. He is most famous, however, for presiding over the Senate Select Committee on Presidential Campaign Activities, popularly known as the Watergate Committee.

Ervin was born September 27, 1896, in Morganton, North Carolina. He received an A.B. from the University of North Carolina in 1917 and served as an infantryman in France during World War I. When he returned from France, he went to Harvard Law School where he received an LL.B. in 1922.

After law school, Ervin returned to North Carolina where for the next thirty years he practiced law, ventured into politics, and served as a county and state judge. Ervin's political career began in 1923 when he was elected to the North Carolina General Assembly; he served two more terms in the legislature in 1925 and 1931. His most notable achievement in the legislature came in 1925 when he helped defeat a bill that would have prohibited the teaching of the theory of evolution in North Carolina public schools.

From 1935 until 1937, Ervin served as a judge in the Burke County Criminal Court and, from 1937 until 1943, in the Superior Court. He resigned the latter post to return to his law practice. In 1946–47 he served part of a term in the U.S. House of Representatives, completing the term of his brother who had died after being elected to office. Ervin chose not to run for reelection when the term was over and returned to North Carolina. In 1948 he became a judge on the North Carolina Supreme Court, a position that he held until 1954.

In 1954 the governor of North Carolina appointed Ervin to complete the term of a U.S. senator who had died. Ervin continued to be elected to the Senate until his retirement in 1974.

SENATE HISTORICAL OFFICE

Samuel James Ervin, Jr.

"THERE IS NOTHING IN THE CONSTITUTION THAT AUTHORIZES OR MAKES IT THE OFFICIAL DUTY OF A PRESIDENT TO HAVE ANYTHING TO DO WITH CRIMINAL ACTIVITIES."

As a senator, Ervin fought against measures that he believed would endanger individual liberty. This led him to oppose most civil rights legislation—which he believed would confer freedom on some at the expense of others—as well as to be instrumental in stopping a proposed constitutional amendment that would have permitted prayer in the public schools. For the same reason, he opposed a government proposal to maintain computerized files on persons who participated in political protests. Such records, said Ervin, raised the specter of a police state. On social issues, he usually voted with the more conservative members of the Senate. He opposed the EQUAL RIGHTS AMENDMENT, and, as a member of the Senate Armed Services Committee, he supported U.S. involvement in Vietnam.

Ervin was widely respected in the Senate for his knowledge of the Constitution, which he described as one of the greatest works in the English language and said should be taken like mountain whiskey—undiluted and untaxed. Nonetheless, he might not have become a national figure had it not been for his role in the Senate WATERGATE hearings in 1973. As Ervin presided over the nationally televised hearings, he became familiar to millions of viewers.

Known among his fellow senators for his wit and erudition, Ervin liked to describe himself as "just an ol' country lawyer." He published several books including *The Whole Truth: The Watergate Conspiracy* (1980); *Humor of a Country Lawyer* (1983); and an autobiography titled *Preserving the Constitution* (1984). Ervin died April 23, 1985, in Winston-Salem, North Carolina.

See also NIXON, RICHARD MILHOUS.

ESCALATOR CLAUSE 📖 A stipulation contained in a union CONTRACT stating that wages will be raised or lowered, based upon an external standard such as the cost of living index. A term, ordinarily in a contract or LEASE, that provides for an increase in the money to be paid under certain conditions. 📖

Escalator clauses frequently appear in business contracts to raise prices if the individual providing a particular service or type of mer-

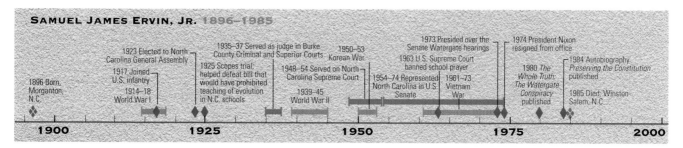

SAMUEL JAMES ERVIN, JR. 1896–1985

1896 Born, Morganton, N.C.

1914–18 World War I

1917 Joined U.S. infantry

1923 Elected to North Carolina General Assembly

1925 Scopes trial; helped defeat bill that would have prohibited teaching of evolution in N.C. schools

1935–37 Served as judge in Burke County Criminal and Superior Courts

1939–45 World War II

1948–54 Served on North Carolina Supreme Court

1950–53 Korean War

1954–74 Represented North Carolina in U.S. Senate

1961–73 Vietnam War

1963 U.S. Supreme Court banned school prayer

1973 Presided over the Senate Watergate hearings

1974 President Nixon resigned from office

1980 *The Whole Truth: The Watergate Conspiracy* published

1984 Autobiography *Preserving the Constitution* published

1985 Died, Winston-Salem, N.C.

1900   1925   1950   1975   2000

chandise is forced to pay more for labor or materials.

Such clauses are also often part of contracts or leases executed subject to price-control regulations. When this type of provision is in a lease, a LANDLORD has the power to collect the maximum amount of rent allowed under rent regulations that are in effect at the time of the lease. The escalator clause provides that if the rent regulations are altered during the time of the lease, the TENANT must pay the new rental fee computed pursuant to the revised regulations.

ESCAPE 📖 The criminal offense of fleeing legal CUSTODY without authority or consent. 📖

In order for an individual who has been accused of escape to be convicted, all elements of the crime must be proved. Such elements are governed by the specific language of each state statute. The general COMMON-LAW principles may be incorporated within a statute, or the law may depart from them in various ways. Federal statutes also make it a crime to escape from federal custody.

Ordinarily, the crime of escape is committed either by the prisoner or by the individual who has the responsibility for keeping the prisoner in custody. The custodian of the prisoner is not ordinarily a warden for the entire PRISON, but is generally the person who has immediate responsibility for guarding the prisoner. Certain states currently punish negligent guards administratively, such as by divesting them of their rank or seniority, or by firing them. Criminal punishment is generally reserved for guards who actively cooperate in facilitating a prisoner's escape.

Charles Jones, an alleged escapee of a Kansas prison, was captured in Wichita. He was serving a twenty-five-year sentence for kidnapping and robbery.

AP/WIDE WORLD PHOTOS

An escape takes place when the prisoner is able to remove himself or herself from the lawful control of an authorized custodian. An individual can be found guilty of escape even in the event that his or her initial arrest was wrongful, since an unlawful arrest must properly be argued in court. The theory is that in order for the process of justice to operate in an orderly manner, a prisoner must not be given the privilege of determining whether or not he or she should be confined. If an arrest is totally unlawful, however, an individual cannot be guilty of escape. This might occur, for example, if a store security guard has no grounds to arrest a shoplifter but does so anyway.

In order to prove that a criminal escape took place, it is ordinarily unnecessary to show that the accused party was actually confined within prison walls. Once an arrest has taken place, the prisoner cannot leave of his or her own volition. Frequently, the degree of the crime is increased when the escape is from a particular kind of confinement. For example, the law might deal more harshly with an individual who escapes from armed prison guards while working on a chain gang than with an individual who runs away while an arresting officer interrogates witnesses. In other JURISDICTIONS, the degree of criminal escape is dependent upon the nature of the crime that initially precipitated the prisoner's confinement.

It is ordinarily necessary to prove that an escaped prisoner was actually attempting to evade legal confinement. For example, if the prisoner went to the wrong place by mistake, he or she will probably not be found guilty of a criminal escape.

Other crimes are related to escape, such as the offense of *aiding escape*, which is committed by a person who, for example, smuggles a prisoner out of jail. Ordinarily a conviction for aiding escape is punishable by a sentence for the number of years specified by the criminal statute.

In some states it is a separate crime to *harbor or conceal an escaped prisoner.* To obtain a conviction against the individual accused of this crime, it must be shown that the individual believed that he or she was aiding an escaped prisoner with the intent to help him or her get clear of lawful custody. It does not constitute a defense to assert that the prisoner never should have been arrested.

Prison breach is an escape committed through the use of force and is more heinous than simple escape. It is not a separate crime, however, and the state may regard it as a more serious degree of criminal escape.

An ATTEMPT to commit escape or any of the related crimes is punishable, even though such an attempt might not have been successful.

ESCHEAT 📖 The power of a state to acquire TITLE to PROPERTY for which there is no owner. 📖

The most common reason that an escheat takes place is that an individual dies INTESTATE, without a valid WILL indicating who is to INHERIT his or her property, and without relatives who are legally entitled to inherit in the absence of a will. A state legislature has the authority to enact an escheat statute.

In feudal England, escheat was a privilege exclusively given to the kings. The policy then was to preserve the wealth of noble families by permitting one individual to inherit an entire ESTATE. There was no right to write a will leaving that property to several HEIRS because that would have the effect of breaking up the estate. In addition, the law designated certain heirs who were in line to inherit the estate. If there was no living person of a designated class to inherit, the king took the property by escheat.

Historically, reasons existed for escheat apart from the absence of heirs to inherit a decedent's property. When CORPORATIONS were subject to strict regulation, it was unlawful for a corporation to own property in any way not permitted by its state-granted CHARTER. Any property beyond that needed by the corporation for the operation of its business, or in excess of the amount designated in its charter or held for a period of time beyond that which was permitted, was subject to escheat.

Certain states mandated escheat of property belonging to religious societies that either promoted POLYGAMY or neglected to incorporate as required by law. Additionally, where public lands were provided for settlers, statutes frequently made provisions for escheat when one individual took possession of more than the permitted acreage or did not properly cultivate the HOMESTEAD. Property that still might be subject to escheat is that belonging to persons who die in a state institution, such as a prison, mental hospital, or veteran's home.

Dissimilarities Escheat is distinguishable from FORFEITURE since, in spite of the fact that the effect is identical under some statutes, forfeiture can be for any type of property interest, including POSSESSION, the right to inherit, or the right of REVERSION if a certain condition was violated by the present owners. Escheat means total relinquishment of ownership. Whereas a forfeiture operates against the individual who has an interest in the forfeited property, an escheat takes place due to the lack of any person with a valid interest in the property.

Property left in a safety deposit box may become the property of the state government through an escheat if the owner dies intestate and has no heirs.

Forfeiture is often used as a penalty for an illegal act, while escheat is not currently linked to any illegality.

Escheat is also distinguishable from reversion, although such distinction has not always been made. A reversion arises only where some remnant of ownership remains in the individual claiming a right to get back the land. The right of reversion can be asserted when some specific condition arises to trigger the right to reclaim. An escheat can occur even though the owner's title is in FEE SIMPLE—that is, complete and unconditional.

SUCCESSION is the passing of a decedent's property to his or her heirs. Escheat is not treated in law like succession; it is completely separate from succession.

The law does not favor escheat. Courts actively seek to avoid it and, as a result, have abandoned most of the grounds for escheat that were recognized centuries ago in England.

Federal law proscribes CORRUPTION OF BLOOD and forfeiture of an entire estate as penalties for convicted criminals.

Property Subject to Escheat Ordinarily, the property subject to escheat is all the property within the state belonging to the original owner upon his or her death. Although initially the doctrine was applicable solely to REAL PROPERTY, it presently extends to PERSONAL PROPERTY, including such INTANGIBLES as bank accounts and shares of STOCK.

A state cannot appropriate property by escheat merely because that property is within its boundaries. Laws in each state prescribe directives for deciding when a deceased person's property is subject to escheat.

Certain other types of property can be the subject of escheat for lack of a known owner. The determination is contingent upon state law.

Certain statutes specify that the property of charitable or religious institutions escheats upon dissolution if its donors have not retained the right to recover it when it is no longer used for religious or charitable objectives.

At common law, any property that belonged to ALIENS was subject to escheat. Laws preserving this rule are considered constitutional.

Unclaimed or abandoned property escheats to the state under some statutes. However, the state cannot merely declare property abandoned and appropriate it. Such laws must function within constitutional limits by observing the requirements imposed by DUE PROCESS. The state is required to adopt a routine procedure for notifying the public and must provide potential claimants an opportunity to argue that the property might belong to them. Without declaring that certain abandoned property has been escheated, the state may lawfully possess the property and hold it for a period of time so that claims can be asserted. A state is not mandated to take over unclaimed property but may choose to exercise the power to escheat only when the value of the property does not exceed the expense of legal proceedings.

Items subject to escheat under various statutes include abandoned bank accounts, deposits left with utility companies, stock DIVIDENDS whose owners cannot be found; unpaid wages; unclaimed LEGACIES from the estate of a deceased relative; INSURANCE money to unknown beneficiaries; and unclaimed money retained by employers or public officials.

Procedure   Escheat statutes prescribe a procedure for location of the rightful owner. If such effort is unsuccessful the property should be applied for the benefit of the public rather than merely the individual who is holding it when it becomes apparent that no owner can be found.

In some states title to some property automatically passes to the state when it escheats for lack of a proper claimant. In other states, a certain period of time must elapse prior to the commencement of escheat proceedings. This does not bar a claimant from stating his or her claim before completion of the escheat proceedings. Some laws require claimants to assert their rights within a period of time or forfeit

them. Often, states mandate that individuals administering estates notify the state government of the existence of property that might be subject to escheat. If the state is not notified when it is required, the time within which the state must start an escheat action is extended accordingly.

The primary burden of proving that there is no proper individual entitled to own the property in question vests in the state, and the general rules regarding the admissibility of EVIDENCE are applicable. Rules of PRESUMPTION, such as the COMMON-LAW presumption of death after a seven-year disappearance, can be used to support the case of the state. After the state has proved a legally sufficient case, any individual claiming a right to the property has an opportunity to go forward and argue against the evidence submitted by the state.

Some states offer money to *informers* who notify the state of property that might be subject to escheat. Informers might be required to provide evidence and pursue the case to a conclusion before they will be entitled to a fee. Other states provide compensation for an *escheater*, a person appointed by the court to manage the claim of the state for escheat. An escheater is entitled to be paid a reasonable amount even if he or she does not succeed in recovering the property for the state.

Property that is either bound over or paid into court for any reason is meant to be held for safekeeping and, therefore, is only in the possession of the court. Escheated property, conversely, is possessed and owned by the state, and the state takes title of such property subject to all other LIENS, MORTGAGES, or ENCUMBRANCES.

Federal law provides that the property of veterans who die without a will or heirs escheats to the United States in certain cases, but ordinarily escheated property goes to the state in which it is situated. Even land that was granted to its owner by the federal government becomes the property of the state if it is subject to escheat. A state law may give escheated property to a COUNTY or TOWN, but this is rare.

ESCROW   Something of value, such as a DEED, STOCK, money, or written instrument, that is put into the CUSTODY of a third person by its owner, a GRANTOR, an OBLIGOR, or a promisor, to be retained until the occurrence of a contingency or performance of a condition.

An escrow also refers to a writing deposited with someone until the performance of an act or the occurrence of an event specified in that writing. The directions given to the person who accepts delivery of the document are called the *escrow agreement* and are binding between the person who promises and the person to whom the promise is made. The writing is held *in escrow* by a third person until the purpose of the underlying agreement is accomplished. When the condition specified in the escrow agreement is performed, the individual holding the writing gives it over to the party entitled to receive it. This is known as the *second delivery.*

Any written document that is executed in accordance with all requisite legal formalities may properly be deposited in escrow. Documents that can be put in escrow include a DEED, a MORTGAGE, a PROMISE to pay money, a BOND, a CHECK, a LICENSE, a PATENT, or a CONTRACT for the sale of REAL PROPERTY. The term *escrow* initially applied solely to the deposit of a formal instrument or document; however, it is popularly used to describe a deposit of money.

The escrow agreement is a contract. The parties to such an agreement determine when the agreement should be released prior to making the deposit. After the escrow agreement has been entered, the terms for holding and releasing the document or money cannot be altered in the absence of an agreement by all the parties.

A *depositary* is not a party to the escrow agreement, but rather a custodian of the deposit who has no right to alter the terms of the agreement or prevent the parties from altering them if they so agree. The only agreement that the depositary must make is to hold the deposit, subject to the terms and conditions of the agreement. Ordinarily, the depositary has no involvement with the underlying agreement; however, an interested party may, in a few states, be selected to be a depositary if all parties are in agreement. In all cases, a depositary is bound by the duty to act according to the trust placed in him or her. If the depositary makes a delivery to the wrong person or at the wrong time, he or she is liable to the depositor.

The document or the money is only in escrow upon actual delivery to the depositary. Ordinarily, courts are strict in their requirement that the terms of the agreement be completely performed before the deposit is released. A reasonable amount of time must generally be allotted for performance. Parties may, however, make the agreement that TIME IS OF THE ESSENCE, and in such a case, any delay beyond the period specified in the agreement makes the individual who is obligated to act FORFEIT all his or her rights in the property in escrow.

ESPIONAGE   The act of securing information of a military or political nature that a competing nation holds secret. It can involve the analysis of diplomatic reports, publications, statistics, and broadcasts, as well as spying, a clandestine activity carried out by an individual or individuals working under a secret identity for the benefit of a nation's information gathering techniques. In the United States, the organization that heads most activities dedicated to espionage is the CENTRAL INTELLIGENCE AGENCY.

Espionage, commonly known as spying, is the practice of secretly gathering information about a foreign government or a competing industry, with the purpose of placing one's own government or corporation at some strategic or financial advantage. Federal law prohibits espionage when it jeopardizes the national defense or benefits a foreign nation (18 U.S.C.A. § 793). Criminal espionage involves betraying U.S. government secrets to other nations.

Despite its illegal status, espionage is commonplace. Through much of the twentieth century, international agreements have implicitly accepted espionage as a natural political activity. This gathering of intelligence has benefited competing nations that wish to stay one step ahead of each other. The general public never hears of espionage activities that are carried out correctly. However, espionage blunders can receive national attention, jeopardizing the security of the nation or the lives of individuals.

Espionage is unlikely to disappear. Since the late nineteenth century, nations have allowed each other to station so-called military attachés in their overseas embassies. These "attachés" collect intelligence secrets about the armed forces of their host country. Attachés have worked toward the subversion of governments, the destabilization of economies, and the ASSASSINATION of declared enemies. Many of these activities remain secret in order to protect national interests and reputations.

The centerpiece of U.S. espionage is the Central Intelligence Agency (CIA), created by the National Security Act of 1947 (50 U.S.C.A. § 402 et seq.) to conduct covert activity. The CIA protects national security interests by spying on foreign governments. The CIA also attempts to recruit foreign agents to work on behalf of U.S. interests. Other nations do the same, seeking to recruit CIA agents or others who will betray sensitive information. Sometimes a foreign power is successful in procuring U.S. government secrets.

One of the most damaging cases of criminal espionage in U.S. history was uncovered in the late 1980s with the exposure of the Walker spy ring, which operated from 1967 to 1985. John A. Walker, Jr., and his son, Michael L. Walker, brother, Arthur J. Walker, and friend, Jerry A.

John Walker sold sensitive navy codes and other data to the Soviet Union from 1967 to 1985. After he was caught the armed forces rebuilt its entire communications system at a cost of nearly $1 billion in order to avoid such problems in the future.

Whitworth, supplied the Soviets with confidential U.S. data including codes from the U.S. Navy that allowed the Soviets to decipher over a million Navy messages. The Walker ring also sold the Soviets classified material concerning Yuri Andropov, secretary general of the Communist party until 1984; the Soviet shooting of a Korean Airlines jet in 1983; and U.S. offensives during the Vietnam War.

John Walker pleaded guilty to three counts of espionage. He claimed that he had become an undercover informant for the thrill of it, rather than fc · the money. He was sentenced to a life term in federal prison, with eligibility for parole in ten years. Michael Walker pleaded guilty to aiding in the supply of classified documents to the Soviets. He was able to reach a plea-bargain under which he was sentenced to twenty-five years in prison. Arthur Walker was convicted of espionage in Norfolk, Virginia. His conviction was affirmed in *United States v. Walker*, 796 F.2d 43 (4th Cir. 1986). Like John Walker, he was sentenced to a life term in federal prison. Jerry Whitworth received a sentence of 365 years for stealing and selling Navy coding secrets (upheld in *United States v. Whitworth*, 856 F.2d 1268 [9th Cir. 1988]).

The ring's ample opportunity to exploit the lax security of the Navy left a legacy of damage. The armed forces frantically scrapped and rebuilt their entire communications system, at a cost to taxpayers of nearly $1 billion. The U.S. Department of Defense (DOD) had to withdraw security clearances from approximately 2 million military and civilian personnel worldwide. The DOD also reduced the number of classified documents in order to limit the number of remaining security clearances.

These reforms only touched the tip of larger, underlying problems. The exploits of Aldrich Hazen Ames brought security problems within the CIA to the fore. As a double agent, Ames sold secrets to Moscow from 1985 to the end of the COLD WAR and beyond. As a CIA agent and later a CIA official, Ames was responsible for, among other things, recruiting Soviet officials to do undercover work for the United States. His position put him in contact with Soviet officials at their embassy in Washington, D.C. While in the embassy, he discussed secret matters related to U.S. intelligence. The CIA's lack of security measures, which usually consisted of no more than the collection of questionable lie detector data, gave Ames the opportunity to illegally acquire a fortune.

In 1986, the CIA suspected the presence of a mole (a double agent with the objective of rising to a key position) in the system. Investigators could not be certain of the mole's identity but determined that something in their operations had gone awry. Two officers at the Soviet Embassy who had been recruited as double agents by the FEDERAL BUREAU OF INVESTIGATION (FBI) had been recalled to Moscow, arrested, tried, and executed. Years later, a major blunder on Ames's part led the CIA to suspect him of leaking information that may have contributed to the death of the agents. Ames had told his superiors in October 1992 that he was going to visit his mother-in-law in Colombia. He actually went to Venezuela, where he met a Soviet contact. His travels were under surveillance, and the CIA took note of the discrepancy.

By May 1993, Ames had become the focus of a criminal investigation dubbed Nightmover. Investigators found that Ames's continued activity with the Soviets had led to the execution of at least ten more agents. Ames's continuing financial struggle necessitated that he continue to sell secrets. While criminal espionage brought him more than $2.5 million from the Kremlin, Ames's carelessness with the money led to his demise. According to court documents, Ames and his wife spent nearly $1.4 million from April 1985 to November 1993. Ames's annual CIA salary never exceeded $70,000.

When Ames pleaded guilty on April 28, 1994, to a two-count criminal INDICTMENT for espionage and TAX EVASION, government prosecutors sought to negotiate the plea to avoid a long trial. A trial, they feared, could force intelligence agencies to disclose secrets about the Ames case, which had already embarrassed the CIA. Escaping the ordeal of a drawn-out trial, Ames was sentenced to life in prison.

As a result of the Ames case, the CIA made a number of changes, including requiring CIA employees to make annual financial disclosures and tightening the requirements for top security clearance.

CROSS-REFERENCES

Hiss, Alger; Rosenberg, Julius and Ethel.

ESQ. An abbreviation for esquire, which is a title used by attorneys in the United States. The term *esquire* has a different meaning in English law. It is used to signify a title of dignity, which ranks above *gentleman* and directly below *knight*.

In the United States, Esq. is written after a lawyer's name, for example: John Smith, Esq.

ESSEX JUNTO In April 1778, a number of men gathered at Ipswich in Essex County, Massachusetts, to discuss the drafting of a new Massachusetts constitution. Composed of lawyers and merchants, the majority of the group were residents of Essex County, from which the assembly derived its name. Included among its members were politicians George Cabot and Timothy Pickering, and jurist THEOPHILUS PARSONS.

The Essex Junto began as a small, independent faction of prominent, educated men but developed into a strong section of the Federalist party, which exerted political influence for many years. It advocated the acceptance of the U.S. Constitution and the financial policies of ALEXANDER HAMILTON. The junto staunchly opposed the ideologies of President THOMAS JEFFERSON, and the Embargo Act of 1807, which prohibited the exportation of American goods to France and England in an effort to compel those countries to ease their restrictions on U.S. trade. The opposition to this act was so vehement that it was repealed.

The Essex Junto was opposed to the War of 1812. It convened, in secrecy, the Hartford Convention in 1814, which proved to be nothing but an airing of grievances without any serious solutions. The war ended shortly thereafter, and many of the junto members were ridiculed and threatened with treason for the closed-door tactics at the Hartford Convention. The junto soon lost much of its power with the signing of the Treaty of Ghent, which signified the end of the much-opposed War of 1812.

CROSS-REFERENCES

Constitution of the United States *In Focus:* Federalists vs. Anti-federalists; Massachusetts Constitution of 1780.

ESTABLISH This word occurs frequently in the CONSTITUTION OF THE UNITED STATES, and it is used there in different meanings: (1) to settle firmly, to fix unalterably; as in to establish justice, which is the avowed object of the Constitution; (2) to make or form; as in to establish uniform laws governing naturalization or bankruptcy; (3) to found, to create, to regulate; as in "Congress shall have power to establish post offices"; (4) to found, recognize, confirm, or admit; as in "Congress shall make no law respecting an establishment of religion"; and (5) to create, to ratify, or confirm, as in "We, the people . . . do ordain and establish this Constitution."

To settle, make, or fix firmly; place on a permanent footing; found; create; put beyond doubt or dispute; prove; convince. To enact permanently. To bring about or into existence.

ESTABLISHMENT CLAUSE See RELIGION.

ESTATE The degree, quantity, nature, and extent of interest that a person has in real and personal property. An estate in lands, TENEMENTS, and HEREDITAMENTS signifies such interest as the tenant has therein. *Estate* is commonly used in CONVEYANCES in connection with the words *right, title,* and *interest,* and is, to a great degree, synonymous with all of them.

When used in connection with PROBATE proceedings, the term encompasses the total PROPERTY of whatever kind that is owned by a DECEDENT prior to the distribution of that property in accordance with the terms of a WILL, or when there is no will, by the laws of INHERITANCE in the state of domicile of the decedent. It means, ordinarily, the whole of the property owned by anyone, the realty as well as the PERSONALTY.

In its broadest sense, the social, civic, or political condition or standing of a person; or a class of persons considered as grouped for social, civic, or political purposes.

There are several types of estates that govern interests in REAL PROPERTY. They are freehold estates, nonfreehold estates, CONCURRENT ESTATES, specialty estates, future INTERESTS, and incorporeal interests.

Freehold Estates A freehold estate is a right of TITLE to land that is characterized by two essential elements: *immobility*, meaning that the property involved is either land or an interest affixed or derived therefrom, and *indeterminate duration*.

There are three kinds of freehold estates: a FEE SIMPLE, a FEE TAIL, and a LIFE ESTATE.

Fee Simple Absolute A fee simple absolute is the most extensive interest in real property that an individual can possess, since it is limited

If this mansion and the surrounding land had a deed that granted a fee simple absolute, upon the death of the owner the land would automatically be inherited by the owner's heirs unless a different provision for it was made in a will.

completely to the individual and his or her HEIRS and ASSIGNS forever, and it is not subject to any limitations or CONDITIONS.

For example, an individual might purchase a plot of land for which the DEED states that the GRANTOR transfers the property "to GRANTEE and his or her heirs," which would have the legal effect of creating a fee simple absolute. The grantee has the right to immediate and exclusive possession of the land, and he or she can do whatever he or she wants with it, such as grow CROPS, remove trees, build on it, sell it, or dispose of it by will. This type of estate is deemed to be perpetual. Upon the death of the owner, if no provision has been made for its distribution, the land will automatically be inherited by the owner's heirs.

Fee Simple Determinable A fee simple determinable, which is also referred to as a *base fee* or *qualified fee*, is one that is created to continue until the occurrence of a specified event. When such an event occurs, the estate will terminate automatically by OPERATION OF LAW, at which time the ownership reverts to the grantor or his or her heirs.

For example, a grantor makes the following conveyance: "To grantee and his or her heirs so long as it is used for school purposes." The grantor's intent is clearly indicated when he or she creates the estate. When the grantee ceases to use the land for school purposes, the grantor has the right to immediate possession. The grantee's estate is restricted to the period during which the land is used for school purposes.

The interest of the grantor is known as a *possibility of reverter.* Ordinarily the words *until* or *as long as* indicate the creation of a special limitation. See also REVERSIONS; REVERTER, POSSIBILITY OF.

Fee Simple Subject to a Condition Subsequent A fee simple subject to a condition subsequent is an estate that terminates only upon the exercise of the power of termination, or RIGHT OF REENTRY, for the violation of a particular condition. It differs from a fee simple determinable in that the latter expires automatically, by operation of law, upon the happening of the event specified. A fee simple subject to a condition subsequent continues even after the occurrence of the event until the grantor DIVESTS the estate or ends it through the exercise of his or her power to terminate.

For example, the grantor conveys land "to grantee and his or her heirs, but if the premises are used for commercial purposes other than the sale of antiques, then the grantor has the right to reenter and repossess the property."

The grantor has the power to end the grantee's fee through his or her reentry onto the premises if the condition is violated. Reentry, however, is totally at the option of the grantor. The grantee's estate continues until the grantor either enters the land or brings an action to recover POSSESSION. When the grantor does reenter the land, the remaining portion of the grantee's estate is FORFEITED.

Ordinarily, the words used in conveyance to create an estate subject to a condition subsequent are *upon condition that, provided that,* or *but if,* together with a provision for reentry by the grantor.

Fee Simple Subject to Executory Limitation At English COMMON LAW, a grantor was not able to create a freehold estate that was to begin in futuro, at a subsequent time, because LIVERY OF SEISIN (actual possession) was essential. If actual possession of the land was given to the grantee, the estate would be immediately effective, contrary to the grantor's intent. The only manner in which an estate that was to begin in the future could be created was through the use of a REMAINDER. For example, if a grantor wished to give the grantee a future interest in the land, he might make the following conveyance, "to transferee for life, remainder to grantee and his or her heirs." Livery of seisin was thereby made to the transferee, who held the estate for life, and upon the transferee's death the SEISIN passed to the grantee.

In 1535, however, the STATUTE OF USES was passed, which allowed the creation, by deed, of *springing interests,* or *executory interests.* A grantor could, thereby, give the grantee a present right to the future interest in the land. The grantor might, for example, convey the land "to grantee and his heirs, grantee's interest to commence five years from the date of the deed."

A grantor can also convey an estate subject to a shifting interest. For example, the grantor might make the following conveyance: "To grantee and his or her heirs, but in the event that grantee dies without ISSUE upon his or her death, then to transferee and his or her heirs." The grantee is thereby given a fee simple subject to an executory limitation, which is the interest of the transferee.

Fee Tail A fee tail is an estate subject to limitations concerning who may inherit the property, which is ordinarily created by a deed or a will.

Two significant historical developments were instrumental in the creation of this type of freehold estate. The first was recognition by the court of the fee simple conditional, and the second was the passing of the Statute De Donis Conditionalibus, commonly known as the Statute De Donis, in 1285 by Parliament.

Prior to 1285, the provision "to grantee and the heirs of his body" was interpreted by the courts as providing the grantee with the power to convey a fee simple in the property if and when he sired a child. An estate of this nature was referred to as a fee simple conditional, since it was a fee simple contingent upon offspring being born to the grantee. The grantee was thereby able to terminate any rights that the heirs of his body might have in the land. In addition, he was able to terminate the possibility of reverter which the grantor had in the land.

The Statute De Donis was subsequently passed in order to keep family land in a family, provided there was a family or issue. A grantee could not convey land in such manner as to terminate the right of heirs of his body to inherit the land upon his death nor could he convey so as to terminate the grantor's reversionary interest. If the grantee conveyed property "to transferee and his heirs," and then died, leaving a child, the child could take the land from the transferee. If the grantee died with no surviving heirs of the body, the grantor could take the land away from the transferee.

The grantor of a fee tail was permitted to limit the inheritance to a specific group of LINEAL descendants of the grantee. He could create a fee tail general, for example, to transferee and "the heirs of his body begotten," regardless of the number of wives by whom the transferee had children. Alternatively, he could create a fee tail special, to transferee and "the heirs of his body on Ann, his now wife, to be begotten," which specifies that only issue of the marriage of the transferee and Ann, and no other marriage, could inherit. A grant to a man and his male bodily heirs, for example, created a fee tail male while a fee tail female restricted transfer of land to the transferee and the female heirs of his or her body only.

Life Estate A life estate is an interest in property that does not amount to ownership, since it is limited by a term of life, either of the individual in whom the right is vested or some other person, or it lasts until the occurrence or nonoccurrence of an uncertain event. A life

A life estate is an interest in property that is not ownership because it lasts only as long as the life of the person who holds it. The life tenant may use the land, grow crops there, and even rent or mortgage the property.

DENNIS MACDONALD/PHOTOEDIT

estate *pur autre vie* is an estate that the grantee holds for the life of another person.

A life estate is generally created by deed but can be created by LEASE. No special language is required provided the grantor's intent to create such an estate is clear. The grantee of a life estate is called the *life tenant.*

A life tenant can use the land, take any fruits stemming therefrom, such as crops, and dispose of his or her interest to another person. The power to dispose includes the right to MORTGAGE the property, and to create LIENS, EASEMENTS, or other rights in the property, provided they do not extend beyond the period of the tenant's life.

The holder of a life estate cannot do anything that would injure the property or cause WASTE, or in any way interfere with the reversionary interest of the grantee. The life tenant has the right to exclusive possession subject to the rights of the grantor to (1) enter the property to ascertain whether or not waste has been committed or is in the process of being committed; (2) collect any rent that is due; (3) come upon the property to make any necessary repairs; (4) move timber that has been severed and belongs to him or her; and (5) do any acts that will prevent the termination of his or her reversion.

The life tenant is permitted to use the property in the same manner as the owner of a fee simple, except that he or she must leave the property in reasonably good condition for the individual who will succeed to the possession. The life tenant has an obligation to maintain the property in good repair and must pay taxes and interest on any mortgage on the premises when the life estate begins. The life tenant has the right to the issues and profits from the land, and any crop planted prior to the termination of the life estate can be harvested by the tenant's personal representative. In addition, any FIXTURES placed on the ground by the tenant can be removed by him or her. If the property is harmed, the life tenant can obtain a recovery for the injury to his or her interest.

1996 Federal Tax Rate on Estates and Trusts	
Taxable income	**Tax Rate**
$0 to $1,600	15%
$1,601 to $3,800	28%*
$3,801 to $5,800	31%
$5,801 to $7,900	36%
more than $7,900	39.6%

*The maximum income tax rate on net long-term capital gains for estates is 28%.
Source: Internal Revenue Service.

In a typical life estate for the life of an individual other than the tenant, the grantor conveys the property "to grantee for the life of A." The grantee is thereby given an estate for the life span of another person. In this type of conveyance, A is the measuring life. At common law, if the grantee died before the individual whose life measured the estate, the property was regarded as being without an owner. The first individual to obtain possession, known as the *common occupant,* was entitled to the estate until the death of the person whose life measured the duration of the estate. An estate pur autre vie could not be inherited by the heirs of the deceased grantee, nor could it be reclaimed by the grantor since he or she had conveyed his or her interest for the life of another person who was still living. No one had the right to evict the common occupant. Some grantors made conveyances that provided for the heirs of the grantee. For example, "to grantee and his heirs for the life of A." If the grantee died during A's lifetime, an heir of the grantee would take as a *special occupant* rather than by descent. Some modern statutes have made the property interest between the death of the grantee and the measuring life a CHATTEL real, making the provision that the grantee's PERSONAL REPRESENTATIVE takes the property as PERSONAL PROPERTY.

A life estate is ALIENABLE, and therefore, the life tenant can convey his or her estate. The grantee of the life tenant would thereby be given an estate pur autre vie. The life tenant is unable, however, to convey an estate that is greater than his or her own.

Nonfreehold Estates Nonfreehold estates are interests in real property without seisin and which are not inheritable. The four main types of nonfreehold estates are an estate for years, an estate from year to year, a tenancy at will, and a tenancy at sufferance.

Estate for Years The most significant feature of an estate for years is that it must be of definite duration, that is, it is required to have a definite beginning and a definite ending. The most common example of an estate for years is the arrangement existing between a LANDLORD and TENANT whereby property is leased or rented for a specific amount of time. In this type of estate the transferor leases the property to the transferee for a certain designated period, for example: "Transferor leases Blackacre to transferee for the period of January 1, 1998, to January 1, 2003, a period of five years."

The conveyance mentioned in the preceding paragraph would last for a specific period of five years. During that period, the transferee has the right to possess Blackacre and use and enjoy the fruits that stem therefrom. He or she is required to pay rent according to the terms of the rental agreement and is not permitted to commit waste on the premises. If the transferee dies during the term of the lease, the remainder of such term will pass to the transferee's personal representative for distribution pursuant to a will or the laws of DESCENT AND DISTRIBUTION, since a leasehold interest is regarded as personal property or a chattel real.

Estate from Year to Year The essential distinguishing characteristic of an estate from year to year is that it is of indefinite duration. For example, a landlord might lease Blackacre to a tenant for a two-year period, from January 1, 1998, to January 1, 2000, at a rental of $600 per month, payable in advance on or before the ninth day of each month. The tenant might hold possession beyond January 1, 2000, and on or before January 9, 2000, give the landlord $600. If the landlord accepts the rent, the tenant has thereby been made a tenant from year to year. An estate of this nature continues indefinitely until one of the parties gives notice of termination. The terms of the original lease are implied to carry over to the year-to-year lease, except for the term that set forth the period of the lease.

Notice of termination is an important component of this type of periodic tenancy. In the preceding example, either party would be able to terminate the tenancy by providing notice at least six months preceding the end of the yearly period. Statutory provisions often abridge the length of notice required to end periodic tenancies. Such tenancies may come within requirements set forth by the STATUTE OF FRAUDS.

Tenancy at Will A tenancy at will is a rental relationship between two parties that is of indefinite duration, since either may end the relationship at anytime. It can be created either by agreement, or by failure to effectively create a tenancy for years.

A tenancy at will is terminated by either individual without notice and ends automatically by the death of either party or by the commission of voluntary waste by the lessee. It is not assignable and is categorized as the lowest type of chattel interest in land.

Tenancy at Sufferance A tenancy at sufferance is an estate that ordinarily arises when a tenant for years or a tenant from period to period retains possession of the premises without the landlord's consent. This type of interest is regarded as naked and wrongful possession.

In this type of estate, the tenant is essentially a TRESPASSER except that his or her original entry onto the property was not wrongful. If the

Federal Estate and Gift Tax Receipts: 1980 to 1994

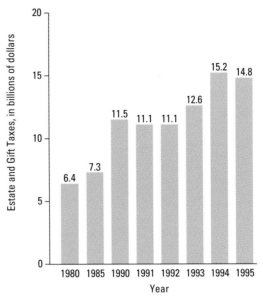

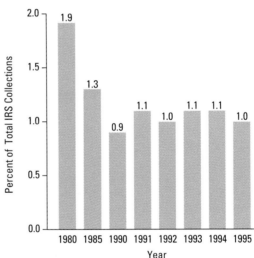

Source: U.S. Office of Management and Budget, *Historical Tables*, annual.

landlord consents, a tenant at sufferance may be transformed into a tenant from period to period, upon acceptance of rent.

Concurrent Estates Concurrent estates are those that are either owned or possessed by two or more individuals simultaneously. The three most common types of concurrent estates are JOINT TENANCY, TENANCY BY THE ENTIRETY, and TENANCY IN COMMON.

Joint Tenancy A joint tenancy is a type of concurrent ownership whereby property is acquired by two or more persons at the same time and by the same instrument. A typical conveyance of such a tenancy would be "Grantor conveys Blackacre to A, B, and C and their heirs in fee simple absolute." The main feature of a

DEL MULKEY/PHOTO RESEARCHERS

A tenancy by the entirety is a form of joint tenancy between a husband and wife. Neither may sell or otherwise dispose of his or her interest in the property.

joint tenancy is the RIGHT OF SURVIVORSHIP. If any one of the joint tenants dies, the remainder goes to the survivors, and the entire estate goes to the last survivor.

In a joint tenancy, there are four UNITIES, those of interest, time, title, and possession.

Unity of interest means that each joint tenant owns an undivided interest in the property as a whole. No one joint tenant can have a larger share than any of the others.

Unity of time signifies that the estates of each of the joint tenants is vested for exactly the same period.

Unity of title indicates that the joint tenants hold their property under the same title.

Unity of possession requires that each of the joint tenants must take the same undivided possession of the property as a whole and enjoy the same rights until one of the joint tenants dies.

Tenancy by the Entirety A tenancy by the entirety is a form of *joint tenancy* arising between a HUSBAND AND WIFE, whereby each spouse owns the undivided whole of the property, with the *right of survivorship.*

A tenancy by the entirety can be created by will or deed but not by descent and distribution. It is distinguishable from a joint tenancy in that neither party can voluntarily dispose of his or her interest in the property. There is unity of title, possession, interest, time, and person.

Tenancy in Common A tenancy in common is a form of concurrent ownership that can be created by deed or will, or by operation of law, in which two or more individuals possess property simultaneously. A typical conveyance of this type of tenancy would be "Grantor, owner of Blackacre in fee simple absolute, grants to A, B, and C, and their heirs—each taking one-third interest in the property."

In the preceding illustration, A, B, and C are tenants in common. There is no right of survivorship in such a tenancy, and each grantee has the right to dispose of his or her share by deed or by will.

In a tenancy in common, one of the tenants may have a larger share of the property than the others. In addition, the tenants in common may take the same property by several titles. The only unity present in a tenancy in common is unity of possession.

Future Interests Future interests are interests in real or personal property, a gift or trust, or other things in which the privilege of possession or of enjoyment is in the future and not the present. They are interests that will come into being at a future point in time. There are five classes of future interests: *reversions; possibilities of reverter; powers of termination,* also known as *rights of re-entry for condition broken; remainders,* and *executory interests.*

Incorporeal Interests Incorporeal interests in REAL PROPERTY are those that cannot be possessed physically, since they consist of rights of a particular user, or the right to enforce an agreement concerning use. The five major types of incorporeal interests are easements, PROFITS, COVENANTS running with the land, equitable servitudes, and LICENSES. See also EQUITY; SERVITUDE.

ESTATE AND GIFT TAXES When PROPERTY interests are given away during life or at death, taxes are imposed on the transfer. These taxes, known as estate and gift taxes, apply to the total transfers an individual may make over a lifetime.

Estate and gift tax law is primarily statutory. Although the Treasury Department issues regulations governing the interpretation of the revenue laws, and although state and federal courts contribute their interpretations of statutory law, the foundation of the TRANSFER TAXES rests in chapters 11 and 12 of the INTERNAL REVENUE CODE. To understand the complex statutory framework requires a basic understanding of the concepts underlying the estate and gift tax system. The transfer tax laws apply to all GRATUITOUS shifts in property interests. But although administered similarly, the estate tax and gift tax have somewhat different goals. The gift tax reaches the gratuitous abandonment of ownership or control in favor of another person during life, whereas the estate tax extends to transfers that take place at death, or before death, as substitutes for dispositions at death. Both taxes are intended to limit the concentration of familial or dynastic wealth.

Even though the potential tax rate is quite high, at 55 percent, most individuals never pay any estate or gift tax. Under the tax system that has been in place since 1986, every person may transfer a combined $600,000 worth of property during life and at death without paying tax. This tax-free allowance corresponds to $192,800 worth of federal tax savings and is known as the unified credit against estate tax. This unified credit is sufficient to satisfy taxes on transfers by all but the richest five percent of U.S. citizens. Accordingly, the estate and gift taxes are motivated primarily by a policy against the concentration of dynastic wealth rather than by a policy of revenue enhancement. In fact, estate tax collections typically constitute less than two percent of total INTERNAL REVENUE SERVICE collections.

With few exceptions, the individual making the transfer is responsible for any transfer tax owed (whereas, in contrast, the individual receiving income is responsible for any income tax owed). Thus, the EXECUTOR of an ESTATE, as the estate's representative, is responsible for paying any estate tax due, and the DONOR of a GIFT is responsible for paying any gift tax due.

Gifts The Internal Revenue Code defines a gift as a "transfer ... in trust or otherwise, whether the gift is direct or indirect, and whether the property is real or personal, tangible or intangible." Generally, a gift is any completed transfer of an interest in property to the extent that the donor has not received something of value in return, with the exception of a transfer that results from an ordinary business transaction or the discharge of legal obligations, such as the obligation to support minor children. This definition of gifts does not require the intent to make a gift. An individual may make gifts of both present interests (such as life estates) and future interests (such as REMAINDERS) in property (26 U.S.C.A. § 2503(b)).

From a tax standpoint, gifts have two principal advantages over transfers at death. First, gifts allow a donor to transfer property while its value is low, allowing future appreciation in property value to pass to others free of additional gift or estate tax. Second, provided the gift is of a present interest in property, a donor may transfer up to $10,000 exempt from tax to each donee every calendar year, which allows the donor to reduce the size of the estate remaining at death without any transfer tax consequences.

To constitute a gift, a transfer must satisfy two basic requirements: it must lack CONSIDER-ATION, in whole or in part (that is, the recipient must give up nothing in return); and the donor must relinquish all control over the transferred interest. To constitute a tax-exempt gift, a transfer also must constitute a present interest in property. (A present interest is something a person owns at the present time, whereas a future interest is something a person will come to own in the future, such as the proceeds of a trust.)

Lack of Consideration A transfer is not a gift if the transferor receives consideration, or something of value, in return for it. For example, if A sells B a used car worth $5,000 and receives $5,000 in exchange, the transfer is not a gift because it is supported by "adequate and full consideration" (26 U.S.C.A. § 2512(b)). But if A sells B the same car for only $2,000, the transfer constitutes a gift of $3,000 because A exchanges $3,000 worth of car for nothing. Finally, if A gives B the car without receiving anything in return, the transfer constitutes a gift of $5,000. Although consideration may be whole or partial, not all transfers for partial or insufficient consideration result in gifts. An arm's-length SALE—that is, a sale free of any special relationship between buyer and seller—will not be considered a gift where no intent to make a gift exists, even if the consideration is not adequate. This limit on the definition of gifts excludes bad business deals and forced sales from gift tax treatment.

The Completeness Requirement A transfer constitutes a gift for tax purposes only if the donor has parted with the ability to exercise "dominion and control" over the property transferred. Many transfers of property satisfy this condition. For example, if A takes B out for a birthday dinner, the act of purchasing the

Giving an antique car as a gift will reduce the estate of the donor without the need to pay transfer taxes.

dinner is a gift because A cannot regain control over the food B consumes or revoke the acts of purchasing and consuming the meal. When the donor has not relinquished absolutely the ability to control or manage the property or its use, however, the "gift" may not be complete for tax purposes. The most common example of an incomplete transfer is a transfer of property to a revocable TRUST, in which the donor retains the right, as TRUSTEE, to alter, amend, or rescind the trust. The gift is not completed because the donor could restore ownership in the trust property to himself or herself, or change his or her mind about who will enjoy or later receive the property.

This distinction between complete and incomplete transfers determines whether property will be included in an estate at death, as well as the value of that property. The value of property that was incompletely transferred during life will be included in the GROSS ESTATE at death (26 U.S.C.A. §§ 2035–2038). Therefore, any appreciation in the value of incompletely transferred property will be included and taxed in the estate, whereas none of the value of completely transferred property will be included in the estate. Accordingly, if A transfers one thousand shares of XYZ stock outright to B when it is worth $10 a share, the value of the transfer subject to tax equals zero because A can take advantage of the annual exclusion described in the following section. If A transfers the same stock to a revocable trust for B's benefit, however, and that stock is worth $100 a share on the date of A's death, the entire $100,000 is included and taxable in A's estate. Moreover, any income distributions from the trust after the transfer of property to the revocable trust are taxable gifts to B for which A must pay tax.

Sometimes people make incomplete transfers rather than completed gifts in order to retain control over the property, even though appreciation in property value is taxed as a consequence of an incomplete transfer. For various reasons, a person may not want to give up that control. An individual may wish to control the distribution of income from a gift to a trust, or even to receive the income distributions from a trust. Or an individual may create a trust for nongift reasons, such as to ensure property or investment management. Parents may not trust their children to manage gifts of stock or cash effectively, and may thus retain control to ensure that transfers are not squandered. Occasionally, donors mistakenly believe that revocable trusts are effective devices to avoid paying estate taxes, and simply do not realize that transfers to revocable trusts are incomplete for gift purposes.

Present versus Future Interests: The Annual Exclusion Each individual may make tax-exempt gifts of up to $10,000 to each donee every year. To qualify for this so-called annual exclusion, a gift must be of a present interest in property (26 U.S.C.A. § 2503(b)). Completed transfers of future interests, such as remainder interests in REAL ESTATE or the vested right to the distribution of trust principal on the donor's death, constitute gifts for tax purposes but do not qualify for the annual exclusion.

Only the unrestricted right to use, enjoy, or possess property in whole or in part constitutes a present interest. For example, if A transfers a LIFE ESTATE in his home to B, with a remainder to C, only the life estate to B, which is a present interest in the home, qualifies for the annual exclusion. The remainder interest to C is a completed gift, but does not qualify for the annual exclusion because it is a gift of a future interest. A more subtle and common illustration of this principle involves trust property. For example, A creates an IRREVOCABLE trust giving B, the trustee, complete discretion over the distribution of income to C for ten years, at which time the trust will terminate and the entire trust corpus and accumulated income will be paid to C. In this case, A has made a completed gift of the entire trust corpus, but the gift does not qualify for the annual exclusion because C has no present right to the trust income.

Testamentary Transfers The gross estate is the measure of the interests an individual is considered capable of transferring at the time of death, and provides the starting point for computing the estate tax (26 U.S.C.A. § 2031). The gross estate is an artificial concept in part, because it may include interests that the individual did not actually own at death (§§ 2035–2038). From the gross estate are deducted expenses of administering the estate, the decedent's legal obligations at death, the value of property passing to a surviving spouse, and the value of BEQUESTS to charity (§§ 2053–2056). The remainder is known as the taxable estate and is the value on which the estate tax is computed.

Conventional interests in property, such as ownership of real estate, STOCKS and BONDS, cash, automobiles, art, and PERSONAL PROPERTY, must be included in the gross estate and valued at their FAIR MARKET VALUE on the date of death. In addition, interests in life INSURANCE, annuities, and certain death benefits are included to the extent that the DECEDENT was able to confer

an interest in them on another person. Finally, three somewhat artificial ownership attributes, including the power to change beneficial enjoyment and the power to revoke or change the type and time of enjoyment, are included in the gross estate to the full extent of the property to which the power applies. The value of property included in the gross estate is equal to its fair market value on the date of death.

Personal property, such as this house, camper, and automobile, are included in the gross estate and valued at the fair market value on the date of the death of the owner.

Designation of Beneficiaries Life insurance, ANNUITIES, and certain death benefits are substitutes for dispositions at death, and are included in the gross estate to the extent that the decedent owned or could exercise "INCIDENTS OF OWNERSHIP" over them until the time of death. Thus, the value of a life insurance policy payable to the decedent's estate on death is included in the decedent's gross estate (26 U.S.C.A. § 2042(a)(1)). In addition, life insurance is includable in the gross estate even though neither the decedent nor the decedent's estate actually owned it, if the decedent possessed any incidents of ownership over the policy. Incidents of ownership encompass the rights to change the distribution of the economic benefit flowing from the insurance policy. For example, if A purchases a life insurance policy payable to B on A's death, the value of that policy is includable in A's gross estate if she retained, at the time of her death, the ability to change the policy BENEFICIARY to C. If the decedent had no rights to direct or affect economic benefits at the time of her death, then the proceeds of the policy are not includable in the gross estate.

Powers of Appointment Frequently, an individual owns the power to designate who will enjoy an item of property. This power may be considered an attribute of ownership sufficient to be included in the gross estate. The provi-

sion 26 U.S.C.A. § 2038, discussed later under retained power, addresses these powers of appointment that individuals reserve to themselves when creating property rights for another individual. Section 2041, in contrast, includes in the gross estate the value of property subject to a "general" power of appointment that the decedent acquired from another person. A general power of appointment is one that individuals may exercise in their own favor or in favor of their estate, their CREDITORS, or the creditors of their estate. If the decedent may only exercise the power in conjunction with either the creator of the power or a person having an adverse interest in the property subject to the exercise of the power, the power is not considered a general power of appointment because the decedent cannot freely control the transfer of the property at the decedent's death, and the property subject to the power is not included in the gross estate. For example, if A dies and leaves B the right to income in a trust, as well as the right to appoint the trust in whatever manner he wishes, then the entire value of the trust is included in B's estate when B dies. If, in contrast, A leaves B the right to income from the trust as well as the right to appoint the trust only to C or C's heirs, then no portion of the trust is includable in B's estate when B dies.

A power that is limited by an ascertainable standard is not a general power, even if it otherwise appears to be a general power. Ascertainable standards include health, education, support, and maintenance. Accordingly, if A dies and leaves B the power to appoint trust principal to herself if it is required for her health, education, support, or maintenance, B's power is limited by an ascertainable standard, and the value of the trust is not included in the gross estate. But if B may invade the trust principal for her "comfort and happiness," B's power is not limited by an ascertainable standard, and the value of the trust is included in B's estate.

Artificial Aspects of the Estate Tax System Before 1976, the gross estate included the value of all gifts made in contemplation of death. Because determining whether a gift was in contemplation of death turned out to be subjective, difficult to prove, and somewhat morbid, a 1976 amendment to the estate tax law automatically included any gift that a decedent made within three years of death (26 U.S.C.A. § 2035(a)). Unfortunately, the effect of § 2035(a) was to include in the gross estate the full value of the transferred property at the date of death, including any appreciation in value since the transfer. Thus, if A transferred $3,000 worth of

Before 1981 a piano or other item given away in contemplation of death would still have been included in the gross estate of the decedent.

stock to B in 1978 and died in 1980, when the stock was worth $25,000, the stock's full value of $25,000 was included in the gross estate, defeating much of A's predeath tax planning.

In 1981, sweeping tax changes eliminated from the gross estate most transfers made within three years of death. Even so, three specific types of transfers—transfers with a retained life estate, transfers with retained powers, and transfers effective on death— are included in the gross estate because the decedent owned an interest in the property at the time of death. Moreover, the value of property once subject to certain retained interests is included in the gross estate if the release or lapse of the retained interest takes place within three years of death, because the disposition of the retained interest is considered a substitute for disposition at death.

Transfers with a retained life estate Transfers with a retained life estate are covered in 26 U.S.C.A. § 2036. For purposes of the estate tax laws, the term *life estate* includes more than just an expressly retained life interest in property. For example, if A creates a trust for the benefit of B but retains the right to receive the income from the trust for the rest of her life, her retained income interest clearly is a retained life estate in the property. But the retention of the right to change the economic benefit derived from the property also constitutes a retained life estate, as when A reserves the right to change the trustee and appoint herself the trustee. It also may include retained life estates by tacit agreement, as when A transfers her home to B, with the understanding that A and not B will live there for the rest of her life.

The mere *possession* of a life estate in property is insufficient to bring it into the gross estate under § 2036. The life interest must be retained

by the decedent and must apply to an interest in property that the decedent transferred. Thus, a life income interest created by someone other than the decedent is not includable in the gross estate under § 2036.

Transfers with retained powers Transfers in which the decedent owns, at the time of death, the power to alter, amend, revoke, or terminate the enjoyment of the property are covered in 26 U.S.C.A. § 2038(a)(1). In contrast to § 2041, which allows general powers of appointment, § 2038 includes only powers associated with a property interest that the decedent gave away during his or her lifetime. The most commonly encountered retained powers are the powers applicable to a revocable trust. A revocable trust is a legal instrument through which an individual relinquishes legal ownership over the property to the trustee of a trust, either retaining to himself or herself beneficial enjoyment of the property, such as the right to income, or granting it to another individual. As its name indicates, the revocable trust is set up so that the creator, known as the GRANTOR, the SETTLOR, or the trustor, may revoke the trust entirely, may change the terms of the trust, or may change the beneficial ownership in the trust.

The creation of or an addition to a revocable trust almost never constitutes a gift. A gift must be completed to be taxable; the creation of or an addition of property to a revocable trust is, by definition, incomplete because the creator may change the beneficial enjoyment at some time, effectively withdrawing the "gift." Distributions from a revocable trust may, however, constitute completed gifts. For example, if A transfers $2 million to a revocable trust that pays income to B, the transfer of the $2 million is not a completed gift, but the annual payment of $100,000 in interest to B is a taxable gift when it takes place. Upon A's death, the entire value of the property subject to the power, including both the trust corpus and undistributed income payable to B, is included in the gross estate. And, because the property is valued as of the date of death, any increases or decreases in the value of the property since the transfer will appear in the gross estate.

Transfers effective on death The provision 26 U.S.C.A. § 2037 includes in the gross estate the value of transfers that take effect on death. Although at a distance § 2037 seems to apply to all property transfers that occur as a result of an individual's death, the stipulated transfers are rarely encountered. To meet the requirements of § 2037, the beneficiary must be able to acquire an interest in the property *only* by surviving the decedent. Furthermore, the decedent must have expressly retained a reversionary interest in the property that is worth at least five percent of the property's value at the time of death. Both conditions are difficult to meet. In the first place, the requirement that the beneficiary obtain an interest in the property solely by surviving the decedent is exclusive: if the beneficiary could have obtained an interest in any other way, such as by surviving another individual, satisfying a condition, or outlasting a term of years, the property is not includable under § 2037. In the second place, the requirement that the decedent's retained reversionary interest exceed five percent of the property's value is difficult to satisfy because most retained REVERSIONS represent remote interests that reach fruition only if the primary, secondary, and all contingent beneficiaries die first or fail to satisfy the conditions of ownership.

Release or lapse of rights The gratuitous relinquishment or lapse, within three years of death, of a retained life estate under 26 U.S.C.A. § 2036, a retained reversion under § 2037, a retained power under § 2038, or an interest in life insurance under § 2042 will subject the value of the property, subject to the retained interest, to inclusion in the gross estate. This result is a remnant of the pre-1981 policy that transfers "in contemplation of death" should be included in the gross estate. Under § 2035(d)(2), the release or relinquishment of a retained interest within three years of death is conclusively presumed to be "in contemplation of death." Thus, if A transfers his home to B in 1985, retaining the right to live there for life, but abandons that right at the end of 1991, a gift of the remainder interest in the property takes place in 1985, followed by a gift of the relinquished life estate in 1991. But if A dies before the end of 1994, both the 1985 and 1991 gift tax returns will be ignored for estate tax purposes, and the entire value of the home will be included in A's gross estate.

As with the retained life estate, the relinquishment or release within three years of death of a power of appointment retained under § 2038 will cause inclusion of the full value of the property at its date-of-death value. For example, if A creates a revocable trust in 1982, then amends it to make it irrevocable at the end of 1992, a gift will result in 1992 when the trust becomes irrevocable. If A dies before the end of 1995, the entire value of the trust, including any appreciation in value, will be included in A's estate, and the 1992 gift will be ignored. Finally, the release or lapse of ownership or any incidents of ownership over a life insurance policy

When a married person dies, the value of certain property that is transferred to the surviving spouse is deducted from the gross estate. That property will be taxed upon the death of the second spouse.

will cause the entire value of that policy to be included in the gross estate.

Deductions Once the value of the gross estate has been computed, the estate is entitled to take deductions. Expenses associated with administering the estate, such as funeral expenses, executors' commissions, and attorneys' fees, as well as debts the decedent owed at death, are deductible because they necessarily reduce the value of the property that the decedent actually is capable of transferring (26 U.S.C.A. § 2053(a), (b)). The two most important deductions for tax purposes are the marital deduction and the charitable deduction.

The Marital Deduction The marital deduction applies to certain interests in property passing from the first spouse to die, to the surviving spouse. It permits an estate to deduct the value of certain property included in the estate from the value of the gross estate, thus eliminating the estate tax with respect to that property. The rationale behind the marital deduction is simple: that a husband and a wife should be considered a single unit for purposes of wealth transfer. Accordingly, as a general rule, the marital deduction will be allowed with respect to certain property passing to a surviving spouse, provided that it will be included and taxed in the estate of that spouse on his or her death.

To qualify for the marital deduction, property must satisfy three basic requirements. First, the surviving spouse must be a U.S. citizen. Second, the interest in the property must pass directly from the first spouse to die, to the surviving spouse. And third, the interest generally must not be terminable (26 U.S.C.A. § 2056). The concept of a terminable interest is complex and technical, but for the most part, an interest is terminable for tax purposes if another interest in the same property passes to someone other than the surviving spouse by reason of the decedent's death, allowing that other person to enjoy the property after the surviving spouse's interest terminates. For example, if A leaves her husband, B, a life estate in her property, with remainder to their children, her bequest to B does not qualify for the marital deduction. B's interest terminates automatically on his death, and the children, by reason of the termination, will then enjoy the property.

If no one else can enjoy the property following the termination of the surviving spouse's interest, the property interest is not considered terminable for tax purposes, and a deduction will be allowed. For example, if A leaves her husband, B, her interest in a patent, and dies while the patent has ten years of life left, the patent interest qualifies for the marital deduction, because no one else will enjoy it after it expires.

Whether an interest is terminable must be determined at the time of death. Therefore, even if an event following the first spouse's death makes the termination of the surviving spouse's interest impossible, the marital deduction will not be allowed if it technically was terminable at the time of death.

Congress in 1981 created an important exception to the general rule that a terminable interest does not qualify for the marital deduction. This exception, called the qualified terminable interest property (QTIP) exception, is a sophisticated statutory rule allowing the estate to deduct the value of a terminable interest that passes to the surviving spouse as long as the transfer meets five requirements:

- the surviving spouse receives all or a specific portion of the income for life from the interest
- the income from the QTIP . . . is paid at least annually
- the surviving spouse has the power to appoint the interest to himself or his estate
- the power must be exercisable in all events
- no other person has the power to appoint the interest to anyone other than the surviving spouse

(26 U.S.C.A. § 2056(b)(7))

In return for the marital deduction, the estate must agree that the QTIP will be included in the estate of the surviving spouse at death, to the extent that the surviving spouse has not disposed of the property during his or her life (§ 2044).

The Charitable Deduction The charitable deduction permits an estate to deduct the entire value of bequests to any of a number of public purposes, including the following:

The estate of a person includes every item owned at the time of death, including tea sets, dishes, flatware, and the like.

- any corporation or association organized for religious, charitable, scientific, literary, or educational purposes
- the United States
- a state or its political subdivisions, and the District of Columbia
- a foreign government, if the bequest is to be used for charitable purposes
- selected amateur sports organizations

(26 U.S.C.A. § 2055(a))

The charitable deduction is intended to provide wealthy individuals a tax incentive to benefit the public interest. Only bequests passing directly from the decedent's estate to the charitable entity qualify for the deduction. Therefore, if A leaves $100,000 to her son C, who gives $50,000 to the Red Cross immediately after A's death, A's estate cannot receive a charitable deduction for the sum given to the charity (§ 2518(b)(4)).

Computation of Tax The estate and gift taxes are progressive and unified taxes, meaning that each taxable transfer taking place after 1976 is taken into consideration when computing the tax on subsequent transfers. For example, if A makes a taxable gift of $500,000 in 1990, the marginal tax rate on the gift is 34 percent. If A makes another taxable gift of $200,000 in 1992, the tax is computed on $700,000, the sum of the post-1976 gifts. Because the first $600,000 of transfers during life and at death are tax free, a unified credit of $192,800 is deducted from the tax on A's 1992 gift. If A dies in 1995 leaving an estate worth $2 million, the tax is computed on $2.7 million, the sum of the value of the estate and the lifetime gifts; the value of the unified credit and the taxes actually paid on the 1992 gift are deducted.

Progressivity in the estate and gift tax system ensures that individuals cannot avoid increased tax rates by making a series of small transfers. If the taxes were not progressive, then $1 million parceled out into ten annual gifts of $100,000 would be taxed at the marginal rate of 26 percent for each gift, whereas under the progressive tax system, the gifts are taxed at the marginal rate of 39 percent. Similarly, unification between the transfer tax systems ensures that individuals cannot avoid paying higher estate tax rates at death simply by giving away most of their property interests during life. Thus, in the case of A above, the marginal tax rate on A's estate is 49 percent, computed on $2.7 million of total lifetime and death transfers, rather than 45 percent, computed only on the value of the gross estate.

ESTIMATED TAX 📖 Federal and state tax laws require a quarterly payment of estimated taxes due from CORPORATIONS, TRUSTS, ESTATES, non-wage employees, and wage employees with income not subject to withholding. Individuals must remit at least 100 percent of their prior year tax liability or 90 percent of their current year tax liability in order to avoid an underpayment penalty. Corporations must pay at least 90 percent of their current year tax liability in order to avoid an underpayment penalty. Additional taxes due, if any, are paid on taxpayer's annual tax return. 📖

Typically, non-wage earners pay estimated tax since their INCOMES are not subject to WITHHOLDING TAX to the same extent as the income of a salaried worker. Persons who receive a certain level of additional income, apart from their salaries, must also pay estimated tax.

The calculation and payment of estimated tax are preliminary stages to the filing of a final INCOME TAX return. Under federal and most state laws, estimated tax is paid in quarterly installments. The tax paid is applied to the tax owed when the taxpayer files a final return. Any overpayment of estimated tax will be refunded after the filing of the final return. If no tax is owed, a taxpayer is still required under federal law, and many state laws, to file a final return. When tax is due upon the filing of the final return, the taxpayer must pay the outstanding amount. Depending upon the amount due and the reasons for the miscalculation, a taxpayer might be liable under federal and state law for interest imposed upon the deficiency, as well as being subject to a penalty.

ESTOPPEL 📖 A legal principle that precludes a PARTY from denying or alleging a certain fact owing to that party's previous conduct, ALLEGATION, or denial. 📖

The rationale behind estoppel is to prevent injustice owing to inconsistency or FRAUD. There are two general types of estoppel: equitable and legal.

Equitable Estoppel Equitable estoppel, sometimes known as estoppel in pais, protects a party who relies detrimentally on another's voluntary conduct—action, silence, acquiescence, or concealment of material facts. One example of equitable estoppel due to a party's acquiescence is found in *Lambertini v. Lambertini*, 655 So. 2d 142 (Fla. 3d Dist. Ct. App. 1995). In the late 1950s, Olga, who was married to another man, and Frank Lambertini met and began living together in Argentina. Olga and Frank hired an attorney in Buenos Aires, who purported to divorce Olga from her first husband and marry her to Frank pursuant to Mexican law. The Lambertinis began what they thought was a married life together, and soon produced two children. In 1968, they moved to the United States and became Florida residents.

In 1992, Olga sought a divorce from Frank. She petitioned the Florida court for sole possession of the marital home and temporary alimony, which the court granted. Frank sought a rehearing, arguing that the Mexican marriage was not a valid legal marriage and was therefore void. Though Frank won with this argument in the trial court, the APPELLATE COURT reversed, holding that Frank was equitably estopped from arguing that the Mexican marriage was invalid. According to the appellate court, Frank and Olga had held themselves out as a married couple for more than thirty years, lived together, raised two children, and owned property jointly. Both Frank and Olga apparently believed all along that the Mexican marriage was legal, and it was only when Olga filed for divorce that Frank discovered and chose to rely on its invalidity. The appellate court granted Olga her divorce, the house, and the temporary alimony. Frank's acquiescence for three decades—holding himself out as being married to Olga—prevented him from denying the marriage's existence.

There are several specific types of equitable estoppel. PROMISSORY ESTOPPEL is a CONTRACT law doctrine. It occurs when a party reasonably relies on the promise of another party, and because of the reliance is injured or damaged. For example, suppose a restaurant agrees to pay a bakery to make fifty pies. The bakery has only two employees. It takes them two days to make the pies, and they are unable to bake or sell anything else during that time. Then, the restaurant decides not to buy the pies, leaving the bakery with many more pies than it can sell and a loss of profit from the time spent baking them. A court will likely apply the promissory estoppel doctrine and require the restaurant to fulfill its promise and pay for the pies.

An estoppel certificate is a written declaration signed by a party who ATTESTS, for the benefit of another party, to the accuracy of certain facts described in the declaration. The estoppel certificate prevents the party who signs it from later challenging the validity of those facts. This type of document is perhaps most common in the context of MORTGAGES, or home loans. If one bank seeks to purchase mortgages owned by another bank, the purchasing bank may request the borrowers, or homeowners, to sign an estoppel certificate establishing (1) that the mortgage is valid, (2) the amount of principal and interest due as of the date of the certificate, and (3) that no defenses exist that would affect the value of the mortgage. After signing this certificate, the borrower cannot dispute those facts.

Estoppel by LACHES precludes a party from bringing an ACTION when the party knowingly failed to claim or enforce a legal right at the proper time. This doctrine is closely related to the concept of STATUTES OF LIMITATIONS, except that statutes of limitations set specific time limits for legal actions, whereas under laches, generally there is no prescribed time that courts consider "proper." A defendant seeking the protection of laches must demonstrate that the plaintiff's inaction, misrepresentation, or silence prejudiced the defendant or induced the defendant to change positions for the worse.

The court applied the doctrine of laches in *People v. Heirens*, 648 N.E.2d 260 (Ill. 1st Dist. Ct. App. 1995). William Heirens pleaded guilty in 1946 to three murders, for which he received three consecutive life terms in prison. Heirens sought court relief numerous times in the ensuing years. In 1989, forty-three years after his conviction, Heirens filed his second postconviction petition seeking, among other things, relief from his prison sentence due to ineffective counsel and the denial of DUE PROCESS at the time of his arrest. The court found that all the witnesses and attorneys involved in Heirens's case had since died. Laches precluded Heirens from bringing his action because, according to the court, it would be "difficult to imagine a case where the facts are more remote and where

the state might be more prejudiced by the passage of time."

Legal Estoppel Legal estoppel consists of estoppel by deed and estoppel by record. Under the doctrine of estoppel by deed, a party to a property DEED is precluded from asserting, as against another party to the deed, any right or TITLE in DEROGATION of the deed, or from denying the truth of any material fact asserted in the deed. For example, suppose a father conveys a plot of land to his son by deed. Unbeknownst to the son, the father actually does not own the plot of land at the time of the CONVEYANCE; the father acquires title to the property only after the conveyance. Technically, the son is not the legal owner of the property because his father did not own and did not have the right to transfer the real estate at the time of the conveyance. But under the doctrine of estoppel by deed, the court may "make good" the imperfection of the poorly timed conveyance by finding the son to be the rightful owner of the plot of land (*Zayka v. Giambro*, 32 Mass. App. Ct. 748, 594 N.E.2d 894 [1992]).

The doctrine of estoppel by record precludes a party from denying the issues adjudicated by a court of competent JURISDICTION (collateral estoppel) or any matter spelled out in a judicial record (judicial estoppel). Estoppel by record exists only between the same parties on the same issues. The doctrine prevents a party from relitigating a matter or from litigating what it might have litigated in a previous case.

COLLATERAL ESTOPPEL, sometimes known as estoppel by judgment, prevents the reargument of a factual or legal issue that has already been determined by a valid JUDGMENT in a prior case involving the same parties. For example, suppose Ms. Jones, who owns a business next to Mr. Smith's, sues Mr. Smith for damage to her property caused by the digging of a hole. Mr. Smith defends by arguing that the hole is on his land. After considering all the evidence, the court determines that Mr. Smith owns the land. Later that year, after a late night at work, Mr. Smith cuts across the back lot, falls into the hole, and is injured. He then sues Ms. Jones for negligent maintenance of her property. In this situation, the court will apply collateral estoppel, preventing Mr. Smith from relitigating an issue that was already decided between the same parties in a prior proceeding—the issue of who owns the land.

The related doctrine of judicial estoppel binds a party to her or his judicial declarations, such as allegations contained in the lawsuit COMPLAINT or TESTIMONY given under oath at a previous trial. Judicial estoppel protects courts from litigants' using opposing theories in the attempt to prevail twice. For instance, a tenant trying to avoid liability to a property owner may not, in the tenant's bankruptcy case, successfully represent to a court that the property agreement is a LEASE and then later, when the property owner sues for nonpayment of rent, declare that the agreement is a mortgage rather than a lease (*Port Authority v. Harstad*, 531 N.W.2d 496 [Minn. Ct. App. 1995]).

Estoppel by record is frequently confused with the related doctrine of RES JUDICATA ("a matter adjudged"), which bars relitigation of the same CAUSE OF ACTION between the same parties once there has been a judgment. For example, if Mr. Chen sues Ms. Lopez for breach of contract and the court returns a decision, Ms. Lopez cannot later sue Mr. Chen for breach of the same contract. Ms. Lopez has the right to APPEAL the first decision, but she cannot bring a new lawsuit that raises the same claim.

ET AL. An abbreviated form of *et alia*, Latin for "and others." When affixed after the name of a person, *et al.* indicates that additional persons are acting in the same manner, such as several plaintiffs or GRANTORS.

When *et al.* is used in a judgment against defendants, it means that the quoted words are applicable to all the defendants.

See also COURT OPINIONS.

ETHICS The branch of philosophy that defines what is good for the individual and for society and establishes the nature of obligations, or duties, that people owe themselves and one another.

The word *ethics* is derived from the Greek word *ethos*, which means "character," and from the Latin word *mores*, which means "customs." In modern society, it defines how individuals, business professionals, and corporations choose to interact with one another.

ARISTOTLE was one of the first great philosophers to study the subject. To him, ethics was more than a moral, religious, or legal concept. He believed that the most important element in ethical behavior is knowledge that actions are accomplished for the betterment of the common good. He asked whether actions performed by an individual or group are good both for that individual or a group and for society. To determine what is ethically good for the individual and for society, Aristotle said, it is necessary to possess three virtues of practical wisdom: temperance, courage, and justice.

Making ethical decisions in business is often difficult because business ethics is not simply an extension of an individual's personal ethics or a society's standards of right and wrong. Just being a good person with high ethical standards may not be enough to handle the tough choices that frequently arise in the workplace. Persons with limited business experience are often called upon to answer troublesome questions about complex issues, such as Can a professional breach client confidentiality? When can a professional permit harm to a client for the sake of the welfare of another person or the public? Can a professional deceive a client for the client's own good?

Business executives are faced with two types of ethical issues in conducting their day-to-day affairs. Micromanagement issues include CONFLICTS OF INTEREST, employee rights, fair performance appraisals, SEXUAL HARASSMENT, proprietary information, DISCRIMINATION, and accepting or offering gifts. Macromanagement issues include corporate social responsibility, PRODUCT LIABILITY, environmental ethics, COMPARABLE WORTH, layoffs and downsizings, employee screening tests, employee rights to PRIVACY in the workplace, and corporate accountability.

The need to control, regulate, and legislate ethical conduct on the individual, corporate, and government levels has ancient roots. For example, one of the first law codes developed, the CODE OF HAMMURABI, made BRIBERY a crime in Babylon during the eighteenth century B.C. Most societies share certain features in their ethical codes, such as forbidding murder, bodily injury, and attacks on personal honor and reputation. In modern societies, the systems of law and public justice are closely related to ethics in that they determine and enforce definite rights and duties. They also attempt to repress and punish deviations from these standards.

Medical professionals must adhere to a high standard of ethics. The American Medical Association has a written code of ethics that is enforceable.

Laws can be neutral on ethical issues, or they can be used to endorse ethics. The prologue to the U.S. Constitution says that ensuring domestic tranquility is an objective of government, which is an ethically neutral statement. CIVIL RIGHTS laws, on the other hand, promote an ethical as well as legal commitment. Often laws and the courts are required to resolve strong ethical dilemmas in society, as in the controversial issues of ABORTION (*Roe v. Wade*, 410 U.S. 113, 93 S. Ct. 705, 35 L. Ed. 2d 147), AFFIRMATIVE ACTION (*University of California v. Bakke*, 438 U.S. 265, 98 S. Ct. 2733, 57 L. Ed. 2d 750), and segregation (*Brown v. Board of Education*, 347 U.S. 483, 74 S. Ct. 686, 98 L. Ed. 873).

Laws also permit many actions that will not bear ethical scrutiny. In other words, what the law permits or requires is not necessarily what is ethically right. For instance, laws allow disloyalty toward friends, the breaking of PROMISES that do not have the stature of legal CONTRACTS, and a variety of deceptions. Laws sometimes require gross immoralities, as did the FUGITIVE SLAVE ACT OF 1850, which required citizens to return runaway slaves to their masters, and the U.S. Supreme Court's *Dred Scott* decision, which seven years later declared that slaves were not citizens but property (60 U.S. 393, 19 How. 393, 15 L. Ed. 691).

Although local, state, and federal regulatory acts do influence the conduct of some professions, many ethical issues cannot be settled by the courts. The ethics of a particular act is many times determined independently of the legality of the conduct. In fact, decisive answers cannot always be given for many ethical issues because there are no enforceable standards or reliable theories for resolving ethical conflicts.

The response of many professions to the challenging and demanding problem of institutionalizing business ethics is to implement codes of ethics, develop statements of corporate goals, sponsor training and educational programs in ethics, install internal judiciary bodies that hear cases of improprieties, and create telephone hot lines through which employees can anonymously report possible ethical violations.

A code of ethics provides members of a profession with standards of behavior and principles to be observed regarding their moral and professional obligations toward one another, their clients, and society in general. A code of ethics is generally developed by a professional society within a particular profession. The higher the degree of professionalism required of society members, the stronger and therefore more enforceable the code. For instance, in medicine, the behavior required is more specific and the consequences are more stringent in the code of ethics for PHYSICIANS than in the code of ethics for nurses.

In addition, professions that require licensure from a state-authorized board, which guarantees both the competency and the moral efficacy of its members, place a duty on the licensed professional to help prevent unauthorized practice by unlicensed providers as a means of protecting the public.

The primary function of a code of ethics is to provide guidance to employers and employees in ethical dilemmas, especially those that are particularly ambiguous. Decisions in such situations can be made more easily if the code is specific, gives detailed directions on what actions should or should not be taken, and spells out explicit penalties for unethical behavior.

Some large and influential professional associations have developed highly detailed and enforceable codes for their membership. The American Medical Association's (AMA's) Principles of Medical Ethics has seven provisions, supplemented by numerous interpretive opinions of a judicial council. The Model Rules of Professional Conduct of the AMERICAN BAR ASSOCIATION (ABA) contains eight sections, construed according to 138 ethical considerations and implemented by a comparable number of parallel disciplinary rules. The Rules of Conduct of the American Institute of Certified Public Accountants has six major principles, each with numerous specifications. The American Psychological Association's Ethical Principles of Psychologists and Code of Conduct contains six principles, with several provisions under each.

Other professions with codes of responsibility include dentistry, social work, education, government service, engineering, journalism, real estate, advertising, architecture, banking, insurance, and human resources management. However, because some of these professions are not licensed, anyone can claim their title and perform their function—thus making it difficult to find legal recourse to claims of unethical conduct.

All professional codes can be considered quasi-public because of the effect they may have on legal judgments during litigation. Many states adopt accrediting associations' codes of ethics, thereby establishing those standards as public codifications. Failure to comply with a code can, in some professions, result in expulsion from the profession. The AMA's Principles of Medical Ethics, for example, are not laws per se, but the maximum penalty for violation of the principles is expulsion from the AMA. In addition, the ABA's Model Rules of Professional Conduct provide evidence of professional standards of loyalty and care, and they become directly enforceable PUBLIC LAW when they or their variants are adopted as binding upon lawyers admitted to practice within a state.

The most common violations of ethics codes that are brought before state professional associations and the legal system are breach of contract, including that resulting from incompetent behavior or decisions or from failure to exercise GOOD FAITH; FRAUD, or an intent to deceive; and professional MALPRACTICE or NEGLIGENCE, which include incompetence and the performance of unnecessary services.

Since the legal profession is more self-regulating (i.e., regulated by ATTORNEYS and JUDGES themselves rather than by government or outside agencies) than most professions, every state supreme court or legislature has a committee authorized to enforce the state rules of professional legal conduct. The state conduct committees make factual determinations on whether to privately reprimand a lawyer, publicly censure him or her, suspend the attorney's LICENSE to practice, or permanently revoke the license (i.e., DISBAR the attorney, or permanently disqualify the attorney from practicing law in the state).

Specific procedures on professional discipline vary from state to state, but every state allows for court review of the conduct committee's recommendations. If a license is revoked, the lawyer may petition the committee for readmission to the bar after a period of time specified by the state rules. Not every violation results in disbarment. This drastic measure is most commonly reserved for theft or misuse of client funds.

Besides laws based on professional bar association codes of ethics, separate federal and state laws define ATTORNEY MISCONDUCT and empower judges to discipline unethical conduct by attorneys. For example, rule 11 of the Federal Rules of Civil Procedure (28 U.S.C.A.) requires sanctions for lawyers and clients who file FRIVOLOUS or abusive claims in court.

Finally, attorneys can be seriously disciplined, such as by suspension from the practice of law for a certain time period, for failing to report misconduct of other lawyers to the ABA.

Judges must comply with the CODE OF JUDICIAL CONDUCT, which was formulated by the ABA in 1972. This code is not considered law; however, federal and state governments have adopted it, and its violations are used as the

basis for punitive action against judges. Any person may lodge a complaint of misconduct against a judge with the appropriate judicial review council. Punitive actions include public or private reprimand and suspension from office.

Interest in ethics has resurged with the rapid social change and technological developments of modern society. For instance, physicians, who have taken the Hippocratic Oath to save life, cure disease, and alleviate suffering, are now faced with whether to use medical devices that can prolong life at the cost of increasing suffering, or to follow patients' requests to be allowed to die without extraordinary lifesaving precautions or to be provided with medications or devices that will end life. See also DEATH AND DYING.

New fields of ethics, such as bioethics, engineering ethics, and environmental ethics, have opened up new areas of concern, not just for the professions involved but for society as well. As these professions grapple with expanding their codes of responsibility to keep up with technological advances and societal pressures for stricter business ethics, changes in laws governing business ethics are bound to change too. Since societal ethics have evolved through the law, they mirror the ethical norms agreed on by the majority.

Renewed interest in more government regulation of business, in teaching ethics in academic institutions, and in extensive corporate involvement in establishing ethics committees and codes of responsibility suggests that business ethics is emerging not only as a major intellectual and legal concern but as a full-fledged social movement.

As society and the moral dilemmas facing businesses have become more sophisticated and complex, some leaders in business ethics have

Attorneys are guided in ethical decisions by the ABA's Model Rules of Professional Conduct. If those rules have been adopted by the state in which the attorney practices, they are enforceable as public law.

referred appropriately to Mark Twain's age-old axiom, "Always do right. This will gratify some people, and astonish the rest."

ET SEQ. 📖 An abbreviation for the Latin *et sequentes* or *et sequentia*, meaning "and the following." 📖

The phrase *et seq.* is used in references made to particular pages or sections of cases, articles, regulations, or statutes to indicate that the desired information is continued on the pages or in the sections following a designated page or section, as "p. 238 *et seq.*" or "section 43 *et seq.*"

The abbreviation *et seq.* is sometimes used to denote a reference to more than one following page or section.

See also COURT OPINIONS.

ETTELBRICK, PAULA LOUISE Paula Louise Ettelbrick is a lawyer and activist for lesbian and gay rights, the first staff attorney for Lambda Legal Defense and Education Fund, and a lifelong advocate of public service.

Ettelbrick was born October 2, 1955, on a U.S. Army base in Stuttgart, Germany. Growing up in a devout Catholic family, she was taught by her parents that each person has an obligation to society and to the greater world, and that all people should be treated equally.

Ettelbrick's convictions initially led her to social work after she had graduated from Northern Illinois University in 1978 with a bachelor of arts degree in history. She held several social services positions, working primarily for the women's shelter at the Harbor Light Center, in Boston, which assists alcoholic and homeless adults. Through her work, in which she sought public benefits, housing, and employment for low- and no-income women, Ettelbrick came to believe that the system doesn't work for the underrepresented—namely, the poor.

With an interest in labor and employment law, Ettelbrick enrolled in law school at Wayne State University, in Detroit, where she wrote for the *Wayne Law Review* and clerked for several legal employers, including the United Auto Workers (UAW) Union. Working for the UAW's international union, located in Detroit,

BIOGRAPHY

Paula Louise Ettelbrick

"WE'RE TALKING ABOUT OVERHAULING A WHOLE SYSTEM THAT WAS BASED ON THE 1930S FAMILY CONSISTING OF A MALE WAGE-EARNER, A NONWORKING WIFE, AND SOME KIDS."

Ettelbrick was exposed to a variety of LABOR LAW and PUBLIC POLICY issues, and helped draft a statement from the union's vice president to the U.S. Congress on why the EQUAL RIGHTS AMENDMENT should be reintroduced to Congress—a meaningful assignment in light of her growing interest in feminist and lesbian issues. In 1984 she graduated cum laude and took an associate position doing commercial litigation at Miller, Canfield, Paddock, and Stone, a large law firm in Detroit.

Two years later, in keeping with her original desire to do public interest work, she left the law firm and joined the Lambda Legal Defense and Education Fund, an organization founded in New York City in 1973 that advocates gay and lesbian civil rights.

Hoping to challenge legal assumptions about gay and lesbian people, Ettelbrick litigated a variety of cases, many related to the heightening legal crisis accompanying AIDS. Within a year, Lambda hired a second staff attorney to do AIDS work, and Ettelbrick was freed up to develop what Lambda called its Sexual Orientation Docket, working with cases involving families, employment, and the military. In 1988, with a staff of seven, she was appointed Lambda's legal director. Soon after, under Ettelbrick's guidance and vision, Lambda opened an office in Los Angeles and created a network of four hundred cooperating attorneys around the United States.

After seven years of high-intensity work at Lambda, Ettelbrick was ready for a change, and in March 1993, she left the organization. Shortly thereafter, the National Center for Lesbian Rights hired her as its director of public policy, where she continued her work on family issues. One of her many accomplishments in this position was helping to draft a new employment discrimination bill introduced in Congress to add sexual orientation to the list of prohibited categories under employment and housing laws. She also worked to develop policies for lesbian health care.

Ettelbrick continued to litigate on behalf of lesbians, and in 1993 and 1994 was involved in the high-profile custody case *Bottoms v. Bottoms*,

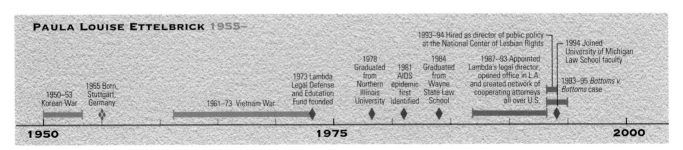

PAULA LOUISE ETTELBRICK 1955–

1950–53 Korean War

1955 Born, Stuttgart, Germany

1961–73 Vietnam War

1973 Lambda Legal Defense and Education Fund founded

1978 Graduated from Northern Illinois University

1981 AIDS epidemic first identified

1984 Graduated from Wayne State Law School

1987–93 Appointed Lambda's legal director; opened office in L.A. and created network of cooperating attorneys all over U.S.

1993–94 Hired as director of public policy at the National Center of Lesbian Rights

1994 Joined University of Michigan Law School faculty

1993–95 *Bottoms v. Bottoms* case

1950   1975   2000

18 Va. App. 481, 444 S.E.2d 276 (1994). The case involved a lesbian, Sharon Lynne Bottoms, whose mother, Pamela Kay Bottoms, had petitioned for custody of Sharon's child owing to Sharon's admitted homosexuality. After Sharon lost custody of the child at the trial court level, she and Ettelbrick appealed and won custody in the Court of Appeals of Virginia. The appeals court held that the mere fact that Sharon was a lesbian and had a live-in female companion did not render her an unfit parent. In a split decision, the Supreme Court of Virginia reversed the court of appeals, reinstating custody in the child's grandmother (457 S.E.2d 102 [1995]).

Beginning in 1990, Ettelbrick taught a course at New York Law School on sexuality and the law, in addition to continuing her other work. In 1994 Ettelbrick left the National Center for Lesbian Rights to teach at the University of Michigan Law School. There she offered "Sexuality and the Law," a survey course that asked questions such as What are the commonalities between the way the law treats prostitution, rape, and gay and lesbian issues? and How far is the government entitled to go to reach into these areas? The course was designed to bridge the gap between the way feminist jurisprudence or women-in-the-law courses are taught and the way sexual orientation in the law is taught.

Ettelbrick's professional successes are many, as a teacher, a litigator, and an advocate for a segment of the population that has been historically marginalized and denied rights taken for granted by the rest of society.

See also ACQUIRED IMMUNE DEFICIENCY SYNDROME; GAY AND LESBIAN RIGHTS.

EVARTS, WILLIAM MAXWELL

William Maxwell Evarts served as attorney general of the United States during the last year of the administration of President ANDREW JOHNSON. Evarts was a distinguished and powerful New York attorney who successfully defended President Johnson at his impeachment trial, represented the Republican party before an electoral commission during the disputed presidential

"TRUTH IS TO THE MORAL WORLD WHAT GRAVITATION IS TO THE MATERIAL."

BIOGRAPHY

LIBRARY OF CONGRESS

William Maxwell Evarts

election of 1876, served as secretary of state during the administration of President RUTHERFORD B. HAYES, and ended his public career as a U.S. senator.

Evarts was born February 16, 1818, in Boston. He graduated from Yale University in 1837 and then attended Harvard Law School. He was admitted to the New York bar in 1841 and subsequently established a successful legal practice. From 1849 to 1853, Evarts acted as assistant district attorney for the New York District.

Evarts entered public service during the Civil War. He participated in diplomatic activities as a member of the Secretary of Defense Committee for the Union. In 1863 he went to England as a Union delegate to convince England to stop providing war vessels and equipment to the Confederacy.

Following the end of the Civil War, Evarts returned to his law practice. He was drawn back to Washington, D.C., in 1868 to help defend President Johnson at his impeachment trial. The charges against Johnson were weak and politically motivated, yet the mood in the Senate appeared to favor conviction. Evarts proved instrumental in obtaining an acquittal, though by a margin of only one vote. Johnson rewarded Evarts by appointing him attorney general. Evarts served in that position until the end of the Johnson administration in March 1869.

Evarts then returned to New York government. He led the New York City Bar Association for ten years and was an advocate for political reform in the city, which was dominated by the corrupt Democratic political machine led by the "Tweed Ring." The ring was named after William Marcy Tweed, the New York City Democratic party leader who ran the party organization popularly known as Tammany Hall. Tweed and his associates used their political connections and political offices to gain a foothold in city and county government. Once formed, the Tweed Ring misappropriated government funds through such devices as faked leases, padded bills, false vouchers, unnecessary repairs, and overpriced goods and

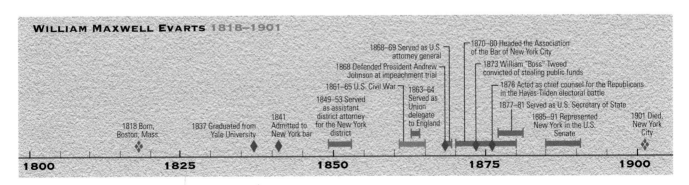

WILLIAM MAXWELL EVARTS 1818–1901

1818 Born, Boston, Mass.

1837 Graduated from Yale University

1841 Admitted to New York bar

1849–53 Served as assistant district attorney for the New York district

1861–65 U.S. Civil War

1863–64 Served as Union delegate to England

1868 Defended President Andrew Johnson at impeachment trial

1868–69 Served as U.S. attorney general

1870–80 Headed the Association of the Bar of New York City

1873 William "Boss" Tweed convicted of stealing public funds

1876 Acted as chief counsel for the Republicans in the Hayes-Tilden electoral battle

1877–81 Served as U.S. Secretary of State

1885–91 Represented New York in the U.S. Senate

1901 Died, New York City

1800   1825   1850   1875   1900

services bought from suppliers controlled by the ring.

In 1876 Evarts reentered the national political arena, this time as the chief counsel of the national Republican party. The presidential election of 1876 between Democrat Samuel J. Tilden and Republican Rutherford B. Hayes ended in disputes involving the voting returns of Florida, Louisiana, and South Carolina. Two sets of returns were submitted from each of these states, one favoring Tilden, the other Hayes. If Hayes were awarded the electoral votes from these states, and one more from a disputed Oregon elector, he would defeat Tilden in a vote of 185–184.

Congress appointed an electoral commission to decide which returns to accept. In the end Evarts and the Republican members of the commission were able to convince commission member and Supreme Court Justice Joseph P. Bradley to cast his vote, which was the deciding vote, for the Hayes electors and Hayes was awarded the presidency. Tilden agreed to the result out of fear that violence would ensue if he disputed it. In return the Republicans made a side agreement with southern Democrats that led to President Hayes in 1877 removing federal occupation troops from the former states of the Confederacy. Evarts was also a key player in these affairs.

President Hayes, like President Johnson before him, rewarded Evarts, appointing him secretary of state in 1877. Evarts served in this capacity during the four years of the Hayes administration. In 1885 he was elected a U.S. senator from New York. He served in the Senate until 1889. In failing health he retired from politics and the law in 1891.

Evarts died February 28, 1901, in New York City.

EVERS, MEDGAR WILEY Shortly before his death, CIVIL RIGHTS activist Medgar Wiley Evers was described in the *New York Times* as the movement's "quiet integrationist." Although his contemporary MARTIN LUTHER KING, JR., achieved greater fame for organizing non-violent demonstrations and BOYCOTTS, Evers was an equally dedicated reformer, whose reports of civil rights abuses in Mississippi helped force social and political changes in the Deep South.

From 1954 to 1963, Evers was state field secretary for the NATIONAL ASSOCIATION FOR THE ADVANCEMENT OF COLORED PEOPLE (NAACP). Courageous, methodical, and devoted to his work, Evers sought to dismantle a decades-old system of segregation. His approach was to create public outrage over the treatment of African Americans by documenting cases of brutality and injustice. Although Evers fought tirelessly against discriminatory laws and conduct, he rejected violence as a means of improving the plight of his people.

By antagonizing powerful white supremacists, Evers put himself in constant danger in his home state. When he was shot and killed by a sniper on June 12, 1963, many Mississippians were not surprised. At his death, Evers became an early martyr in the African American struggle for equal rights. More than thirty years later, when Byron de la Beckwith finally was convicted of his ASSASSINATION, Evers became a symbol of U.S. justice—delayed, but not denied.

Evers was born July 2, 1925, in Decatur, Mississippi, the younger of two sons born to James Evers, a sawmill worker, and Jessie Evers, a devout Christian who encouraged young Evers to succeed. The Evers family was hardworking but poor. Townspeople remember Evers as an upright, sympathetic young man who chafed under the inequities of segregation.

During World War II, Evers served in an all–African American unit of the U.S. Army. Although the military's racial policies infuriated him, he fought with distinction and was decorated for his bravery in the Normandy Invasion. During his tour of duty, Evers experienced in Europe a more tolerant, racially integrated society, which inspired hope for changes in his native Mississippi.

After the war, Evers attended Mississippi's Alcorn A&M College, where he participated in

BIOGRAPHY

Medgar Wiley Evers

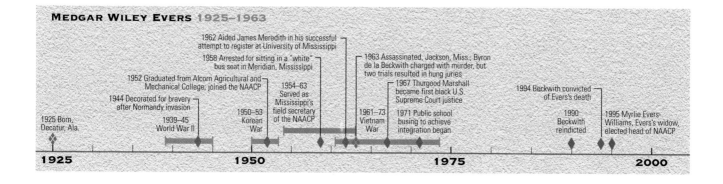

MEDGAR WILEY EVERS 1925–1963

1925 Born, Decatur, Ala.

1939–45 World War II

1944 Decorated for bravery after Normandy invasion

1950–53 Korean War

1952 Graduated from Alcorn Agricultural and Mechanical College; joined the NAACP

1954–63 Served as Mississippi's field secretary of the NAACP

1958 Arrested for sitting in a "white" bus seat in Meridian, Mississippi

1961–73 Vietnam War

1962 Aided James Meredith in his successful attempt to register at University of Mississippi

1963 Assassinated, Jackson, Miss.; Byron de la Beckwith charged with murder, but two trials resulted in hung juries

1967 Thurgood Marshall became first black U.S. Supreme Court justice

1971 Public school busing to achieve integration began

1990 Beckwith reindicted

1994 Beckwith convicted of Evers's death

1995 Myrlie Evers-Williams, Evers's widow, elected head of NAACP

1925 1950 1975 2000

football, track, debate, and choir. He also met his wife, Myrlie Evers, with whom he had three children. After graduation, Evers worked as a sales agent for Magnolia Mutual, an African American–owned life insurance company. Assigned a rural territory, Evers witnessed African American poverty and debasement on such a large scale that he could no longer abide Mississippi's racial DISCRIMINATION. He took a job with the NAACP in 1954, determined to make a difference.

As an NAACP field representative, Evers handled routine administrative duties such as setting up chapters, recruiting new members, and collecting dues. But more important, Evers filed detailed public reports of lynchings, beatings, and other race-related atrocities in Mississippi. His work attracted national attention. Evers also encouraged voter registration for African Americans and, in some instances, boycotts.

Because he signaled the end of the era of white power, Evers was despised by southern bigots. He bravely endured their taunts and death threats. Organizations opposed to integration, such as the White Citizens Council, branded Evers an enemy. Ironically, as African Americans became impatient with the slow pace of social change, Evers's work was overshadowed by more militant civil rights strategies.

On the night of his murder, Evers attended a local rally. Around midnight, he returned to his Jackson, Mississippi, home, where an assassin waited for him in nearby honeysuckle bushes. Evers got out of his car and walked up the driveway, carrying shirts that read Jim Crow Must Go, a reference to laws conferring second-class citizenship on African Americans. The assassin shot him in the back with an Enfield 30.06 rifle. Evers's wife and their young children, Darrell, Reena, and James, heard the gunshot and rushed to his side. Evers could not be saved.

As news of Evers's death spread, riots erupted in Jackson. The United States was stunned by the killing. President JOHN F. KENNEDY denounced the assassination, sending Evers's wife his condolences and praising Evers's devotion to civil rights. The Federal Bureau of Investigation (FBI) was called in to conduct a criminal investigation. Evers was buried in Arlington National Cemetery, in Washington, D.C.

The trail of the FBI's investigation led quickly to white supremacist Byron de la Beckwith, a fertilizer sales representative affiliated with the Ku Klux Klan. Charged with murder, de la Beckwith appeared guilty to most observers, but the racial climate in Mississippi prevented a sure conviction. During his trial, de la Beckwith acted clownish and unrepentant. At one point, Mississippi governor Ross Barnett entered the courtroom and hugged the defendant in full view of the all-white jury. Despite compelling evidence from the prosecution—de la Beckwith's public boasting about the murder, his fingerprints on the rifle scope, his well-known ability as a marksman, and reports that his white Valiant was parked near Evers's home at the time of the killing—the trial resulted in a HUNG JURY. Astonishingly, a second trial also ended in a hung jury.

Evers's widow, who had remarried, refused to let the matter drop. MYRLIE EVERS-WILLIAMS lobbied long and hard to have de la Beckwith tried for a third time for Evers's death. A third prosecution was possible in this case for two reasons. First, there is no STATUTE OF LIMITATIONS for murder, so the passage of time was not a consideration. Second, de la Beckwith had not been exonerated (with a hung jury, the defendant is neither acquitted nor convicted), so DOUBLE JEOPARDY, the constitutional guarantee against multiple prosecutions, was not an issue. Evers-Williams's determination to see justice done, as well as a change in Mississippi politics, made a third trial of de la Beckwith possible.

Facing testimony from new and former witnesses, de la Beckwith was reindicted in 1990. A trial was conducted by District Attorney Ed Peters. On February 21, 1994, a jury of eight African Americans and four whites in Hinds County, Mississippi, found de la Beckwith, now seventy-three years old, guilty of the 1963 murder of Evers. Although the third trial was a painful experience for Evers-Williams, she was relieved that the Mississippi criminal justice system had finally brought closure to a personal and public tragedy.

In life and death, Evers played an important role in the fight for racial equality. He inspired in others, including his family, a commitment to the same social, political, and economic goals for African Americans. Evers's brother, Charles Evers, was elected mayor of Fayette, Mississippi, in 1969, and ran unsuccessfully for governor of the state in 1971. In 1995, Evers-Williams was elected to head the NAACP, the organization to which Evers had dedicated his life.

See also CIVIL RIGHTS MOVEMENT.

EVERS-WILLIAMS, MYRLIE Myrlie Evers-Williams has achieved national prominence as the chairwoman of the NATIONAL ASSOCIATION FOR THE ADVANCEMENT OF COLORED PEOPLE (NAACP). Evers-Williams was narrowly elected to the post in 1995 as part of an effort to

"YOU CAN KILL A MAN BUT YOU CAN'T KILL AN IDEA."

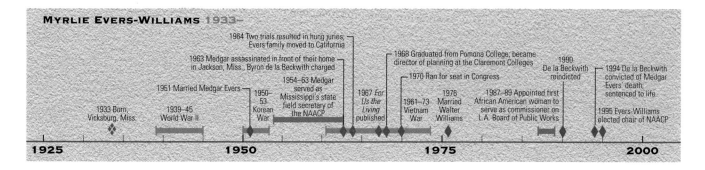

MYRLIE EVERS-WILLIAMS 1933–

1964 Two trials resulted in hung juries;
Evers family moved to California

1963 Medgar assassinated in front of their home
in Jackson, Miss., Byron de la Beckwith charged

1968 Graduated from Pomona College; became
director of planning at the Claremont Colleges

1990
De la Beckwith
reindicted

1994 De la Beckwith
convicted of Medgar
Evers' death,
sentenced to life

1954–63 Medgar
served as
Mississippi's state
field secretary of
the NAACP

1967 For
Us the
Living
published

1970 Ran for seat in Congress

1987–89 Appointed first
African American woman to
serve as commissioner on
L.A. Board of Public Works

1961 Married Medgar Evers

1950–
53
Korean
War

1961–73
Vietnam
War

1976
Married
Walter
Williams

1995 Evers-Williams
elected chair of NAACP

1933 Born,
Vicksburg, Miss.

1939–45
World War II

1925   1950   1975   2000

reform an organization rocked by scandal and allegations of financial mismanagement.

Evers-Williams was born March 17, 1933, in Vicksburg, Mississippi. She became part of the modern CIVIL RIGHTS MOVEMENT through her marriage to MEDGAR EVERS, who was the state field secretary for the Mississippi NAACP. Her world changed dramatically on June 12, 1963, when her husband was shot to death at their home in Jackson, Mississippi. White supremacist Byron de la Beckwith was charged with the murder, but two trials in the 1960s ended in HUNG JURIES. After the second trial, Evers-Williams vowed to bring de la Beckwith to justice.

Following her husband's assassination, Evers-Williams assumed his position as NAACP field secretary. Then, in 1964 she decided to move with her three young children to Claremont, California, and begin a new life. In 1967 she published *For Us the Living*, a memoir of her life with her late husband. She earned a degree in sociology at Pomona College in 1968 and then became director of planning at the Claremont Colleges.

In 1970 she ran for a seat in Congress in what was then the twenty-fourth congressional district in California. Though she lost the election, it was a turning point for Evers-Williams. She was publicly transformed from Mrs. Medgar Evers to Myrlie Evers. In the 1970s and 1980s, she worked in the corporate arena, serving as director of consumer affairs for the Atlantic Richfield Company. In 1976 she married Walter Williams, a California longshoreman and civil rights activist.

In 1987 Evers-Willams became the first African American woman to serve on the Los Angeles Board of Public Works. She and her husband moved to Bend, Oregon, in 1989.

When Mississippi prosecutors failed to try de la Beckwith a third time for the murder of Medgar Evers, Evers-Williams mounted a campaign to generate public opinion in favor of a retrial. In 1994 her efforts succeeded, and de la Beckwith was convicted of the 1963 crime.

CHRISTENSEN/LIAISON

*Myrlie
Evers-Williams*

"NEVER LOSE SIGHT OF YOUR GOALS. WE ARE LIVING IN A TIME WHEN WE MUST TAKE INTO OUR HANDS OUR DESTINIES AND OUR FUTURES."

Despite the many changes and activities in her life, Evers-Williams remained committed to the NAACP. Serving on the national board of directors in the 1990s, she observed firsthand the problems that were engulfing the once dominant civil rights organization. Dissatisfaction with the leadership of Executive Director Benjamin F. Chavis, Jr., culminated in his firing in August 1994 for committing more than $330,000 in NAACP funds without the board's approval to settle a SEX DISCRIMINATION suit filed against him. The focus then shifted to Chairman William F. Gibson, who was accused of misappropriating NAACP funds for personal use.

Evers-Williams was approached to challenge Gibson at the 1995 board election. She hesitated to run because her husband was dying from prostate cancer. However, Walter Williams urged her to take up the fight. She was elected to the chair in February 1995, winning by a one-vote margin. Her husband died shortly after her election.

The precarious state of the NAACP soon became clear to Evers-Williams. Membership had declined from five hundred thousand to three hundred thousand, while the organization's debt had risen to over $4 million. Corporate support had also dropped, forcing severe staff reductions at the national headquarters in Baltimore.

Evers-Williams moved quickly to restore trust. The board hired an accounting firm to audit financial records and directed its attorney to seek restitution from Gibson. Evers-Williams renewed contact with financial contributors, crisscrossing the United States in search of support. By the end of 1995, she had substantially reduced the NAACP's debt. New programs were started with the goal of reinvigorating the NAACP and attracting younger members. In December 1995 the board approved the appointment of Representative Kweisi Mfume (D-Md.) as executive director, capping a frenetic year for Evers-Williams.

EVICTION ▥ The removal of a TENANT from possession of premises in which he or she resides or has a property interest done by a LANDLORD either by reentry upon the premises or through a court action. 📖

Eviction may be in the form of a physical removal of a person from the premises or a disturbance of the tenant's enjoyment of the premises by disrupting the services and amenities that contribute to the HABITABILITY of the premises, such as by cutting off all utilities services to an apartment. The latter method is known as CONSTRUCTIVE EVICTION. An action of EJECTMENT is a legal process by which a landlord or owner of land may seek the eviction of his or her tenant.

EVIDENCE 📖 Any MATTER OF FACT that a party to a lawsuit offers to prove or disprove an issue in the case. A system of rules and standards used to determine which facts may be admitted, and to what extent a JUDGE or JURY may consider those facts, as proof of a particular issue in a lawsuit. 📖

Until 1975, the law of evidence was a creature of the COMMON LAW: evidence rules in most JURISDICTIONS were established by cases rather than by organized, official codifications. Legal scholars long pushed for legislation to provide uniformity and predictability to the evidentiary issues that arise during litigation. Following a lengthy campaign begun by the American Law Institute, which drafted its Model Rules of Evidence in 1942, and the National Conference of Commissioners on Uniform State Rules, which drafted the Uniform Rules of Evidence in 1953, Congress in 1975 adopted the Federal Rules of Evidence. The Federal Rules of Evidence are the official rules in FEDERAL COURT proceedings. Most states now also have codified rules of evidence based on the federal rules. Both state and federal rules of evidence serve as a guide for judges and attorneys so that they can determine whether to admit evidence—that is, whether to allow evidence to be observed by the judge or jury making factual conclusions in a trial.

One important benchmark of admissibility is relevance. Federal Rule of Evidence 402 states, in part, "All relevant evidence is admissible, except as otherwise provided." The goal of this rule is to allow parties to present all the evidence that bears on the issue to be decided, and to keep out all evidence that is IMMATERIAL or lacks probative value. Evidence offered to help prove something that is not at issue is immaterial. For example, the fact that a defendant attends church every week is immaterial, and thus irrelevant, to a charge of running a red light. Probative value is a tendency to make the existence of any material fact more or less probable. For instance, evidence that a murder defendant ate spaghetti on the day of the murder would normally be irrelevant because people who eat spaghetti are not more or less likely to commit murder compared with other people. However, if spaghetti sauce was found at the murder scene, the fact that the defendant ate spaghetti that day would have probative value and would thus be relevant evidence.

Witnesses The most common form of evidence is the TESTIMONY of WITNESSES. A witness can be a person who actually viewed the crime or other event at issue. Or a witness can be a person with other relevant information— someone who heard a dog bark near the time of a murder, saw an allegedly injured plaintiff lifting weights the day after his accident, or shared an office with the defendant and can describe her character and personality. Any COMPETENT person can TESTIFY as a witness provided the testimony meets other requirements, such as relevancy.

The Federal Rules of Evidence contain very broad competence requirements. To testify, a witness must swear or affirm that she or he will testify truthfully; possess personal knowledge of the subject matter of the testimony; have the physical and mental capacity to accurately perceive, record, and recollect fact impressions; and possess the capacity to understand questions and communicate understandably, with an interpreter if necessary. When an issue of state law is being determined, the state rules of evidence govern the competency of a witness. States that have not adopted the Federal Rules

A member of the FBI–New York Police Department Terrorist Task Force gathered bits of physical evidence from the World Trade Center in 1993 after a bombing there.

Objections

Evidentiary objections

At every trial or hearing requiring the admission of evidence, attorneys have the duty to object to evidence that the rules of court deem inadmissible. Objections must be made in a timely fashion, as soon as the witness or opposing party attempts to improperly introduce evidence. An attorney who fails to immediately recognize and object to inadmissible evidence faces serious consequences: the evidence may be admitted for the judge or jury to consider, and should the case be appealed, the appellate court will allow it to stand as admitted. On the other hand, an attorney who makes frequent objections to proper, admissible evidence runs the risk of alienating the jury or angering the judge. A trial lawyer therefore must learn to quickly recognize and correctly object to inadmissible evidence.

Once an attorney objects, the judge must decide whether to sustain the objection and disallow the evidence, or overrule the objection and permit the evidence. To assist this decision, the attorney must generally tell the judge the legal basis for the objection.

Objection	Legal Basis
Objections to questions	
Calls for an *irrelevant* answer	The answer to the question would not make the existence of any consequential fact more or less probable.
Calls for an *immaterial* answer	The answer to the question would have no logical bearing on an issue in the case.
Is asked of an *incompetent* witness	The witness is disqualified by statute from testifying, owing to age, lack of knowledge, or mental illness.
Violates the *best evidence rule*	The original document, rather than testimony, contains the best evidence.
Calls for *privileged communication*	The information sought is privileged communication, such as that between attorney and client, physician and patient, or husband and wife, and is barred from disclosure.
Calls for a *conclusion*	The question improperly asks the witness to reach a legal conclusion, which is a job reserved for the judge or jury.
Calls for an *opinion*	Generally, only expert witnesses may render their opinions; lay witnesses must testify only regarding their observations.
Calls for a *narrative answer*	Witnesses must respond concisely to individual questions, not give a long, rambling explanation.
Calls for *hearsay*	The answer would be inadmissible hearsay.
Is *leading*	The questioning attorney may not frame a question in such a way that it suggests the answer.
Is *repetitive* (or has already been *asked and answered*)	The question has already been asked and answered.
Is *beyond the scope*	On cross-examination, questions normally may not address matters not covered on direct examination.
Assumes *facts not in evidence*	Part of the question assumes that certain facts are true, when such facts have not been admitted into evidence or their existence is in dispute.
Is *confusing* (or *misleading* or *ambiguous* or *vague* or *unintelligible*)	A question must be posed in a manner that is specific and clear enough that the witness reasonably knows what information the examiner seeks.
Calls for *speculation*	Questions that ask the witness to guess or speculate are improper.
Is *compound*	The question brings up two or more separate facts, and any simple answer would be unclear.
Is *argumentative*	The question is essentially an argument to the judge or jury; it elicits no new information but rather states a conclusion and asks the witness to agree with it.
Is an *improper characterization*	For example, the question calls the defendant a spoiled brat, greedy pig, or frenzied dog; characterization is something the jury or judge, not a witness or attorney, should infer.
Mistakes evidence (or *misquotes the witness*)	Misstating or distorting evidence, or misquoting a witness, is improper.
Is *cumulative*	When numerous witnesses testify to the same facts or numerous exhibits demonstrate the same things, without adding anything new, the evidence is objectionable.

(table continued on next page)

of Evidence may have other grounds for incompetency, such as mental incapacity, immaturity, religious beliefs, and criminal convictions. The Federal Rules of Evidence and most jurisdictions state that jurors and presiding judges are not competent to testify in the case before them.

To be ADMISSIBLE, testimony must be limited to matters of which the witness has personal knowledge, meaning matters the witness learned about using any of his or her senses. Second, the witness must declare under OATH or AFFIRMATION that the testimony will be truthful. The purpose of this requirement is to "awaken the witness' conscience and impress the witness' mind with the duty to [be truthful]" (Fed. R. Evid. 603). The oath or affirmation requirement also serves as a ground for PERJURY if the witness does not testify truthfully. Although the oath frequently invokes the name of God, the witness need not possess any religious beliefs; a secular affirmation is sufficient.

Objections to questions (cont.)

Constitutes an *improper impeachment*	Rules surrounding the impeachment of a person's character or credibility are highly technical. For example, evidence of a prior inconsistent statement made by a witness may be used only if the statement is materially inconsistent and is offered in the proper context.
Violates the *parol evidence rule*	The parol evidence rule bars evidence of oral, or verbal, modifications or contradictions of a written contract that is complete and clear on its face.
Is *unresponsive* (or *volunteered*)	An answer that does not directly respond to a question is objectionable as unresponsive; an answer that goes beyond what is necessary to answer the question is objectionable as volunteered. Only the attorney who called the witness may object on these grounds.

Objections to answers

Is *irrelevant*
Is *immaterial*
Is *privileged*
Is a *conclusion*
Is improper *opinion*
Is *hearsay*
Is *narrative*
Is improper *characterization*

Objections to Exhibits

Lacks proper *foundation* (or lacks *foundation*, or has no *foundation*)	Before exhibits can be admitted into evidence, attorneys must establish the necessary foundation, or the facts that indicate the exhibit is what it purports to be. For a photograph of a crime scene, this might include calling the person who took the picture as a witness and asking whether she was at the crime scene, had a camera, and took a picture, and whether the exhibit is that picture.
Lacks *authentication*	Writings and conversations must be authenticated, or shown to have been executed by a party or that party's agent. For example, before testifying about a telephone conversation, a witness must demonstrate his knowledge of who was speaking on the other end of the telephone.
Is *prejudicial*	The exhibit's prejudicial effect outweighs its probative value. This objection is often raised with photo exhibits. A color photo of a murder victim may so prejudice the jury, without adding information helpful to determining the murderer, that the judge may disallow the photo as evidence.
Contains *inadmissible matter*	Exhibits in the forms of charts, diagrams, and maps must not disclose otherwise inadmissible material to the jury. For example, in most jurisdictions, evidence that a defendant in a personal injury case has insurance that may pay for the plaintiff's damages is inadmissible. A chart, shown to the jury, that conveys the name of the defendant's insurance company is improper and objectionable.

Is *irrelevant*
Is *immaterial*
Contains *hearsay*

Nonevidentiary objections

Attorneys may also object to situations that arise during a trial or hearing that do not concern matters of evidence. During voir dire, or jury selection, attorneys may not argue to prospective jurors the law or the facts that will arise at trial; if they do, they will likely receive an objection from opposing counsel. Likewise, attorneys often object to arguments made during opening statements, because opening statements are limited to a discussion of the evidence that will be presented during the trial. An attorney's personal opinion on any evidentiary matter is also objectionable because it places the attorney's credibility directly at issue. And a personal attack by an attorney against a party, witness, or opposing counsel is unprofessional and will almost always result in a sustainable objection.

Witnesses may be called to testify by any PARTY to the lawsuit. The party calling a witness to testify generally questions the witness first, in what is known as DIRECT EXAMINATION. The judge may exercise reasonable control over the questioning of witnesses in order to "(1) make the interrogation and presentation effective for the ascertainment of the truth, (2) avoid needless consumption of time, and (3) protect the witnesses from harassment, or undue embarrassment" (rule 611(a)). Thus, the judge may prevent a witness from rambling in a narrative fashion, and may require an attorney to ask specific questions in order to quickly and effectively ascertain the truth.

The federal rules and most jurisdictions discourage the use of LEADING QUESTIONS on direct examination. These are questions designed to elicit a particular answer by suggesting it. For example, the question "Didn't the defendant then aim the gun at the police officer?" is a leading question, and normally would not be permitted on direct examination. By contrast, "What did the defendant do next?" is a non-leading question and would be permitted on direct examination. In most cases, questions that can be answered with either "Yes" or "No" are considered to be leading questions. Courts generally will permit leading questions during direct examination if the witness is adverse or hostile toward the questioning party.

Leading questions are permitted, and are common practice, during CROSS-EXAMINATION. Once a party conducts a direct examination, the opposing party is entitled to cross-examine the same witness. The scope of questions asked during cross-examination is limited to the subject matter covered during direct examination, and any issues concerning the witness's CREDIBILITY. Attorneys use cross-examination for many purposes, including eliciting from a witness favorable facts; having the witness modify, explain, or qualify unfavorable versions of disputed facts elicited during direct examination; and impeaching, or discrediting, the witness.

If a witness is a lay witness (not testifying as an expert), the witness generally may testify as to facts and not as to opinions or inferences, unless the opinions or inferences are "(a) rationally based on the perception of the witness and (b) helpful to a clear understanding of the witness' testimony or the determination of a fact in issue" (rule 701). For example, a witness may not testify that she smelled marijuana unless she can sufficiently establish that she knows what marijuana smells like. Lay witnesses commonly testify about such things as the speed a car was going or someone's approximate age, but these types of inferences are less likely to be permitted the more closely they address critical issues in the case.

"If scientific, technical, or other specialized knowledge will assist the trier of fact to understand the evidence or to determine a fact in issue, a witness qualified as an expert by knowledge, skill, experience, training, or education, may testify thereto in the form of an opinion or otherwise" (rule 702). The admissibility of expert testimony hinges on whether such testimony would help the judge or jury, and whether the witness is properly qualified as an expert. Expert witnesses may, and usually do, testify in the form of an opinion. The opinion must be supported by an adequate foundation of relevant facts, data, or opinions, rather than conjecture. Thus, an expert frequently relies on firsthand or secondhand observations of facts, data, or opinions perceived prior to trial, or presented at trial during testimony or during a

hypothetical question posed by an attorney. Courts do not require experts to have firsthand knowledge of facts, data, or opinions because experts in the field do not always rely on such firsthand knowledge. For instance, physicians routinely make diagnoses based on information from several sources, such as hospital records, X-ray reports, and opinions from other physicians.

When an expert offers a scientific fact as substantive evidence or as the basis of his or her opinion, the court must determine the reliability of the scientific fact by looking at such things as the validity of the underlying scientific principle, the validity of the technique applying that principle, adherence to proper procedures, the condition of instruments used in the process, and the qualifications of those who perform the test and interpret the results. Issues frequently arise over such scientific tools and techniques as lie detectors, DNA testing, and hypnosis. Some scientific tests, such as drug tests, radar, and paternity blood tests, generally are accepted as being reliable, and their admissibility may be provided for by statute. See also DNA EVIDENCE; FORENSIC SCIENCE; POLYGRAPH.

Hearsay The credibility of any witness's testimony depends upon three factors: (1) whether the witness accurately perceived what she or he described, (2) whether the witness retained an accurate memory of the perception, and (3) whether the witness's narration accurately conveys the perception. To be allowed to testify, the witness generally must take an oath, must be personally present at the trial, and must be subjected to cross-examination. These conditions promote the factors that lend themselves to the witness's credibility. The rule against HEARSAY further bolsters the oath, personal presence, and cross-examination requirements.

Hearsay is a statement, made out of court, offered in court to prove the truth of the matter asserted. The statement may be oral or written, or it may be nonverbal conduct intended as an assertion, such as pointing to a crime suspect in a police lineup. The act of pointing in response to a request for identification is the same as stating, "He did it." Not all nonverbal conduct is intended as an assertion, of course. For example, a person usually opens an umbrella to stay dry, not to make the assertion, "It is raining."

Sometimes, statements made out of court are not hearsay because they are not offered for the purpose of proving what they assert. For example: A man who claims that a collision between his car and a truck rendered him unconscious files a lawsuit against the truck driver for NEGLIGENCE. The truck driver wishes to introduce as evidence a statement the man made seconds after the accident: "I knew I should have gotten my brakes fixed; they haven't been working for weeks!" If the purpose of offering the statement is only to prove that the man was conscious and talking following the accident, the statement is not hearsay. However, if the statement is offered to prove that the man's brakes were not working and therefore he caused the accident, then the statement is offered for its truth and is hearsay.

The Federal Rules of Evidence state generally that hearsay is not admissible evidence. The reason is that it is impractical, and in most cases simply impossible, to cross-examine the declarant of an out-of-court statement, or to have the declarant take an oath prior to making the statement. Thus, the credibility of an out-of-court statement cannot easily be ascertained. But the hearsay doctrine is extremely complex. Under the federal rules, for example, most admissions of guilt are not considered hearsay and are therefore admissible, even though they might be stated out of court and then offered as evidence. The federal rules list more than twenty-five exceptions to the general hearsay prohibition. These exceptions apply to circumstances believed to produce trustworthy assertions.

Some exceptions to the hearsay rule require that the person who made the statement be unavailable to testify at trial. One example of this is when a person who is mortally wounded makes a statement before dying about the cause of her death. Under this hearsay exception, the victim's statement assigning guilt or causation is made admissible because the victim is not available to testify at trial and the need for the information is given greater weight than the fear that she lied. Some have argued that the DYING DECLARATION exception exists at least in part because of the belief that persons would not waste their last breaths to utter a falsehood. One federal court commented, "More realistically, the dying declaration is admitted because of compelling need for the statement, rather than any inherent trustworthiness" (*United States v. Thevis*, 84 F.R.D. 57 [N.D. Ga. 1979]). This exception proved noteworthy in the October 1995 trial and ultimate conviction of Yolanda Saldivar, accused of gunning down tejana singing star Selena Quintanilla Perez in a Corpus Christi, Texas, motel. Motel employees testified that Selena's last words before collapsing and dying were, "Lock the door! She'll

Claus von Bulow was acquitted of the attempted murder of his wife because the evidence presented at his trial was not conclusive.

shoot me again!" and "Yolanda Saldivar in Room 158." Saldivar received a sentence of life in prison following her conviction of murdering the twenty-three-year-old recording artist.

Under some circumstances, the availability of the declarant to testify is immaterial. For example, the excited utterance exception to the hearsay rule allows the admission of an out-of-court statement "relating to a startling event or condition made while the declarant was under the stress of excitement caused by the event or condition" (rule 803(2)). The premise for this exception is that excitement caused by the event or condition leaves a declarant without sufficient time or capacity for reflection to fabricate, thus the statement is considered truthful. An example of an admissible excited utterance is the statement, "Look out! That green truck is running a red light and is headed toward that school bus!" Other examples of hearsay exceptions include statements of medical diagnosis, birth and marriage certificates, business records, and statements regarding a person's character or reputation.

Authentication and Identification

Evidence is not relevant unless its authenticity can be demonstrated. A letter in which the defendant admits her guilt in a tax fraud trial is inadmissible unless the prosecution can first show that the defendant actually wrote it. Bloodstained clothing is irrelevant without some connection to the issues of the trial, such as evidence that the clothing belonged to the

JOURNALISTS' PRIVILEGE

In 1972, information leaked to the *Washington Post* by a confidential informant set the stage for the fall of a U.S. president. A source they called Deep Throat told journalists Bob Woodward and Carl Bernstein that several improprieties, including a break-in at the Democratic National Committee headquarters in Washington, D.C., had been orchestrated by a committee to reelect President Richard M. Nixon. News articles that Woodward and Bernstein wrote based on that information marked the beginning of Watergate, a scandal that led to Nixon's resignation in 1974 in the face of impeachment. More than twenty years later, the true identity of Deep Throat remained unknown.

Reliance on anonymous news sources can create problems when lawyers, judges, or juries seek information during a judicial proceeding. It is a basic principle in the U.S. legal system that "the public has a right to every [person's] evidence" (8 J. Wigmore, *Evidence* § 2192 [McNaughton rev. 1961]). With very few exceptions, individuals who possess knowledge or information that may help a judge or jury must testify or produce the information in court. Journalistic privilege, where recognized, is the right of journalists to withhold from the court certain sources, notes, or materials used to gather news. It is not among the privileges commonly recognized by courts (such as attorney-client privilege or marital privilege).

Since the 1850s, journalists have sought a privilege to protect the identity of news sources or to protect the news-gathering process from discovery at trial. As the number of reporters subpoenaed (ordered by a court to testify) increased dramatically in the 1960s and 1970s, so did their efforts. Reporters argue that to effectively gather vital information and disseminate it to the public, they must have the legal right to withhold the identity of a source. Without such a privilege, sources who fear the disclosure of their name will be less likely to talk with reporters. Reporters who fear reprisal, or who simply do not wish to testify or hire a lawyer, will be less likely to print or broadcast sensitive information. Journalists argue that this result, known as a chilling effect, will ultimately harm the public, which relies on reporters to relay even the most sensitive and secretive news and information.

In resisting subpoenas, journalists usually invoke the First Amendment, which prohibits laws abridging a free press. Unlike the Fifth Amendment, which explicitly grants individuals the right to refuse to testify against themselves, the First Amendment contains no explicit language protecting journalists from having to testify. Nonetheless, reporters have long argued that the purpose of the First Amendment is to allow the news media to freely gather and report the news, without encumbrances by the government. Forcing reporters to testify, they argue, thus violates the First Amendment.

A divided U.S. Supreme Court rejected this argument in the landmark decision *Branzburg v. Hayes*, 408 U.S. 665, 92 S. Ct. 2646, 33 L. Ed. 2d 626 (1972). *Branzburg* involved the appeals of three reporters who had been ordered in three separate incidents to testify before a grand jury (a jury convened to determine whether to indict a criminal suspect). In all three cases, prosecutors wanted to know what the reporters had observed or to whom they had spoken. One reporter had written an article about the process of converting marijuana into hashish; the other two were covering the militant Black Panther organization, believed to be planning guerrilla warfare to support its cause. In all three cases, the reporters had promised to keep their sources' identities secret or not to divulge their observations. The reporters refused to answer certain questions and provide certain information, arguing that doing so would jeopardize or destroy their working relationships with news sources and, ultimately, their ability to disseminate vital information to the public. The Supreme Court pointed out that the duty to testify has roots as deep as the First Amendment's guarantee of a free press, and refused to find a First Amendment privilege protecting reporters from being forced to testify before a grand jury.

According to the Court in *Branzburg*, the First Amendment does not override all other public interests, or exempt reporters from the same obligations to testify imposed on other citizens, merely because the news-gathering process may become more difficult if confidential sources are revealed. "It is clear that the First Amendment does not invalidate every incidental burdening of the press that may result from the enforcement of civil or criminal statutes of general applicability," the Court stated. The Court also acknowledged the importance of a free press to the country's welfare, and recognized that to be effective, the First Amendment must protect not only the dissemination of information but the news-gathering process itself. Yet, the Court made the point that a requirement to testify or otherwise disclose information to a judicial body is not a prohibition on the press's ability to employ confidential sources. The Court stated, "[N]o attempt is made to require the press to publish its sources of information or indiscriminately to disclose them on request."

Justices Potter Stewart, William J. Brennan, Jr., and Thurgood Marshall dissented in *Branzburg*, emphasizing that the independence of the press becomes threatened when journalists are called upon as "an investigative arm of government." When reporters are forced to testify in courtrooms, the three justices found, their constitutionally protected functions are impaired. Such impairment will, "in the long run, harm rather than help the administration of justice." The Court's dissenters stressed that the Constitution protects journalists not for the benefit of journalists but for the benefit of society. "Enlightened choice by an informed citizenry is the basic ideal upon which an open society is premised, and a free press is thus indispensable to a free society," stated the dissenting opinion.

The *Branzburg* decision held that the First Amendment does not protect journalists from grand jury subpoenas seeking evidence in criminal cases, and that there is no testimonial privilege for reporters who witness crimes. The decision did not address whether the Constitution protects reporters' notes, tape recordings, or other news-gathering items; whether there can be a privilege if there is no reason to think the reporter observed illegal activity; and whether reporters are entitled to a privilege in civil actions or other legal proceedings besides grand juries.

Despite the uncertainty, reporters since *Branzburg* have successfully invoked privileges. In some jurisdictions, they have been helped by shield laws, which are statutes allowing journalists to withhold certain information. Even in state jurisdictions without shield laws, many courts have upheld a reporter's claim of privilege using a three-part test championed in the *Branzburg* dissent: a reporter may be forced to reveal confidences only when the government demonstrates (1) that there is probable cause to believe that the journalist has information clearly relevant to a specific legal violation, (2) that the same information is not available by alternative means less destructive to the First Amendment, and (3) that there is a compelling and overriding interest in the information. Yet other courts have interpreted *Branzburg* as prohibiting state courts from creating reporter privileges at all (*Caldero v. Tribune Publishing Co.*, 98 Idaho 288, 562 P.2d 791 [1977]; *In re Roche*, 381 Mass. 624, 411 N.E.2d 466 [1980]).

More than half the states have passed shield laws, making the reporters' privilege statutory. Shield laws range in their coverage: some protect only the identities of confidential sources; others protect everything from sources, notes, videotapes, and film negatives to the reporter's thought processes. At least fourteen other states and most federal jurisdictions recognize the privilege based on common law, state constitutional law, or the First Amendment. These jurisdictions generally apply a version of the three-part test outlined in the *Branzburg* dissent. Even where the privilege is recognized, it is rarely absolute. Courts may order reporters to disclose information under certain compelling circumstances, and a reporter who refuses to obey the court faces a charge of contempt and fines or imprisonment.

Journalists react differently to the threat of incarceration. Los Angeles radio station manager Will Lewis in 1973 initially refused to comply with a federal grand jury subpoena seeking the originals of a letter and a tape recording sent to him by radical groups claiming inside knowledge of the kidnapping of Patty Hearst. Lewis was held in contempt and sent to Terminal Island Federal Prison, where he spent sixteen days in solitary confinement before being released pending his appeal. He lost (*In re Lewis*, 377 F. Supp. 297 [C.D. Cal. 1974], *aff'd* 501 F.2d 418 [9th Cir.]). Faced with returning to prison, Lewis turned over the documents.

But William Farr, a reporter for the *Los Angeles Herald-Examiner*, spent two months in jail rather than name his source. Farr had received a copy of a deposition transcript from a prosecuting attorney in the case of serial murderer Charles Manson. The judge in the case had forbidden officers of the court to publicize the case, which contained particularly gruesome facts. When the judge ordered Farr to name the individual who leaked the information, Farr refused (*Farr v. Superior Court of Los Angeles County*, 22 Cal. App. 2d 60, 99 Cal. Rptr. 342 [Ct. App. 1971]).

Many reporters and their attorneys view the threat of contempt as an opportunity to educate the public on the issue. In 1990, Tim Roche was a twenty-one-year-old reporter for a Florida newspaper, the *Stuart News*, when he was subpoenaed to disclose the name of a confidential source who had shown him a sealed (confidential) court order in a child custody battle. Roche refused to comply, maintaining that he had promised the source confidentiality. He was found in contempt of court and received a thirty-day jail sentence.

Attorneys for Roche appealed, but both the Florida Supreme Court and the U.S. Supreme Court declined to hear the case. Roche then sought clemency (an act to lower or moderate the sentence) from Governor Lawton M. Chiles, of Florida. Chiles refused the plea for clemency, but offered Roche three hundred hours of community service as an alternative to jail. Roche declined the offer, stating that he would not compromise his principles, as he had done nothing wrong. The governor retorted that he also would not compromise his principles, and that no one is above the law. On March 16, 1993, Roche entered the Martin County Jail, where he served nineteen days. National publicity surrounding Roche's plight led to the introduction and passage of a Florida bill designed to protect reporters and their confidential sources. But Chiles vetoed the Tim Roche Bill on May 14, 1993.

Journalists risk jail sentences to protect their reputation as well as their sources: a reporter who is known to have identified a source after promising confidentiality may have a difficult time obtaining information from other sources in the future. Opponents of the reporters' privilege argue that journalists who ignore requests for evidentiary information breach other important societal interests. For example, the Sixth Amendment guarantees a criminal defendant the right to a fair trial. This right is lost when a reporter who possesses information that may help prove the defendant's innocence refuses to testify. The same argument applies to society's interest in prosecuting criminals, who may go free when incriminating evidence is withheld by a journalist.

See also First Amendment; Freedom of the Press; Grand Jury; Shield Law.

accused murderer. The process of linking a piece of evidence to a case—of authenticating or identifying the evidence—is frequently referred to as laying a foundation. Under the Federal Rules of Evidence, a foundation is sufficient if a reasonable juror would find it more probably true than not true that the evidence is what the party offering it claims it to be.

The most basic way to lay an evidentiary foundation is to demonstrate that a witness has personal knowledge. For example, the witness may testify that he wrote the letter, or saw the plaintiff sign the contract, or found the bullet in the kitchen. When the evidence is an object, the witness must testify that the object introduced at the trial is in substantially the same condition as it was when it was witnessed.

Objects that are not readily identifiable must often be authenticated through chain-of-command testimony. In the case of a blood sample, a proper foundation would include testimony from each individual who handled the blood—from the nurse who drew the blood, to the lab technician who tested it, to the courier who delivered it to the courthouse for trial. Unless each individual can testify that the blood sample's condition remained substantially the same from the time it was drawn until the time it was offered as evidence (accounting for any loss in amount due to testing), the court could sustain an objection from the other side. The sample would then be inadmissible for lack of AUTHENTICATION.

Under the Federal Rules of Evidence, some evidentiary items are self-authenticating and need no additional authentication before being admitted. Documents containing the official SEAL of a government unit within the United States, and certified copies of public records such as birth certificates, are self-authenticating, as are newspapers and congressional documents.

Best-Evidence Rule *Best-evidence rule* is a misleading name for the courts' preference for original writings, recordings, and photographs over copies when their contents are sought to be proved. The purpose of this rule at common law was to avoid the potential for inaccuracies contained in handmade copies. The current rule contained in the Federal Rules of Evidence requires the use of original writings, recordings, and photographs (including X rays and motion pictures), but the rule defines original to include most photocopies or prints from the same negative. The risk of inaccuracies from these types of duplicates is almost nonexistent. When the original evidence is lost, destroyed, not obtainable, or in the possession of the oppo-

nent, the court will not require a party to produce the original. See also BEST EVIDENCE.

Judicial Notice Some matters relevant to a trial are so obvious that a court will not require evidence to prove them—for example, that it is dark outside at midnight or that April 30, 1995, fell on a Sunday. To prevent wasting a court's time, the rules of evidence permit courts to take judicial notice of such matters, that is, to accept them as true without formal evidentiary proof. Courts may take judicial notice of facts generally known to be true (e.g., that gasoline is flammable) or facts verifiable from dependable sources (e.g., that Des Moines, Iowa, is in Polk County, which can be verified on a map). As a matter of course, courts judicially notice the contents of laws of and within the United States.

Privileges It is a basic tenet in U.S. jurisprudence that "the public . . . has a right to every [person's] evidence," and parties in litigation should avail themselves of all rational means of ascertaining truth (*Trammel v. United States*, 445 U.S. 40, 100 S. Ct. 906, 63 L. Ed. 2d 186 [1980]). Yet courts view certain interests and relationships to be of such importance that they protect those interests and relationships from certain efforts to gather evidence. These protections, or exclusions from the general rule of free access to evidence, are known as PRIVILEGES.

Federal courts recognize several types of privileges. To encourage clients to communicate freely with their lawyers and to fully disclose any information that may enable their lawyers to provide appropriate legal advice, courts allow clients to refuse to disclose and to prevent any other person from disclosing confidential communications made when seeking legal services. This privilege applies to clients' communications with their attorneys and with the attorneys' office staff. It protects only CONFIDENTIAL COMMUNICATIONS, not communications made to friends or acquaintances in addition to an attorney.

The lawyer-client privilege applies to the client, not the lawyer. Thus, the client, but not the lawyer, has the right to waive the privilege and to testify regarding protected communications. The lawyer-client privilege does not terminate even when the lawyer-client relationship does. The privilege does not apply to a client's allegations of a breach of duty by the lawyer.

To promote open communication within marital relationships, the rules of evidence also recognize a marital privilege. In criminal cases, a person has the privilege to refuse to testify against a spouse. This privilege covers only evidentiary matters that would incriminate the nontestifying spouse (the defendant), since other matters are not likely to jeopardize the MARRIAGE relationship. The nontestifying spouse does not have the right to assert the privilege; the privilege belongs only to the testifying spouse.

In criminal and civil cases, testimony about any confidential communications between spouses is also afforded a privilege. Either spouse, not just the testifying spouse, may assert this privilege. Unlike the testifying spouse privilege, the confidential communications spousal privilege survives the termination of the marriage by death or divorce—but it does not apply to permanently separated spouses.

Courts also recognize a political vote privilege, a clergy-penitent privilege, and qualified privileges for TRADE SECRETS, state secrets, and the identity of an informant. Some courts also recognize a PHYSICIAN-PATIENT PRIVILEGE, an accountant-client privilege, and a privilege granted to journalists seeking to protect their news sources.

CROSS-REFERENCES

Attorney-Client Privilege; Character Evidence; Circumstantial Evidence; Cumulative Evidence; Derivative Evidence; Direct Evidence; Documentary Evidence; Exclusionary Rule; Extrinsic Evidence; Parol Evidence; Privileged Communication.

EXAMINATION 📖 A search, inspection, or interrogation.

In CRIMINAL PROCEDURE, the PRELIMINARY HEARING held to decide whether a suspect arrested for a crime should be brought to trial.

In trial practice, the interrogation of a witness to elicit his or her TESTIMONY in a civil or criminal action, so that the facts he or she possesses are presented before the trial of fact for consideration.

In the law governing REAL PROPERTY transactions, an investigation made into the history of the ownership of and conditions that exist upon land so that a purchaser can determine whether a seller is entitled to sell the land free and clear of any claims made by third persons.

In PATENT law, an inquiry made at the Patent and Trademark Office to determine the novelty and utility of an invention for which a patent application has been filed and whether the invention interferes with any other invention. 📖

EXAMINER 📖 An official or other person empowered by another—whether an individual, business, or government agency—to investigate and review specified documents for accuracy and truthfulness.

A court-appointed officer, such as a *master* or REFEREE, who inspects evidence presented to resolve controverted matters and records statements made by witnesses in the particular proceeding pending before that court.

A government employee in the Patent and Trademark Office whose duty it is to scrutinize the application made for a PATENT by an inventor to determine whether the invention meets the statutory requirements of patentability.

A federal employee of the INTERNAL REVENUE SERVICE who reviews INCOME TAX returns for accuracy and truthfulness. 📖

EXCEPTION 📖 The act of excepting or excluding from a number designated or from a description; that which is excepted or separated from others in a general rule or description; a person, thing, or case specified as distinct or not included; an act of excepting, omitting from mention, or leaving out of consideration. Express exclusion of something from operation of CONTRACT or DEED. An *exception* operates to take something out of a thing granted that would otherwise pass or be included.

OBJECTION to an order or ruling of a trial court. A formal objection to the action of the court, during the trial of a case, in refusing a request or overruling an objection; implying that the party excepting does not acquiesce in the decision of the court, but will seek to procure its reversal, and that he or she means to save the benefit of his or her request or objection in some future proceeding. Under rules practiced in the federal and most state courts, the need for claiming an exception to EVIDENCE or to a ruling to preserve appellate rights has been eliminated in favor of an objection. 📖

EXCHANGE 📖 An association, organization, or group of persons, incorporated or unincorporated, that constitutes, maintains, or provides a marketplace or facilities for bringing together purchasers and sellers of SECURITIES or commodities futures. 📖

A security is a written proof of ownership of an investment, usually in the form of shares of STOCK, which are fractional units of ownership in a company. Commodities are raw materials, like wheat, gasoline, or silver, that are sold either on the spot market, where cash is paid "on the spot," or through futures contracts, where a price for a CONTRACT is set in advance, not to be changed even if the market price for the COMMODITY increases or decreases by the time the contract comes due.

Stock Exchanges The New York Stock Exchange (NYSE) and the American Stock Exchange are located on Wall Street, in New York City. Wall Street (named for a stockade built to protect the original settlers) is the busiest hub of securities trading in the United States. There

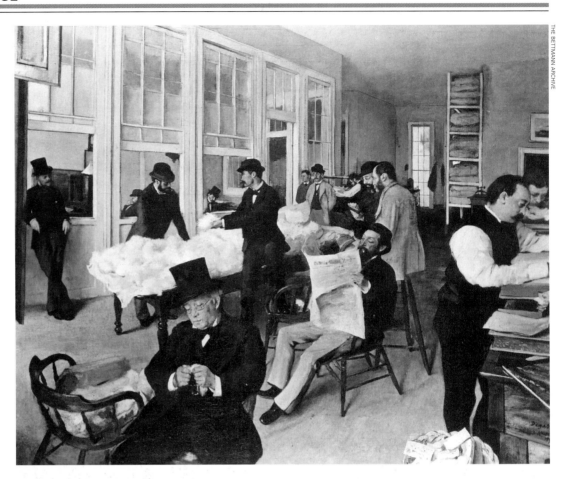

This 1873 painting by Edouard Degas of the cotton market in New Orleans shows brokers testing the quality of cotton and reading the financial news.

are five other, smaller, regional exchanges: the Pacific (in Los Angeles), Cincinnati, Chicago, Philadelphia (at the site of the first stock exchange in the United States), and Boston. These stock exchanges are private associations that sell memberships (seats) for a price, which can fluctuate based on the price of stocks and the volume of trading.

The SECURITIES AND EXCHANGE COMMISSION, which was established pursuant to the Securities Act of 1933 (15 U.S.C.A. §§ 78a et seq., 78d), regulates the activities of securities exchanges (defined at 15 U.S.C.A. § 78c(a)(1)). Private associations such as the NYSE and the National Association of Securities Dealers (NASD) initiate and execute a significant amount of self-regulation and disciplinary activities with the full support of the Securities and Exchange Commission.

Futures Exchanges   Futures contracts for commodities are traded on one of eleven commodities exchanges in the United States, or on other exchanges throughout the world. Each futures contract is tied to the exchange that issued it. Exchanges specialize in various commodities, including currency and financial futures. For example, the Chicago Mercantile Exchange deals in meat, livestock, and currency,

and the Minneapolis Grain Exchange focuses exclusively on grain. Other exchanges include the Chicago Board of Trade and boards of trade and exchanges in Philadelphia; Kansas City, Missouri; and New York City.

The COMMODITIES FUTURES TRADING COMMISSION, which was established pursuant to the Commodity Exchange Act (7 U.S.C.A. §§ 1 et seq., 4a(a)), regulates the activities of boards of trade, defined as associations or exchanges established to trade commodities futures. Private organizations such as the Chicago Board of Trade and the National Futures Association provide significant self-regulation to the commodities futures trading market.

The Auction Market Principle   The floor of a stock or futures exchange operates on the "auction market" principle, whereby BROKERS meet face-to-face on the floor of the exchange to execute buy and sell orders.

Futures exchanges operate on a pure AUCTION system, often referred to as the open outcry system, where all trading takes place on the floor of the exchange, or "in the pit." Buyers and sellers in the pit use hand signals and oral communications to place buy and sell orders simultaneously, acting for themselves and as agents for others.

Securities exchanges operate on an auction-style system, where the market prices for securities are set by buyers and sellers meeting on the floor of the exchange. In contrast to futures exchanges, securities exchanges also employ specialists, who stand ready to buy or sell orders at market prices when there is, for example, a seller and no buyer for a particular security. In this capacity, specialists act as dealers, using their own capital to make bids and offers for stock. They can also act as brokers, holding limit orders (requests to buy or sell a security when it reaches a predetermined market price) for other brokers and executing those orders when the market moves up or down to the desired price. Specialists permit for a more orderly and continuous securities market and prevent wild price fluctuations due to imbalances in supply and demand.

Computerized and Over-the-Counter Trading Computer technology has been introduced in the major exchanges to automate certain aspects of transactions, but the auction process remains the predominant method of trading securities in these forums. In fact, the statutory definition of an exchange in the Securities Exchange Act has been consistently interpreted *not* to include computerized trading.

Stocks not traded on an exchange have historically been termed over-the-counter (OTC) stocks because they are sold over the counter (or desk or telephone) of individual brokers. The NASD once published the quotes of willing buyers and sellers of OTC stocks in what were called pink sheets. In the early 1970s, the NASD computerized this service and called it the National Association of Securities Dealers Automated Quotations System. This decentralized method of trading stocks has grown in efficiency and popularity in the decades since its

The Minneapolis Grain Exchange is one of eleven commodities exchanges in the United States.

introduction, but has never been held to constitute an exchange because it does not facilitate the physical meeting of buyers and sellers. Like specialists in stock exchanges, who often are called upon to "make the market" (purchase and sell securities with their own money) in the absence of willing buyers and sellers, multiple "market makers" in the OTC market use their own capital to respond to fluctuations in the market.

EXCHANGE OF PROPERTY 📖 A transaction wherein parties trade goods, or COMMODITIES, for other goods, in contrast with a SALE or trading of goods for money. 📖

An exchange of property is a type of BARTER contract, applicable only to agreements relating to goods and services, not to agreements involving land.

EXCISE 📖 A tax imposed on the performance of an act, the engaging in an occupation, or the enjoyment of a privilege. A tax on the manufacture, sale, or use of goods or on the carrying on of an occupation or activity, or a tax on the transfer of property. In current usage the term has been extended to include various LICENSE fees and practically every internal revenue tax except the income tax (e.g., federal alcohol and tobacco excise taxes). 📖

EXCLUSIONARY CLAUSE 📖 A term in a SALES contract that limits the remedies available to one or both parties to it in an action for breach of WARRANTY, statements made as to the quality of the goods sold. A provision of an insurance CONTRACT that prohibits recovery pursuant to its terms if certain designated circumstances occur. 📖

The exclusionary clause contains the EXCEPTIONS to INSURANCE coverage upon which the insurer and insured have agreed prior to the execution of the policy.

EXCLUSIONARY RULE 📖 The principle based on federal constitutional law that EVIDENCE illegally seized by law enforcement officers in violation of a suspect's right to be free from unreasonable SEARCHES AND SEIZURES cannot be used against the suspect in a criminal prosecution. 📖

The exclusionary rule is designed to exclude evidence obtained in violation of a criminal defendant's FOURTH AMENDMENT rights. The Fourth Amendment protects against unreasonable searches and seizures by law enforcement personnel. If the search of a criminal suspect is unreasonable, the evidence obtained in the search will be excluded from trial.

The exclusionary rule is a court-made rule. This means that it was created not in statutes passed by legislative bodies but rather by the Supreme Court. The exclusionary rule applies in FEDERAL COURTS by virtue of the Fourth Amendment. The Supreme Court has ruled that it applies in state courts through the Due Process Clause of the FOURTEENTH AMENDMENT. (The Bill of Rights—the first ten amendments—applies to actions by the federal government. The Fourteenth Amendment, the Supreme Court has held, makes most of the protections in the Bill of Rights applicable to actions by the states.) See also INCORPORATION DOCTRINE.

The exclusionary rule has been in existence since the early 1900s. Before the rule was fashioned, any evidence was ADMISSIBLE in a criminal trial if the judge found the evidence to be relevant. The manner in which the evidence had been seized was not an issue.

This began to change in 1914, when the Supreme Court devised a way to enforce the Fourth Amendment. In *Weeks v. United States*, 232 U.S. 383, 34 S. Ct. 341, 58 L. Ed. 652 (1914), a federal agent had conducted a warrantless search for evidence of gambling at the home of Fremont Weeks. The evidence seized in the search was used at trial, and Weeks was convicted. On appeal, the Supreme Court held that the Fourth Amendment barred the use of evidence secured through a warrantless search. Weeks's conviction was reversed, and thus was born the exclusionary rule.

The exclusionary rule established in *Weeks* was constitutionally required only in federal court until *Mapp v. Ohio*, 367 U.S. 643, 81 S. Ct. 1684, 6 L. Ed. 2d 1081 (1961). In *Mapp*, Cleveland police officers had gone to the home of Dollree Mapp to ask her questions regarding a recent bombing. The officers demanded entrance into her home. Mapp called her attorney and then refused to allow the officers in without a warrant. The officers became rough with Mapp, handcuffed her, and searched her home. They found allegedly obscene books, pictures, and photographs.

Mapp was charged with violations of OBSCENITY laws, prosecuted, convicted, and sentenced to seven years in prison. The Ohio Supreme Court affirmed the conviction, but the U.S. Supreme Court overturned it.

In *Mapp*, the Court held that the exclusionary rule applied to state criminal proceedings through the Due Process Clause of the Fourteenth Amendment. Before the *Mapp* ruling, not all states excluded evidence obtained in violation of the Fourth Amendment. Since *Mapp*, a defendant's claim of unreasonable search and seizure has become a matter of course in most criminal prosecutions.

A criminal defendant's claim of unreasonable search and seizure is usually heard in a suppression hearing before the presiding judge. This hearing is conducted before trial to determine what evidence will be suppressed, or excluded from trial.

The exclusionary rule is still regularly invoked by criminal defendants, but its golden age may have passed. Since the 1980s, the Supreme Court has severely limited its application. According to the Court, this rule was not devised to cure all Fourth Amendment violations. Rather, it was designed primarily to deter police misconduct. This construction led to the GOOD FAITH exception to Fourth Amendment violations established in *United States v. Leon*, 468 U.S. 897, 104 S. Ct. 3405, 82 L. Ed. 2d 677 (1984).

In *Leon*, police officers searched the Burbank, California, home of Alberto A. Leon, and arrested Leon after they found a large quantity of drugs in his possession. The search was executed pursuant to a WARRANT that was later determined to be invalid. The information provided by the police in their AFFIDAVIT in support of the warrant had been stale, which meant that too much time had passed between the observations that prompted it and the application for the warrant. No evidence suggested that a police officer had lied about facts. Rather, the staleness of the affidavit had simply been overlooked by the magistrate.

The drug evidence seized from Leon's home was excluded from trial by the U.S. District Court for the Central District of California, and the Ninth Circuit Court of Appeals affirmed the ruling. On appeal, the U.S. Supreme Court reversed, holding that evidence gathered in a search executed pursuant to a warrant later

A Massachusetts state trooper trains a dog to find explosives in airline luggage. Law enforcement officers use many techniques for searching suspects, but if they search without a warrant or probable cause the evidence may not be used at trial under the exclusionary rule.

D. GRECO/STOCK BOSTON

found to be defective should not be excluded from trial.

The majority in *Leon* opened its analysis by noting that the Fourth Amendment "contains no provisions expressly precluding the use of evidence obtained in violation of its commands." The exclusionary rule, according to the majority, was not designed to be a personal right. It was created by the Court "to deter police misconduct rather than to punish the errors of judges and magistrates." Under this interpretation, excluding evidence obtained through an honest mistake would serve no purpose. The Court's ruling in *Leon* meant that evidence obtained in violation of a person's Fourth Amendment rights would not be excluded from trial if the law enforcement officer, though mistaken, acted reasonably.

Justice JOHN PAUL STEVENS dissented, arguing that the facts of the case did not warrant such a sweeping exception to the exclusionary rule. In a separate dissenting opinion, Justices WILLIAM J. BRENNAN, JR., and THURGOOD MARSHALL conceded that, "as critics of the exclusionary rule never tire of repeating," the Fourth Amendment does not contain an express provision calling for the exclusion of evidence seized in violation of its commands. Brennan and Marshall dismissed this argument by noting that the Constitution is stated in general terms, and that the Supreme Court regularly creates doctrines designed to enforce its simple terms.

Brennan and Marshall maintained that "the chief deterrent function of the [exclusionary] rule is," far beyond the simple prevention of police misconduct, "the tendency to promote institutional compliance with Fourth Amendment requirements on the part of law enforcement agencies generally." In other words, if a SEARCH WARRANT is found defective at any point in the prosecution, the evidence should be excluded, even if the defect is due to an honest mistake. This, according to Brennan and Marshall, would preserve the integrity of both law enforcement and the Fourth Amendment. Brennan and Marshall concluded that the majority's reliance on the deterrence rationale "robbed the [exclusionary] rule of legitimacy."

In 1995, the Supreme Court revisited the good faith exception to the exclusionary rule. In *Arizona v. Evans*, 514 U.S. 1, 115 S. Ct. 1185, 131 L. Ed. 2d 34 (1995), the error of a court employee mistakenly listed Isaac Evans as the subject of a misdemeanor ARREST WARRANT. A police officer stopped Evans for a traffic violation, searched Evans pursuant to the faulty warrant information, and found marijuana.

On trial for possession of marijuana, Evans moved to suppress the marijuana evidence. The Maricopa County Superior Court granted the motion. The state of Arizona appealed, and the Arizona Court of Appeals reversed. The Supreme Court of Arizona then heard the case and held that the evidence should be excluded.

On appeal by the state of Arizona, the U.S. Supreme Court reversed, holding that evidence seized in violation of the Fourth Amendment as a result of clerical error need not be excluded from trial. In so holding, the Court emphasized that the Fourth Amendment exists only to guard against unreasonable police intrusions. According to the Court, "[T]he use of the fruits of a past unlawful search or seizure 'works no new Fourth Amendment wrong' " (*Evans*, quoting *Leon*, quoting *United States v. Calandra*, 414 U.S. 338, 94 S. Ct. 613, 38 L. Ed. 2d 561 [1974]).

The good faith exception established in *Leon* is just one exception that renders the exclusionary rule inoperable. Evidence seized by private parties is not excluded from trial if the search was not at the direction of law enforcement officers. If a criminal defendant testifies in her or his own defense, illegally seized evidence may be used to IMPEACH the defendant's testimony. Evidence seized in violation of a person's Fourth Amendment rights may be used in GRAND JURY proceedings and civil proceedings. In a grand jury proceeding, however, illegally seized evidence may not be used if it was obtained in violation of the federal WIRE TAPPING statute (18 U.S.C.A. § 2510 et seq.).

Few legal observers express satisfaction with the exclusionary rule. Some commentators criticize the Supreme Court for limiting the scope of the rule with the good faith exception. Others contend that the rule should be abolished because it impedes law enforcement. Some members of Congress have even proposed legislation to abolish the exclusionary rule in federal court. To date, no such legislation has been adopted.

The exercise of the exclusionary rule can, in some cases, attract enormous public attention. In 1996, U.S. district court judge Harold Baer, Jr., excluded from trial a taped CONFESSION and eighty pounds of cocaine and heroin. New York City police officers had stopped the vehicle of Carol Bayless after seeing four men hurry away from the vehicle when they noticed the police. According to Baer, people in that particular New York City neighborhood naturally fled because they rightfully feared abusive police officers. Thus, the police officers in this case had no PROBABLE CAUSE to believe that the vehicle Bayless was driving held evidence of a crime. After public outcry, Baer reversed his decision and admitted the evidence into trial.

CROSS-REFERENCES

Criminal Law; Criminal Procedure; Fruit of the Poisonous Tree; *Mapp v. Ohio.*

EXCLUSIVE 📖 Pertaining to the subject alone, not including, admitting, or pertaining to any others. Sole. Shutting out; debarring from interference or participation; vested in one person alone. Apart from all others, without the admission of others to participation. 📖

For example, if a court has been granted exclusive JURISDICTION over cases relating to a particular subject matter, no other court is able to entertain cases concerning that particular subject.

EXCLUSIVE AGENCY 📖 Grant to an AGENT of exclusive right to sell within a particular market or area. A CONTRACT to give an *exclusive agency* to deal with property is ordinarily interpreted as not precluding competition by the principal generally, but only as precluding him or her from appointing another agent to accomplish the result. The grant of an *exclusive agency to sell*, that is, the exclusive right to sell the products of a wholesaler in a specified territory, ordinarily is interpreted as precluding competition in any form within the designated area. 📖

EXCULPATE 📖 To clear or excuse from guilt. 📖

An individual who uses the excuse of justification to explain the lawful reason for his or her action might be exculpated from a criminal charge. Exculpatory EVIDENCE is evidence that works to clear an individual from fault.

EXCUSE 📖 The explanation for the performance or nonperformance of a particular act; a reason alleged in court as a basis for exemption or relief from guilt. 📖

An excuse is essentially a DEFENSE for an individual's conduct that is intended to mitigate the individual's blameworthiness for a particular act or to explain why the individual acted in a specific manner. A driver sued for NEGLIGENCE, for example, might raise the defense of excuse if the driver was rushing an injured person to a hospital, or if some unforeseen illness or mechanical failure made safe operation of the vehicle impossible.

EX DIVIDEND 📖 A phrase used by stockbrokers that denotes that a STOCK is sold without the purchaser receiving the right to own its recently declared DIVIDEND which has not yet been paid to the stockholders. 📖

The seller of a stock sold *ex dividend* retains the right to receive payment of the declared dividend. The purchaser of such a stock usually buys it at a price that is reduced by the amount of the dividend to be paid to the seller.

EXECUTE 📖 To complete; to make; to sign; to perform; to do; to carry out according to its terms; to fulfill the command or purpose of. To perform all necessary formalities, as to make and sign a contract, or sign and deliver a note. 📖

Execute is the opposite of EXECUTORY, incomplete or yet to be performed.

EXECUTION 📖 The carrying out of some act or course of conduct to its completion. In criminal law, the carrying out of a death sentence (see also CAPITAL PUNISHMENT).

The process whereby an official, usually a SHERIFF, is directed by an appropriate JUDICIAL WRIT to seize and sell as much of a debtor's nonexempt property as is necessary to satisfy a court's monetary JUDGMENT.

With respect to CONTRACTS, the performance of all acts necessary to render a contract complete as an instrument, which conveys the concept that nothing remains to be done to make a complete and effective contract. 📖

With regard to SEIZURES of property, executions are authorized in any ACTION or proceeding in which a monetary judgment is recoverable and in any other action or proceeding when authorized by statute. For example, the victim of a motor vehicle accident may institute a civil lawsuit seeking DAMAGES from another party. If the plaintiff wins the lawsuit and is awarded money from the defendant as a part of the VERDICT, the court may authorize an execution process to pay the DEBT to the plaintiff.

Ordinarily, execution is achieved through a legal device known as a writ of execution. The writ serves as proof of the property owed by the

Execution includes the gathering of natural resources from land.

INGA SPENCE/THE PICTURE CUBE

defendant, who is called the judgment DEBTOR, to the plaintiff, or judgment CREDITOR. The writ of execution commands an OFFICER OF THE COURT, usually a sheriff, to take the property of the debtor to satisfy the debt. Ordinarily, a writ of execution cannot be issued until after an appropriate court issues a judgment or decree determining the rights and liabilities of the parties involved.

Any type of PERSONAL PROPERTY is subject to seizure under an execution, provided existing laws do not prescribe specific exemptions. Such property may include jewelry, money, and stocks. In most states, REAL PROPERTY, including land, is also subject to execution. INTELLECTUAL PROPERTY, which includes PATENTS, COPYRIGHTS, and TRADEMARKS, is generally immune to execution.

An execution on a judgment is typically issued by the CLERK of the court in which the judgment was rendered. The clerk cannot issue an execution unless directed to do so by the judgment creditor or the judgment creditor's attorney. The time within which an execution must issue varies from one jurisdiction to another. The writ must be delivered to the sheriff or his or her deputy before it can properly be said that the writ has been issued.

The LEVY of the execution is the act by which the officer of the court appropriates the judgment debtor's property to satisfy the command of the writ. The levy must be made by an officer duly qualified to act under the terms of the writ. In most states, the judgment debtor has the right to select and indicate to the officer the property upon which the levy is to be made.

An execution creates a LIEN that gives the judgment creditor qualified control of the judgment debtor's property. In most jurisdictions, an execution lien binds all property, personal or real, that is subject to levy. It is sometimes called a general lien because it attaches to all the defendant's property.

After the sheriff has levied, it is her or his duty to sell the property seized. An execution SALE is a sale of property by a sheriff as an officer acting under the writ of execution. An execution sale should be conducted so as to promote competition and obtain the best price. If necessary, the sheriff can employ an auctioneer as an agent to sell the property, in order to procure the most favorable price and to collect the proceeds.

Body Executions   Execution against a person is by writ of *capias ad satisfaciendum* (Latin for "to take the body to court to pay the debt"). Under this writ, the sheriff arrests and imprisons the defendant until the defendant satisfies the judgment or is discharged from doing so. Such an execution is not intended as punishment for failure to pay the judgment. It is permitted for the purpose of compelling the debtor to reveal property fraudulently withheld from his or her creditor and from which the judgment can be satisfied.

In most jurisdictions, defendants in lawsuits based on contracts are not subject to BODY EXECUTIONS unless they have committed FRAUD. Under the statutes in some JURISDICTIONS, imprisonment for debt has been abolished entirely.

Statutes providing for the issuance of body executions to enforce judgments handed down in civil suits ordinarily do not conflict with provisions against imprisonment for debt. Among the civil, or TORT, actions in which the writ is generally allowed are those involving fraud or deceit, and those for neglect or misconduct in office or professional employment. A body execution is also generally proper in actions to recover for injuries to person or reputation, including LIBEL AND SLANDER, and in actions to recover for MALICIOUS PROSECUTION.

EXECUTIVE BRANCH   The branch of the U.S. government that is composed of the PRESIDENT and all the individuals, agencies, and departments that report to the president, and that is responsible for administering and enforcing the laws that Congress passes.

The U.S. government is composed of three branches: legislative, judicial, and executive. The legislative branch consists of the U.S. Congress, which is responsible for creating laws. The judicial branch is composed of the FEDERAL COURTS, which are responsible for ruling on the validity of the laws that Congress passes and applying them in individual cases. The executive branch differs from both in scope and function.

The Executive Branch and the Constitution   The executive branch has undergone tremendous changes over the years, making it very different from what it was under GEORGE WASHINGTON. Today's executive branch is much larger, more complex, and more powerful than it was when the United States was founded.

When the writers of the Constitution were initially deciding what powers and responsibilities the executive branch—headed by the president—would have, they were heavily influenced by their experience with the British government under King George III. Having seen how the king and other European monarchs tended to abuse their powers, the designers of the Constitution wanted to place strict limits on the power the president would have. At the same time, they wanted to give the president enough power to conduct foreign policy and run the federal government efficiently without being hampered by the squabbling of legislators from individual states. In other words, the Framers wanted to design an executive office that would provide effective and coherent leadership but that could never become a tyranny.

The Framers outlined the powers and duties of the executive branch in Article II of the Constitution. The specific powers given to the president are few, and the language used to describe them is often brief and vague. Specifically, the president has the authority to be commander in chief of the armed forces; to grant PARDONS; to make TREATIES; and to appoint AMBASSADORS, Supreme Court justices, and other government officers. More generally, the president is responsible for making sure "that the Laws be faithfully executed" (§ 3), though the Framers did not specify how the president was to accomplish this goal. The Framers also made no specific provisions for a staff that would assist the president; the Constitution says only that the president may "require the Opinion, in writing, of the principal Officer in each of the executive Departments, upon any Subject relating to the Duties of their respective Offices" (§ 2).

To ensure that the president could never become too powerful, the Framers made many PRESIDENTIAL POWERS dependent upon the will of Congress. For example, the president is given the power to make treaties with foreign countries, but those treaties must be approved by the Senate by a two-thirds majority. Similarly, the power of Congress is limited by the need for presidential approval. Congress can create laws, but those laws must generally be signed by the president; if the president refuses to sign a bill, it can still become law if Congress votes to override the president's VETO by a two-thirds majority. In this way, the Framers did not divide powers between the branches so much as they required the separate branches to share power, resulting in a complex system of checks and balances that prevents any one branch from gaining power over the others.

Modern presidents do have greater powers than did their predecessors, as the executive branch has grown over the years to take on more tasks and responsibilities. For the most part, however, the power of the executive branch at any given time has depended on the leadership skills of the current president; the particular events and crises faced by the president; and the country's desire for, or resistance to, strong executive branch power at that point in history. Though the executive branch does have specific legal powers, the principal power of each president is simply that individual's ability to persuade others—primarily those in Congress—to follow recommendations. Whereas early presidents were selected by a small number of electors, modern presidents are selected by hundreds of ELECTORS who represent citizens nationwide; as a result, they have the advantage of a popular mandate, giving them a bully pulpit that no member of Congress can match.

President Bill Clinton and Vice President Al Gore met with congressional Democrats in 1994. The power of a president can be measured by his or her ability to persuade Congress to promote the agenda of the president and the executive branch.

DIANA WALKER/THE GAMMA LIAISON NETWORK

Divisions of the Executive Branch

The lack of specific, detailed language in the Constitution describing the power and responsibilities of the executive branch has given presidents a great deal of flexibility to increase its size and scope over the years, in terms of both the range of its authority and the number of people, offices, and agencies employed to carry out its responsibilities. Today, the executive branch consists of well over 3 million people who work in one of three general areas: the Executive Office of the President (EOP); the CABINET and fourteen executive departments; and an extensive collection of federal agencies and corporations responsible for specific areas of the government, such as the ENVIRONMENTAL PROTECTION AGENCY and the U.S. Postal Service.

Executive Office of the President The Executive Office of the President is not a single office or department, but a collection of agencies that are all directly responsible for helping the president to deal with Congress and manage the larger executive branch. Specific elements have changed over the years; currently, the EOP consists of nine separate divisions: the White House Office, Office of Management and Budget (OMB), Council of Economic Advisers, National Security Council (NSC), Office of Policy Development, Office of the U.S. Trade Representative, Council on Environmental Quality, Office of Science and Technology Policy, and Office of Administration.

In contrast to modern presidents, early presidents had few people to help them, because the Constitution contained no specific provision or allowance for presidential staff. As a result, presidents became overworked and exhausted. THOMAS JEFFERSON, for example, wrote that the presidency "brings nothing but unceasing drudgery and daily loss of friends." In many cases, presidents used their own money to hire their sons, nephews, or in-laws to work as clerks or secretaries. In 1825, President JAMES MONROE requested that Congress appropriate funds for presidential staff, but Congress was unwilling to spend the money. It was not until 1857 that Congress approved a specific appropriation for the president to hire a private secretary. Throughout the rest of the nineteenth and early twentieth centuries, Congress slowly appropriated more money for presidential staff, allowing the president to hire a greater number of secretaries, clerks, and other assistants, such as stenographers and messengers.

The crisis of the Great Depression in the 1930s created a need for the presidential staff to be fundamentally reorganized and expanded. Whereas presidents of the nineteenth century had functioned with very limited powers, FRANKLIN D. ROOSEVELT took on a much stronger role, developing his collection of New Deal programs to try to grapple with the tremendous social and economic problems facing the country. These programs resulted in a much larger and more complex federal bureaucracy that was difficult to manage, leading Roosevelt to create the Committee on Administrative Management, popularly known as the Brownlow Committee. Headed by Louis Brownlow, the task of the Brownlow Committee was to study the organization of the executive branch and to suggest solutions to the problem of administrative management.

The Brownlow report, completed in 1937, made several recommendations, including the creation of the Executive Office of the President, which would bring together agencies concerned with executive branch activities, such as budgeting, efficiency, personnel, and planning. Though Congress rejected other proposals contained in the Brownlow report, it approved the creation of the EOP, by passing the Reorganization Act in April 1939 (3 U.S.C.A. § 106, 31 U.S.C.A. §§ 701, 1101). As a result, key managerial agencies, such as the Bureau of the Budget and the National Resources Planning Board, were moved into the EOP; the benefit of this move was that crucial management functions could be performed by staff working directly under the president, completing the routine tasks necessary for the government to function. Though the specific elements of the EOP have changed since Roosevelt's presidency, the Brownlow report laid the foundations for the basic administrative structure that allows presidents to manage the numerous and diverse parts of the executive branch.

The Cabinet and Executive Departments The cabinet consists of the president, the VICE PRESIDENT, the heads of the fourteen executive departments, and any other government officials the president wishes to include, such as the head of the OMB or the head of the NSC. In theory, cabinet members are supposed to serve as expert advisers to the president, but in practice, they more often operate as advocates for their department and are seldom involved in actual presidential decision making.

The Constitution makes no specific reference to a president's cabinet; rather, the cabinet is an institution that has evolved over the years. The first executive departments (the Departments of State, War, and the Treasury) were created in 1789 by Washington, who frequently held conferences with their heads (Jefferson,

The cabinet consists of the heads of executive agencies, usually the president's closest advisors. Bill Clinton's first cabinet meeting in January 1993 included (from left) Health Secretary Donna Shalala, Interior Secretary Bruce Babbitt, Secretary of State Warren Christopher, the president, Defense Secretary Les Aspin, the late Commerce Secretary Ron Brown, Transportation Secretary Federico Pena, and EPA Administrator Carol Browner.

Henry Knox, and ALEXANDER HAMILTON, respectively). By 1793, James Madison was using the term *cabinet* to refer to these conferences. The name and the institution stuck, and the cabinet became a fixed element of the executive branch.

Presidents have used their cabinets in widely different ways. In the nineteenth century, cabinet appointments were often made for political reasons, rather than because a president knew or trusted the particular individuals selected. As a result, some presidents had trouble controlling their cabinet, and others met with their cabinet only infrequently. ANDREW JACKSON, for example, virtually ignored his official cabinet in favor of his kitchen cabinet, a close circle of personal friends whom he trusted for information and advice. In the twentieth century, cabinets have most often served as a forum for the president to discuss issues and collect opinions; rarely, if ever, have they served as a decision-making body. Instead, the White House staff members frequently function as primary advisers to the president.

The largest organizational units within the executive branch are the fourteen executive departments: AGRICULTURE, COMMERCE, DEFENSE, EDUCATION, ENERGY, HEALTH AND HUMAN SERVICES, HOUSING AND URBAN DEVELOPMENT, INTERIOR, JUSTICE, LABOR, STATE, TRANSPORTATION, the TREASURY, and VETERANS AFFAIRS. These departments, which vary greatly in size and function, are responsible for administering the great majority of the federal government's activities and programs.

Agencies and Corporations The executive branch includes a large number of AGENCIES for which the president is responsible. Some of

these agencies function independently; others are connected to an executive department but may still function as a largely autonomous unit. These agencies manage specific areas of government operations and have little in common except that they lie outside of the traditional management structure of the executive departments. In general, they come in three types: regulatory agencies, independent executive agencies, and government corporations.

Regulatory agencies and commissions control certain economic activities and consumer affairs. These agencies include the SECURITIES AND EXCHANGE COMMISSION and the Occupational Safety and Health Administration. Regulatory agencies and commissions are created by Congress when members believe that certain economic or commercial activities need to be regulated. They accomplish the task of REGULATION in various ways, depending on their mandate from Congress. Typical methods of regulation include requiring licensing for specific professions and requiring products to be labeled accurately. Some regulatory agencies operate independently, some are governed by bipartisan commissions, and some report to an executive department.

Independent executive agencies are not part of any executive department; rather, they report directly to the president. These agencies include the National Aeronautics and Space Administration (NASA) and the GENERAL SERVICES ADMINISTRATION. Frequently, Congress makes such agencies independent so that they can operate without the burden of bureaucratic regulations or the influence of particular executive departments. For example, NASA was made an independent agency so that it could be created more quickly, function more freely, and avoid the demands and influence of the Defense Department.

Government corporations are a unique type of agency in that they function like businesses, providing necessary public services that would be too expensive or unprofitable for private companies to provide. They include the U.S. Postal Service; Amtrak; and the TENNESSEE VALLEY AUTHORITY, which was created to develop electric power in the Tennessee Valley region. Corporations have more independence than do agencies of any other type. They can buy and sell real estate, and they can sue and be sued. They are not dependent on annual appropriations from Congress, and they retain their own earnings. Congress does provide long-term funding for government corporations, however, so it retains a certain amount of control over their operations.

CROSS-REFERENCES
Administrative Agency; Congress of the United States; Constitution of the United States; Federal Budget; Separation of Powers.

EXECUTIVE ORDERS ◫ Presidential policy directives that implement or interpret a federal statute, a constitutional provision, or a treaty. ◫

The president's power to issue executive orders comes from Congress and the U.S. Constitution. Executive orders differ from presidential PROCLAMATIONS, which are used largely for ceremonial and honorary purposes such as declaring National Newspaper Carrier Appreciation Day.

Executive orders do not require congressional approval. Thus, the PRESIDENT can use them to set policy while avoiding public debate and opposition. Presidents have used executive orders to direct a range of activities, including establishing migratory bird refuges; putting Japanese Americans in internment camps during World War II; discharging civilian government employees who had been disloyal, following World War II; enlarging national forests; prohibiting racial discrimination in housing; pardoning Vietnam War draft evaders; giving federal workers the right to bargain collectively; keeping the federal workplace drug free; and sending U.S. troops to Bosnia.

Historically, executive orders related to routine administrative matters and to the internal operations of federal agencies, such as amending Civil Service Rules and overseeing the administration of public lands. More recently, presidents have used executive orders to carry out legislative policies and programs. As a result, executive orders have become a critical tool in presidential policy making. For example, President JOHN F. KENNEDY used an executive order to eliminate racial DISCRIMINATION in federally funded housing (Exec. Order No. 11,063, 3 C.F.R. 652 [1959–1963], *reprinted in* 42 U.S.C.A. § 1982 app. at 6-8 [1982]); President LYNDON B. JOHNSON acted through an executive order to prohibit discrimination in government contractors' hiring practices (Exec. Order No. 11,246, 3 C.F.R. 339 [1964–1965], *reprinted in* 42 U.S.C.A. § 2000e app. at 28-31 [1982], *amended by* Exec. Order No. 11,375, 3 C.F.R. 684 [1966–1970], *superseded by* Exec. Order No. 11,478, 3 C.F.R. 803 [1966–1970], *reprinted in* 42 U.S.C.A. § 2000e app. at 31-33 [1982]); and President RICHARD M. NIXON used an executive order to set a ninety-day freeze on all prices, rents, wages, and salaries in reaction to rising inflation and unemployment (Exec. Order No. 11,615, 3 C.F.R. 602 [1971–1975], *amended by*

Exec. Order No. 11,617, 3 C.F.R. 609 [1971–1975], *superseded by* Exec. Order No. 11,627, 3 C.F.R. 621 [1971–1975]).

Most executive orders are issued under specific statutory authority from Congress and have the force and effect of law. Such executive orders usually impose sanctions, determine legal rights, limit AGENCY discretion, and require immediate compliance. FEDERAL COURTS consider such orders to be the equivalent of federal statutes. In addition, regulations enacted to carry out these executive orders have the status of law as long as they reasonably relate to the statutory authority. An administrative action carried out under a valid executive order is similar to an agency action carried out under a federal statute. In each case, the agency's authority to enact rules and issue orders comes from Congress.

Absent specific statutory authority, an executive order may have the force and effect of law if Congress has acquiesced in a long-standing executive practice that is well-known to it. For example, in *Dames v. Regan*, 453 U.S. 654, 101 S. Ct. 2972, 69 L. Ed. 2d 918 (1981), the U.S. Supreme Court upheld various executive orders that suspended claims of U.S. nationals arising out of the Iranian hostage crisis, citing Congress's acquiescence in a 180-year-old practice of settling U.S. citizens' claims against foreign governments by executive agreement. In describing the situation before it, the Court stated,

> [W]e freely confess that we are obviously deciding only one more episode in the never-ending tension between the President exercising the executive authority in a world that presents each day some new challenge with which he must deal and the Constitution under which we all live and which no one disputes embodies some sort of system of checks and balances.

Executive orders may also be authorized by the president's independent constitutional authority (*Cunningham v. Neagle*, 135 U.S. 1, 10 S. Ct. 658, 34 L. Ed. 55 [1890]). Various clauses of the U.S. Constitution have been cited to support the issuance of executive orders. Among them are the Vestiture Clause, which states, "The executive Power shall be vested in a President of the United States of America" (art. II, § 1, cl. 1); the Take Care Clause, which states that the president "shall take Care that the Laws be faithfully executed" (art. II, § 3); and the Commander in Chief Clause, which states that the president "shall be Commander in Chief of the Army and Navy of the United

An example of an executive order

Executive Order 12428 of June 28, 1983

PRESIDENT'S COMMISSION ON INDUSTRIAL COMPETITIVENESS

By the authority vested in me as President by the Constitution and laws of the United States of America, and in order to establish, in accordance with the provisions of the Federal Advisory Committee Act, as amended (5 U.S.C. App. I), an advisory committee on industrial competitiveness, it is hereby ordered as follows:

Section 1. *Establishment.* (a) There is established the President's Commission on Industrial Competitiveness. The Commission shall be composed of no more than twenty-five members appointed or designated by the President. These members shall have particular knowledge and expertise concerning the technological factors affecting the ability of United States firms to meet international competition at home and abroad. Members appointed from the private sector shall represent elements of industry, commerce, and labor most affected by high technology, or academic institutions prominent in the field of high technology.

(b) The President shall designate a Chairman from among the members of the Commission.

Sec. 2. *Functions.* The Commission shall review means of increasing the long-term competitiveness of United States industries at home and abroad, with particular emphasis on high technology, and provide appropriate advice to the President, through the Cabinet Council on Commerce and Trade, and the Department of Commerce.

Sec. 3. *Administration.* (a) The heads of Executive agencies shall, to the extent permitted by law, provide the Commission such information as it may require for purposes of carrying out its functions.

(b) Members of the Commission shall serve without compensation for their work on the Commission. However, members appointed from among private citizens of the United States may be allowed travel expenses, including per diem in lieu of subsistence, to the extent permitted by law and to the extent funds are available therefor.

(c) The Secretary of Commerce shall, to the extent permitted by law and subject to the availability of funds, provide the Commission with such administrative services, facilities, staff and other support services as may be necessary for the effective performance of its functions.

Sec. 4. *General.* (a) Notwithstanding any other Executive Order, the functions of the President under the Federal Advisory Committee Act, as amended, except that of reporting to the Congress, which are applicable to the Commission, shall be performed by the Secretary of Commerce, in accordance with guidelines and procedures established by the Administrator of General Services.

(b) The Commission shall terminate on September 30, 1984, unless sooner extended.

[Ronald Reagan]

THE WHITE HOUSE,
June 28, 1983.

States, and of the Militia of the several States, when called into the actual Service of the United States" (art. II, § 2, cl. 1).

Executive orders often omit citing a specific constitutional provision as authority. For example, Executive Order No. 11,246 (3 C.F.R. 339 [1964–1965 Comp.]), which prohibits discrimination in federal employment, simply states, "Under and by virtue of the authority vested in me as President of the United States by the Constitution and statutes of the United States, it is ordered as follows . . ."

Some executive orders issued pursuant to the president's independent constitutional authority have been criticized as implementing what has been called essentially executive managerial policy. Although this type of order is directed to public officials, it may also affect private interests, through the actions of such officials. For example, Executive Order No. 11,246, which prohibits discrimination in federal procurement and employment, affects the interests of federal contractors and their employees; Executive Order No. 10,988 (3 C.F.R. 521 [1959–1963 Comp.]), which extends COLLECTIVE BARGAINING to the federal workforce, affects federal workers; and Executive Order No. 12,291 (3 C.F.R. 127 [1982]), which imposes controls on administrative rule making, affects individuals who are subject to administrative regulations.

Lawsuits brought to force federal agencies to comply with executive orders are usually dismissed by the courts on the ground that the orders do not provide a CAUSE OF ACTION (a right to judicial relief). For example, in *Acevedo v. Nassau County*, 500 F.2d 1078 (2d Cir. 1974), low-income minority groups claimed that the GENERAL SERVICES ADMINISTRATION had violated Executive Order No. 11,512 (35 Fed. Reg. 3,979 [1970]) by planning a federal office building without considering the adequacy of low-income housing in the area. The federal court of appeals refused to decide the claim because the plaintiffs lacked STANDING (a legally protectible interest). In *Manhattan-Bronx Postal Union v. Gronouski*, 350 F.2d 451 (D.C. Cir. 1965), *cert. denied*, 382 U.S. 978, 86 S. Ct. 548, 15 L. Ed. 2d 469 (1966), the court denied a claim against the postmaster general for violating Executive Order No. 10,988 (3 C.F.R. 521 [1959–1963]), because the president did not grant a RIGHT OF ACTION. In *Independent Meat Packers Ass'n v. Butz*, 526 F.2d 228 (8th Cir. 1975), *cert. denied*, *National Ass'n of Meat Purveyors v. Butz*, 424 U.S. 966, 96 S. Ct. 1461, 47 L. Ed. 2d 733 (1976), the appellate court stated that to infer a cause of action would create "a serious risk that a series of protracted lawsuits brought by persons with little at stake would paralyze the rulemaking functions of federal administrative agencies."

Similarly, the courts generally reject claims against private defendants for violations of executive orders. For example, in *Cohen v. Illinois Institute of Technology*, 524 F.2d 818 (7th Cir. 1975), *cert. denied*, 425 U.S. 943, 96 S. Ct. 1683, 48 L. Ed. 2d 187 (1976), the appellate court denied a professor's claim against a university to recover damages for sex discrimination in violation of Executive Order No. 11,246, stating that the executive order could not give rise to an independent private cause of action.

To have the effect of law, executive orders must appear in the *Federal Register*, the daily publication of federal rules and regulations. Executive orders are also compiled annually and published in the *Code of Federal Regulations*. Selected orders are published with related statutes in *U.S. Code Annotated* and *U.S. Code Service*.

Executive orders have been used to influence issues in hundreds of areas. War-related activities are among the most frequently addressed. For example, in September 1939, President Franklin D. Roosevelt prescribed regulations governing the enforcement of the neutrality of the United States "in the war now existing between Germany and France; Poland; and the United Kingdom, India, Australia, and New Zealand" (Exec. Order No. 8,233, 4 Fed. Reg. 3,822). By February 1942, the United States had joined World War II and Roosevelt had ordered the confinement of Japanese Americans to internment camps following the bombing of Pearl Harbor in January 1941 (Exec. Order No. 9,066, 7 Fed. Reg. 1,407). In March 1947, following the war, President HARRY S. TRUMAN established loyalty review boards to discharge civilian government employees who had been disloyal during the war (Exec. Order No. 9835, 3 C.F.R. 627 (1943–1948), *revoked by* Exec. Order No. 10,450, 3 C.F.R. 936 (1949–1953). In January 1977, following the Vietnam War, President JIMMY CARTER directed the U.S. attorney general to cease investigating and indicting Vietnam War draft evaders (Exec. Order No. 11,967, 42 Fed. Reg. 4,393). In December 1995, President BILL CLINTON ordered the U.S. reserve armed forces into active duty to augment the active armed forces' operations in and around the former Yugoslavia (Bosnia) (Exec. Order No. 12,982, 60 Fed. Reg. 63,895).

CROSS-REFERENCES

Administrative Acts; Administrative Agency; Constitution of the United States; Federal Register; Japanese American Evacuation Cases; Presidential Powers.

EXECUTIVE PRIVILEGE 📖 The right of the PRESIDENT of the United States to withhold information from CONGRESS or the courts. 📖

Historically, presidents have claimed the right of executive privilege when they have information they want to keep confidential, either because it would jeopardize national security or because disclosure would be contrary to the interests of the EXECUTIVE BRANCH.

The Constitution does not specifically enumerate the president's right to executive privilege; rather, the concept has evolved over the years as presidents have claimed it. As the courts have ruled on these claims, their decisions have refined the notion of executive privilege and have clarified the instances in which it can be invoked. The courts have ruled that it is implicit in the constitutional SEPARATION OF POWERS, which assigns discrete powers and rights to the legislative, executive, and judicial branches of government. In reality, however, the three branches enjoy not separate but shared powers, and thus are occasionally in conflict. When the president's wish to keep certain information confidential causes such a conflict, the president might claim the right of executive privilege.

The term *executive privilege* emerged in the 1950s, but presidents since GEORGE WASHINGTON have claimed the right to withhold information from Congress and the courts. The issue first arose in 1792, when a congressional committee requested information from Washington regarding a disastrous expedition of General Arthur St. Clair against American Indian tribes along the Ohio River, which resulted in the loss of an entire division of the U.S. Army. Washington, concerned about how to respond to this request and about the legal PRECEDENT his actions would set, called a CABINET meeting. Although no official record was kept of the proceedings, THOMAS JEFFERSON described the deliberations in his diary. The participants, Jefferson wrote, concluded that Congress had the right to request information from the president, and that the president "ought to communicate such papers as the public good would permit & ought to refuse those the disclosure of which would injure the public." In the case at hand, they agreed that "there was not a paper which might not be properly produced," so Washington provided all the documents that Congress had requested. This event, though notable as the first recorded deliberation concerning executive privilege, did not carry precedential value until after 1957, when Jefferson's notes were discovered. In 1958, Attorney General William P. Rogers cited Jefferson's remarks as precedent for an absolute

presidential privilege. Legal scholar Raoul Berger declaimed Rogers's arguments as "at best self-serving assertions by one of the claimants in a constitutional boundary dispute." Instead, Berger argued, Washington's willingness to turn over the requested documents shows his recognition of Congress's right to such materials.

In subsequent incidents, however, Washington and his successors did choose to withhold requested information from Congress, citing various reasons. In 1794, for example, the Senate requested from Washington the correspondence of Gouverneur Morris, the U.S. ambassador to France, who was suspected of aiding the French aristocrats against the revolutionaries despite the United States' official stance of neutrality. Washington provided the letters, but he censored them first, acting on the advice of officials such as Attorney General William Bradford, who said that the president should "communicate to the Senate such parts of the said correspondence as upon examination he shall deem safe and proper to disclose: withholding all such, as any circumstances, may render improper to be communicated." The following year, Washington refused to provide the House with information relating to Ambassador JOHN JAY's negotiation of a treaty with Great Britain, arguing that the House had no constitutional right to participate in the TREATY making process and so had no right to request materials associated with it.

The judiciary, like Congress, can also request information from the president. When AARON BURR was indicted on charges of TREASON, for example, both Congress and the judiciary asked President Jefferson to provide correspondence from General James Wilkinson, a Burr confidant and aide. Jefferson argued that it was wrong to ask him to provide private letters, written to him, containing confidential information. Chief Justice JOHN MARSHALL, presiding over the Burr trial, *United States v. Burr*, 25 Fed. Cas. 187, 191 (C.C. Va. 1807), did not ultimately force Jefferson to turn over each requested document, but he did maintain the right of the judiciary to request such information from the president, writing that "the President of the United States may be . . . required to produce any paper in his possession" and adding that "[t]he occasion for demanding it ought, in such a case, [to] be very strong, and to be fully shown to the court before its production could be insisted on."

As the power of the president's office grew over the nineteenth and twentieth centuries, presidents attempted more frequently to use

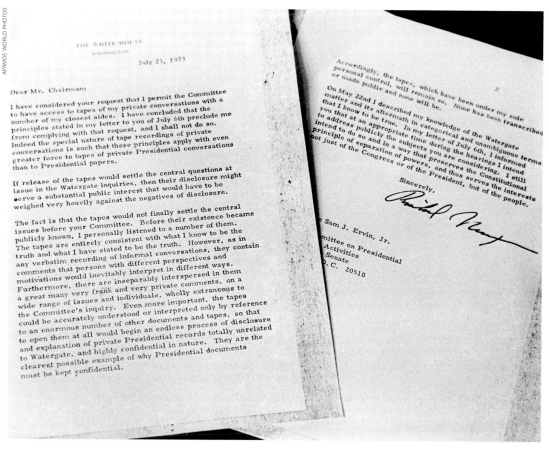

THE WHITE HOUSE
WASHINGTON

July 23, 1973

Dear Mr. Chairman:

I have considered your request that I permit the Committee to have access to tapes of my private conversations with a number of my closest aides. I have concluded that the principles stated in my letter to you of July 6th preclude me from complying with that request, and I shall not do so. Indeed the special nature of tape recordings of private conversations is such that these principles apply with even greater force to tapes of private Presidential conversations than to Presidential papers.

If release of the tapes would settle the central questions at issue in the Watergate inquiries, then their disclosure might serve a substantial public interest that would have to be weighed very heavily against the negatives of disclosure.

The fact is that the tapes would not finally settle the central issues before your Committee. Before their existence became publicly known, I personally listened to a number of them. The tapes are entirely consistent with what I know to be the truth and what I have stated to be the truth. However, as in any verbatim recording of informal conversations, they contain comments that persons with different perspectives and motivations would inevitably interpret in different ways. Furthermore, there are inseparably interspersed in them a great many very frank and very private comments, on a wide range of issues and individuals, wholly extraneous to the Committee's inquiry. Even more important, the tapes could be accurately understood or interpreted only by reference to an enormous number of other documents and tapes, so that to open them at all would begin an endless process of disclosure and explanation of private Presidential records totally unrelated to Watergate, and highly confidential in nature. They are the clearest possible example of why Presidential documents must be kept confidential.

Accordingly, the tapes, which have been under my sole personal control, will remain so. None has been transcribed or made public and none will be.

On May 22nd I described my knowledge of the Watergate matter and its aftermath in categorical and unambiguous terms that I know to be true. In my letter of July 6th, I informed you that at an appropriate time during the hearings I intend to address publicly the subjects you are considering. I still intend to do so and in a way that preserves the Constitutional principle of separation of powers, and thus serves the interests not just of the Congress or of the President, but of the people.

Sincerely,

Richard Nixon

Sam J. Ervin, Jr.
[Com]mittee on Presidential
Activities
Senate
[D].C. 20510

President Richard Nixon cited executive privilege when he refused to release tapes of his conversations to the Senate committee investigating Watergate.

executive privilege to shield themselves and their subordinate officials from investigation. In 1836, for example, a House committee requested personnel rosters and salary information from President ANDREW JACKSON. He declined to fulfill the request, stating that he would "repudiate all attempts to invade the just rights of Executive Departments, and of the individuals composing the same." Similarly, in 1909, President THEODORE ROOSEVELT took personal possession of Federal Trade Commission documents requested by Congress, claiming IMMUNITY for the materials since they were under presidential control. In both cases, Congress failed to pursue its investigations.

During the Eisenhower presidency, executive privilege underwent three major developments. First, in the area of national security, the Supreme Court ruled in *United States v. Reynolds*, 345 U.S. 1, 73 S. Ct. 528, 97 L. Ed. 727 (1953), that the military may refuse to divulge requested information when national security is at stake. While warning that such requests could not be simply left to the "caprice of executive officers," the Court maintained that there would be times when "there is a reasonable danger that the compulsion of the evidence will expose military matters which, in the interest of national security, should not be divulged."

The second development in the use of executive privilege became known as the candid interchange doctrine. In an attempt to shield the executive branch from the bullying investigative tactics of Senator JOSEPH R. MCCARTHY, President DWIGHT D. EISENHOWER directed that executive privilege be applied to all communications and conversations between executive branch employees; without the assurance of confidentiality, he claimed, they could not be completely candid. This doctrine marked a tremendous change in the scope of executive privilege, extending it from the president and the president's top advisers to the myriad offices and agencies that make up the executive branch.

Finally, the third development in executive privilege resulted from *Kaiser Aluminum & Chemical Corp. v. United States*, 157 F. Supp. 939, 141 Ct. Cl. 38 (Cl. Ct. 1958). In this case, Kaiser sought documents containing executive branch employees' opinions regarding the sale of aluminum manufacturing plants. The court ruled that it was ultimately up to the courts "to determine executive privilege in litigation," adding that "the privilege for intradepartmental advice would very rarely have the importance of diplomacy or security." The opinion in this case contains the first recorded use of the phrase *executive privilege*.

The use of executive privilege decreased during the 1960s, but it became the crux of the constitutional crisis created by WATERGATE, a series of scandals involving President RICHARD M. NIXON and his associates. When Congress sought to obtain White House tapes containing Oval Office conversations, Nixon refused to turn them over, claiming that the tapes were subject to absolute executive privilege and asserting that the judiciary had no authority to order their production or inspection. Eventually the dispute reached the Supreme Court, where, in *United States v. Nixon*, 418 U.S. 683, 94 S. Ct. 3090, 41 L. Ed. 2d 1039 (1974), the Court ruled against Nixon. While acknowledging the importance of the president's claims, the Court stated that "neither the doctrine of separation of powers, nor the need for confidentiality of high level communications, without more, can sustain an absolute, unqualified presidential privilege of immunity from judicial process under all circumstances." In its opinion, therefore, the Court explicitly recognized the president's authority to assert executive privilege, but ruled that the use of executive privilege is limited, not absolute. Furthermore, the Court maintained that the judiciary, not the president, has the power to determine the applicability of executive privilege. While the Court affirmed the use of executive privilege, therefore, it determined that in this case, the right of the U.S. people to full disclosure outweighed the president's right to secrecy. This momentous decision soon led to Nixon's resignation from the office of president. See also UNITED STATES V. NIXON.

EXECUTORS AND ADMINISTRATORS

📖 Those who are designated by the terms of a WILL or appointed by a court of PROBATE to manage the ASSETS and LIABILITIES of the ESTATE of the deceased. 📖

When a person dies leaving property, that property, called an estate, is usually settled or administered under the supervision of special courts. Depending on the state, those courts are called probate, surrogate, or orphans' courts. These are typically county courts with jurisdiction and powers defined by state laws.

States have required court supervision for the settlement of estates for a number of reasons. Courts ensure that the assets of an estate will be properly collected, preserved, and assessed; that all relevant DEBTS of the deceased and taxes will be paid; and that remaining assets will be distributed to the HEIRS according to the provisions of the will or applicable laws.

The duty of settling and distributing the estate of a DECEDENT (one who has died) is assigned to PERSONAL REPRESENTATIVES of the

decedent. A personal representative may be an executor (male or female) or executrix (female), or administrator (male or female) or administratrix (female). An executor or executrix is the person named in a will to administer the estate. An administrator or administratrix is a person appointed by the court to administer the estate of someone who died without a will.

Executors and administrators act as OFFICERS OF THE COURT because they derive their authority from court appointments. They are also considered the FIDUCIARIES, or trusted representatives, of the deceased. As such, they have an absolute duty to properly administer the estate solely for its BENEFICIARIES.

Probate is the process by which the court establishes that a will is valid. The first step in the probate process is to file the will in the appropriate court with a petition to admit it to probate and to grant LETTERS TESTAMENTARY to the person designated as executor of the will. Letters testamentary are the formal instruments of authority and appointment given to an executor by the probate court, empowering that person to act as an executor.

If an executor is unable or refuses to serve, if there is no will, or if the will is deemed to be inauthentic or invalid, the court appoints an administrator. Letters of administration are the formal court papers that authorize a person to serve as an administrator of an estate that lacks a valid will.

No administrator is needed if a person dies without a will, possesses no assets, and owes no debts. Where a person dies leaving an estate, but there are no known living heirs, the state usually receives the property under the doctrine of ESCHEAT. In such cases, administration is not required, unless debts must be paid from the estate's assets before the state takes its interest.

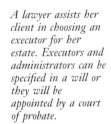

A lawyer assists her client in choosing an executor for her estate. Executors and administrators can be specified in a will or they will be appointed by a court of probate.

Liability Considerations for Executors and Administrators

Your Aunt Lillian has just called to ask if you will serve as executor for her estate after her death. You are honored that she has considered you for this important responsibility, but you also know that there are risks associated with becoming an executor or administrator.

The most potentially damaging risk is liability for actions undertaken on behalf of the estate. The estate's beneficiaries, who are likely your relatives, may sue you if any of the following situations occur:

- You fail to properly secure and insure the assets of the estate, and it suffers a loss as a result.
- You diminish the estate through imprudent investments or inadequate record keeping.
- You fail to pay taxes on the estate, in which case you may be personally liable for interest and penalties.
- You sell an asset of the estate without authority to do so.
- You delay settlement of the estate unnecessarily or are tardy in executing important transactions.
- You engage in actions that constitute a conflict of interest.

- You improperly delegate decisions to others who have no legal authority over the estate.
- You approve a coexecutor's or coadministrator's breach of duty.

Fortunately, you can usually avoid these problems by taking a few simple steps:

- Most important of all, stay in touch with the estate's beneficiaries. Keep them informed of your actions and the general condition of the estate.
- Promptly meet all required deadlines.
- Maintain accurate records of all estate transactions and document all decisions made. Keep receipts of distributions made to beneficiaries.
- Obtain the written consent of all beneficiaries when changing estate investments.
- Obtain a court order from the probate court for significant estate transactions. Petition the court if the will is unclear regarding particular items.
- Keep affairs of the estate confidential.
- Avoid conflicts of interest. Do not put your own interests ahead of the interests of the estate's beneficiaries, and do not use assets of the estate for your own gain or profit.

By using common sense and following these guidelines, you can effectively settle an estate and avoid potential lawsuits.

The administration of a decedent's estate is controlled by statute. The probate court is authorized by statute to determine the fundamental facts essential to the administration of an estate.

As a general rule, the place of the decedent's last legal RESIDENCE determines which probate court shall have JURISDICTION over settlement of the estate.

Appointment of Representatives

Executors A person making a will—called a TESTATOR—should find out whether her or his choice is willing to serve in that role. This small but sensible courtesy can prevent the spending of needless time and money in administration of the estate. A person named as an executor in a will is free to accept or reject the position within a reasonable time following the testator's death. If it is rejected, the court then must appoint another representative, causing a delay in the settlement of the estate and its final distribution to the heirs, and incurring greater legal fees for the estate.

Many people choose their surviving spouse as executor, since that person usually has the greatest knowledge of their financial affairs as well as the family situation. Some people name several persons to serve as coexecutors, to ensure that the estate will be handled fairly and honestly. Frequently, those making a will choose a professional such as an attorney or trust company to act as a coexecutor and to assist with complex issues of the estate.

It is also prudent for a testator to name an alternative executor to serve in the event the designated executor is unable or refuses to serve. A testator may change an executor as long as the change is recorded properly in the will.

Anyone who is capable of making a will is capable of becoming an executor. Courts can disqualify as executors persons who are legally incompetent or unsuitable. When this occurs, the court appoints either an alternative executor, if the will has named one, or an administrator. A person cannot be disqualified as an executor merely because he or she might inherit part of the estate.

A person named as an executor is free to accept or reject the position within a reasonable time following the testator's death.

Administrators A court usually appoints an administrator when a person dies without leaving a will. In most jurisdictions, courts are required by statute to name the spouse of the decedent as administrator. Where no spouse is involved, administration is usually assigned to the next of kin, such as parents, brothers and sisters, nieces and nephews, or cousins. Special laws, called statutes of DESCENT AND DISTRIBUTION, determine the next of kin who are entitled to serve as administrators.

Terms of Office As a general rule, executors and administrators are required to take an OATH as prescribed by statute before beginning their duties. The taking of the oath constitutes acceptance of the office.

In some jurisdictions, statutes require the executor or administrator of an estate to file a BOND to protect those interested in the estate. The amount of an executor's or administrator's bond will be forfeited if the representative is found to deliberately mismanage the estate.

The authority of an executor or administrator terminates only when the estate has been completely administered or the executor dies, resigns, or is suspended or removed. An executor can be removed from office for grounds specified by law, such as mismanagement, WASTE (abuse or destruction of the property), disloyalty, improper administration, NEGLIGENCE, or other misconduct in the administration of the estate. A representative can also be removed for failure to file a proper INVENTORY, accounts, or tax returns within the required time; for failure to comply with a court order requiring him or her to furnish a bond; or for bankrupting the estate. The representative should be removed where personal interests conflict with official duties or where there is such enmity between the personal representative and the beneficiaries as would or might interfere with proper management of the estate.

General Duties The general and primary duties of the administrator or executor are to administer the estate in an orderly and proper manner to the best advantage of all concerned, and to settle and distribute the assets of the estate as quickly and reasonably as is practicable.

Executors must submit the will to probate court, then dispose of the estate according to the will. Both executors and administrators must make an inventory and APPRAISAL of the estate, then file that information with the court.

Executors and administrators are held liable for the debts and taxes of the estate, as well as any losses resulting from unauthorized or improper investments of estate funds.

Executors and administrators are, as a rule, allowed a reasonable compensation for the services they perform in the administration of a decedent's estate. This right arises from and is controlled by statute, unless the will specifically provides the amount of an executor's compensation. Commissions are the most common form of compensation to executors and administrators.

EXECUTORY 📖 That which is yet to be fully executed or performed; that which remains to be carried into operation or effect; incomplete; depending upon a future performance or event. The opposite of *executed*. 📖

EXEMPLIFICATION 📖 An official copy of a document from public records, made in a form to be used as EVIDENCE, and authenticated or certified as a true copy. 📖

Such a duplicate is also referred to as an exemplified copy or a CERTIFIED COPY.

EXERCISE 📖 To put into action, practice, or force; to make use of something, such as a right or option. 📖

To exercise dominion over land is to openly indicate absolute possession and control.

To exercise discretion is to choose between doing and not doing something, the decision being based on sound judgment.

EXHAUSTION OF REMEDIES 📖 The exhaustion-of-remedies doctrine requires that procedures established by statute, COMMON LAW, CONTRACT, or custom must be initiated and followed in certain cases before an aggrieved party may seek relief from the courts. After all other available remedies have been exhausted, a lawsuit may be filed. 📖

Most commonly, exhaustion of remedies applies where an ADMINISTRATIVE AGENCY has been established by Congress to handle grievances that occur under its purview. For example, if a dispute arises over a provision in a labor contract, the parties may be required to follow specific grievance procedures administered by the NATIONAL LABOR RELATIONS BOARD (NLRB). After the parties have satisfied each requirement of the grievance process, and the NLRB has reached its final decision, they may appeal the decision to a higher tribunal.

The rationale behind requiring parties to exhaust their administrative remedies is that the agencies have the specialized personnel, experience, and expertise to sort and decide matters that arise under their JURISDICTION. Also, the doctrine of SEPARATION OF POWERS dictates that an agency created by Congress should be allowed to carry out its duties without undue interference from the judiciary.

The exhaustion-of-remedies doctrine also applies in certain classes of cases where state remedies must be exhausted before a party may pursue a case in FEDERAL COURT. In these situations, exhaustion of remedies is a rule of comity, or courtesy, by which federal courts defer to state courts to make the initial determination as to all claims, federal or state, raised in a case. For example, petitions for HABEAS CORPUS (release from unlawful imprisonment) by an inmate of a state prison are not heard by a federal court until after all state remedies are exhausted (see *Darr v. Burford*, 339 U.S. 200, 70 S. Ct. 587, 94 L. Ed. 761 [1950]).

As with most legal doctrines, there are exceptions to the exhaustion-of-remedies requirement. A party bringing a CIVIL RIGHTS action under 42 U.S.C.A. § 1983 is not required to exhaust state remedies before filing suit in federal court. In *Patsy v. Board of Regents*, 457 U.S. 496, 102 S. Ct. 2557, 73 L. Ed. 2d 172 (1982), the Supreme Court held that the plaintiff—who claimed she was denied employment by a state university because of her race and her sex—was not required to exhaust her state administrative remedies before filing her suit in federal court, because such a requirement would be inconsistent with congressional intent in passing civil rights legislation.

Similarly, a criminal defense exception has been carved out by the Court. It allows a criminal defendant to raise the defense of improper administrative procedure even in cases where the defendant failed to exhaust all available administrative remedies. For example, in *McKart v. United States*, 395 U.S. 185, 89 S. Ct. 1657, 23 L. Ed. 2d 194 (1969), the defendant—who was charged with failure to report for induction into the armed services—was allowed to claim that his draft classification was invalid even though he had failed to pursue administrative remedies.

Finally, courts may allow an exception to the exhaustion-of-remedies doctrine where administrative remedies are inadequate or would cause irreparable harm. In a case involving a claim of wrongful discharge from employment, the Supreme Court held that the plaintiff—who may have had to wait up to ten years to be heard by the administrative agency—was not required to exhaust available administrative remedies before commencing a court action (*Walker v. Southern Ry.*, 385 U.S. 196, 87 S. Ct. 365, 17 L. Ed. 2d 294 [1966]).

See also ADMINISTRATIVE LAW AND PROCEDURE.

EXHIBIT 📖 As a verb, to show or display; to offer or present for inspection. To produce anything in public, so that it may be taken into possession. To present; to offer publicly or officially; to file of record. To administer; to cause to be taken, as medicines. To submit to a court or officer in the course of proceedings.

As a noun, a paper or document produced and exhibited to a court during a trial or hear-

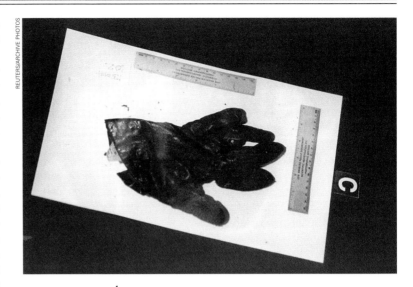

REUTERS/ARCHIVE PHOTOS

An exhibit such as this glove is tangible evidence submitted to a court for inspection during a trial.

ing, or to a person taking DEPOSITIONS, or to auditors or arbitrators as a VOUCHER, or in proof of facts, or as otherwise connected with the subject matter, and which, on being accepted, is marked for identification and annexed to the deposition, report, or other principal document, or filed of record, or otherwise made a part of the case.

A paper, document, chart, map, or the like, referred to and made a part of an AFFIDAVIT, PLEADING, or BRIEF. An item of physical, tangible evidence that is to be or has been offered to the court for inspection. 📖

EX OFFICIO 📖 [*Latin, From office.*] By virtue of the characteristics inherent in the holding of a particular office without the need of specific authorization or appointment. 📖

The phrase *ex officio* refers to powers that, while not expressly conferred upon an official, are necessarily implied in the office. A judge has *ex officio* powers of a CONSERVATOR OF THE PEACE.

EXONERATION 📖 The removal of a burden, charge, responsibility, duty, or blame imposed by law. The right of a party who is secondarily liable for a DEBT, such as a SURETY, to be reimbursed by the party with primary liability for payment of an obligation that should have been paid by the first party. 📖

EX PARTE 📖 [*Latin, On one side only.*] Done by, for, or on the application of one PARTY alone. 📖

An ex parte judicial proceeding is conducted for the benefit of only one party. Ex parte may also describe contact with a person represented by an ATTORNEY, outside the presence of the attorney. The term *ex parte* is used in a case name to signify that the suit was brought by the person whose name follows the term.

Under the FIFTH AMENDMENT to the U.S. Constitution, "No person shall . . . be deprived of life, liberty, or property, without due process of law." A bedrock feature of DUE PROCESS is fair NOTICE to parties who may be affected by legal proceedings. An ex parte judicial proceeding, conducted without notice to, and outside the presence of, affected parties, would appear to violate the Constitution. However, adequate notice of judicial proceedings to concerned parties may at times work irreparable harm to one or more of those parties. In such a case, the threatened party or parties may receive an ex parte court hearing to request temporary judicial relief without notice to, and outside the presence of, other persons affected by the hearing.

Ex parte judicial proceedings are usually reserved for urgent matters where requiring notice would subject one party to irreparable harm. For example, a person suffering abuse at the hands of a spouse or significant other may seek ex parte a TEMPORARY RESTRAINING ORDER from a court, directing the alleged abuser to stay away from him or her. Ex parte judicial proceedings are also used to stop irreparable injury to property. For example, if two neighbors, Reggie and Veronica, disagree over whose property a tree stands on, and Reggie wants to cut down the tree whereas Veronica wants to save it, Veronica can seek an ex parte HEARING before a judge. At the hearing, she will ask the judge for a temporary restraining order preventing Reggie from felling the tree. She will have to show the judge that she had no reasonable opportunity to provide Reggie with formal notice of the hearing, and that she might win the case. The court will then balance the potential hardships to Reggie and Veronica, in considering whether to grant Veronica's request.

A court order from an ex parte hearing is swiftly followed by a full hearing between the interested parties to the dispute. State and federal legislatures maintain laws allowing ex parte proceedings because such hearings balance the right to notice against the right to use the legal system to avert imminent and irreparable harm. Far from violating the Constitution, the ex parte proceeding is a lasting illustration of the elasticity of due process.

Ex parte contact occurs when an attorney communicates with another party outside the presence of that party's attorney. Ex parte contact also describes a judge who communicates with one party to a lawsuit to the exclusion of the other party or parties, or a judge who initiates discussions about a case with disinterested third parties. Canon 3(A)(4) of the American Bar Association (ABA) Model Code of Judicial Conduct discourages judges from such ex parte communications. Under rule 4.2 of the ABA Model Rules of Professional Responsibility, a lawyer should refrain from contacting a party who the lawyer knows is represented by another attorney, unless the lawyer has the consent of the other attorney or is authorized by law to do so.

In a case name, *ex parte* signifies that the suit was initiated by the person whose name follows the term. For example, *Ex parte Williams* means that the case was brought on Williams's request alone. Many JURISDICTIONS have abandoned *ex parte* in case names, preferring English over Latin terms (e.g., *Application of Williams* or *Petition of Williams*). In some jurisdictions, *ex parte* has been replaced by *in re*, which means "in the matter of" (e.g., *In re Williams*). However, most jurisdictions reserve the term *in re* for proceedings concerning property.

EXPATRIATION   📖   The voluntary act of abandoning or renouncing one's country and becoming the citizen or subject of another. 📖

EXPECTANCY 📖 A mere hope, based upon no direct provision, promise, or trust. An expectancy is the possibility of receiving a thing, rather than having a VESTED interest in it. 📖

The term has been applied to situations where an individual hopes and expects to receive something, generally property or money, but has no founded assurance of possession. A person named in a WILL as an HEIR has only an expectancy to INHERIT under the will, since there exists a possibility that the will may be altered so as to DISINHERIT him or her.

EXPLOSIVES   The law of explosives covers dangerously volatile substances, including gasoline, oil, dynamite, and blasting caps filled with highly explosive compounds. Under the police power given to the states through the TENTH AMENDMENT to the U.S. Constitution, state and local governments may regulate the storing, handling, transportation, and use of explosive substances.

All states require a person or business to obtain a permit before using explosives, such as for a fireworks display or the demolition of a building. State laws and local ordinances criminalize the unlicensed use, storage, sale, and transportation of explosives. Most states provide that unlicensed explosives may be subject to forfeiture, and their possessors subject to fines or incarceration, or both.

States delegate some explosives regulation to municipalities. A MUNICIPAL CORPORATION may enact provisions for the inspection of explosives and their storage spaces. It may also prescribe the maximum quantity of particular explosives that are allowed to be kept in a particular location.

The U.S. Congress has the authority to regulate explosives in interstate commerce. Under 18 U.S.C.A. § 841 et seq., Congress requires a LICENSE to import, manufacture, distribute, or store explosive materials that cross state lines. The alcohol, tobacco, and firearms division of the U.S. Treasury is charged with primary enforcement of the federal laws and regulations regarding explosives.

Explosives are a necessity in a developing world. They allow building contractors to excavate land and clear pathways for road building. However, explosives are inherently dangerous, and, despite strict government regulation, even the authorized use of explosives may cause injuries or property damage. When injury or damage occurs, an aggrieved person may seek redress in civil court.

Under TORT law, explosives are considered abnormally hazardous and are subject to STRICT LIABILITY standards. Under strict liability, an explosives operator may be liable for injuries resulting from an explosion regardless of NEGLIGENCE. Not all explosions give rise to this standard. Strict liability may be mandated by statute for injuries resulting from unlicensed explosions. For licensed explosions and accidental explosions, strict liability will be applied where the activity was exceptionally dangerous. For example, a landowner who stores gasoline in a densely populated residential neighborhood may be subject to strict liability, but a business that stores gasoline in an industrial area may not.

Strict liability is not imposed on most licensed explosions. A plaintiff suing for DAMAGES resulting from a licensed explosion must prove that the operator did not observe a standard of care commensurate with the danger. This can be proved by showing that the operator failed to comply with statutes or regulations. The plaintiff must also show that the explosion was the proximate dominant, producing, or moving cause for the injury or property damage.

A seller of explosives may be held liable for damage or injury resulting from their use. Manufacturers are held to a higher standard of care than wholesalers or retailers because they are usually more familiar with the formula of the explosive compound and are thus more capable of giving instructions needed for the safe handling, storage, and use of the product. Manufacturers, wholesalers, and retailers must warn buyers of an explosive's dangerous nature by labeling the packaging and including instructions. A manufacturer, wholesaler, or retailer that sells explosives in violation of a statute may be liable to subsequent purchasers

of the explosives. For example, a manufacturer or merchant that sells to a MINOR will be responsible for any injuries resulting from the explosives.

Transporters of explosives may be held liable for damage or injury caused in transit, if they are negligent. CARRIERS must exercise utmost caution in transporting explosives and follow regulations established by the states. A shipper who hires a carrier for transport may be liable for damage and injury caused by the shipment if the damage and injury were the result of the shipper's negligence. The chain of manufacturer, seller, shipper, and carrier often leads to civil court battles in which each defendant seeks to prove that the others were negligent.

As in any civil case, a defendant in an explosives case may use the defense of "contributory negligence" if the injured party was negligent in some way. For instance, a defendant may invoke contributory negligence if an operator has been adequately instructed but mishandles the explosives. In a small minority of states, contributory negligence by a plaintiff precludes any recovery. In most states, "comparative negligence" statutes allow an amount of recovery reduced by a measure of the plaintiff's negligence. For example, if the plaintiff and defendant were equally at fault, the plaintiff may recover 50 percent of the claim.

A defendant may also seek to argue "assumption of the risk." This means that the injured party was informed of risks but chose to disregard the warnings. For example, a licensed explosives operator who posted notices and warnings according to regulations may escape LIABILITY if the plaintiff ignored the signs and entered the explosion site and was subsequently injured in an explosion on the site.

Fireworks are regulated by state and local governments as explosives, or dangerously volatile substances.

BRUCE HENDERSON/STOCK BOSTON

Fireworks are a popular, colorful form of low-impact explosives whose regulation varies from state to state. Minnesota, for example, bans all fireworks except for licensed displays and toy pistols and toy guns containing a negligible amount of explosive compound (Minn. Stat. Ann. § 624.20 [West]). Other states are more permissive. Alabama, for example, allows fireworks containing up to 130 milligrams of explosive composition for aerial devices and 50 milligrams for nonaerial devices. Sparklers containing chlorate or perchlorate salts may not exceed a weight of five grams (Ala. Code § 8-17-217).

CROSS-REFERENCES

Alcohol, Tobacco, and Firearms, Bureau of; Assumption of Risk; Dominant Cause; Producing Cause; Proximate Cause.

EXPORT-IMPORT BANK OF THE UNITED STATES

The Export-Import Bank of the United States, known as Eximbank, facilitates and helps finance exports of U.S. goods and services. Eximbank has implemented a variety of programs to meet the needs of the U.S. exporting community, according to the size of the transaction. These programs take the form of direct lending, or the issuance of GUARANTEES and INSURANCE so that exporters and private banks can extend appropriate financing without incurring undue risks. The direct lending program of Eximbank is limited to larger sales of U.S. products and services around the world. The guarantees, insurance, and discount programs have been designed to assist exporters in smaller sales of products and services.

Eximbank began as the Export-Import Bank of Washington, authorized in 1934 as a banking corporation organized under the laws of the District of Columbia (Exec. Order No. 6581 [Feb. 2, 1934]), 12 C.F.R. § 401, reprinted in 12 U.S.C.A. § 635. The bank was continued as an agency of the United States by acts of Congress passed in 1935, 1937, 1939, and 1940. It was made an independent agency of the government by the Export-Import Bank Act of 1945 ([12 U.S.C.A. § 635]), which was subsequently amended in 1947 to reincorporate the bank under federal charter. The name was changed to Export-Import Bank of the United States by the Act of March 13, 1968 (82 Stat. 47).

The mission of Eximbank is to help U.S. exporters meet government-supported competition from other countries and to correct market imperfections so that commercial export financing can take place. The bank considers aiding in the export financing of U.S. goods and services when there is a reasonable assurance of repayment. Eximbank does not compete with private financing, but instead supplements it when adequate funds are not available in the private sector. As stated in the Export-Import Act of 1945, as amended, the loans provided are generally for specific purposes and at rates based on the average cost of money to the bank as well as the mandate of the bank to provide competitive financing, and offer reasonable reassurance of repayment. The act further states that financing should be provided for U.S. exports at rates and on terms that are competitive with financing provided by the principal foreign competitors of the United States. Furthermore, in authorizing loans or guarantees, account should be taken of any serious adverse effects upon the competitive position of U.S. industry, the availability of materials that are in short supply in the United States, and employment in the United States.

The bank is authorized to have outstanding at any one time dollar loans, guarantees, and insurance in an aggregate amount not to exceed $75 billion. The bank is also authorized to have a CAPITAL STOCK of $1 billion and may borrow from the U.S. Treasury up to $6 billion outstanding at any one time. Subsidy costs of the bank's programs are appropriated on an annual basis.

Eximbank operates a loan program and a guarantee program for medium- and long-term export transactions. Both programs provide up to 85 percent financing, operate on the basis of preliminary and final commitments, and are open to any responsible party. Eximbank loans also carry the minimum interest rate allowed by the Organization for Economic Cooperation and Development.

To reduce the risks of buyer DEFAULT for U.S. exporters, Eximbank offers a variety of insurance programs. These policies insure against the risk of default in export transactions and are available in a variety of plans that are tailored to the special needs of different types of exporters and financial institutions.

Eximbank offers other programs designed primarily to benefit small-business exporters, including the Working Capital Guarantee Program, a loan guarantee program designed to provide access to working capital loans from commercial lenders. The bank also sponsors the Engineering Multiplier Program, which provides financing to support feasibility studies that have the potential for generating further procurement of U.S. exports.

EXPOSITORY STATUTE

A law executed to explain the actual meaning and intent of a previously enacted statute.

EX POST FACTO LAWS 📖 [*Latin, "After-the-fact" laws.*] Laws that provide for the infliction of punishment upon a person for some prior act that, at the time it was committed, was not illegal. 📖

Ex post facto laws retroactively change the rules of EVIDENCE in a criminal case, retroactively alter the definition of a crime, retroactively increase the punishment for a criminal act, or punish conduct that was legal when committed. They are prohibited by Article I, Section 10, Clause 1, of the U.S. Constitution. An ex post facto law is considered a hallmark of tyranny because it deprives people of a sense of what behavior will or will not be punished and allows for random punishment at the whim of those in power.

The prohibition of ex post facto laws was an imperative in colonial America. The Framers of the Constitution understood the importance of such a prohibition, considering the historical tendency of government leaders to abuse power. As ALEXANDER HAMILTON observed, "[I]t is easy for men . . . to be zealous advocates for the rights of the citizens when they are invaded by others, and as soon as they have it in their power, to become the invaders themselves." The desire to thwart abuses of power also inspired the Framers of the Constitution to prohibit BILLS OF ATTAINDER, which are laws that inflict punishment on named individuals or on easily ascertainable members of a group without the benefit of a trial. Both ex post facto laws and bills of attainder deprive those subject to them of DUE PROCESS OF LAW—that is, of NOTICE and an opportunity to be heard before being deprived of life, liberty, or property.

The Constitution did not provide a definition for ex post facto laws, so the courts have been forced to attach meaning to the concept. In *Calder v. Bull*, 3 U.S. (3 Dall.) 386, 1 L. Ed. 648 (1798), the U.S. Supreme Court provided a first and lasting interpretation of the Ex Post Facto Clause. The focus of the *Calder* case was a May 1795 resolution of the Connecticut legislature that specifically set aside a March 1793 PROBATE court decree. The resolution allowed the defeated party in the probate contest a new hearing on the matter of the WILL. The Court in *Calder* ruled that the Connecticut resolution did not constitute an ex post facto law because it did not affect a VESTED property right. In other words, no one had complete ownership of the property in the will, so depriving persons of the property did not violate the ex post facto clause. The Court went on to list situations that it believed the clause did address. It opined that an ex post facto law was one that rendered new or additional criminal punishment for a prior act or changed the rules of evidence in a criminal case.

In *Calder*, the Court's emphasis on CRIMINAL LAWS seemed to exclude CIVIL LAWS from a definition of ex post facto—that is, it implied that if a statute did not inflict criminal punishment, it did not violate the Ex Post Facto Clause. Twelve years later, the U.S. Supreme Court held that a civil statute that revoked land grants to purchasers violated the Ex Post Facto Clause (*Fletcher v. Peck*, 10 U.S. (6 Cranch) 87, 3 L. Ed. 162 [1810]). However, in 1854, faced with another opportunity to define ex post facto, the Court retreated from *Fletcher* and limited the prohibition to retroactively applied criminal laws (*Carpenter v. Pennsylvania*, 58 U.S. (17 How.) 456, 15 L. Ed. 127 [1854]).

In *Carpenter*, the Court noted that the esteemed legal theorist Sir WILLIAM BLACKSTONE (1723–80) had described ex post facto in criminal terms. According to Blackstone, an ex post facto law has been created when, "after an action (indifferent in itself) is committed, the legislature then for the first time declares it to have been a crime, and inflicts punishment upon the person who has committed it," 1 Sir William Blackstone, *Commentaries on the Laws of England* 45-46 (1765). Using this as the understanding of ex post facto in 1789, the Court reasoned that it must have been the Framers' intent to limit the clause to criminal laws. However, notes from the Constitutional Convention indicate that the clause should cover the retroactive application of all laws, including civil laws. The only exception for ex post facto laws discussed at the Constitutional Convention was in case of "necessity and public safety" (Farrand, 1937).

Since the *Carpenter* ruling, the Supreme Court has struck down some retroactive civil laws, but only those intended to have a punitive intent. This construction of the Ex Post Facto Clause has done little more than raise another question: What is punitive intent? The answer lies, invariably, with the U.S. Supreme Court.

The Court has at times agreed unanimously on ex post facto arguments, but it has also split over the issue. In *California Department of Corrections v. Morales*, 514 U.S. 499, 115 S. Ct. 1597, 131 L. Ed. 2d 588 (1995), Jose Ramon Morales challenged a 1981 amendment (Cal. Penal Code Ann. Sec. 3041 [West 1982]) to California's PAROLE statute that allowed the California Board of Prison Terms to defer for three years the parole hearings of multiple murderers (1977 Cal. Stats. ch. 165, sec. 46). Before the amendment, California law stated that a prisoner eligible for parole was entitled to a parole hearing every year. Morales had two convictions for murder, his second conviction coming in 1980, one year before passage of the amendment.

In 1989, the board denied parole to Morales and scheduled Morales's next hearing for 1992. Morales filed suit, arguing that the amendment was retroactive punishment and therefore unconstitutional. The district court disagreed. However, on appeal, the U.S. Court of Appeals for the Ninth Circuit reversed that decision, holding that the law effectively increased punishment for Morales, thus offending the Ex Post Facto Clause.

By a vote of 7–2, the U.S. Supreme Court reversed the Ninth Circuit. Justice CLARENCE THOMAS, writing for the majority, noted that the law only "introduced the possibility" that a convict would receive fewer parole hearings and serve more prison time than he or she expected. The board was required to formally find "no reasonable probability . . . for parole in the interim period" before it could defer a parole hearing for three years. According to the majority in *Morales*, the evident focus of the California law was " 'to relieve the [board] from the costly and time consuming responsibility of scheduling parole hearings' " (quoting *In re Jackson*, 39 Cal. 3d at 473, 216 Cal. Rptr. at 765, 703 P.2d at 106 [quoting legislative history]). The majority noted further that any assertion that the law might actually increase incarceration for those affected by it was largely "speculative."

Justices JOHN PAUL STEVENS and DAVID H. SOUTER dissented. The dissent warned of legislative OVERREACHING, arguing that "the concerns that animate the Ex Post Facto Clause demand enhanced, and not (as the majority seems to believe) reduced, judicial scrutiny." To Stevens and Souter, the majority's own opinion was speculative, and "not only unpersuasive, but actually perverse."

The debate over ex post facto interpretation continues. Critics of contemporary ex post facto interpretation argue that legislatures circumvent the ex post facto prohibition by casting in civil terms laws that provide additional punishment for convicted criminals. For example, they have passed laws that require certain convicted sex offenders to register with local authorities and thus make public their continued presence in a community. By virtue of the Violent Crime Control and Law Enforcement Act of 1994 (42 U.S.C.A. § 14071(a)(1)(A)), such laws are required of states that wish to receive certain antidrug funds.

Sex offender registration laws, or community notification laws, do not provide for retroactive additional incarceration. They do, however, provide additional consequences for a sex offender who was not, at the time the offense was committed, subject to such a constraint. Courts have held that such laws do not run afoul of the Ex Post Facto Clause, because, in part, the requirement is defined as civil regulation; that is, the law does not require extra prison time or exact an excessive fine. Also, such statutes are enacted for the protection of the public, which is an exception to ex post facto prohibition. Dissenters maintain that sex offender registration laws inflict additional punishment and therefore violate the Ex Post Facto Clause. Only one state, Alaska, has found such a law unconstitutional (*Rowe v. Burton*, 884 F. Supp. 1372 [D. Alaska 1994]).

The line between punitive measure and civil regulation can be thin. So long as legislatures pass laws that provide extra punishment for, or regulation of, conduct already committed, there will be arguments that the government is abusing its power in violation of the Ex Post Facto Clause.

See also FLETCHER V. PECK.

EXPRESS 📖 Clear; definite; explicit; plain; direct; unmistakable; not dubious or ambiguous. Declared in terms; set forth in words. Directly and distinctly stated. Made known distinctly and explicitly, and not left to inference. Manifested by direct and appropriate language, as distinguished from that which is inferred from conduct. The word is usually contrasted with *implied*. 📖

That which is express is laid out in words, such as an *express* WARRANTY, which is an oral or written affirmation from a seller to a buyer of goods that certain standards will be met. Such a warranty may include the promise that any defect which occurs during a certain specified time period will be remedied at the seller's expense. This is distinguishable from an IMPLIED warranty, which is neither written nor based on any specific oral statement from seller to buyer but is implied through the sale itself. A common example is the implied warranty of merchantability, which implies that an item is fit for the usual purposes for which it was purchased.

Express authority is plainly or distinctly delegated power to an AGENT by a PRINCIPAL. For example, the owner of a store may expressly give employees the authority to accept deliveries in the owner's name.

EXPROPRIATION 📖 The taking of private property for public use or in the PUBLIC INTER-

EST. The taking of U.S. industry situated in a foreign country, by a foreign government. 📖

Expropriation is the act of a government taking private property; EMINENT DOMAIN is the legal term describing the government's right to do so. In the United States, this right is granted, indirectly, by the Fifth Amendment to the Constitution, which states, in part, that "private property [shall not] be taken for public use, without just compensation." The courts have interpreted this clause's limitation of the power to expropriate as implying the existence of the power itself.

Two well-known cases of the U.S. government's expropriating private property occurred during labor troubles after World War II. In the spring of 1946, President HARRY S. TRUMAN found it necessary to seize control of the nation's railroads to postpone an imminent STRIKE. He justified this action by declaring that the welfare of the country was at stake. Five days after the president's action, the workers went on strike for three days, until union and management reached an agreement. Truman hastened the agreement by threatening to draft all railway employees who refused to go back to work.

In 1952, faced with an impending strike by steelworkers, President Truman signed Executive Order No. 10340, 17 Fed. Reg. 3139, expropriating eighty-eight steel mills across the country. Again, the president defended his action by declaring that the welfare of the country was at stake. He supported this argument by stressing the demands of the war in Korea. He believed that a steel strike would endanger the lives of U.S. soldiers. This time, Truman's action caused a constitutional crisis that went to the U.S. Supreme Court. In *Youngstown Sheet & Tube Co. v. Sawyer*, 343 U.S. 579, 72 S. Ct. 863, 96 L. Ed. 1153 (1952), the Supreme Court ruled 6–3 that the president did not have the power to take private property to settle a labor dispute. The steelworkers' strike began the same day as the ruling and lasted seven weeks.

INTERNATIONAL LAW recognizes the right of countries to seize private property to further national welfare, but it requires that both CITIZENS and ALIENS be treated in the same manner. The issue of just compensation in return for expropriated property differs from country to country. The United States and most Western countries maintain that the expropriating country should pay prompt, adequate, and effective compensation.

U.S. businesses were expropriated by the governments of both Cuba and Chile during socialist movements in those foreign countries.

In May 1959, after Fidel Castro took over the Cuban government, the seizure of many large U.S. properties began. Before the revolution, U.S. corporations had controlled most of Cuba's resources and over half of its sugar production. In 1960, the first shipment of Soviet oil arrived in Cuba. Under the advice of the U.S. Treasury Department, U.S. oil companies on the island refused to refine it. These refineries were then taken over by the Cuban government. The expropriation of U.S. property in Cuba and Cuba's alliance with the Soviet Union eventually led to the United States' breaking off all diplomatic relations and instituting an EMBARGO.

In 1971, the Chilean people elected a socialist president, Salvador Allende. Soon afterward, the Chilean government began to expropriate U.S. businesses located in Chile. The primary U.S. business in Chile at this time was copper mining. When U.S.-owned mines were seized, in most cases, their owners were provided with adequate and prompt compensation. The El Teniente mine of the Kennecott Company was seized by the government for a much higher price than the BOOK VALUE. In 1970, government control over the industrial sector in Chile had been at 10 percent. One year after the election of President Allende, it was at 40 percent. By 1973, private banks; U.S. copper mines; the steel, cement, and coal industries; and all other vital areas of industry were in the hands of the Chilean state.

In both Cuba and Chile, the seized properties remain under the control of the foreign government.

Twice during labor unrest after World War II President Harry Truman attempted to expropriate railroads including the one in Youngstown, Ohio. The Supreme Court held in 1952 that the president did not have the power to take private property to settle a labor dispute.

CROSS-REFERENCES

Executive Order; Presidential Powers; *Youngstown Sheet & Tube Co. v. Sawyer.*

EXPUNGE 📖 To destroy; blot out; obliterate; erase; efface designedly; strike out wholly. The act of physically destroying information—including criminal records—in files, computers, or other depositories. 📖

EXTENSION 📖 An increase in the length of time specified in a contract.

A part constituting an addition or enlargement, as in an annex to a building or an extension to a house. Addition to existing facilities.

An allowance of additional time for the payment of DEBTS. An agreement between a DEBTOR and his or her CREDITORS, by which they allow the debtor further time for the payment of liabilities. A creditor's indulgence by giving a debtor further time to pay an existing debt.

The word *extension*, when used in its proper and usual sense in connection with a LEASE, means a prolongation of the previous leasehold estate. The distinction between extension and *renewal* of lease is chiefly that, in the case of RENEWAL, a new lease is requisite, while, in the case of extension, the same lease continues in force during an additional period upon performance of a stipulated act. An option for renewal implies giving a new lease on the same terms as those of an old lease, while an option for extension contemplates a continuance of an old lease for a further period.

Request for additional time to file an income tax return beyond the due date. 📖

EXTENUATING CIRCUMSTANCES 📖 Facts surrounding the commission of a CRIME that work to mitigate or lessen it. 📖

Extenuating circumstances render a crime less evil or reprehensible. They do not lower the degree of an offense, although they might reduce the punishment imposed.

Extenuating circumstances might include *extraordinary circumstances*, which are unusual factors surrounding an event, such as the very young age of a defendant in a murder case.

See also MITIGATING CIRCUMSTANCES.

EXTINGUISHMENT 📖 The destruction or cancellation of a right, a power, a contract, or an estate. 📖

Extinguishment is sometimes confused with *merger*, though there is a clear distinction between them. *Merger* is only a mode of extinguishment, and applies to ESTATES only under particular circumstances, but *extinguishment* is a term of general application to rights, as well as estates. *Extinguishment* connotes the end of a thing, precluding the existence of future life therein; in *mergers* there is a carrying on of the substance of the thing, except that it is merged into and becomes a part of a separate thing with a new identity.

Two ways in which the extinguishment of a DEBT can occur are by RELEASE or by payment. *Extinguishment of legacy* takes place where what has been bequeathed by WILL ceases to exist. *Extinguishment of rent* may take place by the tenant purchasing the rented property from the landlord or by grant, release, or surrender of the rental agreement.

EXTORT 📖 To compel or coerce, as in a CONFESSION or information, by any means serving to overcome the other's power of resistance, thus making the confession or admission involuntary. To gain by wrongful methods; to obtain in an unlawful manner, as in to compel payments by means of threats of injury to person, property, or reputation. To exact something wrongfully by threatening or putting in fear. The natural meaning of the word *extort* is to obtain money or other valuable things by compulsion, by actual force, or by the force of motives applied to the will, and often more overpowering and irresistible than physical force. 📖

EXTORTION 📖 The obtaining of property from another induced by wrongful use of actual or threatened force, violence, or fear, or under color of official right. 📖

Under the COMMON LAW, extortion is a MISDEMEANOR consisting of an unlawful taking of money by a government officer. It is an oppressive misuse of the power with which the law clothes a public officer.

Most JURISDICTIONS have statutes governing extortion that broaden the common-law definition. Under such statutes, any person who takes money or property from another by means of illegal compulsion may be guilty of the offense. When used in this sense, extortion is synonymous with BLACKMAIL, which is extortion by a private person. In addition, under some statutes a CORPORATION may be liable for extortion.

Elements of Offense Virtually all extortion statutes require that a threat must be made to the person or property of the victim. THREATS to harm the victim's friends or relatives may also be included. It is not necessary for a threat to involve physical injury. It may be sufficient to threaten to accuse another person of a crime or to expose a secret that would result in public embarrassment or ridicule. The threat does not have to relate to an unlawful act. Extortion may be carried out by a threat to tell the victim's spouse that the victim is having an illicit sexual affair with another.

Other types of threats sufficient to constitute extortion include those to harm the victim's business and those to either TESTIFY against the victim or withhold TESTIMONY necessary to his or her defense or claim in an administrative proceeding or a lawsuit. Many statutes also

Stefano Mazzola, associated with the Genovese crime family, was charged with making money for organized crime through extortion.

provide that any threat to harm another person in his or her career or reputation is extortion.

Under the common law and many statutes, an INTENT to take money or property to which one is not lawfully entitled must exist at the time of the threat in order to establish extortion. Statutes may contain words such as "willful" or "purposeful" in order to indicate the intent element. When this is so, someone who mistakenly believes he or she is entitled to the money or property cannot be guilty of extortion. Some statutes, however, provide that any unauthorized taking of money by an officer constitutes extortion. Under these statutes, a person may be held strictly liable for the act, and an intent need not be proven to establish the crime.

Statutes governing extortion by private persons vary in content. Many hold that a threat accompanied by an intent to acquire the victim's property is sufficient to establish the crime; others require that the property must actually be acquired as a result of the threat. Extortion by officials is treated similarly. Some statutes hold that the crime occurs when there is a MEETING OF THE MINDS between the officer and the party from whom the money is exacted.

Extortion by Public Officers The essence of extortion by a public officer is the oppressive use of official position to obtain a FEE. The officer falsely claims authority to take that to which he or she is not lawfully entitled. This is known as acting under COLOR OF OFFICE. For example, a highway department officer who collects money from a tax delinquent automo-

bile owner in excess of the authorized amount on the pretense of collecting a fine is extorting money under color of office. The victim, although consenting to payment, is not doing so voluntarily but is yielding to official authority.

There are four basic ways in which a public officer commits extortion. The officer might demand a fee not allowed by law and accept it under the guise of performing an official duty. He or she might take a fee greater than that allowed by law. In this case the victim must at least believe that he or she is under an obligation to pay some amount. A third method is for the officer to receive a fee before it is due. The crime is committed regardless of whether the sum taken is likely to become due in the future. It is not criminal, however, for an officer to collect a fee before it is due if the person paying so requests. Finally, extortion may be committed by the officer's taking a fee for services that are not performed. The service refrained from must be one within the official capacity of the officer in order to constitute extortion.

Other Crimes Distinguished As a crime of THEFT, extortion is closely related to ROBBERY and FALSE PRETENSES.

Robbery differs from extortion in that the property is taken against the will and without the consent of the victim, unlike extortion, where the victim consents, although unwillingly, to surrender money or property. Another distinguishing factor is that the nature of the threat for robbery is limited to immediate physical harm to the victim or his or her home. Extortion, on the other hand, encompasses a greater variety of threats.

False pretenses is another crime similar to extortion. The main difference is that for false pretenses the property is obtained by a lie as opposed to a threat.

Defenses A person who acts under a claim of right (an honest belief that he or she has a right to the money or property taken) may allege this factor as an AFFIRMATIVE DEFENSE to an extortion charge. What constitutes a valid claim of right defense may vary from one jurisdiction to another. For example, M, a department store manager, accuses C, a customer, of stealing certain merchandise. M threatens to have C arrested for LARCENY unless C compensates M for the full value of the item. In some jurisdictions it is only necessary for M to prove that he or she had an honest belief that C took the merchandise in order for M to avoid an extortion conviction. Other jurisdictions apply a stricter test, under which M's belief must be based upon circumstances that would cause a reasonable person to believe that C took the item. Another, more stringent, test requires that

C in fact owe the money to M. Finally, some states entirely reject the claim of right defense on the theory that M's threat is an improper means of collecting a debt.

Punishment Extortion is generally punished by a fine or imprisonment, or both. Where the offense is committed by a public officer, the penalty may include forfeiture of office. Under some statutes, the victim of an extortion may bring a CIVIL ACTION and recover pecuniary DAMAGES.

Federal Offenses Extortion is also a federal offense when it interferes with interstate commerce. It is punishable by a fine, imprisonment, or both.

Another federal statute makes it a crime to engage in extortionate CREDIT transactions.

EXTRA [*Latin, Beyond, except, without, out of, outside.*] Additional.

An extra in a CONTRACT would include anything outside of, beyond, or not called for by the contract, such as additional materials.

EXTRADITION The transfer of an ACCUSED from one state or country to another state or country that seeks to place the accused on TRIAL.

Extradition comes into play when a person charged with a crime under state statutes flees the state. An individual charged with a federal crime may be moved from one state to another without any extradition procedures.

Article IV, Section 2, of the U.S. Constitution provides that upon the demand of the governor of the prosecuting state, a state to which a person charged with a crime has fled must remove the accused "to the State having Jurisdiction of the Crime." When extraditing an accused from one state to another, most states follow the procedures set forth in the Uniform Criminal Extradition Act, which has been adopted by most JURISDICTIONS. A newer uniform act, the Uniform Extradition and Rendition Act, is designed to streamline the extradition process and provide additional protections for the person sought, but by 1995, it had been adopted by only one state.

Extradition from one state to another takes place on the order of the governor of the asylum state (the state where the accused is located). The courts in the asylum state have a somewhat limited function in extraditing the accused to the state where she or he is charged with a crime. They determine only whether the extradition documents are in order (e.g., whether they allege that the accused has committed a crime and that she or he is a fugitive)

A sample requisition for extradition

State of _____, Executive Department

[*State Seal*]

To His Excellency, the Governor of _____:

Whereas, it appears by _____ (a copy whereof is hereunto attached and which I certify to be authentic and duly authenticated in accordance with the laws of this State) that _____ stands charged with the crime of _____ committed in the County of _____, in this State (which I certify to be a crime under the laws of this State), and it having been represented and satisfactorily shown to me that said _____ since the commission of said offense _____ fled from the justice of this State and now _____ fugitive from the justice thereof, and may have taken refuge in the State of _____:

Now, therefore, pursuant to the provisions of the Constitution and laws of the United States in such case made and provided, I do hereby request that the said _____ be apprehended and delivered to _____, who is hereby appointed agent to _____ convey to the State of _____, there to be dealt with according to law.

In testimony whereof, I have hereunto set my hand and caused the Great Seal of the State to be affixed at _____, this _____ day of _____, 19___.

[*Seal*]

By the Governor:

Governor of _____

Secretary of State

and do not consider the merits of the charge, since the trial of the accused will take place in the state demanding extradition.

Extradition from one nation to another is handled in a similar manner, with the head of one country demanding the return of a fugitive who is alleged to have committed a crime in that country. Extradition between nations is usually based on a TREATY between the country where the accused is currently located and the country seeking to place him or her on trial for an alleged crime. The United States has entered into extradition treaties with most countries in Europe and Latin America, and with a few countries in Africa and Asia.

To determine whether an individual can be extradited pursuant to a treaty, the language of the particular treaty must be examined. Some treaties list all the offenses for which a person can be extradited; others provide a minimum standard of punishment that will render an offense extraditable. The extradition treaties of most countries fall into the second category, since treaties in the first category must be revised completely if an offense is added to the list.

Even if they do not specifically say so, most treaties contemplate that for an offense to be subject to extradition, it must be a crime under the law in both jurisdictions. This is called the doctrine of double criminality. The name by which the crime is described in the two countries need not be the same, nor must the punishment be the same; simply, the requirement of double criminality is met if the particular act charged is criminal in both jurisdictions

A sample warrant for extradition

State of _____, Executive Department
_____, Governor of the State of _____

To _____ and All Civil Officers of the State of _____:

Whereas, a demand has been made, pursuant to the Constitution and laws of the United States, by _____, Governor of the State of _____, upon the Governor of the State of _____ for the delivery of _____ as a fugitive from justice of the State of _____, and supposed to be within the limits of the State of _____; and whereas, the said _____ stands charged _____ in the County of _____, in the State of _____, with the crime of _____, alleged to have been committed on the _____ day of _____, 19___, in the County of _____, said State of _____, a copy of which was duly produced and annexed to the demand, duly certified to as authentic by the said _____, Governor of the State of _____, which said charge, as set forth in said _____, is made criminal by the laws of such State:

Now, therefore, you are hereby commanded and required to arrest and detain the said _____, if he shall be found within the State of _____, and, after having given him due notice of the demand made for his surrender, the nature of the criminal charge made against him, and an opportunity for a period of twenty-four hours after the arrest under this warrant to apply for a writ of habeas corpus, if he shall claim such right of you, to transport him to the line of said State, and deliver him to _____, who has been appointed by the Governor of the State of _____ agent, to demand and receive the said _____, and this warrant you are to serve at the expense of such agent. And all civil officers of the State of _____ are hereby required to afford all needful assistance in the execution hereof, and that you, and each of you, do and perform all acts required of you, and each of you, by the laws of the United States and of the State of _____ in such case made and provided.

In testimony whereof, I have hereunto set my hand and caused the Great Seal of the State of _____ to be affixed at the Capitol, in the City of _____, this _____ day of _____, in the year of our Lord one thousand nine hundred _____.

[*Seal*]

By the Governor:

Governor of _____

Secretary of State

Manuel Noriega was brought to the United States to stand trial after a U.S. invasion of Panama, not through standard extradition procedures.

(*Collins v. Loisel*, 259 U.S. 309, 42 S. Ct. 469, 66 L. Ed. 956 [1922]).

The doctrine of specialty is also often applied even when not specifically stated in a treaty. It means that once a person has been surrendered, he or she can be prosecuted or punished only for the crimes for which extradition was requested, and not for any other crimes committed prior to the surrender. The doctrine was first established over a hundred years ago, in *United States v. Rauscher,* 119 U.S. 407, 7 S. Ct. 234, 30 L. Ed. 425 (1886). In *Rauscher,* the defendant, a U.S. citizen, was extradited from Great Britain for the beating death of a ship's crew member on a U.S. vessel but was indicted and tried on a charge of CRUEL AND UNUSUAL PUNISHMENT based on the same act. Although the specialty principle was not specifically enumerated in the treaty that allowed the extradition, the U.S. Supreme Court held that an accused "shall not be arrested or tried for any other offense than that with which he was charged in those proceedings."

Extradition treaties often provide exceptions under which a nation can refuse to surrender a fugitive sought by another nation. Many nations will not extradite persons charged with certain political offenses, such as TREASON, SEDITION, and ESPIONAGE. Refusal to extradite under such circumstances is based on the policy that a nation that disagrees with or disapproves of another nation's political system will be reluctant to return for prosecution a dissident who likewise has been critical of the other nation. But, of course, not every criminal act will necessarily be protected. For example, some treaties provide that certain crimes, such as the ASSASSINATION of a head of a foreign government,

do not constitute political offenses that are exempt from extradition. The rise in airplane HIJACKING, TERRORISM, and HOSTAGE taking in the late twentieth century led many nations to enter into multilateral conventions in which the signing countries mutually agreed to extradite individuals who committed such crimes.

Since the 1980s, the international extradition process has been viewed by law enforcement authorities as too time-consuming, expensive, and complicated. It has also been criticized for frequently failing to bring fugitives to justice. As a result, some countries, including the United States, have turned to abduction to return a fugitive to a nation to be tried. Although its legality is questionable, abduction has sometimes been justified to combat drug trafficking and to ensure national security. In 1989, for example, the United States invaded Panama in an attempt to bring General Manuel Noriega to the United States to face charges related to drug trafficking. The Bush administration asserted that the invasion was necessary to protect national interests in the Panama Canal and to prevent an armed attack by Panama. See also PRESIDENTIAL POWERS.

Noriega was eventually brought to the United States to stand trial, where he contested the validity of the federal district court's jurisdiction over him (*United States v. Noriega,* 746 F. Supp. 1506 [S.D. Fla. 1990]). The court rejected his contention, holding that Noriega could be tried in the United States, despite the means that were used to bring him to trial. The court declined to address the underlying legality of Noriega's capture, concluding that, as an unrecognized head of state, Noriega lacked STANDING (the legal right) to challenge the invasion as a violation of international law in the absence of protests from the legitimate government of Panama over the charges leveled against him.

In *United States v. Alvarez-Machain,* 504 U.S. 655, 112 S. Ct. 2188, 119 L. Ed. 2d 441 (1992), the Supreme Court held that Humberto Alvarez-Machain's forcible abduction did not prohibit his criminal trial in the United States. Alvarez, a citizen of Mexico and a physician, was accused by the U.S. government of participating in the kidnapping, torture, and murder of a U.S. Drug Enforcement Administration agent and the agent's airplane pilot, and was indicted for these crimes. Alvarez was later kidnapped from his office and flown by private plane to El Paso, Texas. The Mexican government objected to the abduction and protested it as a violation of the extradition treaty between the United States and Mexico. It asked that the law enforcement agents responsible for the kidnapping be extradited to Mexico, but the United States refused to do so.

Alvarez sought to dismiss the INDICTMENT, claiming that the federal district court lacked jurisdiction to try him because his abduction violated the extradition treaty. The district court agreed and dismissed the indictment. The U.S. Court of Appeals for the Ninth Circuit affirmed, holding that the abduction violated the treaty's underlying purpose of providing a legal means for bringing a person to the United States to face criminal charges. On appeal, the U.S. Supreme Court rejected the lower courts' use of the treaty as the basis for prohibiting Alvarez's trial. Justice WILLIAM H. REHNQUIST, writing for the majority, found in the treaty provisions nothing stating that abductions were forbidden. He further maintained that the treaty was "not the only way in which one country may gain custody of a national of the other country for the purposes of prosecution." Thus, he concluded, the abduction did not prohibit Alvarez's trial in a U.S. court on criminal charges. Justice JOHN PAUL STEVENS, joined by Justices HARRY A. BLACKMUN and SANDRA DAY O'CONNOR, strongly dissented, agreeing with Alvarez and the lower courts that the treaty did set forth limits for dealing with the return of criminal defendants. According to the dissent, Alvarez's abduction was a gross violation of INTERNATIONAL LAW, intruding on the territorial integrity of Mexico.

See also FUGITIVE FROM JUSTICE.

EXTRAJUDICIAL 📖 That which is done, given, or effected outside the course of regular judicial proceedings. Not founded upon, or unconnected with, the action of a court of law, as in extrajudicial evidence or an extrajudicial oath.

That which, though done in the course of regular judicial proceedings, is unnecessary to such proceedings, or interpolated, or beyond their scope, as in an extrajudicial opinion. 📖

An *extrajudicial statement* is an out-of-court utterance, either written or oral. When offered into court as EVIDENCE, it is subject to the HEARSAY rule and its exceptions.

An *extrajudicial oath* is one that is not taken during judicial proceedings but taken formally before a proper officer or MAGISTRATE, such as a NOTARY PUBLIC.

EXTRAORDINARY REMEDY 📖 The designation given to such writs as HABEAS CORPUS, MANDAMUS, and QUO WARRANTO, determined in special proceedings and granted only where

absolutely necessary to protect the legal rights of a party in a particular case, as opposed to the customary relief obtained by the maintenance of an ACTION. 📖

Most states have eliminated extraordinary remedies. The relief formerly provided by them can be sought through an ordinary action.

EXTRATERRITORIALITY 📖 The operation of laws upon persons existing beyond the limits of the enacting state or nation but still amenable to its laws. JURISDICTION exercised by a nation in other countries by TREATY, or by its own ministers or consuls in foreign lands. 📖

In INTERNATIONAL LAW, extraterritoriality exempts certain diplomatic agencies and persons operating in a foreign country from the jurisdiction of the host country. Instead, the agency or individual remains accountable to the laws of the native country. The effects of extraterritoriality extend to troops in passage, passengers on war vessels, individuals on mission premises, and other agencies and persons.

The concept of extraterritoriality stems from the writings of French legal theorist and jurist Pierre Ayraut (1536–1601), who proposed the theory that certain persons and things, while within the territory of a foreign sovereign, remained outside the reach of local judicial process. Classical writers such as HUGO GROTIUS (1583–1645) and Samuel von Pufendorf (1632–94) gave Ayraut's ideas greater circulation. In 1788, the multilingual translation of Georg Friederich von Martens's *Summary of the Law of Nations* put the actual word *extraterritoriality* into the international vocabulary.

Extraterritoriality for AMBASSADORS and other diplomatic representatives gained widespread acceptance during the reign of Queen Anne of Great Britain (1665–1714). In this period, British officials arrested a Russian ambassador who had run up substantial debt to the British government. An international incident ensued as Russian officials and others throughout the world objected to Britain's disregard for the diplomat's immunity. Because of the outcry, Britain passed the Act Preserving the Privileges of Ambassadors in 1708. Other nations followed Britain's example, and the United States enacted a substantially identical statute in 1790.

In the modern world, the UNITED NATIONS has held a key position in upholding extraterritorial law. In a 1961 agreement made in Vienna, the U.N. Conference on Diplomatic Intercourse and Immunities extended exemption from the laws of host countries to the staff and family of DIPLOMATIC AGENTS. In addition, officials of the United Nations and the members of the delegations of its member states receive extensive procedural, fiscal, and other immunities from the jurisdiction of the host country. Separate and special arrangements govern the United States and Switzerland because the United States hosts the U.N. headquarters and Switzerland has U.N. offices in Geneva.

The general laws binding nations to extraterritorial agreements still rest on principle more than established order. The modern, global marketplace has put an additional dimension into extraterritoriality. The United States has consistently held that unless international jurisdiction conflicts are managed or mitigated, they have the potential to interfere seriously with the smooth functioning of international economic relations. The United States has therefore declared that it cannot disclaim its authority to act where needed in defense of its national security, foreign policy, or law enforcement interests.

See also DIPLOMATIC IMMUNITY.

EXTREMIS 📖 A description of the state of being ill beyond the hope of recovery, with DEATH imminent. 📖

An individual who is so seriously ill as to be dying is said to be *in extremis*.

EXTRINSIC EVIDENCE 📖 Facts or information not embodied in a written agreement such as a WILL, TRUST, or CONTRACT. 📖

Extrinsic evidence is similar to *extraneous evidence*, which is not furnished by the document in and of itself but is derived from external sources. In contract law, parol evidence is extrinsic evidence since it is not within a contract but, rather, is oral and outside the instrument. See also PAROL EVIDENCE.

EYEWITNESS 📖 An individual who was present during an event and is called by a party in a lawsuit to TESTIFY as to what he or she observed. 📖

The state and federal rules of EVIDENCE, which govern the admissibility of evidence in CIVIL ACTIONS and criminal proceedings, impose requirements that must be met before the testimony of an eyewitness can be presented during trial. For example, an eyewitness must be COMPETENT (legally fit) and qualified to testify in court. A WITNESS who was intoxicated or insane at the time the controverted event occurred will be prevented from testifying, regardless of whether he or she was the only eyewitness to the occurrence.

FACE 📖 The external appearance or surface of anything; that which is readily observable by a spectator. The words contained in a document in their plain or obvious meaning without regard to external evidence or facts. 📖

The term is applied most frequently in business law to mean the apparent meaning of a CONTRACT, paper, BILL, BOND, record, or other such legal document. A document might appear to be valid on its face, but circumstances may modify or explain it, and its meaning or validity can be altered.

FACE VALUE 📖 A readily ascertainable amount of money determinable from the words of a written instrument alone without the aid of any other source. 📖

The face value of an instrument such as a financial document is only the amount shown on it, without the inclusion of interest or fees customarily added or reference to its actual MARKET VALUE.

FACSIMILE 📖 An exact replica of a document that is copied so as to preserve all its original marks and notations. 📖

FACT 📖 Incident, act, event, or circumstance. A fact is something that has already been done or an action in process. It is an event that has definitely and actually taken place, and is distinguishable from a suspicion, innuendo, or supposition. A fact is a truth as opposed to fiction or mistake. 📖

A QUESTION OF FACT in litigation is concerned with what actually took place. During a TRIAL, questions of fact are generally left for the JURY to determine after each opposing side has presented its case. By contrast, a QUESTION OF LAW is ordinarily decided by a judge, who must deal with applicable legal rules and principles that affect what transpired.

FACTOR 📖 An event, circumstance, influence, or element that plays a part in bringing about a result. 📖

A factor in a case contributes to its causation or outcome. In the area of NEGLIGENCE law, the *factors*, or *chain of causation*, are important in determining whether LIABILITY ensues from a particular action done by the defendant.

FACTORS 📖 People who are employed by others to sell or purchase GOODS, who are entrusted with possession of the goods, and who are compensated by either a commission or a fixed salary. 📖

A factor has possession of the goods offered for SALE, has the goods entrusted to him or her, engages in the business of selling, and receives compensation for these services. A factor is a type of AGENT who sells goods owned by another, called a PRINCIPAL. The factor engages more frequently in the sale of merchandise than the purchase of goods. A factor is distinguished from a mere agent in that a factor must have possession of the principal's property, while an agent need not. The factor-principal relationship is created by a CONTRACT. Both parties are expected to comply with the terms of the agreement. The contract is terminable by the factor, by the principal, or by OPERATION OF LAW.

The merchandise entrusted to the factor is called a CONSIGNMENT, and a factor is often synonymously called a consignee. The factor is sometimes referred to as a commission merchant when his or her compensation is based on a percentage of the sale price. Factorage is defined as the compensation paid to factors.

A home factor is the name given to a factor who resides in the same state or country as the principal; a foreign factor is one who lives in a state or country other than that of the principal.

Factor-Principal Relationship Absent any special authority, a factor can bind the principal only in the ordinary course of business. The factor cannot delegate his or her duty to another individual without the knowledge and consent of the principal, unless custom and usage allow otherwise. He or she has the implied power to do everything reasonably necessary to sell the goods entrusted to him or her, and may even make the sale in his or her own name without disclosing the name of the principal. The factor has the power to receive payment and to give a receipt to the purchaser. There is no authority given to the factor to use the goods for personal benefit, to make an exchange for other merchandise, to cancel a completed sale, or to extend the time of payment after a sale.

A factor must exercise REASONABLE care, skill, and DILIGENCE in selling the goods and is responsible for losses resulting from failure to meet this standard. He or she has a duty to act with good faith and loyalty for the protection and advancement of the interests of the principal and may not make a secret profit for himself or herself. Unless the principal agrees, the factor may not purchase the merchandise.

The factor must faithfully execute the principal's instructions and is liable for any loss resulting from failure to do so. No LIABILITY will be imposed if the instructions are vague, ambiguous, impossible to perform, or illegal, or if the factor is obstructed from following them due to no fault of his or her own. The factor has a duty to inform the principal of any events that necessitate taking protective measures to ensure the safety of the goods; this stems from the obligation to care for the goods. A factor who cares for the merchandise in a reasonable manner is not responsible for business losses not due to his or her fault. He or she must not mingle the principal's goods with his or her own or with those of other people. The factor has the authority to insure the goods and may do so in his or her own name. He or she must obtain INSURANCE when instructed to do so by the principal, by the purchaser, or when custom imposes that obligation and must exercise reasonable prudence and diligence in securing adequate insurance coverage.

In the absence of specific instructions, a factor may sell in such a manner and on such terms as he or she considers appropriate, generally within a reasonable time and at his or her business establishment. When the time and location of the sale are specified in the agreement, the factor must exercise reasonable diligence to sell within the allotted time or at the

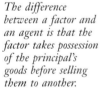

The difference between a factor and an agent is that the factor takes possession of the principal's goods before selling them to another.

authorized place. If the principal fails to designate a desired price, the factor then has an obligation to sell with reasonable skill and diligence so as to obtain the highest price possible in the current market. When instructed to sell at a specified price, he or she must do so, barring some unforeseeable event.

Goods are generally sold for cash upon delivery. When instructed to sell on CREDIT, a factor must exercise reasonable care and secure collateral to ensure payments. He or she is not liable for any loss with regard to payment that occurs through no fault of his or her own, unless specifically made liable in the contract with the principal. Authority to arrange credit terms that are customary in the market in which the goods are sold is implied. The factor must ascertain the financial stability of a purchaser on credit and must diligently advise the principal of any adverse change in the creditor's financial standing. He or she has no duty to divulge the name of a purchaser who buys on credit unless the information is needed for the principal to act on the sale.

Reasonable care and diligence must be taken in collecting the price of merchandise sold on credit. A factor must account to the principal for the proceeds and apply them in the instructed manner. He or she must not commingle the proceeds with his or her own money or with the funds of another, unless there is an existing custom of COMMINGLING to which the principal consents. The proceeds are held subject to the principal's direction and, unless required by agreement or prior course of dealing, it is not necessary for the factor to immediately tender them.

A factor is liable to the principal when he or she deals with the goods in a manner that is inconsistent with the right of the principal. A violation of instructions, breach of duty, misconduct, and FRAUD are grounds upon which the principal may recover for damages incurred. Interest is recoverable if the factor delays in remitting payment for goods after a sale.

There is a duty to keep regular and accurate accounts of all transactions, and the principal has a right to inspect the accounts. A factor has no authority to settle a claim against the principal, to submit a claim to ARBITRATION, or to reship goods to another market in order to sell them. He or she may, however, give a WARRANTY with respect to the quality of the goods.

States regulate the activities of a factor by requiring LICENSES and imposing taxes. To ensure the diligent performance of duties, some states have a factor post a BOND before being allowed to conduct his or her business. The primary purpose of the regulation is to protect persons who deal with factors against dishonest or unscrupulous persons.

Compensation for Services Compensation is a contractual right, and, subject to the terms and conditions of the agreement, commissions are paid when a sale is made. When an express agreement or statute does not fix the amount of compensation, the factor is entitled to the just and reasonable remuneration customarily charged for these services. In the absence of a customary rate, the factor has a right to receive a fee that is fair and reasonable. Acts of fraud, misconduct, GROSS NEGLIGENCE, and breach of contract would cause the factor to forfeit the right to compensation.

The advancement of money due for the cost of freight depends on the contract or course of dealing between the factor and principal. When a factor advances funds in connection with the goods in his or her care and is not reimbursed by the principal, the factor has a right to sell the goods in order to satisfy the expenditures. Any excess must be returned to the principal. The factor is entitled to interest on any advances but forfeits the right to reimbursement and interest if his or her negligence, fraud, or misconduct results in a loss for the principal.

Enforcement A factor has a general LIEN for all commissions due him or her and for all expenditures, including advances plus interest, properly incurred. A factor's lien secures the compensation, expenses, advances, and liabilities incurred by him or her for the principal. A factor is not entitled to a lien unless he or she has fulfilled all contractual and statutory requirements. He or she must have actual or CONSTRUCTIVE possession of the goods before the lien attaches; and if the factor has constructive possession of the goods, he or she must have control over the property before a lien attaches. Once attached, a lien is waived only by express terms or by clear implication, such as when the factor acts in a manner that is inconsistent with its continuance. Fraud or misconduct in transacting the principal's business are other grounds for waiving a lien. A factor may enforce his or her lien by retaining the entrusted property until his or her claims are liquidated, or he or she may sell the goods in order to satisfy his or her claims, returning any excess to the principal.

FACT SITUATION 📖 A concise description of all the occurrences or circumstances of a particular case, without any discussion of their consequences under the law. The fact situation, sometimes referred to as a *fact pattern*, is a summary of what took place in a case for which relief is sought. The fact situation of one case is almost always distinguishable from that of another case.

When one case with a particular fact situation has been decided, an attorney may use it as PRECEDENT and relate it to another similar case on which he or she is currently working.

FACTUM [*Latin, Fact, act, or deed.*] A fact in evidence, which is generally the central or primary fact upon which a controversy will be decided.

FAILURE OF CONSIDERATION

As applied to CONTRACTS, this term does not necessarily mean a want of CONSIDERATION, but implies that a consideration, originally existing and good, has since become worthless or has ceased to exist or been extinguished, partially or entirely. It means that sufficient consideration was contemplated by the parties at the time the contract was entered into, but either on account of some innate defect in the thing to be given, or nonperformance in whole or in part of that which the promisee agreed to do, nothing of value can be or is received by the promisee.

FAILURE OF ISSUE

Dying without having any children or without surviving children.

Children are commonly referred to at law as *issue of a marriage.* Whether or not a person has any issue becomes important in determining the HEIRS upon his or her death.

The Tudor line of English monarchs ended in 1603 when Queen Elizabeth I died without issue. She was succeeded by her relative, King James VI of Scotland, who became James I of England.

LIBRARY OF CONGRESS

FAILURE TO STATE A CLAIM

Failure to state a claim is frequently raised as a defense in civil litigation. This defense asserts that, assuming all the allegations in the plaintiff's COMPLAINT are true, the complaint nevertheless does not establish a CAUSE OF ACTION. In some JURISDICTIONS, such as California, the defense is called a DEMURRER. The successful invocation of this defense will result in the DISMISSAL of the case.

Courts will not dismiss a complaint in which the plaintiff has a legal basis for a CLAIM but has made a technical error that renders the complaint invalid. In such a case, courts allow the petitioner to amend the complaint.

The defense of failure to state a claim is provided for in Federal Rule of Civil Procedure 12(b)(6) and in similar state court rules. Rule 12(b) states that defenses should be presented in the defendant's response to the complaint. However, the rule allows some defenses to be asserted in a separate MOTION to the court, including the defense that the plaintiff does not state a claim upon which relief can be granted. The purpose of these exceptions is to allow a defendant to respond to procedural flaws in the filing of the complaint without responding to the MERITS of the case. Allowing the defendant to respond in a separate motion also allows the court to dismiss quickly civil claims that are without legal merit.

Dawson v. Wilheit, 105 N.M. 734, 737 P.2d 93 (1987), illustrates the dismissal of a suit for failure to state a claim. In *Dawson,* the plaintiff brought suit against Farmington, New Mexico, police officers as well as the city of Farmington and a vehicle towing service. The suit was based on a chain of events that began on November 20, 1983, when the son of the plaintiff was killed by two men, who placed his body in the trunk of a car owned by one of the men. Shortly thereafter the car owner was arrested for driving while intoxicated.

Under police department policy, a police officer should have conducted an inventory of the vehicle with an employee of the towing service, but this did not happen. After his release from jail on the drunk driving charge, the car owner drove away from the lot and dumped the body in a remote area where it was not discovered for six months.

The plaintiffs sued, seeking COMPENSATORY DAMAGES for negligent infliction of emotional distress caused by the failure to conduct an inventory and the resulting delay in finding the body. The district court dismissed the complaint on the ground that the plaintiffs had failed to state a claim. On appeal, the Court of Appeals of New Mexico affirmed the dismissal.

Under basic NEGLIGENCE law, no person may be liable for the injuries of another unless she or he breached a DUTY of care owed to the victim. According to the state high court, the police department's inventory policy was in place to protect the police and towing company from claims of theft, and the police owed no duty to the plaintiffs to find a body when they were unaware of a killing. Thus, the plaintiffs had no basis for their complaint, and their case had been rightly dismissed for failure to state a claim.

FAIR COMMENT 📖 A form of qualified privilege applied to news media publications relating to discussion of matters that are of legitimate concern to the community as a whole because they materially affect the interests of all the community. A term used in the defense of LIBEL actions, applying to statements made by a writer (e.g., in the news media) in an honest belief in their truth, relating to official acts, even though the statements are not true in fact. Fair comment must be based on facts truly stated, must not contain imputations of corrupt or dishonorable motives except as warranted by the facts, and must be an honest expression of the writer's real opinion. 📖

Fair comment is a privilege under the FIRST AMENDMENT to the Constitution and also applies to invasions of the right of PRIVACY.

In order for a statement to fall into the category of a fair comment, it must not extend beyond matters of concern to the public. It must be a mere expression of the opinion of the commentator.

See also FREEDOM OF THE PRESS.

FAIR CREDIT REPORTING ACT 📖 Legislation embodied in title VI of the CONSUMER CREDIT PROTECTION ACT (15 U.S.C.A. § 1681 et seq. [1968]), which was enacted by Congress in 1970 to ensure that reporting activities relating to various consumer transactions are conducted in a manner that is fair to the affected individual, and to protect the consumer's right to PRIVACY against the informational demands of a CREDIT reporting company. 📖

The Fair Credit Reporting Act (FCRA) represents the first federal regulation of the consumer reporting industry, covering all CREDIT BUREAUS, investigative reporting companies, detective and collection agencies, lenders' exchanges, and computerized information reporting companies.

The consumer is guaranteed several rights under the FCRA, including the right to a notice

If a consumer is denied a bank loan, the loan officer must permit the applicant to examine the credit report that the bank received.

of reporting activities, the right of access to information contained in consumer reports, and the right to the correction of erroneous information that may have been the basis for a denial of credit, INSURANCE, or employment. When a consumer is denied an extension of credit, insurance, or employment owing to information contained in a credit report, the consumer must be given the name and address of the credit bureau that furnished the credit report. Consumers are also entitled to see any report that led to a denial, but agencies are not required to disclose risk scores to them. Risk scores (or other numerical evaluation, however named) are assigned by consumer reporting agencies to help clients interpret the agency's report. Credit agencies may not report adverse information older than seven years or BANKRUPTCIES older than ten years.

The provisions of the FCRA apply to any report by an agency relating to a consumer's creditworthiness, credit standing, credit capacity, character, general reputation, personal characteristics, or mode of living. The FCRA covers information that is used or expected to be used in whole or part as a factor in establishing the consumer's eligibility for one of four purposes: (1) employment; (2) credit or insurance for personal, family, or household use; (3) government benefits and LICENSES to operate particular businesses or practice a profession; and (4) other legitimate business needs. Under the FCRA, an agency may also furnish a report in response to a court order or a federal grand jury SUBPOENA, to a written authorization from the consumer, or to a summons from the INTERNAL REVENUE SERVICE.

The FCRA creates civil liability for consumer reporting agencies and users of consumer reports that fail to comply with its requirements. For example, the Joneses, owners and operators of a real estate appraisal business, sued a consumer reporting agency under the FCRA. The Joneses claimed that the agency incorrectly reported a judgment against their business. The Supreme Court of Appeals upheld a jury's award, which included compensatory and punitive damages (*Jones v. Credit Bureau of Huntington, Inc.*, 184 W.Va. 112, 399 S.E.2d 694 [1990]). A consumer reporting agency includes any person or corporation that, for monetary fees, dues, or on a cooperative nonprofit basis, regularly assembles or evaluates credit information or other information on consumers for the purpose of furnishing consumer reports to third parties, and uses any means or facility of interstate commerce for the purpose of preparing or furnishing consumer reports. A retail department store or another comparable business that furnishes information to consumer reporting agencies based on its experience with consumers is not considered a consumer reporting agency under the FCRA (*DiGianni v. Stern's*, 26 F.3d 346 [2d Cir. 1994], *cert. denied*, 513 U.S. 897, 115 S. Ct. 252, 130 L. Ed. 2d 173).

Since its enactment, the FCRA has not undergone major reform. However, legislation has been proposed to address the issues that have arisen from a technological explosion created by a large increase in consumer debt and the information that it generates. In addition, states have enacted comparable statutes covering consumer's rights.

See also CONSUMER CREDIT; CONSUMER PROTECTION.

FAIR HEARING ◨ A judicial proceeding that is conducted in such a manner as to conform to fundamental concepts of justice and equality. ◨

During a fair hearing, authority is exercised according to the principle of DUE PROCESS OF LAW. Fair hearing means that an individual will have an opportunity to present EVIDENCE to support his or her case and to discover what evidence exists against him or her.

In CRIMINAL LAW, when an individual is arrested, a fair hearing means the right to be notified of the charge being brought against him or her and the chance to meet that charge.

In order for a hearing to be fair and comply with due process requirements, it must be held before an impartial tribunal; however, a hearing can be unfair without any intention that it be that way. A fair hearing must provide a reasonable opportunity for an individual to be present at the designated time and place, during which time he or she may offer evidence, cross-examine opposition WITNESSES, and offer a defense. Formalities of a court action need not be strictly complied with in order for a proceeding to be considered a fair hearing.

A fair hearing is not necessarily a fair TRIAL. The hearing might be an administrative one before the Immigration Board or the NATIONAL LABOR RELATIONS BOARD, for example, but fairness is still required. See also ADMINISTRATIVE LAW AND PROCEDURE.

FAIR LABOR STANDARDS ACT ◨ Federal legislation enacted in 1938 by Congress, pursuant to its power under the COMMERCE CLAUSE, that mandated a minimum wage and forty-hour work week for employees of those businesses engaged in interstate commerce. ◨

The Fair Labor Standards Act of 1938 (29 U.S.C.A. § 201 et seq.), popularly known as the "Wages and Hours Law," was one of a number of statutes making up the New Deal program of the presidential administration of FRANKLIN DELANO ROOSEVELT. Aside from setting a maximum number of hours that a person could work for the minimum wage, it also established the right of the eligible worker to "time and a half" or one and one-half times the customary pay for those hours worked in excess of the statutory maximum.

Other provisions of the act forbade the use of CHILD LABOR (those workers under the age of sixteen) in most jobs and prohibited the use of workers under the age of eighteen in those occupations deemed dangerous. The act was

The Fair Labor Standards Act mandates a forty-hour work week and time-and-a-half pay for overtime. Labor activists may protest political policies or specific practices, but the FLSA is still an important element of labor law.

JACK KURTZ/IMPACT VISUALS

also responsible for the creation of the Wage and Hour Division of the Department of Labor.

Over the years, the Fair Labor Standards Act has been subject to amendment but it still continues to play an integral role in the workplace in the United States.

See also EMPLOYMENT LAW; LABOR DEPARTMENT.

FAIR MARKET VALUE 📖 The amount for which REAL PROPERTY or PERSONAL PROPERTY would be sold in a voluntary transaction between a buyer and seller, neither of whom is under any obligation to buy or sell. 📖

The customary test of fair market value in REAL ESTATE transactions is the price that a buyer is willing, but is not under any duty, to pay for a particular property to an owner who is willing, but not obligated, to sell.

Various factors can have an effect on the fair market value of real estate, including the uses to which the property has been adapted and the demand for similar property.

Fair market value can also be referred to as *fair cash value* or *fair value*.

FAIRNESS DOCTRINE 📖 The doctrine that imposes affirmative responsibilities on a broadcaster to provide coverage of issues of public importance that is adequate and fairly reflects differing viewpoints. In fulfilling its fairness doctrine obligations, a broadcaster must provide free time for the presentation of opposing views if a paid sponsor is unavailable and must initiate programming on public issues if no one else seeks to do so. 📖

Between the 1940s and 1980s, federal regulators attempted to guarantee that the BROADCASTING industry would act fairly. The controversial policy adopted to further that attempt was called the fairness doctrine. The fairness doctrine was not a statute, but a set of rules and regulations that imposed controls on the content of the broadcasting media. It viewed radio and TELEVISION as not merely industries but servants of the PUBLIC INTEREST. Enforced by the FEDERAL COMMUNICATIONS COMMISSION (FCC), the fairness doctrine had two main tenets: broadcasters had to cover controversial issues, and they had to carry contrasting viewpoints on such issues. Opponents of the doctrine, chiefly the media themselves, called it unconstitutional. Although it survived court challenges, the fairness doctrine was abolished in 1987 by deregulators in the FCC who deemed it outdated, misguided, and ultimately unfair. Its demise left responsibility for fairness entirely to the media.

The fairness doctrine grew out of early regulation of the radio industry. As the medium of radio expanded in the 1920s, its chaotic growth

caused problems: for one, broadcasters often overlapped on each other's radio frequencies. In 1927, Congress imposed regulation with its passage of the Radio Act (47 U.S.C.A. § 81 et seq.). This landmark law established the Federal Radio Commission (FRC), reestablished in 1934 as the Federal Communications Commission. Empowered to allocate frequencies among broadcasters, the FRC essentially decided who could broadcast, and its mandate to do so contained the seeds of the fairness doctrine. The commission was not only to divvy up the limited number of bands on the radio dial; Congress said it was to do so according to public "convenience, interest, or necessity." Radio was seen as a kind of public trust: individual stations had to meet public expectations in return for access to the nation's airwaves.

In 1949, the first clear definition of the fairness doctrine emerged. The FCC said, in its *Report on Editorializing*, "[T]he public interest requires ample play for the free and fair competition of opposing views, and the commission believes that the principle applies . . . to all discussion of issues of importance to the public." The doctrine had two parts: it required broadcasters (1) to cover vital controversial issues in the community and (2) to provide a reasonable opportunity for the presentation of contrasting viewpoints. In time, additional rules were added. The so-called personal attack rule required broadcasters to allow opportunity for rebuttal to personal attacks made during the discussion of controversial issues. The "political editorializing" rule held that broadcasters who endorsed a candidate for political office had to give the candidate's opponent a reasonable opportunity to respond.

Enforcement was controversial. Complaints alleging violations of the fairness doctrine were

The Fairness Doctrine, which required broadcasters to cover issues of public importance and reflect differing opinions, was abolished in 1987. A discussion between 1992 presidential candidates Bill Clinton and Jerry Brown on the MacNeil/Lehrer News Hour would qualify as such coverage.

to be filed with the FCC by individuals and organizations, such as political parties and unions. Upon review of the complaint, the FCC could take punitive action that included refusing to renew broadcasting LICENSES. Not surprisingly, radio and TV station owners resented this regulatory power. They grumbled that the print media never had to bear such burdens. The fairness doctrine, they argued, infringed upon their FIRST AMENDMENT rights. By the late 1960s, a First Amendment challenge reached the U.S. Supreme Court, in *Red Lion Broadcasting Co. v. FCC*, 395 U.S. 367, 89 S. Ct. 1794, 23 L. Ed. 2d 371 (1969). The Court upheld the constitutionality of the doctrine in a decision that only added to the controversy. The print and broadcast media were inherently different, it ruled. In the broadcast media, the Court said, "it is the right of the viewers and listeners, not the right of the broadcasters, which is paramount... it is the right of the public to receive suitable access to social, political, esthetic, moral, and other ideas and experiences which is crucial here."

Although the fairness doctrine remained in effect for almost two more decades following *Red Lion*, the 1980s saw its abolishment. Antiregulatory fervor in the administration of President RONALD REAGAN brought about its end. The administration, which staffed the FCC with its appointees, favored little or no restrictions on the broadcast industry. In its 1985 *Fairness Report* (102 F.C.C.2d 145), the FCC announced that the doctrine hurt the public interest and violated the First Amendment. Moreover, technology had changed: with the advent of multiple channels on CABLE TELEVISION, no longer could broadcasting be seen as a limited resource. Two years later, in August 1987, the commission abolished the doctrine by a 4–0 vote, intending to extend to radio and television the same First Amendment protections guaranteed to the print media. Congress had tried to stop the FCC from killing the fairness doctrine. Two months earlier, it had sent President Reagan the Fairness in Broadcasting Act of 1987 (S. 742, 100th Cong., 1st Sess. [1987]), which would have codified the doctrine in federal law. The president vetoed it.

President Reagan's VETO of the 1987 congressional bill to establish the fairness doctrine as law did not end the controversy, however. Even into the mid-1990s, proponents continued to call for its reinstatement.

FAIR-TRADE LAWS ▣ State statutes enacted in the first half of the twentieth century permitting manufacturers to set minimum, maximum, or actual selling prices for their products, and thus to prevent retailers from selling products at very low prices. ▣

Manufacturers have an interest in establishing and maintaining GOOD WILL toward their products. This means assuring consumers that the manufacturers' goods are quality products. Good will is promoted by advertising and other sales efforts. Manufacturers in the early 1900s believed that commanding minimum retail prices was necessary to preserve good will, and that uncontrolled price-cutting by retailers would be detrimental to good will. Specifically, manufacturers feared that consumers would become skeptical if a particular retailer began to sell for a lower price a product that had had a relatively consistent price over the years: the lower price would undercut any claim by the manufacturer that the higher price was necessary to maintain the product's quality, and purchasers at the higher price would feel cheated.

The Great Depression following the stock market crash of 1929 started a movement toward state involvement in product price controls. State lawmakers believed that allowing manufacturers to dictate resale prices to retailers would help stabilize price levels and markets.

In 1931, California became the first state to pass fair-trade laws. These laws made it legal for a manufacturer to enter an agreement whereby the purchasing retailer, the signor, could resell a product only at a prescribed minimum price. In 1933, California amended these laws to make such an agreement binding on nonsignors. The amendments made minimum-price agreements enforceable against any retailer who had knowledge of another retailer's agreement with the manufacturer.

The setting of minimum resale prices, which state fair-trade laws legalized, was precisely the

Fair-trade laws permit manufacturers to set prices for their products and to prevent retailers from selling products at very low prices in order to maintain good will toward their products.

MICHAEL NEWMAN/PHOTOEDIT

sort of vertical price-fixing that the federal SHERMAN ANTI-TRUST ACT of 1890 (15 U.S.C.A. § 1) had been intended to prohibit. While the courts wrestled with the conflicting state and federal laws, Congress passed first the Miller-Tydings Act (50 Stat. 693 [Aug. 17, 1935]), which amended the Sherman Act to exempt state fair-trade laws, and then the McGuire Act (66 Stat. 632 [1952]), which allowed states to pass fair-trade laws making minimum price agreements enforceable against nonsignors as well.

After the enactment of Miller-Tydings and McGuire, state fair-trade laws and federal AN-TITRUST LAWS were no longer in conflict, and as many as forty-five states enacted fair-trade laws. As time passed, though, state courts whittled away at the fair-trade laws, often finding them to be in violation of the state's constitution. The perceived importance of allowing manufacturers to set minimum prices deteriorated as it became evident that the laws were harming the free market. In 1975, Congress, with support of the Ford administration, passed the Consumer Goods Pricing Act (Pub. L. No. 94-145), which repealed the Miller-Tydings and McGuire Acts, putting state fair-trade laws back within the prohibitions of the Sherman Act.

Today, the computer and electronics industries face retail price-cutting issues. Volume discount retailers sell name brand computers and electronics at prices far below those initially established in the market. With fair-trade laws off the books, retailers and the market determine at what prices goods will be sold.

FALSE ADVERTISING 📖 "Any advertising or promotion that misrepresents the nature, characteristics, qualities or geographic origin of goods, services or commercial activities" (LAN-HAM ACT, 15 U.S.C.A. § 1125(a)). 📖

Proof Requirement To prove that an advertisement is false, a plaintiff must prove five things: (1) a false statement of fact has been made about the advertiser's own or another person's goods, services, or commercial activity; (2) the statement either deceives or has the potential to deceive a substantial portion of its targeted audience; (3) the deception is also likely to affect the purchasing decisions of its audience; (4) the advertising involves GOODS or services in interstate commerce; and (5) the deception has either resulted in or is likely to result in injury to the plaintiff. The most heavily weighed factor is the advertisement's potential to injure a customer. The injury is usually attributed to money the consumer lost through a purchase that would not have been made had the advertisement not been mislead-

ing. False statements can be defined in two ways: those that are false on their face and those that are implicitly false.

Development of Regulations The five-step proof requirement developed from common law, which allowed a consumer or competitor to bring action against a seller or advertiser for DECEIT or FRAUD if the consumer or competitor could meet all five requirements.

Legislation against false advertising is generally more consumer protective at the state level than it is under COMMON LAW. One early attempt to establish industrywide guidelines was made in 1911 when the trade journal *Printer's Ink* proposed that false advertising be classified as a crime. False advertising became a MISDEMEANOR in the forty-four states that enacted statutes based on the model statute proposed by *Printer's Ink*. These statutes are still in effect; however, they are rarely used because it requires proving that the false advertising exists beyond a reasonable doubt, a difficult standard to meet.

In place of the *Printer's Ink* statute, eleven states have adopted the Uniform Deceptive Trade Practices Act, which lists a dozen different items that make up prohibited trade practices. The only remedy available under this act is injunctive relief—a court order that admonishes the guilty party for its actions—which may explain the low number of states that have adopted it. Other states have different statutes regarding false advertising. Most of these statutes require the courts to interpret the state laws with the federal guidelines later provided by the Federal Trade Commission (FTC) in mind.

The second movement of change in the advertising industry came in 1964 when the FTC amended its standards to help regulate cigarette labeling. The FTC required proof of three elements to show that an advertisement was false or unfair. The ad had to offend PUBLIC POLICY; be immoral, unethical, oppressive, or unscrupulous; and substantially injure consumers. Now, as outlined in the five-step proof guideline, the most important consideration is the potential to injure consumers.

Another gradual change has been seen in the definition of deceptive trade practices. Today, these are defined as practices that will mislead a consumer who is acting reasonably under the circumstances, to that consumer's detriment. Before this formal policy was adopted by the FTC in 1988, deception was determined by a practice's tendency or capacity to deceive and its effect on an ignorant or credulous consumer.

Types of False Advertising Besides advertising that is either false on its face or

False advertising includes false information about competing products as well as false information about one's own product.

implicitly false, today's regulations define three main acts that constitute false advertising: failure to disclose, flawed and insignificant research, and product disparagement.

Failure to Disclose It is considered false advertising under the Lanham Act if a representation is "untrue as a result of the failure to disclose a material fact." Therefore, false advertising can come from both misstatements and partially correct statements that are misleading because they do not disclose something the consumer should know. The Trademark Law Revision Act of 1988 (15 U.S.C.A. § 1051 et seq.), which added several amendments to the Lanham Act, left the creation of the line between sufficient and insufficient disclosure to the discretion of the courts.

American Home Products Corp. v. Johnson & Johnson, 654 F. Supp. 568, S.D.N.Y. 1987, is an example of how the courts use their discretion in determining when a disclosure is insufficient. In this case, Johnson and Johnson was advertis-

ing a drug by comparing its side effects to those of a similar American Home Products drug, leaving out a few of its own side effects in the process. Although the Lanham Act does not require full disclosure, the court held the defendant to a higher standard and ruled the advertisement misleading because of the potential health risks it posed to consumers.

Flawed and Insignificant Research Advertisements based on flawed and insignificant research are defined under section 43(a) of the Lanham Act as "representations found to be unsupported by accepted authority or research or which are contradicted by prevailing authority or research." These advertisements are false on their face.

Alpo Pet Foods v. Ralston Purina Co., 913 F.2d 958 (D.C. Cir. 1990), shows how basing advertising claims on statistically insignificant test results provides sufficient grounds for a false advertising claim. In this case, the Ralston Purina Company claimed that its dog food was beneficial for dogs with canine hip dysplasia, demonstrating the claims with studies and tests. Alpo Pet Foods brought a claim of false advertising against Purina, saying that the test results could not support the claims made in the advertisements. Upon looking at the evidence and the way the tests were conducted by Purina, the court ruled not only that the test results were insignificant but also that the methods used to conduct the tests were inadequate and the results could therefore not support Purina's claims.

Product Disparagement Product disparagement involves discrediting a competitor's product. The 1988 amendment to the Lanham Act extends claims for false advertising to MIS-REPRESENTATIONS about another's products.

Trademark Infringement A topic similar in form to product disparagement is TRADE-MARK infringement, which is listed in section 32(1) of the Lanham Act. This section states that

> anyone who shall, without the consent of the registrant—(a) use in commerce any reproduction, counterfeit, copy or colorable imitation of a registered mark in connection with the sale, offering for sale, distribution or advertising of any goods or services or in connection with which such use is likely to cause confusion, or cause mistake, or to deceive . . . shall be liable in a civil action by the registrant.

The confusion or deceit involved does not have to be in regard to the source of the product; the only requirement is that the public thinks the trademark's owner either sponsored or approved the use of the trademark.

The Polaroid Test For purposes of determining whether there is a likelihood of confusion under the Lanham Act, the courts use the *Polaroid* test, which includes eight factors established in *Polaroid Corp. v. Polara Electronics Corp.*, 287 F. 2d 492 (2nd Cir. 1961). They are the strength of the plaintiff's mark, similarity of uses, proximity of the products, likelihood that the prior owner will expand into the domain of the other, actual confusion, defendant's good or bad faith in using the plaintiff's mark, quality of the junior user's product, and sophistication of consumers. These eight factors do not all have to be satisfied to prove a case; the major factor the courts focus on is the potential to confuse consumers.

The *Polaroid* test is for cases that involve commercial exploitation. When a case raises FIRST AMENDMENT concerns, the *Polaroid* test can become awkward. False advertising cases that raise First Amendment concerns most often involve the use of parody.

Parody For parody cases, a BALANCING test that is more useful than the *Polaroid* test was established by *Cliffs Notes v. Bantam Doubleday Dell Publishing Group*, 886 F.2d 490 (2nd Cir. 1989). In *Cliffs Notes*, the court held that Bantam's production of *Spy Notes*, which was a parody of *Cliffs Notes* study guides, was not a violation of the Lanham Act, because it conveyed not only that it was the original but also that it was not the original and was instead a parody. The balancing test used by the court in *Cliffs Notes* basically requires that a parody have two simultaneous, contradictory messages in order to be protected under the First Amendment. If a parody does not have both messages, it is likely to confuse the consumers, therefore opening itself up to false advertising claims.

Another claim involving parody is the 1995 case of *Hormel Foods Corp. v. Jim Henson Productions*, 73 F.3d 497 (2nd Cir. 1996). In this case, Hormel brought Jim Henson Productions to court for trademark infringement and false advertising under the Lanham Act. At the time the case was initiated, Henson was producing the movie *Muppet Treasure Island* with a new character: an exotic wild boar named Spa'am. Henson's intention was to make the audience laugh at the intended parody between the Muppet's wild boar and Hormel's tame luncheon meat.

Hormel's claims of false advertising and trademark infringement under the Lanham Act and its common-law claims of trademark dilution and deceptive practices were all denied by the court for several reasons, the main one being that Henson had clearly, in all his advertising, identified Spa'am as a character from a Muppet motion picture. This usage was not confusing under the *Polaroid* test and therefore was not a solid basis for a false advertising or trademark infringement claim. Henson's usage also satisfied the balancing test requirements set up by *Cliffs Notes*.

Remedies for False Advertising Had Hormel won its claim against Henson, three remedies would have been available to it: injunctive relief, corrective advertising, and damages.

Injunctive Relief Injunctive relief is granted by the courts upon the satisfaction of two requirements. First, a plaintiff must demonstrate a "likelihood of deception or confusion on the part of the buying public caused by a product's false or misleading description or advertising" (*Alpo*). Second, a plaintiff must demonstrate that an "irreparable harm" has been inflicted, even if such harm is a decrease in sales that cannot be completely attributed to a defendant's false advertising. It is virtually impossible to prove that sales can or will be damaged; therefore, the plaintiff only has to establish that there exists a causal relationship between a decline in its sales and a competitor's false advertising. Furthermore, if a competitor specifically names the plaintiff's product in a false or misleading advertisement, the harm will be presumed (*McNeilab, Inc. v. American Home Products Corp.*, 848 F.2d 34 [2nd. Cir. 1988]). See also INJUNCTION.

Corrective Advertising Corrective advertising can be ruled in two different ways. First, and most commonly, the court can require a defendant to launch a corrective advertising campaign and to make an affirmative, correcting statement in that campaign. For example, in *Alpo*, the court required Purina to distribute a corrective release to all of those who had received the initial, false information.

Second, the courts can award a plaintiff monetary DAMAGES so that the plaintiff can conduct a corrective advertising campaign to counter the defendant's false advertisements. For example, in *U-Haul International v. Jartran, Inc.*, 793 F.2d 1034 (9th Cir. 1986), the plaintiff, U-Haul International, was awarded $13.6 million—the cost of its corrective advertising campaign.

Damages To collect damages, the plaintiff generally has to show either that some consumers were actually deceived or that the defendant used the false advertising in BAD FAITH. Four types of damages are awarded for false advertising: profits the plaintiff loses when sales are diverted to the false advertiser; profits lost by the plaintiff on sales made at prices reduced as a demonstrated result of the false advertising; the cost of any advertising that actually and reasonably responds to the defendant's offending advertisements; and quantifiable harm to the plaintiff's GOOD WILL to the extent that complete and corrective advertising has not repaired that harm (*Alpo*).

Consumer Protection Although most false advertising claims brought against advertisers are by competitors, consumers can also file such claims. No hard-and-fast rules exist for all consumer-initiated cases; courts deal with claims brought by consumers on more of a case-by-case basis than they do with claims brought by competitors. The issues surrounding consumer rights were discussed during the drafting of the 1988 Trademark Law Revision Act, but were not resolved.

In cases where consumers have sued, they have most often been held to the same stan-

Consumers may bring a false advertising claim against a retailer if the seller advertises a product at one price and then sells a similar product at a higher price.

dards as competitors: they need to show that they have a reasonable interest in order to be protected. This standard was demonstrated by the CLASS ACTION lawsuit of *Maguire v. Sandy Mac*, 138 F.R.D. 444 (D.N.J. 1991). In that case, the class included both resellers, who had purchased a ham product from the defendant, and consumers, who had ultimately bought the ham products. The lawsuit claimed that the defendant sold ham products falsely represented as meeting U.S. Department of Agriculture standards. The court ruled for the plaintiffs, saying that "the plaintiff and the proposed class, the consumers, have a reasonable interest in being protected from criminal misrepresentations."

Another way consumers are protected is by state laws on deceptive trade practices. Some such laws define these practices as showing goods or services with the intention of not actually selling them as advertised. In *Affrunti v. Village Ford Sales*, 232 Ill. App. 3d 704, 597 N.E.2d 1242 (3rd. Dist. Ct. App. 1992), a consumer filed a lawsuit against an automobile dealership that sold him a car for more money than it was actually advertised for. Ronald Affrunti went to Village Ford Sales, a used-car lot, and looked at a blue 1986 Celebrity with twenty-nine thousand miles on the odometer. The car did not have a sticker price, so he asked the salesman, Fred Galaraza, for a price. Galaraza answered that he would have to check in his office. After showing Affrunti several other used cars, and without going to his office, Galaraza quoted a price of $8,600 for the Celebrity. Affrunti and Galaraza settled on a final price of $8,524, which included a trade-in and a discount for a front-end alignment. Upon returning home, Affrunti came across an advertisement by Village Ford Sales for a 1986 blue Celebrity with twenty-nine thousand miles on the odometer for $6,995. Affrunti called the dealership. Galaraza checked and said, "By God, it's the same!" Affrunti asked to redo the deal based on the advertised price. Galaraza put him on hold. When Galaraza came back on the line, he said the car in the ad had been sent to auction, and they could not redo the deal because it was not the same car.

At trial, the sales manager testified that prices listed in advertisements are not necessarily the listed cars' actual prices; dealers can sell the cars for higher prices. After hearing the evidence, the judge ruled that the dealer had an obligation to inform the plaintiff of the advertised price of the car, and awarded Affrunti the difference between the purchase price and the advertised price, which amounted to $1,529.00. On appeal, the Illinois Appellate Court ruled that "the defendant's failure to disclose the advertised sale price constituted deceptive conduct under the Consumer Fraud Act." The appellate court also added attorneys' fees to Affrunti's award, bringing the total up to $1,937.50.

See also CONSUMER PROTECTION.

FALSE ARREST 📖 A TORT (a civil wrong) that consists of an unlawful restraint of an individual's personal liberty or freedom of movement by another purporting to act according to the law. 📖

The term *false arrest* is sometimes used interchangeably with that of the tort of FALSE IMPRISONMENT, and a false arrest is one method of committing a false imprisonment. A false arrest must be perpetrated by one who asserts that he or she is acting pursuant to legal authority, whereas a false imprisonment is any unlawful confinement. For example, if a SHERIFF arrests a person without any PROBABLE CAUSE or reasonable basis, the sheriff has committed the torts of false arrest and false imprisonment. The sheriff has acted under the assumption of legal authority to deprive a person unlawfully of his or her liberty of movement. If, however, a driver refuses to allow a passenger to depart from a vehicle, the driver has committed the tort of false imprisonment because he or she unlawfully restrains freedom of movement. The driver has not committed false arrest, however, since he or she is not claiming to act under legal authority. A person who knowingly gives police false information in order to have someone arrested has committed the tort of MALICIOUS PROSECUTION.

An ACTION can be instituted for the damages ensuing from false arrest, such as loss of salary while imprisoned, or injury to reputation that results in a pecuniary loss to the victim. Ill will and MALICE are not elements of the tort, but if

these factors are proven, PUNITIVE DAMAGES can be awarded in addition to COMPENSATORY DAMAGES or NOMINAL DAMAGES.

FALSE DEMONSTRATION 📖 An inaccurate or erroneous description of an individual or item in a written instrument. 📖

With respect to TESTAMENTARY gifts, where the description of an individual or item in a WILL is partly true and partly false, in the event that the true portion describes the subject or object of the gift with adequate certainty, the untrue part may be rejected under the doctrine of false demonstration, and the gift upheld and enforced.

FALSE IMPRISONMENT 📖 The illegal confinement of one individual against his or her will by another individual in such a manner as to violate the confined individual's right to be free from restraint of movement. 📖

To recover DAMAGES for false imprisonment, an individual must be confined to a substantial degree, with her or his freedom of movement totally restrained. Interfering with or obstructing an individual's freedom to go where she or he wishes does not constitute false imprisonment. For example, if Bob enters a room, and Anne prevents him from leaving through one exit but does not prevent him from leaving the way he came in, Bob has not been falsely imprisoned. An accidental or inadvertent confinement, such as when someone is mistakenly locked in a room, also does not constitute false imprisonment; the individual who caused the confinement must have intended the restraint.

False imprisonment often involves the use of physical force, but such force is not required. The threat of force or arrest, or a belief on the part of the person being restrained that force will be used, is sufficient. The restraint can also be imposed by physical barriers or through unreasonable DURESS imposed on the person

This security guard acts under legal authority and so if he were to detain a person unlawfully it would constitute both false arrest and false imprisonment.

being restrained. For example, suppose a shopper is in a room with a security guard, who is questioning her about items she may have taken from the store. If the guard makes statements leading the shopper to believe that she could face arrest if she attempts to leave, the shopper may have a reasonable belief that she is being restrained from leaving, even if no actual force or physical barriers are being used to restrain her. The shopper, depending on the other facts of the case, may therefore have a claim for false imprisonment. False imprisonment has thus sometimes been found in situations where a storekeeper detained an individual to investigate whether the individual shoplifted merchandise. Owing to increasing concerns over shoplifting, many states have adopted laws that allow store personnel to detain a customer suspected of shoplifting for the purpose of investigating the situation. California law, for example, provides that "[a] merchant may detain a person for a reasonable time for the purpose of conducting an investigation . . . whenever the merchant has probable cause to believe the person . . . is attempting to unlawfully take or has unlawfully taken merchandise" (Cal. Penal Code § 490.5 [West 1996]).

FALSE ARREST is a type of false imprisonment in which the individual being held mistakenly believes that the individual restraining him or her possesses the legal authority to do so. A law enforcement officer will not be liable for false arrest where he or she has PROBABLE CAUSE for an arrest. The arresting officer bears the burden of showing that his or her actions were supported by probable cause. Probable cause exists when the facts and the circumstances known by the officer at the time of arrest lead the officer to reasonably believe that a crime has been committed and that the person arrested committed the crime. Thus, suppose that a police officer has learned that a man in his forties with a red beard and a baseball cap has stolen a car. The officer sees a man matching this description on the street and detains him for questioning about the theft. The officer will not be liable for false arrest, even if it is later determined that the man she stopped did not steal the car, since she had probable cause to detain him.

An individual alleging false imprisonment may sue for damages for the interference with her or his right to move freely. An individual who has suffered no actual damages as a result of an illegal confinement may be awarded NOMINAL DAMAGES in recognition of the invasion of rights caused by the defendant's wrongful conduct. A plaintiff who has suffered injuries and can offer proof of them can be compensated for physical injuries, mental suffering, loss of earnings, and attorneys' fees. If the confinement involved MALICE or extreme or needless violence, a plaintiff may also be awarded PUNITIVE DAMAGES.

An individual whose conduct constitutes the TORT of false imprisonment might also be charged with committing the crime of KIDNAPPING, since the same pattern of conduct may provide grounds for both. However, kidnapping may require that other facts be shown, such as the removal of the victim from one place to another.

False imprisonment may constitute a criminal offense in most JURISDICTIONS, with the law providing that a fine or imprisonment, or both, be imposed upon conviction.

FALSE PERSONATION   The crime of falsely assuming the identity of another to gain a benefit or avoid an expense.

The crime of falsely assuming the identity of another person in order to gain a benefit or cause harm to the other person can be referred to as false personation or false impersonation. False personation laws have been enacted at both the state and federal levels to protect the dignity, reputation, and economic well-being of the individual being impersonated. Further, these statutes deter criminals by discouraging the impersonator's pursuit of benefits.

A false impersonator need not alter her or his voice, wear a disguise, or otherwise change her or his characteristics or appearance in order to be found guilty. False personation simply involves passing oneself off as another person. For example, an individual who misrepresents herself to be someone else in order to wrongfully cash that person's paycheck commits false personation.

The person impersonated must be real, not fictitious. If a police officer pulls a driver over for speeding, and the driver pretends to be his brother, the driver is guilty of false personation. His brother is an actual person, and the crime of false personation is designed to take advantage of his brother's reputation and driving record. If the driver pretends to be Dick Tracy, a fictitious person, he is not guilty of false personation. Harming Dick Tracy's fictitious reputation and driving record is not an intended function of the crime. However, in this situation, the driver may be guilty of a different crime such as FRAUD or giving false information to a police officer.

The benefit or harm sought by impersonators may take many forms. Some are obvious, some are not. In the example of the driver who was pulled over for speeding and impersonated his brother, an obvious benefit is to avoid paying a speeding ticket. A less obvious benefit is to keep this offense off the driver's record. Even less obvious, the driver may have set up the whole situation in order to tarnish his brother's driving record or reputation.

False personation statutes may prohibit false personation of another generally, or they may specify a particular group, office, or profession. There are federal statutes that specifically prohibit the false personation of a U.S. citizen; an officer or employee of the United States in pursuit of money or other valuables; an officer or employee of the United States attempting to arrest or search a person or building; a creditor of the . United States; a foreign diplomat or official; a 4-H Club member or agent; or a member or agent of the Red Cross. Many states have statutes prohibiting the impersonation of police officers, firefighters, married people, or voters.

FALSE PRETENSES 📖 False representations of material past or present facts, known by the wrongdoer to be false, made with the intent to DEFRAUD a victim into passing TITLE in property to the wrongdoer. 📖

Suppose Reba tells Alberto that a synthetic gemstone is a valuable diamond that she will give to Alberto in exchange for Alberto's truck. Alberto thinks this sounds like a good deal and transfers title of his truck to Reba. If Reba knows that the stone is a synthetic gemstone, she is guilty of false pretenses.

A truthful statement that causes someone to give up rights in property does not constitute criminal false pretenses. To constitute false pretenses, a representation must be false at the time the potential victim is about to pass title. If the representation was false when made, but changing circumstances made it true by the time the victim passed title, false pretenses did not arise. Also, if the alleged wrongdoer thought his or her statement was a lie, but the statement was in fact true, the crime of false pretenses was not committed. For example, if Reba thinks the stone is synthetic whereas it actually is a diamond, her statement to Alberto claiming that it is a diamond is true, and Reba is not guilty of false pretenses.

A false representation can be a verbal, written, or implied statement. If a statement suggests that the wrongdoer has the authority, power, or ability to perform what is represented, but the wrongdoer does not have that authority, power, or ability, the implication is a false representation.

A false representation can also occur when the wrongdoer says or does nothing. The

If the jewels in this brooch are synthetic and the owner has traded it for a more valuable item by claiming that the stones are real, she is guilty of false pretenses.

knowing concealment of facts that the victim should be made aware of, when undertaken with the intent to defraud the victim, is also a false representation. If Reba tells Alberto that she will trade her valuable sports car for Alberto's truck, knowing that the sports car does not have a motor, she must tell Alberto about the missing motor or her nondisclosure will be a false representation.

The false representation supporting false pretenses must be about a material past or present fact. A material fact is one that would be important to the victim in her or his decision-making process. For example, it is important for Alberto to know that Reba's valuable sports car does not have a motor, because without a motor, the car is less valuable and cannot be driven. It is less important for him to know that the tire pressure is low, because that fact does not affect the value of the car, and thus Reba would not be guilty of false pretenses for failing to mention that the tires need air.

The representation must concern a past or present fact; a false representation of a future fact does not constitute criminal false pretenses. A car salesperson who claims that a car will run great in ten years is representing a future fact. An exaggerated expression of opinion, like a sales pitch, may not be entirely true but is not a criminal false representation. However, a promise about the future that, at the time it is made, the promissor does not intend to keep, is a criminal false representation of a material fact. If the salesperson promises to buy the car back if it is not running great in ten years, but he does not intend to satisfy the promise, the false promise is a false representation.

When a representation is in fact false, the wrongdoer must know it is false. If an alleged wrongdoer believed the statement was true—whether that belief was reasonable or unreasonable—she or he did not commit false pretenses because she or he did not knowingly make a false representation. If Reba believes that the synthetic stone is in fact a diamond, then she does not commit false pretenses when she tells Alberto it is a diamond. However, if the wrongdoer is not sure or does not care if a statement is false, and makes the statement with reckless indifference for truthfulness, the statement is a false representation. The wrongdoer should investigate the veracity of the statement, and not doing so suggests that she or he is acting knowingly and with intent to defraud, and the wrongdoer will therefore be found guilty.

It is important to determine why the wrongdoer told the lie. The wrongdoer must intend the false representation to defraud the victim. Intention to defraud the victim exists where the wrongdoer planned to unjustly acquire title to the victim's property by means of the untruth. That is, the wrongdoer will have planned the false representation in advance and will have calculated to deceive the victim into transferring title by way of the false statement. Telling an untruth, in and of itself, will not subject the liar to prosecution for false pretenses.

The victim of false pretenses must have relied on the false representation. The false representation must be the reason, or one of the reasons, that the victim passed title to the wrongdoer. It does not matter how gullible or naive the victim would seem for believing the representation; the wrongdoer is still guilty. On the other hand, to rely on a false statement, the potential victim must believe it to be true. An individual who does not believe a false representation but passes title to the statement maker anyway does not rely on the representation, and the statement maker will not be guilty.

Conviction of false pretenses requires the wrongdoer to obtain more than POSSESSION of the property; the wrongdoer must also obtain title to the property. A wrongdoer who gains possession of property but not title to the property is guilty of a different crime often referred to as LARCENY. A wrongdoer who breaks a truck's window and hot-wires the truck acquires only possession of the truck and is guilty of larceny.

Other laws may require the delivery of the possession of property in order to complete a transfer of title. In such cases, the wrongdoer may have to obtain title as well as possession of the property to be guilty of false pretenses. Imagine that the laws of the state where Alberto and Reba live require a party to take possession in order to obtain a valid transfer of title. Alberto signs the paper title over to Reba, but before Reba drives the truck away, Alberto figures out the scam, and Reba runs off. No transfer of title has occurred, because the state's laws require possession in addition to paper title, and Reba is not guilty of false pretenses.

Title does not have to pass directly to the wrongdoer. A wrongdoer can cause a victim to pass title to someone other than the wrongdoer and still benefit from the transfer. A transfer of title to a family member or a corporation in which the wrongdoer has an interest constitutes a transfer of title for purposes of false pretenses.

In many states, crimes relating to THEFT of property, including false pretenses, have been combined and consolidated into one signal offense. Statutory consolidation usually does not change the essential elements of false pretenses, but instead ensures smoother prosecution and avoids situations where wrongdoers can avoid criminal consequences by finding legal loopholes to slip through.

A number of crimes are very similar to false pretenses. The crime of bad checks occurs when a wrongdoer, with intent to defraud, obtains money or property by issuing checks from an account that does not exist or has insufficient funds. The wrongdoer falsely represents that the bad checks have value. A confidence game is a more severe version of false pretenses. A wrongdoer in a confidence game preys upon, and takes greater advantage of, the victim's confidence than does a wrongdoer in a case of false pretenses. MAIL FRAUD is a crime reasonably calculated to deceive victims, and accomplishes the deception by using the U.S. mail. A scheme to defraud using the mail is ACTIONABLE whether or not any false representation was made. SECURITIES registration laws prohibit a wrongdoer from knowingly furnishing false information in connection with the sale or registration of securities. FORGERY can be likened to false pretenses in that it is a crime where the genuineness of a document is falsely represented.

In addition to being criminally accountable for obtaining property by false pretenses, the wrongdoer may also be liable in a civil court. LIABILITY for tortuous fraudulent MISREPRESENTATION, or deceit, closely parallels liability for criminal fraudulent misrepresentation. A wrong-doer who fraudulently misrepresents a fact in order to induce another to act or refrain from acting in reliance upon it may be liable for pecuniary loss caused to the victim by the victim's justifiable reliance upon the misrepresentation.

FAMILY CAR DOCTRINE ▥ A rule of law applied in particular cases of NEGLIGENCE that extends LIABILITY to the owner of an automobile for damage done by a family member while using the car. ▥

The family car doctrine, also known as the family purpose doctrine, is based on the premise that a car is provided by the HEAD OF THE HOUSEHOLD for the family's use and, therefore, the operator of the car acts as an AGENT of the owner. If a husband is the owner of a car and his wife uses it for one of the purposes for which it was purchased, such as grocery shopping, then the wife is acting as the husband's agent in carrying out such purpose.

Under the family car doctrine, the individual upon whom liability is sought to be imposed must either own, provide, or maintain an automobile. The car must exist for the general use, pleasure, and convenience of the family.

Liability under this doctrine is contingent upon control and use and is not restricted to the owner or driver of the AUTOMOBILE. In order to successfully initiate an action within the meaning of the doctrine, there must be a showing that the automobile existed for family use and pleasure. If an automobile was purchased and is used for business purposes, it might come

Family Car Doctrine
Licensed Drivers, by Age, in 1994

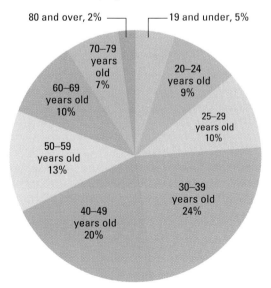

Source: Federal Highway Administration, U.S. Department of Transportation.

within the doctrine, provided it is also used for family purposes and was used for such purposes at the time of the accident.

FAMILY LAW ▥ Statutes, court decisions, and provisions of the federal and state constitutions that relate to family relationships, rights, duties, and finances. ▥

The law relating to family disputes and obligations has grown dramatically since the 1970s, as legislators and judges have reexamined and redefined legal relationships surrounding divorce, child custody, and child support. Family law has become entwined with national debates over the structure of the family, gender bias, and morality. Despite many changes made by state and federal legislators, family law remains a contentious area of U.S. law, generating strong emotions from those who have had to enter the legal process.

Historical Background   Most of the changes made in family law in the late twentieth century have been based on overturning concepts of marriage, family, and gender that go back to European FEUDALISM, canon (church) law, and custom. During Anglo-Saxon times in England, MARRIAGE and DIVORCE were private matters. Following the Norman conquest in 1066, however, the legal status of a married woman was fixed by COMMON LAW, and CANON LAW prescribed various rights and duties. The result was that the identity of the wife was merged into that of the husband; he was a legal person but she was not. Upon marriage, the husband received all the wife's PERSONAL PROPERTY and managed all the property owned by her. In return, the husband was obliged to support the wife and their children.

This legal definition of marriage continued in the United States until the middle of the nineteenth century, when states enacted married women's property acts. These acts conferred legal status upon wives and permitted them to own and transfer property in their own right, to sue and be sued, and to enter into CONTRACTS. Although these acts were significant advances, they dealt only with property a woman inherited. The husband, by placing TITLE in his name, could control most of the assets acquired during marriage, thus forcing the wife to rely on his bounty.

Divorce law has also changed over time. In colonial America, divorce was extremely rare. This was partly because obtaining a divorce decree required legislative action, a process that was time-consuming and costly. Massachusetts in 1780 was the first state to allow judicial divorce. By 1900, every state except South Carolina provided for judicial divorce.

In 1895, when this photo of a pioneer family in Minnesota was taken, the house, barn, crops, wagon, horses, and other possessions were probably all owned by the husband of the family.

Even with availability, divorce remained a highly conflicted area of law. The Catholic Church labeled divorce a sin, and Protestant denominations saw it as a mark of moral degeneration. The adversarial process presented another roadblock to divorce. In the nineteenth century, consensual divorce was not known. For a couple to obtain a divorce, one party to the marriage had to prove that the other had committed a wrong of such weight that the marriage must be ended. The need to find fault was a legacy of family law that was not changed until the 1970s.

Finally, the issue of divorce raised the topic of CHILD CUSTODY. Traditionally, fathers retained custody of their children. This tradition weakened in the nineteenth century, as judges fashioned two doctrines governing child custody. The "best-interests-of-the-child" doctrine balanced a new right of the mother to custody of the child against the assessment of the needs of the child. The "tender years" doctrine arose after the Civil War, giving mothers a presumptive right to their young children.

Divorce Beginning in the 1960s, advocates of divorce reform called for the legal recognition of no-fault divorce. Under this concept, a divorce may be granted on grounds such as INCOMPATIBILITY, IRRECONCILABLE DIFFERENCES, or an IRRETRIEVABLE BREAKDOWN OF THE MARRIAGE relationship. The court examines the condition of the marriage rather than the question of whether either party is at fault. This type of proceeding eliminates the need for one party to accuse the other of a traditional ground for divorce, such as ADULTERY, CRUELTY, alcoholism, or drug addiction.

By 1987, all fifty states had adopted no-fault divorce, exclusively or as an option to traditional fault-grounded divorce. No-fault divorce has become a quick and inexpensive means of ending a marriage, especially when a couple has no children and moderate property assets. In fact, the ability to end a marriage using no-fault procedures has led to criticism that divorce has become too easy to obtain, allowing couples to abandon a marriage at the first sign of marital discord.

The division of marital property has also undergone significant change since the 1970s. Courts now consider the monetary and nonmonetary contributions of a spouse as a homemaker, parent, and helper in advancing the career or career potential of the other party—as, for example, when one spouse works so that the other may go to school. In distributing marital assets and setting ALIMONY and maintenance, the homemaker's contributions are significant factors, although there is disagreement as to their valuation. On the other hand, courts no longer look at alimony as a long-term remedy. Alimony is now often awarded for a fixed term, so as to enable a divorced spouse to acquire education or training before entering the workforce.

Child Custody During a marriage, all custodial rights are exercised by both parents. These include decision-making power over all aspects of upbringing, religion, and education, as long as the parental decisions and conduct stay clear of the neglect, abuse, and dependency laws. Upon divorce, that power traditionally went solely to one parent who obtained custody. Traditionally, the visitation rights given to the noncustodial parent constituted little more than a possessory interest. This made the custody decision upon divorce a significant one: the relationship between the noncustodial parent and her or his children would change, as the parent would lose the ability to shape decisions affecting the children.

In the United States, since the nineteenth century, mothers traditionally gained custody of children. In the late twentieth century, changes in marital and social roles have led to fathers assuming duties once thought to be the exclusive province of mothers. This in turn has led to fathers showing more interest in claiming custody and to courts granting fathers custody. Yet the vast majority of custody dispositions still go to the mother.

From a dissatisfaction with custody decisions has emerged the concept of joint custody. Under joint custody, legal custody (the decision-making power over the child's conduct of life) remains with both parents, and physical custody goes to one or the other or is shared. The concept has met with mixed reactions. If both parents are reasonable, both may be able to participate fully in decisions that would have been denied one of them. On the other hand, joint custody is likely to be harmful if the parents play out any lingering animosity, or confuse the child with conflicting directions, or are simply unwilling to agree on basic issues involving the child's welfare.

Beginning in 1980, the laws governing custody disputes have been guided by federal statutes. A 1980 amendment to the Judiciary Act (28 U.S.C.A. § 1738A) authorized federal rules that control the enforcement and modification of custody decrees. When in conflict, these rules supersede state statutes, including the Uniform Child Custody Jurisdiction Act (UCCJA), which all states have enacted in some version. The UCCJA was created to deal with interstate custody disputes. Before it was passed, a divorced parent who was unhappy with one state's custody decision could sometimes obtain a more favorable ruling from another state. This led to divorced parents' kidnapping their children and moving to another state in order to petition for custody.

Despite the enactment of UCCJA, the problem persisted. In 1980, Congress passed the Parental Kidnapping Prevention Act (28 U.S.C.A. § 1738A), which aids enforcement and promotes finality in child custody decisions, by

Presence of Parents in Home for Children Under 18 Years Old, 1970 and 1994

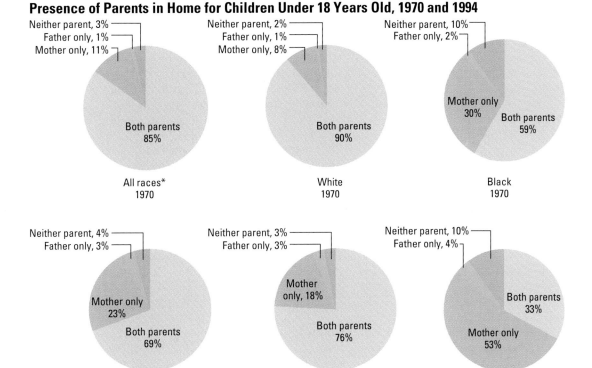

*Includes races not shown separately.

Source: U.S. Bureau of the Census, *Current Population Reports*, P20–450, and earlier reports.

providing that a valid custody decree must be given full legal effect in other states. In an international context, in 1986, the United States adopted the 1980 Hague Convention on the Civil Aspects of International Child Abduction (42 U.S.C.A. § 11603). The convention was designed to facilitate the return of abducted children and the exercise of visitation rights across international boundaries.

Child Support In most cases, a divorce decree will require the noncustodial parent, usually the father, to pay CHILD SUPPORT. The failure of parents to pay child support has significant consequences. Lack of support may force the custodial parent to apply for WELFARE, which in turn affects government budgets and ultimately taxes. This problem has resulted in increasingly more aggressive collection efforts by the government.

The Uniform Reciprocal Enforcement of Support Act (URESA) exists in all states in some form. URESA allows an individual who is due alimony or child support from someone who lives in a different state to bring action for receipt of the payments in the home state. This measure circumvents such problems as expense and inconvenience inherent in traveling from one state to another in pursuit of support.

In response to federal legislation that mandates a more aggressive approach, states have become more creative in extracting money from those who fail to pay child support—who, because they are usually fathers, have come to be labeled deadbeat dads. In 1975, Congress enacted a provision that created the Office of Child Support Enforcement in the Department of Health and Human Services (42 U.S.C.A. § 651). The office was charged with developing ways of collecting child support.

In 1984, the law was amended to strengthen enforcement powers. State laws now must require employers to withhold child support from the paychecks of parents delinquent for one month. Employers are to be held responsible if they do not comply fully. State laws must provide for the imposition of LIENS against the property of those who owe support. Unpaid support must be deducted from federal and state INCOME TAX refunds. Expedited hearings are required in support cases.

Other Areas Family law has grown beyond the boundaries of marriage, divorce, and child custody and support. New areas of law have been created that deal with the legal rights of persons who have not been legally married.

Palimony The colloquial term *palimony* entered the U.S. lexicon in 1976, with the lawsuit *Marvin v. Marvin*, 18 Cal.3d 660, 134 Cal. Rptr. 815, 557 P.2d 106 (Cal.). The term refers to alimony paid out of a nonmarital union. In *Marvin*, the California Supreme Court ruled that although public policy is to encourage and foster the institution of marriage, an equitable distribution of property accumulated during a nonmarital relationship is not precluded. In this case, Michelle Triola Marvin, who had cohabited with film actor Lee Marvin for seven years without a formal marriage, brought an action to enforce an oral contract under which she was entitled to half the property accumulated during the seven-year period, along with support payments. Though the facts of the case ultimately led to Michelle Marvin's not recovering any palimony, the case established the right of a cohabitant to obtain a property settlement. See also COHABITATION.

Same-Sex Marriage Despite court challenges, marriage can occur only between persons of the opposite sex. In *Baker v. Nelson*, 291 Minn. 310, 191 N.W.2d 185 (1971), *cert. denied*, 409 U.S. 810, 93 S. Ct. 37, 34 L. Ed. 2d 65 (1972), the Minnesota Supreme Court sustained a clerk's denial of a marriage license to a homosexual couple.

The possibility of homosexual marriage was revived by the 1993 decision of the Hawaii Supreme Court in *Baehr v. Lewin*, 74 Haw. 530, 852 P.2d 44. In *Baehr*, the court held that a state law restricting legal marriage to parties of the opposite sex establishes a sex-based classification, which is subject to strict constitutional scrutiny when challenged on equal protection grounds. Although the court did not recognize a constitutional right to same-sex marriage, it indicated that if the state prohibited such marriages, it would have a difficult time proving that gay and lesbian couples were not being denied equal protection of the laws. The debate over homosexual marriage continues at both the federal and state levels.

Artificial Conception and Surrogate Motherhood Modern technology has created opportunities for conceiving children through ARTIFICIAL INSEMINATION, in vitro fertilization, and embryo transplantation. Combined with these techniques is the practice of surrogate motherhood. These new techniques have also created legal questions and disputes new to family law.

The most important legal question goes to the child's status, which encompasses the child's rights against, and claims on, the various actors in the typical scenario. These actors might include one or more of the following: the married mother's husband when the child was conceived by artificial insemination with semen donated by a third party; (2) a surrogate mother who carried the child to term and gave birth to the child, where the pregnancy resulted from either (*a*) her artificial insemination or (*b*) her receipt of a fertilized ovum (embryo) from another woman; (3) the donor of the semen; and (4) the donor of the ovum or embryo.

Artificial insemination Where a married woman, with the consent of her husband, has conceived a child by artificial insemination from a donor other than her husband, the law will recognize the child as the husband's LEGITIMATE child.

In vitro fertilization and ovum transplantation The technique of in vitro fertilization gained international attention with the birth of Louise Brown in England in 1978. This technique involves the fertilization of the ovum outside the womb. Where the ovum is donated by another woman, the birth mother will be treated in law as the legitimate mother of the child.

Surrogate motherhood In SURROGATE MOTHERHOOD, women agree to be artificially inseminated or to have a fertilized ovum inserted into their uterus, and to carry the child to term for another party. Where women do this to assist members of their own family, few legal complications arise. However, where women have agreed to the procedure for financial compensation, controversy has followed.

The most famous case involved "Baby M" (*In re Baby M*, 109 N.J. 396, 537 A.2d 1227 [1988]). In 1987, Mary Beth Whitehead agreed to be the surrogate mother for sperm-donor father William Stern. Stern agreed to pay Whitehead $10,000 for carrying the child. Whitehead signed a contract agreeing to turn over the child to Stern and his wife, Elizabeth Stern. When Whitehead refused to turn over the baby she called Melissa, Stern went into court seeking custody of the girl he called Sara. The New Jersey Supreme Court held that the surrogate contract was against public policy and that the right of procreation did not entitle Stern and his wife to custody of the child. Nevertheless, based on the best interests of the child, the court awarded custody to the Sterns and granted Whitehead visitation rights.

Court Procedures Family law has been governed by the adversarial process. This process is geared to produce a winner and a loser. In divorce and child custody cases, the process has increased tensions between the parties, tensions that do not go away after the court process is completed.

States have begun to explore nonadversary alternatives, including family MEDIATION. Court systems are also experimenting with more informal procedures for handling family law cases, in hopes of diffusing the emotions of the parties. See also ADVERSARY SYSTEM; ALTERNATIVE DISPUTE RESOLUTION.

Conclusion Family law has become a major component of the U.S. legal system. Attorneys seeking admission to the bar are being tested on family law subjects, and law schools provide more courses in this field. Many of the social and cultural issues U.S. society debates will ultimately be played out in its family courts.

CROSS-REFERENCES

Child Abuse; Children's Rights; Domestic Violence; Fetal Rights; Gay and Lesbian Rights; Husband and Wife; Parent and Child.

FANNIE MAE See FEDERAL NATIONAL MORTGAGE ASSOCIATION.

FARM CREDIT ADMINISTRATION The Farm Credit Administration (FCA) is an independent agency of the EXECUTIVE BRANCH of the federal government. It supervises and coordinates the Farm Credit System, which is a centralized banking system designed to serve U.S. agricultural interests by granting short- and long-term CREDIT through regional banks and local associations. Although initially capitalized by the federal government, the banks and associations that make up the Farm Credit System are now financed entirely through stock that is owned by members, borrowers, or the associations. The FCA ensures the safe operation of these lending institutions and protects the interests of their borrowers.

The Farm Credit System was established in 1916 in response to the unique credit needs of farmers. Federal land banks were established to provide adequate and dependable credit to farmers, ranchers, producers or harvesters of

William and Elizabeth Stern sued Mary Beth Whitehead, the surrogate mother of "Baby M," for custody of the child. The Sterns won custody of the girl they named Sara.

AP/WIDE WORLD PHOTOS

The Farm Credit Administration was established in 1933 to oversee the entities that grant credit to farmers.

aquatic products, providers of farm services, rural homeowners, and agricultural associations. During the 1930s, the Depression and falling farm prices increased debt delinquencies and led to a serious decline in farm values. Many loan companies and credit institutions failed. In 1933, President FRANKLIN D. ROOSEVELT directed Congress to create the FCA to oversee the entities that grant credit to farmers and ranchers. All government farm credit programs, including the land banks and intermediate credit banks, were unified under the new agency, which was established by the Farm Credit Act of 1933 (U.S. Pub. Law 73-76, 48 Stat. 257).

The modern FCA derives its authority from the Farm Credit Act of 1971 (12 U.S.C.A. § 2241 et seq.), which superseded all prior authorizing legislation. The FCA examines the lending institutions that constitute the Farm Credit System to certify that they are sound. It also ensures compliance with the regulations under which the Farm Credit institutions operate. To that end, it is authorized to issue cease and desist orders, levy civil monetary penalties, remove officers and directors, and impose financial and operating reporting requirements. It may directly intervene in the management of an institution whose practices violate the Farm Credit Act or its regulations. It may also step in to correct an unsafe practice or to assume formal conservatorship over an institution.

The FCA is managed by the Farm Credit Administration Board, whose three full-time members are appointed to six-year terms by the president, with the advice and consent of the Senate. The board meets monthly to set policy

objectives and approve the rules and regulations that govern the FCA's responsibilities.

See also AGRICULTURAL LAW.

FATAL 📖 Deadly or mortal; destructive; devastating. 📖

A *fatal error* in legal procedure is one that is of such a substantial nature as to harm unjustly the person who complains about it. It is synonymous with *reversible error*, which, in appellate practice, warrants the reversal of the judgment before the APPELLATE COURT for review. A fatal error can warrant a new TRIAL.

A *fatal injury* is one that results in death. It is distinguished from a DISABILITY in accident and disability INSURANCE policies, which includes those injuries that prevent the insured from doing his or her regular job but do not result in his or her death.

FAULT 📖 Neglect of care; an act to which blame or censure is attached. Fault implies any NEGLIGENCE, error, or defect of judgment. 📖

Fault has been held to embrace a refusal to perform an action that one is legally obligated to do, such as the failure to make a payment when due.

FEASANCE 📖 The performance of an act. 📖

MALFEASANCE is the commission of an illegal act. MISFEASANCE is the inadequate or improper performance of a lawful act. NONFEASANCE is the neglect of a duty or the failure to perform a required task.

FEDERAL 📖 Relating to the general government or union of the states; based upon, or created pursuant to, the laws of the Constitution of the United States. 📖

The United States has traditionally been named a *federal* government in most political and judicial writings. The term *federal* has not been prescribed by any definite authority but is used to express a broad opinion concerning the nature of the form of government.

A recent tendency has been to use the term *national* in place of *federal* to denote the government of the Union. Neither settles any question regarding the nature of authority of the government.

The term *federal* is generally considered to be more appropriate if the government is to be viewed as a union of the states. *National* is used to reflect the view that individual state governments and the Union as a whole are two distinct and separate systems, each of which is established directly by the population for local and national purposes, respectively.

In a more general sense, *federal* is ordinarily used to refer to a league or compact between two or more states to become joined under one central government.

FEDERAL AVIATION ADMINISTRATION Half a century after Wilbur and Orville Wright flew an airplane for twelve seconds in Kitty Hawk, North Carolina, on December 17, 1903—becoming the first U.S. residents to successfully fly a powered aircraft—Congress established the Federal Aviation Agency, later renamed the Federal Aviation Administration (FAA), with the Federal Aviation Act of 1958 (49 U.S.C.A. § 106). Under the act, the FAA became responsible for all the following:

- Regulating air commerce to promote its development and safety and to meet national defense requirements
- Controlling the use of navigable airspace in the United States and regulating both civil and military operations in that airspace in the interest of safety and efficiency
- Promoting and developing civil aeronautics, which is the science of dealing with the operation of civil, or nonmilitary, aircraft
- Consolidating research and development with respect to air navigation facilities
- Installing and operating air navigation facilities
- Developing and operating a common system of air traffic control and navigation for civil and military aircraft
- Developing and implementing programs and regulations to control aircraft noise, sonic booms, and other environmental effects of civil aviation

A component agency of the Department of Transportation ever since the Department of Transportation Act was passed in 1967 (49 U.S.C.A. § 1651), the FAA engages in a variety of activities to fulfill its responsibilities. One vital activity is safety regulation. The FAA issues and enforces rules, regulations, and minimum standards relating to the manufacture, operation, and maintenance of aircraft. In the interest of safety, the FAA also rates and certifies people working on aircraft, including medical personnel, and certifies airports that serve air CARRIERS. The agency performs flight inspections of air navigation facilities in the United States and, as required, abroad. It also enforces regulations under the Hazardous Materials Transportation Act (49 U.S.C.A. app. 1801) as they apply to air shipments. In 1994, the FAA employed 2,500 safety inspectors, who oversaw 7,300 planes operated by scheduled airlines, 200,000 other planes, 4,700 repair stations, 650 pilot training schools, and 190 maintenance schools. FAA inspectors use a six-inch-thick book called the *Airworthiness Inspector's Handbook* in their work. They have significant power, including the ability to delay or ground aircraft

deemed non-airworthy and to suspend the LICENSE of PILOTS and other flight personnel who break FAA rules.

Another primary activity of the FAA is to manage airspace and air traffic, with the goal being to ensure the safe and efficient use of the United States' navigable airspace. To meet this goal, the agency operates a network of airport traffic control towers, air route traffic control centers, and flight service stations. It develops air traffic rules and regulations and allocates the use of airspace. It also provides for the security control of air traffic to meet national defense requirements.

The FAA also oversees the creation, operation, maintenance, and quality of federal visual and electronic aids to air navigation. The agency operates and maintains voice and data communications equipment, radar facilities, computer systems, and visual display equipment at flight service stations, airport traffic control towers, and air route traffic control centers.

Research, engineering, and development activities of the agency help provide the systems, procedures, facilities, and devices needed for a safe and efficient system of air navigation and air traffic control to meet the needs of civil aviation and the air defense system. The FAA also performs aeromedical research to apply knowledge gained from its work and the work of others to the safety and promotion of civil aviation and the health, safety, and efficiency of agency employees. The agency further supports the development and testing of improved aircraft, engines, propellers, and appliances.

The FAA is authorized to test and evaluate aviation systems, subsystems, equipment, de-

The Federal Aviation Administration manages airspace and air traffic by operating airport traffic control towers such as this one at Washington, D.C.'s National Airport.

AP/WIDE WORLD PHOTOS

vices, materials, concepts, and procedures at any phase in their development, from conception to acceptance and implementation. The agency may assign independent testing at key decision points in the development cycle of these elements.

The agency maintains a national plan of airport requirements and administers a grant program for the development of public-use airports, to ensure safety and to meet current and future capacity needs. The FAA also evaluates the environmental effects of airport development; administers an airport noise compatibility program; develops standards and technical guidance on airport planning, design, safety, and operation; and provides grants to assist public agencies in airport planning and development.

The FAA registers aircraft and records documents related to the title or interest in aircraft, aircraft engines, propellers, appliances, and spare parts.

Under the Federal Aviation Act of 1958 and the International Aviation Facilities Act (49 U.S.C.A. app. 1151), the agency promotes aviation safety and civil aviation abroad by exchanging aeronautical information with foreign aviation authorities; certifying foreign repair stations, aviators, and mechanics; negotiating bilateral airworthiness agreements to facilitate the import and export of aircraft and components; and providing technical assistance and training in all areas of the agency's expertise. The agency provides technical representation at international conferences, including those of the International Civil Aviation Organization and other international organizations.

Finally, the agency conducts miscellaneous activities such as administering the aviation insurance and aircraft loan guarantee programs; assigning priority and allocating materials for civil aircraft and civil aviation operations; developing specifications for the preparation of aeronautical charts; publishing current information on airways and airport services and issuing technical publications for the improvement of safety in flight, airport planning, and design; and serving as the executive administration for the operation and maintenance of the Department of Transportation's automated payroll and personnel systems.

No stranger to controversy, the FAA has been at the center of a variety of national debates during its existence. In the early 1980s, eleven thousand air traffic controllers went on STRIKE to protest stressful working conditions. When President RONALD REAGAN ordered them fired, the FAA pledged to replace many of them

Federal Aviation Administration

Fatal Accidents on Scheduled Commercial Air Carriers*, 1975 to 1995

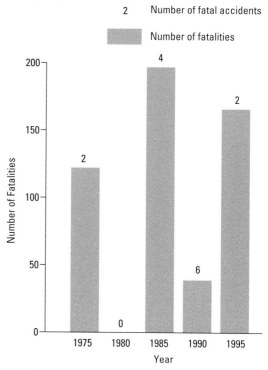

*All scheduled services of U.S. air carriers operating under 14 CFR 121.

Source: Federal Aviation Administration, *FAA Statistical Handbook of Aviation*, annual.

by overhauling and modernizing the system that guides planes from takeoff to landing. Fifteen years later, some critics of the FAA contended that the agency had yet to create a modern air traffic control system, causing delays that cost the airline industry up to $5 billion a year. Speaking on the subject in January 1996, Senator William S. Cohen (R-Me.), a member of the Committee on Governmental Affairs, said, "The FAA is a victim of its own poor management. If the agency devoted more time to managing itself and less time to defending its deficiencies, the air traffic control system would have been replaced years ago."

In the 1980s, the FAA supported drug-testing for commercial airline pilots and air traffic controllers. Though drug-testing is a form of search, implicating Fourth Amendment concerns, these drug tests are routinely upheld as a permissible invasion of privacy in light of the public safety concerns associated with air travel.

With U.S. air traffic increasing by almost 130 percent from 1978 to 1994, fatal aircraft accidents also increased. Critics of the FAA say that the agency failed to increase its number of inspectors at a rate comparable to the rate of growth in air traffic; in fact, the agency had only

12 percent more inspectors in 1994 than it did in 1978. The FAA also came under scrutiny for the safety of smaller aircraft after a succession of fatal commuter jet crashes in the 1980s and early to mid-1990s. In 1988, for example, an AVAir plane crashed in Raleigh, North Carolina, killing twelve people. In the two months before the accident, AVAir had another accident, filed for BANKRUPTCY, shut down, and restarted. In that time, AVAir's FAA inspector never visited the airline's headquarters, observed a pilot check ride, or met the training director.

Together with Federico F. Peña, secretary of the U.S. TRANSPORTATION DEPARTMENT, David R. Hinson, administrator of the FAA, set what he called an ambitious new goal at a January 1995 aviation safety summit: zero accidents. In September of 1995, he defended his agency on the safety issue by saying that of the 173 safety initiatives developed at the summit, more than two-thirds were already complete. Calling perfect safety a shared responsibility, Hinson asked for a "hands-on, eyes-open commitment of every person who designs, builds, flies, maintains and regulates aircraft." The same month, the FAA announced plans to train air traffic controllers with computer simulators. In early 1996, the federal government enacted new rules intended to make small commuter turboprop planes as safe as big jets. As part of the change, the FAA began requiring small AIRLINES to follow the same rules for training and operations as do major airlines.

FEDERAL BANK ACT A statute passed by Congress in 1791 that created the BANK OF THE UNITED STATES as the central bank for the newly formed government.

The National Bank Act, 12 U.S.C.A. § 21 et seq. (1864), was enacted to provide the federal government with an agent to handle its financial affairs through the incorporation of the Bank of the United States, which also carried on general banking business. The bank had a twenty-year charter that expired in 1811, but it was not renewed due to the political climate of the country. The financing problems of the War of 1812, however, highlighted the need for a central bank, motivating Congress to enact legislation to establish the Second Bank of the United States. That bank also had a twenty-year charter, but the bank was closed prior to the charter expiration due to political opposition led by President ANDREW JACKSON.

FEDERAL BAR ASSOCIATION The Federal Bar Association (FBA) was founded in 1920 to advance the science of JURISPRUDENCE and promote the administration of justice; to uphold a high standard for the federal judiciary, attorneys representing the U.S. government, and attorneys appearing before the courts, agencies, and departments of the United States; to encourage friendly relations among members of the legal profession; and to promote the welfare of attorneys. Continuing legal education and professional and community services are among association activities. FBA is affiliated with the National Lawyers Club and the Foundation of the Federal Bar Association. Publications include *Federal Bar News* (monthly), a monthly placement newsletter, *Federal Bar Journal* (quarterly), and *Legislative Update*. The association holds annual meetings in late summer.

FEDERAL BUDGET An annual effort to balance federal spending on such things as forestry, education, space technology, and the national defense, with revenue, which the United States collects largely through federal taxes.

When the federal government spends more money than it collects in a given year, a deficit occurs. U.S. expenditures have exceeded revenue in every year since 1969. By the mid-1990s, annual budget deficits were exceeding $200 billion, alarming the public and fueling debate over how to balance the federal budget.

Of the three branches of the U.S. government, Congress has the power to determine federal spending, pursuant to Article I, Section 9, of the U.S. Constitution, which states, "No money shall be drawn from the Treasury, but in Consequence of Appropriations made by Law." The drafters of the Constitution sought to secure the federal spending power with legislators rather than the PRESIDENT, to keep separate the powers of purse and sword. In *The Federalist* No. 58, JAMES MADISON wrote, "This power of the purse may, in fact, be regarded as the most complete and effectual weapon with which any constitution can arm the immediate representatives of the people."

Still, the Constitution reserved the president some role in legislative decisions regarding federal spending. The president may recommend budget allowances for what he or she considers "necessary and expedient," and if Congress does not heed these recommendations, the president may assert his or her qualified VETO power. But the ultimate determinations of federal expenditures belong to Congress.

To encourage better communication and cooperation between the president and Congress on matters concerning the federal budget, Congress has enacted laws formalizing the budget-making process. The first such law was passed in response to an enormous national debt following World War I. The Budget and Accounting Act of 1921 (31 U.S.C.A. § 501 et seq.) required the president to submit to Congress an annual budget outlining recommendations, or budget aggregates. Within budget aggregates recommended by the president, Congress then was to assign priorities. The 1921 act did not change the balance of powers assigned by the Constitution: Congress retained the right to ignore the president's recommendations, and the president retained the right to veto spending legislation. Rather, the act formalized and codified the roles of each branch.

As may be expected, the president and members of Congress do not always agree on federal budget issues. In the early 1970s, President RICHARD M. NIXON claimed IMPOUNDMENT, which is an executive power to refuse to spend funds appropriated by Congress. Although Nixon argued that he had the right to impound in instances he believed were in the country's best interest, the U.S. Supreme Court affirmed a ruling by the Second Circuit Court of Appeals requiring Nixon to expend federal funds appropriated for the protection of the environment (*Train v. New York*, 420 U.S. 35, 95 S. Ct. 839,

43 L. Ed. 2d 1 [1975]). However, this ruling was based on the terms of a federal water pollution law; the Court declined to address specifically whether the EXECUTIVE BRANCH had the general power to impound funds appropriated by Congress.

Congress responded with the Congressional Budget and Impoundment Control Act of 1974 (2 U.S.C.A. § 190a-1 note et seq.; 31 U.S.C.A. § 702 et seq.). This act sought to restore and strengthen legislative control of the budget by requiring the approval of both the Senate and the House of Representatives for presidential *recisions*, or current-year cuts, of funds appropriated by Congress. The 1974 act also established a budget committee in each congressional house, and the Congressional Budget Office to provide technical information and support. Finally, this act required that Congress adopt budget resolutions setting limits on budget aggregates and allowing debates on spending priorities within those aggregates.

The 1974 act greatly reduced the president's role in the budget process—in particular, the president's responsibility of determining and recommending budget aggregates to Congress. Now, legislators could more readily ignore the president's recommendations, and instead create for themselves, through budget resolutions, generous limits on budget aggregates. This allowed politicians more flexibility in setting spending priorities within the budget aggregates, thus pleasing their constituents. Not surprisingly, federal budget deficits grew.

In 1985, Congress reacted to the rising deficits by enacting the Balanced Budget and Emergency Deficit Control Act (popularly known as the Gramm-Rudman-Hollings Act) (Pub. L. No. 99-177, 99 Stat. 1038) (codified as amended in scattered sections of 2, 31, and 42 U.S.C.A.). The Gramm-Rudman-Hollings Act encouraged congressional conformity to deficit reduction targets specifically prescribed by the act. If, after the budget process has been completed, the budget exceeds deficit reduction targets, spending cuts are ordered by the president's Office of Management and Budget. The Gramm-Rudman-Hollings Act limited this executive power by providing congressionally mandated formulas for the spending cuts.

The Budget Enforcement Act of 1990 (2 U.S.C.A. § 601 et seq.; 15 U.S.C.A. § 1022) revised Gramm-Rudman-Hollings to make deficit targets flexible, not fixed. The 1990 act further required that reductions in defense and foreign spending cannot be used to increase domestic spending, and vice versa. This requirement is known as the *firewall*. In addition,

Federal Budget, 1945–1994

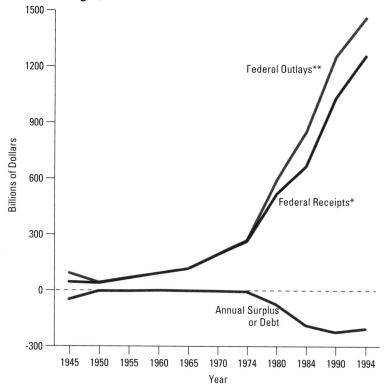

*Includes off- budget receipts.
**Includes off-budget outlays.

Source: U.S. Office of Management and Budget, *Historical Tables,* annual.

the 1990 act required that either revenue increases or spending cuts must balance increases in spending for ENTITLEMENTS, such as Aid to Families with Dependent Children. This requirement is known as *pay-as-you-go*.

The current federal budget process is extremely complex. Confusion and misunderstandings about the process contribute to disagreements over how to resolve the federal deficit. A very basic description of the process follows:

First, the president sends budget recommendations to Congress. Congress, which has the ultimate power to appropriate federal funds, may follow or ignore the president's recommendations.

Second, the House and Senate together devise an overall budget resolution, usually debating their differences at a conference committee. Following the guidelines of the budget resolution, House and Senate committees recommend spending for each of thirteen substantive areas. For the House of Representatives, these committees, which loosely correspond with the thirteen substantive areas, include Agriculture; Banking, Finance and Urban Affairs; Education and Labor; Energy and Commerce; Interior and Insular Affairs; Judiciary; Merchant Marine and Fisheries; Post Office and Civil Service; Public Works and Transportation; Science, Space, and Technology; Veterans Affairs; and Ways and Means. For the Senate, the committees, which also loosely correspond with the thirteen substantive areas, are Agriculture, Nutrition, and Forestry; Banking, Housing, and Urban Affairs; Commerce, Science, and Transportation; Energy and Natural Resources; Environment and Public Works; Finance; Governmental Affairs; Judiciary; Labor and Human Resources; and Veterans' Affairs. The full House and Senate together vote on the recommendations of the committees, following debate in a conference committee if necessary. The House and Senate then jointly send an authorization bill for each of the thirteen substantive areas to the president for signing. These bills merely establish guidelines for spending; they do not actually authorize spending.

Next, the House and Senate Appropriations Committees together draft thirteen separate appropriations bills, which correspond to the authorization bills. The full House and Senate together approve or disapprove each APPROPRIATION, conduct debates in conference committees to resolve differences, and amend appropriations if necessary. They then jointly send the thirteen appropriations bills to the president to be signed. If the bills are signed, spending is approved.

Upon congressional funds appropriations, the branches and agencies of the federal government are required to spend the funds on the functions for which they were appropriated. Congress may supplement budget appropriations if conditions change following the budget process, but supplemental appropriation in excess of authorization bills must be accounted for with spending cuts, amendment of the individual authorization bills, or amendment of the overall budget bill containing all the individual authorization bills.

Several wrinkles complicate the federal budget process. For example, Congress and the president enact as law permanent authorization and spending appropriations for entitlement programs such as Medicare and Medicaid. Thus, appropriations for entitlement programs become automatic, requiring no further congressional action during the annual budget process.

Appropriations funding the principal and interest owed on the national DEBT are, practically speaking, also automatic. Unlike appropriations for entitlement programs, those for the national debt must be approved annually by Congress. But approval for funding this debt is always granted; to allow the United States to DEFAULT would severely damage the national and world economies. In the debate over how to balance the federal budget, politicians and citizens often overlook automatic federal spending.

Also complicating the budget process is the method of ACCOUNTING used by the federal government, known as the *cash method*. The cash method of accounting calculates expenditures based upon the date they are paid. This differs from the *accrual method* of accounting, which calculates expenditures based on the date the obligation is incurred. Although this may seem to be a subtle distinction, the cash method by its nature leaves more room for error in budget appropriations, some of which is corrected by a government statistic called the National Income and Product Accounts. Economists, politicians, and concerned U.S. citizens disagree over which accounting method, cash or accrual, would better serve the U.S. budget and the national economy. Moreover, economics is an inexact science whose complexities are not well understood by the average voter. See also ACCRUAL BASIS; CASH BASIS.

Added to the public's general confusion is the difficulty in estimating the federal budget, both revenues and expenditures, before the start of a fiscal year. Future unemployment, inflation,

Government Shutdown

Legal commentators have argued that by keeping separate the powers of purse and sword, drafters of the U.S. Constitution encouraged battles between Congress and the president. This friction between government branches is part of the constitutionally created system of checks and balances. Discord over federal budget priorities usually resolves in short order; no politician wants the reputation of jeopardizing the national or world economy. But on rare occasions in the 1990s, budget fights led to federal government shutdowns.

In October 1990, when Democrats in Congress sought to reduce the federal deficit by implementing a surtax on the income of millionaires, Republican president George Bush followed through on a threat to veto any budget legislation that included tax increases. The veto effectively shut down several federal agencies. The closures lasted only three days and occurred on a weekend. Fearing negative fallout from a more extensive government shutdown, Congress and the president reached a compromise plan to reduce the federal deficit without the surtax.

Major differences in political ideologies again surfaced in the fall of 1994, when control of Congress shifted from Democrats to Republicans. The new Congress set a goal of balancing the federal budget by the year 2002, a feat that had not occurred since 1969.

Republicans, buoyed by public sentiment favoring this goal, attempted to implement their balanced budget plan in the fall of 1995. But they faced opposition from many Democrats, among them President Bill Clinton. Although agreeing with the necessity of a balanced budget, Clinton opposed proposed cuts to entitlement programs such as Medicare, Medicaid, and welfare. The dispute divided the branches of government as well as political parties, and in November 1995, an impasse led to the expiration of federal funding. Without adequate funding, much of the federal government—including agencies, museums, national parks, and research laboratories—ground to a halt. Some eight hundred thousand government employees deemed "nonessential" were sent home.

Politicians on both sides of the issue faced disapproval from their constituents. Compromises were reached, and a week after it started, the shutdown was over.

But ideological differences continued. Although both Congress and the White House still looked to 2002 as the year of the balanced budget, they could not agree on how to reach that goal. Numerous efforts at negotiation were fruitless. By mid-December 1995, political gridlock caused yet another partial government shutdown. This shutdown, lasting twenty-one days, was longer than any previous one in the United States.

See also Bush, George; Clinton, Bill; Gingrich, Newton.

---

and growth in the gross national product are variables that will affect actual federal spending. And although the Treasury Department and the Senate Finance Committee estimate future revenues, no accurate determination will be available until the fiscal year has already ended.

Largely because the budget process is so complex, there is little agreement as to how to balance the federal budget. As the federal deficit lingers each year, so does public support of a CONSTITUTIONAL AMENDMENT requiring a balanced budget. Yet several attempts at such legislation—in 1984, 1990, 1992, and 1994—have failed to pass in Congress. One vocal proponent of a balanced budget amendment is Texas businessman H. Ross Perot, who ran unsuccessfully for president in 1992. Perot denounced mushrooming deficits, blaming politicians who approve current spending to appease constituents at the expense of future taxpayers: "[I]n 1992 alone we will add over $330 billion to the $4 trillion we've already piled on our children's shoulders.... The weight of that debt may destroy our children's futures." See also INDEPENDENT PARTIES; REFORM PARTY.

Yet a balanced budget amendment would not be without obstacles. One problem is defining a balanced budget, especially given the confusion over federal accounting methods, automatic expenditures, and inaccurate estimates of revenue and spending. For example, a federal budget employing the cash method of accounting may show a far greater deficit than the same budget employing the accrual method of accounting.

Another problem is that of the enforceability of a balanced budget amendment, which hinges in part on taxpayer STANDING, or legal entitlement to sue. Would all taxpayers have standing to enforce a balanced budget amendment, or would only taxpayers who could demonstrate actual damage as a result of an unbalanced budget? Further, courts are reluctant to make determinations of what they consider POLITICAL QUESTIONS, or issues best decided by the legislative or executive branch of government. Many commentators consider the judicial branch incapable of effectively analyzing and deciding issues concerning the federal budget.

Perhaps the greatest impediments to a balanced budget amendment, or any other meaningful reform of the federal budget, are the sacrifices faced by U.S. citizens: to have their taxes raised and their spending programs cut. Whether Congress, the president, and the public will make these sacrifices to reduce and perhaps eliminate the federal deficit is an engaging political question.

CROSS-REFERENCES

Congress of the United States; Constitution of the United States; Office of Management and Budget; Separation of Powers.

FEDERAL BUREAU OF INVESTIGATION

The Federal Bureau of Investigation (FBI) is the principal investigative unit of the U.S. Department of Justice (DOJ). The FBI gathers and reports facts, compiles EVIDENCE, and locates WITNESSES in legal matters in which the United States is or may be a party in interest. In addition, the bureau assists both U.S. and international law enforcement agencies in crime investigation and personnel training.

The FBI investigates all violations of federal law except those specifically assigned to other federal agencies. The bureau's jurisdiction covers a wide range of crimes, from kidnapping and drug trafficking to the unauthorized use of the Woodsy Owl emblem, the U.S. Forest Service's antipollution mascot (18 U.S.C.A. § 711a). The FBI's authority derives from 28 U.S.C.A. § 533, which enables the attorney general to "appoint officials to detect . . . crimes against the United States." The bureau also conducts noncriminal investigations, such as background security checks. The FBI does not prosecute crimes, but assists other law enforcement agencies in investigations that lead to prosecution.

The FBI traces its origins to 1908 when President THEODORE ROOSEVELT instructed Attorney General Charles J. Bonaparte to create a force of special agents to work as investigators within the DOJ. In 1909, Attorney General GEORGE W. WICKERSHAM named the elite group the Bureau of Investigation. In 1935, following a series of name changes, the bureau was officially termed the Federal Bureau of Investigation.

In its early days, the FBI investigated the relatively small number of federal crimes that existed. These included BANKRUPTCY frauds and ANTITRUST violations. During World War I, it was responsible for investigating ESPIONAGE, SABOTAGE, SEDITION, and violations of the Selec-

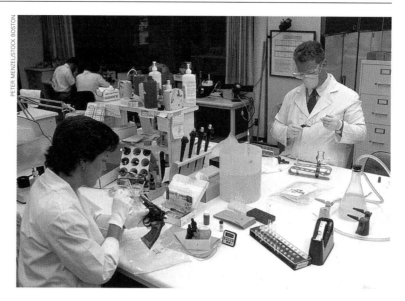

tive Service Act of 1917 (Act May 18, 1917, c. 15, 40 Stat. 76 [Comp. Stat. 1918, § 2044a-2044k]). In 1919, the bureau broadened its scope to include the investigation of motor vehicle THEFTS.

The FBI established its reputation as a tenacious investigative force during Prohibition, in the 1930s. Its many undercover probes throughout that era led to the arrests of notorious crime figures such as John Dillinger and AL CAPONE. With the onset of World War II and the advent of the atomic age, the FBI increased its size and scope to include domestic and foreign intelligence and counterintelligence probes, background security checks, and investigations of internal security matters for the executive branch.

During the 1960s, the bureau's chief concerns were CIVIL RIGHTS violations and ORGANIZED CRIME operations. Counterterrorism, white-collar crimes, illegal drugs, and violent crimes were its focus during the 1970s and 1980s.

The modern FBI divides its investigations among seven major areas: applicant matters (background checks on applicants and candidates for federal positions), civil rights, counterterrorism, foreign counterintelligence, drugs and organized crime, violent crimes and major offenders, and white-collar crimes. It has nine divisions in three offices located at its headquarters in Washington, D.C. These divisions provide program direction and support services to fifty-six field offices, four hundred satellite offices (known as resident agencies), and four specialized field installations within the United States, as well as twenty-two liaison posts outside the United States. The bureau employs approximately ten thousand special agents and over thirteen thousand support personnel.

The Federal Bureau of Investigation gathers and compiles evidence. In its serology lab these scientists test for blood on a .357 magnum and examine liquid blood samples.

J. Edgar Hoover, right, is the most famous of the FBI's directors. He served as director for forty-eight years and under his leadership the bureau grew in size and expertise, though he was criticized for abuse of power and harassment of suspects.

In addition to its investigative work on federal crimes, the FBI provides investigative and training support to other law enforcement agencies. The FBI Laboratory, one of the largest and most comprehensive crime laboratories in the world, is the only full-service federal forensic lab. FBI examiners perform crime scene searches, surveillance, fingerprint examinations, and other scientific and technical services. They also train state and local crime laboratory and law enforcement personnel. Through the Criminal Justice Information Services (CJIS), the FBI provides sophisticated identification and information services to local, state, federal, and international law enforcement agencies. Among the aids available through CJIS is a state-of-the-art automated fingerprint identification system. The bureau also offers extensive training programs to FBI employees and other law enforcement personnel at the FBI Academy, in Quantico, Virginia.

The FBI is headed by a director, the first and most famous of whom was J. EDGAR HOOVER. Appointed in 1924 at the age of twenty-nine, Hoover led the bureau for forty-eight years, until his death in 1972. He is credited with building a highly disciplined force of efficient and respected investigators. During Hoover's tenure, the FBI established its centralized fingerprint file, crime laboratory, and training center for police officers. Hoover was also criticized as an autocrat who wielded his power against anyone he considered a threat to U.S. security. He was obsessively anti-Communist,

and critics charge that his single-minded quest to root out all political dissent led to the harassment of suspects and suspension of their civil liberties.

L. Patrick Gray III became acting director upon Hoover's death. He was succeeded in 1973 by another acting director, William D. Ruckelshaus, who was replaced later that year by Clarence M. Kelley, a former FBI agent. Kelley is credited with modernizing the bureau, curbing arbitrary investigations, and opening the special agent ranks to women and minorities. He presided over the bureau until 1978 when William H. Webster was appointed director. Webster was replaced by acting director John E. Otto in 1987. Otto stepped down later that year and was replaced by William S. Sessions.

During Sessions's tenure, African American and Hispanic agents charged the bureau with racial discrimination and harassment. Sessions settled these claims with the groups and instituted policies to increase the number of women and minorities in the agency. In 1993, Sessions was dismissed from his post by President BILL CLINTON amid allegations of unethical conduct. In his place, Clinton appointed a former FBI agent and federal judge, Louis J. Freeh.

CROSS-REFERENCES

Forensic Science: *Forensic Science in the Federal Bureau of Investigation;* Justice Department.

FEDERAL COMMUNICATIONS COMMISSION   The Federal Communications Commission (FCC) regulates interstate and foreign communications by radio, TELEVISION, wire, satellite, and cable. The FCC oversees the development and operation of broadcast services and the provision of nationwide and worldwide telephone and telegraph services. It also oversees the use of communications for promoting the safety of life and property and for strengthening the national defense.

The FCC was created by the Communications Act of 1934 (47 U.S.C.A. § 151 et seq.) to regulate interstate and foreign communications by wire and radio in the PUBLIC INTEREST. The scope of its regulation includes radio and television BROADCASTING; telephone, telegraph, and cable TV operation; two-way radio and radio operation; and satellite communication. The FCC is composed of five members who are appointed by the president. The commission is assisted by a review board and an office of general counsel. In addition, administrative law judges conduct evidentiary adjudicatory hearings and write initial decisions.

Mass Media Bureau The Mass Media Bureau regulates the following services: amplitude modulation (AM), frequency modulation (FM), television, low-power television, translator, instructional television and related broadcast auxiliary, and direct broadcast satellite. The Mass Media Bureau issues construction permits, operating licenses, and renewals or transfers of such broadcast licenses except for broadcast auxiliary services. The bureau also oversees compliance by broadcasters with statutes and FCC policies.

Common Carrier Bureau The Common Carrier Bureau regulates interstate common carrier communications by telephone. COMMON CARRIERS include companies, organizations, and individuals providing communications services to the public for hire, which must serve all who wish to use them at established rates. In providing interstate communications services, common carriers may employ landline wire or electrical or optical cable facilities.

Wireless Telecommunications Bureau The Wireless Telecommunications Bureau administers all domestic commercial and private wireless telecommunications programs and policies. Commercial wireless services include cellular, paging, personal, specialized mobile radio, air-ground, and basic exchange telecommunications. Private wireless services include land mobile radio (including public safety, industrial, land transportation, and business), broadcast auxiliary, operational fixed microwave and point-to-point microwave, and special radio telecommunications. The Wireless Telecommunications Bureau also implements laws and treaties covering the use of radio for the safety of life and property at sea and in the air, and administers commercial and amateur radio operator programs.

International Bureau The International Bureau manages all FCC international TELE-COMMUNICATIONS and satellite programs and policies, and represents the FCC at international conferences, meetings, and negotiations. The International Bureau consists of three divisions: Telecommunications, Satellite and Radiocommunication, and Planning and Negotiations.

The Telecommunications Division develops and administers policies, rules, and procedures for the regulation of telecommunications facilities and services under section 214 of the Communications Act (47 U.S.C.A. § 153 et seq.) and Cable Landing License Act (47 U.S.C.A. § 34 et seq.). In addition, the division develops and administers regulatory assistance and training programs in conjunction with the administra-tion's Global Information Infrastructure initiative.

The Satellite and Radiocommunication Division develops and administers policies, rules, standards, and procedures for licensing and regulating satellite and earth station facilities, both international and domestic.

The Planning and Negotiations Division represents the FCC in negotiations with Mexico, Canada, and other countries on international agreements that coordinate radio frequency assignments to prevent and resolve international radio interference involving U.S. licensees.

Cable Services Bureau The Cable Services Bureau develops, recommends, and administers policies and programs for the regulation of CABLE TELEVISION systems. The Cable Services Bureau advises the FCC on the development and regulation of cable television. Among its other responsibilities, the bureau investigates complaints from the public; coordinates with state and local authorities in matters involving cable television systems; and advises the public, other government agencies, and industry groups on cable television regulation and related matters.

Office of Engineering and Technology The Office of Engineering and Technology administers the Table of Frequency Allocations, which specifies the frequency ranges that can be used by various radio services. The office also administers the Experimental Radio Service and the Equipment Authorization Program. The Experimental Radio Service permits the public to experiment with new uses of radio frequencies. This allows the development of radio equipment and exploration of new radio techniques prior to licensing under other regulatory programs. The Equipment Authorization Pro-

The Federal Communications Commission regulates communication by radio, television, wire, satellite, and cable.

gram includes procedures for agency approval of radio equipment importation, marketing, and use.

Compliance Much of the investigative and enforcement work of the FCC is carried out by the commission's field staff. The Field Operations Bureau has six regional offices and thirty-five field offices. It also operates a nationwide fleet of mobile radio direction-finding vehicles for technical enforcement purposes. The field staff detects radio violations and enforces rules and regulations. The radio spectrum is under continuous surveillance to detect unlicensed operation and activities or nonconforming transmissions, and to furnish radio bearings on ships and planes in distress. The Field Operations Bureau also administers public service programs aimed at educating FCC licensees, industry, and the general public to improve compliance with FCC rules and regulations.

Telecommunications Act of 1996 In a sweeping overhaul of the Communications Act of 1934, Congress enacted the Telecommunications Act of 1996 (47 U.S.C.A. § 51 et seq.) in February 1996. The legislation was designed to deregulate the $500-billion-a-year telecommunications industry and encourage competition, freeing telephone companies, broadcasters, and cable TV operators to enter one another's markets in order to secure lower prices and higher-quality services for U.S. consumers. Critics of the legislation said it would increase the cost of cable TV and telephone service and would encourage monopolization of the media. Supporters of the legislation said it would foster competition and make available

new services such as advanced wireless communications, home banking, and interactive television.

Despite its intended deregulatory nature, the act requires the FCC to hold hearings on approximately one hundred different issues in order to establish rules implementing parts of the legislation. As a result of legal challenges, certain controversial provisions of the legislation may never go into effect.

For example, title V of the act, known as the Communications Decency Act of 1996 (CDA) (47 U.S.C.A. § 223(a)–(h)), was immediately challenged in court. The CDA forbids the transmission of indecent material over computer networks such as the Internet unless steps are taken to keep the material away from children, and requires that new TV sets be equipped with an electronic block that allows viewers to prevent children from viewing objectionable programming. In February 1996, two separate actions were filed in U.S. district court in Philadelphia challenging the constitutionality of the CDA. The first suit, *ACLU v. Reno*, No. Civ. A. 96-963, 1996 WL 65464 (E.D. Pa.), was filed by the AMERICAN CIVIL LIBERTIES UNION and nineteen other plaintiffs. The second action, *American Library Ass'n v. United States Department of Justice*, No. Civ. A. 96-1458 (E.D. Pa.), was brought by the American Library Association and twenty-six other plaintiffs. The other plaintiffs in both actions included civil libertarians, computer businesses, on-line services, newspapers, and librarians.

The lawsuits were consolidated for hearing before a special three-judge panel, authorized under the CDA and consisting of two federal district court judges and the chief judge of the U.S. Court of Appeals for the Third Circuit. The plaintiffs sought a preliminary INJUNCTION preventing enforcement of the CDA pending the outcome of a trial of their lawsuit. They challenged section 223 of the CDA, which states, in part, that any person in interstate or foreign communications who "by means of a telecommunications device knowingly . . . makes, creates, or solicits and . . . initiates the transmission of . . . any comment, request, suggestion, proposal, image, or other communication which is obscene or indecent, knowing the recipient of the communication is under 18 years of age" may be fined or imprisoned. In addition, section 223 makes it a crime to use an "interactive computer service" to transmit to persons under eighteen years of age any material that, in context, "depicts or describes, in terms patently offensive as measured by contemporary community standards, sexual or excretory activities or

Senators Patrick Leahy (D-Vt.) and Charles Grassley (R-Iowa) confer before the start of testimony on the transmission of indecent material over the Internet.

APWIDE WORLD PHOTOS

organs, regardless of whether the user of such service placed the call or initiated the communication." The plaintiffs argued that the CDA violates the FIRST AMENDMENT because it bans a substantial category of protected speech from most parts of the Internet. The government responded that shielding MINORS from access to indecent materials is a compelling interest that justifies the restrictions imposed by the act.

The court noted that the CDA was not narrowly tailored to further the government's interest in protecting minors, noting that "it is either technologically impossible or economically prohibitive for many of the plaintiffs to comply with the CDA without seriously impeding their posting of online material which adults have a constitutional right to access." According to the court,

> The Internet is a far more speech-enhancing medium than print. . . . Because it would necessarily affect the Internet itself, the CDA would necessarily reduce the speech available for adults on the medium. This is a constitutionally intolerable result. . . . As the most participatory form of mass speech yet developed, the Internet deserves the highest protection from governmental intrusion.

The court granted the plaintiffs' request for a preliminary injunction preventing enforcement of the disputed sections of the CDA pending trial (*Reno*, 929 F. Supp. 824 [E.D. Pa. 1996]).

In another lawsuit, Playboy Entertainment Group, owner of the Playboy cable TV channels, challenged the Telecommunication Act's requirement that cable companies block audio and video transmissions of sexually explicit programs. Section 561 of the act states, in part,

> In providing sexually explicit adult programming or other programming that is indecent on any channel of its service primarily dedicated to sexually-oriented programming, a multichannel video programming distributor shall fully scramble or otherwise fully block the video and audio portion of such channel so that one not a subscriber to such channel or programming does not receive it.

In *Playboy Entertainment Group v. United States*, 918 F. Supp. 813 (D. Del. 1996), the district court issued a temporary restraining order blocking the enforcement of section 561. Playboy had argued that the blocking and time requirements imposed on cable operators violated the First Amendment and Equal Protection. When Playboy applied for an injunction, the same court dissolved the restraining order

and upheld the law. On appeal, the Supreme Court affirmed.

While these legal challenges made their way through the courts, the FCC continued to hold hearings in order to issue rules implementing other parts of the Telecommunications Act.

See also CENSORSHIP; FAIRNESS DOCTRINE.

FEDERAL COURTS 📖 The U.S. judicial tribunals created by Article III of the Constitution, or by Congress, to hear and determine justiciable controversies. 📖

The Constitution created the SUPREME COURT and empowered Congress, in Article I, Section 8, to establish inferior federal courts. The authority of federal courts is limited to that given to them by the federal statutes that created them. Federal courts exist independently of the system of courts in each state that adjudicate controversies that arise pursuant to the laws of that state.

Legislative and Constitutional Courts Constitutional courts are established pursuant to Article III of the Constitution, which states, "The judicial Power of the United States, shall be vested in one supreme Court, and in such inferior Courts as the Congress may from time to time ordain and establish." These courts have only the powers specified in Article III. They can hear only "CASES OR CONTROVERSIES"; their judges hold office for life, as long as they are not guilty of judicial misconduct; and their judges' salary cannot be reduced while those judges serve in office.

The Supreme Court, the U.S. COURTS OF APPEAL (including the U.S. Court of Appeals for the Federal Circuit), the U.S. DISTRICT COURTS, and the Court of International Trade are constitutional, or Article III, courts.

Legislative courts are known as Article I courts because they are created pursuant to the authority given to Congress in Article I, Section 8, Clause 9, of the Constitution. That section empowers Congress "To constitute Tribunals inferior to the supreme Court." No restrictions exist as to the type of court that must be created. Such courts can possess whatever jurisdiction Congress deems appropriate. Judges can be appointed by specific terms of years, and salaries can be adjusted in response to the changing economy.

In earlier times, legislative courts were the best means to bring justice into the territories. TERRITORIAL COURTS heard all kinds of cases that the constitutional courts could not hear, such as DIVORCE cases. Once a territory became a state, cases that fell within the jurisdiction of the federal court would be transferred to the federal court established in the new state; all other

The U.S. Federal Court System

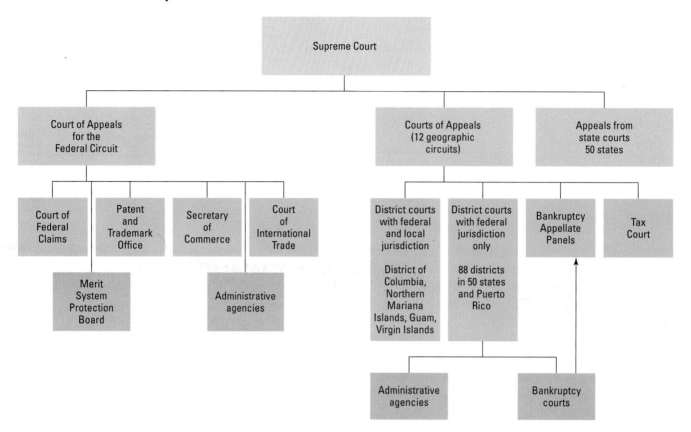

cases would be heard in the courts of the newly created state.

The U.S. Tax Court and the U.S. Court of Federal Claims are legislative courts. Although the Court of Military Appeals was created pursuant to Article I, it is not part of the judiciary but functions as a military tribunal to make rules, to regulate the ARMED SERVICES, and to review COURTS-MARTIAL.

Structure District courts function as general trial-level courts in the federal system. An APPEAL from a judgment rendered in a district court is taken to the court of appeals in the judicial CIRCUIT in which the district court sits. The Supreme Court hears appeals from a court of appeals pursuant to its mandatory jurisdiction, CERTIORARI jurisdiction, and its rarely used jurisdiction to decide questions of law certified to it by the court of appeals. In addition, specialized federal courts such as the U.S. Court of Federal Claims, the U.S. Court of International Trade, the U.S. Court of Appeals for the Federal Circuit, and the U.S. Tax Court entertain and determine cases that involve only certain areas of law.

Geographic Organization Every judicial district has at least one district court judge, and most have from one to three district court judges. The number of judges can be changed by Congress when the need exists. Each judge may preside alone, or, when there are two or more judges, all may hold sessions of court at the same time.

The decisions made in federal district courts are reviewable by the court of appeals in each circuit. All the territory of the United States, Puerto Rico, Guam, and the Virgin Islands is divided into twelve judicial circuits.

These twelve circuits are further subdivided into judicial districts. Every state has at least one judicial district. All the territory of Idaho except Yellowstone National Park makes up one judicial district, for example. All of Yellowstone National Park is within the judicial district of Wyoming, including the parts of the park that are in Idaho. The number of districts in each circuit depends on the size of the area and the number of people living within it. Large states require more than a single district. California, New York, and Texas, for example, include four judicial districts. Judicial districts for large areas are further separated into divisions.

Federal law establishes the number of circuit judges and the place where court is held in each circuit. Congress can change both the number and location at any time, because the courts of appeals, like the district courts, are created by Congress. The Federal Courts Improvement Act of 1982 (Pub. L. 97-164, Apr. 2, 1982, 96 Stat. 25) created the U.S. Court of Appeals for the Federal Circuit, which hears appeals not based on regional boundaries like the other courts of appeal, but involving special topics, such as PUBLIC CONTRACTS and PATENTS, where the uniform application of legal principles nationwide is highly desirable.

The twelve regional courts of appeals hear appeals from the district courts and many decisions of federal ADMINISTRATIVE AGENCIES. Cases are usually heard by three judges, but each circuit arranges to hear some cases EN BANC, with all the circuit judges of that circuit sitting together, hearing or rehearing the case and ruling by majority vote. A majority of the

Federal Courts

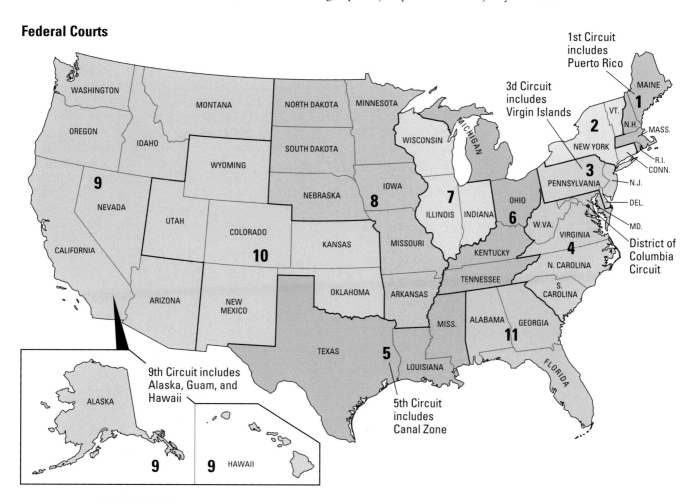

1st Circuit
Maine
Massachusetts
New Hampshire
Rhode Island
Puerto Rico

2d Circuit
Connecticut
New York
Vermont

3d Circuit
Delaware
New Jersey
Pennsylvania
Virgin Islands

4th Circuit
Maryland
North Carolina
South Carolina
Virginia
West Virginia

5th Circuit
Louisiana
Mississippi
Texas
Canal Zone

6th Circuit
Kentucky
Michigan
Ohio
Tennessee

7th Circuit
Illinois
Indiana
Wisconsin

8th Circuit
Arkansas
Iowa
Minnesota
Missouri
Nebraska
North Dakota
South Dakota

District of Columbia
Washington, D.C.

9th Circuit
Alaska
Arizona
California
Hawaii
Idaho
Montana
Nevada
Oregon
Washington
Guam

10th Circuit
Colorado
Kansas
New Mexico
Oklahoma
Utah
Wyoming

11th Circuit
Alabama
Florida
Georgia

judges in regular active service in the circuit can order a case heard en banc at any time. This is usually done if the decision in the case is likely to have a significant effect on issues in pending cases, such as when the case involves an important question of constitutionality, jurisdiction, or the right to appeal.

The Court of Appeals for the Federal Circuit has appellate jurisdiction derived from the merger of the former Court of Claims and the Court of Customs and Patent Appeals in cases involving actions against the government, public contracts, and patents. It also hears appeals from the Court of International Trade, the PATENT AND TRADEMARK OFFICE, the Merit System Protection Board, and other agencies. This court is intended to provide for the uniform application and enforcement of law in cases that Congress deems should be treated uniformly, but which under the former appellate system were often decided differently from circuit to circuit. As a result of its topical appellate jurisdiction, the Court of Appeals for the Federal Circuit significantly reduces the number of appeals from such decisions to the Supreme Court.

The Supreme Court is empowered to hear cases on appeal that originate anywhere in the United States or its territories.

Jurisdiction JURISDICTION is a broad legal term that means the authority of a court to hear and determine a controversy (SUBJECT MATTER JURISDICTION) as well as its authority to bind the parties in the action (PERSONAL JURISDICTION). Before a court can exercise subject matter jurisdiction, it must have personal jurisdiction of the parties; otherwise, any judgment rendered by it is null and void. The jurisdiction of a court is derived from constitutional provisions or from statute. Federal courts are courts of limited jurisdiction. They can exercise only the jurisdiction they were specifically given by the Constitution or federal law. Article III of the Constitution establishes the exclusive jurisdiction of federal courts in all cases, whether based on LAW or EQUITY, that arise under the Constitution or laws or TREATIES of the United States; that involve AMBASSADORS, consuls, and other public ministers, ADMIRALTY and maritime claims, or the United States as a party; or that arise between two or more states, between a state and a citizen of another state, between citizens of the same state claiming lands under grants of different states, or between a state or its citizens and foreign states, citizens, or subjects. This article specifically gives the Supreme Court ORIGINAL JURISDICTION to try cases affecting ambassadors, public ministers, and consuls and

cases in which a state is a party. In all other cases, the Supreme Court has appellate jurisdiction: it can review the decisions rendered by courts in which the action was tried or subsequently heard on appeal.

The power of a federal court to hear matters arising under the Constitution, federal law, or treaty is called FEDERAL QUESTION jurisdiction. Its DIVERSITY-OF-CITIZENSHIP jurisdiction empowers it to determine controversies between parties who are citizens of different states. The controversy must have a value of more than $75,000 in order for the court to exercise either federal question or diversity jurisdiction. The $75,000 figure is known as the jurisdictional amount. Federal district courts have original jurisdiction to try these disputes.

Federal district courts currently have original and exclusive jurisdiction to entertain BANKRUPTCY cases and prize cases, which determine the rights in ships and cargo captured at sea. Other controversies that are within the jurisdiction of federal courts include INTERPLEADER actions involving citizens of different states where the item in dispute is worth $500 or more; postal matters; and COPYRIGHT, patent, and TRADEMARK cases based on federal law. Federal district courts are also authorized by statute to remove actions from state courts to themselves when the disputes could have been brought in such courts originally. See also REMOVAL.

The regional courts of appeals have statutory appellate jurisdiction to review final decisions

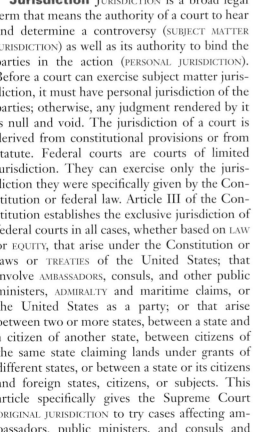

Federal courts, such as the U.S. District Court for the Southern District of Florida, have limited jurisdiction that is specifically established in the Constitution.

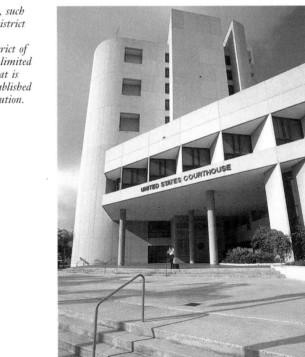

and specified INTERLOCUTORY orders rendered by district courts and administrative determinations made by federal agencies. Interlocutory orders are reviewable in the following situations: when they (1) affect existing INJUNCTIONS in cases where there is no direct review in the Supreme Court; (2) appoint RECEIVERS, refuse to do so, or affect the sale or disposal of property; (3) determine the rights and liabilities of parties in admiralty cases in which appeals from final decree are permissible; or (4) are issued in a bankruptcy action. The courts of appeals also review judgments in CIVIL ACTIONS for patent infringement that are final except for an accounting, and judgments rendered in bankruptcy cases. The U.S. Court of Appeals for the Federal Circuit has specialized appellate jurisdiction.

No federal court has jurisdiction to entertain POLITICAL QUESTIONS or to issue ADVISORY OPINIONS, since neither constitutes a case or a controversy, one of which must exist if a federal court is to exercise its jurisdiction. Federal courts are also powerless to determine matters that are beyond the scope of their jurisdiction, such as cases involving domestic relations or WILLS, which are exclusively within the jurisdiction of state courts.

Bankruptcy Courts In the late 1970s, Congress enacted comprehensive legislation that significantly revised bankruptcy law. Among its various provisions, the Bankruptcy Reform Act of 1978 (11 U.S.C.A. § 101 et seq.) reorganized the structure of the bankruptcy courts. Bankruptcy matters are now heard by a bankruptcy judge. Bankruptcy courts serve as adjuncts to U.S. district courts and have jurisdiction to administer and enforce federal bankruptcy law. A bankruptcy court operates in each federal district. Appeals from this court go to the district court or, if the parties agree, directly to the court of appeals that has jurisdiction over the district.

The Bankruptcy Reform Act of 1994, Pub. L. 103-394, Oct. 22, 1994, 108 Stat. 4106, authorizes bankruptcy judges to hold status conferences to determine the progress of a case and to attempt to expedite the case's conclusion. Pursuant to a status conference, a judge may issue orders that prescribe limitations and conditions necessary to ensure the economic handling of the case. The act also authorizes bankruptcy judges to conduct jury trials with the consent of all parties.

Bankruptcy judges are appointed by the CIRCUIT COURT for the judicial district in which the judges will sit. They serve for a term of fourteen years.

Court of Federal Claims Congress created the former COURT OF CLAIMS to safeguard the financial stability of the government by not permitting a multitude of claims to deplete the public treasury. Traditionally, persons whose rights were violated by the federal government could seek congressional enactment of a PRIVATE BILL authorizing a payment of money to compensate for the loss. Private bills were addressed to the conscience of the government and, therefore, their passage depended on political factors.

Inconsistencies in the passage of private bills and an increase in their number put pressure on legislators and caused serious delay in the completion of the legislative agenda. To ameliorate the situation, Congress enacted a law in 1855 creating the Court of Claims, which was empowered to hear claims against the government and report its findings to Congress along with proposals for solving the problem in each case.

Initially, the Court of Claims could hear only claims and determine whether they had merit. By the end of 1861, Congress was still overburdened by the need to review claims that had already been considered by the Court of Claims. President ABRAHAM LINCOLN recommended that judgments made by the Court of Claims be considered final without any further action on the part of Congress. In 1863, Congress accepted the suggestion. The decisions of the Court of Claims were made final with no further action by Congress necessary to give them effect. Appeals, when permitted, were made directly to the Supreme Court.

In 1982, the Federal Courts Improvement Act (28 U.S.C.A. § 1 et seq.) established the U.S. Claims Court, a trial court that inherited almost all the trial jurisdiction of the former Court of Claims. The court's name was changed to U.S. Court of Federal Claims by the Federal Courts Administration Act of 1992 (106 Stat. 4516 [28 U.S.C.A. § 1 note]). The court hears lawsuits against the United States based on the Constitution, federal laws, or CONTRACTS, or for DAMAGES in actions other than TORTS. It also has jurisdiction to determine cases concerning the salaries of public officers or agents, damages for someone who was unjustly convicted of a federal crime and imprisoned, and some American Indian claims. The Court of Appeals for the Federal Circuit has appellate jurisdiction regarding Court of Federal Claims decisions.

The court's jurisdiction is nationwide. Trials are conducted at locations that are most convenient and least expensive to taxpayers.

Court of International Trade Congress created the Court of International Trade, formerly known as the Customs Court, to have exclusive jurisdiction in actions involving the imposition of CUSTOMS DUTIES by customs officials. The court can consider the classification of merchandise for customs purposes, the rate charged under the applicable TARIFF law, or the refusal of the officials of the Department of the Treasury to make refunds that are allegedly due.

The history and development of the Court of International Trade are intertwined with those of the former Court of Customs and Patent Appeals. At the end of the nineteenth century, the Board of General Appraisers was responsible for the classification of items for import and export and the determination of the rate of customs duties to be imposed. The federal circuit courts, pursuant to their general power to hear appeals, reviewed these decisions from 1890 to 1909. Congress created the Court of Customs Appeals in 1909 to assume the review of appeals from the decisions of the Board of General Appraisers. This specialized court developed expertise in adjudicating the complex and technical issues that arose in customs actions and functioned as a speedy and efficient vehicle to dispense with such matters, since it could not hear any other cases. It provided sure and uniform administration of justice in such matters, since it was the only court in the United States with exclusive jurisdiction over such matters.

The Board of General Appraisers became the U.S. Customs Court in 1926 and was renamed the Court of International Trade in 1981. The Court of Customs Appeals was designated the Court of Customs and Patent Appeals in 1929 because its jurisdiction was expanded to include review of the decisions of the Patent and Trademark Office. The functions of this court were assumed by the U.S. Court of Appeals for the Federal Circuit in 1982.

The Court of International Trade comprises nine judges, who serve for life unless they are guilty of misconduct; one is named chief judge by the president. Although one judge can hear a case, a panel of three judges usually entertains cases that have significant constitutional ramifications in the customs field. The court is located in New York City because of the importance of the city as a port of entry. The chief judge can dispatch any judges to other ports to hear an action when it is economical, efficient, and fair to do so. A hearing can even be held in a foreign country if that country so permits.

District of Columbia Courts Historically, the local District of Columbia courts were considered part of the federal court system, since they were created by an act of Congress. The U.S. district court was the usual forum for the adjudication of controversies that arose under District of Columbia as well as federal laws. Owing to a number of judicial reorganizations, however, the District of Columbia now has its own court system, separate from the federal court system, to hear and determine local disputes. Federal courts still retain authority over any matters that fall within the scope of their designated jurisdiction.

Tax Court The U.S. TAX COURT is a unique tribunal. It was originally created as the U.S. Board of Tax Appeals and functioned as an independent agency in the executive branch of the government. Pursuant to the Tax Reform Act of 1969 (83 Stat. 730), its name was changed to U.S. Tax Court, and it is now an independent judicial body in the legislative branch.

The Tax Court adjudicates various controversies involving overpayments or underpayments of taxes. Unlike the district courts, the Tax Court does not require a citizen to pay the amount of tax in dispute and file a claim for a refund before it will hear and decide the matter. The taxpayer must, however, request and receive from the INTERNAL REVENUE SERVICE a statutory notice of deficiency that states the disputed sum. The Tax Court has no jurisdiction unless the notice has been issued and a petition for a hearing has been filed within a specified time.

Simplified procedures are available for small tax cases where the amount in controversy does not exceed $10,000. The decision of the Tax Court in such a case is final and is not subject to review by any court.

The U.S. Tax Court is an independent judicial body in the legislative branch. Its decisions in small tax cases are final; in larger cases a decision may be reviewed by a court of appeals.

MARK BURNETT/STOCK BOSTON

The Tax Court has jurisdiction to render DECLARATORY JUDGMENTS in many areas, such as the qualification of retirement plans, the tax-exempt status of charitable organizations, and the status of interest on certain government obligations. In addition, the Tax Court may issue injunctions in certain assessment cases and decide taxpayers' appeals from denial of administrative costs by the Internal Revenue Service.

All Tax Court decisions, except those in small tax cases, are subject to review by the courts of appeals and, by writ of certiorari, by the U.S. Supreme Court.

Court of Military Appeals The Court of Military Appeals is the final appellate tribunal that reviews court-martial proceedings of the armed services. Established in 1950 (10 U.S.C.A. § 867), it is presided over by five civilian judges. Rulings of the Court of Military Appeals are subject only to certiorari review by the Supreme Court.

Court of Veterans Appeals The U.S. Court of Veterans Appeals was established in 1988 (102 Stat. 4105 [38 U.S.C.A. § 4051]). It has exclusive jurisdiction to review decisions of the Board of Veterans Appeals. The court may not review the schedule of ratings for disabilities or the policies underlying the schedule. Decisions of the court may be appealed to the U.S. Court of Appeals for the Federal Circuit.

FEDERAL DEPOSIT INSURANCE CORPORATION The Federal Deposit Insurance Corporation (FDIC) was created on June 16, 1933, under the authority of the Federal Reserve Act, section 12B (12 U.S.C.A. § 264(s)). It was signed into law by President FRANKLIN D. ROOSEVELT to promote and preserve public confidence in banks at the time of the most severe banking crisis in U.S. history. From the stock market crash of 1929 to the beginning of Roosevelt's tenure as president in 1933, nine thousand banks closed their doors, resulting in losses to depositors of $1.3 billion. The FDIC was established to provide insurance coverage for bank deposits, thereby maintaining financial stability throughout the United States.

The FDIC is an independent agency of the government. Its management was established by the Banking Act of 1933. It consists of a board of directors numbering three members, one the comptroller of the currency, and two appointed by the president with approval of the Senate. The two appointed members serve six-year terms, and one is elected by the members to serve as chair of the board. The headquarters of the FDIC is located in Washington, D.C., and the corporation has thirteen regional offices. Most employees are bank examiners.

Federal Deposit Insurance Corporation
Bank Insurance Fund-Insured Commercial and Savings Banks Closed or Assisted Due to Financial Difficulties, and Problem Banks: 1980 to 1994

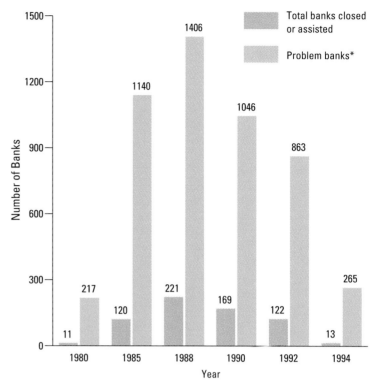

*BIF-insured commercial and savings banks considered to be problem banks by the supervisory authorities at the end of each year.

Source: U.S. Federal Deposit Insurance Corporation, *Annual Report, The FDIC Quarterly Banking Profile.*

The FDIC does not operate on funds from Congress. The capital necessary to start the corporation back in 1933 was provided by the U.S. Treasury and the twelve Federal Reserve banks. Since then, its major sources of income have been assessments on deposits held by insured banks and interest on its portfolio of U.S. Treasury securities.

Besides administering the Bank Insurance Fund, the FDIC is also responsible for the Savings Association Insurance Fund (SAIF), which was established on August 9, 1989, under the authority of the Financial Institutions Reform, Recovery, and Enforcement Act of 1989 (FIRREA) (12 U.S.C.A. § 1821 (2)). The SAIF insures deposits in SAVINGS AND LOAN ASSOCIATIONS.

The FDIC also insures, up to the statutory limitation, deposits in national banks, state banks that are members of the Federal Reserve System, and state banks that apply for federal deposit insurance and meet certain qualifications. If an insured bank fails, the FDIC pays the claim of each depositor, up to $100,000.

The FDIC may make loans to or purchase assets from insured depository institutions in order to facilitate mergers or consolidations, when such action for the protection of depositors will reduce risks or avert threatened loss to the agency. It will prevent the closing of an insured bank when it considers the operation of that institution essential to providing adequate banking.

The FDIC may, after notice and a hearing, terminate the insured status of a bank that continues to engage in unsafe banking practices. The FDIC will regulate the manner in which the depository institution gives the required notice of such a termination to depositors.

From 1980 to 1990, a total of 1,110 banks failed, principally owing to bad loans in a slowly weakening REAL ESTATE market and risky loans to developing countries. The FDIC found itself in such financial straits that in 1990, Chairman L. William Seidman testified before Congress, "The insurance fund is under considerable stress" and is "at the lowest point at anytime in modern history."

The FIRREA and the FDIC Improvement Act of 1991 (codified in scattered sections of 12 U.S.C.A.) came as reactions to the savings and loan crisis and to a banking crisis of the 1980s, which together cost the U.S. taxpayers hundreds of billions of dollars.

FIRREA gave the FDIC authority to administer the SAIF, replacing the Federal Savings and Loan Insurance Corporation (FSLIC) as the insurer of deposits in savings and loan associations. The FDIC Improvement Act placed new restrictions on how the corporation repaid lost deposits. Before the act, the FDIC deemed it necessary to repay all deposits, whether or not they were at an insured bank or over $100,000, in order to protect public confidence in the nation's financial institutions. Since the act, it must take a "least-cost" method of case resolution. The act stipulates that the FDIC will not be permitted to cover uninsured depositors unless the president, the secretary of the treasury, and the FDIC jointly determine that not doing so would have serious adverse effects on the economic conditions of the nation or community.

See also BANKS AND BANKING; FEDERAL RESERVE BOARD.

FEDERAL ELECTION COMMISSION
The Federal Election Commission (FEC) is an independent agency established by the 1974 amendments to the Federal Election Campaign Act of 1971 (88 Stat. § 1280 [2 U.S.C.A. § 431 et seq.]). The 1974 amendments—passed in the wake of President RICHARD M. NIXON's resignation because of the WATERGATE scandals, which included charges of ABUSE OF POWER and obstruction of justice involving campaign contributions—set out financial rules governing campaigns for federal office. The FEC was designed to act both as a clearinghouse for information on federal campaign laws and as the enforcer of campaign laws.

The FEC is composed of six commissioners appointed by the president with the advice and consent of the Senate. The act also provides for three statutory officers—the staff director, the general counsel, and the inspector general—who are appointed by the commission.

The FEC's main responsibility is to enforce federal campaign financing laws. Thus, its scope is limited to overseeing the financing of congressional, senatorial, and presidential ELECTION campaigns. The Federal Election Campaign Act, as amended in 1974, was intended to limit severely the amount of financial contributions made by wealthy individuals, and to place limits on how much candidates could spend on their campaign. In addition, the law required public disclosure of all campaign contributions and established public financing for presidential campaigns.

Since the law was enacted, the FEC has been faced with lawsuits challenging the constitutionality of the law's campaign financing provisions. The U.S. Supreme Court, in *Buckley v. Valeo*, 424 U.S. 1, 96 S. Ct. 612, 46 L. Ed. 2d 659 (1976), complicated the work of the FEC when it ruled that the 1974 act's limitation on

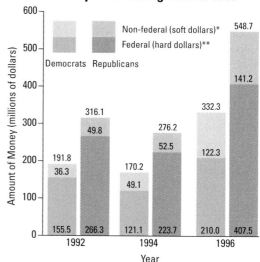

Federal Election Commission: Major Political Party Fundraising 1992 to 1996

* "Soft money" describes funds raised outside the FEC limitations and prohibitions, and is thus prohibited from being used in connection with a federal election.

** "Hard money" describes funds raised under FEC rules.

Source: Federal Election Commission home page.

campaign expenditures was unconstitutional. The Court did uphold the limit of $1,000 for individual contributions, but ruled that candidates could spend as much as they wished of their personal fortune on their campaign.

Because of loopholes in the law and the *Buckley* decision, there has been a tremendous growth in political action committees (PACs) as vehicles for major campaign spending. PACs are special organizations formed by labor, industry, the professions, and other interest groups that are not identified with individual candidates. PACs are not bound by the individual-contribution restriction; therefore, their political influence has risen with their large contributions.

The FEC administers and enforces the law with respect to limits and prohibitions on contributions and expenditures made to influence federal elections. In addition, it enforces the requirement that candidates must disclose where campaign money comes from and how it is spent. This requirement has created a complex set of rules that the FEC must administer. The FEC places reports on the public record within forty-eight hours after they have been received and computerizes the data contained in the reports.

If the FEC discovers irregularities or violations of the law, either through its own internal audits or through a complaint filed by the public, it has the authority to seek civil enforcement of the law. The FEC first seeks compliance through conciliation, but it has brought lawsuits when conciliation fails.

The FEC administers the public funding of presidential elections. It certifies federal payments to primary candidates, general election nominees, and national nominating conventions. It also audits recipients of federal funds and may require repayment to the U.S. Treasury if a candidate makes nonqualified campaign expenditures.

Because of the complexity of the disclosure requirements and the concern that these requirements discourage some individuals from running for federal office, the FEC provides information through a toll-free telephone line; publications; seminars; regulations, which clarify the law; and advisory opinions, which interpret the law in specific, factual situations.

FEDERAL EMERGENCY MANAGEMENT AGENCY

The Federal Emergency Management Agency (FEMA) is the federal agency responsible for coordinating emergency planning, preparedness, risk reduction, response, and recovery. The agency works closely with state and local governments by funding

MICHAEL NEWMAN/PHOTOEDIT

emergency programs and providing technical guidance and training. These coordinated activities at the federal, state, and local levels ensure a broad-based emergency program to protect public safety and property. FEMA is prepared to respond to all types of emergencies, including natural disasters such as hurricanes, floods, and earthquakes, and human-caused events such as toxic chemical spills, problems at nuclear power plants, and nuclear war.

FEMA was established in the executive branch as an independent agency pursuant to Reorganization Plan No. 3 of 1978 (43 Fed. Reg. 41, 943), and Executive Orders No. 12,127 (March 31, 1979) (Federal Emergency Management Agency) and No. 12,148 (July 20, 1979) (Federal Emergency Management).

FEMA has ten regional offices, which are the primary means by which the agency's programs are carried out at the state and local levels. The regional directors are the FEMA director's principal representatives in contacts and relationships with federal, state, regional, and local agencies; industry; and other public and private groups. They are responsible for accomplishing within their region the national program objectives established by the agency, and work with the director to develop national policy.

FEMA has developed the Federal Response Plan, a program for quickly responding to any type of catastrophic disaster. When, for example, an earthquake causes substantial damage and dislocation to a city or region, FEMA moves emergency teams into the area and coordinates efforts to restore public services and to provide food and shelter for those displaced by the natural disaster. FEMA's telecommunications and computer systems are used as a hub operation providing support services for day-to-day emergency activities. FEMA also works

FEMA coordinates emergency planning and works with state and local governments to do things such as providing drinking water at a disaster relief site.

with state and local governments to develop emergency response plans, and to provide training and technical support to these agencies through its Emergency Management Institute.

FEMA includes the Federal Insurance Administration (FIA), which administers the National Flood Insurance Program (NFIP) and the National Crime Insurance Program (NCIP). The NFIP makes flood INSURANCE available to residents of communities that adopt and enforce the program's floodplain management regulations to reduce future flood losses. Over eighteen thousand communities participate in NFIP, a self-supporting program requiring no taxpayer funds to pay claim or operating expenses. The NCIP authorizes the FIA to sell crime insurance at affordable rates in any eligible state. The NCIP offers protection to home and business owners against financial loss from burglary and robbery.

The U.S. Fire Administration (USFA) is another FEMA agency. The USFA provides leadership, coordination, and support for FEMA's activities in the areas of FIRE prevention and control, hazardous materials, and emergency medical services. The USFA develops and disseminates fire safety information to the fire service and the general public. Through its National Fire Academy, the USFA develops and delivers training and education programs to fire service personnel. The USFA is also responsible for the activities of the National Fire Data Center, and for the management of the National Emergency Training Center, in Emmitsburg, Maryland. The USFA works closely with the public and private sectors to reduce fire deaths, injuries, and property losses.

FEMA's External Affairs Directorate serves as the focal point of contact for the public, the media, public interest groups, state and local government organizations, Congress, and foreign governments. The directorate provides the director, the director's staff, and the agencies within FEMA with advice on how to develop and execute programs in the areas of congressional affairs and public and intergovernmental affairs.

FEDERALISM The term *federalism* is derived from the Latin root *foedus*, which means "formal agreement or covenant." It includes the interrelationships between the states as well as between the states and the federal government. Governance in the United States takes place at various levels and branches of government, which all take part in the decision-making process. From the U.S. Supreme Court to the smallest local government, a distribution of power allows all the entities of the system to

work separately while still working together as a nation. Supreme Court justice HUGO L. BLACK wrote that federalism meant

> a proper respect for state functions, a recognition of the fact that the entire country is made up of a Union of separate State governments, and a continuance of the belief that the National Government will fare best if the States and their institutions are left free to perform their separate functions in their separate ways. (*Younger v. Harris*, 401 U.S. 37, 91 S. Ct. 746, 27 L. Ed. 2d 669 [1971])

The Constitution lists the legislative powers of the federal government. The TENTH AMENDMENT protects the residual powers of the states: "The powers not delegated to the United States by the Constitution, nor prohibited by it to the States, are reserved to the States respectively, or to the people."

Checks and Balances In *Texas v. White*, 74 U.S. (7 Wall.) 700, 19 L. Ed. 227 (1868), Justice SALMON CHASE explained the necessity for the constitutional limitations that prevent concentration of power on either the state or national level: "[T]he preservation of the States, and the maintenance of their governments, are as much within the design and care of the Constitution, as the preservation of the Union. . . . The Constitution, in all its provisions, looks to an indestructible Union, composed of indestructible States."

The Federalist Papers: The History of Federalism The strongest arguments for federalism were written during the ratification of the U.S. Constitution. *The Federalist Papers*, a set of eighty-five essays written by ALEXANDER HAMILTON, JAMES MADISON, and JOHN JAY, were originally published in 1787 in New York under the pen name Publius. They were meant to explain the advantages of the Constitution and to persuade New York citizens to ratify it. The essays pointed out that the Constitution not only would allow the principle of popular sovereignty to continue but also would help prevent internal dissolution and uneven distribution of power—problems that contributed to the failure of the ARTICLES OF CONFEDERATION.

The key to the endurance of the Constitution, according to Madison, was that even in a democracy, the majority must not be allowed too much power; it needs to be held in check so that individual and state freedoms will be preserved. Indeed, English writer EDMUND BURKE said that in a "democracy, the majority of citizens is capable of exercising the most cruel oppression on the minority."

The Daily Advertiser.

[Vol. III.]   NEW-YORK: THURSDAY, NOVEMBER 22, 1787.   [No. 8 7]

On November 22, 1787, the New York Daily Advertiser *published* The Federalist, no. 10. *In this essay, James Madison, writing under the pseudonym Publius (see inset, below), argued that in a large republic the worst effects of political and economic factions would be curbed because the very multiplicity of factions would prevent a single group or interest from dominating the national government.*

debts, for an equal division of property, or for any other improper or wicked project, will be less apt to pervade the whole body of the Union, than a particular member of it; in the same proportion as such a malady is more likely to taint a particular county or district, than an entire State.

In the extent and proper structure of the Union, therefore, we behold a Republican remedy for the diseases most incident to Republican Government. And according to the degree of pleasure and pride, we feel in being Republicans, ought to be our zeal in cherishing the spirit, and supporting the character of Federalists.

PUBLIUS.

The check in the political process supported by the Constitution is provided by the SUPREME COURT, which is politically insulated. This check, as explained by Madison, "guarantee[s] the right of individuals, even the most obnoxious, to vote, speak and to be treated fairly and with respect and dignity." The function of the judicial branch, then, was to preserve the liberty of the citizens and the states. The principle of federalism states that the greatest danger to LIBERTY is the majority. These rights were decided "according to the rules of justice and the rights of the minor party, [not] by the superior force of an interested and overbearing majority" (*The Federalist* no. 10, p. 77). Although the Supreme Court is part of the federal government, it is separate from the legislative and executive branches, and it functions as a check on the federal and state governments.

The Constitution was influenced by two major philosophies: federalism and nationalism. The federalists believed in a noncentralized government. They supported the idea of a strong national government that shared authority and power with strong state and local governments. The nationalists, or neofederalists, believed there should be a strong central government with absolute authority over the states.

When the founders were developing the Constitution, they had four goals: First, they wanted the government to be responsive to the citizens. Second, they wanted the political system to enhance, not discourage, interaction between the government and the governed. Third, they wanted the system to allow for the coexistence of political order and liberty. And finally, they wanted the system to provide a fair way of ensuring that civil justice and morality would flourish.

The Constitution as eventually ratified was labeled a bundle of compromises because it allowed for a strong central government but still conceded powers to the individual states. In *The Federalist*, no. 45, Madison said, "The powers delegated by the proposed Constitution to the Federal government are few and defined. Those which are to remain in the State governments are numerous and indefinite."

The constitutional role of the states in the federal government is determined by four factors: (1) the provisions in the federal and state constitutions that either limit or guarantee the powers of the states in relation to the federal government; (2) the provisions in the Constitution that give the states a role in the makeup of the government; (3) the subsequent interpretation of both sets of provisions by the courts, especially the Supreme Court; and (4) the un-written constitutional traditions that have informally evolved and have only recently been recognized by the federal or state constitutions or the courts.

Judicial Review   The development of federalism as a form of government continues. Perhaps the biggest changes have occurred in the judicial branch, with its power of JUDICIAL REVIEW. Judicial review allows the courts to invalidate acts of the legislative or executive branches if the courts determine that the acts are unconstitutional. The Supreme Court first exercised judicial review of national legislation in the landmark case of *Marbury v. Madison*, 5 U.S. (1 Cranch) 137, 2 L. Ed. 60 (1803). The decision, written by Chief Justice JOHN MARSHALL, followed the principles of Publius in *The Federalist*, no. 78. *The Federalist Papers* were based on the principle that the Articles of Confederation were inadequate. The ideas set forth in *The Federalist Papers* challenged those articles and proposed a new governmental style for the new Union.

Judges have five sources of guidance for interpreting the Constitution: the original intention of the founders; arguments based on the theory of the Constitution; arguments based on the Constitution's structure; arguments based on judicial PRECEDENT; and arguments based on moral, social, and political values. Across the centuries, several justices have attempted to interpret the original, often vague intention of a document written in the late 1700s. Justice BENJAMIN N. CARDOZO said, "The great generalities of the constitution have a content and a significance that vary from age to age." Justice JOSEPH MCKENNA wrote, "Time works changes, brings into existence new conditions and purposes. Therefore a principle, to be vital, must be capable of wider application than the mischief which gave it birth. This is peculiarly true of constitutions" (*Weems v. United States*, 217 U.S. 349, 30 S. Ct. 544, 54 L. Ed. 793 [1910]).

Although it may seem unlikely that a federal body would favor STATES' RIGHTS over federal, it is not uncommon. For example, in the 1991 case of *Coleman v. Thompson*, 501 U.S. 722, 111 S. Ct. 2546, 115 L. Ed. 2d 640, the Supreme Court chose not to interfere with a state's JURISDICTION. Roger Keith Coleman had received a death sentence, which he challenged in the Virginia state and FEDERAL COURTS on the basis that he was an innocent man being executed for a crime he did not commit. The case reached the U.S. Supreme Court, where the majority said, "This is a case about federalism. It concerns the respect that federal courts owe the States and the States' procedural rules when reviewing the claims of state prisoners in federal habeas corpus." The Court ruled that because the state court's decision against Coleman was based on independent and adequate state grounds, it would not review the determination. This deference to state laws is based on the idea that states are separate sovereigns with autonomy that must be taken into consideration.

Separation of Powers and Plain Statement Rule Another key element of federalism is the principle of SEPARATION OF POWERS. The Constitution's definition of separation of powers is not specific, and the Supreme Court has struggled to interpret it. Separation of powers is based on the premise that there are three branches of federal government, each with its own enumerated powers. For example, the EXECUTIVE BRANCH, which includes the PRESIDENT, has VETO power; the Senate and Congress make up the legislative branch and have the power of advice and consent over the appointment of executive and judicial officers; and the courts make up the judicial branch and have the power of judicial review.

The separation-of-powers principle has had two interpretations. The first, formalism, is rooted in the idea that the Constitution's goal was to divide the new federal government into three defined categories, each with its own set of powers. The second interpretation, functionalism, is based on the belief that the three branches of government are not clearly delineated. Functionalists believe that the goal of separation of powers is to ensure that each branch retains only as much power as is necessary for it to act as a check on the other branches.

Although the interpretations appear similar, they differ in terms of what constitutes a breach of the separation of powers. A breach under formalism would be a breach under functionalism only if the power in question either infringed on the core function of another branch or increased another branch's power.

In *Gregory v. Ashcroft*, 501 U.S. 452, 111 S. Ct. 2395, 115 L. Ed. 2d 410 (1991), Justice SANDRA DAY O'CONNOR wrote that the Constitution establishes a system of dual sovereignty that balances the power between the states and the federal government. At the same time, however, the SUPREMACY CLAUSE (U.S. Const. art. VI, § 2) gives the federal government "a decided advantage in this delicate balance" by guaranteeing that Congress can make the states do what it wants if it acts within its constitutional delegation of power. O'Connor also said that the Court must assume that Congress does not "exercise lightly" this "extraordinary power" to legislate, even in areas traditionally regulated by the states. The people of a state establish the structure of their government and the qualifications of those who exercise governmental authority. Such decisions are of the most "fundamental sort for a sovereign entity."

The Court in *Gregory* also applied the plain statement rule, requiring Congress to state clearly its intent when creating laws that may interfere with state government functions. The plain statement rule, under *Gregory*, serves as a check against federal regulation of the states. This rule has two tiers of inquiry: (1) Congress must clearly intend to extend a law to the states as states, and (2) Congress must outline which state activities and functions it is targeting within the sweep of federal law.

Conclusion Federalism is the oldest form of government in the United States. The timelessness of the Constitution and the strength of the arguments presented by *The Federalist Papers* offer a clue to its endurance: the Founders wrote the Constitution so that it would always remain open to interpretation. Federalism's ambiguity has contributed to its longevity.

CROSS-REFERENCES

Constitution of the United States; *Federalist Papers*; *Marbury v. Madison*; Original Intent; *Texas v. White*.

FEDERALIST PAPERS A collection of eighty-five essays by ALEXANDER HAMILTON (1755–1804), JAMES MADISON (1751–1836), and JOHN JAY (1745–1829) that explain the philosophy and defend the advantages of the U.S. Constitution.

The essays that constitute *The Federalist Papers* were published in various New York newspapers between October 27, 1787, and August 16, 1788, and appeared in book form in March and May 1788. They remain important statements of U.S. political and legal philosophy as well as a key source for understanding the U.S. Constitution.

The Federalist Papers originated in a contentious debate over RATIFICATION of the U.S. Constitution. After its completion by the Constitutional Convention on September 17, 1787, the Constitution required ratification by nine states before it could become effective. A group known as the Federalists favored passage of the Constitution, and the Anti-Federalists opposed it.

To secure its ratification in New York State, Federalists Hamilton, Madison, and Jay published the *Federalist* essays under the pseudonym Publius, a name taken from Publius Valerius Poplicola, a leading politician of the ancient Roman republic. Their purpose was to

Federalist, No. 78, and the Power of the Judiciary

"We proceed now to an examination of the judiciary department of the proposed government." So begins *Federalist,* no. 78, the first of six essays by Alexander Hamilton on the role of the judiciary in the government established by the U.S. Constitution.

Hamilton made two principal points in the essay. First, he argued for the independence of the judiciary from the other two branches of government, the executive and the legislative. In presenting a case for the judiciary, he reached his second major conclusion: that the judiciary must be empowered to strike down laws passed by Congress that it deems "contrary to the manifest tenor of the Constitution."

In presenting his argument for the independence of the judiciary, Hamilton claimed that it was by far the weakest of the three branches. It did not, he said, have the "sword" of the executive, who is commander in chief of the nation's armed forces, nor the "purse" of the legislature, which approves all the tax and spending measures of the national government. It had, according to Hamilton, "neither FORCE nor WILL but merely judgment."

As a result of this weakness, the U.S. Constitution protects the judiciary from the other two branches by what Hamilton called "permanency in office." Article III, Section 1, of the Constitution declares, "Judges ... shall hold their Offices during good Behaviour." By making the tenure of federal judges permanent and not temporary, Hamilton argued, the Constitution ensures that judges will not be changed according to the interests or whims of another branch of government. According to Hamilton, permanent tenure also recognizes the complexity of the law in a free society. Few people, he believed, will have the knowledge and the integrity to judge the law, and those deemed adequate to the office must be retained rather than replaced.

The judiciary must also be independent, according to Hamilton, so that it may fulfill its main purpose in a constitutional government: the protection of the "particular rights or privileges" of the people as set forth by the Constitution. Here, Hamilton made his second major point. To protect those rights, he proclaimed, the judiciary must be given the power of judicial review to declare as null and void laws that it deems unconstitutional.

Critics of the Constitution claimed that judicial review gave the judiciary power superior to that of the legislative branch. Hamilton responded to them in *Federalist,* no. 78, by arguing that both branches are inferior to the power of the people and that the judiciary's role is to ensure that the legislature remains a "servant" of the Constitution and the people who created it, not a "master":

> There is no position which depends on clearer principles than that every act of a delegated authority, contrary to the tenor of the commission under which it is exercised, is void. No legislative act, therefore, contrary to the Constitution, can be valid. To deny this would be to affirm that the deputy is greater than his principal; that the servant is above his master; that the representatives of the people are superior to the people themselves.

Although judicial review is not explicitly mentioned in the Constitution, the U.S. Supreme Court established the legitimacy of the concept when it struck down an act of Congress in the 1803 case *Marbury v. Madison,* 5 U.S. (1 Cranch) 137, 2 L. Ed. 60. The courts had embraced judicial review by the twentieth century, leading some critics to maintain that the overly active use of judicial review had given the courts too much power. Whether or not the courts have demonstrated "judicial activism" by striking down legislation, Hamilton was correct in foreseeing that the U.S. Supreme Court and lower courts would protect the rights defined by the people in their Constitution.

See also *Marbury v. Madison;* Marshall, John.

---

clarify and explain the provisions of the Constitution, expounding its benefits over the existing system of government under the ARTICLES OF CONFEDERATION.

Hamilton, a New Yorker who served as treasury secretary under President GEORGE WASHINGTON from 1789 to 1795, was the principal architect of *The Federalist Papers.* Hamilton conceived the idea for the book and enlisted the aid of Madison and Jay. He is thought to have written fifty-one of the essays: numbers 1, 6–9, 11–13, 15–17, 21–36, 59–61, and 65–85. Madison, who served two terms as the president of the United States, from 1809 to 1817, probably authored twenty-six of the papers: 10, 14, 37–58, and 62–63. Madison and Hamilton probably wrote papers 18–20 together. Jay, who sat as the first chief justice of the U.S. Supreme Court, from 1789 to 1795, wrote five essays: 2–5 and 64.

The essays presented a number of arguments with great importance for the founding of the

U.S. government. They forcefully made the case for a strong union between the states (numbers 1–14); the ineffectiveness of the Articles of Confederation (15–22); the advantages of a strong, or "energetic," central government (23–36); and a republican government's ability to provide political stability as well as liberty (35–51). The later essays examined the roles of the three branches of government—the legislative (52–66), the executive (67–77), and the judicial (78–83)—as well as the issue of a BILL OF RIGHTS (84). The last essay consists of a closing summary (85). In making their arguments, the authors also discussed the benefits of FEDERALISM, under which the state and federal governments would each have a distinct sphere of power.

Several of the essays have been especially influential in U.S. political history and philosophy. The most famous, *Federalist*, no. 10, by Madison, concerns the dangers and remedies of factionalism for a republican government. Madison, seeking a "republican remedy for the diseases most incident to republican government," argued that a large republic of the kind envisioned by the Constitution will be less likely to fall victim to disputes between different factions than will a small republic. Here and in essay 51, Madison claimed that the diversity, or "plurality," of interests that exist in a large commercial republic will prevent any one faction from uniting to deprive the rights of a smaller faction.

The essays on the role of the federal judiciary have had a lasting influence on U.S. law. Essay 78 contains an important defense of the principle of JUDICIAL REVIEW, the power that allows the U.S. Supreme Court to strike down laws passed by Congress. In number 80, Hamilton argued for the establishment of a system of FEDERAL COURTS separate from state courts, an idea that was realized several years later.

See also CONSTITUTION OF THE UNITED STATES.

FEDERAL JUDICIAL CENTER The Federal Judicial Center (FJC) was created by Congress in 1967 (28 U.S.C.A. § 620) to enhance the growth of judicial administration in the U.S. courts. It has become the judicial branch's agency for planning and policy research, systems development, and continuing education for judges and court personnel. It is located in the Thurgood Marshall Federal Judiciary Building, in Washington, D.C.

Because of increasing caseloads and the growing complexity of the law, court administration has become an important part of the judicial branch. Congress gave the FJC a broad mandate to improve the performance of the COURTS and judges through research, planning, and education.

The FJC conducts research on the operation of the U.S. courts and coordinates similar research with other public and private persons and agencies. The FJC works with its state court counterpart, the National Center for State Courts, which is located in Williamsburg, Virginia, on issues that are common to both state and federal courts. The staff of the FJC has conducted research on the workings of different rules of federal procedure and on topics such as the role of court-appointed experts. The FJC also conducts empirical studies on the courts, analyzing how different FEDERAL COURTS process certain types of cases. In addition, it provides support to judicial systems in foreign countries.

The research and planning efforts of the FJC extend to providing support for the JUDICIAL CONFERENCE OF THE UNITED STATES. The Judicial Conference is composed of the chief justice, the chief judge from each circuit COURT OF APPEAL, the chief judge of the Court of International Trade, and a district judge from each circuit. The conference is the federal judiciary's central policy-making organ and the federal court's chief liaison with Congress. It meets twice a year and functions through a system of twenty-five committees that focus on particular judicial and administrative issues. The FJC's research support to these committees is critical to their effectiveness.

The FJC has also had a role in the introduction of computers and automated data processing to the court system. It has developed materials to help courts around the United States move from tracking cases in large ledger books to using computer database systems.

Continuing education for judges and court personnel is another major responsibility of the FJC. The FJC presents seminars and other types of training that help the federal courts prepare for legislative changes in criminal and civil law. Topical programs in areas such as immigration law and SENTENCING guidelines are among the FJC's educational offerings. The FJC also prepares handbooks and other written materials to teach new judges and court personnel how to carry out their duties fairly and efficiently.

The FJC's basic policies and activities are determined by its board, which includes two judges of the circuit courts of appeals, three judges of the DISTRICT COURTS, and one bankruptcy judge. These members are elected for four-year terms by the Judicial Conference.

The chief justice of the Supreme Court acts as chair, and the director of the ADMINISTRATIVE OFFICE OF THE U.S. COURTS is also a nonelected member.

FEDERAL JURISDICTION See JURISDICTION.

FEDERAL MARITIME COMMISSION

The Federal Maritime Commission (FMC) regulates the waterborne foreign and domestic offshore commerce of the United States; ensures that U.S. international trade is open to all nations on fair and equitable terms; and protects against unauthorized activity in the waterborne commerce of the United States. The FMC reviews agreements made by groups of COMMON CARRIERS (those who operate ships for commercial purposes), ensures that CARRIERS charge rates on file with the FMC, and guarantees equal treatment to carriers and those who ship their goods. The FMC also ensures that adequate levels of financial responsibility are maintained for the indemnification of passengers who sail on commercial passenger ships.

The FMC was established by Reorganization Plan No. 7 of 1961 (5 U.S.C.A. app.), effective August 12, 1961. It is an independent agency that regulates shipping under the following statutes: the Shipping Act of 1984 (46 U.S.C.A. app. at 1701–1720); the Shipping Act, 1916; the Merchant Marine Act, 1920; the Foreign Shipping Practices Act of 1988 (46 U.S.C.A. app. at 1710a); the Intercoastal Shipping Act, 1933 (46 U.S.C.A. app. at 843 et seq.); and certain provisions of the Act of November 6, 1966 (46 U.S.C.A. app. at 817(d), 871(c)).

The commission reviews agreements made by common carriers, terminal operators (those who operate the docking facilities in HARBORS), and other persons subject to the shipping statutes. The FMC also monitors activities under all effective or approved agreements, for compliance with the provisions of the law and its rules, orders, and regulations.

The FMC accepts or rejects TARIFF filings, including filings dealing with service contracts, of common carriers engaged in foreign and domestic offshore commerce of the United States, or conferences of such carriers. The FMC regulates the rate of return of carriers in domestic offshore trades. It has the authority to grant exemptions from tariff requirements.

The commission issues LICENSES to persons, partnerships, corporations, and associations desiring to engage in ocean FREIGHT FORWARDING activities. Shipowners and the operators of passenger ships that carry more than fifty passengers are required to obtain certificates from the FMC that demonstrate that they have the financial resources and responsibility to pay judgments for personal injury or death, or to refund fares in the event that voyages are canceled.

When a violation of the SHIPPING LAWS is alleged or suspected, the FMC is authorized to investigate and may take administrative action to start formal proceedings, to refer matters to other government agencies, or to bring about voluntary agreement between the parties. It may also conduct formal investigations and hearings on its own motion and may adjudicate formal complaints.

The FMC promulgates rules and regulations to interpret, enforce, and ensure compliance with shipping and related statutes by common carriers and other persons subject to those statutes.

The staff of the FMC administers programs to ensure compliance with the provisions of the shipping statutes. These programs include the submission of information, and field investigations and audits of activities and practices of common carriers, terminal operators, and others subject to the shipping statutes. The FMC also conducts rate analyses, studies, and economic reviews of current and future trade conditions, including the extent and nature of competition in various trade areas.

The FMC conducts investigations of practices by foreign governments and foreign carriers that adversely affect the U.S. shipping trade. The commission works with the Department of State to eliminate discriminatory practices on the part of foreign governments against U.S.-flag shipping and to promote fairness between the United States and its trading partners.

The commission comprises a chairman and four commissioners, who are appointed by the president.

The Federal Maritime Commission regulates waterborne commerce of the United States. Ships leaving the port of Sacramento, California, en route to Japan would come under the commission's jurisdiction.

INGA SPENCE/THE PICTURE CUBE

FEDERAL MEDIATION AND CONCILIA-TION SERVICE The Federal Mediation and Conciliation Service (FMCS) is an independent agency of the U.S. government that seeks to prevent or settle disputes between LABOR UNIONS and management that affect interstate COMMERCE. The FMCS was established by the 1947 Labor-Management Relations Act (61 Stat. 153 [29 U.S.C.A. § 172]), better known as the Taft-Hartley Act. Mediators for the FMCS have no law enforcement authority and must rely on their own persuasive techniques.

The LABOR-MANAGEMENT RELATIONS ACT requires that parties to a labor contract must file a notice with the FMCS if agreement is not reached thirty days before a CONTRACT termination or reopening date. The FMCS is required by the act to avoid MEDIATION of disputes that would have only a minor effect on interstate commerce. However, in seeking to promote labor peace through the encouragement and development of long-term, stable relationships between labor and management, the FMCS has taken a broad view of its statutory mandate and has involved itself in disputes that have little effect on interstate commerce.

The FMCS provides both mediation and CONCILIATION services. Most of its interventions involve mediation, which is a voluntary, non-binding form of dispute resolution. A mediator attempts to facilitate an agreement by conducting meetings and coordinating discussions. A mediator may make substantive suggestions as an active participant to help the parties reach a voluntary agreement.

FMCS mediators must be neutral and must have a minimum of seven years' experience in bargaining methods and tactics. Mediators must maintain strict confidentiality of both sides' positions, and may be removed for bias or a failure to maintain confidences. The FMCS employs over two hundred mediators, who typically handle about thirty thousand cases every year.

Conciliation is a different form of dispute resolution. A conciliator acts as a neutral third party, serving as a resource person for both sides. Generally, a conciliator will not participate in any joint meetings between the parties. Instead, a conciliator will present each party's position to the other in separate sessions. The conciliator may also suggest solutions, especially when negotiations have reached a stalemate.

The FMCS will also provide ARBITRATION support. Arbitration is an informal method of adjudication, in which both sides present their

side of the case and an arbitrator decides who prevails. Upon the joint request of a union and an employer, the FMCS will help select arbitrators from a roster of private citizens.

The agency also employs preventive mediation techniques once an agreement is reached. These techniques include the organization of or participation in labor-management committees, which serve as outlets for discussing problems, and the training of labor and management in ALTERNATIVE DISPUTE RESOLUTION techniques. This training is often presented through conferences and seminars.

FEDERAL NATIONAL MORTGAGE ASSOCIATION The Federal National Mortgage Association (Fannie Mae) is the United States' largest CORPORATION. With an overall value of nearly $1 trillion, the federally chartered Fannie Mae holds a unique place in the national MORTGAGE market. Established by federal law in 1934, it was originally a New Deal program. Since the 1970s, it has been a privately owned, for-profit corporation that is regulated and overseen by the federal government. Its chief purpose is to buy federally guaranteed home mortgages on the secondary market, thus freeing lending institutions to make more funds available for new mortgages for low- to middle-income home buyers. Tighter federal regulation began in the early 1990s, even as critics in Washington, D.C., argued that Fannie Mae, which earned $2.14 billion in 1996, should be completely privatized.

A broad federal response to the Great Depression gave rise to Fannie Mae. In the 1930s, the national housing market was devastated when a tight supply of money coupled with a failure of banks made mortgage financing ex-

The Federal Mediation and Conciliation Service, in Washington, D.C., works to settle disputes between labor unions and management.

tremely difficult to secure. Congress responded first by creating the Federal Housing Administration (FHA) in 1934, a body charged with stabilizing the mortgage market by insuring home loans (National Housing Act of 1934, subch. II [12 U.S.C.A. §§ 1707–1715z-11 (1980)]). This measure was not enough, however, to salvage the mortgage market. In 1935, lawmakers created the Reconstruction Finance Corporation (15 U.S.C.A. § 601 [1983], *repealed by* Reorganization Plan of 1957 No. 1 [5 U.S.C.A. § 903 note (1977)]), and in 1938, they added a subsidiary, Fannie Mae (Federal National Mortgage Association Charter Act [12 U.S.C.A. §§ 1716–1723h (1980)]). Fannie Mae's federal charter required it to buy FHA-insured loans from mortgage lenders, thus increasing the supply of mortgage funds available for lending.

Fannie Mae played a major role in the post–World War II boom years in housing. Its portfolio grew after it was authorized to purchase Veterans Administration (VA) loans in addition to FHA loans, a measure that fueled an enormous expansion of housing in the late 1940s and 1950s. In 1954, the federal government began issuing stock in Fannie Mae as part of a plan to share responsibility for the corporation's financial health with lending institutions. It issued PREFERRED STOCK to the TREASURY DEPARTMENT and nonvoting COMMON STOCK to mortgage lenders. For the latter, purchase of stock became a prerequisite for selling mortgages to Fannie Mae.

A shift to private ownership began in 1968. First, Congress split Fannie Mae into two entities: one retained the name Fannie Mae, and the other was called the Government National Mortgage Association (GNMA), under authority of title III of the National Housing Act (12 U.S.C.A. §§ 1716–1716b [1983]). Whereas GNMA, also called Ginnie Mae, was chartered to provide funding for federally assisted housing programs, the new Fannie Mae retained its original mission yet with a new source of funding: lawmakers wanted it to become self-sustaining through fees, stocks, and SECURITIES. In 1970, the federal government sold its share of stock to Fannie Mae for $216 million, severing its last financial tie to the corporation. Two years later, Fannie Mae expanded the scope of its investments by purchasing nonfederally guaranteed loans as well.

Despite its financial independence, the corporation remains closely linked by its charter to the federal government. Federal oversight remained, as did Fannie Mae's mission to provide services to low-, moderate-, and middle-income home buyers. During the 1970s and 1980s, the corporation grew enormously, particularly through the securities market, where it sold so-called mortgage-backed securities, which are pools of mortgage loans acquired from lenders for which the acquiring corporation earns guarantee fees. In 1996, Fannie Mae held $600 billion in these securities, had $325 billion in assets, and earned an annual profit of $2 billion. Its stock was actively sought, primarily because of profitability and a sense on Wall Street that the federal government would always back up the corporation in bad times. In fact, the enormous flow of money through Fannie Mae rivaled that of the nation's major lending institutions.

Calls for reform of Fannie Mae began in the 1980s. The antiregulatory administration of RONALD REAGAN suggested privatizing it completely. But action only followed a scandal of the savings and loan industry, in which greed and mismanagement plunged many of the nation's thrifts into insolvency—at a cost to taxpayers of hundreds of billions of dollars.

Motivated to protect the federal government from suffering such losses again, Congress in 1992 passed the Federal Housing Financial

Federal National Mortgage Association

Mortgage Debt Held by Fannie Mae

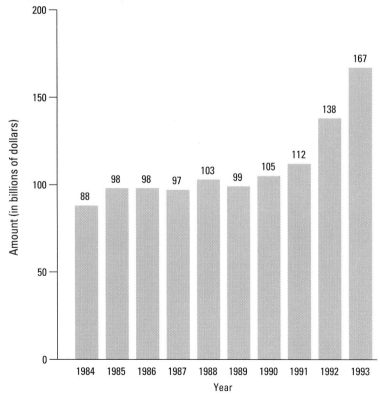

Source: Board of Governors of the Federal Reserve System, *Federal Reserve Bulletin,* monthly.

Enterprises Safety and Soundness Act (Pub. L. No. 102-550, § 1301, 12 U.S.C.A. § 4501). The law tightened regulations governing Fannie Mae and related federally chartered financial institutions. Specifically, it requires that these institutions pass periodic review to ensure that they have adequate capital according to risk criteria determined by Congress. This oversight is conducted by the Office of Federal Housing Enterprise, a part of the Department of Housing and Urban Development. Under law, such a corporation must submit a plan to restore its capital levels if it fails review. Significant under-capitalization can lead to a conservator's being appointed to run the corporation. Congress also prohibited excessive executive and staff salaries. At the same time, it gave Fannie Mae additional responsibility for helping low-income home buyers.

Although Fannie Mae readily passed financial review through 1996, reformers still sought to privatize it fully. Critics argued that under its federal charter, it enjoyed advantages that amounted to $8 billion before taxes in 1995. They also pointed out that a federal bailout of Fannie Mae, in the event that it failed, would be far costlier than the federal rescue of the savings and loan industry had been.

In lieu of privatization, some critics called for charging Fannie Mae a federal user fee. The Congressional Budget Office added support to the reformers' claims in mid-1996 when it charged that Fannie Mae was an expensive means of providing federal subsidies to home buyers, estimating that the corporation "soaked up nearly $1 for every $2 delivered." Fannie Mae attacked the user fee proposal as "a tax on home-ownership" that it would pass on to home buyers (Calmes 1996). Some observers believe that the corporation's political clout will make such drastic reforms difficult to pass.

See also HOUSING AND URBAN DEVELOPMENT DEPARTMENT.

FEDERAL PROCEDURE See CIVIL PROCEDURE.

FEDERAL QUESTION An issue directly involving the U.S. Constitution, federal statutes, or TREATIES between the United States and a foreign country.

Application of these kinds of law to particular cases or interpretation of the meanings of these laws is a power within the authority of the FEDERAL COURTS. The authority to hear lawsuits that turn on a point of federal law is called federal question JURISDICTION. Federal district courts can hear federal question cases only if the dispute involves an interest or right worth more than $75,000. If the AMOUNT IN CONTRO-VERSY is less than $75,000, the action must be commenced in a state court.

FEDERAL REGISTER A daily publication that makes available to the public the rules, regulations, and other legal notices issued by federal ADMINISTRATIVE AGENCIES.

EXECUTIVE ORDERS and agency regulations were promulgated at a furious pace in the early days of the New Deal under President FRANKLIN ROOSEVELT, but there was no requirement that these regulations be centrally filed or regularly published. It became increasingly difficult to know which rules were in effect at any one time. Two important cases were pursued all the way to the Supreme Court before it was discovered that the administrative regulations that the defendants were accused of violating were no longer in effect. Newspapers all over the country castigated the government for prosecuting people under nonexistent laws.

The furor led to enactment in 1935 of the Federal Register Act, now part of 44 U.S.C.A. § 1501 et seq., a law that established the *Federal Register* as a daily gazette for the government. Orders from federal agencies or the executive branch cannot become effective until they have been published in the *Federal Register.* In 1937, the act was amended to create the CODE OF FEDERAL REGULATIONS, a set of thick paperback books that arrange effective regulations from the *Federal Register* by subject.

The *Federal Register* includes (1) presidential PROCLAMATIONS and executive orders; (2) other documents that the president from time to time determines to have general applicability and legal effect; (3) documents that are required by an act of Congress to be published; and (4) other documents selected for publication by the director of the *Federal Register.* Documents are placed on file for public inspection at the Office of the Federal Register in Washington, D.C., on the day before they are published, unless an earlier filing is requested by the agency issuing them.

The *Federal Register* has been published continuously since March 14, 1936, and it provides the only complete history of the regulations of the federal government with the text of all changes. Regulations are published in the order in which they are filed, but specific documents can be located by consulting a table of contents in each daily issue or in the monthly index. Separate guides are prepared to note which regulations have been changed in an issue ("List of C.F.R. Parts Affected in This Issue") and the regulations changed at any time since the beginning of the month ("Cumulative List of C.F.R. Parts Affected During April," for example). A separate pamphlet is published along with the monthly index that lists references to all the changes in regulations since the last time the affected title of the Code of Federal Regulations was revised. All references are made to the Code of Federal Regulations because it is the topically organized version of the regulations that are published daily in the *Federal Register.*

The text of any document in the *Federal Register* can be shown as good and sufficient evidence that the document was properly filed and is, therefore, good law. If a regulation has not been published in the *Federal Register,* a governmental agency would have to show that an individual actually knew about it before it could prosecute the person for violating it. This encourages the agencies to be sure their regulations are published in the one place where everyone can expect to find them.

FEDERAL REPORTER® 📖 A legal reference source primarily covering published decisions of federal appellate courts. 📖

The decisions are published in paperback *Federal Reporter* pamphlets (ADVANCE SHEETS) shortly after they are handed down and then are issued in a hardbound volume when enough cases have accumulated to fill a book. The hardbound volumes are consecutively numbered as they are published. After 300 volumes had been issued, a second series was started in 1924. Following the release of 999 volumes in the second series, the third series started in 1993.

A case may be found in the *Federal Reporter* in the volume whose number is that given first in the CITATION for the case. If the case was decided after 1924, the citation will refer to the second series of the *Federal Reporter.* For example, the case of *O'Connor v. Lee-Hy Paving Co.,* decided by the U.S. Court of Appeals for the Second Circuit in 1978, is cited as 579 F.2d 194. It can be located on page 194 of volume 579 in the *Federal Reporter,* second series.

The *Federal Reporter* covers decisions by (1) the circuit court of appeals, the district courts, the former U.S. Court of Customs and Patent Appeals, the former U.S. Court of Claims, and the Court of Appeals of the District of Columbia for the years from 1880 to 1932; (2) the U.S. courts of appeals and the former U.S. Court of Customs and Patent Appeals for the years beginning with 1932; (3) the U.S. Emergency Court of Appeals from 1942 to 1961 and the U.S. Temporary Emergency Court of Appeals from 1972 to the present; and (4) the former U.S. Court of Claims from 1960 to the fall of 1982; thereafter it became the U.S. Claims Court.

CD-ROM format is available. Other federal court opinions are published in a series called the FEDERAL SUPPLEMENT.

See also REPORTER.

FEDERAL RESERVE BOARD The Federal Reserve System, established by the Federal Reserve Act (12 U.S.C.A. § 221), is the central bank of the United States. The Federal Reserve is charged with making and administering policy for the nation's credit and monetary affairs and helps to maintain the banking industry in sound condition.

The Federal Reserve Board of Governors has broad supervisory powers over the functions of the Federal Reserve System. The board of governors determines general monetary, credit, and operating policies for the Federal Reserve System and formulates the rules and regulations necessary to carry out the purposes of the Federal Reserve Act. A primary function of the board is to influence CREDIT conditions, such as interest rates, in the nation's marketplace. The board regulates the amount of credit that may be initially extended and subsequently maintained on any SECURITIES, in order to prevent an excessive use of credit for their purchase or carrying.

The board of governors' office is located in Washington, D.C. The board is composed of seven members, appointed by the president of the United States with the advice and consent of the Senate. The chair of the board must be chosen from among the seven governors and serves a four-year renewable term. Other board members serve one nonrenewable fourteen-year term, with one governor's term expiring every other January. By executive order the chair of the board is also a member of the National Advisory Council on International Monetary and Financial Policies.

Following the passage of the Federal Reserve Act, Congress attempted to claim exclusive control over the management of monetary policy. It asserted that this was the proper function of Congress, as the constitutionally appointed keeper of the nation's purse. The Banking Act of 1935 curbed Congress's claims by increasing the power of the executive branch's appointees to the board. In the 1970s the Humphrey Hawkins Act (Pub. L. No. 95-253, 15 U.S.C.A. § 3101 et seq.) reformed the Federal Reserve to require biannual congressional oversight hearings on monetary policy and the decisions of the board. Reports on these hearings are presented to Congress by the chair of the board of governors.

The board of governors interacts with the other parts of the Federal Reserve System, including the twelve Federal Reserve banks, their twenty-five branches situated throughout the United States, other member commercial banks, the powerful Federal Open Market Committee (FOMC), the Federal Advisory Council, and the Consumer Advisory Council. Through these arms of the Federal Reserve, board members help to maintain a commercial banking system that responds to the needs of the nation.

Federal Reserve Banks and Their Branch Members The twelve Federal Reserve banks are located in Boston, New York, Philadelphia, Cleveland, Richmond, Atlanta, Chicago, St. Louis, Minneapolis, Kansas City, Dallas, and San Francisco. The powers of these central banks include transferring funds, handling government deposits and debt issues, supervising and regulating banks, and acting as lenders of last resort. The twenty-five branches of these banks are located throughout the country. Along with supervising these member banks, the board has jurisdiction over the administration of other state banks and trust companies. The board may also grant authority to member banks to establish branches in foreign countries or dependencies or insular possessions of the United States.

The board of governors elects directors and officers of the Reserve banks. These representatives are divided into three classes. Class A directors and officers represent the Federal Reserve's stockholding member banks. Class B directors and officers are elected from various industries or banks within their districts to represent the interests of their districts' economies. The six Class A and six Class B directors are elected by the stockholding member banks. Class C directors hold no office or position in any bank. They are elected by the board of governors to terms in office that are arranged to expire, in conjunction with the terms of office in the A and B classes, in alternating years. Class C directors work in consultation with the other directors and fill vacancies as necessary.

The Federal Open Market Committee As part of the FOMC, the board works with other bank representatives to develop key policies for the Federal Reserve. The open market operations of the FOMC determine the control of the nation's money supply and the prevailing economic conditions of the country. Twelve voting members form this committee. Seven members are the governors from the board, and five members are presidents of district banks. The board, therefore, has the majority of the votes within the committee. The chair of the board of governors also presides as

STEPHEN JAFFE/THE IMAGE WORKS

Alan Greenspan has served as chair of the Federal Reserve Board since 1987. The board determines monetary and credit policies and influences national interest rates.

the chair of the FOMC. When the FOMC meets, approximately eight times a year, the board makes suggestions and policy surrounding the purchase and sale of securities in the open market. Such transactions supply bank reserves to support the credit and money needed for long-term economic growth, to offset cyclical economic swings, and to accommodate seasonal demands of businesses and consumers for money and credit.

The Federal Advisory Council The board of governors confers with the Federal Advisory Council on general business conditions throughout the nation. The Federal Advisory Council advises the board on matters within the board's jurisdiction. The council is composed of twelve members, one from each Federal Reserve district. The council meets in Washington, D.C., at least four times each year, and more often if the board of governors calls it to do so.

The Consumer Advisory Council The board of governors confers with the Consumer Advisory Council on the responsibilities of the board in the field of CONSUMER CREDIT protection. Congress established the council in 1976 when it restructured the Advisory Committee on Truth in Lending, initially established under the Truth in Lending Act (15 U.S.C.A. § 1601 et seq. [1968]). The council is composed of approximately thirty members from across the country. It represents consumer and creditor interests, and advises the board on its responsibilities under laws such as Truth in Lending, Equal Credit Opportunity (88 Stat. 1521, 15 U.S.C.A. 1691 et seq.), and Home Mortgage Disclosure (89 Stat. 1125, 12 U.S.C.A. 2801 et seq.).

See also BANK OF THE UNITED STATES; BANKS AND BANKING; GLASS-STEAGALL ACT.

FEDERAL RULES DECISION® ▣ A RE-PORTER that reprints decisions rendered by federal DISTRICT COURTS that interpret or apply the Federal Rules of Civil, Criminal, and Appellate Procedure and also the Federal Rules of Evidence. ▣

The full-text decisions that appear in the Federal Rules Decisions, commonly abbreviated F.R.D., are not published in the FEDERAL SUPPLEMENT.

FEDERAL SUPPLEMENT® ▣ A set of legal reference books containing decisions of FEDERAL COURTS in chronological order. ▣

The first volume of the *Federal Supplement* was published in 1933, and successive volumes have been numbered consecutively. Volume 900 was published in 1994. A citation to an opinion printed in the *Federal Supplement* gives, first, the volume and then the page number on which the case begins. For example, 465 F.Supp. 1286 means that the case can be found in volume 465 on page 1286.

The *Federal Supplement* was created as a REPORTER of trial-level decisions by federal DISTRICT COURTS. It contains the decisions of U.S. district courts from 1932 to the present, decisions of the former U.S. Court of Claims between 1932 and 1960, and the decisions of the U.S. Customs Court from 1949 to 1980. The U.S. Customs Court was renamed the U.S. Court of International Trade in 1980, and its decisions will now be carried under its new designation. In 1969, it started carrying rulings of the Judicial Panel on Multidistrict Litigation. Decisions of the U.S. courts of appeals and of the former U.S. Court of Customs and Patent Appeals and certain other federal courts are printed in the FEDERAL REPORTER.

FEDERAL TORT CLAIMS ACT ▣ A federal statute enacted in 1946 that removed the inherent IMMUNITY of the federal government from most TORT actions brought against it and established the conditions for the commencement of such suits. ▣

The Federal Tort Claims Act (FTCA) (60 Stat. 842) permits persons to sue the government of the United States in FEDERAL COURT for money DAMAGES

> for injury or loss of property, or personal injury or death caused by the negligent or wrongful act or omission of any employee of the Government while acting within the scope of his office or employment, under circumstances where the United States, if a private person, would be liable to the claimant in accordance with the law of the place where the act or omission occurred. (28 U.S.C.A. § 1346(b))

In passing the FTCA, Congress allowed the federal government to be sued. Congress also made specific exceptions to the act, and the U.S. Supreme Court has interpreted one provision broadly, both actions resulting in the dismissal of many plaintiffs' lawsuits.

In consenting to be sued, the federal government waived the SOVEREIGN IMMUNITY it had had in the past. Justice OLIVER WENDELL HOLMES, JR., in *Kawananakoa v. Polyblank*, 205 U.S. 349, 27 S. Ct. 526, 51 L. Ed. 834 (1907), explained that "[a] sovereign is exempt from suit, not because of any formal conception or obsolete theory, but on the logical and practical ground that there can be no legal right as against the authority that makes the law on which the right depends." As early as the 1821 case of *Cohens v. Virginia*, 19 U.S. (6 Wheat.) 264, 5 L. Ed. 257, the Supreme Court recognized the sovereign immunity of the United States.

Nevertheless, during the nineteenth century, Congress consented to the federal government's being sued in several CAUSES OF ACTION. Congress established the Court of Claims in 1855 (28 U.S.C.A. § 171) to entertain CONTRACT actions against the United States. The passage of the TUCKER ACT (28 U.S.C.A. § 1346[a] [2], 1491) in 1887 broadened that court's JURISDICTION to include designated nontort actions, including EMINENT DOMAIN cases. But until 1946 there was no readily accessible remedy for tort actions brought by citizens of the United States. The routine recourse was for members of Congress to introduce PRIVATE BILLS for constituents who had been injured by government NEGLIGENCE. Congress eventually recognized that the private bill method was not an effective way to deal with the problem and passed the FTCA.

Now a person who alleges that an employee of the federal government has caused injury must commence a lawsuit pursuant to the FTCA. Once filed, the FTCA lawsuit becomes the plaintiff's exclusive remedy, regardless of any statute that expressly or impliedly permits actions against a designated agency. A federal judge hears the case without a jury.

Congress did not categorically waive sovereign immunity in the FTCA. The act contains thirteen exceptions, which release the federal government from any LIABILITY for enforcing unconstitutional statutes, for losing letters in the post office, for actions of the military in time of war, for damages caused by the fiscal operations of the Treasury Department or regulation of the monetary system, for collecting custom duties, for claims arising in a foreign country, for most intentional torts, and for several other miscellaneous kinds of claims (28 U.S.C.A. § 2680).

The most important and troublesome exception has been the discretionary function exception. Difficulty quickly emerged with the FTCA's provision that the WAIVER of immunity does not apply to any claim "based upon the exercise or performance or the failure to exercise or perform a discretionary function or duty on the part of a federal agency or an employee of the Government, whether or not the discretion involved be abused" (28 U.S.C. § 2680(a)). In *Dalehite v. United States*, 346 U.S. 15, 73 S. Ct. 956, 97 L. Ed. 1427 (1953), the U.S. Supreme Court broadly interpreted the discretionary function exception to include all situations involving the formulation or execution of plans that were drawn at a high level of government and that entailed exercise of judgment. In *Dalehite*, federal government workers in Texas were negligent in packing and shipping explosive material, and their negligence resulted in the death of 536 people. The Court ruled that the workers were following specifications prepared by superiors in Washington, D.C., who were exercising their discretion. Therefore, the discretionary function exception applied and the government was immune from suit. The Court distinguished between decisions made at the planning and policy stage and those conducted at the lower, or "operational," levels that implement the policy decisions, even if some judgment or discretion is exercised in carrying out such decisions.

The *Dalehite* decision has limited the effectiveness of the FTCA for persons injured by the government. Some commentators have criticized the Court for allowing the discretionary function exception to swallow the FTCA. Many cases center on whether the alleged tortious conduct involved the exercise of discretion or was merely ministerial (carrying out a designated act), although virtually any act by a government employee is either directly or indirectly the outcome of an exercise of discretion.

The Supreme Court has placed other limitations on the scope of the FTCA. In *Feres v. United States*, 340 U.S. 135, 71 S. Ct. 153, 95 L. Ed. 152 (1950), the Court interpreted the FTCA to bar claims by members of the armed forces and their families for injuries arising out of or in the course of activity related to military

service. In *Laird v. Nelms*, 406 U.S. 797, 92 S. Ct. 1899, 32 L. Ed. 2d 499 (1972), the Court held that the requirement of a "wrongful" act means the United States is not liable under any state rule imposing STRICT LIABILITY.

The FTCA's exception for intentional torts, such as ASSAULT, BATTERY, FALSE IMPRISONMENT, FALSE ARREST, and LIBEL, was modified in 1974, in response to the Supreme Court's ruling in *Bivens v. Six Unknown Named Agents of Federal Bureau of Narcotics*, 403 U.S. 388, 91 S. Ct. 1999, 29 L. Ed. 2d 619 (1971). In *Bivens* the Court held that federal law enforcement officers could be sued personally for violation of a person's constitutional rights. The FTCA was subsequently amended to make actionable conduct "or omissions of investigative or law enforcement officers of the United States Government" involving assault, battery, false imprisonment, false arrest, ABUSE OF PROCESS, or MALICIOUS PROSECUTION. This inclusion does not repeal the personal liability of the officers themselves, but it does make it more likely that a plaintiff will seek to sue the government, because the government has more money than do its employees. The government is also liable for torts such as TRESPASS and invasion of privacy.

In 1988 the Supreme Court significantly altered the balance between the PUBLIC INTEREST in granting federal employees immunity from personal suits and the right to sue those employees personally for damages caused by their conduct. In *Westfall v. Erwin*, 484 U.S. 292, 108 S. Ct. 580, 98 L. Ed. 2d 619 (1988), the Court ruled that a federal employee is not absolutely immune for official actions "unless the challenged conduct is within the outer perimeter of an official's duties and is discretionary in nature." *Westfall* denied most rank-and-file federal employees immunity from lawsuits against them personally for COMMON-LAW torts committed in the SCOPE OF EMPLOYMENT.

In response Congress quickly passed the Federal Employees Reform and Tort Compensation Act of 1988 (102 Stat. 4563) as an amendment to the FTCA. The act overruled *Westfall* by broadening the class of activities given immunity. Originally limited to the operation of motor vehicles, the act gave immunity to any wrongful or negligent act that an employee commits while acting within the scope of his or her office or employment. Congress required the government to accept sole responsibility for its employees' actions in the scope of employment, leaving those employees free to administer government policies without fear of personal liability.

See also FERES DOCTRINE.

FEDERAL UNEMPLOYMENT COMPEN-SATION ACT 📖 Legislation enacted by Congress to care for workers who in times of economic hardship and through no fault of their own lose their job and are unable to find new employment. 📖

The Federal Unemployment Compensation Act (FUCA) was first enacted in 1939, underwent substantial revision in 1954, and has been amended over the years, most recently in 1988

Federal Unemployment Compensation Act

Unemployment Rate in U.S., 1920 to 1995

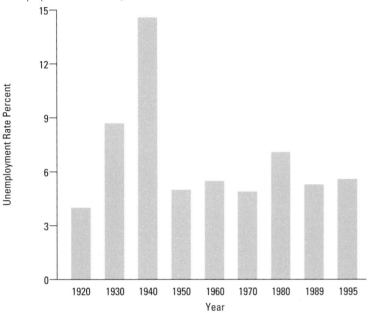

Unemployment statistics specific to the Great Depression

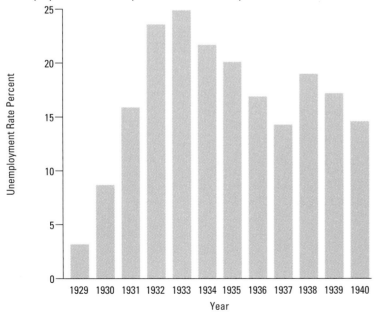

Civilian labor force, persons aged 16 years of age and older.

Source: Bureau of Labor Statistics, U.S. Department of Labor.

(42 U.S.C.A. §§ 501–504, 1101–1105). The act, originally titled the Federal Unemployment Tax Act, is designed to encourage and aid the establishment of state unemployment funds and payments to those funds. The act provides that an employer pay an annual excise tax in the amount of a designated percentage of the total wages paid during that year. Employers with fewer than eight employees, or operating in the field of agricultural labor or domestic service, are exempt from this requirement.

The unemployment insurance system in the United States and FUCA had their origins in the Great Depression of the 1930s, when high unemployment occurred. The unemployment system has three principal objectives. The first is to enhance employment opportunities through a network of employment services where job seekers and job openings can be matched efficiently. The second is to stabilize employment by encouraging employers to retain employees during short periods of economic downturn. The third is to minimize the economic loss of unemployment by paying benefits to persons who are unemployed.

UNEMPLOYMENT COMPENSATION is a joint federal-state program. In 1995, the federal statute imposed a tax of 6.2 percent on payrolls. That tax was reduced to less than one percent if the employer was covered by a state unemployment compensation law that met standards set out in FUCA. These standards address both substantive matters, such as what should be the conditions of eligibility for benefits, and the procedures by which benefits are to be paid.

The typical tax rates paid under state law in 1995 were lower than five percent for most employers, thus creating a substantial incentive for states to participate. An argument that this type of incentive is an unconstitutional coercion of the states by the federal government was rejected by the U.S. Supreme Court in *Chas. C. Steward Machine Co. v. Davis*, 301 U.S. 548, 57 S. Ct. 883, 81 L. Ed. 1279 (1937).

This federal-state sharing of responsibility has generally worked well, but it has made it necessary to work out a number of multistate agreements to handle certain administrative problems.

FEDERATION 📖 A joining together of states or nations in a league or association; the league itself. An unincorporated association of persons for a common purpose. 📖

FEE 📖 A compensation paid for particular acts, services, or labor, generally those that are performed in the line of official duties or a particular profession. An interest in land; an ESTATE of inheritance. 📖

An estate is an interest in land, and a fee, in this sense, is the shortened version of the phrase FEE SIMPLE. A fee simple is the greatest estate that an individual may have in the land because it is total ownership of the land including all structures attached thereto. It is complete ownership absent all conditions, limitations, or restrictions upon alienation, which is its sale or transfer to another.

FEE SIMPLE 📖 The greatest possible ESTATE in land, wherein the owner has the right to use it, exclusively possess it, commit WASTE upon it, dispose of it by DEED or WILL, and take its fruits. A fee simple represents absolute ownership of land, and therefore the owner may do whatever he or she chooses with the land. If an owner of a fee simple dies INTESTATE, the land will descend to the heirs. 📖

The term *fee* used independently is an adequate designation of this type of estate in land. The term *simple* is added to distinguish clearly this estate from other interests in REAL PROPERTY.

FEE TAIL 📖 An ESTATE in land subject to a restriction regarding INHERITANCE. 📖

A fee tail is an interest in REAL PROPERTY that is ordinarily created with words such as "to A and the heirs of his body." It may be limited in various ways, such as to male or female HEIRS only, or to children produced by a particular spouse.

A fee tail is passed by inheritance from generation to generation to the heirs of the body of the initial owner. Since no one is an heir of the living, the children of the owner of a fee tail are merely *heirs apparent.* Such children, therefore, have no transferable interest during their lifetimes.

A fee tail can endure until the holder dies without surviving ISSUE, but it cannot be passed on to COLLATERAL HEIRS. A REVERSION remains in the original owner whenever a fee tail is created. Thus, if a TENANT in fee tail dies without heirs, the property reverts back to the original GRANTOR who initially created the fee tail estate.

The power of the holder of a fee tail is limited, since the holder can use the land during the course of his or her lifetime but cannot prohibit its passing to his or her bodily heirs if any exist upon his or her death.

Many jurisdictions have abolished the fee tail estate since it restricts the ready alienation, or transfer, of property. Such states have transformed it into a FEE SIMPLE through statute.

FELLATIO 📖 A sexual act in which a male places his penis into the mouth of another person. 📖

At COMMON LAW, fellatio was considered a crime against nature. It was classified as a

FELONY and punishable by imprisonment and/or death. Presently it is a crime in some states, sometimes punishable as a form of the more encompassing crime of SODOMY, the act of unnatural sexual relations between two persons or between a person and an animal.

Under both the common law and present-day statutes, there must be actual insertion of the male organ into the mouth of another for the crime to be committed. Any penetration, however slight, is sufficient. Emission is not a necessary element of the offense under most modern statutes.

If the offense is committed by two persons who mutually consent to engage in the act, both are guilty of the offense. If one party is below the AGE OF CONSENT, only the adult is guilty.

The U.S. Supreme Court has held that the regulation of unnatural sexual conduct or activity is within the POLICE POWER of the state. The penalty for fellatio in many states is a fine, imprisonment, or both. Some states, however, do not treat it as an offense. In New York, a penal law prohibiting consensual sodomy was held unconstitutional by the highest state court on the grounds that it violated the constitutional rights of PRIVACY and EQUAL PROTECTION of the law.

Statutory definitions of fellatio may exempt from prosecution spouses who engage in such sexual conduct within the confines of their marriage. Fellatio is among several sexual acts that remain illegal in many jurisdictions, but are rarely prosecuted when consensual and engaged in in private.

FELLOW-SERVANT RULE 📖 A COMMON-LAW rule governing job-related injuries that prevents employees from recovering DAMAGES from employers if an injury was caused by the NEGLIGENCE of a coworker. 📖

In the mid–nineteenth century, a rise in industrial accidents brought to U.S. law an English idea about responsibility. The fellow-servant rule said simply, workers who are hurt by a coworker—a fellow servant—should blame the responsible coworker, not their employer. After first appearing in a U.S. decision in 1842, the rule had a powerful effect on the law for the next century. Its tough-luck notion of fairness protected employers and doomed injured employees, who often had no other hope for recovering damages after serious accidents. In allowing employers to invoke the defense, courts wanted to help the nation's industries grow at a time of vast expansion, when the dangerous jobs of factory work and railroad building needed bodies that could be injured without repercussions to employers. Only in the early and mid-1900s did lawmakers undermine the rule, through passage of federal and state WORKERS' COMPENSATION laws.

The fellow-servant rule broke from general common-law principles of LIABILITY. Traditionally, courts had treated cases of job-related accidents under TORT law (a tort is a civil wrong that causes harm to a person or property). Specifically, these claims came under the tort of negligence—the failure to do what a reasonable person would do under the same circumstances. Certain suits were seen as acceptable: for example, if a man named John were injured by a negligent worker named Bill, and Bill worked for an employer with whom John had no preexisting relationship, John could readily sue the employer for Bill's negligence. But everything changed if John and Bill worked for the same employer; then, the employer could invoke the fellow-servant rule as his defense, and courts would dismiss the suit.

The fellow-servant rule first appeared in 1837, in Great Britain, in *Priestly v. Fowler* (150 Eng. Rep. 1030 [1837]). In that case, an overloaded delivery van driven by one employee overturned and fractured the leg of another employee. The injured employee's lawsuit against their common employer succeeded, but it was overturned by the Court of Exchequer. The magistrate, Lord Abinger, scoldingly held that the injured employee "must have known as well as his master, and probably better" about the risks he undertook in van delivery. Moreover, concerns about the public good steeled the magistrate against the plaintiff. If suits such as *Fowler* were permitted against employers, workers would soon forget about their duty not to hurt themselves.

U.S. law was quick to learn this lesson in employers' immunity to liability. Only five years later, in 1842, the Supreme Judicial Court of Massachusetts announced it in the landmark case *Farwell v. Boston & Worcester R.R.*, 45 Mass. (4 Met.) 49. The nation sat on the verge of its greatest burst in industrial development, led by the expansion of railroads. The transformation of the United States from an agrarian society to an industrial society threw many new problems before the courts. Few state judges appreciated this shift as keenly as the Massachusetts court's chief justice, LEMUEL SHAW (1781–1861). Nearing the end of a remarkable life in law, Shaw grasped economic considerations better than social ones, and his plainspoken opinions were tremendously influential.

Chief Justice Shaw's decision in *Farwell* had blunt logic. Although a railroad employee had lost his hand through the negligence of a fellow

UPI/CORBIS-BETTMANN

The fellow-servant rule was a common-law rule that a worker injured on the job through the negligence of another worker could only recover damages from the coworker, not from the employer. The establishment of workers' compensation laws ended the fellow-servant rule.

worker, Shaw looked beyond the loss of limb to the dangerous PRECEDENT that a finding of employer liability would pose to growing industries at a crucial moment in history. He wanted to encourage this growth. So he imported the fellow-servant rule, justifying it in purely economic terms. Whereas Lord Abinger had reminded employees of their duty to be cautious, Shaw observed that employee alertness was also compensated: workers in more dangerous jobs would be taken care of by the market, through higher wages. Furthermore, employees entered such jobs voluntarily and therefore chose to put themselves at risk. Thus, a CONTRACT of employment existed, and it could not place liability on the employer's shoulders except when the employer was personally responsible—and certainly not when a fellow employee was clearly to blame for the injury.

The reverberations of this decision were felt throughout the rest of the nineteenth century. Shaw was hardly the only judge whose sympathies lay with industry. As more courts adopted the fellow-servant rule, the doctrine had a drastic effect on workers. An 1858 Illinois supreme court decision succinctly echoed Shaw's reasoning: "[E]ach servant, when he engages in a particular service, calculates the hazards incident to it, and contracts accordingly. This we see every day—dangerous service generally receiving higher compensation than a service unattended with danger or any considerable risk of life or limb" (*Illinois Central R.R. v. Cox*, 21 Ill. 20).

The industrial revolution was not an age of safety: laborious work, long hours, crude training, and rough tools led to accidents involving workers. Injured workers sued their employers because employers arguably bore some responsibility and always had deeper pockets (more money) than fellow workers. But employers needed only to point out that a coworker's negligence was partly or wholly the cause of the injury, and the nation's courts stood ready to uphold the fellow-servant rule.

Injured employees could rarely win these suits. A slight hope existed: if an employer was notified of a careless worker's behavior but failed to take disciplinary or corrective action, the employer became directly liable for mishaps that the careless worker caused. But to prove this in court required TESTIMONY. Who would intervene? Worried about losing jobs, few coworkers would testify. Thus, the fellow-servant rule along with two related defenses, contributory negligence and ASSUMPTION OF RISK, came to be dubbed "the three wicked sisters of the common law," because together they left the burden on the injured and powerless employee (48 Vand. L. Rev. 1107 [May 1995]).

The twentieth century brought change. Even by the early 1900s, the fellow-servant rule had begun to crumble. Courts had new ideas. The mere existence of a rule safeguarding employers' interests had failed to stop workers from having accidents and bringing compelling cases. To permit certain lawsuits to proceed, courts created exceptions to the fellow-servant defense. Some courts permitted suits where the coworker was a supervisor; others limited the defense to employees working in the same department. As a result, employers could at last be held liable for some on-the-job injuries caused by coworkers.

Through the efforts of the labor movement, two further reactions against the fellow-servant rule sapped it of most of its force. The first was a change in federal law. In 1908, Congress passed the Federal Employers' Liability Act (45 U.S.C.A. § 51 et seq.), designed to protect railroad employees. Its protections were extended to maritime workers with the Jones Act (46 U.S.C.A. § 688). The major development to

undermine the fellow-servant rule was the passage of workers' compensation laws in states, which ensured that employees would receive compensation for injury or illness incurred at work. By 1949, every state had passed workers' compensation laws.

By the late twentieth century, the fellow-servant rule was largely dead, although a few loopholes remained in some occupations, chiefly farming. At that point, the rule's rare appearance in court provoked surprise, as in the 1989 case of *Pomer v. Schoolman*, 875 F.2d 1262, 7th Cir., which moved federal appellate judge RICHARD A. POSNER to remark in his opinion, "[I]t is up to Illinois to plug what to many observers will seem an anachronistic and even cruel gap in the state's law of industrial accidents."

FELON 📖 An individual who commits a CRIME of a serious nature, such as BURGLARY or MURDER. A person who commits a FELONY. 📖

FELONIOUS 📖 Done with an intent to commit a serious crime or a FELONY; done with an evil heart or purpose; malicious; wicked; villainous. 📖

An AGGRAVATED ASSAULT, such as an ASSAULT with an intent to murder, is a felonious assault. A simple assault, such as one done with an intent to frighten, is not felonious.

FELONY 📖 A serious crime, characterized under federal law and many state statutes as any offense punishable by death or imprisonment in excess of one year. 📖

Under the early common law, felonies were crimes involving MORAL TURPITUDE, those which

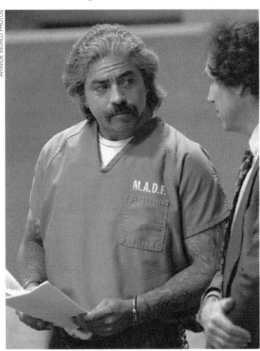

Richard Allen Davis appeared in court to face felony charges of the kidnapping and murder of twelve-year-old Polly Klaas of Petaluma, California.

violated the moral standards of a community. Later, however, crimes that did not involve mortal turpitude became included in the definition of a felony.

Presently many state statutes list various classes of felonies with penalties commensurate with the gravity of the offense. Crimes classified as felonies include, among others, TREASON, ARSON, MURDER, RAPE, ROBBERY, BURGLARY, MANSLAUGHTER, and KIDNAPPING.

FELONY-MURDER RULE   A rule of law that holds that if a killing occurs during the commission or attempted commission of a FELONY (a major crime), the person or persons responsible for the felony can be charged with MURDER.

Generally an intent to kill is not necessary for felony-murder. The rule becomes operative when there is a killing during or a death soon after the felony, and there is some causal connection between the felony and the killing.

The felony-murder rule originated in England under the COMMON LAW. Initially it was strictly applied, encompassing any death that occurred during the course of a felony, regardless of who caused it. Therefore, if a police officer attempting to stop a robbery accidentally shot and killed an innocent passerby, the robber could be charged with murder.

Today most JURISDICTIONS have limited the rule by requiring that the felony must be a dangerous one or that the killing is foreseeable, or both. Statutes that restrict the application of the rule to dangerous felonies usually enumerate the crimes. BURGLARY, KIDNAPPING, RAPE, and ROBBERY are typical felonies that invoke the rule. Under a number of statutes, the felony must be a PROXIMATE CAUSE of the death. In other words, the killing must have been a natural and direct consequence of the felony.

Felony-murder cannot be charged if all the elements of the felony are included in the elements of murder. This is known as the merger doctrine, which holds that if the underlying felony merges with the killing, the felony cannot constitute felony-murder. For example, all of the elements of ASSAULT AND BATTERY with a deadly weapon are included in murder. If a killing, therefore, occurred during the course of this crime, the accused would be charged with murder.

The future of the felony-murder rule is in doubt. Some jurisdictions have abolished the rule and others continue to limit its application. In the 1982 case of *Enmund v. Florida*, 458 U.S. 782, 102 S. Ct. 3368, 73 L. Ed. 2d 1140, the Supreme Court ruled that the imposition of the death penalty upon an accomplice who neither kills, attempts to kill, or intends that a killing occur or lethal force be used in the commission of a felony-murder constitutes CRUEL AND UNUSUAL PUNISHMENT. In those states that have retained the offense, it is usually classified as murder in the first degree, for which the penalty might be death or imprisonment.

FEMINIST JURISPRUDENCE   A philosophy of law based on the political, economic, and social equality of the sexes.

Feminist jurisprudence is a general term that encompasses many theories and approaches based on examining gender, sexuality, and power in relation to the legal system. As a field of legal scholarship and theory, feminist jurisprudence had its beginnings in the 1960s. By the 1990s it had become an important and vital part of the law, informing many debates on sexual and DOMESTIC VIOLENCE, inequality in the workplace, and gender-based discrimination at all levels of U.S. society.

The feminist political movement began in the nineteenth century with a call for female suffrage. At a convention in Seneca Falls, New York, in 1848, a group of women and men drafted and approved the Declaration of Rights and Sentiments. This document, modeled on the language and structure of the DECLARATION OF INDEPENDENCE, was a bill of rights for women, including the right to vote. Throughout the late 1800s, feminist leaders SUSAN B. ANTHONY and ELIZABETH CADY STANTON were persistent critics of male society's refusal to grant women political and social equality. In the mid–nineteenth century, many state legislatures passed married women's separate property acts. These acts gave women the legal right to retain ownership and control of property they brought into the marriage. Until these enactments a husband was permitted to control all property, which often led to the squandering of a wife's estate. Finally, when the NINETEENTH AMENDMENT to the U.S. Constitution was ratified in 1920, women gained voting rights in the United States.

The modern feminist movement began in the 1960s. In 1966 BETTY N. FRIEDAN, author of *The Feminine Mystique* (1963), organized the first meeting of the National Organization for Women (NOW). In 1968 NOW staged a protest at the Miss America Pageant. By 1970 Robin Morgan had enough material on feminism to publish a popular anthology, *Sisterhood Is Powerful*. Women who had become CIVIL RIGHTS and antiwar activists in the 1960s soon turned their attention to gender discrimination and inequality. The decision in *Roe v. Wade*, 410 U.S. 113, 93 S. Ct. 705, 35 L. Ed. 2d 147

(1973), which defined the choice of ABORTION as a fundamental constitutional right, became a touchstone for feminists who argued that women must have reproductive rights.

With the rise of the women's movement and a growing percentage of women attending law school, feminist critiques of the law soon emerged. One centers on the way history was written. According to feminists, traditional historians wrote from the male point of view and excluded the female point of view. These historians did not inquire into women's role in making history, structuring society, and living their own life. Feminists point out that male-written history has created a male bias in the concepts of human nature, gender potential, and social arrangements.

Feminists also criticize mainstream JURISPRUDENCE as patriarchal. They say that male-dominated legal doctrine defines and protects men, not women. By discounting gender differences, the prevailing conceptions of law perpetuate patriarchal power. Because men have most of the social, economic, and political power, they use the system to subordinate women in the public spheres of politics and economics as well as in the private spheres of family and sex. The language, logic, and structure of the law are male created, which reinforces male values. Most troubling, these concepts and values are presented as neutral or objective.

For example, in determining LIABILITY in NEGLIGENCE actions, the law crafted the "reasonable man" test. This "man" was a hypothetical creature whose hypothetical action, reaction, or inaction in any situation was the law's standard of reasonable conduct for real people in similar circumstances. The gender-biased term *man* has been replaced by *person* in the name for this test, which might seem to resolve the problem. But some feminist legal scholars have argued that a gender-neutral label merely avoids the fact that the test is based on assumptions of what a male would do in a situation. They propose that when an action involves a female, a court should apply a "reasonable woman" test. By doing so, the court would recognize the differences in how males and females react to situations.

Feminists challenge biological determinacy, the belief that the biological makeup of men and women is so different that certain behavior can be attributed on the basis of sex. They believe that biological determinacy curtails women's power and their options in society. They argue that gender is created socially, not biologically. Sex determines matters such as genitalia and reproductive capacity but not psychological, moral, or social traits.

In analyzing the workings of gender in the law, feminist scholars share certain common commitments. Politically, they seek equality between men and women. Analytically, they make gender a category to reconstitute legal practices that have excluded women's interests. Methodologically, they use women's experiences to describe the world and to demonstrate the need for change. They rely primarily on an experiential discourse for analyzing gender hierarchy, sexual objectification, and social structures.

Though feminists have much in common, they are not uniform in their approaches. One school of feminist legal thought views women as individual human beings and is based on the desire to promote equal opportunity. Employing the concepts of rationality, rights, and equal opportunity, this school makes arguments similar to those against racial discrimination. It asserts that women are just as rational as men and therefore should have equal opportunity to make their own choices. This school challenges the assumptions of male authority, and it seeks to erase gender based distinctions recognized in the law, thus enabling women to compete equally in the marketplace. It has caused legislatures and the courts to change many discriminatory laws. Its approach works, proponents argue, because it speaks the language the legal system understands. In addition, this approach attracts nonfeminists who agree that non–sex-specific legal solutions are preferable to sex-specific laws. RUTH BADER GINSBURG, first as an attorney and later as a justice of the U.S. Supreme Court, has exemplified supporters of this liberal feminist approach.

Another school of feminist legal thought focuses on the differences between men and women and celebrates those differences. Deeply influenced by the research of psychologist Carol Gilligan, this group of feminist thinkers proposes that men and women speak in different voices. Women emphasize the importance of relationships, contexts, and reconciliation of conflicting interpersonal positions, whereas men emphasize abstract principles of rights and logic. The objective of this school is to give equal recognition to women's moral voice. Proponents seek changes in the existing conditions so that the law will recognize women-valued relationships such as that between mother and child. In expressing this different voice of caring and communal values, this school of feminism criticizes possessive individualism, which, it is claimed, is integral to the maintenance of women in stereotypical roles.

Like the liberal feminist school of thought, radical feminism focuses on inequality. But radical feminism views women as a class, not as individual human beings. It asserts that men, as a class, have dominated women, creating gender inequality. This inequality is the consequence of a systematic subordination rather than irrational discrimination. Thus, heterosexuality is a social arrangement with men dominant and women submissive. For radical feminists, gender is a question of power. Therefore, this school is not satisfied with creating legal categories that promise equal opportunity and fair treatment. It sees these as false categories that mask the entrenched power of the male-dominant structure. What is needed, argue radical feminists, is an abandonment of traditional approaches that take maleness as their reference point: sexual equality must be constructed on the basis of woman's difference from man, not a mere accommodation of that difference.

Radical feminists have targeted sexual and domestic violence. They view PORNOGRAPHY as an instrument of sexual subordination rather than as a creative expression deserving FIRST AMENDMENT protection. In the 1980s law professor CATHARINE A. MACKINNON and writer ANDREA DWORKIN proposed that women be permitted to sue pornographers for damages under civil rights laws. Though their viewpoint has not been accepted by the U.S. courts, their work changed the nature of the debate over pornography.

Through the various approaches of the different schools of feminist legal thought, feminist jurisprudence has changed the way legislators and judges look at issues. By asking the "woman question," feminists have identified gender components and gender implications of laws and practices that are claimed to be neutral. Laws affecting employment, DIVORCE, reproductive rights, RAPE, domestic violence, and SEXUAL HARASSMENT have all benefited from the analysis and insight of feminist jurisprudence. With most law schools teaching the subject, feminist legal analysis holds a significant place in U.S. law and legal thought.

CROSS-REFERENCES

Equal Protection; Equal Rights Amendment; Fetal Rights; Ireland, Patricia; *Roe v. Wade;* Sex Discrimination; Women's Rights.

ABBREVIATIONS

A.	Atlantic Reporter
A. 2d	Atlantic Reporter, Second Series
AAA	American Arbitration Association; Agricultural Adjustment Act of 1933
AAPRP	All African People's Revolutionary Party
ABA	American Bar Association; Architectural Barriers Act, 1968
ABM Treaty	Anti-Ballistic Missile Treaty of 1972; antiballistic missile
ABVP	Anti-Biased Violence Project
A/C	Account
A.C.	Appeal Cases
ACAA	Air Carrier Access Act
ACF	Administration for Children and Families
ACLU	American Civil Liberties Union
ACS	Agricultural Cooperative Service
Act'g Legal Adv.	Acting Legal Advisor
ACUS	Administrative Conference of the United States
ACYF	Administration on Children, Youth, and Families
A.D. 2d	Appellate Division, Second Series, N.Y.
ADA	Americans with Disabilities Act of 1990
ADAMHA	Alcohol, Drug Abuse, and Mental Health Administration
ADC	Aid to Dependent Children
ADD	Administration on Developmental Disabilities
ADEA	Age Discrimination in Employment Act of 1967
ADR	alternative dispute resolution
AEC	Atomic Energy Commission
AECB	Arms Export Control Board
A.E.R.	All England Law Reports
AFDC	Aid to Families with Dependent Children
aff'd per cur.	affirmed by the court
AFIS	automated fingerprint identification system
AFL	American Federation of Labor
AFL-CIO	American Federation of Labor and Congress of Industrial Organizations
AFRes	Air Force Reserve
AFSCME	American Federation of State, County, and Municipal Employees
AGRICOLA	Agricultural Online Access
AIA	Association of Insurance Attorneys
AID	artificial insemination using a third-party donor's sperm; Agency for International Development

AIDS	acquired immune deficiency syndrome
AIH	artificial insemination using the husband's sperm
AIM	American Indian Movement
AIUSA	Amnesty International, U.S.A. Affiliate
AJS	American Judicature Society
ALEC	American Legislative Exchange Council
ALF	Animal Liberation Front
ALI	American Law Institute
ALJ	administrative law judge
All E.R.	All England Law Reports
ALO	Agency Liaison
A.L.R.	American Law Reports
AMA	American Medical Association
Am. Dec.	American Decisions
amdt.	amendment
Amer. St. Papers, For. Rels.	American State Papers, Legislative and Executive Documents of the Congress of the U.S., Class I, Foreign Relations, 1832–1859
AMVETS	American Veterans (of World War II)
ANA	Administration for Native Americans
Ann. Dig.	Annual Digest of Public International Law Cases
ANZUS	Australia–New Zealand–United States Security Treaty Organization
AOA	Administration on Aging
APA	Administrative Procedure Act of 1946
APHIS	Animal and Plant Health Inspection Service
App. Div.	Appellate Division Reports, N.Y. Supreme Court
Arb. Trib., U.S.-British Convention of 1853	Arbitration Tribunal, Claim Convention of 1853, United States and Great Britain
ARS	Advanced Record System
Art.	article
ASCS	Agriculture Stabilization and Conservation Service
ASM	available seatmile
ASPCA	American Society for the Prevention of Cruelty to Animals
Asst. Att. Gen.	Assistant Attorney General
AT&T	American Telephone and Telegraph
ATFD	Alcohol, Tobacco and Firearms Division
ATLA	Association of Trial Lawyers of America
ATTD	Alcohol and Tobacco Tax Division
ATU	Alcohol Tax Unit
AZT	azidothymidine
BALSA	Black-American Law Student Association
BATF	Bureau of Alcohol, Tobacco and Firearms
BCCI	Bank of Credit and Commerce International
BEA	Bureau of Economic Analysis
Bell's Cr. C.	Bell's English Crown Cases
Bevans	United States Treaties, etc. *Treaties and Other International Agreements of the United States of America, 1776–1949* (compiled under the direction of Charles I. Bevans) (1968–76)
BFOQ	bona fide occupational qualification
BI	Bureau of Investigation
BIA	Bureau of Indian Affairs; Board of Immigration Appeals
BJS	Bureau of Justice Statistics
Black.	Black's United States Supreme Court Reports
Blatchf.	Blatchford's United States Circuit Court Reports
BLM	Bureau of Land Management
BLS	Bureau of Labor Statistics
BMD	ballistic missile defense
BOCA	Building Officials and Code Administrators International
BPP	Black Panther Party for Self-Defense

Brit. and For.	British and Foreign State Papers
Burr.	James Burrows, *Report of Cases Argued and Determined in the Court of King's Bench during the Time of Lord Mansfield* (1766–1780)
BVA	Board of Veterans Appeals
c.	Chapter
C³I	Command, Control, Communications, and Intelligence
C.A.	Court of Appeals
CAA	Clean Air Act
CAB	Civil Aeronautics Board
CAFE	corporate average fuel economy
Cal. 2d	California Reports, Second Series
Cal. 3d	California Reports, Third Series
CALR	computer-assisted legal research
Cal. Rptr.	California Reporter
CAP	Common Agricultural Policy
CATV	community antenna television
CBO	Congressional Budget Office
CCC	Commodity Credit Corporation
CCDBG	Child Care and Development Block Grant of 1990
C.C.D. Pa.	Circuit Court Decisions, Pennsylvania
C.C.D. Va.	Circuit Court Decisions, Virginia
CCEA	Cabinet Council on Economic Affairs
CCR	Center for Constitutional Rights
C.C.R.I.	Circuit Court, Rhode Island
CD	certificate of deposit
CDA	Communications Decency Act
CDBG	Community Development Block Grant Program
CDC	Centers for Disease Control and Prevention; Community Development Corporation
CDF	Children's Defense Fund
CDL	Citizens for Decency through Law
CD-ROM	compact disc read-only memory
CDS	Community Dispute Services
CDW	collision damage waiver
CENTO	Central Treaty Organization
CEQ	Council on Environmental Quality
CERCLA	Comprehensive Environmental Response, Compensation, and Liability Act of 1980
cert.	*certiorari*
CETA	Comprehensive Employment and Training Act
C & F	cost and freight
CFC	chlorofluorocarbon
CFE Treaty	Conventional Forces in Europe Treaty of 1990
C.F. & I.	Cost, freight, and insurance
CFNP	Community Food and Nutrition Program
C.F.R.	Code of Federal Regulations
CFTC	Commodity Futures Trading Commission
Ch.	Chancery Division, English Law Reports
CHAMPVA	Civilian Health and Medical Program at the Veterans Administration
CHEP	Cuban/Haitian Entrant Program
CHINS	children in need of supervision
CHIPS	child in need of protective services
Ch.N.Y.	Chancery Reports, New York
Chr. Rob.	Christopher Robinson, *Reports of Cases Argued and Determined in the High Court of Admiralty* (1801–1808)
CIA	Central Intelligence Agency
CID	Commercial Item Descriptions
C.I.F.	Cost, insurance, and freight
CINCNORAD	Commander in Chief, North American Air Defense Command
C.I.O.	Congress of Industrial Organizations

C.J.	chief justice
CJIS	Criminal Justice Information Services
C.J.S.	Corpus Juris Secundum
Claims Arb. under Spec. Conv., Nielsen's Rept.	Frederick Kenelm Nielsen, *American and British Claims Arbitration under the Special Agreement Concluded between the United States and Great Britain, August 18, 1910* (1926)
CLE	Center for Law and Education
CLEO	Council on Legal Education Opportunity
CLP	Communist Labor Party of America
CLS	Christian Legal Society; critical legal studies (movement), Critical Legal Studies (membership organization)
C.M.A.	Court of Military Appeals
CMEA	Council for Mutual Economic Assistance
CMHS	Center for Mental Health Services
C.M.R.	Court of Military Review
CNN	Cable News Network
CNO	Chief of Naval Operations
C.O.D.	cash on delivery
COGP	Commission on Government Procurement
COINTELPRO	Counterintelligence Program
Coke Rep.	Coke's English King's Bench Reports
COLA	cost-of-living adjustment
COMCEN	Federal Communications Center
Comp.	Compilation
Conn.	Connecticut Reports
CONTU	National Commission on New Technological Uses of Copyrighted Works
Conv.	Convention
Corbin	Arthur L. Corbin, *Corbin on Contracts: A Comprehensive Treatise on the Rules of Contract Law* (1950)
CORE	Congress of Racial Equality
Cox's Crim. Cases	Cox's Criminal Cases (England)
CPA	certified public accountant
CPB	Corporation for Public Broadcasting, the
CPI	Consumer Price Index
CPSC	Consumer Product Safety Commission
Cranch	Cranch's United States Supreme Court Reports
CRF	Constitutional Rights Foundation
CRS	Congressional Research Service; Community Relations Service
CRT	critical race theory
CSA	Community Services Administration
CSAP	Center for Substance Abuse Prevention
CSAT	Center for Substance Abuse Treatment
CSC	Civil Service Commission
CSCE	Conference on Security and Cooperation in Europe
CSG	Council of State Governments
CSO	Community Service Organization
CSP	Center for the Study of the Presidency
C-SPAN	Cable-Satellite Public Affairs Network
CSRS	Cooperative State Research Service
CSWPL	Center on Social Welfare Policy and Law
CTA	*cum testamento annexo* (with the will attached)
Ct. Ap. D.C.	Court of Appeals, District of Columbia
Ct. App. No. Ireland	Court of Appeals, Northern Ireland
Ct. Cl.	Court of Claims, United States
Ct. Crim. Apps.	Court of Criminal Appeals (England)
Ct. of Sess., Scot.	Court of Sessions, Scotland
CU	credit union

CUNY	City University of New York
Cush.	Cushing's Massachusetts Reports
CWA	Civil Works Administration; Clean Water Act
Dall.	Dallas' Pennsylvania and United States Reports
DAR	Daughter of the American Revolution
DARPA	Defense Advanced Research Projects Agency
DAVA	Defense Audiovisual Agency
D.C.	United States District Court
D.C. Del.	United States District Court, Delaware
D.C. Mass.	United States District Court, Massachusetts
D.C. Md.	United States District Court, Maryland
D.C.N.D.Cal.	United States District Court, Northern District, California
D.C.N.Y.	United States District Court, New York
D.C.Pa.	United States District Court, Pennsylvania
DCS	Deputy Chiefs of Staff
DCZ	District of the Canal Zone
DDT	dichlorodiphenyltricloroethane
DEA	Drug Enforcement Administration
Decl. Lond.	Declaration of London, February 26, 1909
Dev. & B.	Devereux & Battle's North Carolina Reports
Dig. U.S. Practice in Intl. Law	Digest of U.S. Practice in International Law
Dist. Ct. D.C.	United States District Court, District of Columbia
D.L.R.	Dominion Law Reports (Canada)
DNA	deoxyribonucleic acid
DNase	deoxyribonuclease
DNC	Democratic National Committee
DOC	Department of Commerce
DOD	Department of Defense
Dodson	Dodson's Reports, English Admiralty Courts
DOE	Department of Energy
DOER	Department of Employee Relations
DOJ	Department of Justice
DOS	disk operating system
DOT	Department of Transportation
DPT	diphtheria, pertussis, and tetanus
DRI	Defense Research Institute
DSAA	Defense Security Assistance Agency
DUI	driving under the influence; driving under intoxication
DWI	driving while intoxicated
EAHCA	Education for All Handicapped Children Act of 1975
EBT	examination before trial
ECPA	Electronic Communications Privacy Act of 1986
ECSC	Treaty of the European Coal and Steel Community
EDA	Economic Development Administration
EDF	Environmental Defense Fund
E.D.N.Y.	Eastern District, New York
EDP	electronic data processing
E.D. Pa.	Eastern District, Pennsylvania
EDSC	Eastern District, South Carolina
E.D. Va.	Eastern District, Virginia
EEC	European Economic Community; European Economic Community Treaty
EEOC	Equal Employment Opportunity Commission
EFF	Electronic Frontier Foundation
EFT	electronic funds transfer
Eliz.	Queen Elizabeth (Great Britain)
Em. App.	Temporary Emergency Court of Appeals

ENE	early neutral evaluation
Eng. Rep.	English Reports
EOP	Executive Office of the President
EPA	Environmental Protection Agency; Equal Pay Act of 1963
ERA	Equal Rights Amendment
ERISA	Employee Retirement Income Security Act of 1974
ERS	Economic Research Service
ESF	emergency support function; Economic Support Fund
ESRD	End-Stage Renal Disease Program
ETA	Employment and Training Administration
ETS	environmental tobacco smoke
et seq.	*et sequentes* or *et sequentia;* "and the following"
EU	European Union
Euratom	European Atomic Energy Community
Eur. Ct. H.R.	European Court of Human Rights
Ex.	English Exchequer Reports, Welsby, Hurlstone & Gordon
Exch.	Exchequer Reports (Welsby, Hurlstone & Gordon)
Eximbank	Export-Import Bank of the United States
F.	Federal Reporter
F. 2d	Federal Reporter, Second Series
FAA	Federal Aviation Administration; Federal Arbitration Act
FAAA	Federal Alcohol Administration Act
FACE	Freedom of Access to Clinic Entrances Act of 1994
FACT	Feminist Anti-Censorship Task Force
FAO	Food and Agriculture Organization of the United Nations
FAR	Federal Acquisition Regulations
FAS	Foreign Agricultural Service
FBA	Federal Bar Association
FBI	Federal Bureau of Investigation
FCA	Farm Credit Administration
F. Cas.	Federal Cases
FCC	Federal Communications Commission
FCIA	Foreign Credit Insurance Association
FCIC	Federal Crop Insurance Corporation
FCRA	Fair Credit Reporting Act
FCU	Federal credit unions
FDA	Food and Drug Administration
FDIC	Federal Deposit Insurance Corporation
FDPC	Federal Data Processing Center
FEC	Federal Election Commission
Fed. Cas.	Federal Cases
FEMA	Federal Emergency Management Agency
FFB	Federal Financing Bank
FGIS	Federal Grain Inspection Service
FHA	Federal Housing Authority
FHWA	Federal Highway Administration
FIA	Federal Insurance Administration
FIC	Federal Information Centers; Federation of Insurance Counsel
FICA	Federal Insurance Contributions Act
FIFRA	Federal Insecticide, Fungicide, and Rodenticide Act
FIP	Forestry Incentives Program
FIRREA	Financial Institutions Reform, Recovery, and Enforcement Act
FISA	Foreign Intelligence Surveillance Act of 1978
FMCS	Federal Mediation and Conciliation Service
FmHA	Farmers Home Administration
FMLA	Family and Medical Leave Act of 1993
FNMA	Federal National Mortgage Association, "Fannie Mae"
F.O.B.	free on board

FOIA	Freedom of Information Act
FPC	Federal Power Commission
FPMR	Federal Property Management Regulations
FPRS	Federal Property Resources Service
FR	Federal Register
FRA	Federal Railroad Administration
FRB	Federal Reserve Board
FRC	Federal Radio Commission
F.R.D.	Federal Rules Decisions
FSA	Family Support Act
FSLIC	Federal Savings and Loan Insurance Corporation
FSQS	Food Safety and Quality Service
FSS	Federal Supply Service
F. Supp.	Federal Supplement
FTA	U.S.-Canada Free Trade Agreement, 1988
FTC	Federal Trade Commission
FTS	Federal Telecommunications System
FUTA	Federal Unemployment Tax Act
FWPCA	Federal Water Pollution Control Act of 1948
GAO	General Accounting Office; Governmental Affairs Office
GAOR	General Assembly Official Records, United Nations
GA Res.	General Assembly Resolution (United Nations)
GATT	General Agreement on Tariffs and Trade
Gen. Cls. Comm.	General Claims Commission, United States and Panama; General Claims Commission, United States and Mexico
Geo. II	King George II (Great Britain)
Geo. III	King George III (Great Britain)
GM	General Motors
GNMA	Government National Mortgage Association, "Ginnie Mae"
GNP	gross national product
GOP	Grand Old Party (Republican)
GOPAC	Grand Old Party Action Committee
GPA	Office of Governmental and Public Affairs
GPO	Government Printing Office
GRAS	generally recognized as safe
Gr. Br., Crim. Ct. App.	Great Britain, Court of Criminal Appeals
GRNL	Gay Rights National Lobby
GSA	General Services Administration
Hackworth	Green Haywood Hackworth, *Digest of International Law* (1940–44)
Hay and Marriott	Great Britain. High Court of Admiralty, *Decisions in the High Court of Admiralty during the Time of Sir George Hay and of Sir James Marriott, Late Judges of That Court* (1801)
HBO	Home Box Office
HCFA	Health Care Financing Administration
H.Ct.	High Court
HDS	Office of Human Development Services
Hen. & M.	Hening & Munford's Virginia Reports
HEW	Department of Health, Education, and Welfare
HHS	Department of Health and Human Services
Hill	Hill's New York Reports
HIRE	Help through Industry Retraining and Employment
HIV	human immunodeficiency virus
H.L.	House of Lords Cases (England)
H. Lords	House of Lords (England)
HNIS	Human Nutrition Information Service
Hong Kong L.R.	Hong Kong Law Reports
How.	Howard's United States Supreme Court Reports
How. St. Trials	Howell's English State Trials
HUAC	House Un-American Activities Committee

HUD	Department of Housing and Urban Development
Hudson, Internatl. Legis.	Manley O. Hudson, ed., *International Legislation: A Collection of the Texts of Multipartite International Instruments of General Interest Beginning with the Covenant of the League of Nations* (1931)
Hudson, World Court Reps.	Manley Ottmer Hudson, ed., *World Court Reports* (1934–)
Hun	Hun's New York Supreme Court Reports
Hunt's Rept.	Bert L. Hunt, *Report of the American and Panamanian General Claims Arbitration* (1934)
IAEA	International Atomic Energy Agency
IALL	International Association of Law Libraries
IBA	International Bar Association
IBM	International Business Machines
ICBM	intercontinental ballistic missile
ICC	Interstate Commerce Commission
ICJ	International Court of Justice
IDEA	Individuals with Disabilities Education Act, 1975
IEP	individualized educational program
IFC	International Finance Corporation
IGRA	Indian Gaming Regulatory Act, 1988
IJA	Institute of Judicial Administration
IJC	International Joint Commission
ILC	International Law Commission
ILD	International Labor Defense
Ill. Dec.	Illinois Decisions
ILO	International Labor Organization
IMF	International Monetary Fund
INA	Immigration and Nationality Act
IND	investigational new drug
INF Treaty	Intermediate-Range Nuclear Forces Treaty of 1987
INS	Immigration and Naturalization Service
INTELSAT	International Telecommunications Satellite Organization
Interpol	International Criminal Police Organization
Int'l. Law Reps.	International Law Reports
Intl. Legal Mats.	International Legal Materials
IPDC	International Program for the Development of Communication
IPO	Intellectual Property Owners
IPP	independent power producer
IQ	intelligence quotient
I.R.	Irish Reports
IRA	individual retirement account; Irish Republican Army
IRCA	Immigration Reform and Control Act of 1986
IRS	Internal Revenue Service
ISO	independent service organization
ISSN	International Standard Serial Numbers
ITA	International Trade Administration
ITI	Information Technology Integration
ITO	International Trade Organization
ITS	Information Technology Service
ITU	International Telecommunication Union
IUD	intrauterine device
IWC	International Whaling Commission
IWW	Industrial Workers of the World
JCS	Joint Chiefs of Staff
JDL	Jewish Defense League
JOBS	Jobs Opportunity and Basic Skills
John. Ch.	Johnson's New York Chancery Reports
Johns.	Johnson's Reports (New York)
JP	justice of the peace

K.B.	King's Bench Reports (England)
KGB	Komitet Gosudarstvennoi Bezopasnosti (the State Security Committee for countries in the former Soviet Union)
KKK	Ku Klux Klan
KMT	Kuomintang
LAPD	Los Angeles Police Department
LC	Library of Congress
LD50	lethal dose 50
LDEF	Legal Defense and Education Fund (NOW)
LDF	Legal Defense Fund, Legal Defense and Educational Fund of the NAACP
LEAA	Law Enforcement Assistance Administration
L.Ed.	Lawyers' Edition Supreme Court Reports
LMSA	Labor-Management Services Administration
LNTS	League of Nations Treaty Series
Lofft's Rep.	Lofft's English King's Bench Reports
L.R.	Law Reports (English)
LSAS	Law School Admission Service
LSAT	Law School Aptitude Test
LSC	Legal Services Corporation; Legal Services for Children
LSD	lysergic acid diethylamide
LSDAS	Law School Data Assembly Service
LTBT	Limited Test Ban Treaty
LTC	Long Term Care
MAD	mutual assured destruction
MADD	Mothers against Drunk Driving
MALDEF	Mexican American Legal Defense and Educational Fund
Malloy	William M. Malloy, ed., *Treaties, Conventions, International Acts, Protocols, and Agreements between the United States of America and Other Powers* (1910–38)
Martens	Georg Friedrich von Martens, ed., *Noveau recueil général de traités et autres act es relatifs aux rapports de droit international* (Series I, 20 vols. [1843–75]; Series II, 35 vols. [1876–1908]; Series III [1909–])
Mass.	Massachusetts Reports
MCH	Maternal and Child Health Bureau
Md. App.	Maryland, Appeal Cases
M.D. Ga.	Middle District, Georgia
Mercy	Movement Ensuring the Right to Choose for Yourself
Metc.	Metcalf's Massachusetts Reports
MFDP	Mississippi Freedom Democratic party
MGT	Management
MHSS	Military Health Services System
Miller	David Hunter Miller, ed., *Treaties and Other International Acts of the United States of America* (1931–1948)
Minn.	Minnesota Reports
MINS	minors in need of supervision
MIRV	multiple independently targetable reentry vehicle
Misc.	Miscellaneous Reports, New York
Mixed Claims Comm., Report of Decs.	Mixed Claims Commission, United States and Germany, Report of Decisions
M.J.	Military Justice Reporter
MLAP	Migrant Legal Action Program
MLB	major league baseball
MLDP	Mississippi Loyalist Democratic party
Mo.	Missouri Reports
Mod.	Modern Reports, English King's Bench, etc.
Moore, Dig. Intl. Law	John Bassett Moore, *A Digest of International Law*, 8 vols. (1906)
Moore, Intl. Arbs.	John Bassett Moore, *History and Digest of the International Arbitrations to Which the United States Has Been a Party*, 6 vols. (1898)

Morison	William Maxwell Morison, *The Scots Revised Report: Morison's Dictionary of Decisions* (1908–09)
M.P.	member of Parliament
MPAA	Motion Picture Association of America
mpg	miles per gallon
MPRSA	Marine Protection, Research, and Sanctuaries Act of 1972
M.R.	Master of the Rolls
MS-DOS	Microsoft Disk Operating System
MSHA	Mine Safety and Health Administration
NAACP	National Association for the Advancement of Colored People
NAAQS	National Ambient Air Quality Standards
NABSW	National Association of Black Social Workers
NAFTA	North American Free Trade Agreement, 1993
NARAL	National Abortion Rights Action League
NARF	Native American Rights Fund
NARS	National Archives and Record Service
NASA	National Aeronautics and Space Administration
NASD	National Association of Securities Dealers
NATO	North Atlantic Treaty Organization
NAVINFO	Navy Information Offices
NAWSA	National American Woman's Suffrage Association
NBA	National Bar Association
NBC	National Broadcasting Company
NBLSA	National Black Law Student Association
NBS	National Bureau of Standards
NCA	Noise Control Act; National Command Authorities
NCAA	National Collegiate Athletic Association
NCAC	National Coalition against Censorship
NCCB	National Consumer Cooperative Bank
NCE	Northwest Community Exchange
NCJA	National Criminal Justice Association
NCLB	National Civil Liberties Bureau
NCP	national contingency plan
NCSC	National Center for State Courts
NCUA	National Credit Union Administration
NDA	new drug application
N.D. Ill.	Northern District, Illinois
NDU	National Defense University
N.D. Wash.	Northern District, Washington
N.E.	North Eastern Reporter
N.E. 2d	North Eastern Reporter, Second Series
NEA	National Endowment for the Arts
NEH	National Endowment for the Humanities
NEPA	National Environmental Protection Act; National Endowment Policy Act
NFIP	National Flood Insurance Program
NGTF	National Gay Task Force
NHRA	Nursing Home Reform Act, 1987
NHTSA	National Highway Traffic Safety Administration
Nielsen's Rept.	Frederick Kenelm Nielsen, *American and British Claims Arbitration under the Special Agreement Concluded between the United States and Great Britain, August 18, 1910* (1926)
NIEO	New International Economic Order
NIH	National Institutes of Health, the NIH
NIJ	National Institute of Justice
NIRA	National Industrial Recovery Act; National Industrial Recovery Administration
NIST	National Institute of Standards and Technology, the NIST
NITA	National Telecommunications and Information Administration
N.J.	New Jersey Reports

N.J. Super.	New Jersey Superior Court Reports
NLRA	National Labor Relations Act
NLRB	National Labor Relations Board
No.	Number
NOAA	National Oceanic and Atmospheric Administration
NOW	National Organization for Women
NOW LDEF	National Organization for Women Legal Defense and Education Fund
NOW/PAC	National Organization for Women Political Action Committee
NPDES	National Pollutant Discharge Elimination System
NPL	national priorities list
NPR	National Public Radio
NPT	Non-Proliferation Treaty
NRA	National Rifle Association; National Recovery Act
NRC	Nuclear Regulatory Commission
NSC	National Security Council
NSCLC	National Senior Citizens Law Center
NSF	National Science Foundation
NSFNET	National Science Foundation Network
NTIA	National Telecommunications and Information Administration
NTID	National Technical Institute for the Deaf
NTIS	National Technical Information Service
NTS	Naval Telecommunications System
NTSB	National Transportation Safety Board
N.W.	North Western Reporter
N.W. 2d	North Western Reporter, Second Series
NWSA	National Woman Suffrage Association
N.Y.	New York Court of Appeals Reports
N.Y. 2d	New York Court of Appeals Reports, Second Series
N.Y.S.	New York Supplement Reporter
N.Y.S. 2d	New York Supplement Reporter, Second Series
NYSE	New York Stock Exchange
N.Y. Sup.	New York Supreme Court Reports
NYU	New York University
OAAU	Organization of Afro American Unity
OAP	Office of Administrative Procedure
OAS	Organization of American States
OASDI	Old-age, Survivors, and Disability Insurance Benefits
OASHDS	Office of the Assistant Secretary for Human Development Services
OCED	Office of Comprehensive Employment Development
OCHAMPUS	Office of Civilian Health and Medical Program of the Uniformed Services
OCSE	Office of Child Support Enforcement
OEA	Organización de los Estados Americanos
OFCCP	Office of Federal Contract Compliance Programs
OFPP	Office of Federal Procurement Policy
OICD	Office of International Cooperation and Development
OIG	Office of the Inspector General
OJARS	Office of Justice Assistance, Research, and Statistics
OMB	Office of Management and Budget
OMPC	Office of Management, Planning, and Communications
ONP	Office of National Programs
OPD	Office of Policy Development
OPEC	Organization of Petroleum Exporting Countries
OPIC	Overseas Private Investment Corporation
Ops. Atts. Gen.	Opinions of the Attorneys-General of the United States
Ops. Comms.	Opinions of the Commissioners
OPSP	Office of Product Standards Policy
O.R.	Ontario Reports
OR	Official Records

OSHA	Occupational Safety and Health Administration
OSHRC	Occupational Safety and Health Review Commission
OSM	Office of Surface Mining
OSS	Office of Strategic Services
OST	Office of the Secretary
OT	Office of Transportation
OTA	Office of Technology Assessment
OTC	over-the-counter
OUI	operating under the influence
OWBPA	Older Workers Benefit Protection Act
OWRT	Office of Water Research and Technology
P.	Pacific Reporter
P. 2d	Pacific Reporter, Second Series
PAC	political action committee
Pa. Oyer and Terminer	Pennsylvania Oyer and Terminer Reports
PATCO	Professional Air Traffic Controllers Organization
PBGC	Pension Benefit Guaranty Corporation
PBS	Public Broadcasting Service; Public Buildings Service
P.C.	Privy Council (English Law Reports); personal computer
PCIJ	Permanent Court of International Justice
	Series A—Judgments and Orders (1922–30)
	Series B—Advisory Opinions (1922–30)
	Series A/B—Judgments, Orders, and Advisory Opinions (1931–40)
	Series C—Pleadings, Oral Statements, and Documents relating to Judgments and Advisory Opinions (1923–42)
	Series D—Acts and Documents concerning the Organization of the World Court (1922–47)
	Series E—Annual Reports (1925–45)
PCP	phencyclidine (no need to spell out)
P.D.	Probate Division, English Law Reports (1876–1890)
PDA	Pregnancy Discrimination Act of 1978
PD & R	Policy Development and Research
Perm. Ct. of Arb.	Permanent Court of Arbitration
Pet.	Peters' United States Supreme Court Reports
PETA	People for the Ethical Treatment of Animals
PGM	Program
PHA	Public Housing Agency
Phila. Ct. of Oyer and Terminer	Philadelphia Court of Oyer and Terminer
PHS	Public Health Service
PIC	Private Industry Council
Pick.	Pickering's Massachusetts Reports
PIK	Payment in Kind
PINS	persons in need of supervision
PIRG	Public Interest Research Group
P.L.	Public Laws
PLAN	Pro-Life Action Network
PLI	Practicing Law Institute
PLO	Palestine Liberation Organization
PNET	Peaceful Nuclear Explosions Treaty
POW-MIA	prisoner of war–missing in action
Pratt	Frederic Thomas Pratt, *Law of Contraband of War, with a Selection of Cases from the Papers of the Right Honourable Sir George Lee* (1856)
Proc.	Proceedings
PRP	potentially responsible party
PSRO	Professional Standards Review Organization
PTO	Patents and Trademark Office
PURPA	Public Utilities Regulatory Policies Act

PUSH	People United to Serve Humanity
PWA	Public Works Administration
PWSA	Ports and Waterways Safety Act of 1972
Q.B.	Queen's Bench (England)
Ralston's Rept.	Jackson Harvey Ralston, ed., *Venezuelan Arbitrations of 1903* (1904)
RC	Regional Commissioner
RCRA	Resource Conservation and Recovery Act
RCWP	Rural Clean Water Program
RDA	Rural Development Administration
REA	Rural Electrification Administration
Rec. des Decs. des Trib. Arb. Mixtes	G. Gidel, ed., *Recueil des décisions des tribunaux arbitraux mixtes, institués par les traités de paix* (1922–30)
Redmond	Vol. 3 of Charles I. Bevans, *Treaties and Other International Agreements of the United States of America, 1776–1949* (compiled by C. F. Redmond) (1969)
RESPA	Real Estate Settlement Procedure Act of 1974
RFRA	Religious Freedom Restoration Act
RICO	Racketeer Influenced and Corrupt Organizations
RNC	Republican National Committee
Roscoe	Edward Stanley Roscoe, ed., *Reports of Prize Cases Determined in the High Court of Admiralty before the Lords Commissioners of Appeals in Prize Causes and before the Judicial Committee of the Privy Council from 1745 to 1859* (1905)
ROTC	Reserve Officers' Training Corps
RPP	Representative Payee Program
R.S.	Revised Statutes
RTC	Resolution Trust Company
Ryan White CARE Act	Ryan White Comprehensive AIDS Research Emergency Act of 1990
SAC	Strategic Air Command
SACB	Subversive Activities Control Board
SADD	Students against Drunk Driving
SAF	Student Activities Fund
SAIF	Savings Association Insurance Fund
SALT I	Strategic Arms Limitation Talks of 1969–72
SAMHSA	Substance Abuse and Mental Health Services Administration
Sandf.	Sandford's New York Superior Court Reports
S and L	savings and loan
SARA	Superfund Amendment and Reauthorization Act
Sawy.	Sawyer's United States Circuit Court Reports
SBA	Small Business Administration
SCLC	Southern Christian Leadership Conference
Scott's Repts.	James Brown Scott, ed., *The Hague Court Reports*, 2 vols. (1916–32)
SCS	Soil Conservation Service
SCSEP	Senior Community Service Employment Program
S.Ct.	Supreme Court Reporter
S.D. Cal.	Southern District, California
S.D. Fla.	Southern District, Florida
S.D. Ga.	Southern District, Georgia
SDI	Strategic Defense Initiative
S.D. Me.	Southern District, Maine
S.D.N.Y.	Southern District, New York
SDS	Students for a Democratic Society
S.E.	South Eastern Reporter
S.E. 2d	South Eastern Reporter, Second Series
SEA	Science and Education Administration
SEATO	Southeast Asia Treaty Organization
SEC	Securities and Exchange Commission
Sec.	Section
SEEK	Search for Elevation, Education and Knowledge
SEOO	State Economic Opportunity Office

SEP	simplified employee pension plan
Ser.	Series
Sess.	Session
SGLI	Servicemen's Group Life Insurance
SIP	state implementation plan
SLA	Symbionese Liberation Army
SLBM	submarine-launched ballistic missile
SNCC	Student Nonviolent Coordinating Committee
So.	Southern Reporter
So. 2d	Southern Reporter, Second Series
SPA	Software Publisher's Association
Spec. Sess.	Special Session
SRA	Sentencing Reform Act of 1984
SS	Schutzstaffel (German for Protection Echelon)
SSA	Social Security Administration
SSI	Supplemental Security Income
START I	Strategic Arms Reduction Treaty of 1991
START II	Strategic Arms Reduction Treaty of 1993
Stat.	United States Statutes at Large
STS	Space Transportation Systems
St. Tr.	State Trials, English
STURAA	Surface Transportation and Uniform Relocation Assistance Act of 1987
Sup. Ct. of Justice, Mexico	Supreme Court of Justice, Mexico
Supp.	Supplement
S.W.	South Western Reporter
S.W. 2d	South Western Reporter, Second Series
SWAPO	South-West Africa People's Organization
SWAT	Special Weapons and Tactics
SWP	Socialist Workers party
TDP	Trade and Development Program
Tex. Sup.	Texas Supreme Court Reports
THAAD	Theater High-Altitude Area Defense System
TIA	Trust Indenture Act of 1939
TIAS	Treaties and Other International Acts Series (United States)
TNT	trinitrotoluene
TOP	Targeted Outreach Program
TPUS	Transportation and Public Utilities Service
Tripartite Claims Comm., Decs. and Ops.	Tripartite Claims Commission (United States, Austria, and Hungary), Decisions and Opinions
TRI-TAC	Joint Tactical Communications
TRO	temporary restraining order
TS	Treaty Series, United States
TSCA	Toxic Substance Control Act
TSDs	transporters, storers, and disposers
TTBT	Threshold Test Ban Treaty
TVA	Tennessee Valley Authority
UAW	United Auto Workers; United Automobile, Aerospace, and Agricultural Implements Workers of America
U.C.C.	Uniform Commercial Code; Universal Copyright Convention
U.C.C.C.	Uniform Consumer Credit Code
UCCJA	Uniform Child Custody Jurisdiction Act
UCMJ	Uniform Code of Military Justice
UCPP	Urban Crime Prevention Program
UCS	United Counseling Service
UDC	United Daughters of the Confederacy
UFW	United Farm Workers
UHF	ultrahigh frequency
UIFSA	Uniform Interstate Family Support Act

UIS	Unemployment Insurance Service
UMDA	Uniform Marriage and Divorce Act
UMTA	Urban Mass Transportation Administration
UNCITRAL	United Nations Commission on International Trade Law
UNCTAD	United Nations Conference on Trade and Development
UN Doc.	United Nations Documents
UNDP	United Nations Development Program
UNEF	United Nations Emergency Force
UNESCO	United Nations Educational, Scientific, and Cultural Organization
UNICEF	United Nations Children's Fund
UNIDO	United Nations Industrial and Development Organization
Unif. L. Ann.	Uniform Laws Annotated
UN Repts. Intl. Arb. Awards	United Nations Reports of International Arbitral Awards
UNTS	United Nations Treaty Series
UPI	United Press International
URESA	Uniform Reciprocal Enforcement of Support Act
U.S.	United States Reports
USAF	United States Air Force
U.S. App. D.C.	United States Court of Appeals for the District of Columbia
U.S.C.	United States Code
U.S.C.A.	United States Code Annotated
U.S.C.C.A.N.	United States Code Congressional and Administrative News
USCMA	United States Court of Military Appeals
USDA	U.S. Department of Agriculture
USES	United States Employment Service
USFA	United States Fire Administration
USICA	International Communication Agency, United States
USSC	U.S. Sentencing Commission
U.S.S.R.	Union of Soviet Socialist Republics
UST	United States Treaties
USTS	United States Travel Service
v.	*versus*
VA	Veterans Administration, the VA
VGLI	Veterans Group Life Insurance
Vict.	Queen Victoria (Great Britain)
VIN	vehicle identification number
VISTA	Volunteers in Service to America
VJRA	Veterans Judicial Review Act of 1988
V.L.A.	Volunteer Lawyers for the Arts
VMI	Virginia Military Institute
VMLI	Veterans Mortgage Life Insurance
VOCAL	Victims of Child Abuse Laws
WAC	Women's Army Corps
Wall.	Wallace's United States Supreme Court Reports
Wash. 2d	Washington Reports, Second Series
WAVES	Women Accepted for Volunteer Service
WCTU	Women's Christian Temperance Union
W.D. Wash.	Western District, Washington
W.D. Wis.	Western District, Wisconsin
WEAL	West's Encyclopedia of American Law, Women's Equity Action League
Wend.	Wendell's New York Reports
WFSE	Washington Federation of State Employees
Wheat.	Wheaton's United States Supreme Court Reports
Wheel. Cr. Cases	Wheeler's New York Criminal Cases
Whiteman	Marjorie Millace Whiteman, *Digest of International Law*, 15 vols. (1963–73)
WHO	World Health Organization
WIC	Women, Infants, and Children program
Will. and Mar.	King William and Queen Mary (Great Britain)

WIN	WESTLAW Is Natural; Whip Inflation Now; Work Incentive Program
WIU	Workers' Industrial Union
W.L.R.	Weekly Law Reports, England
WPA	Works Progress Administration
WPPDA	Welfare and Pension Plans Disclosure Act
WWI	World War I
WWII	World War II
Yates Sel. Cas.	Yates' New York Select Cases

BIBLIOGRAPHY

DANIEL, PETER VIVIAN

Stephens, Otis H., Jr., and John M. Scheb II. 1993. *American Constitutional Law.* St. Paul: West.

Hall, Kermit L. 1989. *The Magic Mirror.* New York: Oxford Univ. Press.

DARROW, CLARENCE

Cowan, Geoffrey. 1993. *The People v. Clarence Darrow.* New York: Times Books.

Darrow, Clarence. 1932. *The Story of My Life.* Da Caps. Press.

Driemen, John E. 1992. *Clarence Darrow.* New York: Chelsea House.

Tierney, Kevin. 1979. *Darrow: A Biography.* New York: Crowell.

Weinberg, Arthur, and Lila Weinberg. 1987. *Clarence Darrow: A Sentimental Rebel.* New York: Atheneum.

DAVIS, ANGELA YVONNE

Davis, Angela. 1974. *Angela Davis: An Autobiography.* New York: International Publishers.

DAVIS, DAVID

Stephens, Otis H., Jr., and John M. Scheb II. 1993. *American Constitutional Law.* St. Paul: West.

Hall, Kermit L. 1989. *The Magic Mirror.* New York: Oxford Univ. Press.

DAY, WILLIAM RUFUS

Stephens, Otis H., Jr., and John M. Scheb II. 1993. *American Constitutional Law.* St. Paul: West.

Hall, Kermit L. 1989. *The Magic Mirror.* New York: Oxford Univ. Press.

DEADLY FORCE

Griffin, Thomas J. 1971. "Private Person's Authority, in Making Arrest for Felony, to Shoot or Kill Alleged Felon." *American Law Reports 3d* 32:1078.

Pearson, James O., Jr. 1978. "Modern Status: Right of Peace Officer to Use Deadly Force in Attempting to Arrest Fleeing Felon." *American Law Reports 3d* 83:174.

Pearson, James O., Jr. 1978. "Peace Officer's Civil Liability for Death or Personal Injuries Caused by Intentional Force in Arresting Misdemeanant." *American Law Reports 3d* 83:238.

Belli, Melvin, and Allen P. Wilkinson. 1986. *Everybody's Guide to the Law.* New York: Harcourt Brace Jovanovich.

Sullivan, G. Russell. 1985. "Constitutional Law—Deadly Force and the Fourth Amendment: *Tennessee v. Garner.*" *Suffolk University Law Review* 20.

DEATH AND DYING

Callahan, Daniel. 1990. "Current Trends in Biomedical Ethics in the United States." *Bioethics: Issues and Perspectives.* Washington, D.C.: Pan American Health Organization.

Council on Ethical and Judicial Affairs, American Medical Association. 1994. *Code of Medical Ethics.* Chicago: American Medical Association.

Humphry, Derek. 1991. *Final Exit.* Eugene, Or.: Hemlock Society.

———. 1993. *Lawful Exit: The Limits of Freedom for Help in Dying.* Junction City, Or.: Norris Lane Press.

Monagle, John F., and David C. Thomasma. 1994. *Health Care Ethics: Critical Issues.* Gaithersburg, Md.: Aspen.

DECLARATION OF INDEPENDENCE

Levy, Michael B. 1982. *Political Thought in America.* Homewood, Ill.: Dorsey Press.

DECLARATORY JUDGMENT

Howard, Davis J. 1994. "Declaratory Judgment Coverage Actions." *Ohio Northern University Law Review* 13.

DEFAMATION

Friedman, Jessica R. 1995. "Defamation." *Fordham Law Review* 64 (December).

DEFENSE DEPARTMENT

United States Government Manual, 1994–1995. Washington, D.C.: U.S. Government Printing Office.

DEMOCRATIC PARTY

Wilson, James Q. 1992. *American Government: Institutions and Policies.* Lexington, Mass.: Heath.

DEMONSTRATIVE EVIDENCE

Brain, Robert D., and Daniel J. Broderick. 1992. "The Derivative Relevance of Demonstrative Evidence: Charting Its Proper Evidentiary Status." *University of California at Davis Law Review* 25.

Branson, Frank L. 1989. "Innovative Techniques in Demonstrative Evidence." *American Law Institute-American Bar Association* C396 (January 19).

Heffernan, Thomas A. 1987. "Effective Use of Demonstrative Evidence—'Seeing Is Believing.' " *American Jury Trial Advocate* 10.

O'Callaghan, Richard M. 1988. "Introduction and Use of Demonstrative Evidence." *Practising Law Institute/Litigation* 360 (October 1).

Reuben, Richard. 1995. "Stuntpersons Add Drama to Cases." *American Bar Association Journal* (November).

Taub, Theodore C. "Demonstrative Evidence." *American Law Institute-American Bar Association* C432 (August 14).

DEPOSITION

Balabanian, David M. 1987. "Medium v. Tedium: Video Depositions Come of Age." *Practising Law Institute/Litigation* 328.

Montoya, Jean. 1995. "A Theory of Compulsory Process Clause Discovery Rights." *Indiana Law Journal* 70.

Zweifach, Lawrence J., and Gerson Zweifach. 1994. "Preparing to Take and Taking the Deposition." *Practising Law Institute/Litigation* 507.

DEPRECIATION

Brestoff, Nelson E. 1985. *How to Write Off Your Down Payment.* New York: Putnam.

Hudson, David M., and Stephen A. Lind. 1994. *Federal Income Taxation.* 5th ed. St. Paul: West.

DETERMINATE SENTENCE

Sauer, Kristen K. 1995. "Informed Conviction: Instructing the Jury about Mandatory Sentencing Consequences." *Columbia Law Review* 95:1232.

Forer, Lois G. 1994. *A Rage to Punish.* New York: Norton.

"Mandatory Sentencing: Do Tough Sentencing Laws Reduce Crime?" 1995. *CQ Researcher* (May 26).

O'Connell, John P. 1995. "Throwing Away the Key (and State Money)." *Spectrum: the Journal of State Government* (winter).

Reske, Henry J. 1994. "Judges Irked by Tough-on-Crime Laws." *American Bar Association Journal* (October).

Sklansky, David A. 1995. "Cocaine, Race, and Equal Protection." *Stanford Law Review* 47:1283.

DISABLED PERSONS

Gaskill, Ricca. 1994. *Americans with Disabilities Act: An Analysis of Developments Relating to Disability Law.* New York: Practising Law Institute.

Poston, Sarah. 1994. "Developments in Federal Disability Discrimination Law: An Emerging Resolution to the Section 504 Damages Issue." *1992/1993 Annual Survey of American Law* 419.

DISASTER RELIEF

Copelan, John J., Jr. 1995. "Disaster Law and Hurricane Andrew: Government Lawyers Leading the Way to Recovery." *Urban Lawyer* 27 (winter).

Stratton, Ruth M. 1989. *Disaster Relief: The Politics of Intergovernmental Relations.* Lanham, Md.: Univ. Press of America.

United States Government Manual, 1993–1994. Washington, D.C.: U.S. Government Printing Office.

DISCRETION IN DECISION MAKING

Feinstein, Mary S. 1986. "American Cetacean Society v. Baldrige: Executive Agreements and the Constitutional Limits of Executive Branch Discretion in American Foreign Policy." *Brooklyn Journal of International Law* 12.

Heyman, Michael G. 1994. "Judicial Review of Discretionary Immigration Decisionmaking." *San Diego Law Review* 31.

Koch, Charles H. 1986. "Judicial Review of Administrative Discretion." *George Washington Law Review* 54.

Maranville, Deborah. 1986. "Nonacquiescence: Outlaw Agencies, Imperial Courts, and the Perils of Pluralism." *Vanderbilt Law Review* 39.

Neuren, Cathy S. 1984. "Addressing the Resurgence of Presidential Budgetmaking Initiative: A Proposal to Reform the Impoundment Control Act of 1974." *Texas Law Review* 63.

Shapiro, Sidney A., and Robert L. Glicksman. 1988. "Congress, the Supreme Court, and the Quiet Revolution in Administrative Law." *Duke Law Journal.*

DISFRANCHISEMENT

Belknap, Michael, ed. 1991. *Civil Rights, the White House, and the Justice Department.* New York: Garland.

Reitman, Alan, and Robert B. Davidson. 1972. *The Election Process: Voting Laws and Procedures.* Dobbs Ferry, N.Y.: Oceana.

Schmidt, Benno C., Jr. 1982. "Black Disfranchisement from the KKK to the Grandfather Clause." *Columbia Law Review* 82 (June).

Shapiro, Andrew L. 1993. "Challenging Criminal Disenfranchisement under the Voting Rights Act." *Yale Law Journal* 103 (November).

DISSENT

Mello, Michael. 1995. "Adhering to Our Views: Justices Brennan and Marshall and the Relentless Dissent to Death as a Punishment." *Florida State University Law Review* 22 (winter).

DISTRICT OF COLUMBIA

Harris, Charles Wesley. 1995. *The Conflict of Federal and Local Interests.* Washington D.C.: Georgetown Univ. Press.

Schrag, Philip G. 1985. *Behind the Scenes: The Politics of a Constitutional Convention.* Washington D.C.: Georgetown Univ. Press.

DIVORCE

American Bar Association Standing Committee on the Delivery of Legal Services. 1994. "Responding to the Needs of the Self-Represented Divorce Litigant." Chicago: American Bar Association.

Boumil, Marcia M., et al. 1994. *Law and Gender Bias.* Littleton, Colo.: Rothman.

Phillips, Roderick. 1991. *Untying the Knot.* Cambridge, England: Cambridge Univ. Press.

Wadlington, Walter. 1990. *Domestic Relations: Cases and Materials.* 2d ed. Westbury, N.Y.: Foundation Press.

Warle, Lynn D. 1994. "Divorce Violence and the No-Fault Divorce Culture." *Utah Law Review* (spring).

Woodhouse, Barbara Bennet. 1994. "Sex, Lies, and Dissipation: The Discourse of Fault in a No-Fault Era." *Georgetown Law Journal* 82.

DNA EVIDENCE

Bennett, Margann. 1995. "Admissibility Issues of Forensic DNA Evidence." *University of Kansas Law Review* 44 (November).

"Confronting the New Challenges of Scientific Evidence: DNA Evidence and the Criminal Defense." 1995. *Harvard Law Review* 108 (May).

Federal Bureau of Investigation. 1994. *Handbook of Forensic Science.* Washington, D.C.: U.S. Government Printing Office.

National Research Council. 1992. *DNA Technology in Forensic Science.* Washington, D.C.: National Academy Press.

Wright, Eric E. 1995. "DNA Evidence: Where We've Been, Where We Are, and Where We Are Going." *Maine Bar Journal* 10 (July).

DOMESTIC VIOLENCE

Rohr, Janelle, ed. 1990. *Violence in America: Opposing Viewpoints.* San Diego: Greenhaven Press.

Sommers, Christina Hoff. 1994. *Who Stole Feminism?* New York: Simon & Schuster.

Straus, Murray, and Richard Gelles. 1988. *Intimate Violence.* New York: Simon & Schuster.

DOUBLE JEOPARDY

"Constitutional Law—Goodbye Grady! Blockburger Wins the Double Jeopardy Rematch: *United States v. Dixon.*" 1994. *University of Arkansas at Little Rock Law Journal* 17.

"Continuing Criminal Enterprise, Conspiracy, and the Multiple Punishment Doctrine." 1993. *Michigan Law Review* 91.

Henning, Peter J. 1993. "Precedents in a Vacuum: The Supreme Court Continues to Tinker with Double Jeopardy." *American Criminal Law Review* 31.

Hoffman, Paul. 1994. "Double Jeopardy Wars: The Case for a Civil Rights Exception." *UCLA Law Review* 1.

"Increased Double Jeopardy Protection for the Criminal Defendant: *Grady v. Corbin.*" 1991. *Willamette Law Review* 27.

Kotler, Bradley E., Brian J. Leske, and Benjamin Lieber. 1994. "Double Jeopardy." *Georgetown Law Review* 82.

LaFave, Wayne R., and Jerold H. Israel. 1985. *Criminal Procedure* (student ed.). St. Paul, Minn.: West Publishing.

McAninch, William S. 1993. "Unfolding the Law of Double Jeopardy." *South Carolina Law Review* 44.

Richardson, Eli J. 1994. "Eliminating Double-Talk from the Law of Double Jeopardy." *Florida State University Law Review* 22.

DOUGLAS, WILLIAM ORVILLE

Douglas, William O. 1954. *Almanac of Freedom.*

———. 1974. *Go East, Young Man.* New York: Random House.

———. 1980. *The Court Years: The Autobiography of William O. Douglas.* New York: Random House.

Simon, James F. 1980. *Independent Journey: The Life of William O. Douglas.* New York: Harper & Row.

Woodward, Bob, and Scott Armstrong. 1979. *The Brethren: Inside the Supreme Court.* New York: Simon & Schuster.

DOUGLASS, FREDERICK

Douglass, Frederick. 1845. *Narrative of the Life of Frederick Douglass.* Reprint, New York: Penguin Books, 1986.

Miller, Douglas T. 1988. *Frederick Douglass and the Fight for Freedom.* New York: Facts on File.

DRAMSHOP ACTS

Allen, Jeffrey Wynn. 1994. "Illinois Dram Shop Reform." *John Marshall Law Review* 28 (fall).

Fancher, Catherine. 1993. "One Too Many? . . . Dram Shop Act. . . ." *Texas Tech Law Review* 25.

DRED SCOTT V. SANDFORD

Bernstein, Richard, and Jerome Agel. 1989. *Into the Third Generation: the Supreme Court.* New York: Walker.

Weiss, Ann E. 1987. *The Supreme Court.* Springfield, N.J.: Enslow.

DRUGS AND NARCOTICS

Brickey, Kathleen F. 1995. "Criminal Mischief: The Federalization of American Criminal Law." *Hastings Law Journal* (April).

Contrera, Joseph G. 1995. "The Food and Drug Administration and the International Conference on Harmonization." *Administrative Law Journal of the American University* 8 (winter).

Duke, Steven B. 1995. "Drug Prohibition: An Unnatural Disaster." *Connecticut Law Review* (winter).

"Executive Summary: Mandatory Sentencing." 1995. *CQ Researcher* (May 26).

Inciardi, James A. 1986. *The War on Drugs.* Palo Alto, Cal.: Mayfield.

Justice Department. Bureau of Justice Statistics. 1993. *Sentencing in the Federal Courts: Does Race Matter? The Transition to Sentencing Guidelines, 1986–1990.* December.

Lowney, Knoll D. 1994. "Smoked Not Snorted: Is Racism Inherent in Our Crack Cocaine Laws?" *Washington University Journal of Urban and Contemporary Law* 45 (winter).

Lusane, Clarence. 1991. *Pipe Dream Blues.* Boston: South End Press.

National Clearinghouse for Alcohol and Drug Information. 1992. *A Short History of the Drug Laws.*

Powell, John A., and Eileen Hershenov. 1991. "Hostage to the Drug War: The National Purse, the Constitution, and the Black Community." *University of California at Davis Law Review* 24.

"Report of the Special Committee on Race and Ethnicity to the D.C. Circuit Task Force on Gender, Race, and Ethnic Bias." 1996. *George Washington Law Review* 64 (January).

U.S. Sentencing Commission. 1992. *Monitoring Data Files, April 1–July 1, 1992.*

White House Conference for a Drug Free America. 1988. Final report. Washington, D.C.: U.S. Government Printing Office.

DU BOIS, WILLIAM EDWARD BURGHARDT

Clarke, John Henrik, et al., eds. 1970. *Black Titan: W. E. B. Du Bois.* Boston: Beacon Press.

Du Bois, W. E. B. 1968. *The Autobiography of W. E. B. Du Bois.* International Publishers.

Logan, Rayford Whittingham, ed. 1971. *W. E. B. Du Bois: A Profile.* New York: Hill and Wang.

Marable, Manning. 1986. *W. E. B. Du Bois: Black Radical Democrat.* Boston: Twayne.

DUELING

Baldick, Robert. *The Duel.* 1965. London: Chapman & Hall.

Billacois, Francois. *The Duel.* 1990. New Haven, Conn.: Yale Univ. Press.

Burr, Samuel Engle, Jr. 1971. *The Burr-Hamilton Duel.* San Antonio: Naylor.

Cochran, Hamilton. 1963. *Noted American Duels and Hostile Encounters.* Philadelphia and New York: Chilton Books.

Hussey, Jeannette. 1980. *The Code Duello in America.* Washington, D.C.: Smithsonian Institution Press.

Kiernan, V. G. 1988. *The Duel in European History.* New York: Oxford Univ. Press.

McAleer, Kevin. *Dueling.* 1994. Princeton, N.J.: Princeton Univ. Press.

Rush, Philip. *The Book of Duels.* 1964. London: Harrp.

DULLES, JOHN FOSTER

Halberstam, David. 1993. *The Fifties.* New York: Villard Books.

Merry, Robert W. *Taking on the World: Joseph and Stewart Alsop—Guardians of the American Century.* New York: Viking.

DWORKIN, ANDREA

"Anti-Porn Legal Theorists Gather in Chicago." 1993. *National Law Journal* (March 22).

EDELMAN, MARIAN WRIGHT

Igus, Toyomi, ed. 1991. *Book of Black Heroes. Vol. 2: Great Women in the Struggle.* New York: Scholastic.

EDUCATION DEPARTMENT

U.S. Department of Education. 1992. *Information about the U.S. Department of Education.* Washington, D.C.: Government Printing Office.

———. 1994. *National Education Goals Report.* Washington, D.C.: Government Printing Office.

———. September 5, 1995. "U.S. Department of Education Staff Organization." U.S. Department of Education site. World Wide Web.

———. October 20, 1995. "How We Help America Learn: A Summary of Major Activities." National Library of Education site. World Wide Web.

EDUCATION LAW

Alexander, Kern, and M. David Alexander. 1992. *American Public School Law.* 3d ed. St. Paul: West.

Yudof, Mark G., David L. Kirp, and Betsy Levin. 1992. *Educational Policy and the Law.* 3d ed. St. Paul: West.

EIGHTH AMENDMENT

Bork, Robert. 1990. *The Tempting of America: The Political Seduction of the Law.* Free Press.

Dworkin, Ronald. 1977. *Taking Rights Seriously.* Cambridge, Mass.: Harvard University Press.

ELDER LAW

Flint, Margaret M. 1995. "Nursing Homes." *Practising Law Institute/Estate Planning and Administration* 239.

Frolik, Lawrence A., and Richard L. Kaplan. 1995. *Elder Law.* St. Paul: West.

Hilgers, Gerri, chair, Elder Law Section, Minnesota State Bar Association. 1995. Telephone interview, December 29.

Kass, Richard G. 1986. "Early Retirement Incentives and the Age Discrimination in Employment Act." *Hofstra Labor Law Journal* 4.

Lofton, F. Douglas. 1995. "Determining Legal Mental Capacity." *National Bar Association Magazine* 9 (June).

McCue, Judith W. 1995. "Disability Planning for the Senior Citizen." *American Law Institute-American Bar Association* C126.

Sandahl, Susan. 1995. Telephone interview, December 20.

ELECTION CAMPAIGN FINANCING

Eisner, Keith D. 1993. "Non-Major Party Candidates and Televised Presidential Debates: The Merits of Legislative Inclusion." *University of Pennsylvania Law Review* 141.

Federal Election Commission, Washington, D.C. 1996. Telephone interview, August 23.

Hesse, Richard, professor, Franklin Pierce Law Center, Concord, New Hampshire. 1996. Telephone interview, August 23.

Smith, Bradley A. 1996. "Faulty Assumptions and Undemocratic Consequences of Campaign Finance Reform." *Yale Law Journal* 105.

ELECTORAL COLLEGE

Abbott, David W., and James P. Levine. 1991. *Wrong Winner.* New York: Praeger.

Glennon, Michael J. 1992. *When No Majority Rules: The Electoral College and Presidential Succession.* Washington D.C.: Congressional Quarterly.

Hardaway, Robert M. 1994. *The Electoral College and the Constitution.* New York: Praeger.

Kuroda, Tadahisa. 1994. *The Origins of the Twelfth Amendment.* Westport, Conn.: Greenwood Press.

Rose, Gary L. 1994. *Controversial Issues in Presidential Selection.* Albany, N.Y.: State Univ. of New York Press.

Wayne, Stephen J. 1988. *The Road to the White House.* New York: St. Martin's Press.

ELECTRICITY

Atterbury, Mark S. 1995. "The Strict Liability of Power Companies for Cancer Caused by Electromagnetic Fields." *Southern Illinois University Law Journal* 19.

Handmaker, Robert S. 1989. "Deregulating the Transmission of Electricity: Wheeling under PURPA sections 203, 204 and 205." *Washington University Law Journal* 67.

Laitos, Jan G., and Joseph P. Tomain. 1992. *Energy and Natural Resources Law.* St. Paul: West.

Yelkovac, Peter G. 1994. "Homogenizing the Law of Stray Voltage: An Electrifying Attempt to Corral the Controversy." *Valparaiso University Law Review* 28.

ELECTRONIC SURVEILLANCE

Cavico, Frank J. 1993. "Invasion of Privacy in the Private Employment Sector: Tortious and Ethical Aspects." *Houston Law Review* 30.

Flanagan, Julie A. 1994. "Restricting Electronic Monitoring in the Private Workplace." *Duke Law Journal* 43.

LaFave, Wayne R., and Jerold H. Israel. 1985. *Criminal Procedure*. St. Paul, Minn.: West Publishing.

Lee, Laurie Thomas. 1994. "Watch Your E-mail! Employee E-mail Monitoring and Privacy Law in the Age of the 'Electronic Sweatshop.' " *John Marshall Law Review* 28.

Levy, Leonard. 1988. *Original Intent and the Framers' Constitution*. New York: MacMillan Publishing Co.

Posner, Richard. 1981. *The Economics of Justice*. Cambridge, Mass.: Harvard University Press.

Sheffer, Martin S. 1989. "Nixon, Mitchell, and Warrantless Wiretaps: A Presidential Attempt to Suspend the Fourth Amendment." *Ohio Northern University Law Review* 16.

Wright, Charles A., and Arthur R. Miller. 1990. *Federal Practice and Procedure*. 2d ed.

ELEVENTH AMENDMENT

Fletcher, William A. 1983. "A Historical Interpretation of the Eleventh Amendment: A Narrow Construction of an Affirmative Grant of Jurisdiction Rather than a Prohibition against Jurisdiction." *Stanford Law Review* 35.

Marshall, Lawrence C. 1989. "Fighting Words of the Eleventh Amendment." *Harvard Law Review* 102.

ELLSWORTH, OLIVER

Stephens, Otis H., Jr., and John M. Scheb II. 1993. *American Constitutional Law*. St. Paul: West.

EMANCIPATION PROCLAMATION

Franklin, John Hope. 1993. *The Emancipation Proclamation: Milestone Documents in the National Archives*. National Archives.

————. 1995. *The Emancipation Proclamation*. Davidson.

EMINENT DOMAIN

Berger, Michael M. 1994. "Recent Takings and Eminent Domain Cases." *American Law Institute-American Bar Association* C930 (August).

Harris, David. 1995. "The Battle for Black Land: Fighting Eminent Domain." *NBA National Bar Association Magazine* 9 (March–April).

Kimsey, Paul. 1994. "Eminent Domain." *Stetson Law Review* 23 (spring).

Kruse, Patrick. 1995. "Constitutional Law–Eminent Domain–Riparian Landowners." *University of Detroit Mercy Law Review* 72 (spring).

Mancini, Vincent B. 1993. "Land Use Regulatory 'Takings' and the Eminent Domain Code." *Pennsylvania Bar Association Quarterly* 64 (October).

McCurdy, Claire K., and Nina M. Thompson. 1992. "What Is Eminent Domain and How Do You Do It?" *Journal of the Kansas Bar Association* 61 (December).

Richardson, Mark A. 1995. "A Symposium on Regulatory Takings." *Detroit College of Law Review* (spring).

Salley, Sara T. 1988. "Eminent Domain: Supreme Court Regulatory Takings Analysis: How *Nollan v. California Coastal Commission* Fit In?" *Oklahoma Law Review* 41 (fall).

Searles, Sidney Z. 1995. "The Law of Eminent Domain in the U.S.A." *American Law Institute-American Bar Association* C975 (January).

EMPLOYMENT LAW

Hall, Kermit L. 1989. *The Magic Mirror*. New York: Oxford Univ. Press.

Stephens, Otis H., Jr., and John M. Scheb II. 1993. *American Constitutional Law*. St. Paul: West.

ENDANGERED SPECIES ACT

Cheever, Federico. 1996. "The Road to Recovery: A New Way of Thinking about the Endangered Species Act." *Ecology Law Quarterly* 23.

Craig, Barbara. "The Federal Endangered Species Act." *Advocate (Idaho)* 38:12 (October).

"Endangered Species Act—Judicial Deference to Agency Decision." 1995. *Harvard Law Review* 109.

Moore, Robert C. 1995. "The Pack Is Back: The Political, Social, and Ecological Effects of the Reintroduction of the Gray Wolf to Yellowstone National Park and Central Idaho." *Cooley Law Review* 12.

Wolok, Mimi S. 1996. "Experimenting with Experimental Populations." *Environmental Law Reporter* 26 (January).

ENDOWMENT

Dobris, Joel C. 1993. "Real Return . . . on Annual Spending from Endowments." *Real Property, Probate and Trust Journal* 28 (spring).

ENERGY

Laitos, Jan G., and Tomain, Joseph. 1992. *Energy and Natural Resources Law*. St. Paul: West.

Miller, Alan S. 1995. "Energy Policy from Nixon to Clinton: From Grand Provider to Market Facilitator." *Environmental Law* 25.

Reilly, Kathleen C. 1995. "Global Benefits versus Local Concerns: The Need for a Bird's Eye View of Nuclear Energy." *Indiana Law Journal* 70.

Tomain, Joseph P. 1990. "The Dominant Model of United States Energy Policy." *University of Colorado Law Review* 61.

ENERGY DEPARTMENT

United States Government Manual, 1994–1995. Washington, D.C.: U.S. Government Printing Office.

ENGEL V. VITALE

Blanshard, Paul. 1963. *Religion and the Schools: The Great Controversy*. Boston: Beacon Press.

Castle, Marie, co-chair, Minnesota Atheists. Telephone interview.

"The Establishment Clause and Public Schools." 1993. ACLU Reading Room site. World Wide Web.

"Religion and Schools." 1994. *Congressional Quarterly Researcher* (February 18).

ENGLISH LAW

Bailyn, Bernard. 1992. *Ideological Origins of the American Revolution*. Enl. ed. Boston: Harvard Univ. Press.

Blackstone, William. 1765. *Commentaries on the Laws of England.* Reprint, Chicago: Univ. of Chicago Press, 1979.

Christenson, Ron. 1986. *Political Trials: Gordian Knots in the Law.* New Brunswick, N.J.: Transaction.

———. 1991. *Political Trials in History: From Antiquity to the Present.* New Brunswick, N.J.: Transaction.

Landsman, Stephen. 1983. "A Brief Survey of the Development of the Adversary System." *Ohio State Law Journal* 44.

Levy, Leonard. 1986. *Origins of the Fifth Amendment* New York: Macmillan.

Plucknett, Theodore F. T. 1926. "Bonham's Case and Judicial Review." *Harvard Law Review* 40.

———. 1956. *A Concise History of the Common Law.* Boston: Little, Brown.

Smith, George P., II. 1966. "Dr. Bonham's Case and the Modern Significance of Lord Coke's Influence." *Washington Law Review* 41.

Stoner, James R., Jr. 1992. *Common Law and Liberal Theory: Coke, Hobbes, and the Origins of American Constitutionalism.* Univ. Press of Kansas.

Thorne, Samuel. 1938. "Dr. Bonham's Case." *Law Quarterly Review* 54.

Trevelyan, G. M. 1982. *A Shortened History of England.* New York: Penguin Books.

Wood, Gordon S. 1969. *The Creation of the American Republic.* New York: Norton.

ENVIRONMENTAL LAW

Rogers, William H., Jr. 1977. *Environmental Law Hornbook.* St. Paul: West.

———. 1986. *Environmental Law: Air and Water Pollution.* St. Paul: West.

EQUAL EMPLOYMENT OPPORTUNITY COMMISSION

Player, Mack A. 1988. *Employment Discrimination Law.* St. Paul: West.

United States Government Manual, 1994–1995. Washington, D.C.: U.S. Government Printing Office.

Williams, Douglas L. 1995. "Handling the EEOC Investigation." *American Law Institute-American Bar Association* C983.

EQUAL PROTECTION

Bailyn, Bernard. 1967. *The Ideological Origins of the American Revolution.* Belknap Press.

Berman, Harold J. 1983. *Law and Revolution.* Cambridge, Mass.: Harvard University Press.

Friedman, Lawrence M. 1985. *A History of American Law.* 2d ed. New York: Simon & Schuster.

Hall, Kermit L. 1989. *The Magic Mirror.* New York: Oxford Univ. Press.

Rotunda, Ronald D., et al. 1986. *Treatise on Constitutional Law: Substance and Procedure.* Volume 3. St. Paul, Minn.: West Publishing.

Wills, Garry. 1978. *Inventing America: Jefferson's Declaration of Independence.* New York: Doubleday.

EQUAL RIGHTS AMENDMENT

Corwin, Edward S. 1978. *The Constitution and What it Means Today.* 14th ed. Princeton, N.J.: Princeton Univ. Press.

EQUITY

Laycock, Douglas. 1993. "The Triumph of Equity." *SUM Law and Contemporary Problems* 56:53 (summer).

ESPIONAGE

Adams, James. 1994. *The New Spies.* London: Hutchinson.

Gerolymatos, Andre. 1986. *Espionage and Treason.* Amsterdam: Gieben.

Hartman, John D. 1993. *Legal Guidelines for Covert Surveillance Operations in the Private Sector.* Boston: Butterworth-Heinemann.

Udell, Gilman G. 1971. *Laws Relating to Espionage, Sabotage, Etc.* Washington, D.C.: U.S. Government Printing Office.

U.S. House Permanent Select Committee on Intelligence. 1995. *Legislative Proposals Relating to Counterintelligence: Hearing before the Permanent Select Committee on Intelligence House of Representatives.* Washington, D.C.: U.S. Government Printing Office.

Volkman, Ernest. 1995. *Espionage.* New York: Wiley.

———. 1994. *Spies.* New York: Wiley.

ESTATE AND GIFT TAXES

"The Revocable Living Trust as an Estate Planning Tool." 1972. *Real Property, Probate, and Trust Journal* 11.

Stephens, R., et al., eds. 1991. *Federal Estate and Gift Taxation.* 6th ed. Warren Gorham & Lamont, Publisher.

ETHICS

Callahan, Joan C., ed. 1988. *Ethical Issues in Professional Life.* New York: Oxford Univ. Press.

Gorlin, Rena A., ed. 1994. *Codes of Professional Responsibility.* Washington, D.C.: Bureau of National Affairs.

Madsen, Peter, and Jay M. Shafritz. 1990. *Essentials of Business Ethics.* New York: Penguin Books.

McDowell, Banks. 1991. *Ethical Conduct and the Professional's Dilemma: Choosing between Service and Success.* New York: Quorum Books.

Salbu, Steven. "True Codes versus Voluntary Codes of Ethics in International Markets: Towards the Preservation of Colloquy in Emerging Global Communities." *University of Pennsylvania Journal of International Business Law* 15 (fall).

Twain, Mark. 1901. Correspondence to Young Peoples' Society, Greenpoint Presbyterian Church, Brooklyn, N.Y. (February 16).

ETTELBRICK, PAULA LOUISE

"Braschi v. Stahl Associates Co.: In Praise of Family." 1991. *New England Law Review* (summer).

"Domestic Relations Law: Visitation Rights of Lesbian Companion." 1991. *New York Law Journal* (May 7).

"Family Ties." 1991. *Brooklyn Journal of International Law* 17.

"Litigating for Lesbian and Gay Rights: A Legal History." 1993. *Virginia Law Review* 79 (October).

"Lov(h)ers: Lesbians as Intimate Partners and Lesbian Legal Theory." 1990. *Temple Law Review* 63 (fall).

"Mother's Lesbian Partner Denied Visitation Rights." 1991. *New York Law Journal* (May 3).

"New Law on Medical Treatment Decisions Urged by Task Force." 1992. *New York Law Journal* (March 24).

"On the Prudence of Discussing Affirmative Action for Lesbians and Gay Men." 1993. *Stanford Law & Policy Review* 5 (fall).

"Panel to Air Benefits for Domestic Partners." 1993. *New York Law Journal* (October 27).

Ettelbrick, Paula. 1994. *Custody/Visitation Issues (Legal Issues Facing the Non-Traditional Family)*. Practising Law Institute Tax Law and Estate Planning Course Handbook series (April–May).

"Removing Bricks from a Wall of Discrimination: State Constitutional Challenges of Sodomy Laws." 1992. *Hastings Constitutional Law Quarterly* 19 (winter).

"Same-Sex Marriage and the Right of Privacy." 1994. *Yale Law Journal* 103 (April).

"Statutory Protection of the Other Mother." 1991. *Hastings Constitutional Law Quarterly* 43 (November).

"Summaries of Court Opinions." 1991. *New York Law Journal* (October 15).

"Today's News." 1992. *New York Law Journal* (November 13).

"Towards a Revitalization of Family Law." 1990. *Texas Law Review* 69 (November).

Ettelbrick, Paula. "Who Is a Parent?: The Need to Develop a Lesbian Conscious Family Law." 1993. *New York Law School Journal of Human Rights* 10 (spring).

"Women Denied Partnerships Revisited." 1990. *Hofstra Labor Law Journal* 8 (fall).

EVERS, MEDGAR WILEY

Evers, Myrlie, with William Peters. 1967. *For Us, the Living*. Garden City, N.Y.: Doubleday.

Massengill, Reed. 1994. *Portrait of a Racist: The Man Who Killed Medgar Evers?* New York: St. Martin's Press.

Nossiter, Adam. 1994. *Of Long Memory: Mississippi and the Murder of Medgar Evers*. Reading, Mass.: Addison-Wesley.

EVIDENCE

Gillmor, Barron, and Terry Simon. 1990. *Mass Communication Law Cases and Comment*. 5th ed. St. Paul: West.

Leonard, David P. 1995. "Foreword: Twenty Years of the Federal Rules of Evidence." *Loyola of Los Angeles Law Review* 28 (June).

Mauet, Thomas A. 1988. *Fundamentals of Trial Techniques*. 2d ed. Boston: Little, Brown.

McCormick on Evidence. 3d ed. 1984 and Supp. 1987. St. Paul: West.

EXCHANGE

Booth, Richard A. 1994. "The Uncertain Case for Regulating Program Trading." *Columbia Business Law Review* 1.

Maynard, Therese H. 1992. "What is an 'Exchange?'—Proprietary Securities Trading Systems and the Statutory Definition of an Exchange." *Washington & Lee Law Review* 49.

Morris, Kenneth M., and Alan M. Siegel. 1993. *The Wall Street Journal Guide to Understanding Money & Investing*. Lightbulb Press.

Romano, Roberta. 1996. "A Thumbnail Sketch of Derivative Securities and Their Regulation." *Maryland Law Review* 55.

EXCLUSIONARY RULE

"Criminal Procedure." 1993. *The Conviser Mini Review*. Orlando, Fla.: Harcourt Brace Jovanovich Legal & Professional Publications.

Eiben, Valerie L. 1987. "The Good Faith Exception to the Exclusionary Rule: The New Federalism and a Texas Proposal." *St. Mary's Law Journal* 18.

Israel, Jerold H., Yale Kamisar, and Wayne R. LaFave. 1993. *Criminal Procedure and the Constitution*. St. Paul: West.

EXECUTION

Gridley, Doreen J. 1995. "The Immunity of Intangible Assets from a Writ of Execution." *Indiana Law Review* 28.

EXECUTIVE BRANCH

Congressional Quarterly. 1989. *Cabinets and Counselors: The President and the Executive Branch*. Washington, D.C.: Congressional Quarterly.

Hart, John. 1987. *The Presidential Branch*. New York: Pergamon Press.

Hodgson, Godfrey, ed. 1992. *The United States*. Vol. 2. New York: Facts on File.

Nelson, Michael, ed. 1988. *The Presidency and the Political System*. Washington, D.C.: CQ Press.

Pfiffner, James P. 1994. *The Modern Presidency*. New York: St. Martin's Press.

Shaw, Malcolm, ed. 1987. *The Modern Presidency*. New York: Harper & Row.

EXECUTIVE ORDERS

Ostrow, Steven. 1987. "Enforcing Executive Orders: Judicial Review of Agency Action under the Administrative Procedure Act." *George Washington Law Review* 55.

Raven-Hansen, Peter. 1983. "Making Agencies Follow Orders: Judicial Review of Agency Violations of Executive Order 12,291." *Duke Law Journal*.

EXECUTORS AND ADMINISTRATORS

Plotnick, Charles K., and Stephen R. Leimberg. 1991. *How to Settle an Estate: A Manual for Executors and Trustees*. Consumer Reports Books.

EX PARTE

Gottlieb, Henry. 1995. "ABA Limits Ex-Parte Contacts; N. J. Lawyer Dissents." *New Jersey Law Journal* (September 4).

Harhut, C. T. 1995. "Ex Parte Communication Initiated by a Presiding Judge." *Temple Law Review* 68.

EXPORT-IMPORT BANK OF THE UNITED STATES

United States Government Manual, 1994–1995. Washington, D.C.: U.S. Government Printing Office.

EX POST FACTO LAWS

Aiken, Jane Harris. 1992. "Ex Post Facto in the Civil Context: Unbridled Punishment." *Kentucky Law Journal* 81.

Booth, Michael. 1995. "State, U.S. Rift Leaves Megan's Law Fate Unclear." *New Jersey Law Journal* (July 31).

EXPROPRIATION
Angell, Allan. 1971. "Chile: From Christian Democracy to Marxism?" *Current History* (February).
_____. 1973. "Problems in Allende's Chile." *Current History* (February).
Chaffee, Wilber A. 1989. *Cuba: A Different America.* Rowman and Littlefield.
Marcus, Maeva. 1977. *Truman and the Steel Seizure Case.* New York: Columbia Univ. Press.
McCullough, David. 1992. *Truman.* New York: Simon & Schuster.

EXTRADITION
"Abduction as an Alternative to Extradition—A Dangerous Method to Obtain Jurisdiction over Criminal Defendants." 1993. *Wake Forest Law Review* 28.

EXTRATERRITORIALITY
Castel, J. G. 1988. *Extraterritoriality in International Trade.* Toronto and Vancouver: Butterworths.
Hermann, A. H. 1982. *Conflicts of National Laws with International Business Activity: Issues of Extraterritoriality.* London: British-North American Committee.

FAIR CREDIT REPORTING ACT
American Marketplace Business Publishers. 1992. *House Panel Approves Overhaul of Fair Credit. . . ."*
"Bank's Reporting to a Local Credit Bureau of Its Own Credit Experience with a Delinquent Borrower Was Not Covered by the Fair Credit Reporting Act." 1995. *The Banking Law Journal.*
Jacquez, Albert S., and Amy S. Friend. 1993. "The Fair Credit Reporting Act: Is It Fair for Consumers?" *Loyola Consumer Law Reporter.*
Smith, Nancy. 1996. "The SEC Speaks." *Practising Law Institute. Corporate Law and Practice Course Handbook Series.* 949:487.
Porter, J. Isaac. 1994. "Protecting against Disclosure of Consumer Data: A Complicated Issue." *Banking Policy Report.*
Blair, Roger D., and Virginia Maurer. 1984. "Statute Law and Common Law: The Fair Credit Reporting Act." *Missouri Law Review.*

FAIRNESS DOCTRINE
Barron, Jerome A. 1989. "What Does the Fairness Doctrine Controversy Really Mean?" *Hastings Communications and Entertainment Law Journal* (winter).
Hall, Roland F. L. 1994. "The Fairness Doctrine and the First Amendment: Phoenix Rising." *Mercer Law Review* (winter).
Harowitz, Linda. 1990. "Laying the Fairness Doctrine to Rest: Was the Doctrine's Elimination Really Fair?" *George Washington Law Review* (June).

FAIR-TRADE LAWS
Areeda, Phillip, and Louis Kaplow. 1988. *Antitrust Analysis.* 4th ed.
Posner, R. 1976. *Antitrust Law: An Economic Perspective.* University of Chicago Press.

FALSE ADVERTISING
Jacobs-Meadway, Roberta. 1995. "False Advertising." *American Law Institute-American Bar Association* C122 (April 3).
Postel, Theodore. 1993. "Consumer Fraud Act: False Advertising of Used Cars." *Chicago Daily Law Bulletin* (February 5).

FALSE PRETENSES
Bishop, Joel Prentiss. 1986. *Commentaries on the Criminal Law.* Buffalo: Hein.
Lafave, Wayne R., and Austin W. Scott, Jr. 1986. *Substantive Criminal Law.* St. Paul: West.
Torcia, Charles E. 1995. *Wharton's Criminal Law.* New York: Clark Boardman Callaghan.

FAMILY LAW
Hall, Kermit L. 1989. *The Magic Mirror.* New York: Oxford Univ. Press.

FEDERAL AVIATION ADMINISTRATION
Boswell, J., and A. Coats. 1994. "Saving the General Aviation Industry: Putting Tort Reform to the Test." *Journal of Air Law and Commerce* 60 (December-January).

FEDERAL BUDGET
Bowen, James W. 1994. "Enforcing the Balanced Budget Amendment." *Seton Hall Constitutional Law Journal* 4:565.
Devins, Neal. 1990. "Budget Reform and the Balance of Powers." *William and Mary Law Review* 31.

FEDERAL BUREAU OF INVESTIGATION
FBI site. World Wide Web.
Jeffreys, Diarmuid. 1995. *The Bureau.* Boston: Houghton Mifflin.
Kessler, Ronald. 1993. *The FBI.* New York: Pocket Books.
Shapiro, Howard M. 1994. "The FBI in the 21st Century." *Cornell International Law Journal* 28.

FEDERAL DEPOSIT INSURANCE CORPORATION
Seidman, William L. 1993. *Full Faith and Credit.* New York: Random House.
White, Lawrence J. 1991. *The S & L Debacle.* New York: Oxford Univ. Press.

FEDERAL ELECTION COMMISSION
United States Government Manual, 1995–1996. Washington, D.C.: U.S. Government Printing Office.

FEDERAL EMERGENCY MANAGEMENT AGENCY
United States Government Manual, 1995–1996. Washington, D.C.: U.S. Government Printing Office.

FEDERALISM
Burke, Edmund. 1989. *Reflections on the Revolution in France.* Garden City, N.Y.: Doubleday.
Cardozo, Benjamin N. 1921. *The Nation of the Judicial Process.* New Haven, Conn.: Yale Univ. Press.
Dorsen, Norman. 1994. "How American Judges Interpret the Bill of Rights." *Constitutional Commentary* 11 (fall).

"Federalism—Clear Congressional Mandate Required to Preempt State Law: *Gregory v. Ashcroft.*" 1991. *Harvard Law Review* 105 (November).

McManamon, Mary Brigid. 1993. "Felix Frankfurter: The Architect of 'Our Federalism.'" *Georgia Law Review* 27 (spring).

Savage, David G. 1995. "The Supreme Court Goes Back to Work." *American Bar Association Journal* 81 (October).

Tanielian, Matthew J. 1995. "Separation of Powers and the Supreme Court: One Doctrine, Two Visions." *Administrative Law Journal of the American University.* 8 (winter).

Vause, W. Gary. 1995. "The Subsidiarity Principle in European Union Law—American Federalism Compared." *Case Western Reserve Journal of International Law* 27 (winter).

Wiessner, Siegfried. 1993. "Federalism: An Architecture for Freedom." *New Europe Law Review* 1 (spring).

FEDERALIST PAPERS

Hamilton, Alexander, James Madison, and John Jay. 1787–88. *The Federalist Papers.* Reprint, New York: New American Library of World Literature, 1961.

FEDERAL JUDICIAL CENTER

United States Government Manual, 1995–1996. Washington, D.C.: U.S. Government Printing Office.

FEDERAL MARITIME COMMISSION

United States Government Manual, 1995–1996. Washington, D.C.: U.S. Government Printing Office.

FEDERAL MEDIATION AND CONCILIATION SERVICE

Newman, William A. 1990. "Use of Non-Adjudicative Third-Party Dispute Resolution Methods by Dispute Resolution Agencies of the United States Government." *Ohio Northern University Law Review* 17.

United States Government Manual, 1995–1996. Washington, D.C.: U.S. Government Printing Office.

FEDERAL NATIONAL MORTGAGE ASSOCIATION

Fannie Mae site. World Wide Web.

Froomkin, A. Michael. 1995. "Reinventing the Government Corporation." *University of Illinois Law Review.*

Malloy, Robin Paul. 1986. "The Secondary Mortgage Market: A Catalyst for Change in Real Estate." *Southern Methodist University Law Review* (February).

FEDERAL RESERVE BOARD

Colander, David C., and Dewy Daane. 1994. *The Art of Monetary Policy.* New York: Sharpe.

Federal Reserve Subcommittee on Economic Growth and Credit Formation of the Committee on Bank-ing, Finance, and Urban Affairs. 1994. *Conduct of Monetary Policy: Report of the Federal Reserve Pursuant to the Full Employment and Balanced Growth Act of 1978, P.L. 95–523, and the State of the Economy: Hearing before the Subcommittee on Economic Growth and Credit Formation of the Committee on Banking, Finance, and Urban Affairs* (February 22).

Harvrilesky, Thomas. 1995. *The Pressures on American Monetary Policy.* Boston: Kluwer Academic.

Mankiw, Gregory N. 1994. *Monetary Policy.* Chicago: Univ. of Chicago Press.

U.S. Senate. 1993. *The Federal Reserve President's Views on Monetary Policy and Economic Conditions: Hearing before the Committee on Banking, Housing, and Urban Affairs.* S. Hr'g No. 103-98 (March 10).

———. 1994. *Federal Reserve: Recent Monetary Policy Actions: Hearing before the Committee on Banking, Housing, and Urban Affairs.* S. Hr'g No. 103-901 (May 27).

———. 1995. *Federal Reserve's First Monetary Policy Report for 1995: Hearing before the Committee on Banking, Housing, and Urban Affairs.* S. Hr'g No. 104-62 (February 22).

FEDERAL TORT CLAIMS ACT

Morris, Daniel A. 1991. "Federal Employees' Liability Since the Federal Employees Liability Reform and Tort Compensation Act of 1988 (The Westfall Act)." *Creighton Law Review* 25.

Reynolds, Osborne M., Jr. 1989. "The Discretionary Function Exception of the Federal Tort Claims Act: Time for Reconsideration." *Oklahoma Law Review* 42.

FELLOW-SERVANT RULE

Cahill, Kelly Ann. 1995. "Hooters: Should There Be an Assumption of Risk Defense to Some Hostile Work Environment Sexual Harassment Claims?" *Vanderbilt Law Review* (May).

Chase, Anthony R. 1995. "Race, Culture, and Contract Law: From the Cottonfield to the Courtroom." *Connecticut Law Review* (fall).

Irwin, Shirley A. 1994. "Glass v. City of Chattanooga: The Abolishment of the Fellow Servant Doctrine in Tennessee." *University of Memphis Law Review* (fall).

Wertheim, Frederick. 1986. "Slavery and the Fellow Servant Rule: An Antebellum Dilemma." *New York University Law Review* (December).

FEMINIST JURISPRUDENCE

Becker, Mary, Cynthia G. Bowman, and Morrison Torrey. 1994. *Feminist Jurisprudence: Taking Rights Seriously.* St. Paul: West.

Hayman, Robert L., and Nancy Levit. 1995. *Jurisprudence.* St. Paul: West.

TABLE OF CASES CITED

INDEX

BY NAME

453

454 INDEX BY NAME

INDEX

References that include photos or exhibits are printed in italic type.